W9-BAL-119

Guatemala

Lucas Vidgen

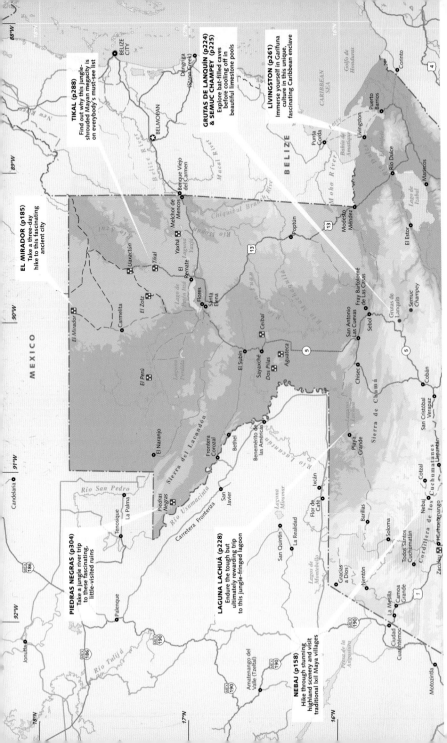

EL MIRADOR (p185)
Take a three-day hike to this fascinating ancient city

TIKAL (p288)
Find out why this jungle-shrouded Mayan megacity is on everybody's must-see list

GRUTAS DE LANQUÍN (p224) & SEMUC CHAMPEY (p225)
Explore bat-filled caves before cooling off in beautiful limestone pools

LIVINGSTON (p261)
Immerse yourself in Garífuna culture in this unique, fascinating Caribbean enclave

PIEDRAS NEGRAS (p304)
Take a jungle river trip to these fascinating, little-visited ruins

LAGUNA LACHUÁ (p228)
Endure the tough but ultimately rewarding trip to this jungle-fringed lagoon

NEBAJ (p158)
Hike through stunning highland scenery and visit traditional Ixil Maya villages

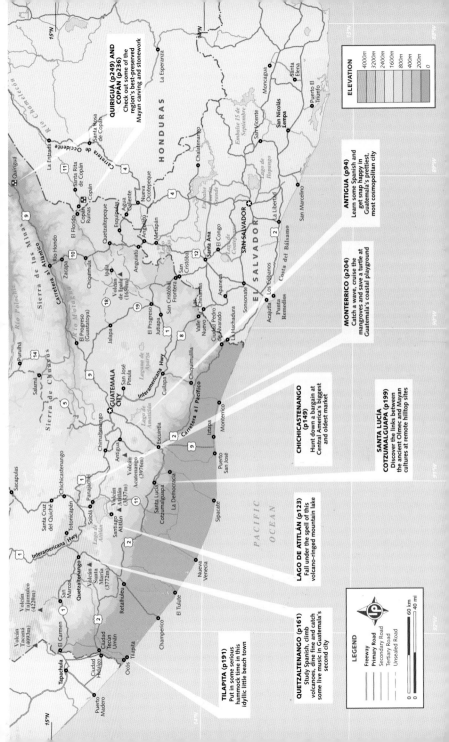

QUIRIGUÁ (p249) AND COPÁN (p236)
Check out one of the region's best-preserved Mayan carving and stonework

ANTIGUA (p94)
Learn some Spanish and get snap happy in Guatemala's prettiest, most cosmopolitan city

MONTERRICO (p204)
Catch a wave, cruise the mangroves and save a turtle at Guatemala's coastal playground

CHICHICASTENANGO (p149)
Hunt down a bargain at Central America's biggest and oldest market

SANTA LUCÍA COTZUMALGUAPA (p199)
Discover the links between the ancient Olmec and Mayan cultures at remote hilltop sites

LAGO DE ATITLÁN (p123)
Fall under the spell of this volcano-ringed mountain lake

TILAPITA (p191)
Put in some serious hammock time in this idyllic little beach town

QUETZALTENANGO (p161)
Study Spanish, climb volcanoes, dine fine and catch some live music in Guatemala's second city

ELEVATION

| 4000m |
| 3200m |
| 2400m |
| 1600m |
| 800m |
| 400m |
| 200m |
| 0 |

LEGEND

Freeway
Primary Road
Secondary Road
Tertiary Road
Unsealed Road

0   60 km
0   40 mi

On the Road

LUCAS VIDGEN Coordinating Author

Roadside (again!), high in the Cuchumatanes mountains. This is probably the most beautiful bus stop in the world. While here, I started thinking about how random change is in Guatemala. This road (in the middle of nowhere) was a nightmarish dirt track a few years ago – now it's one of the best in the country.

MY FAVORITE TRIP

I live in the mountains, so when I'm up for some serious culture shock, I head for the coast, to **Tilapita** (p191), then down the highway and through the back door to **Lago de Atitlán** (p123) and **San Marcos La Laguna** (p146).

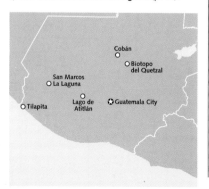

A city boy at heart, I actually like **Guatemala City** (p70) for its restaurants, cultural centers and nightlife. Next its up to **Cobán** (p216), and the **Biotopo del Quetzal** (p215), before heading back home through the Cuchumatanes.

ABOUT THE AUTHOR

Lucas has been traveling and working in Latin America for more than a decade. He currently lives in Quetzaltenango, Guatemala, where he is a director of the NGO EntreMundos and publishes the city's leading culture and nightlife magazine, *XelaWho*.

Lucas has contributed to Lonely Planet's *Central America on a Shoestring*, as well as *Guatemala, Belize & Yucatán*, *Argentina* and *South America on a Shoestring*. His Spanish is OK, but he misses potato cakes and his mum.

UNRAVELLING GUATEMALA

Guatemala is a magical place. If you're into the Maya, the mountains, the markets or a million other things, you're bound to be captivated.

People come and they stay. Or they leave and return. There's almost too much going on here, and even the shortest trip takes you completely different places, with new challenges and surprises. Don't be surprised if you hear yourself saying 'we'll have to come back and do that, *next time.*'

Guatemala's got its problems, but it isn't the scary place your mother fears it is. Travel here, once dangerous and uncomfortable, is now characterized by ease – you can do pretty much whatever you want, and will only be limited by your imagination.

Natural Wonders

Lack of development in Guatemala brings at least one blessing – huge areas of unspoilt forests, mangroves and waterways. The Cobán area is literally dotted with caves and waterfalls and the Highlands consist of a chain of volcanoes just begging to be climbed. Up north in El Petén, the thick jungle is still home to an incredible array of wildlife.

1 Lago de Atitlán
Surrounded by volcanoes and traditional villages, this **mountain lake** (p123) exudes a timeless beauty. Kayaking, trekking or simply sunset-gazing are just some of the ways to experience its charms.

2 Semuc Champey
Regularly earning the accolade 'the most beautiful place in Guatemala', these **limestone pools** (p225) are fed by a series of waterfalls and surrounded by lush jungle.

3 El Petén
A huge, sparsely populated region, El Petén's remote **archaeological sites** (p303) share space with a dazzling array of wildlife, including jaguars, ocelots, pumas and over 300 species of birds.

4 Refugio Bocas del Polochic
At the western end of the gorgeous Lago de Izabal, one of the country's largest **freshwater wetlands** (p256) is home to alligators, manatees, howler monkeys and even more birds.

5 Biotopo Monterrico-Hawaii
Down on the steamy Pacific coast, this reserve protects coastal mangroves, caimans, several turtle species and other wildlife. A sunset **rowboat tour** (p206) through its canals is a nature lover's delight.

6 Río Dulce
Running from the Lago de Izabal to the Caribbean coast, the **boat ride** (p264) along this river through jungle-walled canyons is a truly unforgettable experience.

Outdoor Adventures

There's no shortage of ways to get out there in Guatemala – adventure tourism operators are springing up all the time and there are also plenty of opportunities to go it alone. Trekking in the Highlands and through the jungle, rafting the country's many waterways, paragliding, zip lining and sailing are just some of your options here.

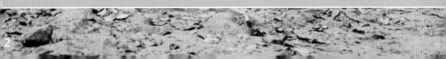

① Volcano treks

Nothing beats a sunrise seen from the top of a volcano. Experienced guides operate out of **Quetzaltenango** (p166), **Antigua** (p104) and **San Pedro La Laguna** (p142) and there are other peaks to be conquered around **Chiquimula** (p231) and **Cuilapa** (p209).

② Jungle treks

Like it or not, the only way to reach some of the remote **Mayan sites** (p303) is on foot – a rugged, exhausting and rewarding way to get off the tourist trail.

③ Paragliding

For a truly bird's-eye view of the fascinating and beautiful **Lago de Atitlán** (p147), there's nothing quite like jumping off a mountain with a parachute strapped to your back.

④ Sailing

The town of **Río Dulce** (p251) is bustling with yachties ready to take you out to the cays (or further afield) on a Caribbean adventure.

⑤ Rafting

The **Cahabón** (p225), **Naranjo** (p194) and **Chiquibul** (p274) rivers offer various degrees of difficulty and are the perfect place for a paddle, stopping off at Mayan ruins and hot springs along the way.

⑥ Zip lining

Zipping over the jungle near **Tikal** (p285) or **Lago de Atitlán** (p137) is yet another way to experience Guatemala's beauty – it's serious fun, but not for the fainthearted.

Festivals & Markets

If there are two things that Guatemalans
know how to do, they would be celebrate
and sell stuff. Every town, no matter how
small, has at least one annual festival and
one weekly market. Some are fairly ordinary;
others are absolutely unmissable – heady
combinations of age-old tradition and
modern-day life.

1 Semana Santa
Easter is serious business in Guatemala. The most picturesque place for street processions is in **Antigua** (p107).

2 Chichicastenango
The country's biggest **market** (p150) literally takes over the town and Guatemalans and foreigners flood in to browse and haggle over the handicrafts and weavings on offer.

3 Day of the Dead
All Saints' Day (November 1) is celebrated all over the country, but the place to be is in **Santiago Sacatepéquez** (p120) or **Sumpango** (p120), where giant kites are flown to honor the dead.

4 Garífuna National Day
November 26 sees the Garífuna celebrate their unique cultural heritage with live music, traditional dancing and storytelling in the Garífuna town of **Lívingston** (p264).

5 Totonicapán
This **artisans' village** (p178) near Quetzal-tenango is famed for its ceramics, leather-work, textiles and carpentry. There aren't many tourists, meaning there are a whole lot of bargains.

6 Día de la Independencia
The annual festival at **Quetzaltenango** (p169) coincides with Independence Day celebrations – live concerts, markets, food stalls, games and rides are just some of the attractions on offer.

Ancient Mayan Culture

Dr Allen J Christenson

Templo I (p292), the Temple of the Grand Jaguar, Tikal, El Petén

RICHARD I'ANSON

The foundations of the Maya world-view date back more than 2000 years, and core elements of their beliefs and rituals continue to be practiced in traditional Mayan communities today. It is a part of who the Maya are, and significant numbers have steadfastly held to their unique perspective despite the Spanish conquest and the immense pressure to abandon their traditional faith that followed.

THE CREATION STORY

The date of creation that appears in inscriptions throughout the Maya world is 13.0.0.0.0, 4 Ahaw, 8 Kumk'u, or August 13, 3114 BC on our calendar.

On that day the creator gods set three stones in the dark waters that covered the primordial world. These formed a cosmic hearth at the center of the universe. They then struck divine fire by means of lightning, charging the world with life.

This account of creation is echoed in the first chapters of the *Popol Vuh,* a book compiled by members of the Maya nobility soon after the Spanish Conquest.

This is the account of when all is still silent and placid. All is silent and calm. Hushed and empty is the womb of the sky. These then are the first words, the first speech. There is not yet one person, one animal, bird, fish, crab, tree, rock, hollow, canyon, meadow, or forest...

All alone are the Framer and the Shaper, Sovereign and Quetzal Serpent, They Who Have Borne Children and They Who Have Begotten Sons... There is also Heart of Sky [a lightning god], which is said to be the name of the god...

Then they called forth the mountains from the water. Straightaway the great mountains came to be. It was merely their spirit essence, their miraculous power, that brought about the conception of the mountains.

WORLD-TREE & XIBALBÁ

For the Maya, the sky, the surface of the earth and the mysterious 'unseen world' beneath the earth called Xibalbá (shee-bahl-*bah*) were all one unified structure. Transcending the three layers of the cosmos was a World-Tree, the first life to emerge out of the primordial chaos. The Maya linked this World-Tree with the ceiba, whose branches grow straight out from the trunk – such cross-like trees appear frequently in Mayan art. In the 16th century Christian missionary friars arrived and required the Maya to venerate the cross, which soon became linked with the World-Tree in the eyes of the Maya, an association that continues today.

Ceiba tree, Tikal (p288), El Petén
JOHN ELK III

ANONYMOUS

The authors of the *Popol Vuh* did not sign their names, likely because doing so would have endangered their lives. The *Popol Vuh* contains descriptions of ancient Maya gods and deified ancestors. Those found in possession of the book were often tortured or killed by the Spanish.

MAYAN CITIES AS THE CENTER OF CREATION

The ancient Maya built their communities to reflect sacred geography, often choosing a lakeside site overlooked by three volcanoes.

The lowland Maya didn't have mountains so they built them in the form of plaza-temple complexes. In hieroglyphic inscriptions the central plazas of Mayan cities were called *nab'* (sea) or *lakam ja'* (great water). Rising above were massive pyramid-temples, often in groups of three, representing the first mountains to emerge out of the 'waters' of the plaza.

THE CREATION OF HUMANKIND

The gods made three attempts at creating people before getting it right. First they made deer and other animals, but not being able to speak properly to honor the gods, the animals were condemned to be eaten.

Next was a person made from mud. At first, the mud person spoke, 'but without knowledge and understanding,' and he soon dissolved back into the mud.

The gods' third attempt was people carved from wood. These too were imperfect and also destroyed. The *Popol Vuh* says that the survivors of these wooden people are the monkeys that inhabit the forests.

The gods finally got it right when they discovered maize, and made mankind:

Thus their frame and shape were given expression by our first Mother and our first Father. Their flesh was merely yellow ears of maize and white ears of maize...

Signature red *huipiles* (p138) of Chimaltenango, the Highlands

ERIC WHEATER

THE PEOPLE OF MAIZE

The Maya refer to themselves as 'true people' and consider themselves literally of a different flesh from those who do not eat maize. Traditionalist mothers in the Highlands place an ear of maize into the palm of newborns, and eat only dishes made from maize while breastfeeding to ensure that the child grows 'true flesh.'

No Maya raised in the traditional way would eat a meal that didn't include maize. Women do not let grains of maize fall on the ground or into an open fire. If it happens accidentally, the woman will gently pick up the grains and apologize to them.

KINGSHIP

For the Maya, creation wasn't a one-time event. They constantly repeated the primordial events through ceremonies timed to the sacred calendar. They saw the universe as a living thing that grows old, weakens and ultimately dies. Everything needed to be periodically recharged with life-bearing power. Mayan kings were seen as mediators to this renewal.

Relief carving of Mayan god

ERIC WHEATER

The Maize God is the most sacred of the deities because he gives his flesh so that humans may live, but this sacrifice must be repaid. A king was thus required to periodically give his own blood, which was believed to contain the essence of godhood itself.

Royal blood was collected on sheets of bark paper, then burned to release its divine essence. At times of crisis, such as the end of a calendar cycle, or upon the death of a king, the sacrifice had to be greater. This generally involved capturing nobles or royals from a neighboring Maya state and sacrificing them.

HIEROGLYPHIC WRITING

During the Classic period, the Mayan lowlands were divided into two major linguistic groups. In the Yucatán Peninsula and Belize people spoke Yucatec, and in the eastern highlands and Motagua Valley of Guatemala they spoke a language related to Chol. People in El Petén likely spoke both languages. Scholars have suggested that the written language throughout the Maya world was a form of Chol.

Long before the Spanish conquest, the Maya developed a sophisticated hieroglyphic script which is partly phonetic (glyphs representing sounds), and partly logographic (glyphs representing words).

Vibrant Mayan textiles are woven in Zunil (175), the Highlands

Contents

On the Road   4

Unravelling
Guatemala   5

Ancient Mayan
Culture   12

Getting Started   19

Itineraries   23

History   28

The Culture   42

Food & Drink   55

Environment   63

Guatemala City   70
History   71
Orientation   71
Information   71
Dangers & Annoyances   76
Sights   76
Walking Tour   79
Guatemala City for
Children   81
Tours   81
Sleeping   81
Eating   85
Drinking   87
Entertainment   88
Shopping   90
Getting There & Away   90
Getting Around   92

Antigua   94
History   95
Orientation   95

Information   99
Dangers & Annoyances   101
Sights   101
Activities   104
Language Courses   106
Tours   107
Festivals & Events   107
Sleeping   108
Eating   112
Drinking   115
Entertainment   115
Shopping   116
Getting There & Around   116
AROUND ANTIGUA   117
Jocotenango   117
San Lorenzo El Tejar   118
El Hato   118
Ciudad Vieja   118
San Antonio Aguas
Calientes   119
San Juan Comalapa   119
Santiago Sacatepéquez
& Sumpango   120

The Highlands   121
Climate   122
Getting Around   122
LAGO DE ATITLÁN   123
Tecpán   123
Sololá   125
Panajachel   125
Around Panajachel   136
Santiago Atitlán   137
San Pedro La Laguna   141
San Juan La Laguna   146
San Marcos La Laguna   146
Jaibalito   148
Santa Cruz La Laguna   148
QUICHÉ   149
Chichicastenango   149
Santa Cruz del Quiché   155
Sacapulas   157
Uspantán   157
Nebaj   158
WESTERN HIGHLANDS   160
Cuatro Caminos   161
Quetzaltenango   161
Around Quetzaltenango   174
Huehuetenango   181
Around Huehuetenango   185
La Mesilla   189

Regional Map Contents

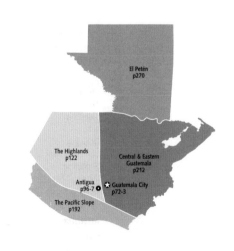

El Petén p270

The Highlands p122

Central & Eastern Guatemala p212

Antigua p96-7

Guatemala City p72-3

The Pacific Slope p192

Getting Started

Traveling in Guatemala requires little detailed planning. Bus transportation is plentiful – for many trips all you need do is show up and hop on the next bus. Accommodations are equally easy: unless you have your heart set on one hotel, booking ahead isn't usually necessary. The major exception is Semana Santa (Easter week), when the whole country takes a holiday and you need to book rooms, and often transportation, in advance.

See the Directory (p307) for more details on climate, festivals and events.

Guatemala is a country for any budget. It's popular with backpackers because you can survive on a few dollars a day, but also has many midrange lodgings and restaurants offering comfort and quality at good prices.

WHEN TO GO

There's no bad time for visiting Guatemala, though the rainy season – called *invierno* (winter) – makes unpaved roads more difficult from mid-May to mid-October, and into November and December in the north and east. In the lowland jungles of El Petén, the mud at this time will slow you down, guaranteed. Humidity – never low on the coasts or in El Petén – increases during the rainy season, too. In the highlands things get cold and damp during *invierno*, especially at night. It doesn't rain all day during the rainy season, but you can expect daily showers (downpours in the north) at the very least. The dry season – *verano* (summer) – is from about November to April, and this means sweltering heat in El Petén and along the coasts and comfortably warm days in the highlands. In the eastern parts of the country, rain is possible at any time.

HOW MUCH?

Three-hour, 2nd-class bus ride US$3

A week of Spanish classes with homestay US$100-200

Admission to Tikal US$7

Taxi from Guatemala City airport to city center US$10

Comfortable lakeside double with bathroom, Lago de Atitlán US$25-35

The height of the foreign tourist season is from Christmas to Easter. Things become acute around Christmas, New Year's and Easter, when Guatemalans take holidays too– in many places you'll need to book ahead. Another high season runs June to August, when throngs of North Americans descend on Guatemala to study Spanish and travel.

COSTS & MONEY

Prices in Guatemala are among the best in Central America. Beds in *hospedajes* (budget hotels) normally cost US$4 to US$5 per person. Markets

---

DON'T LEAVE HOME WITHOUT...

- Checking the visa situation (p318).
- Checking travel advisories (p310).
- Warm clothes for chilly highland nights.
- A flashlight (torch) for exploring caves, ruins, and your room when the electricity fails.
- Getting the whole 'it's OK to see other people while I'm away' thing absolutely straight with your partner.
- A mosquito net, if you're planning on hitting the jungle or sleeping in cheap rooms without screens.
- Insect repellent containing DEET (p331), for wet-season travels. You may want to take medication against malaria, too (p329).
- A small towel, for rooms without one.
- Telling your mother not to worry.

sell fruit and snacks for pennies, cheap eateries called *comedores* offer one-or two-course meals for US$3 to US$4, and bus trips cost around US$1 per hour. It's completely realistic to spend US$15 a day in Guatemala without too much hardship. If you want more comfort – nice rooms with private hot-water bathrooms and well-prepared food in pleasant surroundings, you'll still only pay around US$35 per person for a room and two – or even three – meals. Add in transportation, admission fees, some shopping and a few beers and you're looking at a total of around US$60 a day.

There are few bargains for solo travelers, as there often isn't much price difference between a single and double room. If it's practical, hook up with some other folks to defray room costs. Many places have rooms for three or four people, where the per-person price drops dramatically. In restaurants, you can save money by opting for set two- or three-course meals (the *menú del día*). On the road, public buses are far cheaper than the more comfortable tourist shuttle buses.

ATTENTION: THIS IS NOT GOD SPEAKING

We regret to inform you that some of the best experiences you have while traveling will have absolutely nothing to do with this book.

Travel at its best is discovery – people, places, foods and experiences – and it's very hard to get that when you're mentally chained to somebody else's opinions, no matter how knowledge-able they are.

Guatemala, to wheel out an old cliché, is a land of contrasts. Some towns in this book haven't changed in years. Others move so fast that what was true today will be kind of suspect next week and seriously outdated next year. The best, most updated information you're going to get is from locals and travelers on the scene. Talk it up.

We know there's a thing called the Lonely Planet Trail – the same faces in the same kinds of places from Mexico to Patagonia – and we're doing our best to diminish its excesses. Through-out this book you'll find 'Explore More' boxes, designed to give you just enough information to get off the trail without getting into trouble. We also try to put in back-door routes whenever feasible, for the adventurous types who can do without the shuttle bus and want to get into the thick of it.

But you people have to do your bit, too. The restaurants and hotels listed in this book appear because they were the best on offer at the time of research. By now there may well be better ones. If you like the look of a place that's not listed, go in and ask to see a room or a menu. You can always walk straight back out again. Guatemalans are used to foreigners doing far crazier things than that. If, on the other hand, you like what you see, then Bam! You've made a discovery, and that's guaranteed to feel better than following the pack around. It's great to hang out with other travelers, but nothing compares to doing your own thing.

Go with your instincts. If there's one restaurant full of foreigners and another beside it full of locals, it's an easy bet which is going to have the better food (and the better prices).

Independent travelers rock for many reasons, but mostly because they interact with the country they're in – they get to know the people, the history, the language and the culture and their travel becomes what it should be – a cultural exchange.

By spreading the money around, supporting a range of small, locally owned businesses and shying away from corporate multinationals, independent travelers can do far more for a country than tour groups and cruise ships ever will.

Anyway. It's just something to think about. No doubt you're here to have fun and maybe learn something. We hope this book helps. It *is* a guidebook, though – with the emphasis on guide. Look at it as a list of options – a leaping off point to help you create your own adventure. It's not a checklist of things you have to do, or (much as we appreciate the compliment) the Bible.

Happy travels, and if you *do* find something new and fantastic, shoot us an email.

TOP **10**

GUATEMALA

Guatemala City

Honduras

CELESTIAL EVENTS

The stars, moon and sun were important to the Maya, so while you're here, you might find yourself looking to the heavens for inspiration. Here are some good places to start:

1 Sunrise from Tajumulco volcano (p166)

2 Sunset with a daiquiri in hand from a hammock in Monterrico (p204)

3 Full moon parties in San Pedro La Laguna (p141)

4 Stargazing from El Mirador, deep in the Petén jungle (p303)

5 Watching the sun set over the Lago de Petén Itzá in Flores (p272)

6 Hiking the Santa María (p166) volcano by the light of the full moon

7 Aligning your chakras by starlight in a pyramid in San Marcos La Laguna (p146)

8 Bathing by the light of the moon in Quetzaltenango (p161), a moon so inspiring it had a song written about it (*La Luna de Xelajú*)

9 Catching the sunrise from Temple IV in Tikal (p288)

10 Listening to jazz in the Sunset Café (p134) in Panajachel as the sun disappears behind the volcanoes

BEST MAYAN READS

The Maya, past and present, are the theme of whole libraries of writing. Here are our 10 favorite books on them:

1 *The Maya,* Michael D Coe (p29)

2 *The Blood of Kings: Dynasty & Ritual in Maya Art,* Linda Schele and Mary Ellen Miller (p28)

3 *Scandals in the House of Birds: Shamans and Priests on Lake Atitlán,* Nathaniel Tarn (p49)

4 *I, Rigoberta Menchú: An Indian Woman in Guatemala,* Rigoberta Menchú (p38)

5 *Maya of Guatemala – Life and Dress,* Carmen L Pettersen (p53)

6 *Chronicle of the Maya Kings and Queens,* Simon Martin and Nikolai Grube (p32)

7 *Unfinished Conquest: The Guatemalan Tragedy,* Víctor Perera (p33)

8 *The Maya Textile Tradition,* Margot Blum Schevill (ed) (p53)

9 *Breaking the Maya Code,* Michael D Coe (p29)

10 *The Ancient Maya,* Robert J Sharer (p28)

PLACES TO DO SWEET FA

This book is full of stuff *to do,* and one option is getting out there and *doing it.* It is your holiday, though – don't forget the tried and trusted combination of a beer, a hammock and a good book (book optional). Here are our top 10 places to get a little down time:

1 El Remate (p285)

2 Tilapita (p191)

3 San Juan La Laguna (p146)

4 El Retiro (p225)

5 San Pedro (p141)

6 El Estor (p255

7 Luna Jaguar Spa Resort (p248)

8 The Río Sotzil (p224)

9 Finca Ixobel (p269)

10 Las Cumbres (p176)

TRAVEL LITERATURE

Ronald Wright's *Time among the Maya* is a story of travels through the whole Mayan region – Guatemala, Mexico, Belize and Honduras – delving into the glorious past and exploited present of the Maya and their obsession with time. Wright visits many of the places you'll visit, and his book is a fascinating read, even though written in the troubled 1980s.

Guatemalan Journey, by Stephen Benz, casts an honest and funny modern traveler's eye on the country. So does Anthony Daniels' *Sweet Waist of America*, also published as *South of the Border: Guatemalan Days*, where the medic author pinpoints some of the country's contradictions.

In *Sacred Monkey River*, Christopher Shaw explores by canoe the jungle-clad basin of the Río Usumacinta, a cradle of ancient Mayan civilization along the Mexico–Guatemala border.

Bird of Life, Bird of Death, by Jonathan Evan Maslow, subtitled *A Naturalist's Journey Through a Land of Political Turmoil*, tells of the author's searches for the resplendent quetzal (the 'bird of life') – which he found to be increasingly endangered, while the *zopilote* (vulture; the 'bird of death') flourished.

The 19th-century classic *Incidents of Travel in Central America, Chiapas and Yucatan*, by John L Stephens (illustrated by Frederick Catherwood), was the first serious look at many Mayan archaeological sites. It's a laborious but interesting read.

INTERNET RESOURCES

Gringo's Guide (www.thegringosguide.com) Useful info on the country's main travel destinations.

Guatemala (www.visitguatemala.com) Moderately interesting official site of Inguat, the national tourism institute.

La Ruta Maya Online (www.larutamayaonline.com) Reasonably useful mixed bag.

Lanic Guatemala (http://lanic.utexas.edu/la/ca/guatemala) The University of Texas' magnificent set of Guatemala links.

Lonely Planet (www.lonelyplanet.com) Succinct summaries on Guatemala travel; the popular Thorn Tree forum; and links to the most useful travel resources elsewhere on the web.

Xela Pages (www.xelapages.com) Good information on the highlands and coast and an excellent forum where you can get answers to even your most obscure questions.

Itineraries

CLASSIC ROUTES

HIGHLAND FLING   10 days/Guatemala City to Quetzaltenango

Guatemala's most spectacular scenery and strongest Mayan traditions await you along this well-traveled route.

From the capital head first to gorgeous **Antigua** (p94), enjoying the country's finest colonial architecture, the great restaurants and the big traveler and language-student scene. Several volcanoes wait to be climbed here. From Antigua move on to **Panajachel** (p125) on volcano-ringed **Lago de Atitlán** (p123). Hop in a boat to check out some of the quieter, more traditional Mayan villages around the lake such as **Santiago Atitlán** (p137), **San Pedro La Laguna** (p141), **San Marcos La Laguna** (p146) or **Santa Cruz La Laguna** (p148). Now head north to **Chichicastenango** (p149) for its huge Thursday and Sunday market. If you have extra time, detour north to **Nebaj** (p158), where you'll find great walking and a strong Mayan way of life amid stunning scenery.

From Chichicastenango follow the Interamericana Hwy west along the mountain ridges to **Quetzaltenango** (p161), Guatemala's clean, orderly, second city, with a host of intriguing villages, markets and natural wonders waiting within short bus rides away. From Quetzaltenango you can head south, or on to Mexico – perhaps via **Todos Santos Cuchumatán** (p185), a fascinating Mayan mountain town with great walking possibilities.

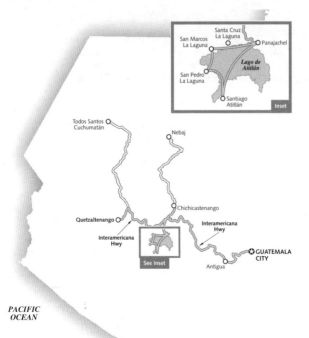

This 320km jaunt could take a few months if you stop off to learn some Spanish in Antigua, Panajachel, San Pedro La Laguna or Quetzaltenango, and you could more than double the distance with detours to Nebaj and Todos Santos Cuchumatán.

THE BIG LOOP   3 weeks

This trip takes you to the best of Guatemala's Mayan ruins, into its dense jungles and to some of its spectacular natural marvels.

Start out northeastward from Guatemala City and detour south into Honduras to see the great Mayan site of **Copán** (p236). Return to Guatemala and continue northeastward to another fine Mayan site, **Quiriguá** (p249) and on to the curious Garífuna enclave of **Lívingston** (p261) on the sweaty Caribbean coast. Take a boat up the jungle-lined **Río Dulce** (p264) to **Río Dulce town** (p251), then turn north up Hwy 13 to stay and chill out at **Finca Ixobel** (p269) before continuing to **Flores** (p272), a quaint small town on an island in the Lago de Petén Itzá. From Flores, head for **Tikal** (p288), the most majestic of all Mayan sites. Spend a night at Tikal itself or nearby **El Remate** (p285). While in the Flores–Tikal area, you should have time to take in further impressive Mayan sites such as **Yaxhá** (p297) and **Uaxactún** (p296).

From Flores head southwest to the relaxed riverside town of **Sayaxché** (p299), which is at the center of another group of intriguing Mayan sites – **Ceibal** (p300), **Aguateca** (p302) and **Dos Pilas** (p302). The road south from Sayaxché is now nearly all paved to **Chisec** (p227) and **Cobán** (p216), jumping-off points for a whole series of pristine natural wonders such as jungle-ringed **Laguna Lachuá** (p228), the **Grutas de Lanquín** (p224) and the turquoise lagoons and waterfalls of **Semuc Champey** (p225).

This 1900km round trip takes you to all the top destinations in the center, east and north of the country. Really pushing, you might do it in two weeks, but if you have four, you'll enjoy it more.

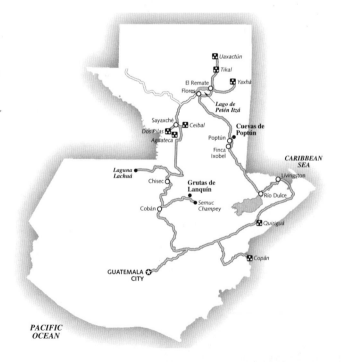

HAMMOCK FRENZY   1 week

The beaches in Guatemala take some getting used to. Black volcanic sand makes them look dirty (and some are), but there are plenty of small, laid-back towns that are great for splashing around, surfing, cruising the mangroves and just generally chilling out. There's no coast road as such, so you'll find yourself popping in and out from the main highway all the way down the coast.

Starting way up near the Mexican border, make your way to **Tilapita** (p191), not to be confused with Tilapa – the former is far prettier, with exactly one hotel at the time of writing.

From there it's back out onto the highway, east to Mazatenango and on another bus for **Tulate** (p198), the best beach along here for swimming and bodysurfing. From Tulate, there's no need to go back to the main highway – just catch a bus back to La Máquina, then another on to **Chiquistepeque** (p199), a lovely, untouched stretch of beach where you can volunteer with the French-Guatemalan NGO, Proyecto Hamaca y Pescado, working with the local community.

Moving on, it's back out to the highway, heading east with a bus change in Siquinala for the surfers' haven of **Sipacate** (p203).

The road could end at your next stop, **Monterrico** (p204), favorite of Guatemalan weekenders and Antigua language students alike. If you haven't had enough yet, make your way to **Las Lisas** (p208), where a gorgeous, exclusive island getaway near the Salvadoran border awaits.

It's only 220km as the turtle swims from the Mexican to the Salvadoran border – you could do it in a week, but what's the rush?

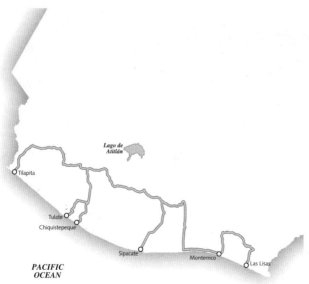

ROADS LESS TRAVELED

ACROSS THE IXCÁN   2 days/Huehuetenango to Laguna Lachuá

Now that the road from Huehuetenango to Cobán is an easy one-day jaunt, adventure junkies and chicken-bus lovers have been bemoaning the loss of a difficult-but-rewarding trip.

Fear not. The route from Huehue to Laguna Lachuá pushes all the same buttons – bad roads, stunning scenery, fascinating villages and very, very few tourists.

Buses run, but less frequently than elsewhere. If you're thinking about going this route, you should have some spare time and be prepared to rumble around in the back of a pickup truck now and then.

Starting from **Huehuetenango** (p181) it's an easy, scenic ride up into the Cuchumatanes on a good road to **Soloma** (p187). Say goodbye to the asphalt here. From Soloma the road undulates over hills before reaching **Santa Eulalia** (p188), a pretty and interesting town where you may want to pause for a couple of hours.

Then it's up again, through pastures and pine forests to the town of **San Mateo Ixtatán** (p188), a good place to break for the night because transport drops off in the late afternoon and there are a few interesting sights around town.

Next day, it's a slow cruise downhill to **Barillas** (p189), from where you should be able to grab a bus or at least a pickup for the terrible-roads-but-great-scenery ride across to Playa Grande and **Laguna Lachuá** (p228).

There are serious plans to put in a highway along this 150km stretch between Huehue and Playa Grande – get in while the adventure's still alive!

TAILORED TRIPS

THE MAYA THEN & NOW

In **Guatemala City** (p70), your start and finish, don't miss the museums dedicated to Mayan archaeology and textiles. Head west to the ruins at **Iximché** (p123), and on to **Lago de Atitlán** (p123), surrounded by traditional villages such as **Santiago Atitlán** (p137). Don't miss the big Mayan markets at **Sololá** (p125) and at **Chichicastenango** (p149), also the scene of unique religious practices. Northward, visit the old K'iche' Mayan capital **K'umarcaaj** (p155), still an important center for Mayan rites. Westward, **Quetzaltenango** (p161) is a base for visiting many traditional villages (for example, **Zunil**, p175) and the sacred **Laguna Chicabal** (p180). Further north, see the old Mam Mayan capital, **Zaculeu** (p181), en route to **Todos Santos Cuchumatán** (p185), a mountain village with strong traditions and uniquely striking costumes.

Next, head east along mountain roads to **Nebaj** (p158), a center of the colorful Ixil Maya, and to **San Cristóbal Verapaz** (p223). Head north through Cobán to **Sayaxché** (p299), close to the ancient Mayan sites **Ceibal** (p300), **Aguateca** (p302) and **Dos Pilas** (p302), then on to **Flores** (p272) and the mother of all Mayan cities, **Tikal** (p288). In the Petén jungles, you can explore remoter archaeological sites such as **Yaxhá** (p297), **Uaxactún** (p296), **El Zotz** (p305) and (if you have stamina for four or five days' walking) **El Mirador** (p306).

Head back to Guatemala City via **Quiriguá** (p249) and, just over the Honduras border, **Copán** (p236).

NATURAL WONDERS

Tone up your muscles by climbing a couple of the volcanoes around Antigua: the active **Pacaya** (p104) and the mighty **Acatenango** (p105). Move on to **Lago de Atitlán** (p123), certainly one of the most beautiful lakes in the world. Continue westward to bag more volcanoes around Quetzaltenango – say, **Santa María** (p166) and **Tajumulco** (p166), the highest peak in Central America. Head north to experience the beauty of the Cuchumatanes mountains around **Todos Santos Cuchumatán** (p185) and **Nebaj** (p158). East from Nebaj is **Cobán** (p216), stepping stone for the lovely lagoons and waterfalls of **Semuc Champey** (p225), the extensive cave system of the **Grutas de Lanquín** (p224), the forest trails of the **Biotopo del Quetzal** (p215) and the jungle-surrounded **Laguna Lachuá** (p228). Move north to the thick jungles of El Petén, exploring the rich bird and plant life of **Laguna Petexbatún** (p301). The magnificent ancient Mayan city **Tikal** (p288) and the area around **El Perú** ruins (p303) are two of the finest spots in the country for observing tropical wildlife. On your way back south, pause for cave exploration at **Finca Ixobel** (p269), a boat ride along the beautiful, jungle-shrouded **Río Dulce** (p264) and a side trip to the **Refugio Bocas del Polochic** (p256), which supports over 300 bird species.

History

ARCHAIC PERIOD (UP TO 2000 BC)

It's accepted that, barring a few Vikings in the north and conceivable direct transpacific contact with Southeast Asia, the prehispanic inhabitants of the Americas arrived from Siberia. They came in several migrations between perhaps 60,000 and 8000 BC, during the last ice age, crossing land that is now submerged beneath the Bering Strait, then gradually moving southward.

These early inhabitants hunted mammoths, fished and gathered wild foods. The ice age was followed by a hot, dry period in which the mammoths' natural pastureland disappeared and the wild nuts and berries became scarce. The primitive inhabitants had to find some other way to survive, so they sought out favorable microclimates and invented agriculture, in which maize (corn) became king. The inhabitants of what are now Guatemala and Mexico successfully hybridized this native grass and planted it alongside beans, tomatoes, chili peppers and squash (marrow). They wove baskets to carry in the harvest, and they domesticated turkeys and dogs for food. These early homebodies used crude stone tools and primitive pottery, and shaped simple clay fertility figurines.

PRECLASSIC PERIOD (2000 BC–AD 250)

The improvement in the food supply led to an increase in population, a higher standard of living and more time to experiment with agricultural techniques and artistic niceties. Decorative pots and healthier, fatter corn strains were produced. Even at the beginning of the Preclassic period, people in Guatemala spoke an early form of the Mayan language. These early Maya also decided that living in caves and under palm fronds was passé, so they invented the *na*, or thatched Mayan hut – still used today throughout much of the country. Where spring floods were a problem, a family would build its *na* on a mound of earth. When a family member died, burial took place right there in the living room, after which the deceased attained the rank of honored ancestor.

The Copán Valley (in present-day Honduras) had its first proto-Mayan settlers by about 1100 BC, and a century later settlements on the Guatemalan Pacific coast were developing a hierarchical society.

By the middle Preclassic period (800–300 BC) there were rich villages in the Copán Valley, and villages had been founded at what came to be the majestic city (and modern Guatemala's number one tourist attraction), Tikal, amid the jungles of El Petén, northern Guatemala. Trade routes developed, with coastal peoples exchanging salt and seashells for highland tribes' tool-grade obsidian. A brisk trade in ceramic pots and vessels flourished throughout the region.

As the Maya honed their agricultural techniques, including using fertilizer and elevated fields to boost production, a rich, noble class emerged that indulged in such extravagances as resident scribes and artists – and temples, which consisted of raised platforms of earth topped by a thatch-roofed shelter very much like a normal *na*. The local potentate was buried beneath the shelter, increasing the site's sacred power. Pyramid E-VII-sub at Uaxactún, 23km north of Tikal, was a good example of this; others have been found at Tikal itself and El Mirador, another Petén site that flourished during the

The Ancient Maya, by Robert J Sharer, is a 1990s update of Sylvanus G Morley's classic 1940s tome of the same name. The first half of the book treats the Mayan story chronologically; the second half discusses different aspects of their culture. The book is admirably clear and uncomplicated.

The Blood of Kings: Dynasty & Ritual in Maya Art, by Linda Schele and Mary Ellen Miller, is a heavily and fascinatingly illustrated guide to the art and culture of the ancient Maya, with particular emphasis on sacrifices, bloodletting, the ball game, torture of captives and other macabre aspects of Mayan culture.

TIMELINE	11,000 BC or earlier	Around 250 BC to AD 100
	First human occupation of Guatemala	Early Mayan cities El Mirador and Kaminaljuyú flourish

late Preclassic period (300 BC–AD 250). Kaminaljuyú, in Guatemala City, reached its peak from about 400 BC to AD 100, with thousands of inhabitants and scores of temples built on earth mounds.

In El Petén, where limestone was abundant, the Maya began to build platform temples from stone. As each succeeding local potentate had to have a bigger temple, larger and larger platforms were built over existing platforms, eventually forming huge pyramids with a *na*-style shelter on top. The potentate was buried deep within the stack of platforms. El Tigre pyramid at El Mirador, 18 stories high, is believed to be the largest ever built by the Maya. More and more pyramids were built around large plazas, in much the same way that the common people clustered their thatched houses in family compounds facing a communal open space. The stage was set for the flowering of classic Mayan civilization.

Mayan priests used a variety of drugs during divination rituals – ranging from fermented maize and wild tobacco to hallucinogenic mushrooms.

CLASSIC PERIOD (AD 250–900)

During the Classic period the Maya produced prehispanic America's most brilliant civilization in an area stretching from Copán, in modern Honduras, through Guatemala and Belize to Mexico's Yucatán Peninsula. The great ceremonial and cultural centers included Copán; Quiriguá in southern Guatemala; Kaminaljuyú; Tikal, Uaxactún, Río Azul, El Perú, Yaxhá, Dos Pilas and Piedras Negras, all in El Petén; Caracol in Belize; Yaxchilán and Palenque in Chiapas, Mexico; and Calakmul, Uxmal and Chichén Itzá on the Yucatán Peninsula. All these sites can be visited, with varying degrees of difficulty, today. Around the beginning of the Classic period, Mayan astronomers began using the elaborate Long Count calendar to date all of human history (see p31).

While Tikal began to assume a primary role in Guatemalan history around AD 250, El Mirador had been mysteriously abandoned about a century earlier. Some scholars believe a severe drought hastened this great city's demise.

The Classic Maya were organized into numerous city-states. Each city-state had its noble house, headed by a priestly king who placated the gods by shedding his blood in ceremonies during which he pierced his tongue, penis or ears with sharp objects. (For more on these rites and other Mayan beliefs, see p47.) As sacred head of his community, the king also had to lead his soldiers into battle against rival cities, capturing prisoners for use in human sacrifices. Many a king perished in a battle he was too old to fight. A typical Mayan city functioned as the religious, political and market hub for the surrounding farming hamlets. Its ceremonial center focused on plazas surrounded by tall temple pyramids and lower buildings – so-called palaces – with warrens of small rooms. Stelae and altars were carved with dates, histories and elaborate human and divine figures. Stone causeways called *sacbeob*, probably built for ceremonial use, led out from the plazas.

The Maya, by Michael D Coe, is probably the best single-volume, not-too-long telling of the ancient Maya story – learned and careful, yet readable and well illustrated. Coe's *Breaking the Maya Code* recounts the modern decipherment of ancient Mayan writing, and his *Reading the Maya Glyphs* will help you read ancient inscriptions.

MAYAN BEAUTY

The ancient Maya considered flat foreheads and crossed eyes beautiful. To achieve these effects, children would have boards bound tight to their heads and wax beads tied to dangle before their eyes. Both men and women made cuts in their skin to gain much-desired scar markings, and women sharpened their teeth to points, another mark of beauty – which may also have helped them to keep their men in line!

AD 230	**562**
King Yax Moch Xoc of Tikal establishes the dynasty that will make Tikal the dominant city of the southern Mayan world	Leading Mayan city Tikal defeated by rivals Calakmul and Caracol

In the first part of the Classic period, most of the city-states were probably grouped into two loose military alliances centered on Calakmul, in Mexico's Campeche state, and Tikal. Like Kaminaljuyú and Copán, Tikal had strong connections with the powerful city of Teotihuacán, near modern Mexico City. When Teotihuacán declined, Tikal's rival Calakmul allied with Caracol to defeat a weakened Tikal in 562. However, Tikal returned to prominence under a resolute and militarily successful king named Moon Double Comb, also known as Ah Cacau (Lord Chocolate), who ruled from 682 to 734. Tikal conquered Calakmul in 695.

> Archaeologists estimate that only 10% of Tikal – one of the country's biggest and most famous Mayan sites – has been uncovered.

In the late 8th century, trade between Mayan states started to shrink and conflict began to grow. By the early 10th century the cities of Tikal, Yaxchilán, Copán, Quiriguá and Piedras Negras had reverted to little more than minor towns or even villages, and much of El Petén was abandoned. Many explanations, including population pressure and ecological damage, have been offered for the Classic Mayan collapse. Current theories point to three droughts, each lasting several years, around 810, 860 and 910, as major culprits.

POSTCLASSIC PERIOD (900–1524)

Some of the Maya who abandoned El Petén must have moved southwest into the highlands of Guatemala. In the 13th and 14th centuries they were joined by Maya-Toltec migrants or invaders from the Tabasco or Yucatán areas of Mexico (the Toltecs were a militaristic culture from central Mexico with powerful, wide-ranging influence). Groups of these newcomers set up a series of rival states in the Guatemalan highlands: the most prominent were the K'iche' (or Quiché; capital, K'umarcaaj, near modern Santa Cruz del Quiché), the Kaqchiquels (capital, Iximché, near Tecpán); the Mam (capital, Zaculeu, near Huehuetenango); the Tz'utujil (capital, Chuitinamit, near Santiago Atitlán); and the Poqomam (capital, Mixco Viejo, north of Guatemala City). All these sites can be visited today. Another group from the Yucatán, the Itzáes, wound up at Lago Petén Itzá in the Petén region, settling in part on the island that is today called Flores.

> During the late Classic period, population density in Guatemala was over 950 people per square kilometer.

SPANISH CONQUEST

Spaniards under Hernán Cortés defeated the Aztec Empire based at Tenochtitlán (modern Mexico City) in 1521. It only took a couple of years for the conquistadors to turn to Guatemala in their search for wealth. Pedro de Alvarado, one of Cortés' most brutal lieutenants, entered Guatemala in 1524 with about 600 Spanish and Mexican soldiers and the unanswerable advantages of firearms and horses. Alvarado defeated a small K'iche' force

---

PLAYTIME WITH THE MAYA

The recreation most favored by the Maya was *juego de pelota* (a ball game), courts for which can still be seen at many archaeological sites. It's thought that the players had to try to keep a hard rubber ball airborne using any part of their body other than their hands, head or feet. A wooden bat may also have been used. In some regions, a team was victorious if one of its players hit the ball through stone rings with holes little larger than the ball itself.

The ball game was taken very seriously and was often used to settle disputes between rival communities. On occasion, it is thought, the captain of the losing team was punished by execution.

682

King Moon Double Comb, or Lord Chocolate, ascends Tikal's throne, launching a revival for Tikal

695

Tikal conquers Calakmul

> **MAYAN COUNTING SYSTEM**
>
> The Mayan counting system's most important use – and the one you will encounter during your travels – was in writing dates. It's an elegantly simple system: dots are used to count from one to four; a horizontal bar signifies five; a bar with one dot above it is six, a bar with two dots is seven, and so forth. Two bars signifies 10, three bars 15. Nineteen, the highest common number, is three bars stacked up and topped by four dots.
>
> To signify larger numbers the Maya stack numbers from zero to 19 on top of each other. Thus the lowest number in the stack shows values from one to 19, the next position up signifies 20 times its face value, the third position up signifies 20 times 20 times its face value. The three positions together can signify numbers up to 7999. By adding more positions one can count as high as needed. Zero is represented by a stylized picture of a shell or some other object.
>
> The Maya likely used the counting system from day to day by writing on the ground, the tip of the finger creating a dot, and using the edge of the hand to make a bar.

on the Pacific Slope and then the much larger main K'iche' army near Xelajú (modern Quetzaltenango) soon afterwards – killing the K'iche' leader Tecún Umán in hand-to-hand combat, or so legend has it. Alvarado then sacked the K'iche' capital, K'umarcaaj. The K'iche' had failed to persuade their traditional local enemies, the Kaqchiquels, to join forces against the invaders. Instead, the Kaqchiquels allied with the Spanish against the K'iche' and Tz'utujils, and so the Spanish set up their first Guatemalan headquarters next door to the Kaqchiquel capital, Iximché. The name Guatemala is a Spanish corruption of Quauhtlemallan, the name Alvarado's Mexican allies gave to Iximché (Land of Many Trees).

The romance between the Spanish and the Kaqchiquels soured when the latter couldn't meet the ever-increasing demands for gold, and Alvarado – not surprisingly – turned on them, burning Iximché to the ground. And so it went throughout Guatemala as the megalomaniacal Alvarado sought fortune and renown by murdering and subjugating the Mayan population. The one notable exception was the Rabinal of present-day Baja Verapaz, who survived with their preconquest identity intact and remain one of Guatemala's most traditional groups to this day.

Mesoweb (www.mesoweb .com) is a great resource on the Maya, past and present.

Alvarado moved his base from Tecpán to Santiago de los Caballeros (now called Ciudad Vieja) in 1527, but shortly after his death while in Mexico in 1541, Ciudad Vieja was destroyed by a flood. The Spanish capital was relocated under the same name to a new site nearby, known today as Antigua.

COLONIAL PERIOD (1524–1821)

The Spanish effectively enslaved Guatemala's indigenous people to work what had been their own land for the benefit of the invaders, just as they did throughout the hemisphere. Refusal to work the land meant death. With the most fertile land and a labor force to work it firmly in hand, the colonists believed themselves omnipotent and behaved accordingly. That is to say, badly.

Enter the Catholic Church and Dominican friar Bartolomé de Las Casas. Las Casas had been in the Caribbean and Latin America since 1502 and had witnessed firsthand the near complete genocide of the indigenous populations of Cuba and Hispaniola. Convinced he could catch more flies with honey

To translate a date using the Mayan calendar, visit the Mayan Date Calculator at www.pauahtun .org/Calendar/tools.

9th century	**13th & 14th centuries**
The collapse of Classic Mayan civilization	Toltec-Maya migrants from southeast Mexico establish kingdoms in the Guatemalan highlands

THE MAYAN CALENDAR

The ancient Maya's astronomical observations and calculations were uncannily accurate. They could pinpoint eclipses and their Venus cycle erred by only two hours for periods covering 500 years.

Time was, in fact, the basis of the Mayan religion. They believed the current world to be just one of a succession of worlds, each destined to end in cataclysm and be succeeded by another. This cyclicity enabled the future to be predicted by looking at the past. Most Mayan cities were constructed in strict accordance with celestial movements, and observatories were not uncommon.

Perhaps the best analog to the Mayan calendar is the gears of a mechanical watch, where small wheels mesh with larger wheels, which in turn mesh with other sets of wheels to record the passage of time.

Tzolkin or Cholq'ij or Tonalamatl

The two smallest wheels in this Mayan calendar 'watch' were two cycles of 13 days and 20 days. Each of the 13 days bore a number from one to 13; each of the 20 days bore a name such as Imix, Ik, Akbal or Xan. As these two 'wheels' meshed, the passing days received unique names. For example, when day one of the 13-day cycle fell on the day named Imix in the 20-day cycle, the day was called 1 Imix. Next came 2 Ik, then 3 Akbal etc. After 13 days, the first cycle began again at one, even though the 20-day name cycle still had seven days to run, so the 14th day was 1 Ix, followed by 2 Men, 3 Cib etc. When the 20-day name cycle was finished, it began again with 8 Imix, 9 Ik, 10 Akbal etc. The permutations continued for a total of 260 days, ending on 13 Ahau, before beginning again on 1 Imix.

The two small 'wheels' of 13 and 20 days thus created a larger 'wheel' of 260 days, called a *tzolkin, cholq'ij* or *tonalamatl.*

Visitors interested in Mayan culture might want to head to one of the towns still observing the *tzolkin* calendar (such as Momostenango or Todos Santos Cuchumatán) for Wajshakib Batz, the start of the *tzolkin* year. It falls on December 19, 2007; September 4, 2008; May 22, 2009; February 6, 2010; October 24, 2010; and July 11, 2011. Outsiders are not necessarily invited to join in the ceremonies, as they tend to be sacred affairs, but it's still a good time to be in one of these traditional towns.

Vague Year (Haab)

Another set of wheels in the Mayan calendar watch comprised 18 'months' of 20 days each, which formed the basis of the solar year or *haab* (or *ab'*). Each month had a name – Pop, Uo, Zip, Zotz, Tzec etc – and each day had a number from zero (the first day, or 'seating', of the month) to 19.

Chronicle of the Maya Kings and Queens, by Simon Martin and Nikolai Grube (2000), tells in superbly illustrated detail the histories of 11 of the most important Mayan city-states and their rulers.

than vinegar and horrified at what he saw in the Indies, Las Casas appealed to Carlos V of Spain to stop the violence. Las Casas described the fatal treatment of the population in his influential tract *A Very Brief Account of the Destruction of the Indies.* The king agreed with Las Casas that the indigenous people should no longer be regarded as chattels and should be considered vassals of the king (in this way they could also pay taxes). Carlos V immediately enacted the New Laws of 1542, which technically ended the system of forced labor. In reality, forced labor continued, but wanton waste of Mayan lives ceased. Las Casas and other Dominican, Franciscan and Augustinian friars went about converting the Maya to Christianity – a Christianity that became imbued with many aspects of animism and ceremony from the indigenous belief system.

A large portion of the Church's conversion 'success' can be attributed to the pacifism with which it approached Mayan communities, the relative

---

1524

Spaniards under Pedro de Alvarado conquer Guatemala

1527

Alvarado establishes his capital at Santiago de los Caballeros (modern Ciudad Vieja, near Antigua)

So the month Pop ran from 0 Pop (the 'seating' of the month Pop), 1 Pop, 2 Pop and so forth to 19 Pop, and was followed by 0 Uo, 1 Uo and so on.

Eighteen months, each of 20 days, equals 360 days, a period known as a *tun;* the Maya added a special omen-filled five-day period called the *uayeb* at the end of this cycle in order to produce a solar calendar of 365 days. Anthropologists today call this the Vague Year, its vagueness coming from the fact that the solar year is actually 365.24 days long (the reason for the extra day in leap years of our Gregorian calendar).

Calendar Round

The huge wheels of the *tzolkin* and the *haab* also meshed, so that each day actually had a *tzolkin* name-and-number and a *haab* name-and-number used together: 1 Imix 5 Pop, 2 Ik 6 Pop, 3 Akbal 7 Pop and so on – a total of 18,980 day-name permutations. These repeated every 52 solar years, a period called the Calendar Round. The Calendar Round was the dating system used not only by the Maya but also by the Olmecs, Aztecs and Zapotecs of ancient Mexico. It's still in use in some traditional Guatemalan villages, and you can see why a special Mayan elder has to be designated to keep track of it and alert his community to important days in this complex system.

Long Count

For a people as obsessed with counting time as the Maya, the Calendar Round has one serious limitation: it only lasts 52 years. After that, it starts again, and there is no way to distinguish a day named 1 Imix 5 Pop in one 52-year Calendar Round cycle from the identically named day in the next cycle.

Hence the Long Count, which the Maya developed around the start of the Classic period (about AD 250). The Long Count uses the *tun*, the year of 18 20-day months, but ignores the *uayeb*, the final five-day period that follows the *tun* in the Vague Year. In Long Count terminology, a day was a *kin* (meaning 'sun'). A 20-*kin* 'month' is called a *uinal,* and 18 *uinals* make a *tun*. Twenty *tuns* make a *katun* (7200 days, nearly 20 of our Gregorian solar years), and 20 *katuns* make a *baktun* (144,000 days, about 394 years). Further gigantic units above *baktun* were only used for grandiose effect, as when a very self-important king wanted to note exactly when his extremely important reign took place in the awesome expanse of time. Curiously for us today, 13 *baktuns* (1,872,000 days, or 5125 Gregorian solar years) form something called a Great Cycle, and the first Great Cycle began on August 11, 3114 BC (some authorities say August 13) – which means it will end on December 23 (or 25), AD 2012. The end of a Great Cycle was a time fraught with great significance – usually fearsome. Stay tuned around Christmas 2012.

respect it extended to traditional beliefs, and the education it provided in indigenous languages. In short, the Catholic Church became extremely powerful in Guatemala quite quickly. No clearer evidence existed of this than the 38 houses of worship (including a cathedral) built in Antigua, which became the colonial capital of all Central America from Chiapas to Costa Rica. But Antigua was razed by a devastating earthquake on July 29, 1773. The capital was moved 25km east to its present site, Guatemala City.

INDEPENDENCE

By the time thoughts of independence from Spain began stirring among Guatemalans, society was already rigidly stratified. At the very top of the colonial hierarchy were the European-born Spaniards; next were the *criollos*, people born in Guatemala of Spanish blood; below them were the ladinos

Unfinished Conquest: The Guatemalan Tragedy, by Guatemalan Víctor Perera, interweaves personal experiences with an exploration of the current situation of the Guatemalan Maya and the long history preceding it.

1541	**1542**
Santiago de los Caballeros destroyed by flood; a new city (now Antigua) is founded.	Spain enacts the New Laws, officially banning forced labor in its colonies

or *mestizos,* people of mixed Spanish and Mayan blood; and at the bottom were the Maya and black slaves. Only the European-born Spaniards had any real power, but the *criollos* lorded it over the ladinos, who in turn exploited the indigenous population who, as you read this, still remain on the bottom rung of the socioeconomic ladder.

In their remote hideaway at Flores, the Itzáes managed to remain unconquered by the Spanish until 1697, far later than any other people in Guatemala or Mexico.

Angered at being repeatedly passed over for advancement, Guatemalan *criollos* took advantage of Spanish weakness following a Napoleonic invasion in 1808, and in 1821 successfully rose in revolt. Unfortunately, independence changed little for Guatemala's indigenous communities, who remained under the control of the church and the landowning elite. Despite cuddly-sounding democratic institutions and constitutions, Guatemalan politics has continued to this day to be dominated almost without pause by corrupt, brutal strongmen in the Pedro de Alvarado tradition, for the benefit of the commercial, military, landowning and bureaucratic ruling classes. While the niceties of democracy are observed, real government often takes place by means of intimidation and secret military activities.

Mexico, which was recently independent, quickly annexed Guatemala, but in 1823 Guatemala reasserted its independence and led the formation

---

UNCLE SAM GOES SOUTH

The United States' role in the 1954 coup that brought down democratically elected president Jacobo Arbenz is well-known, but that's not all, folks. Here's a little sampler of some of the work that's been done since then, in the name of freedom, justice and anticommunism:

- **1962** Conservative Guatemala City newspaper *El Imparcial* reports that US Military presence in Izabal and Zacapa is expanded in response to popular protests against the Fuentes government. Forces are lead by Green Berets of Puerto Rican and Mexican descent to make the US presence less conspicuous.

- **1963** General Ydigoras is overthrown in a coup by Colonel Peralta Azurdia. Veteran Latin American correspondent Georgie Anne Geyer reports that 'Top sources within the Kennedy administration have revealed the U.S. instigated and supported the 1963 coup.'

- **1966** US Colonel John D Webber Jr takes command of the American military mission in Guatemala. *Time* magazine reports that Webber expands counterinsurgency training and brings in US Jeeps, trucks, communications equipment and helicopters to give the army more firepower and mobility, and breathes new life into the army's 'civic-action' program.

- **1968–72** Anticommunist violence intensifies. Amnesty International estimates that in this period, between 3000 and 80,000 Guatemalans are killed by the police, the military and right-wing 'death squads'. Tortured, mutilated or burned bodies are found in mass graves or dropped into the Pacific from airplanes; whole villages are rounded up, suspected of supporting the guerrillas, the adult males taken away, never to be seen again.

- **1970** By now, according to the US Agency for International Development, over 30,000 Guatemalan police personnel have received training from the US's Office of Public Safety (OPS). The OPS trained officers in 'interrogation techniques' such as putting an insecticide-filled hood over the victim's head, or electrocuting their testicles.

- **1981** General Vernon Walters, former deputy director of the CIA, on a visit to Guatemala claims that the US hopes to help the Guatemalan government defend 'peace and liberty'. The *New York Times* and *Washington Post* report that Guatemalan security forces, official and

---

of the United Provinces of Central America (July 1, 1823), along with El Salvador, Nicaragua, Honduras and Costa Rica. Their union, torn by civil strife from the start, lasted only until 1840 before breaking up into its constituent states. This era brought prosperity to the *criollos* but worsened the lot of the Guatemalan Maya. The end of Spanish rule meant that the crown's few liberal safeguards, which had afforded the Maya a minimal protection, were abandoned. Mayan claims to ancestral lands were largely ignored and huge tobacco, sugar-cane and henequen (agave rope fiber) plantations were set up. The Maya, though technically and legally free, were enslaved by debt peonage to the big landowners.

THE LIBERALS & CARRERA

The ruling classes of independent Central America split into two camps: the elite conservatives, including the Catholic church and the large land-owners, and the liberals, who had been the first to advocate independence and who opposed the vested interests of the conservatives.

During the short existence of the United Provinces of Central America, liberal president Francisco Morazán (1830–39) from Honduras instituted

Guatemala in the Spanish Colonial Period, by Oakah L Jones Jr, is a comprehensive assessment of the 300 years of Spanish dominance. Where this book leaves off, Paul Dosal's Doing Business with the Dictators: A Political History of United Fruit in Guatemala, 1899–1944 takes over.

---

unofficial, massacre at least 2000 peasants (accompanied by the usual syndrome of torture, mutilation and decapitation), destroy several villages, assassinate 76 officials of the opposition Christian Democratic Party, scores of trade unionists, and at least six Catholic priests.

■ **1982** Using the loopholes in legislation against supporting dictators, the Reagan administration supplies $13 million worth of military supplies, according to the *New York Times*. The Green Berets continue instructing Guatemalan Army officers in the finer points of warfare.

■ **1981–83** Despite the continuing embargo, the *London Guardian* reports that the Guatemala's Air Force helicopter fleet increases from eight to 27, all of them American made. The *Guardian* also reports that Guatemalan officers are once again being trained at the notorious US School of the Americas, then based in Panama.

■ **1982** General Efraín Ríos Montt seizes power. The *New York Times* reports that in the next six months, 2600 peasants are massacred. Amnesty International estimates that during his 17-month reign, more than 400 villages are brutally wiped off the map. In December 1982 Reagan, referring to allegations of human-rights abuses, is quoted in the *New York Times* as saying that the Guatemalan leader is receiving 'a bad deal'.

■ **1988** Newly opened Guatemalan newspaper *La Época* is blown up by US-backed government terrorists. Julio Godoy, a journalist from the paper, says 'One is tempted to believe that some people in the White House worship Aztec gods – with the offering of Central American blood.'

■ **1989** Sister Dianna Ortiz, a nun, is kidnapped, burned with cigarettes, raped repeatedly, and lowered into a pit full of corpses and rats. The *Los Angeles Times* reports her claims that a fair-skinned man who spoke with an American accent seemed to be in charge.

■ **1990** The Bush administration, in a show of public anger over the state-backed killing of a US businessman, cuts off military aid to Guatemala, but according to the *New York Times* secretly allows the CIA to provide millions of dollars to the military government to make up for the loss. The annual payments of $5 million to $7 million continue into the Clinton administration. Combined sources put the murder toll since Arbenz's overthrow at around 200,000.

1823–40	1870s
Guatemala is part of the United Provinces of Central America	Liberal governments modernize Guatemala but turn indigenous lands over to coffee plantations

reforms aimed at ending the overwhelming power of the church, the division of society into a *criollo* upper class and an indigenous lower class, and the region's impotence in world markets. This liberal program was echoed by Guatemalan chief of state Mariano Gálvez (1831–38).

But unpopular economic policies, heavy taxes and a cholera epidemic led to an indigenous uprising that brought its leader, a conservative ladino pig farmer, Rafael Carrera, to power. Carrera held power from 1844 to 1865 and undid much of what Morazán and Gálvez had achieved. He also naively allowed Britain to take control of Belize in exchange for construction of a road between Guatemala City and Belize City. The road was never built, and Guatemala's claims for compensation were never resolved, leading to a quarrel that festers to this day.

LIBERAL REFORMS OF BARRIOS

The liberals returned to power in the 1870s, first under Miguel García Granados, next under Justo Rufino Barrios, a rich young coffee plantation owner who held the title of president, but ruled as a dictator (1873–79). Under Barrios, Guatemala made strides toward modernization, with construction of roads, railways, schools and a modern banking system. Everything possible was done to stimulate coffee production. Peasants in good coffee-growing areas (up to a 1400m altitude on the Pacific Slope) were forced off their land to make way for new coffee *fincas* (plantations), while those living above 1400m (mostly Maya) were forced to work on the *fincas*. This created migrant labor patterns that still exist among some highland groups. Under Barrios' successors a small group of landowning and commercial families came to control the economy, foreign companies were given generous concessions, and political opponents were censored, imprisoned or exiled by the extensive police force.

ESTRADA CABRERA & MINERVA

Manuel Estrada Cabrera ruled from 1898 to 1920, and his dictatorial style, while bringing progress in technical matters, placed a heavy burden on all but the ruling oligarchy. He fancied himself a bringer of light and culture to a backward land, styling himself the 'Teacher and Protector of Guatemalan Youth.'

Daniel Wilkinson, in *Silence on the Mountain*, uncovers in microcosm the social background to the civil war as he delves into the reasons for the burning of a coffee estate by guerrillas.

He sponsored Fiestas de Minerva (Festivals of Minerva) in the cities, inspired by the Roman goddess of wisdom, invention and technology, and ordered construction of temples to Minerva, some of which still stand (as in Quetzaltenango). Guatemala was to become a 'tropical Athens.' At the same time, however, Estrada Cabrera looted the treasury, ignored the schools and spent extravagantly to beef up the armed forces. He was also responsible for courting the US-owned United Fruit Company, a business of gross hegemonic proportions that set up shop in Guatemala in 1901.

JORGE UBICO

When Estrada Cabrera was overthrown in 1920, Guatemala entered a period of instability, which ended in 1931 with the election of General Jorge Ubico as president. Ubico had a Napoleon complex and ruled as Estrada Cabrera had, but more efficiently. He insisted on honesty in

1945–54	1954
Enlightened, progressive government by presidents Juan José Arévalo and Jacobo Arbenz	Arbenz appropriates Guatemalan lands of the US-owned United Fruit Company and is deposed in US-orchestrated coup

government, and modernized the country's health and social welfare infrastructure. Debt peonage was outlawed, but a new bondage of compulsory labor contributions to the government road-building program was established in its place. His reign ended when he was forced into exile in 1944.

ARÉVALO & ARBENZ

Just when it appeared that Guatemala was doomed to a succession of harsh dictators, the elections of 1945 brought a philosopher – Juan José Arévalo – to the presidential palace. Arévalo, in power from 1945 to 1951, established the nation's social security system, a government bureau to look after indigenous concerns, a modern public health system and liberal labor laws. He also survived 25 coup attempts by conservative military forces.

Arévalo was succeeded by Colonel Jacobo Arbenz, who continued Arévalo's policies, instituting an agrarian reform law that was meant to break up the large estates and foster high productivity on small, individually owned farms. He also expropriated vast lands conceded to the United Fruit Company during the Estrada Cabrera and Ubico years that were being held fallow. Compensation was paid at the value that the company had declared for tax purposes (far below its real value), and Arbenz announced that the lands were to be redistributed to peasants and put into cultivation for food. But the expropriation set off alarms in Washington, which (surprise! surprise!) supported United Fruit. In 1954 the US, in one of the first documented covert operations by the Central Intelligence Agency (CIA), orchestrated an invasion from Honduras led by two exiled Guatemalan military officers. Arbenz was forced to step down, and the land reform never took place.

Arbenz was succeeded by a series of military presidents elected with the support of the officer corps, business leaders, compliant political parties and the Catholic Church. Violence became a staple of political life. Opponents of the government regularly turned up dead or not at all. Land reform measures were reversed, voting was made dependent on literacy (which disenfranchised around 75% of the population), the secret police force was revived and military repression was common.

In 1960, left-wing guerrilla groups began to form.

Searching for Everardo, by US attorney Jennifer K Harbury, tells how she fell in love with and married a URNG guerrilla leader who then disappeared in combat, and of her dedicated and internationally publicized struggles with the US and Guatemalan governments – including a hunger strike outside the White House – to discover his fate.

1960S & 1970S

Guatemalan industry developed fast, but the social fabric became increasingly stressed as most profits from the boom flowed upwards, labor unions organized, and migration to the cities, especially the capital, produced urban sprawl and slums. A cycle of violent repression and protest took hold, leading to the total politicization of society. Everyone took sides; usually it was the poorer classes in the rural areas versus the power elite in the cities. By 1979 Amnesty International estimated that 50,000 to 60,000 people had been killed during the political violence of the 1970s alone.

A severe earthquake in 1976 killed about 22,000 people and left around a million homeless. Most of the aid sent for the people in need never reached them.

1960s	1976
Left-wing guerrilla groups form in opposition to military governments; civil war starts	Earthquake kills 22,000 in Guatemala

RIGOBERTA MENCHÚ TUM

Of all the unlikely candidates for the Nobel Prize throughout history, a rural indigenous Guatemalan woman would have to be near the top of the list.

Rigoberta Menchú was born in 1959 near Uspantán in the highlands of Quiché department and lived the life of a typical young Mayan woman until the late 1970s, when the country's civil war affected her tragically and drove her into the left-wing guerrilla camp. Her father, mother and brother were killed in the slaughter carried out by the Guatemalan military in the name of 'pacification' of the countryside and repression of communism.

Menchú fled to exile in Mexico, where her story *I, Rigoberta Menchú: An Indian Woman in Guatemala*, based on a series of interviews, was published and translated throughout the world, bringing the plight of Guatemala's indigenous population to international attention. In 1992 Rigoberta Menchú was awarded the Nobel Prize for peace, which provided her and her cause with international stature and support. The Rigoberta Menchú Tum Foundation, which she founded with the US$1.2 million Nobel Prize money, works for conflict resolution, plurality, and human, indigenous and women's rights in Guatemala and internationally.

Guatemalans, especially the Maya, were proud that one of their own had been recognized by the Nobel committee. In the circles of power, however, Menchú's renown was unwelcome, as she was seen as a troublemaker.

Anthropologist David Stoll's book *Rigoberta Menchú and the Story of All Poor Guatemalans* (1999) contested the truth of many aspects of Menchú's book, including some central facts. The *New York Times* claimed that Menchú had received a Nobel Prize for lying, and of course her detractors had a field day.

Menchú took the controversy in stride, not addressing the specific allegations, and the Nobel Institute made it clear that the prize was given for Menchú's work on behalf of the indigenous, not the content of her book. More than anything, the scandal solidified support for Menchú and her cause while calling Stoll's motives into question.

In 1999, before a Spanish court, the Rigoberta Menchú Tum Foundation formally accused former dictators General Oscar Humberto Mejía Victores (1983–86) and Efraín Ríos Montt (1982–83) of genocide. Menchú pressed for extradition proceedings. At the time of writing, however, the case is bogged down in jurisdictional arguments. Menchú has since returned to Guatemala and works alongside the Berger government as a goodwill ambassador for the Peace Accords, a move that has caused some of her previous supporters to question her commitment to leftist politics.

1980S

Guatemala finally recognized Belizean independence in 1992, but the exact border remained in dispute till 2002, when the two countries agreed on a draft settlement, subject to referenda in both countries.

In the early 1980s, military suppression of antigovernment elements in the countryside reached a peak, especially under the presidency of General Efraín Ríos Montt, an evangelical Christian who came to power by coup in March 1982. Huge numbers of people, mostly indigenous men, were murdered in the name of anti-insurgency, stabilization and anticommunism. Guatemalans refer to this scorched-earth strategy as *la escoba*, the broom, because of the way the reign of terror swept over the country. While officials did not know the identities of the rebels, they did know which areas were bases of rebel activity – chiefly poor, rural, indigenous areas – so the government decided to terrorize the populations of those areas to kill off support for the rebels. Over 400 villages were razed, and most of their inhabitants massacred (often tortured as well).

It was later estimated that 15,000 civilian deaths occurred as a result of counter-insurgency operations during Ríos Montt's term of office alone,

1982–83	1992
State terror against rural indigenous communities peaks during the rule of General Efraín Ríos Montt	Guatemalan Maya Rigoberta Menchú awarded the Nobel Prize for peace

not to mention the estimated 100,000 refugees (again, mostly Maya) who fled to Mexico. The government forced villagers to form Patrullas de Autodefensa Civil (PACs; Civil Defense Patrols) to do much of the army's dirty work: the PACs were ultimately responsible for some of the worst human-rights abuses during Ríos Montt's rule.

In February 1982 four powerful guerrilla organizations had united to form the URNG (Guatemalan National Revolutionary Unity). Perhaps half a million people, mostly peasants in the western and central highlands and El Petén, actively supported the guerrilla movement, but as the civil war dragged on and both sides committed atrocities, more and more rural people came to feel caught in the crossfire. They were damned if they supported the insurgents and damned if they didn't.

In August 1983 Ríos Montt was deposed by General Oscar Humberto Mejía Victores, but the abuses continued. It was estimated that over 100 political assassinations and 40 abductions occurred each and every month under his rule. Survivors of *la escoba* were herded into remote 'model villages' known as *polos de desarrollo* (poles of development) surrounded by army encampments. The bloodbath led the US to cut off military assistance to Guatemala, which in turn resulted in the 1986 election of a civilian president, Marco Vinicio Cerezo Arévalo of the Christian Democratic Party.

Before turning over power to the civilians, the military established formal mechanisms for its continued control of the countryside. There was hope that Cerezo Arévalo's administration would temper the excesses of the power elite and the military and establish a basis for true democracy. But armed conflict festered on in remote areas and when Cerezo Arévalo's term ended in 1990, many people wondered whether any real progress had been made.

> *La Hija del Puma* (The Daughter of the Puma), directed by Ulf Hultberg, is a powerful 1995 film, based on a true story, about a K'iche' Mayan girl who survives the army massacre of her fellow villagers and sees her brother captured. She escapes to Mexico but then returns to Guatemala in search of her brother.

EARLY 1990S

President Jorge Serrano (1990–93) was an evangelical Christian representing the conservative Movimiento de Acción Solidaria (Solidarity Action Movement). Serrano reopened a dialogue with the URNG, hoping to bring the decades-long civil war to an end. When the talks collapsed, the mediator from the Catholic church blamed both sides for intransigence.

Massacres and other human-rights abuses continued during this period despite the country's return to democratic rule. In one dramatic case in 1990, Guatemalan anthropologist Myrna Mack, who had documented army violence against the rural Maya, was fatally wounded after being stabbed dozens of times by a military death squad. Later that same year, the army massacred 13 Tz'utujil Maya (including three children) in Santiago Atitlán. Outraged, the people of Santiago fought back, becoming the first town to succeed in expelling the army by popular demand. That unprecedented success was a watershed event for the Mayan and human-rights causes in Guatemala.

Serrano's presidency came to depend more on the army for support. In 1993 he tried to seize absolute power, but after a tense few days was forced to flee into exile. Congress elected Ramiro de León Carpio, an outspoken critic of the army's strong-arm tactics, as president to complete Serrano's term.

> *Guatemala: Nunca Mas* (1998) published by ODHAG and REMHI details many of the human rights abuses – with moving personal testimonials – committed during Guatemala's civil war.

1996	1998
Peace Accords are signed to end the 36-year civil war in which an estimated 200,000 Guatemalans died	Odhag declares the army responsible for most civil war deaths; two days later Odhag's coordinator, Bishop Gerardi, is murdered

PEACE ACCORDS

President de León's elected successor, Álvaro Arzú of the center-right Partido de Avanzada Nacional (PAN), took office in 1996. Arzú continued negotiations with the URNG and, finally, on December 29, 1996, 'A Firm and Lasting Peace Agreement' was signed at the National Palace in Guatemala City. During the 36 years of civil war, an estimated 200,000 Guatemalans had been killed, a million made homeless, and untold thousands had disappeared. The Peace Accords, as the agreement is known, contained provisions for accountability for the human-rights violations perpetrated by the armed forces during the war and the resettlement of Guatemala's one million displaced people. They also addressed the rights of indigenous peoples and women, health care, education and other basic social services, and the abolition of obligatory military service. Many of these provisions remain unfulfilled.

90% of drug raids in Guatemala fail due to information leaks.

GUATEMALA SINCE THE PEACE ACCORDS

Any hopes that Guatemala might become a truly just and democratic society have looked increasingly frayed as the years have passed since 1996. A national referendum in 1999 (in which only 18% of registered voters turned out) voted down constitutional reforms formally legislating the rights of indigenous people, adding checks and balances to the executive office and retooling the national security apparatus.

The single most notorious and tragic flouting of peace, justice and democracy came in 1998 when Bishop Juan Gerardi, coordinator of the Guatemalan Archbishop's Human Rights Office (Odhag), was beaten to death outside his home. Two days previously, Bishop Gerardi had announced Odhag's findings that the army was responsible for most of the 200,000 civil war deaths and many other atrocities.

The 1999 presidential elections were won by Alfonso Portillo of the conservative Frente Republicano Guatemalteco (FRG; colloquially known as the Mano Azul – Blue Hand – for its symbol daubed on lampposts, rocks and trees countrywide). Portillo was just a front man for the FRG leader, ex-president General Efraín Ríos Montt, author of the early 1980s scorched-earth state terror campaign. As one common jibe had it, when the two men discussed important decisions, civilian president Portillo always had the last word – 'Yes, general.'

See www.amnesty.org for Amnesty International reports on Guatemala.

President Portillo did pay out $1.8 million in compensation in 2001 to the families of 226 men, women and children killed by soldiers and paramilitaries in the northern village of Las Dos Erres in 1982, but implementation of the Peace Accords stalled and then went into reverse. In 2002 the UN representative for indigenous peoples, after an 11-day Guatemalan tour, stated that 60% of Guatemalan Maya were still marginalized by discrimination and violence. The UN human development index for 2002, comparing countries on criteria such as income, life expectancy, school enrolment and literacy, ranked Guatemala 120th of the world's 173 countries, the lowest of any North, Central or South American country. Poverty, illiteracy, lack of education and poor medical facilities are all much more common in rural areas, where the Mayan population is concentrated.

International organizations, from the European Parliament to the Inter-American Commission on Human Rights, queued up to criticize the state of human rights in Guatemala. Those brave souls who tried to protect

2000–2004	2005
Presidency of Alfonso Portillo of the FRG party, led by Efraín Ríos Montt	Hurricane Stan hits southwest Guatemala. Landslides and flooding leave a death toll in the hundreds and leave thousands homeless

human rights and expose abuses were being subjected to threats and killings, the perpetrators of which seemed able to act with impunity. The URNG guerrillas had disarmed in compliance with the Peace Accords, but President Portillo failed to carry out a promise to disband the presidential guard (whose soldiers killed Bishop Gerardi and whose chief had ordered the 1990 Myrna Mack killing), and he doubled the defense budget, taking it beyond the maximum level fixed in the Peace Accords.

Lawlessness and violent crime increased horrifyingly. The US 'decertified' Guatemala – meaning it no longer considered it an ally in the battle against the drugs trade – in 2002. The same year, Amnesty International reported that criminals were colluding with sectors of the police and military and local affiliates of multinational corporations to flout human rights. According to police figures, 3630 people died violent deaths in 2002. Lynchings were not uncommon as people increasingly took the law into their own hands.

El Periódico newspaper printed an article in 2003 arguing that a 'parallel power structure' involving Efraín Ríos Montt had effectively run Guatemala ever since he had been ousted as president 20 years previously. Within days, the paper's publisher and his family were attacked in their home by an armed gang of 12. Days later, Ríos Montt himself was, incredibly, granted permission by Guatemala's constitutional court to stand in the elections for Portillo's successor in late 2003, despite the fact that the constitution banned presidents who had in the past taken power by coup, as Ríos Montt had in 1982. In the end Guatemala's voters dealt Ríos Montt a resounding defeat, electing Oscar Berger, of the moderately conservative Gran Alianza Nacional, as president till 2008.

The national anticorruption prosecutor, Karen Fischer, fled the country in 2003 in the face of threats received when she investigated Panamanian bank accounts allegedly opened for President Portillo.

The FRG showed its colors fairly blatantly in the run-up to the election by making sizeable 'compensation' payments to the former members of the PACs (Civil Defense Patrols), who had carried out many atrocities during the civil war.

For the latest on the progress (or otherwise) of human rights in Guatemala, visit the Guatemala Human Rights Commission/USA website (www.ghrc-usa.org) or click on 'Human Rights' on the website of the US embassy in Guatemala City (http://usembassy .state.gov/guatemala).

2006	2007
Guatemala ratifies Cafta, a free trade agreement between the US and Central America	US President George W Bush visits Guatemala to discuss CAFTA, the war on drugs and immigration. Massive street protests

The Culture

THE NATIONAL PSYCHE

You will be amazed when you first reach Guatemala by just how helpful, polite and unhurried Guatemalans are. Everyone has time to stop and chat and explain what you want to know. This is apparent even if you've just crossed the border from Mexico, where things aren't exactly rushed either. Most Guatemalans like to get to know other people without haste, feeling for common ground and things to agree on, rather than making blunt assertions and engaging in adversarial dialectic. Some observers explain this mild manner as a reaction to centuries of repression and violence by the ruling class, but whatever the truth of that, it makes most Guatemalans a pleasure to deal with.

What goes on behind this outward politeness is harder to encapsulate. Few Guatemalans exhibit the stress, worry and hurry of the 'developed' nations, but this obviously isn't because they don't have to worry about money or employment. They're a long-suffering people who don't expect wealth or good government but make the best of what comes their way – friendship, their family, a good meal, a bit of good company.

Outwardly, it appears that family ties are strong, but beneath the surface you may find that the real reason that three generations live together in one house has more to do with economics than affection.

Guatemalans are a religious bunch – atheists and agnostics are very thin on the ground. People will often ask what religion you are quite early in a conversation. Unless you really want to get into it, saying 'Christian' generally satisfies.

Orthodox Catholicism is gradually giving way to evangelical Protestantism amongst the ladinos, with the animist-Catholic syncretism of the traditional Maya always present. People's faiths give them hope, not only of better things in the afterlife but also of improvements in the here and now – whether through answered prayers or, in the evangelicals' case, of a more sober, more gainful and happier existence without alcohol, gambling or domestic violence.

The tales of violence – domestic violence, civil-war violence, criminal violence – that one inevitably hears in Guatemala sit strangely with the mild-mannered approach you will encounter from nearly everybody. Whatever the explanation, it helps to show why a little caution is in order when strangers meet.

It has been said that Guatemala has no middle class, that it just has a ruling class and an exploited class. It's true that Guatemala has a small, rich, ladino ruling elite whose main goal seems to be to maintain wealth and power at almost any cost. It also has an indigenous Mayan population, comprising more than half the people in the country, that tends to be poor, poorly educated and poorly provided for and has always been kept in a secondary role by the ruling elite. The Mayan villagers' strengths lie in their strong family and community ties, and their traditions. Those who do break out of the poverty cycle, through business or education, do not turn their backs on their communities. But as well as these two groups at the extremes, there is also a large group of working-class and middle-class ladinos, typically Catholic and family-oriented but with aspirations influenced by education, TV, international popular music and North America (of which many Guatemalans have direct experience as migrant workers) – and maybe by liberal ideas of equality and social tolerance. This segment of society has its bohemian/student/artist

Gregory Nava's tragic film *El Norte* (The North) brings home not only the tragedy of Guatemala's civil war but also the illusory nature of many Guatemalans' 'American dream' as it follows an orphaned brother and sister who head north to the US to look for a living.

circles whose overlap with educated, forward-looking Maya may hold the greatest hope for progress toward an equitable society.

LIFESTYLE

The majority of Guatemalans live in one-room houses of brick, concrete blocks or traditional *bajareque* (a construction of stones, wooden poles and mud), with roofs of tin, tiles or thatch. They have earth floors, a fireplace (but usually no chimney) and minimal possessions – often just a couple of bare beds and a few pots. These small homes are often grouped in compounds with several others, all housing members of one extended family. Thus live most of Guatemala's great Mayan majority, in the countryside, in villages and in towns.

The few wealthier Maya and most ladino families have larger houses in towns and the bigger villages, but their homes may still not be much more than one or two bedrooms and a kitchen that also serves as a living area. Possessions, adornments and decorations may be sparse. Of course, some families have bigger, more comfortable and impressive homes. Middle-class families in the wealthier suburbs of Guatemala City live in good-sized one- or two-story houses with gardens. The most select residences will have their gardens walled for security and privacy. The elite few possess rural as well as urban properties – for example, a coffee *finca* (ranch/plantation) on the Pacific Slope with a comfortable farmhouse, or a seaside villa on the Pacific or Caribbean coast.

While many rural houses now have running water, the village *pila* (communal laundry trough) remains a place to get together and exchange gossip.

Despite modernizing influences – education, cable TV, contact with foreign travelers in Guatemala, international popular music, time spent as migrant workers in the USA – traditional family ties remain strong at all levels of society. Large extended-family groups gather for weekend meals and holidays. Old-fashioned gender roles are strong too: many women have jobs to increase the family income but relatively few have positions of much responsibility. Homosexuality barely peeks its head above the parapet: only in Guatemala City is there anything approaching an open gay scene, and that is pretty much for men only.

Traveling in Guatemala you will encounter a much wider cross-section of Guatemalans than many Guatemalans ever do as they live their lives within relatively narrow worlds. The Guatemalans you'll meet will also tend to be among the most worldly and open-minded, as a result of their contact with tourists and travelers from around the globe. Guatemala has a broad web of people, often young, who are interested in learning, in other cultures, in human rights, in music and the arts, in improving the position of women, the indigenous and the poor, in helping others. You only need to peel away one or two layers of the onion to uncover them.

ECONOMY

With a young population and an abundance of natural resources, you'd expect the Guatemalan economy to be at least vaguely healthy, but almost all the indicators point in the other direction. By UN figures, 6.4 million Guatemalans – more than half the population – live in poverty. The official national minimum wage is only US$235 a month in urban areas and US$173 in rural areas – and not everyone is entitled even to this. A typical school teacher earns around US$192 a month. Poverty is most prevalent in rural, indigenous areas, especially the highlands. Wealth, industry and commerce are concentrated overwhelmingly in sprawling, polluted Guatemala City, the country's only large city, and home to about 25% of its people.

Guatemala has the highest private ownership per capita of helicopters in the world – a fact many ascribe to the poor state of the highways and the healthy state of drug dealers' bank accounts.

What little industry that does exist is mostly foreign-owned, or is on such a small scale that it provides limited employment opportunities. A large stumbling block for foreign investors is Guatemala's relative insecurity – even

GETTING ALONG WITH GUATEMALANS

Guatemalans are easy to get along with, as long as you follow a few simple guidelines. The pace of life here is slower, and people rarely launch into whatever they're doing – even in such routine situations as entering a store or taking a bus seat – without a simple greeting: *buenos días* (good morning) or *buenas tardes* (good afternoon) and a smile will get conversations off to a positive start. The same holds true when you enter a room, including public places such as a restaurant or waiting room; make a general greeting to everyone in the room – the requisite *buenos días* or *buenas tardes* will do. When leaving a restaurant, it is common to wish the other diners *buen provecho* (bon appétit). Handshakes are another friendly gesture and are used frequently.

Many Maya, especially in villages, speak only their indigenous language. Try first in Spanish, but if that doesn't work, you may as well be speaking English (or Swahili). Sign and body language are your best friends here.

In recent years, stories circulated in Guatemala that some foreign visitors (particularly white women) were kidnapping Maya children, perhaps to raise them as their own, or even for the grisly purpose of selling their bodily organs. Some local people are extremely suspicious of foreigners who make friendly overtures toward children, especially foreigners who photograph indigenous children. Women traveling alone are treated most distrustfully in this regard, but in 2000, two men (a Japanese tourist and his Guatemalan driver) were beaten to death by a mob in Todos Santos Cuchumatán after the tourist picked up a small child to comfort it.

Many Maya are *very* touchy about having their photo taken. Always ask permission before taking pictures. Sometimes your request will be denied, often you'll be asked for a quetzal or two, and maybe in a few special instances you'll make new friends.

Many Maya women prefer to avoid contact with foreign men; in their culture, talking with strange men is not something that a virtuous woman does. Male travelers in need of directions or information should find another man to ask. In general the Maya are a fairly private people, and outsiders need to treat them with sensitivity. Some Mayan communities are still very much in a recovery phase from the nightmare of the civil war. Once you get to know someone, they may be willing to share their war stories, which are probably horrific – but don't dig for information, let your hosts offer it. On the language front, using the term *indio* (Indian) to refer to a Maya person carries racist undertones. The preferred term is *indígena*.

Pay attention to your appearance. It's difficult for Guatemalans to understand why a foreign traveler, who is naturally assumed to be rich, would go around looking scruffy when even poor Guatemalans do their best to look neat. When dealing with officialdom (police, border officials, immigration officers), it's a good idea to appear as conservative and respectable as possible.

General standards of modesty in dress have relaxed somewhat; some women wear miniskirts in towns and cities, where formerly this would have been unthinkable. Coastal dwellers tend to show a lot more skin than highland types. Nevertheless, not all locals appreciate this type of attire. Dress modestly when entering churches. Shorts are usually worn, by men or women, only at the beach and in coastal towns. Also think about safety in connection with your appearance. Particularly in the capital, locals will warn you against wearing even cheap imitation jewelry: you could be mugged for it. If you have any wealth, take care not to flaunt it.

the smallest stores are obliged to hire security guards (you'll see them out on the sidewalk toting heavy weaponry), making the cost of doing business in Guatemala relatively high.

POPULATION

Of Guatemala's 13.1 million people, some 50% to 60% are indigenous. Nearly all of this indigenous population is Mayan, although there is a very small population of non-Mayan indigenous people called the Chinka' (Xinca) in the southeastern corner of the country. The rest of Guatemala's population are nearly all ladinos – descended from both the Maya and from European (mostly Spanish) settlers. There are also a few thousand

For more than 40,000 entries in 31 Mayan languages, check out http://maya.hum.sdu.dk.

Garífuna (descended from Caribbean islanders and shipwrecked African slaves) around the Caribbean town of Lívingston.

The Maya are spread throughout the country but are most densely concentrated in the highlands, which are home to the four biggest Mayan groups, the K'iche' (Quiché), Mam, Q'eqchi' (Kekchí) and Kaqchiquel (Cakchiquel). Mayan languages are still the way most Maya communicate, with approximately 20 separate (and often mutually unintelligible) Mayan languages spoken in different regions of the country. It's language

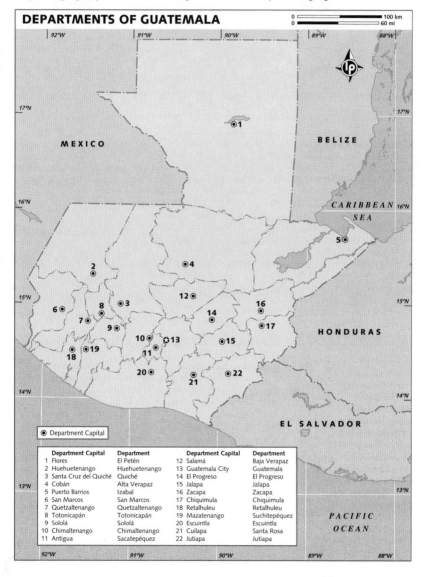

DEPARTMENTS OF GUATEMALA

	Department Capital	Department		Department Capital	Department
1	Flores	El Petén	12	Salamá	Baja Verapaz
2	Huehuetenango	Huehuetenango	13	Guatemala City	Guatemala
3	Santa Cruz del Quiché	Quiché	14	El Progreso	El Progreso
4	Cobán	Alta Verapaz	15	Jalapa	Jalapa
5	Puerto Barrios	Izabal	16	Zacapa	Zacapa
6	San Marcos	San Marcos	17	Chiquimula	Chiquimula
7	Quetzaltenango	Quetzaltenango	18	Retalhuleu	Retalhuleu
8	Totonicapán	Totonicapán	19	Mazatenango	Suchitepéquez
9	Sololá	Sololá	20	Escuintla	Escuintla
10	Chimaltenango	Chimaltenango	21	Cuilapa	Santa Rosa
11	Antigua	Sacatepéquez	22	Jutiapa	Jutiapa

● Department Capital

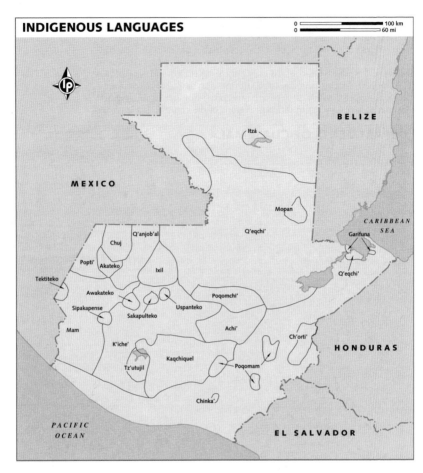

INDIGENOUS LANGUAGES

that primarily defines which Mayan people someone belongs to. Though many Maya speak some Spanish, it's always a second language to them – and there are many who don't speak any Spanish.

The population as a whole is densest in the highland strip from Guatemala City to Quetzaltenango, the country's two biggest cities. Many towns and large villages are dotted around this region. Some 45% of the population lives in towns and cities, and 41% are aged under 15.

SPORTS

The sport that most ignites Guatemalans' passion and enthusiasm is football (soccer). Though Guatemalan teams always flop in international competition, the 10-club Liga Mayor (Major League) is keenly followed by reasonably large crowds. Two seasons are played each year: the Torneo de Apertura (Opening Tournament) from July to November, and the Torneo de Clausura (Closing Tournament) from January to May. The two big clubs are Municipal and Comunicaciones, both from Guatemala City. The 'Classico Gringo' is when teams from Quetzaltenango and Antigua

Izabal in the east and El Petén in the north are the most sparsely populated of Guatemala's 22 departments, with 38 and 13 people per square kilometer respectively. The national average density is 120 people per square kilometer.

(the two big tourist towns) play. The national press always has details on upcoming games. Admission to games runs from US$2 to US$3.50 for the cheapest areas and US$12 to US$20 for the best seats.

Guatemala is recognized as a prime sport fishing destination, as the hosting of the annual Presidential Challenge Sport Fishing Championships out of Puerto Quetzal testifies. It's not a sport that has really caught on with mainstream Guatemalans yet, but the Zona 10 crowd from Guatemala City are starting to pick up on it.

For up-to-the-minute news on the football scene in Guatemala, log on to www.guatefutbol.com.

RELIGION
Christian

Roman Catholicism is the predominant religion in Guatemala, but it is not the only religion by any stretch of the imagination. Since the 1980s evangelical Protestant sects, around 75% of them Pentecostal, have surged in popularity, and it is estimated that 30% to 40% of Guatemalans are now Evangelicals. These numbers continue to grow as evangelical churches compete hard for further souls.

Catholicism's fall can also be attributed in part to the Civil War. On occasion, Catholic priests were (and still are) outspoken defenders of human rights, attracting persecution (and worse) from dictators at the time, especially the evangelical Ríos Montt.

The number of new evangelical churches, especially in indigenous Mayan villages, is astonishing. You will undoubtedly hear loud Guatemalan versions of gospel music pouring out of some of them as you walk around, and in some places loudspeakers broadcast the music and its accompanying preaching across entire towns. One reason for the Evangelicals' success is their opposition to alcohol, gambling and domestic violence: many women find that husbands who join evangelical churches become more reliable providers.

Catholicism is fighting back with messages about economic and racial justice, papal visits and new saints – Guatemala's most venerated local Christian figure, the 17th-century Antigua-hospital-founder Hermano Pedro de San José de Betancurt, was canonized in 2002 when Pope John Paul II visited Guatemala. Catholicism in the Mayan areas has never been exactly orthodox. The missionaries who brought Catholicism to the Maya in the 16th century wisely permitted aspects of the existing animistic, shamanistic Mayan religion to continue alongside Christian rites and beliefs. Syncretism was aided by the identification of certain Mayan deities with certain Christian saints, and survives to this day. A notable example is the deity known as Maximón in Santiago Atitlán, San Simón in Zunil and Rilaj Maam in San Andrés Itzapa near Antigua, who seems to be a combination of Mayan gods, the Spanish conquistador Pedro de Alvarado and Judas Iscariot (see the boxed text, p140).

Football club Municipal, nicknamed Los Rojos (the Reds), tends to nurture young Guatemalan talents, while Comunicaciones (Las Cremas, the Creams) likes to import players from other countries.

Mayan
ANCIENT MAYAN BELIEFS

For the ancient Maya, the world, the heavens and the mysterious underworld called Xibalbá were one great, unified structure that operated according to the

---

GUATEMALANS ABROAD

About one in every 10 Guatemalans – over 1.5 million people – lives in the US. There has been a steady northward flow of Guatemalans since the 1980s, peaking in 2000 when 177,000 of them moved to the US. Money sent home by these expatriates amounts to US$3 billion a year, that's US$3,000 million, more than the combined value of traditional exports, including coffee, sugar and bananas. Over 50% of Guatemalans in the US live either in Los Angeles, New York or Miami.

laws of astrology, cyclical time and ancestor worship. (For more on astrology and the calendar, see the Mayan Calendar boxed text, p31) The towering, sacred ceiba tree symbolized the world-tree, which united the heavens (represented by the tree's branches and foliage), the earth (the trunk) and the nine levels of Xibalbá (the roots). The heavens, the earth and the underworld were also all aspects of the single supreme creator, called Itzamná or Hunab Ku or Lizard House. The world-tree had a sort of cruciform shape and was associated with the color green. In the 16th century, when the Franciscan friars came bearing a cross and required the Maya to venerate it, the symbolism meshed easily with the established Mayan belief in the ceiba or world-tree.

Each point of the compass had a color and a special religious significance. East, where the sun was reborn each day, was most important; its color was red. West, where the sun disappeared, was black. North, where the all-important rains came from, was white. South, the 'sunniest' point of the compass, was yellow. Everything in the Mayan world was seen in relation to these cardinal points, with the world-tree at the center.

Just as the great cosmic dragon shed its blood, which fell as rain to the earth, so humans had to shed blood to link themselves with Xibalbá. Bloodletting ceremonies were the most important religious ceremonies, and the blood of kings was seen as the most acceptable for these rituals. Mayan kings often initiated bloodletting rites to heighten the responsiveness of the gods. Thus, when the Christian friars said that the blood of Jesus, the King of the Jews, had been spilled for the common people, the Maya could easily understand and embrace the symbolism.

Mayan ceremonies were performed in natural sacred places as well as their human-made equivalents. Mountains, caves, lakes, cenotes (natural limestone cavern pools), rivers and fields were, and still are, sacred. Pyramids and temples were thought of as stylized mountains. A cave was the mouth of the creature that represented Xibalbá, and to enter it was to enter the spirit of the secret world. This is why some Mayan temples have doorways surrounded by huge masks: as you enter the door of this 'cave' you are entering the mouth of Xibalbá.

Ancestor worship was very important to the ancient Maya, and when they buried a king beneath a pyramid or a commoner beneath the floor

Mayan Folktales, edited by James D Sexton, brings together the myths and legends of the Lake Atitlán area, translated into English.

THE BIGGEST PARTY IN TOWN

It's Friday night in any small town in Guatemala. The music's pumping, there's singing and clapping hands. Have you just stumbled onto a local jam session? Sorry to disappoint, but what you're most likely listening to is an Evangelical church service.

The Evangelicals are the fastest-growing religion in Latin America – one recent estimate put the number of new Latino converts at a staggering 8000 per day.

The Catholic church is worried – this is their heartland, after all, and the reasons that they're losing their grip aren't all that easy to pin down.

Some say it's the Evangelicals' use of radio and TV that brings them wider audiences; for some it's their rejection of rituals and gestures and customs in favor of real human contact. Others say it's the way the newcomers go to the roughest barrios and accept anybody – including 'the drunks and the hookers', as one priest put it.

For some, they're just more fun – they fall into trances and speak in tongues, heal and prophesy. And then there's the singing – not stale old hymns, but often racy pop numbers with the lyrics changed to more spiritual themes.

One thing's for sure – an Evangelical makes a better husband: drinking, smoking, gambling and domestic violence are all severely frowned upon. Maybe, once again in Guatemala, it's the wives who are really calling the shots.

THE MAYA BURY THEIR DEAD

It is the night before the funeral, and the shaman is in the house of the deceased, washing candles in holy water. If he misses one, a family member could go blind or deaf. He has counted off the days, and divined that tomorrow will be propitious for the burial.

He prays to the ancestral spirits, asking for the health of the family and the absence of disaster. The list is long and detailed. Personal objects are placed in the coffin; if they're not, the man's spirit might return home looking for them.

Members of the cofradía bear the coffin to the cemetery, a trail of mourners following. Four stops are made on leaving the house: at the doorway, in the yard, on entering the street, and at the first street corner. At each stop, mourners place coins on the coffin – in reality to buy candles, symbolically so that the spirit can buy its way out of purgatory and into heaven.

As the coffin is lowered into the ground, mourners kiss handfuls of dirt before throwing them on top. Once the coffin is buried, women sprinkle water on top, packing down the soil and protecting the corpse from werewolves and other dark spirits.

Every All Soul's Day (November 2) the family will come to the cemetery to honor their dead. Sometimes this will stretch over three days (beginning on the first). They will come to clean and decorate the grave, and set out food such as roasted corn, sweet potatoes, vegetable pears, and other fresh-picked fruit of the field. The church bells will ring at midday to summon the spirits, who feast on the smells of the food.

---

or courtyard of a *na* (thatched Mayan hut), the sacredness of the location was increased.

MODERN MAYAN RITUALS

Many sites of ancient Mayan ruins – among them Tikal, Kaminaljuyú and K'umarcaaj – still have altars where prayers, offerings and ceremonies continue to take place today. Fertility rites, healing ceremonies and sacred observances to ring in the various Mayan new years are still practiced with gusto. These types of ceremony are directed or overseen by a Mayan priest known as a *tzahorín* and usually involve burning candles and copal (a natural incense from the bark of various tropical trees), making offerings to the gods and praying for whatever the desired outcome may be – a good harvest, a healthy child or a prosperous new year, for example. Some ceremonies involve chicken sacrifices as well. Each place has its own set of gods – or at least different names for similar gods.

Visitors may also be able to observe traditional Mayan ceremonies in places such as the Pascual Abaj shrine at Chichicastenango (p149), the altars on the shore of Laguna Chicabal outside Quetzaltenango (p180), or El Baúl near Santa Lucía Cotzumalguapa (p200), but a lot of traditional rites are off-limits to foreigners.

Maya Cosmos – Three Thousand Years of the Shaman's Path, by David Freidel, Linda Schele and Joy Parker, traces Mayan creation myths from the past to the present with a dose of lively personal experience.

WOMEN IN GUATEMALA

One of the goals of the 1996 Peace Accords was to improve women's rights in Guatemala. By 2003 the Inter-American Commission on Human Rights had to report that laws discriminating against women had yet to be repealed. Women got the vote and the right to stand for election in 1946, but by 2003 only eight of the 113 congressional deputies were women. Women's leaders repeatedly criticize Guatemala's *machista* culture, which believes a woman's place is in the home (unless she's out washing the clothes or at the market or collecting firewood). The situation is, if anything, worse for indigenous women in rural areas, who also have to live with most of the country's direst poverty.

To get a handle on Maximón and shamanism around Lago de Atitlán, check out *Scandals in the House of Birds: Shamans and Priests on Lake Atitlán* by anthropologist and poet Nathaniel Tarn.

The international organization Human Rights Watch reported in 2002 that women working in private households were persistently discriminated against. Domestic workers, many of whom are from Mayan communities, lack certain basic rights, including the rights to be paid the minimum wage and to work an eight-hour day and a 48-hour week. Many domestic workers begin working as young adolescents, but Guatemalan labor laws do not provide adequate protection for domestic workers under the age of 18.

Probably of greatest concern have been the reports of escalating violence against women, accompanied by a steadily rising murder rate. These victims were once brushed off as being 'just' gang members or prostitutes, but it is now clear that murder, rape and kidnapping of women is a serious issue. The international community has begun to put pressure on Guatemala to act, but the realities of *machista* society mean that crimes against women are seldom investigated and rarely solved.

> For information on Guatemalan women's organizations (and much, much more) visit EntreMundos (www .entremundos.org).

ARTS
Literature

> Despite men taking the lead in Guatemala's *machista* culture, women live longer, averaging 71 years against 67 for men.

A great source of national pride is the Nobel Prize for Literature that was bestowed on Guatemalan Miguel Ángel Asturias (1899–1974) in 1967. Best known for *Men of Maize,* his magical-realist epic on the theme of European conquest and the Maya, and for his thinly veiled vilification of Latin American dictators in *The President,* Asturias also wrote poetry (collected in the early volume *Sien de Alondra,* published in English as *Temple of the Lark*). He also served in various diplomatic capacities for the Guatemalan government. Other celebrated Guatemalan authors include short-story master Augusto Monterroso (1921–2003) – look for his *The Black Sheep and Other Fables* – and Luis Cardoza y Aragón (1901–92), principally known for his poetry and for fighting in the revolutionary movement that deposed dictator Jorge Ubico in 1944. Gaspar Pedro Gonzáles' *A Mayan Life* is claimed to be the first novel written by a Mayan author.

Music

The marimba is considered the national instrument, although scholars cannot agree whether this xylophone-type instrument already existed in Africa before slaves brought it to Guatemala. Marimbas can be heard throughout the country, often in restaurants or in plazas in the cool of an evening. The very earliest marimbas used a succession of increasingly large gourds as the

---

WHO'S YOUR DADDY?

You might have noticed by now that Guatemalans have no problem with long names. Four is the norm – five is not out of the ordinary. As well as being tradition, it's also a form of social control – you can always tell who somebody's parents were, and thus which level of society they come from.

It may not sound like a big deal, but in status-conscious Guatemala, it certainly is. There have been cases of doctors and lawyers denied membership to country clubs here just because they have the wrong (ie indigenous) surname.

Here's how it works: when you're born, you get two first names, much like we do. Next comes your father's family name, then your mother's family name, both these names being from the father's side of the family.

When a woman marries, she often changes the mother's family part of her surname to that of her husband's family, with a 'de' in front of it.

For everyday use, Guatemalans often use their first name, followed by their father's family name.

resonator pipes, but modern marimbas are more commonly outfitted with wooden pipes, though you may see the former type in more traditional settings. The instrument is usually played by three men and there is a carnival-like quality to its sound and traditional compositions.

Guatemalan festivals provide great opportunities for hearing traditional music featuring instruments such as cane flutes, square drums and the *chirimía*, a reed instrument of Moorish roots related to the oboe.

Guatemalan tastes in pop music are greatly influenced by the products of other Latin American countries. Reggaeton is huge – current favorites being Daddy Yankee, Don Omar and Calle 13.

Guatemalan rock went through its golden age in the '80s and early '90s. Bands from this era like Razones de Cambio, Bohemia Suburbana and Viernes Verde still have their diehard fans. The most famous Guatemalan-born musician is Ricardo Arjona, who has lived in Mexico since the '90s.

La Casa de Enfrente, an award-winning film directed by Tonatiúh Martínez, is said to represent the new wave of smart, sophisticated Guatemalan film making.

Architecture

Modern Guatemalan architecture, apart from a few flashy bank and office buildings along Av La Reforma in Guatemala City, is chiefly characterized by expanses of drab concrete. Some humbler rural dwellings still use a traditional wall construction known as *bajareque,* where a core of stones is held in place by poles of bamboo or other wood, which is faced with stucco or mud. Village houses are increasingly roofed with sheets of tin instead of tiles or thatch – less aesthetically pleasing but also less expensive.

The marimba became hip in the 1940s when jazz greats like Glenn Miller started to include it in their compositions.

MAYAN ARCHITECTURE

Ancient Mayan architecture is a mixed bag of incredible accomplishments and severe limitations. The Maya's great buildings are both awesome and beautiful, with their aesthetic attention to intricately patterned facades, delicate 'combs' on temple roofs, and sinuous carvings. These magnificent structures, such as the ones found in the sophisticated urban centers of Tikal, El Mirador and Copán, were created without beasts of burden (except for humans) or the luxury of the wheel. Nor did Mayan builders ever devise the arch: instead, they used what is known as a corbeled arch, consisting of two walls leaning toward one another, nearly meeting at the top and surmounted by a capstone. This created a triangular rather than rounded arch and did not allow any great width or make for much strength. Instead, the building's

www.rockrepublik.net is the best place to go to find out about up and coming Guatemalan rock bands.

EDUCATION IN GUATEMALA

Education is free and in theory compulsory between the ages of seven and 14. Primary education lasts for six years, but in reality only 78% of children reach grade five, according to 2005 UN figures. Secondary school begins at age 13 and comprises two cycles of three years each, called *básico* and *magisterio*. Not all secondary education is free – a major deterrent for many. Some people continue studying for their *magisterio* well into adulthood. Completing *magisterio* qualifies you to become a school teacher yourself. It's estimated that only about 34% of children of the 13-to-18 age group are in secondary school. Guatemala has five universities. The Universidad de San Carlos, founded in 1676 in Antigua (later moved to Guatemala City), was the first university in Central America.

Overall, adult literacy is around 70% in Guatemala, but it's lower among women (63%) and rural people. Mayan children who do seasonal migrant work with their families are least likely to get an education, as the time the families go away to work falls during the school year. A limited amount of school teaching is done in Mayan languages – chiefly the big four, K'iche', Mam, Kaqchiquel and Q'eqchi' – but this rarely goes beyond the first couple of years of primary school. Spanish remains the necessary tongue for anyone who wants to get ahead in life.

foundations and substructure needed to be very strong. Once structures were completed, experts hypothesize, they were covered with stucco and painted red with a mixture of hematite and most probably water.

Although formal studies and excavations of Mayan sites in Guatemala have been ongoing for more than a century, much of their architectural how and why remains a mystery. For example, the purpose of *chultunes,* underground chambers carved from bedrock and filled with offerings, continues to baffle scholars. And while we know that the Maya habitually built one temple on top of another to bury successive leaders, we have little idea how they actually erected these symbols of power. All the limestone used to erect the great Mayan cities had to be moved and set in place by hand – an engineering feat that must have demanded astronomical amounts of human labor. Try to imagine mining, shaping, transporting and hefting two million cubic meters of limestone blocks: this is the amount of rock scholars estimate was used in the construction of the Danta complex at El Mirador.

For a 3D representation of the Tikal archaeological site, check out www .tikalpark.com/map.htm.

COLONIAL ARCHITECTURE

During the colonial period (the early 16th to early 19th centuries) churches, convents, mansions and palaces were all built in the Spanish styles of the day, chiefly Renaissance, Baroque and Neoclassical. But while the architectural concepts were European-inspired, the labor used to realize them was strictly indigenous. Thus, Mayan embellishments – such as the lily blossoms and vegetable motifs that adorn Antigua's La Merced – can be found on many colonial buildings, serving as testament to the countless laborers forced to make the architectural dreams of Guatemala's newcomers a reality. Churches were built high and strong to protect the elite from lower classes in revolt.

Mary Ellen Miller's well illustrated *Maya Art and Architecture* paints the full picture from gigantic temples to intricately painted ceramics.

Guatemala does not have the great colonial architectural heritage of neighboring Mexico, partly because earthquakes destroyed many of its finest buildings. But the architecture of Antigua is particularly striking, as new styles and engineering techniques developed following each successive earthquake. Columns became lower and thicker to provide more stability. Some Antigua buildings, including the Palacio de los Capitanes and Palacio del Ayuntamiento on the central plaza, were given a double-arch construction to strengthen them. With so many colonial buildings in different states of grandeur and decay, from nearly crumbled to completely restored, Antigua was designated a World Heritage Site by Unesco in 1979.

After the 1776 earthquake, which prompted the relocation of the capital from Antigua to Guatemala City, the Neoclassical architecture of the day came to emphasize durability. Decorative flourishes were saved for the interiors of buildings, with elaborate altars and furniture adorning churches and homes. By this time Guatemalan architects were hell-bent on seeing their buildings stay upright, no matter how powerful the next earthquake. Even though several serious quakes have hit Guatemala City since then, many colonial buildings (such as the city's cathedral) have survived. The same cannot be said for the humble abodes of the city's residents, who suffered terribly when the devastating quake of 1976 reduced their homes to rubble.

Weaving

Guatemalans make many traditional handicrafts, both for everyday use and to sell to tourists and collectors. Crafts include basketry, ceramics and wood carving, but the most prominent are weaving, embroidery and other textile arts practiced by Mayan women. The beautiful *traje* (traditional clothing) made and worn by these women is one of the most awe-inspiring expressions of Mayan culture.

WHAT ARE ALL THESE PEOPLE DOING HERE?

There's no doubt that tourism has an impact. Lake Atitlán, for example, is straining under the pressure of its own popularity – the drains for one, just aren't holding up, and every year as more visitors arrive and more hotels are built, more sewerage flows into the lake. Tourists, it seems, kill the thing that they love.

We've all seen tourism at its worst – temples eroded by too many people climbing over them, forests cut down to make way for eco-lodges. Village kids in Nikes leaving their traditional family life to tout hotels or sell drugs.

But there's another side to all this – what looks to the outsider like a culture disappearing often feels to the person living in that culture like progress. And who are we to say that people should stay in their mud huts without electricity while we go home to our plasma screen TVs and microwave dinners?

There are plenty of reasons for the erosion of traditional lifestyles – consumer culture, the lure of big cities, TV and Hollywood to name just a few. Tourism does some terrible stuff, there's no doubt, but managed properly, it can keep cultures alive.

Take backstrap weaving for example. Just about every tourist who comes to Guatemala wants to take a typical fabric home with them. This demand (and the income it generates) means that young people learn to weave, as it offers viable employment. Without the tourists, who knows what they'd be doing for work, or who would be keeping the craft alive.

The most arresting feature of these costumes is their highly colorful weaving and embroidery, which makes many garments true works of art. It's the woman's *huipil*, a long, sleeveless tunic, that receives the most painstaking loving care in its creation. Often entire *huipiles* are covered in a multicolored web of stylized animal, human, plant and mythological shapes, which can take months to complete. Each garment identifies the village from which its wearer hails (the Spanish colonists allotted each village a different design in order to distinguish their inhabitants from each other) and within the village style there can be variations according to social status, as well as the creative individual touches that make each garment unique.

The *huipil* is one of several types of garment that have been in use since prehispanic times. Other colorful types include the *tocoyal*, a woven head-covering often decorated with bright tassels; the *corte*, a piece of material 7m or 10m long that is used as a wraparound skirt; and the *faja*, a long, woven waist sash that can be folded to hold what other people might put in pockets. Blouses are colonial innovations. Mayan men's garments owe more to Spanish influence; nudity was discouraged by the church, so shirts, hats and *calzones*, long baggy shorts that evolved into full-length pants in most regions, were introduced in colonial times. Mayan men now generally wear dull Western clothing, except in places such as Sololá and Todos Santos Cuchumatán where they still sport colorful *traje*. For more on the various types of traditional garments, see p138.

Materials and techniques are changing, but the prehispanic backstrap loom is still widely used. The warp (long) threads are stretched between two horizontal bars, one of which is fixed to a post or tree, while the other is attached to a strap that goes round the weaver's lower back. The weft (cross) threads are then woven in. Throughout the highlands you can see women weaving in this manner outside the entrance to their homes. Nowadays, some *huipiles* and *fajas* are machine made, as this method is faster and easier than hand weaving.

Yarn is still hand-spun in many villages. For the well-to-do, silk threads are used to embroider bridal *huipiles* and other important garments. Vegetable dyes are not yet totally out of use, and red dye from cochineal insects and

Well-illustrated books on Mayan textiles will help you to start identifying their wearers' villages. Two fine works are *Maya of Guatemala – Life and Dress*, by Carmen L Pettersen, and *The Maya Textile Tradition*, edited by Margot Blum Schevill.

natural indigo are employed in several areas. Modern luminescent dyes go down very well with the Maya, who are happily addicted to bright colors, as you will see.

It's generally in the highlands, which are heavily populated by Maya, that colorful traditional dress is still most in evidence, though you will see it in all parts of the country. The variety of techniques, materials, styles and designs is bewildering to the newcomer, but you'll see some of the most colorful, intricate, eye-catching and widely worn designs in Sololá and Santiago Atitlán, near the Lago de Atitlán, Nebaj in the Ixil Triangle, Zunil near Quetzaltenango, and Todos Santos and San Mateo Ixtatán in the Cuchumatanes mountains.

You can learn the art of backstrap weaving in weaving schools in Quetzaltenango and San Pedro La Laguna. To see large collections of fine weaving, don't miss the Museo Ixchel in Guatemala City (p78) or the shop Nim Po't in Antigua (p116).

For a wonderful collection of photos of *huipiles* and other Mayan textiles, see the website of Nim Po't (www.nimpot.com).

Food & Drink

What you eat in Guatemala will be a mixture of Guatemalan food, which is nutritious and filling without sending your taste buds into ecstasy, and international traveler-and-tourist food that's available wherever travelers and tourists hang out. Your most satisfying meals in both cases will probably be in smaller eateries where the boss is in the kitchen him- or herself. Guatemalan cuisine reflects both the old foodstuffs of the Maya (such as corn (maize), beans, squashes, potatoes, avocados, chilies and turkey), and the influence of the Spanish (bread, greater amounts of meat, rice and European vegetables). Modern international cuisine comes in considerable variety in places like Antigua, Guatemala City, Quetzaltenango and around Lake Atitlán. In villages and ordinary towns off the tourist trail, food will be strictly Guatemalan.

A woman feeding a family of eight (not unusual in Guatemala) makes around 170 tortillas a day.

STAPLES & SPECIALTIES

Travelers attempting an Atkins diet may have to put it on hold for the duration. Guatemala is carbohydrate heaven – don't be surprised if your plate comes with rice, potatoes and corn and is served up with a healthy stack of tortillas.

The fundamental staple is indeed the tortilla – a thin round patty of corn dough cooked on a griddle called a *comal*. Tortillas can accompany any meal; if you know Mexican tortillas, you'll find that Guatemalan ones are smaller and a little plumper – except if they appear on a menu under the heading 'Tortillas' (with chicken or meat or eggs etc), when they'll be bigger and performing a vaguely pizza-baselike function. Fresh handmade tortillas can be delicious. Tortillas are the exclusive domain of women and you'll see and hear women making them in every corner of the country. Fresh machine-made ones are sold at a *tortillería*. The tortillas sold in restaurants are fairly fresh and kept warm in a hot, moist cloth. These are all right, but will eventually become rubbery. Tortillas accompanying meals are unlimited; if you run out, just ask for more.

Tortillas come in all shapes and sizes – mostly they're made from corn meal, but in the south, flour tortillas are common. Coastal dwellers like 'em thick, whereas mountain folk prefer them thinner.

The second staple is *frijoles* (fri-*hoh*-les), or black beans. These can be eaten boiled, fried, refried, in soups, spread on tortillas or with eggs. *Frijoles* may be served in their own dark sauce, as a runny mass on a plate, or as a thick and almost black paste. No matter how they come, they can be delicious and are always nutritious. The third Mayan staple is the squash.

Bread (*pan*; sold in *panaderías*) replaces tortillas in some tourist restaurants and for some Guatemalans who prefer not to eat *a la indígena*.

The above staples accompany all sorts of things at meal times. There's always a hot sauce on hand, either bottled or homemade: the extra kick it provides can make the difference between a so-so and a tasty meal.

On the coast, seafood is the go. Generally, your fish or shrimp will come fried in oil, but for a little more flavor you can always specify *con ajo* (with garlic). These plates come with salad, fries and tortillas. Also good is *caldo de mariscos*, a seafood stew that generally contains fish, shrimp and mussels.

The Recipe Archives website has fine Guatemalan recipes at http://recipes2.alastra.com/ethnic/guatemalan.html.

Be careful with salads and fruit: if they have been washed in dodgy water or cut with a dirty knife, they can cause you problems. Salads are so common that it can be hard *not* to eat them. If the establishment you're eating in impresses with its cleanliness, the salad is likely to be safe. If vegetables, salads and the like are washed in purified water, then you're home and dry.

Breakfast

Desayuno chapín (Guatemalan breakfast) is a large affair involving (at least) eggs, beans, fried plantains, tortillas and coffee. This will be on offer in any *comedor* (basic eatery). It may be augmented with rice, cheese or *mosh,* an oatmeal/porridge concoction. Scrambled eggs are often made with chopped tomatoes and onions.

Anywhere tourists go, you'll also find a range of other breakfasts on offer, from light continental-style affairs to US-style bacon, eggs, *panqueques* (pancakes), cereals, fruit juice and coffee. Breakfast is usually eaten between 6am and 10am.

To find out more about Guatemalan food on the internet, visit 1try.com's links at www.1try.com /recipes_g/Guatemalan _Cuisine.html.

Lunch

This is the biggest meal of the day and is eaten between noon and 2pm. Eateries usually offer a fixed-price meal of several courses called an *almuerzo* or *menú del día,* which may include from one to four courses and is usually great value. A simple *almuerzo* may consist of soup and a main course featuring meat with rice or potatoes and a little salad or vegetables, or just a *plato típico:* meat or chicken, rice, beans, cheese, salad and tortillas. More expensive versions may have a fancy soup or *ceviche* (a choice main course such as steak or fish), salad, dessert and coffee. You can also choose à la carte from the restaurant's menu, but it will be more expensive.

Most Guatemalans who eat cornflakes like them with hot milk. Specify *leche fría* (cold milk) if you don't fancy this!

Dinner & Supper

La cena is, for Guatemalans, a lighter version of lunch, usually eaten between 7pm and 9pm. Even in cities, few restaurants will serve you after 10pm. In rural areas, sit down no later than 8pm to avoid disappointment. In local and village eateries supper may be the same as breakfast: eggs, beans and plantains. In restaurants catering to tourists, dinner might be anything from pepper steak to vegetarian Thai curry.

DRINKS
Coffee, Tea & Chocolate

While Guatemala grows some of the world's richest coffee, a good cup is only generally available in top-end and (some) tourist restaurants and cafés, because most of the quality beans are exported. Guatemalans tend to drink weak percolated or instant coffee with plenty of sugar. Sometimes sugar is added before it reaches the table, so make sure you specify in advance if you don't want it. Black tea *(té negro),* usually made from bags, can be disappointing. Herbal teas are much better. Chamomile tea *(té de*

TRAVEL YOUR TASTE BUDS

Guatemala's most sensational flavors can be sampled on the Caribbean coast where the speciality is *tapado,* a mouth-watering casserole of seafood, plantain, coconut milk, spices and a few vegetables. Yummmmm!

Less tongue-tingling but filling and warming on chilly mountain mornings is *mosh,* a breakfast dish that sounds just like what it is, an oatmeal/porridge that ranges from sloppy to glutinous.

More flavorsome, and found widely around the country, is *pepián* – chicken or turkey in a spicy sesame-seed and tomato sauce. Keep your fingers crossed that the bird under the sauce has some flesh on it. *Jocón* is a green stew of chicken or pork with green vegetables and herbs.

In Cobán and the Alta Verapaz department, try *kac-cik* (*kak-ik* or *sack'ik*), a turkey soup/stew with ingredients such as pepper (capsicum), garlic, tomato and chili.

In the Ixil Triangle the local favorite is *boxbol* – maize dough and chopped meat or chicken, wrapped tightly in leaves of the *güisquil* squash and boiled. It's served with salsa.

ONES TO AVOID

Guatemalans, particularly in El Petén, eat a lot of wild game, much of which ends up on the menu at restaurants. You may come across armadillo, *venado* (venison), paca or *tepescuintle* (agouti), *tortuga* or *caguama* (turtle), and iguana (lizard). Don't order them: they may well be endangered species. The same applies here to the humble *conejo* (rabbit).

Down on the coast, a local favorite is *sopa de tortuga* (turtle soup). The same applies here – it may be delicious, but you're eating something into extinction.

---

manzanilla), common on restaurant and café menus, is a good remedy for a queasy gut.

Hot chocolate or cocoa was the royal stimulant during the Classic period of Mayan civilization, being drunk on ceremonial occasions by the kings and nobility. Their version was unsweetened and dreadfully bitter. Today it's sweetened and, if less authentic, at least more palatable. Hot chocolate can be ordered *simple* (with water) or *con leche* (with milk).

Juices & Licuados

Fresh fruit and vegetable juices *(jugos),* milkshakes *(licuados)* and long, cool, fruit-flavored water drinks *(aguas de frutas)* are wildly popular. Many cafés and eateries offer them and almost every village market and bus station has a stand with a battalion of blenders. The basic *licuado* is a blend of fruit or juice with water and sugar. A *licuado con leche* uses milk instead of water.

Limonada is a delicious thirst-quencher made with lime juice, water and sugar. Try a *limonada con soda,* which adds a fizzy dimension, and you may have a new drink of choice. *Naranjada* is the same thing made with orange juice.

On the coast, the most refreshing nonalcoholic option is a green coconut – you'll see them piled up roadside. The vendor simply slices the top off with a machete and sticks a straw in. If you've never drunk green coconut juice, you *have* to give it a go – it's delicious!

Alcoholic Drinks

Breweries were established in Guatemala by German immigrants in the late 19th century, but they didn't bring a heap of flavor with them. The two most widely distributed beers are Gallo (rooster; pronounced '*gah*-yoh') and Cabro. The distribution prize goes to Gallo – you'll find it everywhere – but Cabro is darker and more flavorful. Moza is the darkest local beer, but its distribution is limited. Brahva, the Guatemalan-produced version of the Brazilian Brahma beer, is preferred by many foreigners (and some locals) and is becoming more widely available, as are 'boutique' imported beers like Heineken and Quilmes. Up north, Mexican beers, especially Tecate, are more readily available and sometimes cheaper than domestic brands.

Rum *(ron)* is one of Guatemala's favorite strong drinks, and though most is cheap in price and taste, some local products are exceptionally fine. Zacapa Centenario is a smooth, aged Guatemalan rum made in Zacapa. It should be sipped slowly and neat, like fine cognac. Ron Botrán Añejo, another dark rum, is also good. Cheaper rums like Venado are often mixed with soft drinks to make potent but cooling drinks such as the *Cuba libre* of rum and Coke. On the coast you'll find *cocos locos*, green coconuts with the top sliced off and rum mixed with the coconut water.

Aguardiente is a sugarcane firewater that flows in cantinas and on the streets. Look for the signs advertising Quetzalteca Especial. This is the *aguardiente* of choice.

Guavas are so common on the coast that most people don't even eat them – they just feed them to their pigs.

Guatemalans celebrate All Saints' Day (*Día de Todos los Santos*, November 1) by eating *fiambre*, a large salad-type dish made from meats and/or seafood and a huge range of vegetables and herbs, all prepared in a vinegar base.

For classic Guatemalan recipes collected by a French-trained chef, try tracking down a copy of *Favorite Recipes from Guatemala* by Laura Lynn Woodward.

Ponche is a potent potable made from pineapple (or coconut) juice and rum and served hot.

Water & Soft Drinks

Purified water *(agua pura)* is widely available in hotels, shops and restaurants (see p332). Salvavida is a universally trusted brand. You can order safe-to-drink carbonated water by saying *'soda.'*

Soft drinks are known as *aguas* (waters). If you want straight unflavored water, say *'agua pura'*, or you may be asked *'¿Qué sabor?'* ('What flavor?').

Hibiscus (*jamaica*; pronounced 'hah-*my*-cah') flowers are the basis of two refreshing drinks. *Agua de jamaica* is a long, cool thirst-quencher. *Té de rosa de jamaica* is a tasty herbal tea.

WHERE TO EAT & DRINK

A *comedor* is a basic, no-fuss eatery serving straightforward local food in plain surroundings for low prices. If the place looks clean and busy, it will likely be hygienic and good value; the best *comedor* food is equivalent to good home cooking. There is unlikely to be a printed or written menu or even much choice: the staple fare is set breakfasts, set lunches and set suppers, each for around US$2 to US$4. The cheapest *comedores* of all are tables and benches set up in markets, with the cooking done on the spot.

A *restaurante* is at least a little fancier than a *comedor*. It will have pretensions (at least) to decor, staff might wear some kind of uniform, and there'll be a menu – a selection from soups, salads, sandwiches, *antojitos* (snacks), burgers, pasta, pizza, chicken, meat and fish dishes, and desserts. A typical set meal in a decent restaurant costs US$3 to US$6, à la carte a little more. In Guatemala City, Antigua, Quetzaltenango and around Lake Atitlán you can eat at specialist and ethnic restaurants and some quite classy, moderately expensive establishments. But even in the capital's most exclusive spots you'll find it hard to leave more than US$30 lighter.

The biggest internet collection of Guatemalan recipes is for readers of Spanish only, at www .quetzalnet.com/recetas.

Comedores and *restaurantes* typically open from 7am to 9pm, but the hours can vary by up to a couple of hours either way. Places close earlier in small towns and villages, later in cities and tourist destinations. A few fancier city places may not open until 11am or noon and close from 3pm to 6pm. If a restaurant has a closing day, it is usually Sunday, with Antigua restaurants being the exception – if they close it will usually be on Mondays or Tuesdays.

A *café* or *cafetería* will offer, apart from the coffee, food of some kind. This might be light snacks or it might be a fuller range akin to a restaurant. A *pastelería* is a cake shop, and often it will provide tables and chairs where you can sit down and enjoy its baked goods with a drink.

Guatemala has plenty of fast-food restaurants, but most ubiquitous is the local chicken franchise, Pollo Campero.

Bars are open long hours, typically from 10am or 11am to 10pm or 11pm. If they have a closing day, it's usually Sunday. Officially, no alcohol may be served in Guatemala after 1am, but the smaller the town (and the lower the police presence), the less likely this rule is adhered to.

THE FREE MARKET

The market in Guatemala is not just a place to buy your fruit and veg – it's a meeting point, and in most small towns, the social center.

Guatemalan markets can be overwhelming – they're noisy, smelly, packed out places that seem chaotic. There is *some* kind of order, though. Generally, the more perishable the product, the deeper inside the market you'll find it. So if you're looking for pigs' feet or goats' heads, you're going to have to delve deep. If you're just on the lookout for a pair of socks, you'll find them on the periphery.

DOS & DON'TS

■ When you sit down to eat, it's polite to say *'buenos días'* (good morning) or *'buenas tardes'* (good afternoon), as appropriate, to the people at the next table.

■ When you leave a restaurant it's polite to say *'buen provecho'* (bon appétit) to those near you. They may say the same to you, which is a way of wishing you good digestion!

■ Always tip, around 10%: the wages of the people who cook and serve your food are often pitifully low.

Quick Eats

Bus snacks can become an important part of your Guatemalan diet, as long bus rides with early departures are not uncommon. Women and girls come on the bus proclaiming '¡*Hay comida!'* ('I've got food!'). This is usually a small meal of tortillas smeared with beans, accompanied by a piece of chicken or a hard-boiled egg. Other snacks include fried plantains, ice cream, peanuts, *chocobananos* (chocolate-covered bananas), *hocotes* (a tropical fruit eaten with salt, lime and nutmeg) and *chuchitos* (small parcels of corn dough filled with meat or beans and steamed inside a corn husk). *Elotes* are grilled ears of corn on the cob eaten with salt and lime.

Much the same cheap fare is doled out by street stalls around bus stations, markets, street corners and so on. It's rare for any of these items to cost as much as US$1, and if you're on a tight budget you may do quite a lot of your eating at street stalls. On buses and streets alike, take a good look at the cleanliness of the vendor and stall: this is a good indication of how hygienic the food will be.

Up for an appetite killer? Have a browse through the US Food and Drug Administration's *Bad Bug Book*. You can also download it free at www.cfsan.fda.gov/~mow/intro.html.

VEGETARIANS & VEGANS

Given that meat is a bit of a luxury for many Guatemalans, it's not too hard to get by without it. The basic Mayan combination of tortillas, beans and vegetables is fairly nutritious. If you request a set lunch or *plato típico* without meat at a *comedor* you'll still get soup, rice, beans, cheese, salad and tortillas. Indeed some restaurants offer just this combination of items under the name *plato vegetariano*. Be careful with soups: even if they contain no pieces of meat, they may be made with meat stock. Beans, if fried, may have been fried in lard. If you eat eggs, dairy products or fish, you can eat more or less the same breakfast as anyone else, and your options for other meals increase greatly. In most places that travelers go, many restaurants – especially ethnic ones – have nonmeat items on the menu. There are even a few dedicated vegetarian restaurants in cities and tourist haunts. Chinese restaurants are also a good bet for nonmeat food. Plenty of fruit, vegetables and nuts are always available in markets.

For more Guatemalan recipes, log on to Guatemalan Recipes at www.mayantraditions.com

EAT YOUR WORDS

Communicating successfully with restaurant staff is halfway to eating well. For further guidance on pronouncing Spanish words, see p334.

Useful Phrases
Do you have a menu (in English)?
  ¿*Hay una carta (en inglés)?*   ai *oo*-na *kar*-ta (en een-*gles*)?

What is there for breakfast/lunch/dinner?
  ¿*Qué hay para el desayuno/*   ke ai *pa*-ra el de-sa-*yoo*-no/
  el almuerzo/la cena?   el al-*mwer*-so/la *se*-na?

Is this water purified?
    ¿El agua es purificada?   El a-gwa es poo-ree-fee-ka-da?
I'm a vegetarian.
    Soy vegetariano/a. (m/f)   soy ve-khe-te-rya-no/a
I don't eat meat or chicken or fish or eggs.
    No como carne ni pollo ni   no ko-mo kar-ne nee po-yo nee
    pescado ni huevos.   pes-ka-do nee we-vos
I'd like the set lunch.
    Quisiera el menú del día.   kee-sye-ra el me-noo del dee-a
Is it spicy-hot?
    ¿Es picante?   es pee-kan-te?
The bill, please.
    La cuenta, por favor.   la kwen-ta, por fa-vor

Menu Decoder

a la parrilla	a la pa-ree-lya	grilled, perhaps over charcoal
a la plancha	a la plan-cha	grilled on a hotplate
aguacate	a-gwa-ka-te	avocado
ajo	a-kho	garlic
antojitos	an-to-khee-tos	literally 'little whims,' these are snacks or light dishes such as burritos, chiles rellenos, chuchitos, enchiladas, quesadillas, tacos and tamales. They can be eaten at any time, on their own or as part of a larger meal.
arroz	a-ros	rice
atole	a-to-le	a hot gruel made with maize, milk, cinnamon and sugar
aves	a-ves	poultry
banano	ba-na-no	banana
bistec or **bistec de res**	bees-tek/bees-tek de res	beefsteak
burrito	boo-ree-to	any combination of beans, cheese, meat, chicken or seafood, seasoned with salsa or chili and wrapped in a wheat-flour tortilla
café (negro/con leche)	ka-fe (ne-gro/kon le-che)	coffee (black/with milk)
calabaza	ka-la-ba-sa	squash, marrow or pumpkin
caldo	kal-do	broth, often meat-based
camarones	ka-ma-ro-nes	shrimps
camarones gigantes	ka-ma-ro-nes khee-gan-tes	prawns
carne	kar-ne	meat
carne asada	kar-ne a-sa-da	tough but tasty grilled beef
cebolla	se-bo-lya	onion
cerveza	ser-ve-sa	beer
ceviche	se-vee-che	raw seafood marinated in lime juice and mixed with onions, chilies, garlic, tomatoes and cilantro (coriander leaf)
coco	ko-ko	coconut
chicharrón	chee-cha-ron	pork crackling
chile relleno	chee-le re-lye-no	a large chili stuffed with cheese, meat, rice or other foods, dipped in egg whites, fried and baked in sauce
chuchito	choo-chee-to	small tamal
chuletas (de puerco)	choo-le-tas (de pwer-ko)	(pork) chops
churrasco	choo-ras-ko	slab of grilled meat

enchilada	en-chee-*la*-da	ingredients similar to those in a *burrito* rolled up in a tortilla, dipped in sauce and then baked or partly fried
ensalada	en-sa-*la*-da	salad
fajita	fa-*khee*-ta	grilled meat served on a flour tortilla with condiments
filete de pescado	fee-*le*-te de pes-*ka*-do	fish fillet
flan	flan	custard, crème caramel
fresas	*fre*-sas	strawberries
frijoles	free-*kho*-les	black beans
frutas	*froo*-tas	fruit
guacamole	gwa-ka-*mo*-le	avocados mashed with onion, chili sauce, lemon and tomato
guajolote	gwa-kho-*lo*-te	turkey
güisquil	gwees-*keel*	type of squash
hamburguesa	am-boor-*gwe*-sa	hamburger
helado	e-*la*-do	ice cream
huachinango	wa-chee-*nang*-go	red snapper
huevos fritos/revueltos	*we*-vos *free*-tos/re-*vwel*-tos	fried/scrambled eggs
jamón	kha-*mon*	ham
jícama	*khee*-ka-ma	a popular root vegetable resembling a potato crossed with an apple; eaten fresh with a sprinkling of lime, chili and salt, or cooked like a potato
jocón	kho-*kon*	green stew of chicken or pork with green vegetables and herbs
lechuga	le-*choo*-ga	lettuce
legumbres	le-*goom*-bres	root vegetables
licuado	lee-*kwa*-do	milkshake made with fresh fruit, sugar and milk or water
limón	lee-*mon*	lime or lemon
limonada	lee-mo-*na*-da	drink made from lime juice; *limonada con soda* is made with carbonated water
mariscos	ma-*rees*-kos	seafood
melocotón	me-lo-ko-*ton*	peach
miel	myel	honey
milanesa	mee-la-*ne*-sa	crumbed, breaded
mojarra	mo-*kha*-ra	perch
mosh	mosh	hot oatmeal/porridge
naranja	na-*ran*-kha	orange
naranjada	na-ran-*kha*-da	drink made from orange juice and fizzy water
pacaya	pa-*ka*-ya	a squash-like staple
papa	*pa*-pa	potato
papaya	pa-*pa*-ya	pawpaw
pastel	pas-*tel*	cake
pato	*pa*-to	duck
pavo	*pa*-vo	turkey
pepián	pe-pee-*an*	chicken and vegetables in a piquant sesame and pumpkin seed sauce
pescado **(al mojo de ajo)**	pes-*ka*-do (al *mo*-kho de *a*-kho)	fish (fried in butter and garlic)
piña	*pee*-nya	pineapple
plátano	*pla*-ta-no	plantain (green banana), edible when cooked (usually fried)

plato típico	*pla*-to tee-*pee*-ko	meat or chicken, rice, beans, cheese, salad, tortillas and maybe a soup to start
pollo (asado/frito)	*po*-lyo (a-*sa*-do/*free*-to)	(grilled/fried) chicken
postre	*pos*-tre	dessert
puerco	*pwer*-ko	pork
puyaso	poo-*ya*-so	a choice cut of steak
quesadilla	ke-sa-*dee*-ya	flour tortilla topped or filled with cheese and occasionally other ingredients and then heated
queso	*ke*-so	cheese
refacciones	re-fa-chee-*o*-nes	light meals; see *antojitos*
salchicha	sal-*chee*-cha	sausage
salsa	*sal*-sa	sauce made with chilies, onion, tomato, lemon or lime juice and spices
sopa	*so*-pa	soup
taco	*ta*-ko	a soft or crisp corn tortilla wrapped or folded around the same filling as a burrito
tamal	ta-*mal*	corn dough stuffed with meat, beans, chilies or nothing at all, wrapped in banana leaf or corn husks and steamed
tapado	ta-*pa*-do	a seafood, coconut milk and plantain casserole
tarta	*tar*-ta	cake
tocino	to-*see*-no	bacon or salt pork
tomate	to-*ma*-te	tomato
tostada	tos-*ta*-da	flat, crisp tortilla topped with meat or cheese, tomatoes, beans and lettuce
verduras	ver-*doo*-ras	green vegetables
zanahoria	sa-na-o-rya	carrot

English–Spanish Glossary

butter	*mantequilla*	man-te-*kee*-yah
cup	*taza*	*ta*-sa
drink	*bebida*	be-*bee*-da
fork	*tenedor*	te-ne-*dor*
glass	*vaso*	*va*-so
knife	*cuchillo*	koo-*chee*-yo
lunch	*almuerzo*	al-*mwer*-so
margarine	*margarina*	mar-ga-*ree*-na
milk	*leche*	*le*-che
pepper (black)	*pimienta*	pee-*myen*-ta
plate	*plato*	*pla*-to
salt	*sal*	sal
spoon	*cuchara*	koo-*cha*-ra
sugar	*azúcar*	a-*soo*-kar
table	*mesa*	*me*-sa
tip	*propina*	pro-*pee*-na

Environment

THE LAND

Guatemala covers an area of 109,000 sq km – a little less than the US state of Louisiana; a little more than England. Geologically, most of the country lies atop the North American tectonic plate, but this abuts the Cocos plate along Guatemala's Pacific coast and the Caribbean plate in the far south of the country. When any of these plates gets frisky, earthquakes and volcanic eruptions ensue. Hence the major quakes of 1773, 1917 and 1976 and the spectacular chain of 30 volcanoes – some of them active – running parallel to the Pacific coast from the Mexican border to the Salvadoran border. North of the volcanic chain rises the Cuchumatanes range.

Tajumulco (4220m), west of Quetzaltenango, is the highest peak in Central America. La Torre (3837m), north of Huehuetenango, is the highest nonvolcanic peak in Central America.

North of Guatemala City, the highlands of Alta Verapaz gradually decline to the lowland of El Petén, occupying northern Guatemala. El Petén is hot and humid or hot and dry, depending on the season. Central America's largest tracts of virgin rain forest straddle El Petén's borders with Mexico and Belize, although this may cease to be true if conservation efforts are not successful.

Northeast of Guatemala City, the valley of the Río Motagua (dry in some areas, moist in others) runs down to Guatemala's short, very hot Caribbean coast. Bananas and sugarcane thrive in the Motagua valley.

Between the volcanic chain and the Pacific Ocean is the Pacific Slope, with rich coffee, cotton, rubber, fruit and sugar plantations, cattle ranches, beaches of black volcanic sand and a sweltering climate.

Guatemala sits at the confluence of three tectonic plates – hence its 30 volcanoes and frequent earthquakes.

Guatemala's unique geology also includes tremendous systems of caves. Water coursing for eons over a limestone base created aquifers and conduits that eventually gave way to subterranean caves, rivers and sinkholes when the surface water drained into underground caverns and streams. This type of terrain (known as karst) is found throughout the Verapaces region and makes Guatemala a killer spelunking destination.

DON'T LET YOUR MOM READ THIS

We don't want to worry you, but Guatemala, along with being Land of the Eternal Spring, the Land of Smiles, and Land of the Trees also seems to be the Land of the Natural Disaster. Don't panic – there are really only three biggies you have to worry about:

- Earthquakes – Sitting on top of three tectonic plates hasn't really worked out that well for Guatemala. The present day capital was founded after Antigua got flattened, but Guatemala City still got pummeled in 1917, 1918 and 1976. This last one left 23,000 people dead.

- Hurricanes – Nobody likes a hurricane. They're windy and noisy and get mud and water everywhere. Guatemala's got two coastlines, so theoretically the hit could come from either angle, although it's statistically more likely to come from the Pacific side. Hurricane Stan was the worst the country's seen, killing more than 1500 and affecting nearly half a million people. Hurricane season runs June to November – for the latest news, you can check with the National Hurricane Center and Tropical Prediction Center (www.nhc.noaa.gov).

- Volcanoes – Great to look at, fun to climb, scary when they erupt. Guatemala's got four active volcanoes: Pacaya, Volcán de Fuego, Santiaguito and Tacaná. The nastiest to date was back in 1902, when Santa María erupted, taking 6000 lives. Since late 2006, Pacaya (in between Guatemala City and Escuintla) has been acting up, with increased lava flow and ash. If you feel you need to keep an eye on it, log on to the Humanitarian Early Warning website (www.hewsweb.org/volcanoes).

WILDLIFE

Guatemala's natural beauty, from volcanoes and lakes to jungles and wetlands, is one of its great attractions. With its 19 different ecosystems, the variety of fauna and flora is great – and if you know where to go, opportunities for seeing exciting species are plentiful.

The black bass, introduced into Lake Atitlán for sport fishing in 1958, took over quickly and is now the dominant fish species in the lake.

Animals

Estimates point to 250 species of mammals, 600 species of birds, 200 species of reptiles and amphibians and many species of butterflies and other insects.

The national bird, the resplendent quetzal (for which the national currency is named) is small but exceptionally beautiful. The male sports a bright-red breast, brilliant blue-green neck, head, back and wings, and a blue-green tail several times as long as the body, which stands only around 15cm tall. The female has far duller plumage. The quetzal's main habitat is the cloud forests of Alta Verapaz. For more on the quetzal, see p215.

Bird-lovers must get hold of either *The Birds of Tikal: An Annotated Checklist*, by Randell A Beavers, or *The Birds of Tikal*, by Frank B Smythe. If you can't find them elsewhere, at least one should be on sale at Tikal itself, and both are useful much further afield.

Exotic birds of the lowland jungles include toucans, macaws and parrots. If you visit Tikal, you can't miss the ocellated turkey, also called the Petén turkey, a large, multicolored bird reminiscent of a peacock. Tikal is an all-round wildlife hot spot: you stand a good chance of spotting howler and spider monkeys, coatis (locally called *pisotes*) and other mammals, plus toucans, parrots and many other birds. Some 300 endemic and migratory bird species have been recorded at Tikal, among them nine hummingbirds and four trogons. Good areas for sighting waterfowl – including the jabiru stork, the biggest flying bird in the western hemisphere – are Laguna Petexbatún and the lakes near Yaxhá ruins, both in El Petén, and the Río Dulce between the Lago de Izabal and Lívingston.

Guatemala's forests still host many mammal and reptile species. Petén residents include jaguars, ocelots, pumas, two species of peccary, opossums, tapirs, kinkajous, agoutis (*tepescuintles*; rodents 60cm to 70cm long), white-tailed and red brocket deer, and armadillos. Guatemala is home to at least five species of sea turtle (the loggerhead, hawksbill and green ridley on the Caribbean coast, and the leatherback and olive ridley on the Pacific) and at least two species of crocodile (one found in El Petén, the other in the Río Dulce). Manatees exist in the Río Dulce, though they're notoriously hard to spot.

Plants

Guatemala has more than 8000 species of plants in 19 different ecosystems ranging from mangrove forests and wetlands on both coasts to the tropical rain forest of El Petén and the pine forests, open grasslands and cloud forests of the mountains. The cloud forests, with their epiphytes, bromeliads and dangling old-man's-beard, are most abundant in Alta Verapaz department. Trees of El Petén include the sapodilla, wild rubber trees, mahogany, several useful palms and the ceiba (Guatemala's national tree for its manifold symbolism to the Maya, also called the kapok or silk-cotton tree in English).

To see rare scarlet macaws in the wild, the place to head is La Ruta Guacamaya (the Scarlet Macaw Trail) of El Perú ruins in El Petén (p303).

The national flower, the *monja blanca* (white nun orchid), is said to have been picked so much that it's now rarely seen in the wild; nevertheless, with 550 species of orchid (one third of them endemic to Guatemala), you

---

SNAKE IN THE GRASS

The Central American or common lancehead, also called the fer-de-lance (locally known as *barba amarilla*, 'yellow beard') is a highly poisonous viper with a diamond-pattern back and an arrow-shaped head. The *cascabel* (tropical rattlesnake) is the most poisonous of all rattlers. Both inhabit jungles and savanna.

SAVING THE RAINFOREST

The Reserva de Biosfera Maya, in northern Guatemala, along with the adjoining Calakmul reserve in southern Mexico, comprises 3.9 million acres of tropical forest – the largest such area in the Americas after the Amazon.

The forest is shrinking daily, under the strain of human immigration from other parts of Guatemala, illegal logging, oil exploration and the spread of the agricultural frontier.

Wildlife here is particularly vulnerable, too – a victim of habitat loss, unsustainable hunting, and capture for the illegal pet trade. Species that were once abundant, such as scarlet macaws, Baird's tapirs, jaguars, giant anteaters and the Harpy eagle, are becoming rare. Some are presumed extinct.

If you'd like to help save the forest and the habitat of these animals, some well established organizations in the Petén accept volunteers:

Arcas (www.arcasguatemala.com) This animal rescue center has a cooperative agreement with the Guatemalan government and is recognized as the official destination for all confiscated wildlife taken from smugglers in the Reserva de Biosfera Maya.

Rainforest Alliance (www.rainforest-alliance.org) An organization that works to promote the sustainable use of the forest and green products.

The Equilibrium Fund (www.theequilibriumfund.org) An alliance of US, Guatemalan and Nicaraguan professionals who work with indigenous and marginalized women to produce food, earn income and raise healthy families without destroying their environment. They focus on the uses and processing techniques for the Maya nut (*Brosimum alicastrum*), a nutritious and easy-to-harvest rain-forest tree food that was once abundant and is now threatened with extinction by logging and land conversion for pasture and agriculture.

---

shouldn't have any trouble spotting some. If you're interested in orchids, be sure to visit the Vivero Verapaz orchid nursery at Cobán (p219).

Domesticated plants, of course, contribute at least as much to the landscape as wild ones. The *milpa* (maize field) is the backbone of agricultural subsistence everywhere. *Milpas* are, however, usually cleared by the slash-and-burn method, which is a major factor in the diminution of Guatemala's forests. Cities such as Antigua become glorious with the lilac blooms of jacaranda trees in the early months of the year.

PARKS & PROTECTED AREAS

Guatemala has 92 protected areas, including *reservas de biosfera* (biosphere reserves), *parques nacionales* (national parks), *biotopos protegidos* (protected biotopes), *refugios de vida silvestre* (wildlife refuges) and *reservas naturales privadas* (private nature reserves). Even though some areas are contained within other, larger ones, they amount to 28% of the national territory. Many of the protected areas are remote and hard to access for the independent traveler; the table (p67) shows those that are easiest to reach and/or most interesting to visitors (but excludes volcanoes, nearly all of which are protected, and areas of mainly archaeological interest).

ENVIRONMENTAL ISSUES

Environmental consciousness is not enormously developed in Guatemala, as the vast amounts of garbage strewn across the country and the choking clouds of diesel gas pumped out by its buses and trucks will quickly tell you. Despite the impressive list of parks and protected areas, genuine protection for those areas is harder to achieve, partly because of official collusion to ignore the regulations and partly because of pressure from poor Guatemalans in need of land.

Guatemala's popularity as a tourist destination leads to a few environmental problems – the question of sewerage and trash disposal around Lake

For some gorgeous watercolor illustrations and a fascinating account of a woman's travels through Guatemala in the late 1800s, look out for *A Pocket Eden*, by Caroline Selvin

To see rare scarlet macaws in the wild, the place to head is La Ruta Guacamaya (the Scarlet Macaw Trail) to El Perú ruins in El Petén (p303).

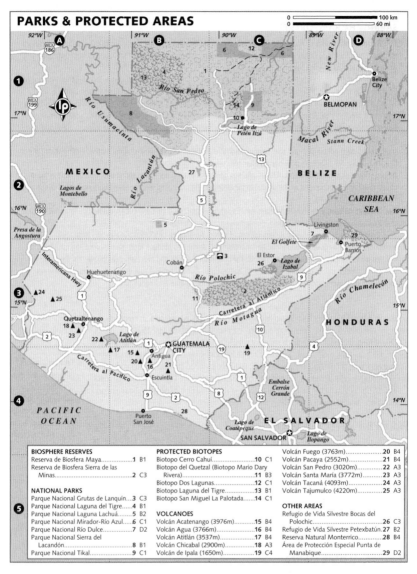

PARKS & PROTECTED AREAS

BIOSPHERE RESERVES
Reserva de Biosfera Maya.................**1** B1
Reserva de Biosfera Sierra de las
    Minas...**2** C3

NATIONAL PARKS
Parque Nacional Grutas de Lanquín...**3** C3
Parque Nacional Laguna del Tigre......**4** B1
Parque Nacional Laguna Lachuá........**5** B2
Parque Nacional Mirador-Río Azul.....**6** C1
Parque Nacional Río Dulce................**7** D2
Parque Nacional Sierra del
    Lacandón..**8** B1
Parque Nacional Tikal.......................**9** C1

PROTECTED BIOTOPES
Biotopo Cerro Cahuí.........................**10** C1
Biotopo del Quetzal (Biotopo Mario Dary
    Rivera)..**11** B3
Biotopo Dos Lagunas........................**12** C1
Biotopo Laguna del Tigre..................**13** B1
Biotopo San Miguel La Palotada.......**14** C1

VOLCANOES
Volcán Acatenango (3976m)............**15** B4
Volcán Agua (3766m)......................**16** B4
Volcán Atitlán (3537m)...................**17** B4
Volcán Chicabal (2900m)................**18** A3
Volcán de Ipala (1650m)................**19** C4

Volcán Fuego (3763m)....................**20** B4
Volcán Pacaya (2552m)..................**21** B4
Volcán San Pedro (3020m).............**22** A3
Volcán Santa María (3772m)..........**23** A3
Volcán Tacaná (4093m)..................**24** A3
Volcán Tajumulco (4220m).............**25** A3

OTHER AREAS
Refugio de Vida Silvestre Bocas del
    Polochic...**26** C3
Refugio de Vida Silvestre Petexbatún..**27** B2
Reserva Natural Monterrico..............**28** B4
Área de Protección Especial Punta de
    Manabique.....................................**29** D2

Ecotravels in Guatemala (www.planeta.com /guatemala.html) has arresting articles, good reference material and numerous links.

Atitlán being a major one, and some inappropriate development in the rain forests of the Petén being another. Infrastructure development in Guatemala is moving at such a pace, though, that these problems seem minor compared to some of the other challenges that environmentalists face.

Deforestation is a problem in many areas, especially El Petén, where jungle is being felled at an alarming rate not just for timber but also to make way for cattle ranches, oil pipelines, clandestine airstrips, new settlements and new maize fields cleared by the slash-and-burn method.

PARKS & PROTECTED AREAS

Protected Area	Features	Activities	Best Time to Visit	Page
Área de Protección Especial Punta de Manabique	large Caribbean wetland reserve; beaches, mangroves, lagoons, birds, crocodiles, possible manatee sightings	boat trips, wildlife observation, fishing, beach	any	p260
Biotopo Cerro Cahuí	forest reserve beside Lago de Petén Itzá; Petén wildlife including monkeys	walking trails	any	p285
Biotopo del Quetzal (Biotopo Mario Dary Rivera)	easy-access cloud-forest reserve; howler monkeys, birds	nature trails, bird watching, possible quetzal sightings	any	p215
Biotopo San Miguel La Palotada	adjoins Parque Nacional Tikal; dense Petén forest with millions of bats	jungle walks, visits to El Zotz archaeological site and bat caves	any, drier November–May	p271
Parque Nacional Grutas de Lanquín	large cave system 61km from Cobán	seeing bats; don't miss the nearby Semuc Champey lagoons and waterfalls	any	p224
Parque Nacional Laguna del Tigre	remote, large park within Reserva Maya; freshwater wetlands, Petén flora and fauna	spotting wildlife including scarlet macaws, monkeys, crocodiles; visiting El Perú archaeological site; volunteer opportunities at Las Guacamayas biological station	any, drier November–May	p303
Parque Nacional Laguna Lachuá	circular, jungle-surrounded, turquoise lake, 220m deep; many fish, occasional jaguars and tapir	camping, swimming, guided walks	any	p228
Parque Nacional Mirador-Río Azul	national park within Reserva Maya; Petén flora and fauna	jungle treks to El Mirador archaeological site	any, drier November–May	p305
Parque Nacional Río Dulce	beautiful jungle-lined lower Río Dulce between Lago de Izabal and the Caribbean; manatee refuge	boat trips	any	p264
Parque Nacional Tikal	diverse jungle wildlife among Guatemala's most magnificent Mayan ruins	wildlife spotting, seeing Mayan city	any, drier November–May	p291
Refugio Bocas del Polochic	delta of Río Polochic at western end of Lago de Izabal; Guatemala's second-largest freshwater wetlands	bird-watching (more than 300 species), howler monkey observation	any	p256
Refugio de Vida Silvestre Petexbatún	lake near Sayaxché; water birds	boat trips, fishing, visiting several archaeological sites	any	p301
Biotopo Monterrico-Hawaii	Pacific beaches and wetlands; birdlife, turtles	boat tours, bird and turtle watching	June–November (turtle nesting)	p206
Reserva de Biosfera Maya	vast 21,000 sq km area stretching across northern Petén; includes four national parks	jungle treks, wildlife spotting	any, drier November–May	p271
Reserva de Biosfera Sierra de las Minas	cloud-forest reserve of great biodiversity; key quetzal habitat	hiking, wildlife spotting	any	p256

Oil exploration is a concern all over the country – the Guatemalans are scrambling to start drilling in El Petén, as the Mexicans have been doing for years, tapping into a vast subterranean reserve that runs across the border. In his short stint in office, then-president Alfonso Portillo came up with the crazy idea of drilling for oil in the middle of Lago Izabal. The plan was only shelved after massive outcry from international and local environmental agencies and some not too subtle pressure from Guatemala's trading partners. It's a project that's gone but unfortunately not forgotten.

Large-scale infrastructure projects are being announced with frightening regularity, often in environmentally sensitive areas. The two latest involve highways – one from Río Dulce to Tactic, which will take the bulk of the truck traffic once the Belizeans put their own highway through to the southern border. This road will pass through the Polochic region – previously well-preserved and one of the few remaining habitats for the quetzal in Guatemala.

The other megaproject is the upgrading of the road from Playa Grande to Barillas and the flooding of 12 sq km for the construction of the Xalalá dam, a hydroelectric project. The construction will displace local communities, affect water quality downstream and alter the ecology of the area through habitat loss.

The road here, called the Northern Transversal, will eventually lead into Mexico. Local environmental groups fear that the real reason for its construction is to facilitate oil exploration in the Ixcán.

Transnational mining companies are moving in, most notably in San Marcos in the western highlands and the Sierra de las Minas in the southeast. Without the proper community consultation called for by law, the government has granted these companies license to operate open cut mines in search of silver and gold. Chemical runoff, deforestation, eviction of local communities and water pollution are the main issues here. Police have been used to forcibly evict residents and quash community groups' peaceful protests.

On the Pacific side of the country, where most of the population of Guatemala lives, the land is mostly agricultural or given over to industrial interests. The remaining forests in the Pacific coastal and highland areas are not long for this world, as local communities cut down the remaining trees for heating and cooking.

Nevertheless, a number of Guatemalan organizations are doing valiant work to protect their country's environment and biodiversity. The following are good resources for finding out more about Guatemala's natural and protected areas:

Alianza Verde (www.alianzaverde.org in Spanish; Parque Central, Flores, Petén) Association of organizations, businesses and people involved in conservation and tourism in El Petén; provides information services such as *Destination Petén* magazine, and Cincap, the Centro de Información Sobre la Naturaleza, Cultura y Artesanía de Petén, in Flores.

Arcas (Asociación de Rescate y Conservación de Vida Silvestre; ☎ /fax 2478 4096; www.arcas guatemala.com; 4 Av 2-47, Sector B5, Zona 8 Mixco, San Cristobal, Guatemala) NGO working with volunteers in sea turtle conservation and rehabilitation of Petén wildlife (see also p206 and p283).

Asociación Ak' Tenamit (www.aktenamit.org) Guatemala City (☎ 2254 1560; 11a Av A 9-39, Zona 2) Río Dulce (☎ 7908 3392) Maya-run NGO working to reduce poverty and promote conservation and ecotourism in the rainforests of eastern Guatemala.

Cecon (Centro de Estudios Conservacionistas de la Universidad de San Carlos; ☎ 3361 6065; www.usac.edu.gt/cecon in Spanish; Av La Reforma 0-63, Zona 10, Guatemala City) Manages six public *biotopos* and one *reserva natural*.

Conap (Consejo Nacional de Áreas Protegidas; ☎ 2238 0000; http://conap.online.fr; Edificio IPM, 5a Av 6-06, Zona 1, Guatemala City) The government arm in charge of protected areas.

Find out about the Yaxhá Private Reserve and what you can do to protect it at www.yaxhanatural.org.

Timber, Tourists, and Temples, edited by Richard Primack and others, brings together experts on the Mayan forests of Guatemala, Mexico and Belize for an in-depth look at the problems of balancing conservation with local people's aspirations.

For information about the spectacular Chelemhá cloud forest, check out www.chelemha.org.

Fundación Defensores de la Naturaleza (☎ 2440 8138; www.defensores.org.gt in Spanish; 7a Av 7-09, Zona 13, Guatemala City) NGO that owns and administers several protected areas.

Green Deal (www.greendeal.org) Certifies and promotes ecologically friendly and low-impact businesses, mostly in the Petén.

Planeta (www.planeta.com/guatemala.html) Focuses on sustainable tourism in Guatemala.

ProPetén (☎ 7926 1370; www.propeten.org; Calle Central, Flores, Petén) NGO that works in conservation and natural resources management in Parque Nacional Laguna del Tigre.

Proyecto Ecoquetzal (☎ /fax 7952 1047; www.ecoquetzal.org; 2a Calle 14-36, Zona 1, Cobán, Alta Verapaz) Works in forest conservation and ecotourism.

Les D Beletsky's *Belize & Northern Guatemala: The Ecotravellers' Wildlife Guide* provides detailed, almost encyclopedic information on the area's flora and fauna.

Guatemala City

Guatemala's capital city, the largest urban agglomeration in Central America, spreads across a flattened mountain range run through by deep ravines. Let's just say that there are more beautiful places on earth.

Depending on who you talk to, Guate (as it's known) is either big, dirty, dangerous and utterly forgettable or big, dirty, dangerous and fascinating. Either way, there's no doubt that there's an energy here unlike that found in the rest of Guatemala, and the extremes that categorize the whole country are in plain view.

It's a place where dilapidated buses belch fumes next to Beamers and Hummers, where skyscrapers drop shadows on shantytowns and immigrants from the countryside and the rest of Central America eke out a meager existence, barely noticed by the country's elite.

This is the real cultural capital of Guatemala – the writers, the thinkers, the artists mostly live and work here. All the best museum pieces go to the capital, and while nearly every city dweller dreams of getting away to Antigua or Monterrico for the weekend, this is where they spend most of their time, a fact reflected in the growing sophistication of the restaurant and bar scene.

Many travelers skip the city altogether, preferring to make Antigua their base. Still, you may want, or need, to get acquainted with the capital because this is the hub of the country, where all transportation lines meet and all services are available.

TOP FIVE

- Visiting the country's best **museums** (p79) and **zoo** (p79)
- Hitting the bars in Zona 10's **Zona Viva** (p88)
- Getting amongst the thick of it in busy **Zona 1** (p76)
- Gazing on Guatemala from above at the **Mapa en Relieve** (p78)
- Soaking up some culture in Zona 4's **Cuatro Grados Norte** (p89)

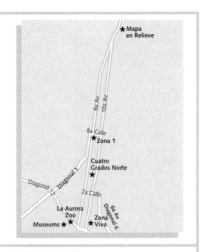

| ▪ POPULATION: 3.1 MILLION | ▪ ELEVATION: 1500M |

HISTORY

Kaminaljuyú, one of the first important cities in the Mayan region, flourished two millennia ago in what's now the western part of Guatemala City. By the time Spanish conquistadors arrived in the 16th century, only overgrown mounds were left. The site remained insignificant until the earthquake of July 29, 1773, razed much of the then Spanish colonial capital, Antigua. The authorities decided to move their headquarters to La Ermita valley, hoping to escape further destruction, and on September 27, 1775, King Carlos III of Spain signed a royal charter for the founding of La Nueva Guatemala de la Asunción. Guatemala City was officially born.

Unfortunately, the colonial powers didn't move the capital far enough, for earthquakes in 1917, 1918 and 1976 rocked the capital and beyond, reducing buildings to rubble. The 1976 quake killed nearly 23,000, injured another 75,000 and left an estimated one million homeless.

ORIENTATION

The formal and ceremonial center of Guatemala City is the Parque Central at the heart of Zona 1, which is home to most of the city's better budget and midrange hotels, many of its bus stations and a lot of commerce. South down 6a or 7a Av from Zona 1 is Zona 4. Straddling the border of the two zones is the Centro Cívico (Civic Center), with several large, modern government and institutional buildings, including the main tourist information office. Southwestern Zona 4 is a chaotic area where the city's local market district and the biggest 2nd-class bus station, the Terminal de Autobuses, fuse into one overcrowded mess.

South from the southeast corner of Zona 4 runs Av La Reforma, a broad boulevard forming the boundary between Zonas 9 and 10. These zones are among the city's poshest residential and office areas, especially Zona 10 with its Zona Viva (Lively Zone) where deluxe hotels, fancy restaurants and nightclubs, and glitzy malls all congregate.

The city's airport, Aeropuerto La Aurora, is in Zona 13, just south of Zona 9 and a 6km drive or bus ride from the heart of Zona 1. Zona 13 has several museums and the parklike La Aurora Zoo.

Maps

Intelimapas' *Mapa Turístico Guatemala,* Inguat's *Mapa Vial Turístico* and International Travel Maps' *Guatemala* all contain useful maps of Guatemala City (see p315). Sophos (below) is one of the most reliable sources of maps. The **Instituto Geográfico Nacional** (IGN; ☎ 2332 2611; www.ign.gob.gt in Spanish; Av Las Américas 5-76, Zona 13; ☉ 9am-5pm Mon-Fri) sells 1:50,000 and 1:250,000 topographical sheets of all parts of Guatemala, costing US$6 each.

INFORMATION
Airline Offices

American Airlines (www.aa.com) airport (☎ 2260 6550; Aeropuerto Internacional La Aurora); city (☎ 2422 0000; Guatemala City Marriott Hotel, 7a Av 15-45, Zona 9)

Continental Airlines (www.continental.com) airport (☎ 2331 2051; Aeropuerto Internacional La Aurora); city (☎ 2385 9601; Edificio Unicentro, 18a Calle 5-56, Zona 10)

Copa Airlines (☎ 2385 5555; www.copaair.com; 1a Av 10-17, Zona 10)

Cubana (☎ 2367 2288/89/90; www.cubana.cu; Local 29, Edificio Atlantis, 13a Calle 3-40, Zona 10)

Delta Air Lines airport (☎ 2260 6439; Aeropuerto Internacional La Aurora); city (☎ 1 800 300 0005; Edificio Centro Ejecutivo, 15a Calle 3-20, Zona 10)

Grupo TACA (Aviateca, Inter, LACSA, Nica, TACA; www.taca.com) airport (☎ 2260 6497; Aeropuerto Internacional La Aurora); city (☎ 2470 8222; Avenida Hincapié 12-22, Zona 13)

Iberia (www.iberia.com) airport (☎ 2260 6337; Aeropuerto Internacional La Aurora); city (☎ 2332 0911, 2332 3913; Oficina 507, Edificio Galerías Reforma, Av La Reforma 8-00, Zona 9)

Mexicana (www.mexicana.com) airport (☎ 2260 6335; Aeropuerto Internacional La Aurora); city (☎ 2333 6001; Local 104, Edificio Edyma Plaza, 13a Calle 8-44, Zona 10)

United Airlines (www.unitedguatemala.com) airport (☎ 2660 6481; Aeropuerto Internacional La Aurora); city (☎ 2336 9900; Oficina 201, Edificio El Reformador, Av La Reforma 1-50, Zona 9)

Bookstores

Geminis Bookstore (☎ 2366 1031; Casa Alta, 3a Av 17-05, Zona 14) Good range of books in English, but rather far from the center of things.

Sophos (☎ 2334 6797; Av La Reforma 13-89, Zona 10) Relaxed place to have a coffee and read while in the Zona Viva, with a good selection of books in English on Guatemala and the Maya, including Lonely Planet guides, and maps.

Vista Hermosa Book Shop (☎ 2369 1003; 2a Calle 18-50, Zona 15) Ditto.

GUATEMALA CITY

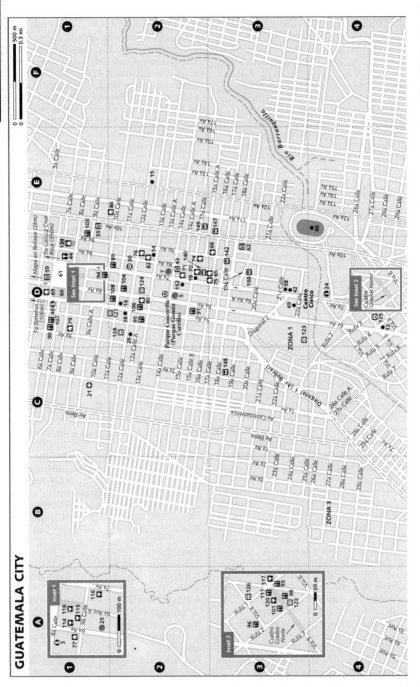

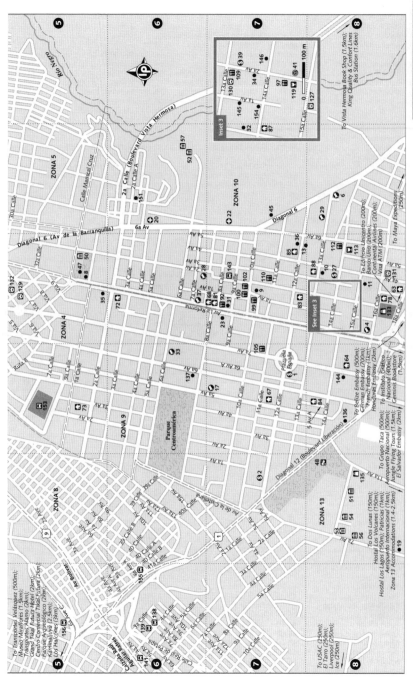

Internet Access

Zona 1 throngs with inexpensive internet cafés. Elsewhere, rates tend to be higher.

Café Internet Navigator (14a Calle, Zona 1; per hr US$0.80; ☾ 8am-8pm) East of 6a Av.

Carambolo Café Internet (14a Calle, Zona 1; per hr US$1.30; ☾ 8:30am-8:30pm) East of 7a Av.

Internet (Local 5, 6a Av 9-27, Zona 1; per hr US$0.65; ☾ 8am-7pm)

Web Station (2a Av 14-63, Zona 10; per hr US$2.60; ☾ 10am-midnight Mon-Sat, noon-midnight Sun) One of the cheapest in the Zona Viva.

Laundry

Lavandería El Siglo (12a Calle 3-42, Zona 1; ☾ 8am-6pm Mon-Sat) Charges US$4 for up to 12lb (5.5kg).

Medical Services

Guatemala City has many private hospitals and clinics. Public hospitals and clinics provide free consultations but can be busy: to reduce waiting time, get there before 7am.

Clínica Cruz Roja (Red Cross Clinic; 3a Calle 8-40, Zona 1; ☾ 8am-5:30pm Mon-Fri, 8am-noon Sat) This public clinic charges for consultations but is inexpensive.

Farmacia del Ejecutivo (☎ 2338 1447; 7a Av 15-01, Zona 1) Public pharmacy. Open 24 hours and accepts Visa and MasterCard.

Hospital Centro Médico (☎ 2332 3555, 2334 2157; 6a Av 3-47, Zona 10) Recommended. This private hospital has some English-speaking doctors.

Hospital General San Juan de Dios (☎ 2253 0443/7; 1a Av at 10a Calle, Zona 1) One of the city's best public hospitals.

Hospital Herrera Llerandi (☎ 2334 5959, emergencies 2334 5955; 6a Av 8-71, Zona 10) Another recommended private hospital with some English-speaking doctors.

Money

Take normal precautions when using ATMs.

ABM (☎ 2361 5602; Plazuela España, Zona 9) Changes euros into quetzals.

American Express Zona 9 (☎ 2331 7422; Centro Comercial Montufar, 12a Calle 0-35; ☾ 8am-5pm Mon-Fri, 8am-noon Sat) In an office of Clark Tours.

Banco Agromercantil (8a Calle Zona 1; ☾ 9am-7pm Mon-Fri, 9am-1pm Sat) Facing Parque Centenario. Changes US-dollar cash (not traveler's checks).

Banco Uno (☎ 2366 2191; Edificio Unicentro, 18a Calle 5-56, Zona 10) Changes cash euros into quetzals.

Banquetzal airport arrivals hall (☾ 6am-9pm) Changes US dollars and American Express traveler's checks into quetzals, and has a MasterCard and American Express ATM; airport departures level (☾ 6am-8pm Mon-Fri, 6am-6pm Sat & Sun) Currency exchange services and a MasterCard ATM.

Credomatic (Edificio Testa; cnr 5a Av & 11a Calle, Zona 1; ☾ 8am-7pm Mon-Fri, 9am-1pm Sat) Gives cash advances on Visa and MasterCard – take your passport.

Edificio Testa (cnr 5a Av & 11a Calle, Zona 1) Visa, MasterCard and American Express ATMs. There's another Visa ATM across the street.

Lloyds TSB (14a Calle 3-51, Zona 10) Changes euro traveler's checks.

MasterCard ATM (Hotel Stofella, 2a Av 12-28, Zona 10)

Visa ATMs (cnr 5a Av & 6a Calle, Zona 1) Opposite Parque Centenario; (2a Av, Zona 10) South of 13a Calle; (Edificio Unicentro, 18a Calle 5-56, Zona 10); (Guatemala City Marriott Hotel, 7a Av 15-45, Zona 9); there's also a Visa ATM at the airport arrivals hall, by the exit doors.

Post

DHL (☎ 2332 7547; www.dhl.com; 12a Calle 5-12, Zona 10) Courier service.

Post office (Palacio de Correos; 7a Av 11-67, Zona 1; ☾ 8:30am-5pm Mon-Fri, 8:30am-1pm Sat) In a huge

---

KNOWING EXACTLY WHERE YOU ARE

Guatemala City, like (almost) all Guatemalan towns, is laid out on a logical street grid. Avenidas run north–south; calles run east–west. Each avenida and calle has a number, with the numbers usually rising as you move from west to east and north to south. Addresses enable you to pinpoint exactly which block a building is in, and which side of the street it's on. The address 9a Av 15-24 means building No 24 on 9a Av in the block after 15a Calle; 9a Av 16-19 refers to building No 19 on 9a Av in the block after 16a Calle; 4a Calle 7-3 is building No 3 on 4a Calle in the block after 7a Av. Odd-numbered buildings are on the left-hand side as you move in the rising-numbers direction; even numbers are on the right.

In addition, most cities and towns are divided into a number of zonas – 21 in Guatemala City, fewer in other places. You need to know the zona as well as the street address, for in some places the numbers of avenidas and calles are repeated in more than one zona. Beware, too, a couple of other minor wrinkles in the system. Short streets may be suffixed 'A,' as in 14a Calle A, which will be found between 14a Calle and 15a Calle. In some smaller towns and villages no one uses street names, even when they're posted on signs.

pink building at the Palacio de Correos. There's also a small post office at the airport.

UPS (☎ 2360 6460; www.ups.com; 12a Calle 5-53, Zona 10) Courier service.

Telephone

Telgua street card-phones are plentiful.

Telefónica office (2a Av, Zona 10) Between 13a and 14a Calles. Telefónica street card-phones are fairly common too; cards can be bought at the Telefónica office.

Tourist Information

Disetur (Tourist Police; ☎ 2232 0202; 11 calle 12-06, Zona 1).

Inguat Centro Cívico (☎ 2331 1333, 2331 1347; informacion@inguat.gob.gt; 7a Av 1-17, Zona 4; ☷ 8am-4pm Mon-Fri) Located in the lobby of the Inguat (Guatemalan Tourism Institute) headquarters in the Centro Cívico. This main office has limited handout material, but staff are extremely helpful. Aeropuerto La Aurora (☎ 2331 4256; arrivals hall; ☷ 6am-9pm).

Travel Agencies

Servisa (☎ /fax 332-7526; Av La Reforma 8-33, Zona 10) An efficient agency.

Viajes Tivoli (☎ 238-4771/2/3; centro@tivoli.com.gt; 12a Calle 4-55, Edificio Herrera, Zona 1) Housed in a building with several other travel agencies; take your pick.

DANGERS & ANNOYANCES

Street crime, including armed robbery, has increased in recent years. Use normal urban caution (behaving as you would in, say, Manhattan or Rome): don't walk down the street with your wallet bulging out of your back pocket, and avoid walking downtown alone late at night. Work out your route before you start so that you're not standing on corners looking lost or peering at a map. It's safe to walk downtown in early evening, as long as you stick to streets with plenty of lighting and people. Stay alert and leave your valuables in your hotel. Don't flaunt anything of value, and be aware that women and children swell the ranks of thieves here. The incidence of robbery increases around the 15th and the end of each month, when workers get paid.

The area around 18a Calle in Zona 1 has many bus stations, and hosts the lowlife and hustlers who tend to lurk around them. Nearly half of Zona 1 robberies happen here, the worst black spots being the intersections with 4a, 6a and 9a Avs. This part of town (also a red-light district) is notoriously dangerous at night; if you are arriving by bus at night

or must go someplace on 18a Calle at night, take a taxi.

The more affluent sections of the city – Zona 9 and Zona 10, for example – are much safer. The Zona Viva, in Zona 10, has police patrols at night. But even here, going in pairs is better than going alone.

All buses are the turf of adroit pickpockets. Some armed robberies happen on buses, too, though mainly in the city's outlying zones.

Never try to resist if you are confronted by a robber.

SIGHTS

The major sights are in Zona 1 (the historic center) and Zonas 10 and 13, where the museums are grouped.

Zona 1

The main sights here are grouped around the **Parque Central** (officially the Plaza de la Constitución). The standard colonial urban-planning scheme required every town in the New World to have a large plaza for military exercises and ceremonies. On the north side of the plaza was usually the *palacio de gobierno* (colonial government headquarters). On another side, preferably the east, would be a church (or cathedral). On the other sides of the square there could be additional civic buildings or the imposing mansions of wealthy citizens. Guatemala City's Parque Central is a classic example of the plan.

The Parque Central and adjoining Parque Centenario are never empty during daylight hours, with shoeshine boys, ice-cream vendors and sometimes open-air political meetings adding to the general bustle.

On the north side of the Parque Central is the imposing **Palacio Nacional de la Cultura** (☎ 2253 0748; 6a Calle; ☷ 9-11:45am & 2-4:45pm Mon-Fri, 9-10:45am & 2-3:45pm Sat & Sun), built as a presidential palace between 1936 and 1943 during the dictatorial rule of General Jorge Ubico at enormous cost to the lives of the prisoners who were forced to labor here. It's the third palace to stand on the site. Despite its tragic background, architecturally the palace is one of the country's most interesting constructions, a mélange of multiple earlier styles from Spanish Renaissance to neoclassical. Today, most government offices have been removed from here and it's open as a museum and for a few ceremonial events.

Visits are by guided tour (available in English), lasting about 45 minutes – the tours are free, but a tip to your guide is a good idea. You pass through a labyrinth of gleaming brass, polished wood, carved stone and frescoed arches. Features include an optimistic mural of Guatemalan history by Alberto Gálvez Suárez above the main stairway, and a two-ton gold, bronze and Bohemian-crystal chandelier in the reception hall. The banqueting hall sports stained-glass panels depicting – with delicious irony – the virtues of good government. From here your guide will probably take you out onto the presidential balcony, where you can imagine yourself a banana-republic dictator reviewing your troops. In the western courtyard, the Patio de la Paz, a monument depicting two hands stands where Guatemala's Peace Accords were signed in 1996; each day at 11am the rose held by the hands is changed by a military guard and tossed to a woman among the spectators.

On the first floor of the Palacio de Correos you'll find the **Centro Cultural Metropolitano** (cnr 12a Calle & 7 Av; 9am-5pm Mon-Fri), a surprisingly avant-garde cultural center, hosting art exhibitions, book launches, handicraft workshops and film nights.

The **Casa MIMA** (cnr 8a Av & 14a Calle; 9am-12:30pm, 2-6pm Mon-Fri, 9am-5pm Sat) is a wonderfully presented museum and cultural center set in a house dating from the late 1800s. The owners of the house were collectors with eclectic tastes ranging from French neo-Rococo, Chinese, and art deco to indigenous artifacts. The place is set up like a functioning house, filled with curios and furniture spanning the centuries.

The **Railway Museum** (Museo de Ferrocarril; 18a Calle; 9am-4:30pm Tue-Fri, 10am-4:30pm Sat & Sun) is one of the city's more intriguing museums (and the only one with a Domino's Pizza attached). Documented here are the glory days of the troubled Guatemalan rail system, along with some quirky artifacts, like hand-drawn diagrams of derailments and a kitchen set up with items used in dining cars. You can go climbing around the passenger carriages, but not the locomotives. It's between 9a and 10a Avs.

The **Catedral Metropolitana** (7a Av; 6am-noon & 2-7pm), facing Parque Central, was constructed

---

WHAT'S A HUELGA?

If you're around Guatemala in the time leading up to Easter, no doubt you'll see groups of university students out in colorful robes and hoods. They could be mistaken for penitents, but in fact they're participating in one of Guatemala's oldest political traditions.

The Huelga de Dolores (strike of sorrows) started in 1898 as a protest against the corrupt rule of dictator Manuel Estrada Cabrera. Students from Guatemala's public Universidad de San Carlos wear hoods – color coded by the faculty they belong to – a traditional defense against state reprisals.

The Huelga takes place over Lent, the forty days leading up to Easter. The most colorful part of it is the Desfile de Bufos (parade of ridicule), a massive street parade featuring floats and banners, which generally takes the opportunity to mock political leaders on a general theme. Past parades have focused on the war in Iraq and Guatemala's involvement in the Central America Free Trade Agreement.

Another unique aspect of the Huelga is the collecting of *talachas*, a tax that is placed on businesses and motorists. In the past, money collected from the *talachas* was used to fund social projects. Now, as rumor has it, it is used to fund university parties and keep the organizers of the Huelga in employment year-round. Some estimate that *talachas* bring in millions of dollars per year. No accounts are kept, so nobody really knows.

Businesses that don't pay the *talachas* are likely to have their shop front painted in burnt motor oil, the Thursday before Easter, on a night called Noche de las pintas (the Night of the paints). Motorists who don't pay have had their cars vandalized and tires slashed.

Every year newspaper editorials and business owners speak out against the *talachas,* the students say they are simply redistributing money from those who have to those who don't, and the police say they don't have the resources to stand up to the students.

Supporters of the Huelga say it is an important tradition and one of the few times in the year that popular opinion is heard. Critics say, in a country like Guatemala, the last thing graduating students need to learn is that extortion, violence and lack of accountability can be so profitable.

between 1782 and 1815 (the towers were finished in 1867). It has survived earthquake and fire well, though the quake of 1917 did substantial damage and the one in 1976 did even more. Its heavy proportions and sparse ornamentation don't make for a particularly beautiful building, but it does have a certain stateliness, and the altars are worth a look.

The **Mercado Central**, behind the cathedral, was one of the city's major markets for food and other daily necessities until the building was destroyed by the 1976 earthquake. Reconstructed in the late 1970s, it now specializes in tourist-oriented handicrafts.

The **Museo Nacional de Historia** (☎ 2253 6149; 9a Calle 9-70; admission US$4; ☉ 8:30am-4pm Mon-Fri) is a jumble of historical relics with an emphasis on photography and portraits. Check the carefully manicured hairstyles of the 19th-century generals and politicos.

Zona 2

North of Zona 1, Zona 2 is mostly a middle-class residential district, but it's worth venturing along to Parque Minerva to see the **Mapa en Relieve** (Relief Map; admission US$4; ☉ 9am-5pm), a huge open-air map of Guatemala showing the country at a scale of 1:10,000. The vertical scale is exaggerated to 1:2000 to make the volcanoes and mountains appear dramatically higher and steeper than they really are. Constructed in 1905 under the direction of Francisco Vela, the Mapa was fully restored and repainted in 1999. Viewing towers afford a panoramic view. This is an odd but fun place, and it's curious to observe that Belize is still represented as part of Guatemala. To get there take bus V-21 northbound on 7a Av just north or south of the Parque Central.

Zona 4

Pride of Zona 4 (actually straddling its borders with Zonas 1 and 5) is the **Centro Cívico**, a set of large government and institutional buildings constructed during the 1950s and '60s. One is the headquarters of **Inguat** (Guatemalan Tourist Institute; see p76), housing the city's main tourist office. Nearby are the **Palacio de Justicia** (High Court; cnr 7a Av & 21a Calle, Zona 1), the **Banco de Guatemala** (7a Av, Zona 1) and the **Municipalidad de Guatemala** (City Hall; 22a Calle, Zona 1). The bank building bears relief sculptures by Dagoberto Vásquez depicting his country's history; the city hall contains a huge mosaic by Carlos Mérida, completed in 1959.

Behind Inguat is the national stadium, **Estadio Nacional Mateo Flores** (10a Av, Zona 5).

Zona 7

The **Parque Arqueológico Kaminaljuyú** (☎ 2253 1570; 11a Calle, Zona 7; admission US$4; ☉ 9am-4pm), with remnants of one of the first important cities in the Mayan region, is just west of 23a Av and is some 4km west of the city center. At its peak, from about 400 BC to AD 100, ancient Kaminaljuyú (kah-mih-nahl-huh-yuh)had thousands of inhabitants and scores of temples built on earth mounds, and probably dominated much of highland Guatemala. Large-scale carvings found here were the forerunners of Classic Mayan carving, and Kaminaljuyú had a literate elite before anywhere else in the Mayan world. The city fell into ruin before being reoccupied around AD 400 by invaders from Teotihuacán in central Mexico, who rebuilt it in Teotihuacán's *talud-tablero* style, with buildings stepped in alternating vertical *(tablero)* and sloping *(talud)* sections. Unfortunately, most of Kaminaljuyú has been covered by urban sprawl: the *parque arqueológico* is but a small portion of the ancient city and even here the remnants consist chiefly of grassy mounds. To the left from the entrance is La Acrópolis, where you can inspect excavations of a ball court and *talud-tablero* buildings from AD 450 to 550. The best carvings from the site are in the new Museo Nacional de Arqueología y Etnología (opposite).

You can get here by bus No 35 from 4a Av, Zona 1, but check that the bus is going to the *ruinas de Kaminaljuyú* – not all do. A taxi from Zona 1 costs around US$4.50.

Zona 10

Two of the country's best museums are housed in large, modern buildings at the Universidad Francisco Marroquín, 1km east of Av La Reforma.

The **Museo Ixchel** (☎ 2331 3634/8; 6a Calle Final; admission US$3; ☉ 9am-5pm Mon-Fri, 9am-1pm Sat) is named for the Mayan goddess of the moon, women, reproduction and, of course, textiles. Photographs and exhibits of indigenous costumes and other crafts show the incredible richness of traditional arts in Guatemala's highland towns. If you enjoy Guatemalan textiles at all, you must visit this museum. It has disabled access, a section for children, a café, a shop and a library, and guided tours are available in English or Spanish.

Behind it is **Museo Popol Vuh** (☎ 2361 2301; www
.popolvuh.ufm.edu; 6a Calle Final; adult/child US$3/1; ☯ 9am-
5pm Mon-Fri, 9am-1pm Sat), where well-displayed
pre-Hispanic figurines, incense burners and
burial urns, plus carved wooden masks and
traditional textiles, fill several rooms. Other
rooms hold colonial paintings and gilded
wood and silver artifacts. A faithful copy
of the Dresden Codex, one of the precious
'painted books' of the Maya, is among the
most interesting pieces, and there's a colorful
display of animals in Mayan art.

The Universidad de San Carlos has a large,
lush **Jardín Botánico** (Botanical Garden; Calle Mariscal Cruz
1-56; admission US$0.80; ☯ 8am-3:30pm Mon-Fri, 8am-
noon Sat) on the northern edge of Zona 10. The
admission includes the university's **Museo de
Historia Natural** (Natural History Museum; ☯ 8am-3:30pm
Mon-Fri, 8am-noon Sat) at the site.

Zona 11

Museo Miraflores (☎ 2470 3415; www.museomiraflores
.org; 7a Calle 21-55, Zona 11; admission US$2; ☯ 9am-7pm) is
an excellent, modern museum inauspiciously
jammed between two shopping malls a few
kilometers out of town. Downstairs focuses on
objects found at Kaminaljuyú (see opposite),
with fascinating trade route maps showing the
site's importance.

Upstairs there are displays on textiles and
indigenous clothing, separated by region,
from around the country. Signs are in Spanish
and (mostly) English. Out back is a pleasant
grassy area with paths and seating – a good
place to take a breather. To get there, catch
any bus from the center going to Tikal Futura and get off there. The museum is 250m
down the road between it and the Miraflores
shopping center.

Zona 13

The attractions here in the city's southern
reaches are all ranged along 5a Calle in the
Finca Aurora area, northwest of the airport.
While here you can also drop into the **Mercado
de Artesanías** (Crafts Market; ☎ 2472 0208; cnr 5a Calle &
11a Av; ☯ 9:30am-6pm).

La Aurora Zoo (☎ 2472 0894; 5a Calle; adult/child
US$2.50/1; ☯ 9am-5pm Tue-Sun) is not badly kept
as zoos go, and the lovely, parklike grounds
alone are worth the admission fee.

Almost opposite the zoo entrance is the
Museo de los Niños (Children's Museum; ☎ 5475 5076;
5a Calle 10-00; admission US$4.50; ☯ 8am-noon & 1-5pm
Tue-Thu, 8am-noon & 2-6pm Fri, 10am-1:30pm & 2:30-6pm Sat

& Sun), a hands-on affair that is a sure success if
you have kids to keep happy. The fun ranges
from a giant jigsaw-map of Guatemala to a
Lego room and, most popular of all, a room
of original and entertaining ball games.

The **Museo Nacional de Arqueología y Etnología**
(☎ 2472 0489; Sala 5, Finca La Aurora; admission US$4;
☯ 9am-4pm Tue-Fri, 9am-noon & 1:30-4pm Sat & Sun)
has the country's biggest collection of ancient
Mayan artifacts, but explanatory information
is very sparse. There's a great wealth of monumental stone sculpture, including Classic-period stelae from Tikal, Uaxactún and Piedras
Negras, a superb throne from Piedras Negras
and animal representations from preclassic
Kaminaljuyú. Also here are rare wooden lintels from temples at Tikal and El Zotz, and a
room of beautiful jade necklaces and masks.
Don't miss the large-scale model of Tikal. The
ethnology section has displays on the languages, costumes, dances, masks and homes
of Guatemala's indigenous peoples.

Next door is the **Museo Nacional de Arte Mod-
erno** (☎ 2472 0467; Sala 6, Finca La Aurora; admission
US$1.30; ☯ 9am-4pm Tue-Fri, 9am-noon & 2-4pm Sat & Sun),
with a collection of 20th-century Guatemalan
art including works by well-known Guatemalan artists such as Carlos Mérida, Carlos
Valente and Humberto Gavarito. Behind the
archaeology museum is the **Museo Nacional de
Historia Natural Jorge Ibarra** (☎ 2472 0468; 6a Calle
7-30; admission US$1.30; ☯ 9am-4pm Tue-Fri, 9am-noon &
2-4pm Sat & Sun), whose claim to fame is its large
collection of dissected animals.

WALKING TOUR

Walking is not generally considered a recreational activity in Guatemala City. Poorly
maintained sidewalks, high levels of pollution
and the odd spot of street crime make the city
a difficult and sometimes dangerous place to
take a stroll.

That being true, the historical center of
Zona 1 has a tight concentration of interesting sights, and the best way to see them all in
one hit is on foot.

The best place to start is at the **Parque
Concordia (1)**, which has some interesting cast
bronze statues dotted around and is always
full of local characters taking a breather on
the shady seats.

To the northeast you'll be able to see the
mock battlements of the **National Police Headquarters (2)**. Head towards it, trying not to
think about what went on inside back in the

Bad Old Days – chances are it'll ruin the rest of your walk.

Heading north on 6a Av, you'll be engaged in a time-honored Guate tradition. This is the main shopping strip, and before the big shopping malls went up, there was even a verb for window-shopping along here – 'sexteando' (see p90). Right next to the police station is the **Iglesia de San Francisco (3)**, filled with artifacts brought here when Antigua was abandoned.

Keep moving north, alternating between the road and the sidewalk, whichever is less congested. On the next block, to the right is the **Capitol Shopping Center (4)**, site of the first ever electric escalators in the city. Every now and then you can still see country folk in town for the day, getting their kicks on them.

As you reach the next corner, make sure you look to the right – down the hill is one of the city's most photographed sights, the yellow and white arch of the **Main Post Office** (**5**; Palacio de Correos). You'll be coming back this way later, but this is the best angle to photograph it from.

From here it's another four blocks of dodging buyers and sellers of everything from cheap socks to probably not designer shoes until you reach the Central Park. If it's beer o'clock already, pull up just short of the park and duck into the Portal de Comercio arcade on your right. Deep in the bowels you'll find **El Portal (6)**, where Che Guevara blew the suds off a few in his time.

Back out on the **Central Park (7)**, you should have a wander around just to take it all in. If you're here on a weekend, the place will be packed out with families, and on Sundays with young (mostly indigenous) girls who work as maids in the city and use their day off to come here and canoodle with their boyfriends. Any day of the week there's generally buskers, snake charmers, Polaroid photographers and the occasional raving evangelist to liven up the scene.

WALK FACTS

Start point Parque Concordia
End Point Museo de Ferrocarril
Distance 2km
Duration 3 hours

Guatemala City Walking Tour

Moving clockwise from your entrance to the park on 6a Av, you'll see the Parque del Centenario – another concrete expanse, really, with the **Biblioteca Nacional** (8; National Library) at its western edge.

If you're up for coffee and cake at this point, make a short detour up 6a Calle to **Café de Imeri (9)**, one of Zona 1's finest cafés.

Suitably recharged, head back down to the park. On the northern end is the **Palacio Nacional (10)**, always worth a look in for its revolving exhibitions of modern and classical art, as well as its charming courtyards and colonial architecture.

If you've really got your walking shoes on, you can head further north on 6a Av, to the Mapa en Relieve (p78), which is an easy 2km walk straight ahead. If you want to cheat, a taxi should cost about US$4, and we won't tell anybody.

Moving south from the Palacio Nacional, on the eastern edge of the park you'll find the city's main **cathedral (11**; p77), a once-impressive blend of Neoclassical and baroque styles that is most notable for the twelve pillars out front, inscribed with the names of thousands of people who were 'disappeared' during the civil war.

Leaving the park, exiting on 8a Calle heading west, you'll come to the **Mercado Central (12)**. Once the city's main fruit and veg supplier, it's now about 75% souvenirs (haggle hard), but the basement level keeps it real with a thriving mass of vendors hawking flowers, vegetables, prayer candles, fresh meat, underpants, etc.

Back out in the daylight, follow 8a Av south for six blocks until you reach **Casa MIMA (13**; p77), a well-restored and intriguing private museum with a good little café out in the patio.

From there, it's another four blocks south, then one block east on 18a Calle to the **Museo de Ferrocarril (14**; p77), where you can scramble around passenger carriages, check out derailment diagrams and grab a slice of pizza.

GUATEMALA CITY FOR CHILDREN

Guatemala City has enough children's attractions to make it worth considering as an outing from Antigua if you have kids to please. The **Museo de los Niños** (p79) and **La Aurora Zoo** (p79), conveniently over the road from each other in Zona 13, top the list. Kids might also relish the dead animals in various states of preservation at the nearby **Museo Nacional de Historia Natural Jorge Ibarra** (p79). It shouldn't be too hard to find some food that the littl'uns are willing to eat at the food courts in the malls **Centro Comercial Los Próceres** (16a Calle, Zona 10) or **Centro Comercial Tikal Futura** (Calzada Roosevelt 22-43, Zona 11), where everyone can also enjoy a little air-conditioning and shopping (window or otherwise). The **Mapa en Relieve** (p78), too, amuses most ages, and there are a few swings and climbing frames in the adjacent park.

TOURS

Clark Tours (☎ 2337 7777; www.clarktours.com.gt; Torre II, Centro Gerencial Las Margaritas, Diagonal 6 No 10-01, Zona 10; morning tours per person US$26, Mon-Wed & Fri-Sat; day tours up to four people US$260-280) Guatemala's longest-established tour operator offers morning and full-day city tours. The morning tour visits the Palacio Nacional de la Cultura, cathedral, Mapa en Relieve and Centro Cívico. The day tour adds three of the city's best museums and Kaminaljuyú. Clark tours also has branches at the Westin Camino Real (cnr 14a Av & Av La Reforma, Zona 10), Holiday Inn and Guatemala City Marriott Hotel (p83).

Maya Expeditions (☎ 2363 4955; www.mayaexpeditions.com; 15 Calle A 14-07, Zona 10) Guatemala's most respected adventure tourism company specializes in white-water rafting and trekking, but also offers archaeological trips, wildlife viewing expeditions and a whole lot more, mostly in the Alta Verapaz and Petén regions.

SLEEPING

For budget and many midrange hotels, make a beeline for Zona 1. If you have just flown in or are about to fly out, a few guesthouses near the airport are as convenient as you could get. Top-end hotels are mostly around Zona 10. Many have desks in the airport arrivals area, where you can book a room and/or obtain transportation (often free) to the hotel.

Zona 1
BUDGET

Many of the city's cheaper lodgings are clustered in the area between 6a and 9a Avs and 14a and 17a Calles, 10 to 15 minutes' walk south from the Parque Central. Keep street noise in mind as you look for a room.

Hotel San Martin (☎ 2238 0319; 16a Calle 7-65; r with/without bathroom US$9/7) If you're on a serious budget, the San Martin's the one to go for – nothing fancy, but good solid value and reasonably clean.

Pensión Meza (☎ 2232 3177; 10a Calle 10-17; s/d US$7/8, with bathroom US$9/11) The rooms are grimy

---

DAY TRIPPER

Guatemala City may not be your dream destination, but if you do have to hang around for a while, there are plenty of good day trips to make that are just outside of town:

■ Heavily polluted and shunned for many years, **Lago de Amatitlán** (p210) is making a comeback, thanks to community groups.

■ Where else but **Volcán de Pacaya** (p104), visible from the capital, are you going to get a chance to get up close and personal with flowing lava?

■ A privately owned reserve on the slopes of Pacaya, **Parque Natural Canopy Calderas** (☎ 5538 5531; www.parquenaturalcalderas.com; ☺ 9am-5pm) protects a lake and a patch of rainforest – you can go horse riding or zip lining or simply enjoy the peaceful setting.

■ The old capital of the Poqomam Maya, **Mixco Viejo** (p215), has the most dramatic setting of any ruins in the country.

■ The pretty little flower-growing town of **San Juan Sacatepéquez** – come on a Friday when the market is in full swing.

---

and the beds are spongy, but the courtyard's pretty, with plenty of places to hang out, and the management is very friendly. It's a long-time backpackers' favorite, with table tennis, a book exchange and a big notice board.

Hotel Fenix (☎ 2251 6625; 7a Av 15-81; r US$8, with private bathroom & TV US$11) For Zona 1 budget digs, the Fenix does alright, with a fair bit of charm (most of it crumbling off the walls). The high ceilings, spacious rooms and old-timey feel keep this hotel a popular option. The hotel has a café and spacious hang-out areas.

Hotel Capri (☎ 2232 8191; 9a Av 15-63; s/d US$9/14, with bathroom US$14/21; P) This modern three-story number is in a decent location and rooms are set back from the street, so they're quiet. Big windows looking onto patios and light wells keep the place sunny and airy.

Hotel Ajau (☎ 2232 0488; hotelajau@hotmail.com; 8a Av 15-62; s/d US$10/14, with bathroom US$16/20; ☐) If you're coming or going to Cobán, the Ajau's the obvious choice, being right next-door to the Monja Blanca bus station. Otherwise it's still a pretty good deal, with lovely polished floor tiles and cool, clean rooms.

Hotel Spring (☎ 2230 2858; hotelspring@hotmail .com; 8a Av 12-65; s/d/tr US$12/17/22, with bathroom s US$17-25 d US$22-31 tr US$26-37; P ☐) With a beautiful courtyard setting, the Spring has a lot more style than other Zona 1 joints. It has central but quiet sunny patios. The 43 rooms vary greatly, but most are tall, spacious and clean. Have a look around if you can. All rooms have cable TV; some of the more expensive ones are wheelchair accessible.

It's worth booking ahead. A *cafetería* serves meals from 6:30am to 1:30pm.

Hotel Clariss (☎ 2232 1113; 8a Av 15-14; s/d US$14/20, with bathroom US$22/25; P ☐) This friendly place next to the Cobán bus terminal is in a modern building. There are some good-sized rooms (and other, smaller ones). Those at the front get more air and light, but also the bulk of the street noise.

MIDRANGE

Hotel Colonial (☎ 2232 6722; www.hotelcolonial.net; 7a Av 14-19; s/d/tr US$17/22/27, with bathroom US$25/30/35; P) This is a large old house converted to a hotel with spacious communal areas and heavy, dark, colonial decor. It's a very well-run establishment whose 42 rooms are clean, good-sized and adequately furnished. Nearly all have a private bathroom and TV.

Hotel Quality Service (☎ 2251 8005; www.quality guate.com; 8a Calle 3-18; s/d US$22/28; P ☐) There's a pleasing, old-timey feel about this place, which is balanced perfectly by the modern-but-not-overly-so rooms. The pick of the bunch near the park.

Hotel Excel (☎ 2253 2709; hotelexcel@hotmail.com; 9a Av 15-12; s/d US$22/28) The Excel's bright, modern motel-style may be a bit bland for some, but the rooms are spotless and the showers blast hot water.

Hotel Centenario (☎ 2338 0381; centenario@itelgua .com; 6a Calle 5-33; s/d US$30/36) Although it's looking a bit worn around the edges (and not that flash in the middle, either), the Centenario offers a pretty good deal, right on the park. Rooms are basic and unrenovated, with TV and hot showers.

Hotel Fortuna Royal (☎ 2238 2484; hotelfortuna royal@yahoo.com.ar; 12a Calle 8-42; s/d US$35/40; P) The 21 rooms are large, with good tiled bathrooms and big mirrors and wardrobes. Cable TV, phone, and touches such as oriental-style reading lamps, alarm clock and minibar help make it one of the best downtown deals in this range. There's a restaurant too.

TOP END

Hotel Royal Palace (☎ 2232 5125, 2220 8970; www .hotelroyalpalace.com; 6a Av 12-66; s/d US$48/57; P ⚡) A little island of glamour amidst the rough and tumble of 6a Av, this place offers most comforts. The style is modern-reconstruction, with plenty of dark woods and fancy tiling around the place. Rooms are large, sparkling clean and wheelchair-accessible. Those at the front have balconies overlooking the street – a fascinating, if noisy, spectacle. Facilities include a restaurant, bar, gym, sauna, and free airport transfers.

Hotel Pan American (☎ 2232 6807; www.hotelpan american.com.gt; 9a Calle 5-63; s/d US$50/55; P 💻) Guatemala City's luxury hotel before WWII, the Pan American is still run by its founding family and is one of the few hotels in the city with any air of history. There's a fine, Art Deco lobby that's filled with plants and a not-too-shabby restaurant. Rooms are spacious and simple, often with three or more beds. The bathrooms are stylish and modern, with good-sized tubs. Avoid rooms facing the noisy street.

Zona 9
MIDRANGE

Hotel del Istmo (☎ 2332 4389; 3a Av 1-38; s/d with TV US$20/24, s/d without TV US$18/22) If you are arriving by Melva bus from San Salvador, this hotel at the terminal is clean, comfortable and convenient. All the rooms have a hot-water bathroom and a cable TV.

Hotel Carrillon (☎ 2332 4036; hcarrillon@guate.net .gt; 5 Av 11-25; s/d US$30/36; P) In a fairly ordinary section of Zona 9 (but within walking distance of all the Zona 10 action), this hotel offers a reasonable deal. Rooms are smallish, wood-paneled affairs. Ask to see a few.

Mi Casa (☎ 2339 2247; www.hotelmicasa.com; 5a Av A 13-51; s/d US$40/50; P 💻) Set in a family house on a quiet street, these rooms are big and sunny, with private bathrooms, lino floors,

standard acrylic paintings, fans and reading lamps. Prices include breakfast, which is served in a leafy little patio out back. You can call them and they'll pick you up from the airport.

TOP END

Guatemala City Marriott Hotel (☎ 2339 7777; www .marriott.com; 7a Av 15-45; s & d US$122; P ✗ ⚡ 💻 📺) For that big, corporate I'd-rather-not-be-here hotel experience, it's hard to go past the Marriot.

Hotel Cortijo Reforma (☎ 2332 0712; fax 2331 8876; Av La Reforma 2-18; s/d US$60/65; P) The 130 suites here, though far from modern or flashy, each feature a large living room, bedroom, good tiled bathroom, phone and TV. Some (a little costlier) also have kitchens.

Zona 10
BUDGET

Xamanek Inn (☎ 2360 8345; www.mayaworld.net; 13a Calle 3-57; dm US$14, r with bathroom US$35; 💻) A welcome newcomer in the often-overpriced Zona Viva area is this comfy little hostel. Dorms are spacious and airy, separated into male and female. Rates include a light breakfast and free internet. There's a book exchange, kitchen use and Skype calling for US$0.30 per minute.

MIDRANGE

Eco Hotel los Próceres (☎ 2337 3250; www.ecohotel proceres.com; 18a Calle 3-03; s/d US$40/50; P ⚡) The spotless, brightly painted rooms here are a pretty good deal. They're a bit cramped, but tasteful decoration and modern bathrooms (with tub!) make up for that.

Hotel Posada de los Próceres (☎ 2363-0744; www.ecohotelproceres.com; 16a Calle 2-40; s/d US$40/50; P 💻 ⚡) Twenty brightly decorated, if slightly tatty, rooms right on the edge of the Zona Viva. They're surprisingly large, with attractive tiled bathrooms, phone, clock, cable TV, wooden furniture and mini-fridge. Prices include a light breakfast.

TOP END

Hotel Casa Grande (☎ 2332 0914; www.casagrande-gua .com; Av La Reforma 7-89; s/d US$60/67; P ⚡ 💻) Located within spitting distance of the US embassy (not that we're trying to give you any ideas), this is a refined option that mostly caters to the business crowd. Several patio areas and a log fire in the lounge area crank up the comfort factor.

GUATEMALA CITY

Hotel San Carlos (☎ 2362 9076; www.hsancarlos.com; Av La Reforma 7-89; r US$72, apt from US$120; ☒ ☐ ☒) OK, so it goes a little heavy on the baroque furnishings, but this place is still a good deal. Set well back from the busy street, it's quiet, and the well-appointed rooms and apartments are spacious and comfortable.

Hotel Stofella (☎ 2410 8600; www.bestwestern.com; 2a Av 12-28; s/d US$75/80; ☒ ☒ ☒ ☐) This pleasant, medium-sized Zona Viva hotel is part of the international Best Western chain, and provides quality rooms – with air-conditioning, safes, and phones in bedroom and bathroom – at reasonable prices. Rates include breakfast and one hour of free internet usage daily. You can hook up a computer in your room for US$5 a day.

our pick **Otelito** (☎ 2339 1811; www.otelito.com; 12a Calle 4-51; s/d US$90/100; ☒ ☒ ☐) Screaming with Zen tranquility, this place bustles with bamboo, mood lighting and polished steel. Rooms are spacious and minimalist and bathrooms modern, with big glassed-in shower stalls. There's a garden restaurant/café out front. Book ahead.

Zona 11

Grand Tikal Futura Hotel (☎ 2410 0800; www.grandtikal futura.com.gt; Calzada Roosevelt 22-43; s & d from US$250; ☒ ☒ ☐ ☒) The towering glass architecture here is a contemporary reinterpretation of the grandiose concepts of ancient Tikal. The 205 luxurious rooms and suites all enjoy spectacular views and have their own safes.

Hook up with a Guatemalan and you can take advantage of hefty 'local discounts.' On the lower levels of the complex, you'll find one the city's biggest shopping malls, 10 cinemas and a bowling alley. It's in the west of the city on the road to Antigua, 3km from Zona 1, Zona 10 or the airport.

Zona 13

Four dependable guesthouses in a middle-class residential area in Zona 13 are very convenient for the airport. All their room rates include breakfast and airport transfers (call from the airport on arrival). There are no restaurants out here, but these places offer breakfast and have the complete lowdown on fast-food home delivery in the area.

BUDGET

Patricia's Guest House (☎ 2261 4251, 5402 3256 in English; 19 Calle 10-65; r per person US$12) The most relaxed and comfortable option is in this family house with a sweet little backyard where guests can hang out. They also offer private transport around the city and shuttles to bus stations.

Dos Lunas (☎ /fax 2261 4248; www.xelapages.com /doslunas; 21a Calle 10-92; dm US$12, s/d US$15/30; ☒ ☐) An old faithful, the Dos Lunas has excellent common areas, a cramped dorm and a couple of very nice private rooms. Book through the website. Dos Lunas also offers onward-travel packages and Flores flights at good prices.

ADOPTION CENTRAL

In your travels around Guatemala City you're likely to see a surprising sight: young, hopeful couples from the US with brand-new Guatemalan babies.

The number of Guatemalan children adopted by foreign couples in 2006 was 4359, and 95% of these went to couples from the US. Adopting a child is a surprisingly simple process, due to the largely unregulated nature of Guatemala's adoption laws – a fact that has many observers worried.

There has been so much concern over kidnapping and baby selling (the lawyers alone on these transactions make an average of US$15,000 per adoption) that the US, British and Canadian embassies now require a DNA test to make sure that the woman giving up the baby is in fact the birth mother.

Critics say this does little. Babies can be swapped between the embassy and the airport and there is no guarantee that the birth mother is not being coerced to give up her baby.

One thing is sure – with 20,000 Guatemalan children living in orphanages and another 5000 living on the streets of Guatemala City, something has to be done.

For years now, activists have been trying to get Congress to pass 'The Children's Code' – a piece of legislation designed to protect the rights of children. It seems that the political will is not there, and until it is, maybe the best hope these kids have is for a ticket out of the country.

MIDRANGE

Rates at both these places include breakfast and airport transfers (call from the airport on arrival).

Hostal Los Lagos (☎ 2261 2909; www.loslagoshostal .com; 8a Av 15-85; dm US$15, s/d with bathroom US$30/60; **P** 💻) This is the most hostellike of the near-the-airport options. Rooms are mostly set aside for dorms, which are airy and spacious, but there are a couple of reasonable-value private rooms. The whole place is extremely comfortable, with big indoor and outdoor sitting areas.

Hostal Los Volcanes (☎ 2261 3040; www.hostallos volcanes.com; 16a Calle 8-00; dm US$15, s/d US$20/30, with bathroom & TV US$25/40; 💻) A cozy place with big, clean, shared bathrooms and some decent rooms with private bathroom. There's plenty of Nahual furniture and *tipica* fabrics around, giving the place a good atmosphere.

EATING

Cheap eats are easy to find in Zona 1. Fine dining is more prevalent in Zona 10.

Zona 1
BUDGET

Dozens of restaurants and fast-food shops are strung along and just off 6a Av between 8a and 15a Calles. American fast-food chains like McDonald's and Burger King are sprinkled liberally throughout Zona 1 and the rest of the city. They're open long hours, often from 7am to 10pm. Pollo Campero is Guatemala's KFC clone: a serve of chicken, fries, Pepsi and bread costs around US$4.

Café de Imeri (6a Calle 3-34; mains US$3-5; 🕑 8am-7pm Tue-Sat) Completely out of step with the majority of Zona 1 eateries, this place offers interesting breakfasts, soups and pastas. The list of sandwiches is impressive and there's a beautiful little courtyard area out back.

Doner Kebab (10 Calle 6-35; kebabs US$3; 🕑 breakfast, lunch & dinner) For a quick Turkish-food fix in the center, it's hard to beat the authentic flavors in this place. Nothing fancy in the decor, but you *can* get six beers for US$7.

Parrillada Doña Sara (cnr 9a Calle & 9a Av; mains US$3.50-5; 🕑 lunch & dinner) A lot of places call themselves Argentine steakhouses, but this one recreates the atmosphere almost exactly, with photo-covered walls, cheap wine and good (but not great) steaks.

Café-Restaurante Hamburgo (15a Calle 5-34; set lunch or dinner US$4-6; 🕑 7am-9:30pm) This bustling

spot facing the south side of Parque Concordia serves good Guatemalan food, with chefs at work along one side and orange-aproned waitresses scurrying about. At weekends a marimba band adds atmosphere.

Restaurante Rey Sol (11a Calle 5-51; meals around US$4; 🕑 8am-5pm Mon-Sat) Good, fresh ingredients and some innovative cooking keep this strictly vegetarian restaurant busy at lunchtimes.

Restaurante Long Wah (6a Calle 3-70; dishes US$4-6; 🕑 11am-10pm) With friendly service and decorative red-painted arches, the Long Wah is a good choice from Zona 1's other concentration of Chinese eateries, in the blocks west of Parque Centenario.

Picadily (cnr 6 Av & 11a Calle; mains US$4-8; 🕑 lunch, dinner) Right in the thick of the 6a Av action, this bustling restaurant does OK pizzas and pastas and good steak dishes. The place is clean and street views out of the big front windows are mesmerizing.

Bagel Factory (cnr 7a Av & 10 Calle; bagels US$4; 🕑 breakfast, lunch & dinner) Anywhere outside of NYC, bagels can be a dodgy proposition, but these guys do OK. Fresh ingredients, plenty of options, a super-clean environment and a sunny courtyard make this place a winner.

Bar-Restaurante Europa (Local 201, Edificio Testa, 11a Calle 5-16; mains US$4-6; 🕑 8am-8:30pm Mon-Sat) The Europa is a comfortable, relaxed, 11-table restaurant, bar and gathering place for locals and foreigners alike (the bar stays open till midnight). A sign on the door says 'English spoken, but not understood.' It has international cable TV and good-value food – try chicken cordon bleu for dinner, or eggs, hash browns, bacon and toast for breakfast.

MIDRANGE

Hotel Pan American (☎ 2232 6807; 9a Calle 5-63; breakfast US$6-10, lunch US$8-12; 🕑 breakfast, lunch & dinner) The restaurant at this venerable hotel (see p83) is high on ambience. It has highly experienced and polished waiters sporting traditional Mayan regalia. The food (Guatemalan, Italian and American) is fine, although it is a little on the expensive side.

El Gran Pavo de Don Neto (☎ 2232-9912; 13a Calle 4-41; mains US$8-11; 🕑 breakfast, lunch & dinner) Big and bright, the Gran Pavo serves almost every Mexican dish imaginable. The *birria*, a spicy-hot soup of meat, onions, peppers and *cilantro* (coriander leaf), served with tortillas, is a meal in itself for US$4.

TOP END

Restaurante Altuna (☎ 2232 0669; 5a Av 12-31; mains US$10-15; ⏰ lunch & dinner Tue-Sat, lunch Sun) This large and classy restaurant has the atmosphere of a private club. It has tables in several rooms that are off a skylighted patio. The specialities are seafood and Spanish dishes; service is both professional and welcoming.

Zona 4
MIDRANGE

Cuatro Grados Norte, situated on Vía 5 between Rutas 1 and 3, is the name for a two-block pedestrianized strip of restaurants and cafés with sidewalk tables and relaxed café society. Inaugurated in 2002, and the only place of its kind in Guatemala City, it is conveniently close to the main Inguat tourist office. It gets lively in the evening, particularly around weekends. You can choose from a dozen or so establishments, some of which double as galleries, bookstores or music venues.

Del Paseo (Vía 5 1-81, Cuatro Grados Norte; mains US$5-8.50; ⏰ lunch & dinner Tue-Sun) This spacious, artsy, Mediterranean-style bistro is one of Cuatro Grados Norte's most popular spots. Relaxed jazz plays in the background unless there's a live band (try Thursdays from 9pm). You might select roast chicken breast with tropical fruits and grated coconut – or spinach-and-ricotta filo pastry parcels? Wine goes for US$3 a glass.

Tarboosh (Vía 5, Cuatro Grados Norte; mains US$6-15; ⏰ lunch & dinner Tue-Sun) Done out like a harem (but tastefully), this place offers authentic Middle Eastern fare like falafel (US$6.50), *kibellah* and delicious *mezzeh* platters (US$20).

ourpick L'Osteria (cnr Vía 5 & Ruta 2, Cuatro Grados Norte; mains US$7-10; ⏰ lunch & dinner Tue-Sun) Excellent Italian dishes – mostly pizzas and pastas – and a good wine list. The shady terrace out front earns top marks for people watching.

Flamenco (Vía 4, Cuatro Grados Norte; tapas US$6, mains US$10; ⏰ lunch & dinner Tue-Sun) Catch a breeze and take a breather on the upstairs balcony at this tapas bar/Spanish restaurant.

Kampai (Vía 5, Cuatro Grados Norte; mains US$10-15; ⏰ lunch & dinner Tue-Sun) Apart from some atrocious music selections, this is a surprisingly good Japanese restaurant. All your faves are here – sashimi, teppanyaki, tempura, plus a range of 'novelty rolls' – California rolls shaped like cars, scorpions, etc.

Zona 9

Puerto Barrios (☎ 2334-1302; 7a Av 10-65; mains US$12-16; ⏰ noon-3pm & 7-11pm) The Puerto Barrios specializes in tasty prawn and fish dishes and is awash in nautical themes – paintings of buccaneers, portholes for windows, a big compass by the door. If you're having trouble finding it, just look for the big pirate ship that it's housed in.

Zona 10
BUDGET

A string of (mostly) nameless *comedores* opposite the Los Proceres mall serve up the cheapest eats in Zona 10. There's nothing fancy going on here – just good, filling eats at rock bottom prices.

Cafetería Patsy (Av La Reforma 8-01; set lunch US$3.50; ⏰ 7:30am-8pm) A bright, cheerful place popular with local office workers, offering subs, sandwiches and good value set lunches.

San Martín & Company (13a Calle 1-62; light meals US$3-5; ⏰ 6am-8pm Mon-Sat) Cool and clean, with ceiling fans inside and a small terrace outside, this Zona Viva café and bakery is great at any time of day. For breakfast try a scrumptious omelet and croissant (the former arrives inside the latter). Later there are tempting and original sandwiches, soups and salads. The entrance is on 2a Av.

La Chapinita (1 Av 10-24; mains US$4-6; ⏰ breakfast, lunch & dinner) Down-home Guatemalan food served in more or less formal surrounds can be hard to come by in Zona 10, but this place does it well at good prices. Tables out front on the shady terrace are cool and breezy.

Los Alpes (10a Calle 1-09; breakfast US$4-6; ⏰ breakfast & lunch) A relaxing garden restaurant/bakery. It's set well back from the road, behind a wall of vegetation, giving it a feeling of deep seclusion. The freshly made sandwiches and cakes really hit the spot.

MIDRANGE

Inka Grill (☎ 2363 3013; 2a Av 14-22; mains US$8-15; ⏰ lunch & dinner Tues-Sun) Peruvian artifacts adorn the pink and yellow walls; tasty Peruvian food makes the tables a treat. Try the specialty *arroz con mariscos* (rice with seafood). There's a good international wine list too.

TOP END

Marea Alta (10a Calle 1-89; mains US$10-20, buffet US$13; ⏰ lunch & dinner; buffet Mon-Wed) Specializing in imported seafood, this place has some good

---

LOCAL LORE: THE WIDOW AND THE DEVIL

There was once a wise widow with three beautiful daughters. Every day, men would arrive, trying to woo them, but the widow saw through them and sent them away.

Then one day a handsome, charming man arrived and began to win the hearts of all three daughters.

He showed them magic tricks, turning potatoes into gold coins and pulling jewels from their hair. The daughters were enchanted. The next day he returned and his tricks became more fabulous – he turned himself into an eagle and a jaguar and a peacock.

The widow became suspicious, and went to see the priest, who came up with a plan. The next day, when the stranger returned and began his tricks again, the widow said, 'If you're so powerful, why don't you shrink yourself down into this bottle?'

In an instant he did, and the widow plugged the bottle with a cork that had been blessed by the priest.

The devil could not escape – he needed a human to release him, and the widow and the priest buried the bottle in the forest.

Years passed, and then one day Alfonso, a drunk, was walking by the spot and fell over. 'Release me,' said the devil, 'and I will make you rich.'

So Alfonso uncorked the bottle, and the devil proposed a plan. They would go from town to town and the devil would go into people's stomachs, making them sick, and Alfonso would sell them the cure.

One day they arrived in the capital, and decided to fool the governor. The devil went into his stomach and soon Alfonso was called for.

But when Alfonso entered the governor's house he was distracted by the beauty of the governor's daughter and gave the governor a glass of acid to drink by mistake. The acid burnt the devil, who refused to come out.

Alfonso began to repent his evildoing and confessed to the governor, who organized for a loud noise to be made.

Alfonso told the devil that the noise was the widow who had trapped him in the bottle.

The devil got scared and ran away. The governor got better and Alfonso was soon engaged to his daughter.

---

prices considering the location. The lunchtime buffet is a winner, as is the surf 'n' turf platter for US$10.

Txoco (13a Calle 5-17; mains US$10-25; ☺ lunch & dinner Tue-Sun) Good, hearty Spanish and Basque food in a relaxed and informal atmosphere. The tapas list is long and varied and the wine list features bottles from Italy, Spain and Chile. Thursday to Sunday there are daily specials like paella and seafood stew.

Tamarindos (☎ 2360 2815; 11a Calle 2-19A; mains US$15-20; ☺ lunch Mon-Fri, dinner Mon-Sat) A chic and delicious Thai and Italian restaurant with a Guatemalan twist. The four-cheese gnocchi is irresistible, and the vegetarian pad Thai blends a thousand flavors. The stylish decor recalls New York – but the prices are Guatemalan.

DRINKING
Zona 1
Staggering from bar to bar about the darkened streets of Zona 1 is not recommended, but fortunately there's a clutch of good drinking places all within half a block of each other just south of the Parque Central.

Las Cien Puertas (Pasaje Aycinena 8-44, 9a Calle 6-45) This superhip (but not studiously so) little watering hole is a gathering place for all manner of local creative types (and a few travelers) who may be debating politics, strumming a guitar or refining the graffiti when you show up. Tasty snacks such as tacos and quesadillas are served. It's in a shabby colonial arcade that's said to have a hundred doors (hence the name) and is sometimes closed off for live bands.

La Arcada (7 Av 9-10) Drop into this friendly little neighborhood bar for a few drinks – they'll let you pick the music, or spin some of their own – anything from Guat rock to ambient trance.

El Portal (Portal del Comercio, 6a Av; ☺ 10am-10pm Mon-Sat) This atmospheric old drinking den serves fine draft beer (around US$2 a mug)

THE BIG NIGHT OUT

Guatemalans love going out and you shouldn't have any trouble finding a place to grab a beer anywhere you go in the country. The only question remains where. Generally speaking, you can go anywhere without too much trouble, but you should be aware that there are a couple of significant differences in the way that nightspots get named here.

Cantinas, for example, are generally the roughest of the drinking establishments – this is where you go to get falling down drunk, and listen to *ranchera* (Mexican cowboy) music. It's an all-male atmosphere, and while women are most certainly welcome, they won't feel comfortable.

Bars are a tricky one. In big cities, a bar can be exactly what we understand it to be – a place with music, mixed drinks and a mixed crowd. In smaller towns, however, a bar generally has the same atmosphere as a cantina, except it doubles as a brothel.

Nightclubs (or, as most of these places would have it, 'Nigthclubs') ar e not at all the same here as they are back home. These places are basically strip joints, with prostitutes working.

Discotecas are more what we think of when we say nightclub. They have big dance floors, dress codes and sometimes charge an entry fee.

---

and free tapas. Che Guevara was once a patron. Sit at the long wooden bar or one of the wooden tables. Clients are mostly, but not exclusively, men. To find it, enter the Portal del Comercio arcade from 6a Av a few steps south of the Parque Central.

El Rincón del Centro (9a Calle 6-37) In every way a halfway house between El Portal and Pasaje Aycinena, this bar attracts a mixed crowd, from students to 30- and 40-somethings, all enjoying a few beers to recorded rock.

Zona 4

Guate's restaurant/bar precinct, Cuatro Grados Norte, is taking over from Zona 10 as *the* place to go out. You can just have a drink at any of the restaurants along here, but there are a couple of good bars.

Suae (Vía 5, Cuatro Grados Norte) Hip, but not exclusive, this bar has a great, laidback ambience in the day and heats up at night. Rotating art exhibitions, a funky clothes boutique and guest DJs all add to the appeal.

La Playa (cnr Vía 5 & Ruata 1, Cuatro Grados Norte) With a heap of pool tables and cheap beer on tap, this upstairs bar is as good a place as any to start your night.

Zona 10

The best place to go bar hopping is around the corner of 2a Av and 15a Calle – there are plenty of places to choose from – check and see who's got the crowd tonight.

Mi Guajira (2 Av 14-42) This happening little disco/bar has a pretty good atmosphere and goes fairly light on the snob factor. Music varies depending on the night, but be pre-

pared for anything from salsa to reggaeton to trance.

El Establo (14a Calle 5-08) This mellow watering hole attracts both foreigners and locals with its pub-style layout, three-sided, brass-topped bar, good pub food and enormous range of music spun by the German owners. Not cheap, though, at US$3 a Gallo beer.

Zona 12

For a seriously down to earth night out, you should go out partying with the students from USAC, Guatemala's public university. The strip of bars along 31a Calle at the corner of 11a Av, just near the main entrance to the university, all offer cheap beer, loud music and bar/junk food. Like student bars all over the world, they're busy any time of day, but nights and weekends are best. A taxi out here from the center should cost about US$6 if it's not too late, or you can catch any bus that says 'USAC' that doesn't go along Av Petapa.

El Tarro (31a Calle 13-08) The most formal of the bunch (in that it has menus, vaguely comfortable seats and draft beer) has a dance floor out back.

Liverpool (31a Calle 11-53) Plenty of pool tables and cheap drinks keep this place swinging.

Ice (31a Calle 13-39) This one heats up later into the night, when the dance floor fills up with students dancing salsa, merengue and *reggaeton*.

ENTERTAINMENT
Cinema

Various multiscreen cinema complexes show Hollywood blockbuster movies, often in

English with Spanish subtitles. Unless they're kids movies, in which case they'll most likely be dubbed into Spanish. Most convenient are **Cines Tikal Futura** (Centro Comercial Tikal Futura; ☎ 2440-3297; Calzada Roosevelt 22-43, Zona 11) or **Cines Próceres** (Centro Comercial Los Próceres; ☎ 2332-8508; 16a Calle, Zona 10). Tickets cost between US$2 and US$4. Movie listings can be found in the *Prensa Libre* newspaper.

Gay Venues

Don't get too excited about this heading: there are only a couple of places worthy of mention for men, and nothing much for women.

Genetic (Ruta 3 No 3-08, Zona 4; ⏱ 9pm-1am Fri & Sat) This used to be called Pandora's Box, and has been hosting Guatemala's gay crowd since the '70s, although it gets a mixed crowd and is one of the best places in town to go for trance/dance music. It has two dance floors, a rooftop patio and a relaxed atmosphere with a mainly under-30 crowd.

Ephebus (4a Calle 5-30, Zona 1; ⏱ 9pm-1am Thu-Sat) A well-established gay disco-bar in a former private house near the city center, often with strippers.

El Encuentro (Local 229, Centro Capitol, 6a Av 12-51, Zona 1; ⏱ 5pm-midnight Mon-Sat) This quiet bar, in the back of a noisy downtown mall, is another gay meeting place.

Theater

Two very good cultural centers in Cuatro Grados Norte host regular theatrical performances and other artistic events. It's always worth dropping in or checking their websites to see what's on.

The English language magazine *Revue* (www.revuemag.com) has events details, although it focuses more on Antigua. Your hotel should have a copy, or know where to get one. Free events mags in Spanish come and go. At the time of writing, *El Azar* (elazarcultural@yahoo.es) had the best info. Pick up a copy at any cultural center listed below.

IGA Cultural Center (www.iga.edu; Ruta 1, 4-05, Zona 4) The Instituto Guatemalteco Americano hosts art exhibitions and live theater.

Centro Cultural de España (www.centroculturalespana.com.gt; Vía 5 1-23, Zona 4) The Spanish Cultural center hosts an excellent range of events, including live music, film nights and art exhibitions, mostly with free admission.

Centro Cultural Miguel Ángel Asturias (☎ 232 4042; 24a Calle 3-81, Zona 1) Cultural events are also held here.

Live Music

La Bodeguita del Centro (12a Calle 3-55, Zona 1) There's a hopping, creative local scene in Guatemala City, and this large, bohemian hangout is one of the best places to connect with it. Posters featuring the likes of Che, Marley, Lennon, Víctor Jara, Van Gogh and Pablo Neruda cover the walls from floor to ceiling. There's live music

---

LOCAL VOICES: PEDRO MENDEZ, TROVADOR

Spend any time out and about in a big city in Guatemala and you're bound to hear some Guatemalan folk music, or *trova*. We caught up with *trovador* Pedro Mendez to find out what all the fuss is about.

When did you start playing *trova*?

I started playing seriously when I was about 15. Before I just played around, but my friends told me I was good so I got more serious about it.

Did you study music?

A little bit in school, but *trova* is a very street thing. We say that school for *trovadores* is in the street. Most of what I learnt was just from playing with people and listening.

What is trova for you?

At its most simple, *trova* is one person with a guitar, singing. But it's more complicated than that. *Trova* songs are rougher, they're not like pop songs – they speak about the hardships of life – poverty, broken hearts, bad luck…

Trova has a political side…

There's a lot of different types of *trova* – pop, alternative, romantic, but it really got big here as a political expression. There was a time in Guatemala when the *trovadores* were the only ones that could really talk about what was going on, and even they had to be careful. I guess it's still kind of like that.

of some kind almost every night from Tuesday to Saturday, usually starting at 9pm, plus occasional poetry readings, films or forums. Entry is usually free Tuesday to Thursday, with a charge of US$2.50 to US$5 on Friday and Saturday nights. Food and drinks are served. Pick up a monthly schedule of events.

Rattle & Hum (4a Av & 16a Calle, Zona 10) One of the last places in Zona 10 to still be hosting live music, this Australian-owned place has a warm and friendly atmosphere.

Blue Town Café Bar (11a Calle 4-51, Zona 1) If La Bodeguita doesn't suit you, check out this nearby youthful spot with live bands.

TrovaJazz (Vía 6 No 3-55, Zona 4) Jazz, blues and folk fans should look into what's happening here.

Dancing

La Estación Norte (Ruta 4, 6-32, Zona 4) As far as mega discos go, this one around the corner from Cuatro Grados Norte is kind of interesting. It's done out in a train theme, with carriages for bars and platforms for dance floors. Dress well, but not over the top.

Zona 10 has a bunch of clubs attracting twenty-something local crowds along 13a Calle and adjacent streets such as 1a Av. The area's exclusivity means that door staff are well versed in the old 'members only' and 'sorry, we're full' routines. If you want to try your luck, the universal rules apply: dress up, go before 11pm and make sure your group has more women than men in it. Check flyers around town for special nights. Here are a couple to get you started:

Kahlua (15a Calle & 1a Av, Zona 10) For electronica and bright young things.

Mr Jerry (13a Calle 1-26, Zona 10) For salsa and merengue.

SHOPPING

Mercado Central (9a Av btwn 6a & 8a Calles; ⏰ 9am-6pm Mon-Sat, 9am-noon Sun) Until the quake of 1976, Mercado Central, behind the cathedral, was where locals shopped for food and other necessities. Reconstructed after the earthquake, it now deals in colorful Guatemalan handicrafts such as textiles, carved wood, metalwork, pottery, leather goods and basketry, and is a pretty good place to shop for these kinds of things, with reasonable prices.

Mercado de Artesanías (Crafts Market; cnr 5a Calle & 11a Av, Zona 13; ⏰ 9:30am-6pm) This sleepy official market near the museums and zoo sells similar goods in less-crowded conditions.

For fashion boutiques, electronic goods and other first-world paraphernalia, head for the large shopping malls such as **Centro Comercial Los Próceres** (16a Calle, Zona 10) or **Centro Comercial Tikal Futura** (Calzada Roosevelt 22-43, Zona 11).

For a more everyday Guatemalan experience, take a walk along 6a Av between 8a and 16a Calles in Zona 1. Back in the '70s, before the big shopping malls started stealing all the customers away, there was a verb 'sexteando,' which meant going for a stroll along the 6a Av (La Sexta) to see what was on offer. The scene has quietened down a bit, but it's still ground central for cheap copied CDs, shoes, underwear, overalls and pretty much everything else under the sun.

GETTING THERE & AWAY

Air

Guatemala City's **Aeropuerto La Aurora** (☎ 2334 7680) is the country's major airport. All international flights to Guatemala City land and take off here. At the time of writing, the country's only *scheduled* domestic flights are between Guatemala City and Flores. The major carrier, Grupo TACA, makes two round-trip flights daily (one in the morning, one in the afternoon), plus an extra flight four mornings a week which continues from Flores to Cancún (Mexico) and flies back from there via Flores in the afternoon. See p71 for contact details.

Tickets to Flores cost around US$127/204 one-way/round-trip with Grupo TACA, but some travel agents, especially in Antigua, offer large discounts on these prices.

Bus

Buses from here run all over Guatemala and into Mexico, Belize, Honduras, El Salvador and beyond. Most bus companies have their own terminals, some of which are in Zona 1. The Terminal de Autobuses, in Zona 4, is used only by some 2nd-class buses. The city council has been on a campaign to get long-distance bus companies out of the city center, so it may be wise to double check with Inguat or your hotel owner about the office location before heading out there.

PULLMAN BUS SERVICES

The following bus companies have Pullman services:

Escobar y Monja Blanca (☎ 2238 1409; 8a Av 15-16, Zona 1)

Fortaleza del Sur (☎ 2230 3390; Calzada Raúl Aguilar Batres 4-15, Zona 12)
Fuente del Norte (☎ 2251 3817; 17a Calle 8-46, Zona 1)
Hedman Alas (☎ 2362 5072/5; 2a Av 8-73, Zona 10)
King Quality & Confort Lines (☎ 2369 0404/56; 18a Av 1-96, Zona 15)
Línea Dorada (☎ 2232 9658; cnr 10a Av & 16 Calle, Zona 1)
Líneas América (☎ 2232-1432; 2a Av 18-47, Zona 1)
Litegua (☎ 2253 8169; 15a Calle 10-40, Zona 1)
Los Halcones (☎ 2439 2780; Calzada Rosevelt 37-47, Zona 11)
Melva Internacional (☎ 2331 0874; 3a Av 1-38, Zona 9)
Pullmantur (☎ 2332 9785/6; Holiday Inn, 1a Av 13-22, Zona 10)
Rutas Orientales (☎ 2253 7282; 19 Calle 8-18, Zona 1)
Tica Bus (☎ 2366 4038; Blvd Los Proceres 26-55, Zona 10)
Transportes Álamo (☎ 2251 4838; 12 Av 'A' 0-65, Zona 7)
Transportes Galgos (☎ 2253 4868; 7a Av 19-44, Zona 1)
Transportes Velásquez (☎ 2440 3316; Calzada Roosevelt 9-56, Zona 7)

Pullman Bus Departures

Belize City (US$40, 16 hours) Línea Dorada has first class buses, with a few hours' wait in Flores. Alternatively, take a bus to Flores/Santa Elena and an onward bus from there.
Biotopo del Quetzal (US$4, 3½ hours) Escobar y Monja Blanca has hourly buses from 4am to 5pm, via El Rancho and Purulhá.
Chetumal (Mexico) Take a bus to Flores/Santa Elena, where daily buses leave for Chetumal (see p281).
Chiquimula (US$2.60, three hours) Rutas Orientales departs every 30 minutes, from 4:30am to 6pm.
Ciudad Tecún Umán/Ciudad Hidalgo (Mexican border) (US$8, six hours) Fortaleza del Sur has 20 daily buses, from12:15am to 6:30pm.
Cobán (US$4.25; 4½ hours) Escobar y Monja Blanca has buses hourly, from 4am to 5pm, stopping at El Rancho and the Biotopo del Quetzal.
Copán (Honduras) (US$36, five hours) Hedman Alas departs at 5am daily with 1st-class buses, which continue to San Pedro Sula and La Ceiba. It's cheaper, and slower, to take a bus to Chiquimula, then another to the border at El Florido, then another on to Copán.
El Carmen/Talismán (Mexican border) (US$6.50, seven hours) Fortaleza del Sur has 20 daily buses, from 12:15am to 6:30pm.
Esquipulas (US$4, 4½ hours) Rutas Orientales departs every 30 minutes, from 4:30am to 6pm
Flores/Santa Elena (eight to 10 hours) Fuente del Norte runs 18 daily buses (US$9 to US$17 depending on the service) Línea Dorada has buses at 9am, 9pm and 10pm (US$23).
Fuente del Norte goes hourly, with a special Maya de Oro service (US$17) at 10:30pm.

Huehuetenango (US$6.50, five hours) Los Halcones departs at 7am, 2pm and 5pm. Transportes Velásquez also stops at Huehuetenango. All go by the Interamericana.
La Mesilla/Ciudad Cuauhtémoc (Mexican border) (US$9, seven hours) Transportes Velásquez departs every 30 minutes, from 8am to 11am. From Ciudad Cuauhtémoc there are fairly frequent buses and vans on to Comitán & San Cristóbal de Las Casas.
Lívingston See Puerto Barrios (p260) and Río Dulce (p254); from either place you can reach Lívingston by boat.
Melchor de Mencos (Belizean border) (US$10.50, 11 hours)
Poptún Take a bus headed to Flores.
Puerto Barrios (First Class/Standard Pullman US$11/5.50, five hours) Litegua departs every half hour, from 4:30am to 6pm.
Quetzaltenango (US$6, five hours) Transportes Álamo has six buses from 8am to 5:30pm. Líneas América has seven buses from 5am to 7:30pm. Línea Dorada departs at 8am and 3pm (US$8). Transportes Galgos has seven buses from 5:30am to 5pm.
Quiriguá Take a Puerto Barrios bus (see p250 for details on getting from the Carretera al Atlántico to Quiriguá ruins).
Retalhuleu (US$6, three hours) Fortaleza del Sur has 20 buses from 12:10am to 7:10pm.
Río Dulce (US$6, six hours) Litegua departs at 6am, 9am, 11:30am and 1pm. Flores-bound buses stop at Río Dulce too.
San Salvador (El Salvador) (five to six hours) Melva Internacional runs buses via the border at Valle Nuevo hourly, from 5:15am to 4:15pm (US$10). Tica Bus departs 12:30pm daily (US$9.50). From San Salvador, Tica Bus services all other Central American capitals except Belize City. King Quality & Confort Lines runs luxury buses at 6:30am, 8am, 2pm and & 3:30pm (US$20), with connections to Tegucigalpa and Managua. Pullmantur has luxury buses at 7am, 1pm and 3pm.
Sayaxché (11 hours) Fuente del Norte departs at 4pm (US$12) and 7pm (US$15) via Río Dulce & Flores, and at 5:30pm via Cobán (US$12).
Tapachula (Mexico) (six to seven hours) Transportes Galgos departs at 7:30am and 1:30pm (US$21.50). Línea Dorada departs at 7am and 4pm (US$33). Tica Bus departs at noon (US$19). From Tapachula buses run to many points in Mexico.
Tegucigalpa (Honduras) (US$54; 12 hours) Hedman Alas departs at 5am with 1st-class buses.
Tikal Take a bus to Flores/Santa Elena and onward transportation from there.

SECOND-CLASS BUS SERVICES

The following are all second-class bus services:
Antigua (US$0.65, 1¼ hours, 45km) Buses depart from 1a Av between 3a and 4a Calle, Zona 7, every few minutes from 5am to 9pm. See p117 for details on shuttle minibuses.

Chichicastenango (US$1.55, three hours, 145km) Veloz Quichelense (☎ 41a Calle btwn 6a & 7a Calle, Zona 8) Has hourly buses from 5am to 8pm.

Ciudad Pedro de Alvarado/La Hachadura (Salvadoran border) (US$2, two hours) Buses to Taxisco depart from the Terminal de Autobuses every 30 minutes, from 5am to 4pm. Some continue to the border; otherwise change at Taxisco where buses leave for the border every 15 minutes until 5pm.

Escuintla (US$1.25, one hour, 57km) See La Democracia & Puerto San José.

La Democracia (US$1.50, two hours, 92km) Chatía Gomerana (cnr 4a Calle & 8a Av, Zona 12) Has buses every 30 minutes, from 6am to 4:30pm, stopping at Escuintla.

Monterrico Take one of the half-hourly buses, from 5am to 4pm, from the Terminal de Autobuses to Taxisco (US$1.50, two hours). Change there for a bus to La Avellana (US$1, one hour, 12 daily, from 7am to 6pm) and from there take a boat (see p208).

Nebaj Take a bus to Santa Cruz del Quiché & another onto Nebaj from there.

Panajachel (US$2, 3½ hours, 150km) Transportes Rébuli (☎ 2230 2748; 41a Calle btwn 6a & 7a Calle, Zona 8) Departs hourly, from 7am to 4pm, with a Pullman bus (US$4.25) at 9:30am.

Puerto San José (US$2, 2½ hours, 90km) Various companies run via Escuintla about every 15 minutes, from 5am to 6pm, from 4a Calle between 7a and 8a Avs, Zona 12.

Salamá (US$3, three hours, 150km) Transportes Dulce María (☎ 2253 4618; 17a Calle 11-32, Zona 1) Departs every hour, from 5am to 5pm.

Santa Cruz del Quiché (US$3.50, 3½ hours, 163km) Buses depart from the Terminal de Autobuses every 15 to 20 minutes, from 5am to 5pm.

Santa Elena See Flores/Santa Elena.

Santa Lucía Cotzumalguapa Take a bus to Escuintla and another from there.

Santiago Atitlán (US$3.50, four hours, 165km) Various companies depart from 4a Calle between 8a and 9a Avs, Zona 12, every half hour from 4am to 5pm.

Tecpán (US$1, two hours, 92km) Veloz Poaquileña (1a Av btwn 3a & 4a Calles, Zona 7) Departs every 15 minutes, from 5:30am to 7pm.

Car

Most major rental companies have offices both at La Aurora airport (in the arrivals area) and in Zona 9 or 10. Companies include the following:

Ahorrent (www.ahorrent.com) Aeropuerto Internacional La Aurora (☎ 2362 8921/2); Zona 9 (☎ 2361 5661; Blvd Liberación 4-83)

Avis (www.avisenlinea.com in Spanish) Aeropuerto Internacional La Aurora (☎ 2260 6242); Zona 9 (☎ 2339 3249; 6a Av 7-64)

Dollar (www.dollar.com) Aeropuerto Internacional La Aurora (☎ 2261 3257); Zona 10 (☎ 2332 7525; Av La Reforma 8-33)

Hertz (www.hertz.com.gt) Aeropuerto Internacional La Aurora (☎ 2470 3800, 2470 3838); Guatemala City Marriott Hotel (☎ 2339 7777); Holiday Inn (☎ 2332 2555); Hotel Real Inter-Continental Guatemala (☎ 2379 4444); Westin Camino Real (☎ 2368 0107); Zona 9 (☎ 2332 2242; 7a Av 14-76)

Tabarini (www.tabarini.com) Aeropuerto Internacional La Aurora (☎ 2260 6343); Zona 10 (☎ 2331 6108; 2a Calle A 7-30)

Tally Renta Autos (www.tallyrentaautos.com) Aeropuerto Internacional La Aurora (☎ 2277 9072); Zona 1 (☎ 2232 0421/3327; 7a Av 14-60)

Thrifty (☎ 2379 8747; thrifty@intelnet.gt; 1a Av 13-74, Zona 10)

Shuttle Minibus

Door-to-door minibuses run from the airport to any address in Antigua (usually US$10 per person, one hour). Look for signs in the airport exit hall or people holding up 'Antigua Shuttle' signs. The first shuttle leaves for Antigua about 7am and the last around 8pm or 9pm. Shuttle services from Guatemala City to popular destinations such as Panajachel and Chichicastenango (both around US$25) are offered by travel agencies in Antigua such as Sin Fronteras – see p100 for contact details.

GETTING AROUND
To/From the Airport

Aeropuerto La Aurora is in Zona 13, in the southern part of the city, 10 to 15 minutes from Zona 1 by taxi, half an hour by bus.

For the city bus, cross the road outside the arrivals exit and climb the steps. At the top, with your back to the terminal building, walk to the left down the approach road (about 100m), then turn right to the bus stop. Buses 83 'Terminal' and 83 'Bolívar' go to the Parque Central in Zona 1, passing through Zonas 9 and 4 en route: you can get off at any corner along the way. The 83 'Terminal' goes up 7a Av through Zonas 9, 4 and 1; the 83 'Bolívar' goes via Av Bolívar and then 5a Av. Both run about every 15 minutes, from 6am to 9pm, and cost US$0.15. Going from the city center to the airport, bus 83 'Aeropuerto' goes south through Zona 1 on 10a Av, south through Zonas 4 and 9 on 6a Av, passes by the west end of La Aurora Zoo and the Zona 13 museums and stops right in front of the international terminal. It then continues southward, passing close to all the Zona 13 guesthouses. For information on shuttle minibuses to/from the airport, see opposite.

Taxis wait outside the airport's arrivals exit. Official fares are posted on a sign here (US$8 to US$9 to Zona 9 or 10, US$10 to Zona 1, US$30 to Antigua), but in reality you may have to pay a bit more – US$9 to US$10 to Zona 1, US$35 to Antigua. Be sure to establish the destination and price before getting in. A tip is expected. Prices for taxis *to* the airport, hailed on the street, are likely to be lower – around US$6 from Zona 1. For Antigua, shuttle minibuses are more economical than taxis if there's only one or two of you.

Bus & Minibus

If you spend any time out and about in Guatemala City, especially Zona 1, its buses will become a major feature of your existence as they roar along in large numbers belching great clouds of black smoke. Jets flying low over the city center intermittently intensify the cacophony. Still, Guatemala City buses are cheap, frequent and, though often very crowded, useful. They are not, however, always safe. Theft and robbery are not unusual; there have even been murders on board. Buses cost US$0.15 per ride: you pay the driver as you get on.

To get from Zona 1 to Zona 10, take bus 82 or 101 southbound on 10a Av between 8a and 13a Calles. These buses swing west to travel south down 6a Av for 1km or so before swinging southeast along Ruta 6 (Zona 4) then south along Av La Reforma. For the main Inguat tourist office, get off on 6a Av at 22a Calle (Zona 1) and walk east along 22a Calle, then south down the far (east) side of 7a Av.

Traveling north *to* Zona 1, buses 82 and 101 go along Av La Reforma then 7a Av, Zona 4 (passing right by Inguat) and 9a Av, Zona 1.

To get to the Terminal de Autobuses in Zona 4 by city bus, it makes sense simply to get any bus that's going south through Zona 4 on 6a Av (such as bus 83 'Aeropuerto') or north through Zona 4 on 7a Av (such as bus 83 'Terminal'), then walk a few blocks west to the terminal. This saves you getting caught in the snarl-ups around the terminal itself. The same holds true in reverse if you want to get away from the Terminal de Autobuses by city bus.

City buses stop running about 9pm, and *ruteleros* (minibuses) begin to run up and down the main avenues. They run all night, until the buses resume their rattling rides at 5am. Hold up your hand at a street corner to stop a minibus or bus.

Taxi

Plenty of taxis cruise most parts of the city. Fares are negotiable; always establish your destination and fare before getting in. Zona 1 to Zona 10, or vice-versa, costs around US$5.50 to US$8. If you want to phone for a taxi, **Taxi Amarillo Express** (☎ 2232 1515) has metered cabs that often work out cheaper than others, although true *capitaleños* (capital city residents) will tell you that taximeters are all rigged and you get a better deal bargaining.

Antigua

In all the long, boring discussions about where the 'real Guatemala' is, you can be sure the word Antigua has never come up. This is fantasyland – what the country would look like if the Scandinavians came in and took over for a couple of years. It's a place where power lines run underground, building codes are adhered to, rubbish is collected, traffic diverted and stray dogs 'disappear' mysteriously in the middle of the night.

But you'd be a fool to miss it. Antigua's setting is gorgeous, nestled between three volcanoes: Agua (3766m), Fuego (3763m) and Acatenango (3976m), and its streetscapes – with sprays of bougainvillea bursting from crumbling ruins, and pastel facades under terracotta roofs – offer photo opportunities at every turn. The language school scene is thriving, the hostels offer colonial-chic accommodations and the dining is some of the best in the country.

The most exciting time to visit Antigua is during Holy Week – especially Good Friday. It takes planning (reserve hotels at least four months in advance), as this is the busiest week of the year. Other busy times are June through August and November to April.

Antigua is cold after sunset, especially between September and March, so bring warm clothes, a sleeping bag or a blanket. Antigua residents are known by the nickname *panza verde* (green belly), as they are said to eat lots of avocados, which grow abundantly here.

TOP FIVE

- Catching the views of active Volcán Fuego from the 3976m summit of **Acatenango** (p105)
- Dusting off your high-school Spanish with well-trained teachers at one of the city's many highly-regarded language schools, such as the **Escuela de Español Cooperacion** (p106)
- Dining fine in **El Sabor del Tiempo** (p114), just one from the excellent range of restaurants – the widest variety that Guatemala has to offer
- Getting historical in Antigua's museums, monasteries, mansions, churches and convents, like **Iglesia y Convento de Santo Domingo** (p103)
- Snapping up bargains at **Diez Mil Pueblitos** (p116) while shopping for Mayan crafts, fine jewelry, home wares, etc

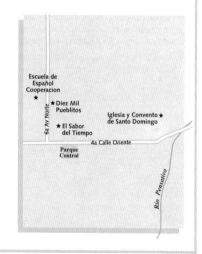

- POPULATION: 45,200
- ELEVATION: 1530M

HISTORY

Antigua wasn't the Spaniards' first choice for a capital city. The first place they tried was in Iximché, which was settled in 1524 in order to keep an eye on the Kaqchiquel, with whom they had an uneasy truce. Things got uneasier in 1527 when the Kaqchiquel rebelled, so the city was moved to present-day Ciudad Vieja (p118) on the flanks of Volcán Agua. That didn't work out, either – the town practically disappeared under a mudslide in 1541 and everybody packed up and moved again. And so it was that on March 10, 1543, La muy Noble y muy Leal Ciudad de Santiago de los Caballeros de Goathemala, the Spanish colonial capital of Guatemala (for the time being), was founded.

Antigua was once the epicenter of power throughout Central America, and during the 17th and 18th centuries little expense was spared on the city's magnificent architecture, despite the fact that the ground rumbled ominously on a regular basis. Schools, hospitals, churches and monasteries sprang up, their grandeur only rivaled by the houses of the upper clergy and the politically connected.

At its peak Antigua had no fewer than 38 churches, including a cathedral, as well as a university, printing presses, a newspaper and a lively cultural and political scene. Those rumblings never stopped, though, and for a year the city was shaken by earthquakes and tremors of varying degrees until the great earthquake of July 29, 1773, destroyed the city (which had already suffered considerable damage). In 1776 the capital was transferred again, this time to Guatemala City. Antigua was evacuated and plundered for building materials, but, despite official decrees, it never completely emptied of people, and began to grow again around 1830, by then known as La Antigua Guatemala (Old Guatemala). Renovation of battered old buildings helped maintain the city's colonial character. In 1944 President Jorge Ubico declared Antigua a national monument, and in 1979 Unesco designated it a World Heritage site.

ORIENTATION

Volcán Agua is south of the city and visible from most points within it; Volcán Fuego and Volcán Acatenango are to the southwest (Acatenango is the more northerly of the two). These three volcanoes provide easy reference points.

Antigua's focal point is the broad and beautiful Parque Central. Few places in town are more than 15 minutes' walk from here. The city's street-naming system is unusual in that it has no *zonas* (zones), and compass points are added to the numbered Calles and

---

ANTIGUA IN...

Two Days

Start with breakfast in colonial surroundings at **Café La Escudilla** (p112), then drop by one of our recommended agencies to set up a volcano trip for tomorrow – Acatenango if you can afford it, Pacaya otherwise. Spend the day exploring some of Antigua's colonial buildings – the **cathedral** (p101), **Santo Domingo** (p103), **Las Capuchinas** (p103), **La Merced** (p102) – with a light lunch along the way. Eat a hearty typical dinner at **Cuevita de las Urquizas** (p113) then check out **Café No Sé** (p115). Don't stay out too late: in the morning you leave early for your **volcano** (p104). Afterwards enjoy the dinner you've earned at **Mesón Panza Verde** (p114) (or **Nokiate**, p114, if you're jonesing for a little sushi), followed by a couple of drinks at **El Muro** (p115), **Sangre** (p115) or **Fridas** (p114). Round things off, if you still can, with a shimmy at **La Casbah** (p115).

Four Days

Follow the two-day itinerary, then visit the **Centro Cultural La Azotea** (p118) at Jocotenango on day three. At night catch a dinner show at **La Peña de Sol Latino** (p113), the best **movie** (p115) you can find, and a drink at **Gaia** (p114) – in any order!.On day four reactivate with an out-of-town **guided walk** (p107), **bike ride** (p105) or **horse ride** (p105). Watch the sun go down from **Café Sky** (p115) before enjoying food and the lounge scene at **Estudio 35** (p113). Then revisit your favorite bar...

ANTIGUA

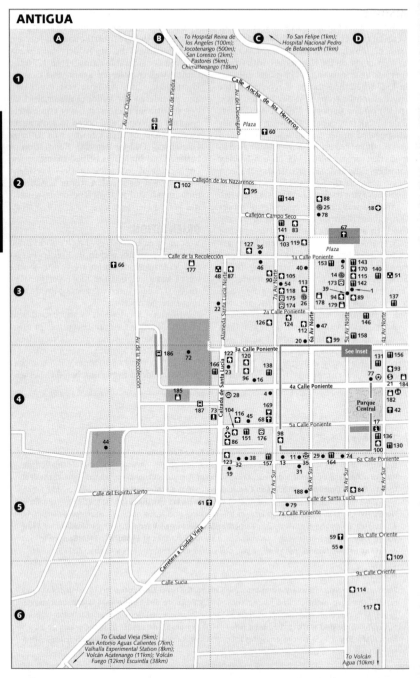

ANTIGUA

To Hospital Reina de
los Angeles (100m);
Jocotenango (500m);
San Lorenzo (2km);
Pastorés (5km);
Chimaltenango (18km)

To San Felipe (1km);
Hospital Nacional Pedro
de Betancourth (1km)

Calle Ancha de los Herreros

Av. de Chajón

Calle Cruz de Piedra

Av del Desengaño

Plaza

63

60

Callejón de los Nazarenos

102

95

144

88
@ 25
78

18

Callejón Campo Seco

141 83

67

Plaza

127 36

103 119

153 5

143
170
140

Calle de la Recolección

177

1a Calle Poniente

14 @
173

115
142

Alameda Santa Lucía Norte

48 87

46

40

105

90

54

113

39

94

89

1

51

137

118
175
174

26

178 179

7a Av Norte

2a Calle Poniente

22

126

124

112

47

6a Av Norte

5a Av Norte

146

4a Av Norte

158

Av de la Recolección

186

72

20

99

See Inset

131

156

3a Calle Poniente

122
120
23

93

166

138

77

21 184

96 16

4a Calle Poniente

182

185

28

4

169

Parque
Central

42

187

73

104

116 45

68

17

136

130

Calzada de Santa Lucía

9

86

151 176

98

5a Calle Poniente

100

123

32 38

19

157

13 11 29 164 74

31

35

6a Calle Poniente

7a Av Sur

8a Av Sur

5a Av Sur

4a Av Sur

Calle del Espíritu Santo

44

188

84

79

Calle de Santa Lucía

61

7a Calle Poniente

Carretera a Ciudad Vieja

59

55

8a Calle Oriente

109

9a Calle Oriente

Calle Sucia

114

117

To Ciudad Vieja (5km);
San Antonio Aguas Calientes (7km);
Valhalla Experimental Station (8km);
Volcán Acatenango (11km); Volcán
Fuego (12km) Escuintla (38km)

To Volcán
Agua (10km)

ANTIGUA

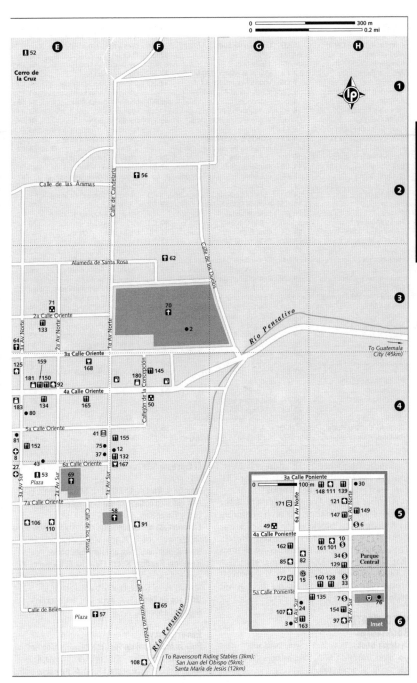

Avs, indicating whether an address is *Norte* (north), *Sur* (south), *Poniente* (west) or *Oriente* (east) of the Parque Central.

Another famous Antigua landmark is the Arco de Santa Catalina, an arch spanning 5a Av Norte, 2½ blocks north of the Parque Central, on the way to La Merced church. This is one of the few Antigua constructions that withstood the 1773 earthquake.

Buses arrive at and depart from the streets around the large open-air market, about 400m west of the Parque Central.

INFORMATION
Bookstores
Dyslexia Books (1a Av Sur 11) Secondhand and new books, mainly in English. Some politics and a good selection on indigenous culture.

El Cofre (6a Calle Poniente 26) Secondhand books, mainly in English.

Hamlin y White (☎ 832-7075; 4a Calle Oriente 12A) New and used books in several languages, including many Lonely Planet titles.

Librería Casa del Conde (Portal del Comercio 4) New books on Guatemala and the Maya in several languages; carries International Travel Maps and some used books.

Rainbow Reading Room (7a Av Sur 8) Thousands of used books in English and Spanish for sale, rent or trade. Also has one of the best notice boards in town.

Un Poco de Todo (5a Av Norte 10A) New books in English and Spanish.

Emergency
Policía Municipal de Turismo (Municipal Tourism Police; ☎ 7832 7290; Palacio del Ayuntamiento, 4a Av Norte; ☾ 24hr). The helpful tourism police will go with

you to the national police and assist with the formalities, including any translating that needs to be done.

Policía Nacional Civil (National Civil Police; ☎ 7832 0251; Palacio de los Capitanes, Parque Central) Formal reports to the police about a crime or loss should be made to the Policía Nacional Civil.

Internet Access

Antigua has a large number of affordable internet services. Among the best for price, connection quality and convenience are the following:

Aló Internet (5a Calle Ponient 28; per hr US$0.80)

Conexion (Centro Comercial La Fuente, 4a Calle Oriente 14; per hr US$0.80; 🕑 8:30am-7:30pm) All-purpose communications center; charges US$2 per hour to hook up your laptop; plus printing, photocopying and CD-burning services.

El Cofre (6a Calle Poniente 26; per hr US$1)

El Naufrago (5a Av Norte 30A; per hr US$1.30; 🕑 8:30am-10pm)

Enlaces (☎ 7832 5555; 6a Av Norte 1; per hr US$0.80; 🕑 8am-7:30pm Mon-Sat, 8am-1pm Sun) Good connections, smoking and nonsmoking areas.

Enlínea (5a Av Sur 12; per hr US$1)

Funky Monkey (5a Av Sur 6, Pasaje El Corregidor; per hr US$1) Inside Monoloco.

Internet Café (Hotel Convento Santa Catalina Mártir, 5a Av Norte 28; per hr US$1.20; 🕑 8am-10pm) Some of the most reliable connections in town.

Nueva Er@ (6a Av Norte 34 & 39; per hr US$1)

Laundry

Laundries are everywhere, especially along 6a Calle Poniente.

Lavandería Dry Clean (6a Calle Poniente 49; 🕑 7am-7pm Mon-Sat, 9am-6pm Sun) Charges US$3.75 a load.

Quick Laundry (6a Calle Poniente 14; ⏰ 8am-5pm Mon-Sat) Fast and reliable; charges US$3.25 to wash and dry a 5lb (2.25kg) load.

Media

The Antigua-based **Revue Magazine** (www .revuemag.com) runs about 90% ads, but has reasonable cultural events information. It's available everywhere.

La Cuadra, also Antigua-based, is a much more underground publication, which mixes politics with irreverent commentary. You should be able to get onto a copy at Café No Sé (see p115).

Medical Services

Casa de los Nahuales (☎ 7832 0068; 3a Av Sur 6) Offers alternative medical and spiritual services, including Mayan horoscopes, massages, aromatherapy and Bach flower remedies.

Casa de Salud Santa Lucía (☎ 7832 3122; Calzada de Santa Lucía Sur 7) If possible, you're probably best going to a private hospital such as this one.

Hospital Nacional Pedro de Betancourth (☎ 7832 2801) This public hospital in San Felipe, 2km north of the center, has an emergency service.

Hospital Reina de los Ángeles (☎ 7832 2258; Calle Ancha de los Herreros 59) Another private hospital.

Ixmucane (☎ 7832 5539; womanway@aol.com; 4a Av Norte 32) Provides a complete range of gynecological and obstetrical services, from dispensing birth control to delivering babies. Herbal supplements, treatment and information are available here too, in English and Spanish.

Obras Sociales de Hermano Pedro (Hospital San Pedro; ☎ 7832 0883; 6a Calle Oriente 20) This is the more central of Antigua's two public hospitals, but it has no emergency service. It's primarily a refuge for the handicapped, elderly and abused, but does give medical consultations.

Money

Banco del Quetzal (4a Calle; ⏰ 8:30am-7pm Mon-Fri, 9am-1pm Sat & Sun) Facing Parque Central. Often has the best rates; has a MasterCard ATM outside. Also changes US dollars (cash and traveler's checks).

Banco Industrial (5a Av Sur 4; ⏰ 9am-7pm Mon-Fri, 9am-5pm Sat) Has a Visa ATM and changes US dollars (cash and traveler's checks).

Credomatic (Portal del Comercio; ⏰ 9am-7pm Mon-Fri, 9am-1pm Sat) Gives Visa and MasterCard cash advances. Changes US dollars (cash and traveler's checks).

LAX Travel (☎ /fax 7832 1621; laxantigua@intelnet.net .gt; 3a Calle Poniente 12) You can change cash euros here.

Lloyds TSB (cnr 4a Calle Oriente & 4a Av Norte; ⏰ 9am-3:30pm Mon-Fri, 9:30am-12:30pm Sat) Gives Visa and MasterCard cash advances. Changes US dollars (cash and traveler's checks).

Visa & MasterCard ATM (5a Av Norte) Facing Parque Central.

Post

DHL (☎ 7832 0073; 6a Calle Poniente 34) Offers door-to-door service.

Post office (cnr 4a Calle Poniente & Calzada de Santa Lucía) West of Parque Central, near the market.

Telephone & Fax

Many businesses, including several internet cafés, offer cut-rate international calls. Some of these are by internet telephone – very cheap, but line quality is unpredictable.

Funky Monkey (5a Av Sur 6, Pasaje El Corregidor) Offers internet calls anywhere in the world, from US$0.15 to US$0.40 per minute. Inside Monoloco.

Guatemala Ventures (1a Av Sur 15) Rents cell phones on which you can call the US for US$0.10 per minute or Europe for US$0.20 per minute, for US$10 per week (with a US$50 deposit).

Western Union Kall Shop (6a Av Sur 12; ⏰ 8.30am-6pm Mon-Fri, 8.30am-4pm Sat) Pay US$0.30 per minute to call the US or Canada, US$0.45 to Mexico, Central America or Europe, US$0.55 to South America and US$0.60 to anywhere else.

Tourist Information

Inguat (☎ 7832 0763; Palacio de los Capitanes, Parque Central; ⏰ 8am-12:30pm & 2:30-5pm Mon-Fri, 9am-12:30pm & 2:30-5pm Sat & Sun) This tourist office has free city maps, bus information and schedules of Semana Santa events, and the staff will try to find the answers to any poser you might throw at them.

Travel Agencies

Everywhere you go in Antigua, you'll come across travel agencies. These agencies offer international flights, shuttle minibuses, tours to interesting sites around Antigua and elsewhere in Guatemala, and more. Reputable travel agencies include the following:

Adrenalina Tours (☎ 7832 1108; www.adrenalinatours .com; 5a Av Norte 31) Specialists in the western Highlands; can arrange everything from tours and shuttles to domestic and international flights.

Adventure Travel Center (☎ /fax 7832 0162; viareal@guate.net; 5a Av Norte 25B)

Antigua Tours (☎ /fax 7832 5821; www.antiguatours .net; Portal de Santo Domingo, 3a Calle Oriente 28) Inside the Casa Santo Domingo Hotel.

Atitrans (☎ 7832 3371; www.mundo-guatemala.com; 6a Av Sur 8)

Aviatur (☎ /fax 7832 5989; aviaturfer@yahoo.com.mx; 5a Av Norte 34)

LAX Travel (☎ /fax 7832 1621; laxantigua@intelnet.net
.gt; 3a Calle Poniente 12) An international flight specialist.

Monarcas Travel (☎ 7832 1939; Calzada de Santa
Lucía 7) Operates shuttles to Copán and elsewhere.

National Travel (☎ 7832 8383; antigua@nationalgua
.com; 6a Av Sur 1A) Offers one-way flights, including
student and teacher fares.

Rainbow Travel Center (☎ /fax 7832 4202; rainbow
travel@gua.gbm.net; 7a Av Sur 8) Student and teacher air
fares are a specialty here.

Sin Fronteras (☎ 7832 1017; www.sinfront.com; 5a Av
Norte 15A) Sells one-way international air tickets; issues
student and youth cards for US$8; sells International Travel
Maps; runs tours to Cuba, among other destinations.

STA Travel (☎ 7832 4080; www.isyta.com; 6a Calle
Poniente 21) Offers student and teacher air fares and a
change-of-date and lost-ticket-replacement service for
tickets issued by student/youth travel agencies. Issues
student, teacher and youth cards for US$8.

Viajes Tivoli (☎ 7832 1370, 7832 4274; antigua@tivoli
.com.gt; 4a Calle Oriente 10, local 3)

Vision Travel & Information Services (☎ 7832
3293; Casa de Mito, 3a Av Norte 3) Tours to places ranging
from Tikal to local coffee *fincas* (plantations) are offered
here, as are shuttle services and many guidebooks (including Lonely Planet titles) to buy or simply read on the spot.

Voyageur Tours (☎ 7832 4237; www.travel.net.gt;
Centro Comercial La Fuente, 4a Calle Oriente 14) Operates
some good-value shuttle minibus services.

Volunteer Work

Many of Antigua's language schools can
help you find volunteer work. See p106 for
more details.

AmeriSpan Guatemala (☎ 7832 0164; www.amerispan
.com; 6a Av Norte 40A) Can hook you up with volunteer
opportunities all over Guatemala. It charges a US$60
registration fee.

Proyecto Mosaico Guatemala (☎ /fax 7932 0955;
www.promosaico.org; Casa de Mito, 3a Av Norte 3; ☯ 2-
4pm Mon-Fri) This is a nonprofit organization providing
volunteers and resources to over 60 projects in Guatemala.
Its resource center in the Casa de Mito has information on
these projects and matches up volunteers with projects.
It's very interested in people with medical experience but
there's work for periods from one week to one year doing
things as varied as carpentry, teaching, environmental
protection, helping HIV-positive kids, and organic farming.
You need to be at least 18 and fit.

DANGERS & ANNOYANCES

Though you'll probably never have a problem, be wary when walking empty streets late
at night, especially away from the center, as
robberies have taken place. Pick pocketing is

rife during Semana Santa: even more than
at other times of year, don't carry anything
you don't immediately need. Armed robberies
have occurred in the past on Cerro de la Cruz
and in the Cementerio General, but crime in
these places has effectively ceased since the
formation in 1996 of the Policía Municipal
de Turismo (p99), who provide free escorts
to both sites and to some of the ruins around
town. Some of the volcanoes visited from Antigua, especially Pacaya and Agua (p104), have
also been the scene of robberies.

SIGHTS
Parque Central

This broad and beautiful plaza, easily the love-
liest in the country, is the gathering place for
Antigüeños and visitors alike – a fine, verdant
place to sit or stroll and observe Antigua happening around you, from hawkers and shoe
shiners to school kids and groups of tourists.
The famous central fountain is a 1936 reconstruction of the original 1738 version.

PALACIO DE LOS CAPITANES

Dating from 1558, the **Captain-Generals' Palace**
was the governmental center of all Central
America from Chiapas to Costa Rica until
1773. It didn't gain its stately double-arcaded
facade, which marches proudly along the
southern side of the park, until the early 1760s,
however. Today the palace houses the Inguat
tourist office, the national police and the office
of the governor of Sacatepéquez department.

CATEDRAL DE SANTIAGO

On the east side of the park, **Catedral de Santiago** (☯ 9am-5pm) was begun in 1542, demol-
ished in 1668, rebuilt between 1669 and 1680,
repeatedly damaged by earthquakes, wrecked
in 1773, and only partly rebuilt between 1780
and 1820. The present cathedral, without its
expensive original decoration, occupies only
the entrance hall of the 17th-century edifice,
and strictly speaking is not a cathedral but
the Parroquia (Parish Church) de San José.
It's most striking at night when it is tastefully
lit. More interesting by day are the **remains**
(admission US$0.40; ☯ 9am-5pm) of the main part of
the cathedral, entered from 5a Calle Oriente.
Slightly overhyping itself as 'the most important monument in the country,' it's nonethe-
less an impressive place with sweeping brick
archways, massive columns and underground
crypts (according to graffiti, inveterate Latino

ANTIGUA

ANTIGUA

traveler Paco was here). Some statues and plasterwork remain and vegetation sprouts from cracks in walls – it's a good place to take photos for the CD cover of your goth band.

Conquistador Pedro de Alvarado, his wife Beatriz de la Cueva, their daughter Leonora de Alvarado, Guatemala's first bishop Francisco Marroquín, and the conquistador (and historian of the Spanish conquest) Bernal Díaz del Castillo, were all buried beneath the main altar, though their bones went astray at some stage in history. Behind the main altar, steps lead down to a former crypt now serving as a chapel, with a smoke-blackened Christ.

PALACIO DEL AYUNTAMIENTO

The **City Hall**, on the north side of the park, dates mostly from 1743. In addition to town offices, it houses the **Museo de Santiago** (☎ 7832 2868; admission US$1.50; ☼ 9am-4pm Tue-Fri, 9am-noon & 2-4pm Sat & Sun), in the former town jail. The mermaid statues that once graced the fountain in the Central Park are here, along with a room full of creepy portraits whose eyes follow you everywhere. Also on exhibit are canons from the Castillo San Felipe (see p254) and some good examples of colonial era pottery. Next door is the **Museo del Libro Antiguo** (Old Book Museum; ☎ 7832 5511; admission US$1.50 Mon-Sat, by donation Sun; ☼ 9am-4pm Tue-Fri, 9am-noon & 2-4pm Sat & Sun), showcasing the greatest hits of the early days of Guatemalan printing, plus a replica of Guatemala's first printing press, which began work here in the 1660s. There is an entire room dedicated to the process of making marbled paper.

UNIVERSIDAD DE SAN CARLOS

The **San Carlos University**, now in Guatemala City, was founded in Antigua in 1676; what used to be its main building (built in 1763), half a block east of the park, houses the **Museo de Arte Colonial** (☎ 7832 0429; 5a Calle Oriente 5; admission US$3.25; ☼ 9am-4pm Tue-Fri, 9am-noon & 2-4pm Sat & Sun), with sculptures of saints and paintings by leading Mexican artists of the colonial era, such as Miguel Cabrera and Juan de Correa.

Churches & Monasteries

Once glorious in their gilded baroque finery, Antigua's churches have suffered indignities from both nature and humankind. Rebuilding after earthquakes gave the churches thicker walls, lower towers and belfries and unem-

bellished interiors, and moving the capital to Guatemala City deprived Antigua of the population needed to maintain the churches in their traditional richness. Still, they are impressive. In addition to those churches mentioned below, you'll find many others scattered around town in various states of decay. The Policía Municipal de Turismo (p99) will provide free escorts to some of the outlying monuments, where robberies have sometimes occurred.

IGLESIA Y CONVENTO DE NUESTRA SEÑORA DE LA MERCED

From the Parque Central, walk three long blocks along 5a Av Norte, passing beneath the **Arco de Santa Catalina**, which was built in 1694 (to enable nuns to cross the street without being seen) and rebuilt with its clock tower in the 19th century. At the northern end of 5a Av is La Merced – Antigua's most striking colonial church.

La Merced's construction began in 1548. The most recent of its several bouts of rebuilding has taken place since the 1976 earthquake, and the place is in pretty good shape. Inside the **monastery ruins** (admission US$0.80; ☼ 9am-6:30pm) is a fountain 27m in diameter, said to be the largest in Hispanic America. It's in the shape of a water lily (traditionally a symbol of power for Mayan lords), and lily motifs also appear on the church's entrance arch, suggesting the influence of indigenous laborers used to construct La Merced. Go upstairs for a bird's-eye view of the fountain and the town. A candlelit procession, accompanied by much bell ringing and firecrackers, starts and ends here on the last Thursday evening of each month.

IGLESIA DE SAN FRANCISCO

Little of the original 16th-century **Iglesia de San Francisco** (cnr 8a Calle Oriente & Calle do los Pasos) remains, but reconstruction and restoration over the centuries have produced a handsome structure. In the north transept is the tomb of Santo Hermano Pedro de San José de Betancurt (1626–67), a Franciscan monk who founded a hospital for the poor in Antigua and earned the gratitude of generations. He's Guatemala's most venerated local Christian figure, and was made a saint in 2002 when Pope John Paul II visited Guatemala. His intercession is still sought by the ill, who pray fervently by the tomb. On the south side of the church are the **Museo del Hermano Pedro** and the ruins of the adjoining **monastery** (joint admission US$0.80; ☺ 8am-5pm Tue-Sun). The museum houses relics from the church and Santo Hermano's curiously well-preserved personal belongings, including some spectacularly uncomfortable-looking underwear. The *pasillo de los milagros* is a corridor jam-packed with testimonials, photos, plaques and crutches donated by people who claim to have been healed by the Hermano.

LAS CAPUCHINAS

Inaugurated in 1736 by nuns from Madrid, **Las Capuchinas** (Iglesia y Convento de Nuestra Señora del Pilar de Zaragoza; cnr 2a Av Norte & 2a Calle Oriente; adult/student US$4/2; ☺ 9am-5pm) was seriously damaged by the 1773 earthquake and thereafter abandoned. Restoration began in 1943 and continues today. Looking around at the high, arched passageways, pretty gardens and stately courtyards, it's tempting to think that the nuns who lived here were onto a good thing. The building has many unusual features, including a unique towerlike building of 18 nuns' cells built around a circular patio.

IGLESIA Y CONVENTO DE LA RECOLECCIÓN

The massive **La Recolección** (Av de la Recolección; adult/student US$4/2; ☺ 9am-5pm) is among Antigua's most impressive monuments. It's set a little ways out of town, and a serene air pervades the site. Built between 1701 and 1715, the church was inaugurated in 1717, but suffered considerable damage from an earthquake that same year. The buildings were destroyed in the earthquake of 1773: enormous chunks of masonry still lie jumbled around the ruined church. You can clamber up to the second story for better views, but watch your step.

COLEGIO DE SAN JERÓNIMO

Built in 1757, the **Colegio de San Jerónimo** (Real Aduana; cnr Calzada de Santa Lucía & 1a Calle Poniente; adult/student US$4/2; ☺ 9am-5pm) was used as a school by friars of the Merced order, but because it did not have royal authorization, it was taken over in 1761 by Spain's Carlos III, and in 1765 designated for use as the Real Aduana (Royal Customs House). Today it's a tranquil, mostly open-air site. The handsome cloister centers on a lovely octagonal fountain, which operates most days – it's an evocative setting for various dance and other cultural performances. Make your way upstairs for

some excellent photo angles of Volcán Agua through stone archways.

IGLESIA Y CONVENTO DE SANTA CLARA

Santa Clara (2a Av Sur 27; adult/student US$4/2; ☺ 9am-5pm) was first completed in 1702, and the existing construction, inaugurated in 1734, was wrecked in 1773 but remains large and impressive.

In front of the church is one of Antigua's prettiest plazas, lined with palm trees. At the eastern end are public clothes-washing sinks, where some women still come to do their washing, spreading their laundry out on the ground to dry. Also in the plaza stands a gift made to Antigua (formally Santiago de los Caballeros de Guatemala) in 1988 by the city of Santiago de Compostela in Galicia, Spain: a *cruceiro*, a typically Galician stone cross carved with biblical scenes.

IGLESIA Y CONVENTO DE SANTO DOMINGO

Founded in 1542, **Santo Domingo** (☎ 7832 0140; 3a Calle Oriente 28; archaeological area guests/nonguests US$free/6; ☺ 9am-6pm Mon-Sat, 10am-6pm Sun) became the biggest and richest monastery in Antigua. Its large church was completed in 1666. Damaged by three 18th-century earthquakes, the buildings were further depleted when pillaged for construction material in the 20th century. The site is currently occupied by the Hotel Casa Santo Domingo. You can visit the hotel's public spaces, which are tastefully dotted with colonial statuary and archaeological pieces, any time. The *áreas arqueológicas* (archaeological areas) form part of the *paseo de museos* (museum walk). It includes the very picturesque ruined monastery church (cleared of a 5m layer of rubble in the 1990s and now used for mass and weddings), the adjacent cloister with its large fountain created in 1618, and two crypts discovered in the 1990s – one, the Cripta del Calvario, boasts a pristine mural of the Crucifixion; the other holds two graves with human bones. The *paseo* also includes museums dedicated to colonial and contemporary art, archaeology, handicrafts and even a pharmacological museum. The price for all this may seem steep, but the entire complex is very well done – with excellent, evocative lighting and signage, it's just modern enough to let the pieces speak for themselves. Without doubt the leading museum in Antigua.

Casa Popenoe

The beautiful **Casa Popenoe** (☎ 7832-3087; 1a Av Sur 2; admission US$1.30; ☺ 2-4pm Mon-Sat) was built in 1636 by Don Luis de las Infantas Mendoza. After the 1773 earthquake the house stood desolate for 150 years until it was bought in 1929 by agricultural scientist William Popenoe and his wife Dorothy. Their painstaking, authentic restoration yields a fascinating glimpse into how a royal official lived in 17th-century Antigua.

Monumento a Landívar

Commemorating Jesuit priest and poet Rafael Landívar (1731–93), **Monumento a Landívar** (cnr Calzada de Santa Lucía & 5a Calle Poniente) is a structure of five colonial-style arches set in a pristine little park. Landívar lived and wrote in Antigua for some time, and his poetry is esteemed as the best of the colonial period, even though much of it was written in Italy after the Jesuits were expelled from Guatemala. Landívar's ruined house is behind the monument.

Market

Antigua's **market** (btwn Calzada de Santa Lucía & Av de la Recolección; ☺ Mon, Thu & Sat) – chaotic, colorful and always busy – sprawls north of 4a Calle. Morning, when villagers from the Antigua vicinity are actively buying and selling, is the best time to come. On the official market days Mayan women spread their wares over open-air areas north and west of the covered market area. Like many Guatemalan markets, Antigua market is cheek-by-jowl with the bus terminal, adding to the crowds, noise and dirt.

Cementerio General

Antigua's **Cementerio General** (☺ 7am-noon & 2-6pm), southwest of the market and bus terminal, is a beautiful conglomeration of tombs and mausoleums decked with wreaths, exotic flowers and other signs of mourning. There have been robberies here, so go with the free escort from the Policía Municipal de Turismo (see p99).

Cerro de la Cruz

Overlooking Antigua from the north is Cerro de la Cruz (Hill of the Cross), which provides fine views looking south over town toward Volcán Agua. In the past this hill was famous for muggers waiting to pounce on unsuspecting visitors, and Antigua's tourism police were formed precisely to counter this threat. The Policía Municipal de Turismo (see p99) offer a free escort, and it's still best to go with them.

ACTIVITIES

Two professional, established and friendly outfits offering a big range of activities are **Old Town Outfitters** (☎ /fax 7832 4171; www.bike guatemala.com; 5a Av Sur 12C) and **Guatemala Ventures/Mayan Bike Tours** (☎ /fax 7832 3383; www.guatemalaventures.com; 1a Av Sur 15). Drop by either place to chat about possibilities.

Ox Expeditions (☎ 7832 0074; www.guatemala volcano.com; 1 Av Sur 4B) is a new outfit offering rigorous climbing opportunities in the area. Part of the company's profits goes to local environmental projects.

Volcano Ascents

All three volcanoes overlooking Antigua are tempting challenges but how close you can get to **Fuego** depends on recent levels of activity. In many ways the twin-peaked Acatenango, the highest of the three and overlooking Fuego, is the most exhilarating summit. For an active-volcano experience many people take tours to **Pacaya** (2552m), 25km southeast of Antigua (a 1½-hour drive). In general the weather and the views on all the volcanoes are better in the morning. In the rainy season (May to October) thunderstorms are possible in the afternoon. Get reliable advice about safety before you climb, for example from the Inguat tourist office, or from your embassy in Guatemala City if need be. Take sensible precautions: wear adequate footwear (volcanic rock can be very rough on shoes), warm clothing (it can be very cold up there) and, in the rainy season, some sort of rain gear. Carry a flashlight (torch) in case the weather changes; it can get as dark as night when it rains on the mountain – though it's better not to go at all if rain is expected. Don't neglect food and water.

In view of the possible dangers not only from volcanic activity and the elements but also from armed robbers preying on tourists on some volcano trails, it's safest to go with a reputable agency. People like Old Town Outfitters, Guatemala Ventures and Ox Expeditions (see above) know what's happening on the mountains and will keep you clear of trouble. **Agua** trips with Guatemala Ventures (US$49) drive to the end of the dirt road, well

LOCAL LORE: LA LLORONA

There was once a beautiful peasant woman who lived in Antigua, back when it was the capital. She fell in love with a nobleman, and bore him two children.

Predictably enough, he never married her, and one day announced that he was going to Spain, where he would marry a noblewoman his family had chosen for him.

The woman was stricken with grief, and in a jealous rage took the two children to the Río Pensativo and drowned them.

When she came to her senses and realized what she had done, she let out a fearful wail and threw herself into the river to drown.

The legend goes that La Llorona (the wailer) appears near water, and there have been reports of her appearing all over the country, near rivers, lakes, fountains – even *pilas* (laundry troughs). They say that, if you are near water and you hear wailing late at night, it is La Llorona, lamenting the loss of her children.

beyond the village of Santa María de Jesús, in whose vicinity hikers have been robbed. The summit is about two hours' walk from the end of the road (against five hours from the village).

Trips of varying difficulty are available. A trek to within two hours' walk of the top of **Acatenango** with Old Town Outfitters costs US$49 for a day trip, US$80 with a night camping on the mountain.

One-day Pacaya trips, with 1½ to two hours' walking uphill and one to 1½ hours down, cost around US$60. With luck you'll be able to look down into the crater of this active volcano. Various companies run bargain-basement, seven-hour Pacaya trips daily for US$8 (leaving Antigua at 6am) or US$6 (leaving at 1pm). Extra costs include food, drinks and US$3.25 admission to the Pacaya protected area. The installation of park rangers on Pacaya has made this volcano, once notorious for robberies of tourists, much more secure.

Another possibility in these areas are hike-and-bike trips (see right).

Other Hikes

Old Town Outfitters (☎ /fax 7832-4171; www.bike guatemala.com; 5a Av Sur 12C) has a popular range of guided half-day walks (US$30) in the hills around Antigua. It can also take you to any summit in the country or on a three-day trek through eastern Guatemala's Sierra de las Minas, with its cloud forests. It rents out and sells camping gear too. **Guatemala Ventures/Mayan Bike Tours** (☎ /fax 7832 3383; www.guatemalaventures.com; 1a Av Sur 15) offers a range of hikes including some interesting cloud-forest, bird-watching and ridge-hiking options.

Cycling

Old Town Outfitters (☎ /fax 7832 4171; www.bike guatemala.com; 5a Av Sur 12C) rents out quality bikes with gloves, helmets and maps for US$8/12 per half/whole day. It also takes a great range of mountain-bike tours at all levels of difficulty, including the two-day Pedal & Paddle Tour (US$140 to US$175), which includes kayaking and hiking at Lago de Atitlán.

Guatemala Ventures/Mayan Bike Tours (☎ /fax 7832 3383; www.guatemalaventures.com; 1a Av Sur 15) also rents out good mountain bikes for US$2/12 per hour/day and offers some tasty bike tours from intermediate to expert levels. It does hike-and-bike tours to Pacaya volcano (US$29) and bike-and-kayak trips to Lago de Atitlán and Monterrico (US$129, both two days). Another, lazier option is its trip up Cerro Alto in a minibus with a coast back down on mountain bike (US$29).

Horse Riding

Ravenscroft Riding Stables (☎ 7832 6229; 2a Av Sur 3, San Juan del Obispo), 3km south of Antigua on the road to Santa María de Jesús, offers English-style riding, with scenic rides of three, four or five hours in the valleys and hills around Antigua, for US$15 per hour per person. You need to be fairly fit. Reservations and information are available through the **Hotel San Jorge** (☎ 7832 3132; 4a Av Sur 13). You can reach the stables on a bus bound for Santa María de Jesús (p116).

You can also ride at La Azotea in Jocotenango (p117).

Cooking Classes

Antigua Cooking School (☎ 5944 8568; www.antigua cookingschool.com; 5a Av Norte 25B; 4-hr class US$50) offers classes in traditional Guatemalan cooking, preparing classics like corn tamales, *subanik*, *pepian* and *chuchitos*. Classes are available Tuesday through Saturday.

Spa & Massage

Mayan Spa (☎ 7832 3537; Alameda Santa Lucía Norte 20) Offers massage, facials, exfoliations, manicures, Pilates and yoga.

LANGUAGE COURSES

Antigua's famous Spanish-language schools attract students from around the world. There are around 75 schools to choose from.

The price, quality of teaching and student satisfaction varies greatly from one school to another. Often the quality of instruction depends upon the particular teacher, and thus may vary even within a single school. Visit a few schools before you choose one and, if possible, talk to people who have studied recently at schools you like the look of – you'll have no trouble running into lots of Spanish students in Antigua. The Inguat tourist office has a list of authorized schools. They include the following:

Academia de Español Antigueña (☎ 7832 7241; www.spanishacademyantiguena.com; 1a Calle Poniente 10) A highly recommended school, only hiring experienced teachers. They can arrange volunteer work in hospitals for social workers, lab assistants and child care workers on request. Also supports an educational project in San Antonio Aguas Calientes.

Academia de Español Sevilla (☎ /fax 7832 5101; www.sevillantigua.com; 1a Av Sur 8) This school has a good free activity program, and offers a shared student house as an accommodation option. Can arrange volunteer work in the local orphanage, home for the aged, hospitals and other community projects.

Academia de Español Tecún Umán (☎ /fax 7832 2792; www.escuelatecun.com; 6a Calle Poniente 34A) Also has a school on Lago de Atitlán. Organizes volunteer placement with Obras Sociales del Hermano Pedro (a local hospital) and the project Familias de Esperanza (doing education and medical work).

Casa de Lenguas Guatemala (☎ 7832 4846; www.casadelenguas.com; 6a Av Norte 40) This school has group classes (US$65 per week) as well as individual classes (US$95 per week). Volunteer opportunities for social workers, teachers, health-care professionals and in environmental, nature and wildlife programs as well as construction of low-cost housing and classrooms.

Centro Lingüístico De La Fuente (☎ 7832 2711; www.delafuenteschool.com; 1a Calle Poniente 27) Offers volunteer positions as classroom assistants, hospital workers and in local orphanages. Supports local projects to fund an ambulance service in Antigua and provide school supplies to economically underprivileged schoolchildren in local villages.

Christian Spanish Academy (☎ 7832 3922; www.learncsa.com; 6a Av Norte 15) Very professional outfit where students get to report on the teachers weekly.

Escuela de Español Cooperacion (☎ 7812 2482; www.geocities.com/escuela_coop; 7 Av Norte, 15 B) A highly recommended school run as a cooperative, ensuring teachers get paid fairly.

Escuela de Español San José el Viejo (☎ 7832 3028; www.sanjoseelviejo.com; 5a Av Sur 34) Professional, 30-teacher school with pool, superb gardens, tennis court and its own tasteful accommodations.

Ixchel Spanish School (☎ /fax 7832 7137; www.ixchelschool.com; 3a Av Sur 6) Comfortable, welcoming school with enjoyable group activities and lush garden. Has information on more than 50 volunteer projects in the area, ranging from helping in hospitals and orphanages to working as an assistant teacher in a local school as well as construction work and reforestation projects.

Probigua (☎ 7832 2998; www.probigua.org; 6a Av Norte 41 B 2) A highly regarded, nonprofit school helping Guatemalan children by donating the school's profits to establish and maintain libraries in the many rural villages where there is no access to books.

Proyecto Lingüístico Francisco Marroquín (☎ /fax 7832 2886; www.langlink.com/plfm; 7a Calle Poniente 31) Antigua's oldest Spanish school, founded in 1971; run by a nonprofit foundation working to preserve Mayan languages and culture. Courses in some of these are also available.

Other recommended schools include the following:

Centro Lingüística Maya (☎ 7832 0656; www.clmmaya.com; 5a Calle Poniente 20)

Centroamerica Spanish Academy (☎ 7832 3297; www.quik.guate.com/spanishacademy; 4a Calle Oriente 14)

Classes start every Monday at most schools, though you can usually be placed with a teacher any day of the week. Most schools cater for all levels and allow you to stay as long as you like. Three or four weeks is typical, though it's perfectly OK to do just one week. The busiest seasons are during January and from April to August, and some schools request advance reservations for these times.

Instruction is nearly always one-on-one and costs US$65 to US$115 per week for four hours of classes daily, five days a week. You can enroll for up to 10 hours a day of instruction, although this may lead to brain meltdown. Most people find that four to five hours a day is plenty. Most schools offer to arrange room and board with local families, where you'll usually have your own room, often with shared bathrooms, for around US$55 per week (including three meals daily except Sunday). Some schools may offer accommodation in guesthouses or their own hostels for similar or slightly higher prices.

Homestays are supposed to promote the total immersion concept of language learning, but often there are several foreigners staying with one family. This can make it more like a hotel than a family atmosphere. Often there are separate mealtimes for students and the family. Make a point of inquiring about such details if you really want to be totally immersed.

Antigua is not for everyone who wants to study Spanish; there are so many foreigners about, it takes some real discipline to converse in Spanish rather than your native tongue. Many enjoy this social scene, but if you think it will bother you, consider studying in Xela, El Petén or elsewhere, where there are fewer foreign students and more opportunities to dive into Spanish.

TOURS

Elizabeth Bell, author of books on Antigua, leads three-hour cultural walking tours of the town (in English and/or Spanish) on Tuesday, Wednesday, Friday and Saturday at 9:30am. On Monday and Thursday, the tours are led by her colleague Roberto Spillari and start at 2pm. The cost is US$18 (US$15 for Spanish students and project volunteers). Reservations are suggested and can be made through **Antigua Tours** (☎ /fax 7832 5821; www.antiguatours.net; Portal de Santo Domingo, 3a Calle Oriente 28) which is inside the Casa Santo Domingo Hotel. Adventure Travel Center, Vision Travel, El Condor Expeditions and Sin Fronteras (see p100) also offer daily city walking tours, visiting a variety of convents, ruins and museums. These firms also do interesting tours of assorted villages and coffee or macadamia plantations for US$20 to US$30. Bell's book, *Antigua Guatemala: The City and Its Heritage,* is well worth picking up at a bookstore: it describes all the city's important buildings and museums, and neatly encapsulates Antigua's history and fiestas.

CATour (☎ 7832 9638; www.catours.co.uk; 6a Calle Oriente 14) offers two-day motorbike tours to Lake Atitlán or Monterrico from US$140.

Numerous travel agencies offer tours to more distant places, including Tikal, Copán, Río Dulce, the Cobán area, Monterrico, Chichicastenango, Guatemala City and Panajachel. Two-day trips to Tikal, flying from Guatemala City to Flores and back, cost between US$150 and US$300, largely depending on where you stay. A hectic one-day Tikal round-trip costs US$150 to US$180. Two-day land tours to Copán (some also including Quiriguá and Río Dulce) are between US$115 and US$150.

On long-distance tours be sure of what you are paying for – some of the cheaper tours simply amount to shuttling you to Guatemala City then popping you on a public bus.

FESTIVALS & EVENTS

The most exciting time to be in Antigua is **Semana Santa** (Easter Week), when hundreds of people dress in deep purple robes to accompany the most revered sculptural images from the city's churches in daily street processions remembering Christ's crucifixion and the events surrounding it. Dense clouds of incense envelop the parades and the streets are covered in breathtakingly elaborate *alfombras* (carpets) of colored sawdust and flower petals. These beautiful but fragile works of art are destroyed as the processions shuffle over them, but are re-created the next morning for another day of parades.

The fervor and the crowds peak on Good Friday, when an early morning procession departs from La Merced, and a late afternoon one leaves from the Escuela de Cristo. There may also be an enactment of the crucifixion in Parque Central. Have ironclad Antigua room reservations well in advance of Semana Santa, or plan to stay in Guatemala City or another town and commute to the festivities.

Processions, *velaciones* (vigils) and other events actually go on every weekend through Lent, the 40-day period prior to Semana Santa. Antigua's tourist office has schedules of everything, and the booklet *Lent and Holy Week in Antigua* by Elizabeth Bell gives explanations.

On a secular note, beware of pickpockets. It seems that Guatemala City's entire population of pickpockets (numbering perhaps in the hundreds) decamps to Antigua for Semana Santa. In the press of the emotion-filled crowds lining the processional routes, they target foreign tourists especially.

SLEEPING

Antigua's climate, combined with the plaster and cement used in construction, means some hotel rooms can be damp and musty, and this holds true for all price ranges, not just the budget places. Rooms on the ground floor and/or with carpet seem to fare worst, so avoid the mildew funk by going for an upstairs room, preferably with wood or tile floors. Upper floors generally get more air and more light.

Book as far ahead as you can for accommodations during Semana Santa, and be prepared for rates to double then.

Some Antigua hotels have desks in the Guatemala City airport arrivals area, where you can book a room and/or obtain transportation (often free) to the hotel.

Budget

When checking a budget establishment, look at several rooms, as some are much better than others. Where hot water is indicated, expect an electric unit taped to the shower head; feel especially blessed if there's actually a separate hot-water tap.

Posada Ruiz 2 (no phone; 2a Calle Poniente 25; s/d US$3/6) The rough-hewn archway over the entrance is by far the most impressive aspect of this super cheapie. The rooms are small rooms

and the bathrooms are moderately clean. It's a fair deal for the price, and some budget travelers stay here, congregating in the courtyard in the evening.

Guest House Los Encuentros (☎ 7832 4232; 7 Av Norte 60; dm/s/d US$5/6/12; ☐) Nothing fancy going on here – the rooms are basic, running down one side of a narrow house and the bathrooms are shared, but this family-run place has a great feel to it in this often impersonal town. Kitchen access and breakfast are available.

Ummagumma (☎ 7832 4413; www.ummagumma hostel.blogspot.com; 7 Av Norte 15; dm/s/d US$5/7/12, s/d with bathroom US$10/20) Slightly tatty at the edges, the Ummagumma has some of the best atmosphere in town – it's a great place to relax, meet people and hang out on the leafy rooftop terrace. A well-stocked kitchen is available for guest use and the owners run a good travel agency downstairs.

Black Cat Hostel (☎ 7832 1229; www.blackcatantigua .com; 6 Av Norte 1A; dm US$6.50) A near-inexplicably happening hostel right in the middle of the action. The dorms are cramped, you can't use the kitchen, but the place is hopping, both as a hostel and at the bar out front for the nightly happy hour. Plenty of tours are on offer, free movies, good local advice and a huge breakfast are included in the price.

Jungle Party Hostal (☎ 7832 0463; www.jungleparty hostal.com; 6a Av Norte 20; dm US$7) One of Antigua's hottest hostels keeps going from strength to strength, with a great hostel atmosphere, bar

---

LOCAL VOICES: EDUARDO VASQUEZ, SHOEMAKER

The small village of Pastores, just outside of Antigua, is famed for its leatherwork. People come from all over the country to buy their cowboy boots and rodeo hats here. We spoke to Eduardo Vasquez about the cobbler's life.

How long have you been making shoes?
About 15 years. When you start, you cut the hides to learn how it's done. Later you do the moldings. Then, if you're good, you start sewing.

Have the techniques changed over the years?
Not really. Hardly anybody in Pastores uses machines – we do pretty much everything by hand.

There are a lot of cheap imports coming in from Asia now. Have they affected business?
We haven't seen that. People come here when they want quality, because they know that hand-made shoes are better. We have people who come from Zacapa, Jalapa, Jutiapa…

What kind of materials do you use?
(Laughs) We can make shoes out of anything. We mostly use leather, but we also work with ostrich, lizard, python, crocodile, manta ray, cobras… anything, really.

You do custom work – what's the strangest order you've had?
A woman came in with a pair of boots that she'd bought in Italy, and wanted us to make a copy of them… We did a pretty good job… I think we did alright.

service, hammock hang-outs and the famous all-you-can-eat Saturday barbecue.

Posada Don Tono (3a Calle Poniente, Lotificación Cofiño, 2o Callejón 4; s/d US$9/13) Next-door to Don Ismael (below), this is another friendly little spot with six simple, clean rooms alongside a small patio, free drinking water, and use of a kitchen.

Yellow House (☎ 7832 6646; main@granjaguar.com; 1a Calle Poniente 24; s/d US$8/16; ✗ 🖳) Rooms here are simple but clean and nonsmoking, with comfy beds, wooden furniture, pastel walls and big mosquito-netted windows. Try to get one upstairs. The shared bathrooms are immaculate and use solar-heated water. Rates include use of the guest kitchen, unlimited internet and drinking water.

Hotel Cristal (☎ 7832 4177; Av el Desengaño 25; s/d US$8/12, s/d with bathroom US$10/14) There's some good solid value on offer here, even if the place is a little out of the center. Rooms at the front can be noisy and the bathrooms aren't huge, but it's well priced by Antigua standards.

Posada Juma Ocag (☎ 7832 3109; Calzada de Santa Lucía Norte 13; s/d/US$12/14) Sun bursts through the patio at this cheerful little hotel – the budget prices belying the tranquil atmosphere. The seven spotless, comfortable rooms have high-quality mattresses and traditional appointments including wrought-iron bed heads, reading lamps and mirrors made by your friendly, attentive host, Juan Ramón. Each room has a private hot shower; there's also a rooftop patio and well-tended little garden. Touches like drinking water and decorative ceramic masks make this great value. It's peaceful, despite the location on a busy street. Reservations are accepted in person only. Grab a room upstairs for even more peace in this central location.

Hotel la Casa de Don Ismael (☎ /fax 7832 1932; www .casadonismael.com; 3a Calle Poniente, Lotificación Cofiño, 20 Callejón 6; s/d US$10/15) Safe, friendly Don Ismael's, hidden down a small side-street, fills up fast. The seven cheerful, comfy rooms share three hot-water bathrooms. There's a pleasant roof terrace, washing sinks, drinking water and breakfast available.

Posada Doña Clara (☎ 5432 6091; 5a Ave Norte 16; s/d US$12/18) The maze of rooms set around leafy patios just keeps unwinding, but persevere and head for the rear upstairs, where they're most spacious and the balconies come with volcano views. The entrance is through the handicrafts store on the street.

Casa Santa Lucía No 1 (☎ 7832 7418; Calzada de Santa Lucía Sur 9; s/d US$13) Of all the Santa Lucías in town, this is probably the nicest, and definitely the most central. Why is it the cheapest? Another mystery of Guatemala... There's an excellent, colonial atmosphere on offer here, at a fraction of what it usually goes for.

Las Golondrinas (☎ 7832 3343; drrios@intel.net.gt; 6a Ave Norte 34 Apt 6; s/d US$12/24, with kitchen US$15/30) An excellent option for serious self-caterers are the apartment-like rooms with balconies (and views) here. They're set around a grassy garden area dotted with trees. The apartments are well set up, with enough furniture to keep long-termers happy. Good weekly and monthly discounts are available.

Casa Cristina (☎ 7832 0623; www.casa-cristina.com; Callejón Camposeco 3A; s/d US$16/20) A near-overdose of quaint in this comfy little two-story hotel – they lay it on thick with the indigenous bedspreads and soft pastel paint job, but it's a quiet spot in a good area and a good deal for the price.

Posada Don Diego (☎ 7832 1401; posadadon_diego @hotmail.com; 6a Av Norte 52; s/d with bathroom US$18/20) Probably the thing that stands out most about this place is the Dunkin' Donuts franchise in the café out front. The handful of rooms are set beside a pretty little patio with wooden pillars, a patch of lawn and a stone fountain. Bathrooms are actually across the hall from the rooms.

Casa Santa Lucía No 2 (☎ 7832 7418; Calzada de Santa Lucía Norte 21; s/d US$19; Ⓟ) Sparklingly clean, light and spacious, the rooms at the second of the four Santa Lucías have terracotta tiled floors waxed to perfection and plenty of colonial charm. The showers are rippers here, too – just make sure you ask what time they turn on the hot water.

Casa Santa Lucía No 3 (☎ 7832 1386; 6 Av Norte; s/d US$19) Stepping way back in time brings you to this grand colonial-style house with arched hallways and heavy wooden exposed beams. Rooms are nothing special, but a good deal for the price and the blasting hot showers do the job.

Midrange

Some of Antigua's midrange hotels allow you to wallow in the city's colonial charms for a moderate outlay of cash.

Hostal el Montañés (☎ 7832 3046; Calle del Hermano Pedro 19B; dm/r US$20/50) Rooms in this modern family home are well-appointed and bright, with spotless bathrooms. The three-bed dorm is a good deal and there are discounts for longer stays.

Hotel Posada La Merced (☎ 7832 3197; www .merced-landivar.com; 7a Av Norte 43; s/d US$20/25, with bathroom US$40/45; P ☒) Deceptively colonial from the outside, La Merced has big wooden doors that open onto a fiendishly modern interior. The whole effect is softened somewhat by plenty of native weaving and Nahuali furniture. Hammocks are hung in a couple of interior patios. Bonuses include a rooftop terrace and a well-appointed guest kitchen.

Posada de Don Valentino (☎ 7832 0384; www.posada donvalentino.com; 5a Calle Poniente 28; s/d US$20/30) The unassuming entranceway here, clogged with internet users, opens onto a charming little hotel with well appointed, spacious rooms. No 109 is best for light and views of the pretty interior patio, but the two right up top have volcano views.

Hotel Posada Landívar (☎ /fax 7832 8819; 5a Calle Poniente 23; s/d US$20/30; P) This is a friendly little place with five of its seven rooms set round a pretty little patio with a fountain. Rooms vary – some are cramped. Colorful weavings and paintings, drinking water, baggage storage and a little roof garden add to the appeal.

Hotel Posada San Vicente (☎ /fax 7832 3311; 6a Av Sur 6; s/d/tr US$20/30) Clean, colorful rooms, all with bathroom, on two stories around a wide patio dominated by a massive ornamental fountain. There's a roof terrace and an in-house travel agency. The upstairs rooms are a bit bigger.

Hotel La Tatuana (☎ 7832 1223; latatuana@hotmail .com; 7a Av Sur 3; s/d US$20/36) This brightly painted, cozy little hotel feels more like a B&B. There's a cute little patio/sitting area and a small roof terrace. Rooms vary greatly – ask to see a few.

Posada Asjemenou (☎ 7832 2670; asjemenou1 @yahoo.com; 5a Av Norte 31; s/d US$20/26, with bathroom US$26/35) Just north of the Arco de Santa Catalina, the Asjemenou is built around two patios, the front one being a lovely grassy courtyard with a fountain, the back one being not quite so impressive. Rooms are sizable and clean, with drinking water provided. Rates include breakfast in the front patio. In quieter seasons prices can be slashed by almost half.

Hotel La Sin Ventura (☎ 7832 0581; www.lasinventura .com; 5a Av Sur 8; s/d US$25/38; P) An impres-

sive hotel on many fronts – the proximity to the park, the tile work and, believe it or not, a great smell. Rooms are spacious and although windows face onto a corridor, they have good views of the park and cathedral. Excellent views are to be had from the small roof terrace.

Casa Rustica (☎ 7832 3709; www.casarusticagt.com; 6a Av Norte 8; s/d US$28/32; ☐) Everything about this place is big, right down to the Texan owner. It's also one of the few hotels in this price range to offer guests full kitchen access, wi-fi, a good bar, double hammocks on the rooftop and a quiet, central location.

Hotel Posada del Sol (☎ 7832 6838; Callejón de los Nazarenos 17; s/d US$28/35; P) Hanging plants and a cheerful little courtyard welcome you to this cute little option a little ways out of town in a peaceful, leafy street. Try to get an upstairs room as the ones below get chilly.

Hotel Plaza Mayor (☎ 7832 0055; juanchew@gmail .com; 4a Calle Poniente 9; s/d US$30/40) A curious blend of rustic and modern styles makes this an interesting option. Rooms are surprisingly spacious, but the big winner here is the location, a few short steps from the park.

Posada Don Ché (☎ 7832 3895; posadadonche@hotmail .com; 7a Av Norte 15; s/d US$30/40) A tranquil little spot not too far from the action. Rooms are well decked out with classic tile work and firm beds. Upstairs rooms are by far the better choice here, for air, light and volcano views.

Hotel Posada San Pedro (☎ 7832 0718; www.posada sanpedro.net; 7a Av Norte 29; s/d US$30/40) Somebody's restored this one with a whole lot of love and attention to detail. Rooms are spacious and well furnished and look out onto two lush patios surrounded by hanging plants.

Hotel Palacio Chico (☎ 7832 0406; www.palaciochico .enantigua.com; 4a Av Sur 4; s/d with breakfast US$30/40) Close to Parque Central and with a friendly reception, this hotel is good value, although the bedspreads may be a little too furry for some. Rooms are spacious, attractively painted with that sponged-over technique that is so fetching in Antigua, and have lots of wood.

our pick **Posada Lazos Fuertes** (☎ 7832 9436; www.posadalazosfuertes.com; Calzada Santa Lucía Sur 5; s/d US$35/42; P ☐) Yet another of Antigua's beautifully restored colonial hotels, the Lazos Fuertes stands out with its location right next to the market and the fact that profits go to the project Safe Passage (www.safepassage.org), which helps rehabilitate kids who work picking through trash in Guatemala City dumps.

Hotel Santa Clara (☎ 7832 4291; santaclara12000 @yahoo.com; 2a Av Sur 20; s/d US$35/45) In a quiet area south of the center, the 19-room Santa Clara has some older rooms with character featuring tiling and brickwork, set around three pretty patios. It also has newer, mostly brighter rooms on two levels at the rear. It's clean, and popular with small groups.

Hotel Posada San Pedro (☎ 7832 3594; www.posada sanpedro.net; 3a Av Sur 15; s/d US$35/45) The 10 rooms here are super-clean and inviting, with pink and white paint, good wooden furniture, cable TV and tiled bathrooms. Two spacious sitting areas and two terraces with great views add to the comfortable, friendly atmosphere. Rooms in the front on the upper floor are bigger and get better light.

Hotel San Jorge (☎ /fax 7832 3132; www.hotelsanjorge .centroamerica.com; 4a Av Sur 13; s/d US$45/50; P) Though in a modern building, this hotel has a rustic reception area and all 14 rooms share a long balcony and overlook a beautiful flower-filled garden replete with an insanely loud fountain and chirping birds. The rooms have a fireplace, cable TV, pretty tiles and a bathroom with a tub. Ask about discounts in low season.

Top End

Hotel Aurora (☎ 7832 0217; www.hotelauroraantigua .com; 4a Calle Oriente 16; s/d US$50/60) The Aurora has a good, old-timey feel to it. The large rooms are centered on a grassy patio that comes replete with tinkling fountain and wicker lawn chairs. Breakfast (included in the price) is served on the wide interior balconies.

Posada San Sebastián (☎ /fax 7832 2621; snsebast @hotmail.com; 3a Av Norte 4; s/d US$50/60) Crammed full of antiques, but still spacious, rooms here are some of the most tranquil in town. Megasized bathrooms with tub are an added bonus, as are the use of a kitchen, roof terrace and a pretty little courtyard garden.

Hotel Uxlabil (☎ 7832 9090; www.uxlabil.com; 3a Poniente 5; s/d US$60/70) The wild (or, to be kind, eclectic) array of colonial and indigenous furnishings somehow hangs together in this medium-sized hotel set around two lush patios. Ask to see a few rooms – styles range from four-poster beds and chandeliers to rough stone and plant-filled, grottolike bathrooms.

Hotel Convento Santa Catalina Mártir (☎ 7832 3080; www.convento.com; 5a Av Norte 28; s/d US$60/70; P 🖵) The Arco de Santa Catalina (right

outside the front door) was built for the nuns of this ex-convent. Of all the fabulously dressed up renovations in this town, this has to be one of the most impressive for the price. Rooms in the colonial section are large and atmospheric. Out back there are newer ones that are larger, face private, leafy gardens and have kitchenettes.

Casa de los Cántaros B&B (☎ 7832 0674; www .travellog.com/guatemala/casa/cantaros.html; 5a Av Sur 5; s/d US$75/95) An excellent balance between rustic and swanky awaits at this exclusive little B&B with only three rooms, a few steps from the park. Pay a bit more for the suite and you basically get a small house.

Hotel Quinta de las Flores (☎ 7832 3721; www .quintadelasflores.com; Calle del Hermano Pedro 6; r from US$70, bungalows US$120; P 🖵 🐾) More like a miniresort than a hotel, this place is bursting with charms – the grounds are carpeted in flowers and dotted with fountains, there's a well-equipped kids playground, a good-sized swimming pool and a restaurant on the premises. There are eight large, luxurious rooms, most with a fireplace, plus five rustic-style, two-story houses each with two bedrooms, a kitchen and living room. Considerable discounts are offered for stays by the week.

Hotel Casa Azul (☎ 7832 0961; www.casazul.guate .com; 4a Av Norte 5; r from US$83; P 🐾) One of Antigua's original boutique hotels, this little place right by the park is almost impossibly stylish, combining a designer's eye with colonial charms. Each room has a unique design, but all are picture-perfect. The upstairs units are spectacular, with sweeping views, luxurious baths, telephones and minibars. The cheaper downstairs rooms are just as impressive, but without views. Still, they give better access to the pool, Jacuzzi and sauna.

Hotel Meson de María (☎ 7832 6068; www.hotelmeson demaria.com; 3a Calle Poniente 8; s/d US$80/100) You'll forgive the rooms for being a bit, ahem, tight on space when you see that the bathrooms feature real live tubs. Everything else is as good as it should be – firm beds, big TVs and a couple of gorgeous patio/breakfast areas.

Hotel Casa Azul (☎ 7832 0961; www.casazul.guate .com; 4a Av Norte 5; r from US$83; P 🐾) One of Antigua's original boutique hotels, this little place right by the park is almost impossibly stylish, combining a designer's eye with colonial charms. Each room has a unique design, but all are picture-perfect. The upstairs units are spectacular, with sweeping views, luxurious baths, telephones and minibars. The cheaper downstairs rooms are just as impressive, but without views. Still, they give better access to the pool, Jacuzzi and sauna.

Cloister (☎ /fax 7832-0712; www.thecloister.com; 5a Av Norte 23; r with breakfast US$90; **P** ✗) A romantic option is this renovated cloister from the 16th century, one of the most exclusive hotels in Antigua. Bubbling fountains highlight the horticultural triumph that is the Cloister's garden courtyard, and guests will likely spend a lot of time relaxing here. All seven rooms and suites have antique furniture, fireplace and library. Prices include breakfast. Credit cards are not accepted.

Casa Santo Domingo Hotel (☎ 7832 0140; www .casasantodomingo.com.gt; 3a Calle Oriente 28; r from US$120; **P** 🖵 🖭) This is quite the most gorgeous large hotel in Antigua, a town well known for its gorgeous hotels. It is set amid the beautiful remains of the Santo Domingo monastery. The 97 rooms and suites are of an international five-star standard, but the public spaces are wonderfully colonial, dotted with antiques and archaeological relics, and include a large swimming pool, fine restaurant, shops and three museums. The Dominican friars never had it so good. A fine place to spend a lot of money, the prices go down from September to November and up during weekends.

Posada del Ángel (☎ 7832 5244; www.posadadel angel.com; 4a Av Sur 24A; s/d US$130/150; **P** ✗ 🖭) The Posada became Antigua's most celebrated B&B when Bill Clinton bedded down here in 1999. It doesn't look like much from the outside, but behind the garage door the luxury just keeps unfolding. If you didn't think it was possible to fit a swimming pool into an Antigua patio, stop by. The three rooms and one suite all have fireplaces, fresh flowers, gorgeous furnishings and highly polished tile floors.

Mesón Panza Verde (☎ 7832 2925; www.panzaverde .com; 5a Av Sur 19; d US$75-250; **P** 🖭) The stunning Panza Verde is an elegant American-owned guesthouse with four rooms and eight suites. It's decked out with sumptuous furniture and fittings, some pieces ever so fashionably tatty due to being semi-outdoors. Upstairs there is an art gallery, reached by a staircase with a beautiful iron balustrade. The atmosphere and restaurant here are among the most appealing in Antigua.

EATING

Within 10 minutes' walk of Parque Central you can dine well and inexpensively on Italian, Spanish, French, Greek, Thai, Indonesian, Vietnamese, Irish, Austrian, German, American, Chinese, Peruvian, Mexican and even Guatemalan food.

Note that most formal restaurants in Antigua whack on a 10% tip before presenting the bill. It should be itemized, but if in doubt, ask.

Budget

The cheapest eating in town is the good, clean, tasty food served from street stalls a block west of Parque Central, in the early evening. Small restaurants north of the bus station on Alameda de Santa Lucia do good-value set lunches for around US$2.50.

Doña María Gordillo Dulces Típicos (4a Calle Oriente 11) This shop opposite Hotel Aurora is filled with traditional Guatemalan sweets, and there's often a crowd of Antigüeños lined up to buy them.

Fernando's Kaffe (cnr 7a Av Norte & Calle Camposeco; breakfast US$1-3; ☖ 7am-8pm) Ignore the shopfront-look from the street and head for the back patio. Antigua has no shortage of coffee or cafés, but Fernando's is the sort of place where you could end up hanging out all day, munching your way through the menu of salads and empanadas and sipping some of the best coffee in town.

Sabe Rico (6a Av Sur 7; sandwiches & salads US$4; ☖ 9am-6pm) This little deli whips up some super-tasty snacks, picnic items, delicious homemade cookies, organic fruit and veg and also sells a range of hard-to-find imported foods like couscous and soba noodles.

Café La Escudilla (4a Av Norte 4; pasta US$2.50-3.25, meat dishes US$3.50-5.50; ☖ 7am-midnight) Hugely popular with travelers and language students, La Escudilla is an inexpensive patio restaurant with tinkling fountain, lush foliage and some tables under the open sky. The food is simple but well prepared and there are plenty of vegetarian options, as well as economical breakfasts and a one-course set lunch or dinner for under US$2.40. At the back is Riki's Bar (see p115).

Restaurante Doña Luisa Xicotencatl (4a Calle Oriente 12; sandwiches & breakfast dishes US$3-4; ☖ 7am-9:30pm) Probably Antigua's best-known restaurant, this is a place to enjoy the colonial patio ambience over breakfast or a light meal. The bakery here sells many kinds of breads, including whole grain. Check out the hot-from-the-oven banana bread daily at around 2pm.

our pick Cuevita de las Urquizas (2 Calle Oriente 9D; mains US$4-5; ☺ lunch & dinner) Sumptuous *típico* food is the draw here, all kept warming in earthenware pots out front – a very dirty trick as the smells wafting out are impossible to go past. Hugely popular with locals, it's worth getting here early to avoid waiting for a table.

Bagel Barn (5a Calle Poniente 2; bagels US$2-3.25; ☺ 6am-9pm) Just off Parque Central, this is popular for bagels with almost anything, and breakfasts and coffee. They also offer decaf espresso, although we fail to see the point.

Restaurante La Estrella (4a Calle Poniente 3; mains US$2.50-4; ☺ lunch & dinner) An efficient, friendly, economical Chinese restaurant, the Estrella has several tofu options.

Jardín Bavaria (7a Av Norte 49; breakfast US$2.20, mains US$2.20-4.50; ☺ high season 7am-1am Mon-Sat, low season 1pm-1am Mon-Sat, 9am-3pm Sun) This is a bar-restaurant with a verdant patio and spacious roof terrace, offering a mixed Guatemalan–German menu including buffalo steak and suckling pig. There's a good range of beers and US$4.50 Sunday buffet lunches.

Weiner (Calzada Santa Lucía Norte 8; mains US$3-7; ☺ lunch & dinner) Possibly the biggest wiener schnitzel you've ever seen, alongside some good-value set lunches and the sort of beer list you'd expect from a German restaurant.

Café No Sé (1 Av Sur 11C; mains US$3-5; ☺ breakfast, lunch & dinner) Advertising uncomfortable seats, confused staff and battered books, this is a pleasantly downbeat option among all of Antigua's finery. There's a little bit of everything here – breakfast (including one option of a shot of mescal and two boiled eggs; US$2.50), burritos, fried chicken, sandwiches, movies, a tequila bar and live music.

El Mix (4a Av Sur 2A; mains US$3-5; ☺ breakfast, lunch & dinner) As the name implies, there's a good mix of things on the menu here – comfort foods, Israeli dishes and a couple of Guatemalan numbers. The star of the show is the mind-boggling array of make-your-own sandwich options.

Rainbow Café (7a Av Sur 8; mains US$4-6; ☺ 7am-midnight) Fill up from an eclectic range of all-day breakfasts, curries, stir-fries, Cajun chicken, guacamole and more, and enjoy the relaxed patio atmosphere. The Rainbow has a bookshop and travel agency on the premises.

Traveler Menu (6a Calle Poniente 14; mains US$4-5; ☺ dinner Tue-Sun) Not nearly as unimaginative as the name would imply, this little bar-restaurant serves up big portions of food that you may have been craving (chow mein, curry etc) in an intimate candlelit environment.

La Fuente (4a Calle Oriente 14; mains US$4; ☺ 7am-7pm) Another pretty courtyard restaurant, tranquil La Fuente has lots of vegetarian selections, good breakfasts and desserts.

Café Condesa (Portal del Comercio 4; snacks US$2.50-5) Walk through the Librería Case del Conde on the west side of the Parque Central to this delightful restaurant around the patio of a 16th-century mansion. On the menu are excellent breakfasts, coffee, salads, sandwiches, quiches, cakes and pies. The Sunday buffet, from 10am to 2pm, a lavish spread for US$7, is an Antigua institution.

Midrange

La Peña de Sol Latino (5a Calle Poniente; mains US$3-8; ☺ lunch & dinner) With good, cheap and innovative food and free live music nightly, this little indoor-outdoor place is fast becoming one of the hottest bar-restaurants in town. Get there before 7pm for a good table.

Café Flor (4a Av Sur 1; mains US$4-8; ☺ 11am-11pm) The Flor makes a good stab at Thai, Indonesian and Chinese cuisine. Dishes come in generous quantity and there's live music nightly.

Los Arcos (1a Calle Poniente 3; mains US$4-10; ☺ breakfast, lunch & dinner) This English-run place has the longest menu in town, from all-day breakfasts to Thai stir-fries, and does a decent job of most of it.

Restaurante Korea (5a Calle Poniente 6; mains US$5-6; ☺ breakfast, lunch & dinner) This little restaurant, plonked in the middle of a hotel courtyard, serves up incredibly tasty, authentic Korean dishes. Wash them down with a Korean beer or some rice wine!

Estudio 35 (5a Av Norte 35; mains US$5-10; ☺ lunch & dinner) A hip little bar-restaurant serving up some good pizzas and crepes. There's a few different, laid-back and loungey sitting areas to choose from.

Perú Café (4a Av Norte 7; mains US$7-11; ☺ lunch & dinner Tue-Sun) Enjoy tasty Peruvian specialties at this pretty patio restaurant. The excellent *causas* are like burgers with layers of mashed potato instead of bread; *ají de gallina* is chicken in yellow chili sauce with baked potatoes, parmesan and rice.

ANTIGUA

El Cafecito (5a Calle Poniente 7A; mains US$8-10; ⏱ lunch & dinner Tue-Sat) Some good, hearty Portuguese food is on offer here, including *feijolada* (US$8), a chunky stew made with beans, vegetables and four kinds of meat.

El Papaturo (2 Calle Oriente 4; mains US$8-11; ⏱ lunch & dinner) If you've got a hankering for Salvadoran food, but you're not likely to make it that far, check this place out for some authentic dishes and good steak plates.

Restaurante Las Palmas (6a Av Norte 14; mains US$6-8; ⏱ lunch & dinner) Twinkling lights and gentle guitar music make this a popular romantic dinner spot. The staples are chicken, seafood, steaks and pasta: try the fettuccine with goat's cheese, shrimps, herbs and garlic.

El Punto (7a Av Norte 8A; mains US$7-9; ⏱ lunch & dinner Tue-Sat, lunch Sun) Highly popular El Punto serves probably Antigua's best Italian food in a neat but animated setting of three adjoining rooms and a patio, each with three or four tables – and some particularly interesting posters on Italian and Guatemalan themes.

Monoloco (5a Av Sur 6, Pasaje El Corregidor; dishes US$4-8; ⏱ lunch & dinner) An old-time tourist hangout (take that as a recommendation or a warning), this place serves up a good blend of comfort foods and local dishes, as well as ice-cold beers in a relaxed environment.

Gaia (5 Av Norte 35; mains US$7-10; ⏱ lunch & dinner) An almost painfully hip Mid East flavored restaurant with an excellent menu, a long wine and cocktail list and *nargilas* (water pipes) for US$6.

Fridas (5a Av Norte 29; snacks US$2.50-4, mains US$6-8; ⏱ lunch & dinner) Dedicated to Ms Kahlo, this bright bar-restaurant serves tasty, if not cheap, Mexican fare and is always busy.

El Sabor del Tiempo (5a Av Norte & 3a Calle; mains US$6-8; ⏱ lunch & dinner) One of the town's more atmospheric eateries, done out in rich woods and antique fittings. The menu features some good Italian-themed dishes like rabbit in white wine (US$7) and there's draft beer on tap.

La Fonda de la Calle Real (mains US$5-8.50) 3a Calle Poniente 7 (☎ 7832 0507; ⏱ noon-10pm); 5a Av Norte 5 (☎ 7832 2629; ⏱ noon-10pm); 5a Av Norte 12 (☎ 7832 3749; ⏱ 8am-10pm) This restaurant with three spacious branches, all in appealing colonial style, has a good, varied menu ranging from generous salads and sandwiches (US$3) to grilled meats (up to US$8.50). The speciality *caldo real*, a hearty chicken soup, makes a good meal. The 5a Av Norte 12 branch is a little cheaper than the others but 3a Calle

Poniente 7 is the most attractive, with several rooms and patios.

Top End

La Casserole (☎ 7832 0219; Callejón de la Concepción 7; 2-course meals US$15-18; ⏱ lunch & dinner Tue-Sat, lunch Sun) This French restaurant with friendly but smooth service is one of Antigua's best. It's great for steak and dessert lovers. There are just a dozen tables in a patio and one side room.

Nokiate (☎ 7821 2896; 1a Av Sur 7; mains US$8-15; ⏱ dinner Wed-Sun) Antigua's most authentic sushi bar has the lot – the tranquil, minimalist atmosphere, the sake and some excellent, fresh sushi.

Mesón Panza Verde (☎ 7832 2925; 5a Av Sur 19; mains US$6-20; ⏱ lunch & dinner) This guesthouse restaurant provides divine continental cuisine in an appealing Antiguan atmosphere. Two courses should cost you about US$20. If you don't have the budget for a full meal but want to check out the great ambience and gorgeous patio, have a drink or snack at the Panza Verde's Café Terraza.

Las Antorchas (3a Av Sur 1; mains US$10-15; ⏱ lunch & dinner Mon-Sat, lunch Sun) This place has a beautiful courtyard to go with its sumptuous steaks. The *pincho gigante* (giant shish kebab; US$15) should be enough for two.

Restaurante Don Rodrigo (☎ 7832 2664; 5a Av Norte 17; mains US$12-16; ⏱ breakfast, lunch & dinner) The food's up to scratch here – lots of meat and seafood with light Guatemalan twists. The real draw is the setting, a gorgeous courtyard with plenty of wrought iron, blossoming flowers and tinkling fountains.

Casa Santo Domingo Hotel (☎ 7832 0140; 3a Calle Oriente 28; 2-course meals US$13-25) The restaurant at this luxurious hotel is another beautiful spot for a splurge, with mixed Guatemalan and international delights served inside or out in the garden.

El Sereno (☎ 7832 0501; 4a Av Norte 16; mains US$15-20; ⏱ lunch & dinner) Another of Antigua's beautiful courtyard restaurants, this one offers a careful blend of Asian, Italian and Guatemalan influences. There's a full bar inside, but outside is the place to be for lunch, under the shade of two big trees.

Welten (☎ 7832 6967; 4a Calle Oriente 21; mains US$15; ⏱ lunch & dinner Wed-Mon) Despite some very snooty service, this is an enjoyable restaurant, lovingly decorated and serving up some of Antigua's more imaginative dishes.

DRINKING

Antigua's bar scene is jumping, except for the nationwide law that says that all bars must close at 1am. Many people roll in from Guatemala City for a spot of Antigua-style revelry on Friday and Saturday. La Peña de Sol Latino (p113), Estudio 35 (p113) and Rainbow Café (p113) are good places to go for drinks.

Riki's Bar (4a Av Norte 4; ☽ until midnight) Behind Café La Escudilla, this old favorite gets packed every evening with Antigua's young, international scene of locals, travelers and language students. For quieter moments, slip through to the low-key Paris Bar in the rear.

Monoloco (5a Av Sur 6, Pasaje El Corregidor) The 'Crazy Monkey' is the place that everybody goes until they get sick of it, so often has a real party atmosphere with plenty of newcomers. It's a two-level place (semi-open-air upstairs, with benches and long tables), with sports on TV and good-value food.

Reilly's (5a Av Norte 31) Guatemala's only Irish bar (so far), Reilly's is sociable and relaxed, with a young international crowd. Sadly, small bottles of Guinness are US$4.50 – more than double the cost of local beers! The Sunday evening quiz is one of Antigua's most enjoyable events.

Sangre (5a Av Norte 33A) Antigua's jet set gathers on the upstairs deck out back of this wine bar, sipping from a choice of over 40 types of wines (from US$4 per glass) and munching on creative *boquitas* (snacks; US$5 to US$7) while checking out the skyline views.

El Muro (3a Calle Oriente 19D) A friendly little neighborhood pub with a good range of beers, some decent snacks and plenty of sofas to lounge out on.

Café No Sé (1 Av Sur 11C) This downbeat little bar has live music most nights and an attached tequila bar where they serve their own brand of mescal.

Onis (7a Av Norte 2) With a back terrace overlooking the illuminated ruins of San Agustín church, Onis is another travelers' and students' haunt. Unlike some Antigua bars, it has a liquor license: shots and cocktails cost US$2 to US$3, but rum, vodka or gin are just US$0.15 for women from 7pm to 10pm on Thursday. There's good, economical food too.

Café Sky (1a Av Sur 15) On the rooftop above the Guatemala Ventures/Mayan Bike Tours office, this is a very popular place for sunset drinks.

Los Arcos (1a Calle Poniente 3) Come here for pool, draft beer and all-drinks-one-price offers.

For a quick caffeine fix, hit **Café Condesa Express** (Portal del Comercio 4; ☽ 6:45am-6:45pm) on the west side of the Parque Central.

ENTERTAINMENT

Proyecto Cultural El Sitio (☎ 7832 3037; www.elsitio cultural.org; 5a Calle Poniente 15) This arts center has lots going on, from music, dance and theater events (including plays in English) to exhibition openings most Saturdays. Stop by to check the schedule.

Classical concerts happen in the **Museo de Arte Colonial** (☎ 7832 0429; 5a Calle Oriente 5) and the **Antiguo Colegio de la Compañía de Jesús** (6a Av Norte), between 3a and 4a Calles.

Cinema, TV & Slide Shows

Several cinema houses show a wide range of Latin American, art-house and general-release movies: some in English, some in Spanish, usually for US$1.25 to US$2. Check the programs of the following:

Bagel Barn (5a Calle Poniente 2) Café with movies at 8pm.

Café 2000 (6a Av Norte 2) Café showing free movies on big screen.

Proyecto Cultural El Sitio (☎ 7832 3037; www.elsitio cultural.org; 5a Calle Poniente 15) Movies usually on Tuesday evening.

For North American and European sports on TV, check the programs posted at Café 2000 (see above), Los Arcos and Monoloco.

For North American and European sports on TV, check the programs that are posted at **Café 2000** (6a Av Norte 2), **Los Arcos** (1a Calle Poniente 3; mains US$4-10; ☽ breakfast, lunch & dinner) and **Monoloco** (5a Av Sur 6, Pasaje El Corregidor).

Writer Elizabeth Bell gives a fascinating one-hour English-language **slide show** (admission US$3; 6pm Tue) about Antigua called *Behind the Walls*. It's in the Christian Spanish Academy (p106).

Dancing

La Casbah (☎ 832 2640; 5a Av Norte 30; admission incl 1 drink US$2.50-4; ☽ 9pm-1am Mon-Sat) This two-level disco near the Santa Catalina arch has a warm atmosphere, is reportedly gay-friendly and quite a party most nights.

La Chimenea (cnr 7a Av Norte & 2a Calle Poniente) This is the latest hot spot for salsa and merengue dancers.

You can learn to salsa at several places around town. **La Salsa** (☎ 5400 0315; www.lasalsadance.com;

7 Av Norte 11) comes highly recommended, both for teaching style and lack of 'sleaze factor.'

SHOPPING

Nim Po't (www.nimpot.com; 5a Av Norte 29) This shop boasts a huge collection of Mayan dress, as well as hundreds of masks and other wood carvings. This sprawling space is packed with *huipiles, cortes, fajas* and more, all arranged according to region, so it makes for a fascinating visit whether you're in the market or not.

Diez Mil Pueblitos (6 Av Norte 21; diezmilpueblitos @yahoo.com) One of the country's few exclusively fair-trade stores (where the majority of profits go to producers) sells an excellent selection of quality handmade products as well as crepes and coffee in the café out back.

Mercado de Artesanías (Handicrafts Market; 4a Calle Poniente; 🕑 8am-8pm) At the west end of town by the main market, this market sells masses of Guatemalan handicrafts. While not at the top end of the quality range, it has a variety of colorful masks, blankets, jewelry, purses and so on. Don't be afraid to bargain.

There are also a number of craft shops on 4a Calle Poniente, between Parque Central and the market. Vendors will also approach you in Parque Central, or while you are drinking a coffee or eating breakfast in a casual dining place. Prices for handicrafts can be much higher in Antigua than elsewhere in Guatemala. Always bargain for a fair price.

Casa del Tejido Antiguo (1a Calle Poniente 51; admission US$0.70; 🕑 9am-5:30pm Mon-Sat) This is another intriguing place for textiles; it's like a museum, market and workshop rolled into one. It claims to be the only place in Antigua managed by indigenous people.

Antigua has some excellent but pricey jewelry and clothes shops. If you're not flush, stay away from these places, but if you have the cash and see something you like, grab it as you probably won't find the same quality elsewhere in Guatemala.

Joyería del Ángel (4a Calle Oriente 5A) This shop has exquisite pieces of imaginative, up-to-the-minute exotic jewelry using shells, semi-precious stones, bone and classy clasps. Many pieces are large and flamboyant; others are daintier with unusual combinations like jade and rose garnets. Some pieces are moderately priced but on the whole this place is quite expensive.

Casa de Arte Popular (4a Calle Oriente 10) One of the interesting art galleries along 4a Calle Oriente, it's in the same building as La Casa del Jade. For information on the distinctive style of art exhibited here, see the boxed text, p142.

GETTING THERE & AROUND
Bus

Buses to Guatemala City, Ciudad Vieja and San Miguel Dueñas arrive and depart from a street just south of the market. Buses to Chimaltenango, Escuintla, San Antonio Aguas Calientes and Santa María de Jesús go from the street outside the west side of the market. If you're heading out to local villages, it's best to go early in the morning and return by mid-afternoon, as bus services drop off dramatically as evening approaches.

TRUE JADE

Jade, beloved of the ancient Maya, isn't always green. It can be lilac, yellow, pink, white or even black. On the other hand, a lot of stones passed off as jade are not the real thing. There are two main forms of genuine jade: nephrite, found in Asia, and jadeite, found in Guatemala. Albite, serpentine, chrysoprase, diopside, chrysolite and aventurine – none of these are true jade. It seems that the ancient Maya themselves had a hard time telling the difference. Many items of Mayan 'jade' in museums have been revealed, on testing, to be one or other of these inferior stones.

To discern quality jade, look for translucency, purity and intensity of color and absence of flaws – and ask if you can scratch the stone with a pocket knife: if it scratches, it's not true jadeite but an inferior stone.

Several Antigua shops specialize in jade, including **La Casa del Jade** (www.lacasadeljade.com; 4a Calle Oriente 10), **Jades SA** (www.jademaya.com; 4a Calle Oriente 1, 4a Calle Oriente 12 & 4a Calle Oriente 34; Hotel Casa Santo Domingo, 3a Calle Oriente 28) and **El Reino del Jade** (cnr 5a Av Norte & 2a Calle Poniente). At La Casa del Jade and Jades SA's 4a Calle Oriente 34 branch, you can visit the workshops in the rear of the showrooms. Jades SA's jade comes from a rediscovered ancient Mayan jade mine in Guatemala's Motagua valley. You should ask about prices at a few places before making any purchase.

To reach highland towns such as Chichicastenango, Quetzaltenango, Huehuetenango or Panajachel (except for the one direct daily bus to Panajachel), take one of the frequent buses to Chimaltenango, on the Interamericana Hwy, and get an onward bus from there. Making connections in Chimaltenango is easy, as many folks will jump to your aid as you alight from one bus looking for another. But stay alert and don't leave your pack unattended, as bag slashing isn't unheard of in Chimal. Alternatively, you can take a bus from Antigua toward Guatemala City, get off at San Lucas Sacatepéquez and change buses there – this takes a bit longer, but you'll be boarding the bus closer to the capital so you're more likely to get a seat.

Chimaltenango (US$0.50, 30 minutes, 19km, every 15 minutes from 5am to 7pm)

Ciudad Vieja (US$0.30, 15 minutes; 7km, take a San Miguel Dueñas bus)

Escuintla (US$0.80, 1 hour, 39km, 16 buses daily from 5:30am to 5pm)

Guatemala City (US$1, 1¼hours, 45km, every few minutes from 6am to 7pm)

Panajachel (US$5, 2½hours, 146km, one Pullman bus daily at 7am) Departs from El Condor Expeditions (☎ 5498 9812; 4a Calle Poniente 34)

San Antonio Aguas Calientes (US$0.30, 30 minutes, 9km, every 20 minutes from 6:30am to 7pm)

San Miguel Dueñas (US$0.25, 30 minutes, 10km, every few minutes from 6am to 7pm). Placards just say 'Dueñas.'

EXPLORE MORE OF ANTIGUA

While Antigua itself is pretty much well-trodden territory from end to end, there are plenty of little villages just outside of town just begging to be explored:

■ Santa María de Jesús is a traditional Guatemalan village, just 30 minutes outside of town.

■ San Juan del Obispo has a wonderful colonial church and sweeping, panoramic views of Antigua.

■ San Felipe, an artisans' village, has some of the finest jade, silver and ceramic work in the area.

■ San Antonio is famed for its weaving and textiles (p119).

■ Pastores is ground zero for leatherwork. This is the place to come for those handmade cowboy boots and stock whips.

Santa María de Jesús (US$0.30, 30 minutes, 12km, every 45 minutes from 6am to 7:30pm)

Shuttle Minibus

Numerous travel agencies and tourist minibus operators offer frequent and convenient shuttle services to places tourists go, including Guatemala City and its airport, Panajachel and Chichicastenango. They go less frequently (usually on weekends) to places further afield. These services cost a lot more than buses, but they are comfortable and convenient, with door-to-door service at both ends. These are some typical one-way prices:

Chichicastenango US$6
Copán (Honduras) US$12
Guatemala City US$5
Monterrico US$8
Panajachel US$6
Quetzaltenango US$15
Río Dulce US$13

Pin down shuttle operators about departure times and whether their trip requires a minimum number of passengers. Be careful of 'shuttles' to Flores or Tikal. This service may just consist of taking you to Guatemala City and putting you on a public bus there.

Car & Motorcycle

Rental companies include the following:

CATour (☎ 7832 9638; www.catours.co.uk; 6a Calle Oriente 14) Rents motorcycles from US$10/45 per hour/day as well as motorcycle tours from US$140.

Dollar (☎ 2219-6848; www.dollar.com; 5a Av Norte 15)

Tabarini (☎ 832-8107; www.tabarini.com; 6a Av Sur 22)

Taxi

Taxis and tuk-tuks wait where the Guatemala City buses stop, and on the east side of Parque Central. A ride in town costs around US$1.60. A taxi to or from Guatemala City usually costs US$30 (US$40 after midnight).

AROUND ANTIGUA

JOCOTENANGO

This village just northwest of Antigua (effectively a suburb) gives you a taste of more typical Guatemalan life than downtown Antigua. Storefronts are occupied by tailors at their sewing machines, school kids throng the streets in the middle of the day, and women linger over their purchases to chat.

ANTIGUA

Sights

Jocotenango's **Centro Cultural La Azotea** (☎ 7832 0907; Calle del Cementerio, Final; adult/child US$3.25/0.65; 🕑 8:30am-4pm Mon-Fri, 8:30am- 2pm Sat) is an excellent three-in-one coffee, music and costume museum. The coffee section includes a 19th-century water wheel–powered processing plant: you get a free cup to drink at the end of the tour. Part two of the center is the Casa K'ojom, a top-class collection of traditional Mayan musical instruments, masks, paintings and other artifacts amassed by dedicated cultural conservationist Samuel Franco. The displays set the objects in the context of the many ceremonies and customs in which they are used, with a particularly interesting section on Maximón, the semipagan deity revered by many highland Maya (see p140). A good audiovisual show illustrating the musical instruments in action is part of the visit. The third exhibit is the Rincón de Sacatepéquez, displaying the colorful costumes and crafts of the Antigua valley. Free tours to all this are available in English and Spanish.

Also at La Azotea are two shops selling quality coffee, local crafts, Mayan instruments and recordings and videos of them, a restaurant with good, moderately priced Guatemalan food. There is also the **Establo La Ronda**, where you can take a one-hour morning horse ride round the grounds for US$3.25 (ring the museum two days ahead).

The **church** dominating the main square is a marvel of crumbling pink stucco that still holds services. About 100m along the street toward Antigua from the square, the **Fraternidad Naturista Antigua** (☎ 7831 0379; Calle Real 30; 🕑 7am-6pm Sun-Thu, 7am-1pm Fri) offers massages, saunas and chiropractic services. It also sells an amazing variety of medicinal herbs. A 45-minute massage with unlimited sauna time costs US$6.50; a sauna alone is US$5. There are separate, very clean, facilities for men and women. The massages can be strenuous, some say rough, and men should be especially careful here as the masseurs are wicked strong!

Getting There & Away

You can also use local buses (US$0.15, 10 minutes) between Jocotenango and Antigua. They run about every 15 minutes during daylight from behind Antigua market and from Jocotenango's square. It's also quite possible to walk: it's less than 1km along Calle Ancha de los Herreros from the north end of Antigua's 6a Av to Jocotenango's square.

Free minibuses to La Azotea leave from Antigua's Parque Central hourly from 9am to 2pm, returning from La Azotea hourly from 10:30am to 2:30pm and at 4pm. You're quite free to explore the village before hopping back on the bus. From La Azotea's ticket office, walk 350m back along the driveway then 350m straight on along the street ahead (1a Calle) to reach Jocotenango's main square.

SAN LORENZO EL TEJAR

These hot springs are a 25-minute ride from Antigua. Catch any bus headed for San Lorenzo (US$0.25) and tell the driver you're going to the *aguas calientes*. You'll get dropped at the signposted turnoff. The **hot springs** (admission US$1; 🕑 7am-5:30pm Mon, Wed-Thu, Sat-Sun, 7am-noon Tue & Fri) are 500m down the narrow valley on a dirt road. The place is best avoided Sundays, when it packs out with family groups.

EL HATO

An excellent getaway from the bustle of Antigua is the **Earth Lodge** (☎ 5664 0713; www .earthlodgeguatemala.com; dm US$4, cabins s/d US$9/14), high in the hills above Jocotenango. This little slice of hippy heaven is set on 40 acres of ex-avocado farm, and the views of the Panchoy valley and volcanoes are truly mesmerizing. There's plenty to do out here – hiking trails, Spanish lessons, a *chuj* (Mayan sauna) as well as just hanging in a hammock and taking it all in. Nutritious and filling meals (US$4 to US$6) are served. You can work on the farm for a reduction in room rates. Accommodation is in comfortable wooden cabins and an eight-bed dorm, and you can camp here for US$3 per person.

Getting here is slightly complicated – your best bet is to call (with plenty of advance warning) to see if the friendly owners can come and pick you up from Antigua. Otherwise, there's a pickup that leaves from outside the basketball court on 1 Av Norte in Antigua that makes the trip to Aldea El Hato. From there it's a 10-minute walk – any villager can give you directions – just ask for *'los gringos.'*

CIUDAD VIEJA

Seven kilometers southwest of Antigua along the Escuintla road is **Ciudad Vieja** (Old City), site of the first capital of the Captaincy General of Guatemala. Founded in 1527, it was destroyed in 1541 when Volcán Agua loosed a flood of water penned up in its crater. The water deluged the town with tons of rock and mud, leaving only a few ruins of La Concepción church.

Java junkies in this neck of the woods will want to check out the coffee plantation **Finca los Nietos** (☎ 7831 5438; www.geocities.com/losnietosfinca; ☻ 8-11am Mon-Fri) for a tour and a taste. The hour-long tour (US$6 per person, minimum two people) will answer all your nitty-gritty coffee questions, from how seedlings are propagated to how beans are roasted. The price includes a bag of coffee. Phone for an appointment and mention then if you want to roast your own beans (minimum 2.5kg or 5lb). The *finca* is 7km from Antigua, just off the bus route to San Antonio Aguas Calientes: you go through Ciudad Vieja and San Lorenzo El Cubo, then get off the bus at the crossroads before the textile shop called Carolina's (bus drivers know this intersection). This is before the road goes downhill to San Antonio. Walk two blocks to the right (toward Volcán Agua) until you come to a white wall with bougainvillea and pine trees showing above it. Ring the bell and you're in.

SAN ANTONIO AGUAS CALIENTES

If you continue on to **San Antonio Aguas Calientes**, you'll see why this village is noted for its textiles as soon as you enter its plaza. Stalls in the plaza sell local woven and embroidered goods, as do shops on side streets (walk to the left of the church to find them). Bargaining is expected.

Valhalla Experimental Station (☎ 7831 5799; exvalhalla@yahoo.com; ☻ 8am-4:40pm), a macadamia farm raising 300 species of this delicious nut, is near the village of San Miguel Dueñas, 4km west of Ciudad Vieja. You can tour this organic, sustainable agriculture project and sample nuts, oils and cosmetics made from the harvest. Bring a picnic and save some room for the stellar, hand-dipped chocolate-covered macadamia nuts for sale at the shop here. To get there take a San Miguel Dueñas bus from Antigua or, if under your own steam, follow the Escuintla road past Ciudad Vieja and turn right at a large cemetery on the right-hand side. From here, the farm is about a 15-minute walk or five-minute drive downhill. This road goes on to San Miguel Dueñas. To continue round to San Antonio Aguas Calientes from here, take the first street on the right – between two houses – after coming to the concrete-block paving in Dueñas (if you reach the Texaco station in the village center, you've missed the road). The road winds through coffee *fincas*, farming hamlets and little vegetable fields.

For information on buses to these villages, see p116.

SAN JUAN COMALAPA

Another interesting day trip from Antigua is this small artisans' village 16km north of Chimaltenango. Set on the side of a deep ravine, it's a relatively modern town, founded by the Spanish when they amalgamated several Kaqchiquel towns.

The plaza's worth a quick look in, where there's a collection of dilapidated pre-Colombian sculptures and a monument to Rafael Alvarez Ovalle, who was born here and composed Guatemala's national anthem.

Most people come, though, for the primitive folk paintings that the town is famous for. San Juan gained its reputation when Andrés Curuchich rose to fame for his paintings of village life and his works ended up on display as far away as New York and Los Angeles.

Curuchich died in 1969, but his legacy lives on, as many villagers have taken up the brush and work in a similar style. Several galleries around the plaza show and sell their work. Some of Curuchich's original works are on display at the Museo Ixchel in Guatemala City (p78).

Also of interest is a mural that runs down the side wall of the cemetery, a collaborative effort on the part of local artists, depicting the Mayan creation story, the Spanish conquest and the events of the civil war.

Painting is (mostly) considered men's work – the women here are recognized as expert weavers, traditionally using silk and *cuyuxcate* (an untreated brown thread distinctive to the region), although these days modern fibers are much more common.

The best time to pick up a weaving (and just about anything else) is on Sunday, when the town's market is in full swing.

Several *comedores* line the plaza, dishing out good, unexciting meals for US$2 to US$4. If you want to stay the night, your best bet is **Hotel Pixcayá** (☎ 7849 8260; 0 Av 1-82; s/d US$5/10, with bathroom US$9/18; P).

Buses (US$0.80, 45 minutes, hourly) run from Chimaltenango, with minibuses and pickups leaving when full.

ANTIGUA

SANTIAGO SACATEPÉQUEZ & SUMPANGO

Throughout Latin America, All Saints' Day (November 1) is a spectacle. In parts of Guatemala they celebrate with the **Feria del Barrilete Gigante** (Festival of the Giant Kite). The two biggest parties happen in Santiago Sacatepéquez and Sumpango, about 20km and 25km north of Antigua respectively. These kites are giants: made from tissue paper with wood or bamboo braces, and with guide ropes as thick as a human arm, most are more than 13m wide and have intricate, colorful designs. They're flown over the cemetery to speak with the souls of the dead. Judges rank the kites according to size, design, color, originality and elevation. Part of the fun is watching the crowd flee when a giant kite takes a nose dive!

Unfortunately, the wind is sometimes insufficient to lift these giant kites, which makes for an anticlimactic festival, despite the plethora of fantastic street food. *Fiambre* (a traditional dish made from meat, seafood and vegetables served cold in vinaigrette) is typically eaten on this day. It's a labor of love to make a decent *fiambre,* and women take pride in their prowess at preparing it. It is, however, an acquired taste.

Many agencies run day trips from Antigua on November 1 for around US$8 per person, though you can easily get there on your own by taking any Guatemala City–bound bus and getting off with the throngs at the junction for Santiago. From here, take one of the scores of buses covering the last few kilometers. The fastest way to Sumpango is to take a bus to Chimaltenango and backtrack to Sumpango; this will bypass all of the Santiago-bound traffic, which is bumper to bumper on fair day.

The Highlands

Guatemala's most dramatic region – the Highlands – stretches from Antigua to the Mexican border northwest of Huehuetenango. Here the verdant hills sport emerald-green grass, cornfields and towering stands of pine, and every town and village has a story.

The traditional values and customs of Guatemala's indigenous peoples are strongest in the Highlands. Mayan dialects are the first language, Spanish a distant second. The age-old culture based on maize (from which the Maya believe that humans were created) is still alive; a sturdy cottage set in the midst of a thriving *milpa* (maize field) is a common sight. And on every road you'll see men, women and children carrying burdens of *leña* (firewood), to be used for heating and cooking.

Most towns here were already populated by the Maya when the Spanish arrived. History turned bloody and inhumane with the beginning of the civil war in 1960, when the Highlands were targeted heavily by guerrillas and the army alike.

The poster child for Guatemala's natural beauty, the volcano-ringed Lago de Atitlán has been attracting tourists for decades. Surrounded by small villages, the lake deals with its popularity well. The only place that feels really played out is Panajachel – the other villages maintain a quiet air, while offering a reasonable degree of comfort. This area was particularly badly hit by Hurricane Stan in late 2005 and the whole village of Panabaj disappeared under a landslide. Reconstruction work – for the most part by local communities and international organizations – is ensuring a slow but sure return to normality for this region.

THE HIGHLANDS

TOP FIVE

- Kicking back or partying hard lakeside around sublime **Lago de Atitlán** (p123)
- Hunting down a bargain at colorful, indigenous markets at **Chichicastenango** (p149) and **Momostenango** (p179)
- Polishing your Spanish and hiking volcanoes around **Quetzaltenango** (p161)
- Taking in the stunning Cuchumatanes scenery and village life around **Nebaj** (p158) or **Todos Santos Cuchumatán** (p185)
- Admiring the colorful costumes in towns such as **Santiago Atitlán** (p137), **Todos Santos Cuchumatán** (p185) and **Nebaj** (p158), and tuning into age-old **Mayan culture** in small towns and villages everywhere

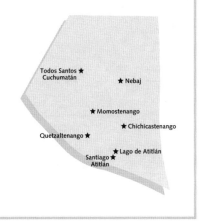

CLIMATE

The emerald-green grass, tall fields of yellow maize (corn) and towering stands of pine that characterize the Highlands all depend on the abundant rain that falls between May and October. If you visit during this rainy season, be prepared for some dreary, chilly, damp days. At high altitudes it can get cold at night at any time of year. But when the sun comes out, this land is stunning to behold.

GETTING AROUND

The meandering Interamericana (Hwy 1), running 345km along the mountain ridges between Guatemala City and the Mexican border at La Mesilla, passes close to all of the region's most important places, and count-

less buses roar up and down it all day, every day. Two key intersections act as major bus interchanges: Los Encuentros for Panajachel and Chichicastenango, and Cuatro Caminos for Quetzaltenango. If you can't find a bus going all the way to your destination, simply get one to Los Encuentros or Cuatro Caminos and change there. These transfers are usually seamless, with not-too-frustrating waiting times and locals who are always ready to help travelers find the right bus.

Travel is easiest in the morning and, for smaller places, on market days. By mid- or late afternoon, buses may be difficult to find, and it's not generally a good idea to be out on the roads after dark. On more-remote routes further off the beaten track, you may

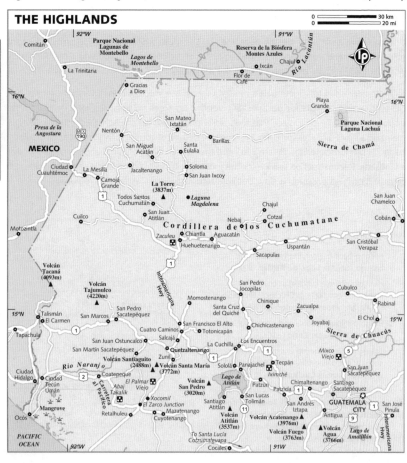

THE HIGHLANDS

be relying more on pickups or trucks than buses for transportation.

Shuttle minibuses ferry tourists between the major destinations of the region and beyond. They travel faster, more comfortably and more expensively than buses. There's a belief that shuttles are more vulnerable to highway robbery, because a vanload of gringos (Westerners) is such a tempting target. In reality, the percentage of shuttles that gets held up is minuscule – but you have to make up your own mind.

LAGO DE ATITLÁN

Surrounded by volcanoes, steep hillsides and villages where traditional Mayan culture meets the international travel scene, Lago de Atitlán – 8km across from north to south, 18km from east to west, and averaging around 300m deep – is one of the world's most beautiful and fascinating bodies of water. Many travelers have fallen in love with it and made their homes here. It's a three-hour bus ride west from Guatemala City or Antigua. The main lakeside town is Panajachel, or 'Gringotenango' as it is sometimes unkindly called, and most people initially head here to launch their Atitlán explorations.

The Maya around the north and northeast sides of the lake are mostly Kaqchiquel, while those on the west, south and southeast are Tz'utujil. When the Spanish arrived in 1524 the Kaqchiquels allied with them against the Tz'utujils, who were defeated in a bloody battle at Tzanajuyú. The Kaqchiquels subsequently rebelled against the Spanish and were themselves subjugated by 1531.

There is an ersatz town at the highway junction of Los Encuentros, based on the presence of throngs of people changing buses. From La Cuchilla junction, 2km further west along the Interamericana, a road descends 12km southward to Sololá, and then a sinuous 8km more, losing 500m in altitude, through pine forests to Panajachel. Sit on the right-hand side of the bus for breathtaking views of the lake and its surrounding volcanoes.

Dangers & Annoyances

Although most visitors never experience any trouble, there have been incidents of robbery, rape and murder in the Highlands. The most frequent sites for robberies are unfortunately some of the most beautiful – the paths that run around Lago de Atitlán. The security situation is forever changing here – some months it's OK to walk between certain villages, then that route suddenly becomes dangerous.

If you do plan to go walking, use common sense – don't take any more money than you need, or anything that you really don't want to lose. Walk in groups of at least six. Locals often take a machete along (for deterrent purposes only, naturally). If you do run into trouble, don't resist – your life is worth more than your camera.

There are persistent rumors about a Japanese tourist who was lynched for taking a photo of a child in the Highlands. This is slightly misleading. What he actually did was pick up a crying child in an effort to comfort it, which led the locals to think that a kidnapping was afoot. Fears of foreigners kidnapping children are common in the Highlands, so exercise restraint. And, of course, ask permission before taking photos of people.

Stay out of the lake in the first couple of weeks of the rainy season, when many months' worth of dry-season garbage and excreta is washed down into it.

TECPÁN

Founded as a Spanish military base during the conquest, Tecpán today is a somewhat dusty town with a couple of small hotels. The ruins of the Kaqchiquel Mayan capital, Iximché (ish-im-*che*), make it worth a visit for history fans.

Overlooking the more northerly of Tecpán's twin central plazas is a fine colonial church, the **Parroquia de San Francisco de Asís**. Tecpán honors San Francisco de Asís (St Francis of Assisi) in its annual **festival** in the first week of October. Market day is Thursday.

Iximché

Founded in 1463 on a flat promontory surrounded by ravines, Iximché was well sited to be the Kaqchiquel capital. At that time, the Kaqchiquel were at war with the K'iche' Maya, and the city's natural defenses served them well.

The Spanish, who arrived in 1524, set up their first Guatemalan headquarters at Tecpán. However, the demands of the Spanish

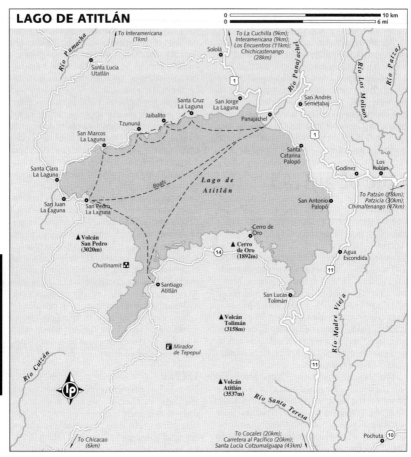

LAGO DE ATITLÁN

THE HIGHLANDS

---

for gold and other loot soon put an end to their alliance with the Kaqchiquel, who were defeated in the ensuing guerrilla war.

Entering the **archaeological site** (admission US$4; ☉ 8am-4:30pm), visit the small museum on the right, then continue to the four ceremonial plazas, which are surrounded by temple structures up to 10m high, and ball courts. Some structures have been uncovered: on a few the original plaster coating is still in place.

Ruinas buses to the site (US$0.20, 10 minutes) leave the north side of the more southerly of Tecpán's plazas at least every hour till 4pm. The last bus back leaves the site no later than 4:30pm.

Sleeping & Eating

Hotel Iximché (☎ 7840 3495; 1a Av A 1-38, Zona 2; s/d US$4/8, with bathroom US$7/13) This hotel will put you up in pink-painted, decent-sized, adequately clean rooms. It's just off the southern plaza.

There are various eateries around the twin plazas.

Getting There & Away

Veloz Poaquileña runs buses to Guatemala City (US$1, two hours) about every 30 minutes, from 5:30am to 7pm, departing in front of the church. Few buses traveling to or from Los Encuentros (US$0.70, 40 minutes), or anywhere else northwest along the Intera-

HOW ATITLÁN WAS BORN

The first volcanoes in the Atitlán region popped up 150,000 years ago, but today's landscape has its origins in the massive Los Chocoyos eruption of 85,000 years ago, which blew volcanic ash as far as Florida and Panama. The quantity of magma expelled from below the earth's crust caused the surface terrain to collapse, forming a huge, roughly circular hollow that soon filled with water – the Lago de Atitlán. Smaller volcanoes rose out of the lake's southern waters thousands of years later: Volcán San Pedro (today 3020m above sea level) about 60,000 years ago, followed by Volcán Atitlán (3537m) and Volcán Tolimán (3158m) some 40,000 to 30,000 years ago. These reduced the lake's surface area but at the same time created the dramatic volcano vistas that make Atitlán what it is. The lake today is around 300m deep and has a surface area of 128 sq km. Its water level fluctuates curiously from year to year.

mericana, go into central Tecpán. It's about a 1km walk (or, if you're lucky, a short ride on a yellow urban bus) to the center from the Tecpán turnoff on the Interamericana.

SOLOLÁ
pop 59,960 / elev 2110m

There was a Kaqchiquel town (called Tzoloyá) here long before the Spanish showed up. Sololá's importance comes from its location on trade routes between the *tierra caliente* (hot lands of the Pacific Slope) and *tierra fría* (the chilly highlands). All the traders meet here, and Sololá's terrific **market** (Tue & Fri) is one of the most authentic in the Highlands. On market mornings the plaza next to the cathedral is ablaze with the colorful costumes of people from a dozen surrounding villages and towns. Displays of meat, vegetables, fruit, house wares and clothing are neatly arranged in every available space, with tides of buyers ebbing and flowing around the vendors. Elaborate stands are well stocked with brightly colored yarn for making the traditional costumes you see around you. This is a local rather than a tourist market.

Every Sunday morning the officers of the traditional *cofradías* (religious brotherhoods) parade ceremoniously to the cathedral. On other days, Sololá sleeps.

You can make a very pleasant walk from Sololá down to the lake, either taking the highway to Panajachel (8km) or the walking track to Santa Cruz La Laguna (10km), but ask around about safety before starting out.

Virtually everyone stays in Panajachel, but if you need a bed in Sololá, **Hotel Belén** (7762 3105; 10a Calle 4-36, Zona 1; s/d US$5/9; P) has eight clean upstairs rooms with hot-water bathroom. It's a block uphill behind the clock tower that overlooks the main square.

All buses between Panajachel and Los Encuentros stop at Sololá. It's US$0.20 and 20 minutes to either place.

PANAJACHEL
pop 15,000 / elev 1560m

The busiest and most built-up lakeside settlement, Panajachel ('Pana' to pretty much the entire country) has developed haphazardly and, some say, in a less than beautiful way.

Several different cultures mingle on Panajachel's dusty streets. Ladinos and gringos control the tourist industry. The Kaqchiquel and Tz'utujil Maya from surrounding villages come to sell their handicrafts to tourists. Tour groups descend on the town by bus for a few hours or overnight.

Panajachel's excellent transportation connections and thumping nightlife make it a favorite destination for weekending Guatemalans. During the week, things quieten down, though the main street, Calle Santander, remains the same – internet café after handicrafts store after restaurant after travel agent. But you need only go down to the lakeshore to understand why Pana attracts so many visitors.

Lago de Atitlán is one of the world's most spectacular locales. Diamond splatters dance across the water, fertile hills dot the landscape, and over everything loom the volcanoes, permeating the entire area with a mysterious beauty. It never looks the same twice.

Lago de Atitlán is often placid and beautiful early in the day, which is the best time for swimming – though Pana's shores aren't the cleanest. (Note that since the lake is a volcanic crater filled with water, the lake bed often drops off sharply very near the shore.) By noon the Xocomil, a southeasterly wind, may have risen to ruffle the water's surface,

THE HIGHLANDS

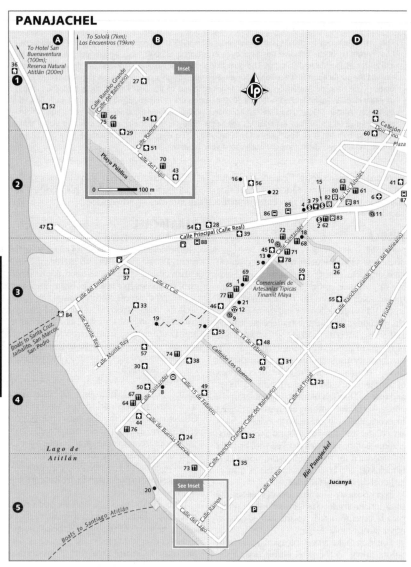

sometimes violently, making it a tough crossing for the small boats plying between the lakeside villages. This is particularly true between November and February, a time known as the windy season in these parts. It's always good to get your traveling done in the morning, when weather conditions are better and there is more traffic.

Orientation

Calle Principal (also called Calle Real) is nominally Pana's main street, although with Calle Santander's plethora of tourist-related businesses, you'll probably find yourself spending much more time there. Many of the establishments here don't use street addresses.

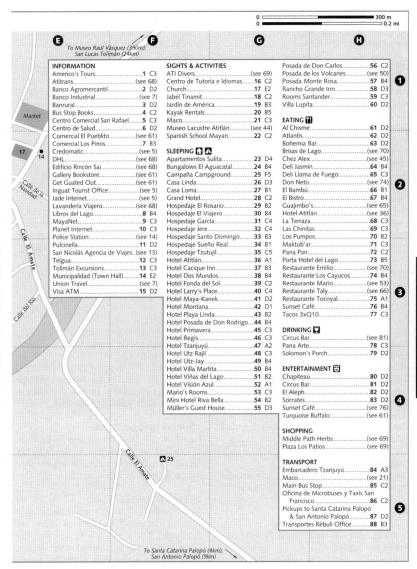

THE HIGHLANDS

Most buses stop at the intersection of Calle Principal and Calle Santander, the main road to the lake. Calle Santander is lined with restaurants, shops, accommodations, cybercafés, travel agencies and other tourist services. Beyond the Calle Santander corner, Calle Principal continues 400m to 500m northeast to the town center, where

you'll find the market (busiest on Sunday and Thursday, but in action daily), church, town hall and a further smattering of places to sleep and eat.

Calle Rancho Grande (also called Calle del Balneario) is the other main road to the beach; it's parallel to, and east of, Calle Santander. The pedestrian Calle del Lago

THE HIGHLANDS

runs along the lakeside between Calle Santander and Calle Rancho Grande; it's a pretty place for strolling.

Information
BOOKSTORES
Bus Stop Books (Centro Comercial El Dorado, Calle Principal) A good range of mainly used books to swap and buy, and a small selection of guidebooks.
Gallery Bookstore (Comercial El Pueblito, Av Los Árboles) Sells and exchanges used books, plus sells a few new ones including some Lonely Planet guides.
Libros del Lago (Calle Santander) Has an excellent stock of books in English and other tongues on Guatemala, the Maya and Mesoamerica, plus maps, English and Latin American literature in English, and Lonely Planet and other guidebooks.

EMERGENCY
Policía de Turismo (Tourist Police) Town Hall (☎ 7762 1120; Municipalidad, Calle Principal; 🕑 9am-5pm); Inguat tourist office (Centro Comercial San Rafael Local 11, Calle Santander; 🕑 9am-5pm) English-speaking; main office in the town hall.

INTERNET ACCESS
As you'd expect, Pana has plenty of places to check your email and surf the web. The standard price is US$1.30 an hour; typical hours are 9am to 10pm, perhaps slightly shorter on Sunday.
Gallery Bookstore (Comercial El Pueblito, Av Los Árboles)
Jade Internet (Centro Comercial San Rafael, Calle Santander) One of several cybercafés on Calle Santander.
MayaNet (Calle Santander 3-62)
Planet Internet (Calle Santander) Has good connections.
Pulcinella (Calle Principal 0-62)

LAUNDRY
Lavandería Viajero (Edificio Rincón Sai, Calle Santander; 🕑 8am-7pm) Reliable place; charges US$0.45 per pound.

MEDICAL SERVICES
The nearest hospital is at Sololá.
Centro de Salud (Clinic; Calle Principal; 🕑 8am-6pm Mon-Fri, 8am-1pm Sat)

MONEY
Banco Agromercantil (cnr Calles Principal & Santander; 🕑 9am-6pm Mon-Fri, 9am-1pm Sat) Changes cash US dollars and traveler's checks, and has a MasterCard ATM.
Banco Industrial (Comercial Los Pinos, Calle Santander; 🕑 9am-4pm Mon-Fri, 9am-1pm Sat) Changes cash US dollars, offers Visa-card cash advances and has a Visa ATM.
Banrural (Calle Principal; 🕑 9am-5pm Mon-Fri, 9am-1pm Sat) Changes cash US dollars and traveler's checks; next door are a Visa ATM and Banco Agromercantil.
Credomatic (Centro Comercial San Rafael, Calle Santander) Visa and MasterCard cash advances and changes cash US dollars.

Some of the travel agencies, restaurants and hotels along Calle Santander will change US dollars or euros cash, but not at the best rates.
Americo's Tours Does Visa and MasterCard cash advances, but charges a 10% commission.
Circus Bar (Av Los Árboles) Changes euros.

POST
DHL (Edificio Rincón Sai, Calle Santander) Courier service.
Get Guated Out (☎ /fax 7762 0595; gguated@c.net.gt; Comercial El Pueblito, Av Los Árboles) English-speaking outfit that can ship your important letters and parcels by air freight or international courier. It will also buy handicrafts for you and ship them for export – handy if you can't come to Panajachel yourself.
Post Office (cnr Calles Santander & 15 de Febrero)

TELEPHONE
Some cybercafés and travel agencies located on Calle Santander offer moderately cheap phone calls – around US$0.15 a minute to North America or Central America and US$0.25 a minute to Europe. Try Jade Internet or Planet Internet. For local calls there is a line of card phones outside **Telgua** (Calle Santander).

TOURIST INFORMATION
Inguat (☎ 5874 9450; Centro Comercial San Rafael Local 11, Calle Santander; 🕑 9am-5pm) This tourist office is on the main street. There are a few brochures available and staff can answer straightforward questions.

TRAVEL AGENCIES
Many of the full-service travel agencies located in Panajachel are scattered along Calle Santander. These establishments offer trips, tours and shuttle services to other destinations around Guatemala. Included among these travel agencies:
Americo's Tours (☎ 7762 2021; Calle Santander)
Atitrans (☎ 7762 2336; Edificio Rincón Sai)
San Nicolás Agencia de Viajes (☎ 7762 0382; Calle Santander 1-71)
Tolimán Excursions (☎ /fax 7762 2455, 7762 0334; Calle Santander 1-77)
Union Travel (☎ 7762 2426; Local 2, Comercial Los Pinos)

Sights

MUSEUMS

Pana has two very worthwhile museums. The **Museo Lacustre Atitlán** (Hotel Posada de Don Rodrigo, Calle Santander; admission US$4.50; 🕑 8am-6pm Sun-Fri, 8am-7pm Sat) has fascinating displays on the history of the Atitlán region and the volcanic eruptions that created its majestic landscape, and a collection of ancient Mayan artifacts recovered from the lake. The **Museo Raúl Vásquez** (5a Calle Peatonal, Calle Principal; admission US$1.30; 🕑 10am-6pm) is the home, studio, and sculpture and meditation garden of the quirky Panajachel artist for which it is named. The garden is filled with Vásquez sculptures of an eclectic selection of deities, from Jesus Christ to Shiva; indoors, you can browse his colorful, abstract paintings. To get there, follow Calle Principal 700m northeast from the market, and follow the museum sign pointing down an alley: the museum is 120m off the road.

RESERVA NATURAL ATITLÁN

A former coffee plantation being retaken by natural vegetation, the **Reserva Natural Atitlán** (☎ 7762 2565; www.atitlanreserva.com; admission US$5; 🕑 8am-5pm) is 200m past the Hotel Atitlán on the northern outskirts of town. It makes a good outing on foot or bicycle. You can walk the main trail at a leisurely pace in an hour: it leads up over swing bridges to a waterfall, then down to a platform for viewing the local population of spider monkeys. You should also see *pisotes* (coatis), relatives of the raccoon with long snouts and long, upright, furry tails. The reserve also includes a herb garden and butterfly enclosure, an interpretive center, zip lines, camping, a small shade coffee plantation and an aviary.

Activities

CYCLING, HIKING, KAYAKING & HORSE RIDING

Lago de Atitlán is a cycling, hiking and riding wonderland, with hill and dale spread among a fantastic setting. You can take a bike to San Santiago Atitlán, San Pedro La Laguna or another village to start a cycling tour around the lake. A few places in Panajachel rent out bikes: equipment varies, so check out a bike before renting it. **Maco** (☎ 7762 0883; Calle Santander) rents motorbikes for around US$8/40 per one/24 hours.

See Santiago Atitlán (p137) and following sections for information on walks around Lago de Atitlán.

Make inquiries about safety before setting out for any hike or ride, and keep asking as you go (see p123). In some cases it's better to go with a guide, and some travel agencies, such as Tolimán Excursions (opposite), offer guided hikes and rides in the lake area.

A one-day walking trip from Panajachel to the top of Volcán San Pedro and back (crossing the lake by boat) should cost around US$25 per person.

Kayaks are available for rent (from US$4 per hour) from the pier at the foot of Calle del Balneario.

DIVING

British- and American-run **ATI Divers** (☎ 7762 2621; www.laiguanaperdida.com; Plaza Los Patios, Calle Santander; 🕑 9:30am-1pm Mon-Sat) leads dive trips from Santa Cruz La Laguna (p148). Professional Association of Diving Instructors (PADI) beginning certification is a four-day affair costing US$205. ATI also offers advanced certification, fun dives for certified divers (US$30/50 for one/two dives), and specialty courses including a two-dive altitude course (US$70). Lago de Atitlán is an interesting dive site because it's a collapsed volcanic cone with bizarre geological formations and some places where hot water vents directly into the lake. There's not much aquatic flora or fauna here. The advantages of doing a dive course here is that it's one of the rare places in the world where you can dive at altitude without having to use a dry suit. Diving at altitude brings its own challenges – you need better control over your buoyancy, and visibility will be reduced. During the rainy season the water clouds up, so the best time to dive is between October and May (in the morning).

ATI Divers also organizes the annual garbage cleanup of the lake, during which several tons of trash are collected. This event, typically held in September, is a great opportunity to give something back to the community and make new friends.

Language Courses

Panajachel has a niche in the language-school scene. Two well-set-up schools are **Jardín de América** (☎ /fax 7762 2637; www.jardindeamerica.com; Calle 14 de Febrero, 3a Av Peatonal 4-44) and **Jabel Tinamit** (☎ 7762 0238; www.jabeltinamit.com; Calle Santander). Both have ample gardens and good atmospheres. Four hours of one-on-one study five days per week, including a homestay with a local family, will cost around US$120 per week at either place. Other schools include **Centro de Tutoría e Idiomas** (CTI; ☎ 7762 0259/1005; 2a Av Peatonal 1-84, Zona 2) and **Spanish School Maya** (☎ 7810 7196; Callejón Santa Elena), both of which teach some Mayan languages as well as Spanish.

Tours

If you're pressed for time, a boat tour of the lake, stopping at a few villages, is a fine idea. Boats leave the Playa Pública quay daily at 8:30am and 9:30am for tours to San Pedro La Laguna (where you stop for about 1½ hours), Santiago Atitlán (1½ hours) and San Antonio Palopó (one hour). Both get back at 3:30pm, so you get a little less shore time on the 9:30am departure. Cost is US$8 for either tour. Many travel agencies (p128) offer more-expensive boat tours (around US$25 per person), which may include weaving demonstrations, visits to the shrine of Maximón in Santiago, and so on. To arrange a tour, head to the pier at the foot of Calle del Balneario and start bargaining. Most travel agencies also arrange boat tours.

Festivals & Events

The **festival of San Francisco de Asís**, October 4, is celebrated with massive drinking and fireworks in Panajachel.

Sleeping

BUDGET

Budget travelers here will rejoice at the profusion of family-run *hospedajes* (budget hotels). They're simple – perhaps two rough beds, a small table and a light bulb in a bare boarding room – but cheap. Most provide clean toilets, and some have hot showers. More-expensive hotels offer generous discounts for longer stays.

Campaña Campground (☎ 7762 2479; Carr a Santa Catarina Palopó; campsites per person US$4) Located 1km out of town on the road to Santa Catarina Palopó. Amenities include a kitchen, a book exchange, luggage storage, clean bathrooms, electrical hookups, free drinking water, basketball, darts and inexpensive international phone calls, all in a pleasant, tree-surrounded setting. To get there, follow the Palopó road 1km from Calle Principal and turn left opposite Calle Cementerio. Three clean little rooms in wooden cabins are available too.

Casa Linda (☎ 7762 0386; Callejón El Capulin; s/d US$5/7, with bathroom US$9/12) Spotless little rooms down an alley off Calle Santander. Upstairs, rooms get a good breeze and the balconies are good for that afternoon siesta.

Rooms Santander (☎ 7762 1304; off Calle Santander; s/d US$5/8, with bathroom US$9/12) One of Pana's longest-running budget hostelries, the Santander is still going strong, with clean rooms on two levels around a small patio full of trees.

Hotel Villa Martita (Calle Santander 5-51; s/d US$5/8) A friendly little three-room place two blocks from the lake. Rooms are basic and clean, and some are the cheapest in town.

Hospedaje Santo Domingo (☎ 7762 0236; off Calle Monte Rey; s/d US$5/8, with bathroom US$10/13) This amicable, tranquil establishment has a variety of rooms. The cheapest are very basic wood-plank affairs, but there are also better shared-bathroom doubles in a newer, two-story block. There's a grassy hangout area here that makes this place.

Hospedaje García (☎ 7762 2787; Calle 14 de Febrero 2-24; s/d US$5/9, with bathroom US$15/20) The rooms with bathroom here are OK – clean enough, but the real winners are the cheaper ones – they're about twice the size and have balconies looking out onto the patio.

Casa Loma (☎ 7762 1447; Calle Rancho Grande; s/d US$5/10, with bathroom US$20/26) Excellent-value, solid wooden rooms are on offer at this place. Most are in a two-story building and have good, firm beds. The huge grassy lawn out the back is a great place to hang out.

Villa Lupita (☎ 5511 0541; Callejón Don Tino; s/d US$6/7.50, with bathroom US$7/8.50) Family-run Lupita is great value if you feel like staying in the town center. The 18 clean, secure rooms have comfortable beds, reading lamps and colorful carpets, and free coffee and drinking water are on offer. The shared hot-water bathrooms are clean, and the roof terrace affords good views.

Mario's Rooms (☎ 7762 2370; Calle Santander; s/d US$6.50/9, with bathroom US$9/13) Offering some of the best budget rooms in town, the smallish rooms at Mario's are ranged on two floors facing a cheery, plant-filled courtyard, and have blasting-hot showers.

Hotel Fonda del Sol (☎ 7762 0407; h_fondadelsol@yahoo.com; Calle Principal, near bus stop; s/d US$7/14, with bathroom US$12/24; **P**) The more expensive rooms here are heavy on stonework and light on other decoration. The cheaper ones are an excellent budget choice – large, wood-paneled rooms with comfy beds and random decorations.

Hospedaje Tzutujil (☎ 7762 0102; off Calle Rancho Grande; s/d US$8/10, with bathroom & cable TV US$14/18) Down a little alley set among cornfields, the Tzutujil is one of the best budget deals in town, with clean, modern rooms, balconies and firm beds. Upstairs rooms all have fantastic mountain views.

Hospedaje El Viajero (☎ 7762 0128; www.sleeprent buy.com/elviajero; s/d US$10/13) Nothing fancy going on here, but the paintwork should wake you up smiling, and the proximity to the lake is a winner. Upstairs rooms are a bit bigger, brighter and airier. El Viajero is at the end of a short lane off lower Calle Santander, making it quiet and peaceful, yet you're near everything. You can use a cooker, microwave and fridge, and there's laundry service and free drinking water.

Hotel Viñas del Lago (☎ 7762 0389; Playa Pública; s/d with bathroom US$10/13; P) Don't let the garish paint job put you off – the big, airy rooms upstairs here have some of the best views in town.

Hospedaje Jere (☎ 7762 2781; jere_armando@yahoo .com; Calle Rancho Grande; s/d with bathroom US$10/13; P ⌨) The Jere's big, tastefully decorated rooms are another class act in this part of town. Everything is enlivened by textiles, photos, maps and informative posters, and you can book shuttle buses and lake tours on the spot.

Hotel Utz Rajil (☎ 7762 0303; gguated@yahoo .com; Calle 14 de Febrero; s/d with bathroom US$13/19) A modern, three-story hotel with bigger rooms than most. Try to snag a front one, as the big balconies have good views.

Posada Monte Rosa (☎ 7762 0055; Calle Monte Rey; s/d with bathroom US$13/20) A short distance off Calle Santander, rooms here are sizable, with colorful Mayan fabric curtains, and fronted by patches of lawn. Unfortunately, this place don't take phone reservations.

Hotel Maya-Kanek (☎ 7762 1104; Calle Principal; s/d with bathroom US$14/18; P) These motel-style rooms in the town center are arranged around a cobbled courtyard filled with flitting hummingbirds. The 20 rooms, though small and simple, are a bit more comfortable than at a *hospedaje,* and they come with hot-water bathroom. Ask for a discount if you stay more than one night.

Posada de Don Carlos (☎ 7762 0658; Callejón Santa Elena 4-45; s/d with bathroom US$15/20) Huge upstairs

rooms face a balcony overlooking a lush courtyard, and the bathrooms, with full-sized tubs, are unbeaten in this price range.

Hotel Larry's Place (☎ 7762 0767; Calle 14 de Febrero; s/d with bathroom US$15/20; P) Set back from the road behind a wall of vegetation, Larry's Place offers good-sized, cool dark rooms. Furnishings are tasteful and the balconies without views are nonetheless welcome.

Hospedaje El Rosario (☎ 7762 1482; Calle del Lago, Playa Pública; s/d with bathroom US$15/20; P) Set around a parking lot, these stone rooms nonetheless have a bit of character and are literally stumbling distance from the lake.

Apartamentos Sulita (☎ 7762 2514; Calle del Frutal 3-42; cabins per week US$125) These cute little one- or two-person cabins are a great option if you're going to be hanging around for a while – they come fully equipped with kitchen, lounge, bathroom and one bedroom. Cable TV is available on request.

MIDRANGE

Midrange lodgings are busiest on weekends. From Sunday to Thursday you may get a discount, and you should definitely get one if you're planning on staying for longer than four days. All provide bathrooms with hot showers.

Hospedaje Sueño Real (☎ 7762 0608; Calle Ramos; s/d US$18/23) Raising its head a little above the budget pack here, the Sueño Real has tasteful, clean rooms with TV, fan and hot-water bathroom. They're well decorated, if slightly cramped. The 2nd-floor terrace with chairs, tables and lake view is a plus.

Mini Hotel Riva Bella (☎ 7762 1348; Calle Principal 2-21; s/d US$18/23; P) This collection of neat two-room bungalows, each with cable TV and its own parking place, is set around lush gardens. They're clean and modern but lack cooking facilities.

Hotel Montana (☎ 7762 0326; Callejón Don Tino; s/d US$25/30; P) Down a narrow street near the church, the Montana has 23 clean, bright rooms. The curvy balconies and Mayan fabrics thrown around the place give it a touch of style. It's in a quiet location with a fine, green, parking courtyard full of birdsong.

Hotel Utz-Jay (☎ 7762 0217; hotelutzjay.com; Calle 15 de Febrero 2-50; s/d incl breakfast US$27/36; P ✗) This excellent-value small hotel, a short distance from the lake and Calle Santander, has eight beautiful mud-brick cottages set separately around a shady yard area. They have traditional fabrics, a hot-water bathroom, cozy sitting areas out front and nice touches such as candles and drinking water. Good breakfasts and laundry service are available and there's a traditional Mayan sauna called a *chuj*. The owners speak Spanish, French and English, have lots of information about the area, and run hiking and camping trips around the lake.

Posada de los Volcanes (☎ 7762 0244; www.posadade losvolcanes.com; Calle Santander 5-51; s/d US$29/39) It may be a bit of an ask, but if you can make it to the 4th floor of this modern hotel, you'll be rewarded with high ceilings and good lake and volcano views. Some rooms have two double beds, some have one; all are brightened by paintings and mirrors.

Hotel Playa Linda (☎ 7762 0097; akennedy@gua .gbm.net; Calle del Lago, Playa Pública; r with/without lake view US$45/30; P) The Playa Linda is a rambling place with 17 assorted rooms, mostly good sized, and welcoming owners and staff. Rooms 1 to 5 and 26 have large balconies with tables, chairs and wonderful lake views. The gardens out front are bursting with rose bushes. All the rooms have a bathroom, most have fireplaces and some have a TV. Rates go up US$5 on Friday and Saturday, and by around 35% (without view) or around 50% (with view) for July, August, Semana Santa (Easter week) and the Christmas–New Year holidays.

Hotel Tzanjuyú (☎ 7762 1318; Calle Principal 4-96; s/d US$30/39; P ☎) Probably quite stylish once, and still appealing in a faded-charm sort of way, this is another hotel that comes alive at holiday times. It's set right on the lakeshore, with large gardens and a good-sized pool. The big bonuses here are the lake views from each room's private balcony and the hippie-free-zone location.

Müller's Guest House (☎ /fax 7762 2442; atmuller@ amigonet.gt; Calle Rancho Grande; s/d incl breakfast US$30/ 40; P) Blending the European and colonial styles, this place has big rooms with wooden floorboards, firm beds and serious-sized TVs. Balconies facing the grassy patio are a great place to while away the hours.

Hotel Primavera (☎ 7762 2052; www.primaveratitlan .com; Calle Santander; s/d US$30/40) This minimally decorated hotel just feels right – there are plant-filled window boxes in the rooms and a wooden decked patio area out back that makes for a relaxing atmosphere. Rates go up about 50% for July, August, Semana Santa and the Christmas–New Year holidays.

Hotel Visión Azul (☎ /fax 7762 1426; Finca San Buenaventura; r US$40; P ☎) Spanish tiles and local carvings mix well here, in a semi-secluded location just outside of town, looking toward the lake. The big, bright rooms in the main building have spacious terraces festooned with bougainvillea and ivy. The private balconies are well furnished, too, and have some great sunset views.

Grand Hotel (☎ 7762 2940; granhotelpanajachel@yahoo .com; Calle Principal; s/d US$40/45; P ☎) The Grand looks grungy from the street, but inside is a garden with lawns, plants and fountains. The 30 rooms are a little tired but adequately clean, with cheery, colored bedspreads. Get one at the back for quietness – there are slightly cheaper rooms that overlook the street. All rooms have TV and hot-water bathroom, and there's a pool and restaurant, so it's a good place to stay if you're traveling with kids.

Hotel Regis (☎ /fax 7762 1152; regisresevaciones@ yahoo.com; Calle Santander 3-47; s/d US$40/50; P ☎) Dinky, pine-paneled rooms that are spacious enough, with sitting room and oddly beautiful tile work. The real attraction here is the grounds – great expanses of lawn peppered with sitting areas, kids playgrounds, and hot tubs with water fed from a volcanic seam. Rates rise during July, August, Semana Santa and the Christmas–New Year holidays.

Hotel Dos Mundos (☎ 7762 2078; www.hoteldos mundos.com; Calle Santander 4-72; s/d US$40/55; P ☎) Italian-owned Dos Mundos has a great location towards the lake end of Calle Santander, but its installations are set well away from the street. The 22 bungalows, all with terracotta floors, woven bedspreads, Italian fittings, cable TV and at least one double and one single bed, are set around tropical gardens with a large pool. Also here are a good Italian restaurant, an in-house travel agency and a clean-cut continental-style bar fronting the street.

Rancho Grande Inn (☎ 7762 2255; www.ranchogrande inn.com; Calle Rancho Grande; d incl breakfast US$45-65; P ☎) Founded in the 1940s, the Rancho Grande has a dozen varied rooms, suites and *cabañas* (cabins) in perfectly maintained German country-style villas. Most rooms are carpeted and some are a little poky. All have TV, phone and carpets, and rates include a filling, delicious breakfast featuring original pancakes and home-grown honey and coffee. The grounds are gorgeous – manicured lawns dotted with fruit trees, and the best part – there's bar service in the swimming pool until 9pm.

Hotel Cacique Inn (☎ /fax 7762 2053; Calle El Cali 3-82; s/d US$50/60; **P** **☲**) Near Embarcadero Tzanjuyú, where boats leave for the lake's western villages, the Cacique is an assemblage of pseudo-rustic red-roofed buildings around verdant gardens with lots of birds and a swimming pool. The 34 comfortable rooms have double beds, fireplaces and weavings.

Bungalows El Aguacatal (☎ 7762 1482; Calle de Buenas Nuevas; bungalows for 4 with/without kitchen US$65/52; **P**) The decorations may strike you as a little drab, but these concrete bungalows are a good deal for groups, especially if you're planning on cooking. Each bungalow has two bedrooms and salon.

TOP END
Hotel San Buenaventura (☎ 7762 2559; www.hotelsan buenaventura.net; Finca San Buenaventura; s/d US$73/105, bungalows for 4/6 people US$173/262; **P** **☲**) The beautifully designed brick cottages here either come as simple rooms, or can be hired entirely, giving you a living room, fully equipped kitchen and terrace with barbecue area.

Hotel Posada de Don Rodrigo (☎ 7762 2326; www .corporacionhotelera.com; Calle Santander; s/d US$80/100; **P** **☲**) In the center of the action, down by the lakeside, the Don Rodrigo's cobblestoned grounds hold all sorts of delights – saunas, restaurants, squash courts, swimming pools. The rooms are big and decorated in the colonial style, and open onto private grassy sitting areas.

Hotel Atitlán (☎ /fax 7762 1441; www.hotelatitlan .com; Finca San Buenaventura; r incl breakfast US$140; **P** **☐** **☲**) Pana's loveliest hotel is on the lakeshore 1.5km northwest of the town center. It's a rambling, three-story, semicolonial-style affair surrounded by large and gorgeous gardens. Decorations go heavy on the religious imagery, wood carvings and wrought iron. The patio has views across the swimming pools to the lake. The 65 rooms all have lakefacing balconies, and the hotel has a restaurant, bar and a well-stocked gift shop.

Eating
BUDGET
Pana Pan (Calle Santander 1-61; pastries US$0.80; ☽ breakfast &lunch) Great cinnamon rolls, banana and chocolate muffins, and whole-wheat bread make a call here obligatory. Take away or sit down with a coffee.

Tacos 3xQ10 (Calle Santander; 3 tacos US$1.30; ☽ 8am-10pm Sun-Thu, 8am-11pm Fri & Sat) Try the yummy *hawaiiano*, with chicken, onion, chili and pineapple.

Deli Jasmín (lower Calle Santander; items US$3-5; ☽ breakfast & lunch Wed-Mon) This tranquil garden restaurant serves a great range of healthy foods and drinks to the strains of soft classical music. Breakfast is served all day, and you can buy whole-wheat or pita bread, hummus or mango chutney to take away.

Deli Llama de Fuego (Calle Santander; items US$3-5; ☽ 7am-6pm Thu-Tue) Has the same excellent menu as Deli Jasmin, in only slightly less peaceful surroundings.

Bohemia Bar (Av Los Árboles; mains US$3-5; ☽ lunch & dinner) The snacks and burgers are OK at this little place, but it really gets cooking with the three-hour happy hour, starting at 6pm, and occasional live-music shows.

Al Chisme (Comercial El Pueblito, Av Los Árboles; mains US$3-5; ☽ breakfast, lunch & dinner) Offers Tex-Mex, vegetarian and pasta dishes, and more-expensive meat and fish as well as down-home food such as biscuits and gravy (US$3). Its streetside patio is most popular in the evening, especially when there's live music.

Las Chinitas (Plaza Los Patios, Calle Santander; mains or set lunches US$4-6.50; ☽ lunch & dinner) Las Chinitas serves up unbelievably delicious, moderately priced food. Try the Malaysian curry with coconut milk or the satay, both with rice, tropical salad and your choice of tofu, tempeh, chicken, pork or prawns.

Guajimbo's (Calle Santander; mains US$4-6; ☽ breakfast, lunch & dinner) This Uruguayan grill is one of Pana's best eateries, serving up generous meat and chicken dishes with vegetables, salad, garlic bread and either rice or boiled potatoes. You won't leave hungry. Try the *chivita Hernandarias*, tenderloin cooked with bacon, mozzarella, peppers and olives. There are vegetarian dishes too, good-value breakfasts, and bottomless cups of coffee for US$0.70.

Atlantis (Calle Principal; mains US$4-9; ☽ breakfast, lunch & dinner) This café-bar serves up some excellent submarines (US$4) alongside more-substantial meals. The beer garden out the back is the place to be on a balmy night.

Maktub'ar (Calle Santander 3-72; mains US$5-7; ☽ breakfast, lunch & dinner) The garden setting here is an excellent, relaxed place to hang out during the day. At night, once happy hour kicks in, things start to liven up. The menu runs from sandwiches and burgers to larger meals, but the real winner is the wood-fired thin-crust pizza.

THE HIGHLANDS

THE HIGHLANDS

Sunset Café (cnr Calles Santander & del Lago; mains US$6-8; ☽ lunch & dinner) This open-air eatery has a great lake vista and serves meat, fish and vegetarian dishes. With a bar and live music nightly, it's quite the place to be to watch the sun go down behind the volcanoes.

El Bistro (Calle Santander; meals US$6-10; ☽ breakfast, lunch & dinner Tue-Sun) It doesn't look like much from the outside, but this is the place for authentic Italian food, including a range of pastas, and treats such as carpaccio and antipasto.

If you're looking for cheap with a view, check out the touristy restaurants overlooking the lake at the east end of Calle del Lago, such as El Bambú and Restaurante Taly (both with breezy upper floors), Los Pumpos, Restaurante Emilio and Brisas de Lago. Most of these places will do breakfast for US$1.50 to US$2 and quite acceptable lunch or dinner mains for US$4.

Cheap meals on Calle Santander? Several places offer bargain set meals:

Restaurante Los Cayucos (breakfast mains US$1-1.50; mains from US$1.70; ☽ breakfast, lunch & dinner) The food is standard, but the prices bring in the crowds.

Don Neto (mains US$2-3.25; ☽ lunch & dinner) The US$2 lunch or dinner gives you a choice of eight or nine meat or fish selections, with fries, salad, rice, tortilla and a soft drink.

Restaurante Mario (lunches US$4; ☽ breakfast, lunch & dinner) The lunch includes soup, a main dish with rice or steamed veggies, and coffee.

MIDRANGE & TOP END

Ristorante La Lanterna (Hotel Dos Mundos, Calle Santander 4-72; mains US$6-10; ☽ 7am-3pm & 6-10pm) This is a good, authentic Italian restaurant with both inside and garden tables; you're welcome to use the swimming pool if you eat here.

La Terraza (☎ 7762 0041; Edificio Rincón Sai, Calle Santander; mains US$6-11; ☽ lunch & dinner) One of Calle Santander's most atmospheric spots, this breezy upstairs restaurant has French, Mexican and Asian influences. It's a good idea to book on weekends.

Porta Hotel del Lago (☎ 7762 1555; cnr Calle Rancho Grande & Calle de Buenas Nuevas; breakfast/dinner buffet US$7/13; ☽ breakfast, lunch & dinner) This luxury hotel offers lavish Sunday buffets when it's fully occupied, which usually happens on weekends and holidays.

Restaurante Tocoyal (Calle del Lago; mains US$8-11; ☽ 8:30am-5pm Sun-Fri, 8:30am-8pm Sat) The Tocoyal is a cut above the other Calle del Lago eateries. Staples are meat, chicken and fish, but there are cheaper vegetarian dishes and *chiles rellenos* (chile stuffed with cheese, meat or rice).

ourpick Chez Alex (☎ 7762 2052; Hotel Primavera, Calle Santander; mains US$10-17; ☽ lunch & dinner) This is some of Pana's finest dining, with plenty of European influence. There's fondue, stuffed trout and a whole range of seafood, among other delicacies.

Hotel Atitlán (☎ 7762 1441; Finca San Buenaventura; lunch or dinner buffet US$15; ☽ breakfast, lunch & dinner) This hotel, on the northern outskirts of town, has a beautiful restaurant with some outdoor tables and magnificent lake views. If you come to eat here, you can use the swimming pool and gardens for free. The Sunday breakfast buffet is US$9. Lunch or dinner buffets are offered when occupancy is high: call ahead. Otherwise, ample set meals are always available for similar prices.

Drinking

Pana's best places to drink are generally the places that also have live music (opposite).

Pana Arte (Calle Santander) This is a good place to start, continue or finish your night, with a seemingly endless happy hour. The classic rock may not be to your liking, but two mixed drinks for under US$2 is hard to argue with.

Circus Bar (Av Los Árboles; ☽ noon-midnight) The best thing about this bar is the double swing doors, so you can go busting in like a real cowboy. Yeehaw! Closely following is the huge list of imported liquors, US$2 Bloody Marys, good pizza and live music most nights.

Solomon's Porch (Calle Principal; ☽ lunch & dinner) The balcony overlooking Calle Santander is a great place for a few drinks, accompanied by big-screen TV, wireless internet and live music.

Entertainment

Panajachel's miniature Zona Viva (party zone) focuses on Av Los Árboles. Things can be quiet from Sunday to Wednesday.

CINEMAS

Turquoise Buffalo (Comercial El Pueblito, Av los Árboles; admission US$2) This cinema shows two movies each evening. If you go earlier in the day, you can choose your own film (minimum two people).

DANCING

Chapiteau (Av Los Árboles) After the music stops at the Circus Bar or Al Chisme, simply cross the street and come here, a disco-bar with billiards upstairs.

El Aleph (Av Los Árboles) Located a couple of doors down from Chapiteau, this bar has occasional trance and hip-hop DJ sessions or live music.

Socrates (Calle Principal) Opposite the start of Av Los Árboles, Socrates is a large disco-bar playing thumping Latin pop, highly popular with the Guatemalan teens and 20-somethings who descend on Pana on weekends and holidays (as well as a smattering of gringos). The assorted folk pictured on the walls run the gamut from Albert Einstein to Jerry García of the Grateful Dead.

LIVE MUSIC

Circus Bar (Av Los Árboles; ✪ noon-midnight) With walls hung with old circus posters, smooth drinks service and food, Circus Bar has live music (normally a Latin combo of some kind) from 8pm to 11pm nightly. An interestingly mixed crowd usually assembles here.

Al Chisme (Comercial El Pueblito, Av Los Árboles) Often serves up neat jazz or piano music on Friday or Saturday nights.

Sunset Café (cnr Calles Santander & del Lago; ✪ 11am-midnight) Head here for sunset (and later) drinks overlooking the lake. It's popular, with great views, food, a bar, and live music nightly.

Shopping

Calle Santander is lined with booths, stores and complexes that sell (among other things) traditional Mayan clothing, jade, Rasta berets with built-in dreadlocks, colorful blankets, leather goods and wood carvings. Freelance vendors and artisans also set up tables or blankets, especially on weekends. Among this is **Comerciales de Artesanías Típicas Tinamit Maya** (✪ 7am-7pm), an extensive handicrafts market, with an impressive variety at dozens of stalls. You can make good buys here if you bargain and take your time. **Middle Path Herbs** (Plaza Los Patios, Calle Santander) sells medicinal herbs and health foods (and can put you in touch with an acupuncturist or masseur).

Some travelers prefer the Pana shopping scene to the well-known market at Chichicastenango because the atmosphere is low-key and you're not bumping into tour groups with video cameras at every turn. The beach end of Calle Rancho Grande is also adorned with booths.

There are also wholesalers in Pana if you want to buy in bulk. If you're interested, check www.panajachel.info for some contacts.

Getting There & Away
BOAT

Passenger boats for Santiago Atitlán depart from the Playa Pública (public beach) at the foot of Calle del Balneario. All other departures leave from the dock at the foot of Calle del Embarcadero. The big, slow ferries are generally only used for the Santiago run, with fast, frequent *lanchas* (small motorboats) going elsewhere. Boats stop running around 4:30pm.

One-way passage anywhere on Lago de Atitlán costs US$1.30, but prepare to get done like a sucker. Generally, foreigners end up paying around US$2.50. You can hold out for the local fare, but you may have to let a few boats go by. One way to keep the cost down is to ignore all middlemen (or boys, as the case may be) and negotiate the fare directly with the captain.

Another route goes counterclockwise around the lake, stopping in Santa Cruz La Laguna (15 minutes), Jaibalito, Tzununá, San Marcos La Laguna (30 minutes), San Juan La Laguna and San Pedro La Laguna (40 minutes). After departing Panajachel from the Calle del Balneario dock, the boats stop at another dock at the foot of Calle del Embarcadero before heading out (or vice versa, when arriving at Panajachel).

Lanchas are also available for private hire from the Playa Pública or Embarcadero Tzanjuyú: expect to pay around US$23 to San Pedro.

To the villages along the lake's eastern shore, there are no public boat services. A privately hired *lancha* from the Playa Pública costs around US$13 to Santa Catarina Palopó, US$23 to San Antonio Palopó and US$40 to San Lucas Tolimán. It's better to go by bus or pickup.

BUS

Panajachel's main bus stop is at the junction of Calle Santander and Calle Principal, across from the Banco Agromercantil. The taxi and shuttle bus booth nearby on Calle Principal can usually give you the general picture on bus schedules, but this is not an exact science. Transportes Rébuli, running buses to Guatemala City, has an office further down Calle Principal, but its buses still usually depart from the Principal/Santander corner. Departures – approximately and subject to change – are as follows:

THE HIGHLANDS

Antigua A direct Pullman bus (US$5, 2½ hours, 146km) departs from the Rébuli office at 10:45am Monday to Saturday. Or take a Guatemala City bus and change at Chimaltenango.

Chichicastenango About eight buses (US$1.50, 1½ hours, 37km) depart 7am to 4pm daily. Or take any bus heading to Los Encuentros and change buses there.

Ciudad Tecún Umán (Mexican border) By the Pacific route (210km), take a bus to Cocales and change there; by the highland route (210km), take a bus to Quetzaltenango and change there.

Cocales (Carr al Pacífico) Eight buses (US$1, 2½ hours, 70km) depart 6:30am to 2:30pm daily.

Guatemala City Transportes Rébuli (US$2.50, 3½ hours, 150km) departs 10 times daily from 5am to 2:30pm. Or take a bus to Los Encuentros and change there.

Huehuetenango Take a bus to Los Encuentros (3½ hours, 140km) and wait there for a bus bound for Huehue or La Mesilla. Or catch a bus heading to Quetzaltenango, alight at Cuatro Caminos and change buses there. There are buses at least hourly from these junctions.

La Mesilla (Mexican border; 6 hours; 225km; see Huehue).

Los Encuentros Take any bus heading towards Guatemala City, Chichicastenango, Quetzaltenango or the Interamericana (US$1; 35 minutes; 20km).

Quetzaltenango Six buses (US$2; 2½ hours; 90km) depart from 5am to 4pm daily. Or take a bus to Los Encuentros and change there.

San Lucas Tolimán There's one bus at 4pm (US$1.20, 1½ hours, 28km) or you can take any bus heading for Cocales, get off at the San Lucas turnoff and walk about 1km into town.

Santa Catarina Palopó Daily buses (US$0.80, 20 minutes, 4km). Or get a pickup at the corner of Calles Real and El Amate.

Sololá Frequent direct local buses (US$0.60; 20 minutes; 8km). Or take any bus heading to Guatemala City, Chichicastenango, Quetzaltenango or Los Encuentros.

MOTORCYCLE

Maco (☎ 7762 0883; Calle Santander) rents motorbikes for around US$8/40 per one/24 hours.

SHUTTLE MINIBUS & TAXI

Tourist shuttle buses take half the time of buses, for several times the price. You can book at a number of travel agencies on Calle Santander (p128). The **Oficina de Microbuses y Taxis San Francisco booth** (Calle Principal near cnr Calle Santander) also sells shuttle bus seats (or can call you a taxi). Despite impressive advertised lists of departures, real shuttle schedules depend on how many customers there are, so try to establish a firm departure time before parting with money. Typical fares: Antigua US$12; Chichicastenango US$6; Guatemala City US$22; La Mesilla US$25; Quetzaltenango US$20; and Ciudad Tecún Umán US$40.

AROUND PANAJACHEL

East of Pana, 5km and 10km respectively along a winding road, lie the lakeside villages of Santa Catarina Palopó and San Antonio Palopó – picturesque places of narrow streets paved in stone blocks and adobe houses with roofs of thatch or tin. Some villagers still go about daily life dressed in their beautiful traditional clothing. There's little in the way of sightseeing, but these are good places to buy the luminescent indigo weavings you see all around Lago de Atitlán. Also out here is a surprising little clutch of midrange and top-end places to stay.

Santa Catarina Palopó

On weekends and holidays, young textile vendors may line the path to the lakeside at Santa Catarina Palopó with their wares, and any day you can step into wooden storefronts hung thick with bright cloth.

Posada Don Vitalino (☎ 7762 2660; s/d US$7/14), a little hotel on the edge of town, offers decent-sized, clean rooms with hot showers. Get a room upstairs – downstairs they get a bit stuffy.

A further 2km along, **San Tomás Bella Vista Ecolodge** (☎ 7762 1566; s/d/tr/q incl breakfast US$45/60/75/90; P R) has vast grounds running down to the lakeshore, with walking trails and even a sandy beach. The 14 rooms, in bungalows, are bright and spacious. Main dishes at lunch and dinner cost US$5 to US$10. This is one of those places that is best on weekends and holidays: midweek, with no one around, it can seem desolate.

If your budget allows, **Villa Santa Catarina** (☎ 7762 1291; www.villasdeguatemala.com; s/d/ste US$61/68/104; P R) is a treat for a drink or a meal. The dining room serves moderately priced table d'hôte meals and the hotel has a big swimming pool and lovely gardens almost on the lakeshore. The 36 neat rooms have wood-beam ceilings, colorful weavings and lake views. Rooms 24, 25, 26 and 27 (partly) and the two suites face across the lake to Volcán San Pedro. Two children under 12 can share with two adults for free.

One kilometer past Santa Catarina, on the hillside above the road to San Antonio Palopó, **Hotel Casa Palopó** (☎ 7762 2270; www.casapalopo.com; r US$153-208; P 🖳 R) is a luxury retreat for the moneyed. It has just seven rooms, furnished in tasteful modern style with Mayan touches, super views, a pool and a classy restaurant.

The open-air **Restaurante Laguna Azul** (mains US$3.25-5), on the lakeshore below the Villa Santa Catarina, serves reasonably priced chicken, fish and meat dishes.

San Antonio Palopó

San Antonio Palopó is a larger (population 3700) but similar village. Entire families clean mountains of scallions by the lakeshore and tend their terraced fields in bursts of color provided by their traditional dress. Up the hillside, the gleaming white church forms the center of attention. **Cerámica Palopó Atitlán** (☎ 7762 2606), to the right along the street just before the lake as you descend from the church, sells attractive blue stoneware pottery.

The excellent **Hotel Terrazas del Lago** (☎ 7762 0157; s/d US$28/31), almost on the lakeshore, has 15 attractive stone-walled rooms with Frederick Crocker prints, small terraces and hot-water bathrooms, and serves good, inexpensive meals (US$5 to US$8) on a terrace looking straight across to Volcán Tolimán.

Getting There & Away

Pickups to both Santa Catarina and San Antonio leave about every half-hour from the corner of Calles Principal and El Amate in Panajachel. It takes 20 minutes to Santa Catarina (US$0.80) and 45 minutes to San Antonio (US$1.20). Frequency is less after about noon, and the last pickup back to Pana leaves San Antonio about 5pm.

San Lucas Tolimán

pop 15,950 / elev 1590m

Further around the lake from San Antonio Palopó, but reached by a different, higher-level road, San Lucas Tolimán is busier and more commercial than most lakeside villages. Set at the foot of the dramatic Volcán Tolimán, it's a coffee-growing town and a transportation point on a route between the Interamericana and the Carretera al Pacífico. Market days are Sunday and Thursday. The 16th-century **Parroquia de San Lucas** parish church has a beautiful children's folk choir, which sings at 10:30am mass most Sundays. The parish, aided by Catholic missionaries from the USA and volunteers from North America and Europe, has been active in redistributing coffee-plantation land, setting up the Juan-Ana fair-trade coffee cooperative and founding schools, a clinic and a reforestation program. For visits to the cooperative, guided volcano hikes and infor-

mation on volunteering, contact the **parish office** (☎ 7722 0112; sanlucas@pronet.net.gt).

From San Lucas, a paved road goes west around Volcán Tolimán to Santiago Atitlán.

An atmospheric choice almost on the waterfront, **Hotel Don Pedro** (☎ 7722 0028; Final de Calle Principal; s/d US$9/17; P) is made entirely of stone and rough-hewn timber beams. Rooms are spacious, and upstairs ones have lake views. There's a restaurant (meals US$5 to US$8) and bar on the premises.

Hotel Tolimán (☎ 7722 0033; www.atitlanhotel.com; Final de Calle Principal; s/d US$36/50; P   ) has 22 rooms and suites in a rustic but comfortable style, with hot-water bathroom, and a restaurant (meals US$6 to US$8), bar and a pool in lush gardens on the lakeshore.

For details on bus and boat transportation, see p141.

Parque Chuiraxamolo

Just off the road between the main highway and Santa Clara, this community-run **adventure park** (admission US$3; 8am-4pm Wed-Sun) offers incredible views of the lake from a few paths that run around the mountains. The big attraction here, though, is the canopy tour and rappelling (US$10) – there are three zip lines set up, the scariest being 400m long and 200m off the ground.

SANTIAGO ATITLÁN

elev 1590m

South across the lake from Panajachel, beside an inlet squeezed between the towering volcanoes of Tolimán and San Pedro, lies Santiago Atitlán. Though Santiago is the most touristy lakeside settlement outside Panajachel, many *atitecos* (as its people are known) cling to a traditional Tz'utujil Mayan lifestyle. Women weave and wear *huipiles* (tunics) embroidered with brilliantly colored birds and flowers, and the town's *cofradías* maintain the ceremonies and rituals of *la costumbre*, the syncretic traditions and practices of Mayan Catholicism. There's a large art and crafts scene here, too. The best days to visit are Friday and Sunday, the main market days, but in fact any day will do.

It's the most workaday of the lake villages, home to Maximón (mah-shee-*mohn*; see the boxed text, p140), who is paraded around during Semana Santa – a good excuse to head this way during Easter. The rest of the year, Maximón resides with a caretaker, receiving

---

TRADITIONAL CLOTHING

Anyone visiting the Highlands can delight in the beautiful *traje indígena* (traditional Mayan clothing). The styles, patterns and colors used by each village – originally devised by the Spanish colonists to distinguish one village from another – are unique, and each garment is the creation of its weaver, with subtle individual differences.

The basic elements of the traditional wardrobe are the *tocoyal* (head covering), *huipil* (tunic), *corte* or *refago* (skirt), *calzones* (trousers), *tzut* or *kaperraj* (cloth), *paz* (belt) or *faja* (sash) and *caïtes* or *xajáp* (sandals).

Women's head coverings are beautiful and elaborate bands of cloth up to several meters long, wound about the head and often decorated with tassels, pom poms and silver ornaments. In some places they are now only worn on ceremonial occasions and for tourist photos.

Women's *huipiles* are worn proudly every day. Though some machine-made fabrics are now being used, many *huipiles* are still made completely by hand. The white blouse is woven on a backstrap loom, then decorated with appliqué and embroidery designs and motifs common to the weaver's village. Many of the motifs are traditional symbols. No doubt all motifs originally had religious or historical significance, but today that meaning is often lost to memory.

Cortes (refagos) are pieces of cloth 7m to 10m long that are wrapped around the body. Traditionally, girls wear theirs above the knee, married women at the knee and old women below the knee, though the style can differ markedly from region to region.

Both men and women wear *fajas,* long strips of backstrap-loom-woven cloth wrapped around the midriff as belts. When they're wrapped with folds upward like a cummerbund, the folds serve as pockets.

Tzutes (for men) or *kaperraj* (for women) are the all-purpose cloths carried by local people and used as head coverings, baby slings, produce sacks, basket covers and shawls. There are also shawls for women called *perraj.*

Before the coming of the Spaniards, the leather thong sandals known as *caïtes* or *xajáp* were commonly only worn by men. Even today, many highland women and children go barefoot, while others wear more elaborate *huarache*-style sandals or modern shoes.

---

offerings. He changes house every year, but he's easy enough to find by asking around. If that's too much work, local children will take you to see him for a small tip.

In the 1980s, left-wing guerrillas had a strong presence in the Santiago area, leading to the killings or disappearance of hundreds of villagers at the hands of the Guatemalan army. Santiago became the first village in the country to succeed in expelling the army, following a notorious massacre of 13 villagers on December 1, 1990.

Orientation & Information

The street straight ahead from the dock leads up to the town center. Every tourist walks up and down this street, so it's lined with craft shops and art galleries.

You'll find a lot of fascinating information about Santiago, in English, at www.santiagoatitlan.com.

About 500m up from the dock, turn left past the Hotel Tzutuhil to reach the central plaza and, behind it, the Catholic church.

You can change cash US dollars and traveler's checks at **Banrural** (☼ 8:30am-5pm Mon-Fri, 9am-1pm Sat) on the plaza.

Dangers & Annoyances

Santiago children may greet you as you disembark at the dock, selling small souvenirs or offering to act as guides. If you hire them, agree on the price beforehand or, as one sage traveler put it, you'll 'be amazed at the bad language some charming little girls can haul out.' Santiago kids have been known to pick tourists' pockets. If a few of them start to crowd you in, watch out.

Muggings of tourists have reportedly occurred, mostly at night, on the outskirts of Santiago, such as the trail between the dock and the Hotel Bambú or the road out to the Posada de Santiago. Take care.

Sights

The huge parish church, the **Iglesia Parroquial Santiago Apóstol**, was built between 1572 and 1581. A memorial plaque on your right just inside the entrance commemorates Father Stanley Francis Rother, a missionary priest from Oklahoma. Beloved by the local people, he was hated by ultrarightist 'death squads,' who murdered him in his study at the church during the troubled year of 1981. Along the walls are wooden statues of the saints, each of whom has new clothes made by local women every year. On the carved wooden pulpit, note the figures of corn (from which humans were formed, according to Mayan religion) and of the angel, quetzal bird, lion and horse (symbols of the four evangelists, with the quetzal replacing the more traditional eagle). Mayanist Allen Christenson writes that in the center of the nave is a hole called the R'muxux Ruchiliew, which traditionalist Tz'utujils believe is an entrance to the underworld. The hole is uncovered only on Good Friday, when a large cross bearing a statue of Christ is lowered into it. At the far end of the church stand three sacred colonial altarpieces that were renovated between 1976 and 1981 by brothers Diego Chávez Petzey and Nicolás Chávez Sojuel. The brothers subtly changed the central altarpiece from a traditional European vision of Heaven to a more Mayan vision representing a sacred mountain with two Santiago *cofradía* members climbing towards a sacred cave. The three altarpieces together symbolize the three volcanoes around Santiago, which are believed to protect the town and also, in a local creation myth, to have been the first dry land that rose

out of the primordial waters. You can read a version of Allen Christenson's interpretation at www.mesoweb.com.

On the subject of religion, you can't fail to notice while wandering around Santiago just how many evangelical churches are now competing with Catholicism and traditional Mayan *costumbre* for the villagers' faith.

The site of the 1990 massacre is now the **Parque de Paz** (Peace Park), about 500m beyond the Posada de Santiago.

Activities

There are several rewarding **day hikes** around Santiago. Unfortunately, owing to robberies and attacks on tourists in the Atitlán area, it's highly advisable to go with a guide and tourist police escort. Ask at your hotel for a recommended guide, or get in touch with the Posada de Santiago (see p141). Prices for hikes up any of the three **volcanoes** usually run at about US$80 per group; to the **Mirador de Tepepul**, about 4km south of Santiago, it's US$30 for two; and to **Cerro de Oro**, some 8km northeast, should be around US$30 for two. The *mirador* (lookout) trip, four to five hours roundtrip, goes through cloud forest populated with many birds, including parakeets, curassows, swifts, boat-tailed grackles and tucanets (if you're lucky you might even glimpse a quetzal), and on to a lookout point with beautiful views all the way to the coast. Cerro de Oro is a small village beneath a hill

THE HIGHLANDS

IN THE PATH OF STAN

In October 2005, Hurricane Stan slammed into the west coast of Guatemala, killing hundreds and leaving thousands homeless. Areas hardest hit were the coastal regions, San Marcos and Huehuetenango province and the area around Lake Atitlán.

Much of the devastation was caused by landslides, as mud from deforested hillsides slid down and buried villages below. This is what happened in Panabaj, a village behind Santiago Atitlán. The slide happened at night, causing many to be buried as they slept.

Exact figures vary, but everybody agrees that there were at least 250 people buried underneath the mudslide.

A frantic, week-long rescue effort began, but had to be abandoned as the land was too unstable and the work became dangerous. President Berger announced that the area, the size of six football fields, would become a burial ground, as the risk of infection from unearthed corpses was too great.

Massive protests from victims' families fell on deaf ears, and the Forensic Anthropology Foundation nongovernment organization (NGO), more experienced at excavating civil war mass graves, moved in to help recover the bodies.

Government relief and reconstruction efforts have been characteristically slow, and more than a year after the tragedy, displaced families were still living in makeshift refuges. To learn more about relief efforts, log on to www.puebloapueblo.org.

of the same name (1892m), about halfway between Santiago and San Lucas Tolimán. The climb up the hill yields great views, and there's a pretty church in town. You could travel at least one way by one of the pickups running between Santiago and San Lucas Tolimán.

Another destination from Santiago is **Chuitinamit**, a small hill across the inlet from Santiago with the ruins of the prehispanic Tz'utujil capital and the site of the Santiago area's first church and Franciscan monastery, founded about 1540. Walking to San Pedro La Laguna is not recommended, unless the security situation improves, since this remote route has a robbery risk.

Jim and Nancy Matison (☎ 7811 5516; wildwest@ amigo.net.gt) offer well-recommended **horse rides** to the Mirador de Tepepul and elsewhere, for US$45 to US$60. Most rides include a meal. They do guided hikes, too.

Dolores Ratzan Pablo is an accomplished guide specializing in **Mayan ceremonies**. This charming, funny Tz'utujil woman can introduce you to the wonders of Mayan birthing and healing ceremonies or take you to weaving demonstrations and art galleries. Dolores speaks English, Spanish, Kaqchiquel and, of course, Tz'utujil. Tours typically last between one and three hours, for US$18 an hour. Contact Dolores through the Posada de Santiago (see opposite).

Sleeping & Eating

Hotel Tzanjuyu (☎ 5590 3980; s/d US$4/6, with bathroom US$6/8) Decent, plain rooms with a choice of volcano or lake views. It is prohibited, as signs point out, to spit on the walls here.

THE HIGHLANDS

THAT'S ONE SMOKIN' GOD

The Spanish called him San Simón, the ladinos (persons of mixed indigenous and European race) named him Maximón and the Maya know him as Rilaj Maam (ree-lah-*mahm*). By any name, he's a deity revered throughout the Guatemalan Highlands. Assumed to be a combination of Mayan gods, Pedro de Alvarado (the Spanish conquistador of Guatemala) and the biblical Judas, San Simón is an effigy to which Guatemalans of every stripe go to make offerings and ask for blessings. The effigy is usually housed by a member of a *cofradía* (Mayan Catholic brotherhood), moving from one place to another from year to year, a custom anthropologists believe was established to maintain the local balance of power. The name, shape and ceremonies associated with this deity vary from town to town, but a visit will be memorable no matter where you encounter him. For a small fee, photography is usually permitted, and offerings of cigarettes, liquor or candles are always appreciated.

In Santiago Atitlán, Maximón is a wooden figure draped in colorful silk scarves and smoking a fat cigar. Locals guard and worship him, singing and managing the offerings made to him (including your US$0.25 entry fee). His favorite gifts are Payaso cigarettes and Venado rum, but he often has to settle for the cheaper firewater Quetzalteca Especial. Fruits and gaudy, flashing electric lights decorate his chamber; effigies of Jesus Christ and Christian saints lie or stand either side of Maximón and his guardians. Fires may be burning in the courtyard outside as offerings are made to him.

In Nahualá, between Los Encuentros and Quetzaltenango, the Maximón effigy is à la Picasso: a simple wooden box with a cigarette protruding from it. Still, the same offerings are made and the same sort of blessings asked for. In Zunil, near Quetzaltenango, the deity is called San Simón but is similar to Santiago's Maximón in custom and form.

San Jorge La Laguna on Lake Atitlán is a very spiritual place for the highland Maya; here they worship Rilaj Maam. It is possible that the first effigy was made near here, carved from the *palo de pito* tree that spoke to the ancient shamans and told them to preserve their culture, language and traditions by carving Rilaj Maam (*palo de pito* flowers can be smoked to induce hallucinations). The effigy in San Jorge looks like a joker, with an absurdly long tongue.

In San Andrés Itzapa near Antigua, Rilaj Maam has a permanent home, and is brought out on October 28 and paraded about in an unparalleled pagan festival. This is an all-night, hedonistic party where dancers grab the staff of Rilaj Maam to harness his power and receive magical visions. San Andrés is less than 10km south of Chimaltenango, so you can easily make the party from Antigua.

Hotel Lago de Atitlán (☎ 7721 7174; s/d US$4/7, with bathroom US$10/12) Go four blocks uphill from the dock, then turn left to this hotel, whose reception is in the *ferretería* (hardware store) next door. It's a modern five-story building, rather an anomaly in this little town. Rooms are bland but mostly bright, many having large windows with decent views. Go up to the rooftop for great sunsets.

Hotel & Restaurant Bambú (☎ 7721 7332; www .ecobambu.com; s/d US$38/52; P) The Bambú is a fine hotel set in wild-yet-manicured grounds. It's run by amiable Spaniard José de Castro, a veteran Latin American traveler. It's 600m from the dock: walk to the left (north) along a path through lakeside vegetable gardens – the hotel's large grass-roofed restaurant building is visible from the dock. The 10 spacious rooms are in grass- or bamboo-roofed buildings, with cypress wood fittings, colorful paint and earthy tile floors. All have a bathroom. The excellent restaurant has big picture windows with sweeping views out over the lake towards the San Pedro Volcano. The incredibly tasty, reasonably priced dishes include an international array of very-well-prepared pasta, meat, seafood and vegetarian main dishes for US$6 to US$11. For those with vehicles, the hotel has an entrance from the Cerro de Oro road on the edge of Santiago.

Posada de Santiago (☎ 7721 7366; www.posadade santiago.com; s/d from US$50/65; P) This is another of the most charming hotels around Lago de Atitlán. Seven cottages and two suites, all with stone walls, fireplaces, porches, hammocks and folk art, are set around beautiful gardens stretching up from the lake. There are also a few budget rooms for US$14 per person, sharing hot-water bathrooms, and two suites for US$85 and US$95. The restaurant has well-prepared Asian, Continental and American food, and a very cozy ambience. The Posada can set you up with hikes and biking trips. It's 1.5km from the dock. Walk up the street ahead all the way to its end, turn left, go to the end of the street, and turn right onto a paved road, which almost immediately becomes dirt. Alternatively, you can arrange for the Posada to pick you up by *lancha* at the Santiago dock (US$3 to US$4) or at Panajachel (US$20).

El Pescador (set lunches US$4.50; ☺ breakfast, lunch & dinner) Two blocks up the street straight ahead from the dock, this is a good, clean restaurant with big windows, white-shirted waiters and neatly laid tables. A typical *menú del día* (set

lunch) might bring you chicken, rice, salad, guacamole, tortillas and a drink.

Shopping

The street leading up from the dock to the town center is lined with shops selling leather belts and hats, carved wooden animals, colorful textiles, masks and paintings.

Getting There & Away

Subject to change (of course!), boats leave Santiago for San Pedro La Laguna (US$1.30, 45 minutes) at 7am, 9am, 10am, 11am, noon, 1pm, 2pm, 3:30pm and 5pm. Pickups to Cerro de Oro and San Lucas Tolimán start outside the Hotel Chi-Nim-Yá. Buses to Guatemala City (US$3.50, three hours) leave about hourly, 4am to 2pm, from the main plaza. For transportation from Panajachel, see p135.

SAN PEDRO LA LAGUNA

pop 10,000 / elev 1610m

It all comes down to what you're looking for – price wars between competing businesses keep San Pedro among the cheapest of the lakeside villages, and the beautiful setting attracts long-term visitors whose interests include (in no particular order) drinking, fire twirling, African drumming, Spanish classes, volcano hiking and hammock swinging.

Right alongside this whirling circus, San Pedro has a very conservative side – there's plenty of traditional dress and subsistence agriculture going on. You'll see coffee being picked and spread out to dry on wide platforms at the beginning of the dry season.

Orientation & Information

San Pedro has two docks, about 1km apart. The one on the southeast side of town serves boats going to and from Santiago Atitlán. The other, around on the northwest side of town, serves boats going to and from Panajachel. From each dock, streets run ahead to meet outside the market in the town center, a few hundred meters uphill. Most of the interest for travelers is in the lower part of town, between the two docks and either side of them. Various minor streets, tracks and paths enable you to walk around this lower area without going up to the town center. To work your way across this lower area from the Panajachel dock, turn left immediately before the Hotel Mansión del Lago, then right opposite Casa Elena, then left at the

THE HIGHLANDS

TZ'UTUJIL OIL PAINTING

Although many of the paintings on display in Santiago's tourist galleries – landscapes, portraits, scenes of local life – use lurid acrylic colors and look very similar to each other, some works by finer Santiago artists such as Martín Reanda Quieju, Nicolás Reanda Quieju, Pedro Miguel Reanda, Miguel Chávez and Martín Ratzan Reanda exude a special energy and talent. Good Tz'utujil painting has a distinctive primitivist style, depicting rural life in vibrant colors. Centered on San Pedro La Laguna and Santiago Atitlán, the style is distinctly Mayan and has been the theme of shows the world over.

Legend has it that Tz'utujil art began one day when Rafael González y González from San Pedro La Laguna noticed some dye that had dripped and mixed with the sap of a tree; he made a paintbrush from his hair and began creating the type of canvases still popular today. His relatives Pedro Rafael González Chavajay, Lorenzo González Chavajay and Mariano González Chavajay are leading exponents of the Tz'utujil style.

The grandfather of Santiago painting was Juan Sisay; success at an international art exhibition in 1969 sparked an explosion of painters working in his style. Juan Sisay was assassinated in 1989, but his sons Manuel, Diego and Juan Francisco carry his banner, chiefly working in photographic-style portraits.

For more on Mayan oil painting, visit the website **Arte Maya Tz'utuhil** (www.artemaya.com).

---

top of that street. From the Santiago dock, turn right immediately before the Hotel Villasol. No one much uses street names or numbers in San Pedro, even though they do officially exist. We give them where it has been possible to discover them.

There is no tourist information office in San Pedro, but the staff at the Alegre Pub near the Pana dock are well informed, and have a folder full of answers to most FAQs.

You can change cash US dollars and traveler's checks at **Banrural** (8:30am-5pm Mon-Fri, 9am-1pm Sat), in the town center, which has a Visa ATM. There's internet access at D'Noz, Casa Verde Internet and the Internet Cafe, all just up the street from the Panajachel dock; the typical rate is around US$0.80 an hour. You can call North America/Europe for US$0.65/0.90 at D'Noz, or anywhere in the world for US$0.65 a minute at Hotel Mansión del Lago, 100m further up the street.

Sights

Two very good museums focusing on local Mayan culture operate in San Pedro. They're both on the path in between the docks.

Museo Maya Tzutujil (admission US$1.50; 9am-1pm, 3-6pm Mon-Sat) is the more humble of the two, but it does have some good displays on the various *trajes* (traditional costumes) used by people around the lake, some great old photographs and a good lending library/bookstore. Once a month or so, a Mayan priest comes to perform ceremonies here, and the

public is welcome to attend – ask for when the next one is.

Museo Tz'unun Ya' (www.descubresanpedro.com; admission US$4; 8am-noon, 2-6pm Tue-Sun) is an excellent, modern museum focusing on culture, folklore and the fascinating geology of the region. Displays are semi-interactive and a free guided tour (in Spanish only at the time of writing) is included in the admission price.

Activities
ASCENDING VOLCÁN SAN PEDRO

Looming above the village, Volcán San Pedro almost asks to be climbed by anyone with a bit of energy and adventurous spirit. The volcano has recently been placed within an **Ecological Park** to minimize environmental damage caused by hikers and also to improve the security situation, which wasn't great before. Guides can take you up here from San Pedro for US$13, including entrance fee.

Excursion Big Foot (7a Av, Zona 2), 50m to the left at the first crossroads up from San Pedro's Panajachel dock, has a track record of responsibility in this respect and goes at 6am when there are at least four people (US$10 each). The ascent is through fields of maize, beans and squash, followed by primary cloud forest. You'll be back in San Pedro about 1pm. Take water, snacks, a hat and sunblock.

OTHER ACTIVITIES

Another popular hike goes up the hill to the west of the village that is generally referred to as **Indian Nose** (its skyline resembles the profile of an ancient Maya dignitary). **Excursion Big Foot** (7a Av, Zona 2) will guide a minimum of four people up there for US$10 each; it also offers horse rides (US$2.50 per hour) and rents bikes (US$1.50/7 per hour/day).

Walking from San Pedro to other lakeside villages is potentially risky. In recent years there have been robberies, at least one armed attack and at least one rape at various places between San Pedro and Jaibalito, and robberies between San Pedro and Santiago. Hopefully this will change, but meanwhile we don't recommend these walks except with a responsible guide who can give convincing safety assurances. It takes about four hours from San Pedro to Santiago, 1½ hours to San Pablo, three hours to San Marcos and six hours to Santa Cruz.

Kayaks are available for hire, turning right from the Pana dock. Prices start at US$1.50 per hour.

After all that activity, you'll probably be in need of a good soak, and one of the best places to do so is in the solar-heated tubs at **Thermal Waters** (9am-9pm; US$3 per person), down a small path next to the Buddha Bar. Book ahead so they have a pool nice and hot for you when you arrive.

Courses

Turning right from the Pana dock and following the 'Yoga and Massage' signs brings you to **La Mysticoteca** (5871 0506; www.freewebs.com/la mysticoteca). This health and wellness center offers courses in Shiatsu massage, reiki and meditation. You can also practice yoga (US$3.50) here or come for reiki (US$10), sound healing (US$17) or massages (from US$15).

On the path between the docks, **Cielo Maya** (5928 6189; 2-5:30pm) is a Tz'utujil women's collective that sells fair-trade woven goods and offers weaving and beading classes from US$2 per hour (materials not included).

LANGUAGE COURSES

San Pedro is making quite a name for itself in the language game, with ultra-economical rates at its Spanish schools, whose numbers are now approaching double figures. Check out a couple of schools before deciding. Some of them are distinctly rustic, rather amateurish affairs; others are professional enterprises with good reputations. Optional extras can range from volcano hikes and dance classes to Mayan culture seminars and volunteer work

opportunities. The standard price for four hours of one-on-one classes, five days a week, is US$50 to US$55. Accommodation with a local family, with three meals daily (except Sunday) usually costs US$40. Schools can also organize other accommodation options.

Run as a cooperative (therefore guaranteeing fair wages for teachers), **Cooperativa Spanish School** (5398 6448; www.cooperativeschoolsanpedro .com) comes highly recommended. A percentage of profits goes to needy families around the lake. After-school activities include videos, conferences, salsa classes, volunteer work, kayaking and hiking. The office is halfway along the path between the two docks.

Down a laneway coming off the street between the two docks, the well-organized **Escuela Mayab** (5556 4785) holds classes under shelters in artistically designed gardens. Activities include videos, kayaking and horse rides, although tuition is cheaper without these things. It is associated with a medical clinic in Nahuala and can organize volunteer work for doctors, nurses and assistants.

Run by respected brothers and teachers Samuel and Vicente Cumes, **Casa Rosario** (5613 6401; www.casarosario.com) holds classes in gardens near the lake. The office is along the first street to the left as you walk up from Santiago dock. Volunteer projects include reforestation, teachers' assistants and environmental awareness campaigns.

Turn first left as you go up from Santiago dock to reach the well established **Corazón Maya** (7721 8160; www.corazonmaya.com). Activities include cooking classes, visits to local artists, and conferences about current political, social and cultural issues in Latin America.

San Pedro Spanish School (7715 4604; www.sanpedro spanishschool.org), a well-organized school on a street between the two docks, consistently gets good reviews. Classes are held under shelters in artistically designed gardens. The school supports Niños del Lago, an organization that sponsors Tz'utujil children to provide them with education, health care and nutrition.

Sleeping

Although San Pedro has a lot of places to stay, you may still find that your first choices are full. In many places in San Pedro it's possible to negotiate deals for longer stays and during low season. For longer stays, it's also possible to rent a room or an entire house in town. Ask around.

THE HIGHLANDS

NEAR THE PANA DOCK

Hotel Xocomil (☎ 5598 4546; xocomil333@yahoo.com; s/d US$2/4) Up the lane to the right just after the Gran Sueño, this place is definitely in the basic backpacker category, with quiet rooms around a cement courtyard.

Hotel Mansión del Lago (☎ 7721 8124; 3a via & 4a Av, Zona 2; s/d US$4/8) Straight up from the Pana dock, you'll see this concrete monster. Rooms are good and big, with wide balconies and lake views. A room at the top costs another US$2.

Gran Sueño (☎ 7221 8110; 8a Calle 4-40 Zona 2; s/d US$5/10) On the street going left from the Mansión del Lago is the Gran Sueño. Rooms here are OK sized, spotless with tiled floors, cable TV and good hot showers. Get one upstairs for glimpses of the lake.

Hotel Nahual Maya (☎ 7721 8158; 6 Av 8 C-12; s/d US$5/10) This modern construction isn't the loveliest piece of architecture you're likely to see in Guatemala, but the rooms are big and homey and have little balconies with hammocks out front.

BETWEEN THE DOCKS

Hostel Jarachik (☎ 5571 8720; 4a Calle 2-95 Zone 2; s/d US$8/10) This happening little hostel is a newcomer in town, and rightly popular. Rooms are clean and bright. Get one on the top floor for light and ventilation.

Hotelito El Amanecer Sak'cari (☎ 8712 1113, 7721 8096; www.hotelsakcari.com; 7a Av 2-12, Zona 2; s/d with bathroom US$8/12; P) On the left just after San Pedro Spanish School, the Sak'cari has clean, tangerine-colored rooms. They vary greatly in size and comfort, so have a look around. Right down the back, rooms have big balcony areas out front with lake views and hammocks.

Hotel Mikaso (☎ 5173 3129; www.mikasohotel.com; 4a Callejon A 1-88; dm/rm with bathroom US$8/30) Fans of Antigua's colonial hotel scene will find some comforting memories here in this built-new-to-look-old construction. Really the only 'fine' hotel in San Pedro, its rooms are big and well furnished and the rooftop bar and Spanish restaurant (mains US$6 to US$8) have lovely lake views. Dorm rooms are spacious and spotless and a good deal for large groups.

NEAR THE SANTIAGO DOCK

Hotel Villa Sol (☎ 7721 8009; cnr 7a Av & Calle Principal; s/d US$3/4, with bathroom US$5/8; P) The 45 rooms here, just 200m up from the Santiago dock, are bare but clean; those with a bathroom look onto a grassy courtyard.

Hotel Peneleu (☎ 5925 0583; 5a Av 2-20, Zona 2; s/d with bathroom US$3/6) It doesn't look like much from the outside, but once you get past the dirt yard, you'll find a clean, modern hotel with some of the best budget rooms in town. Try to get No 1 or 2, which are up top with big windows overlooking the lake. To find it, go 80m up Calle Principal from Hotel Villasol, then along the street to the left.

Hotel Villa Cuba (☎ 5409 1633; www.hotelvillacuba .com; Camino a la finca, Zona 4; s/d US$6/12) A large, modern hotel on grounds that sweep down to the lake, set out in cornfields in a quiet stretch on the road to Santiago. The swimming is good here, but it's definitely a walk to the bar and restaurant scene. To find it, take the first road to the left up from the dock and follow it for 2km.

Eating

There are plenty of places to get your grub on around the Pana dock. Prices are incredibly low lakeside in San Pedro, but if you're still hurting, there are a bunch of *comedores* (cheap eateries) up the hill in the main part of town.

Alegre Pub (8a Calle 4-10; mains US$3-6; ☺ breakfast, lunch & dinner) Near the Pana dock, the Alegre is always, well, *alegre* (happy), with a real British pub feel – drinks specials, a Sunday roast and trivia nights. There are free movies twice a week in the way-laid-back rooftop garden, and loads of free, reliable tourist info. The big breakfast fry-up will make Brits weep with homesickness.

Bistro Nuevo Sol (mains US$3-6; ☺ breakfast, lunch & dinner) This little place serves up some tasty US$3 breakfasts and other gourmet delights such as California pizza (US$6), calzones, focaccias and a mouthwatering spicy tomato soup.

Shanti Shanti (8a Calle 3-93; mains US$4-6; ☺ breakfast, lunch & dinner) By far the best set-up as far as lakeside chilling goes. Falafel, sandwiches and curry are just some of the tempters on the menu here.

Fata Morgana (8a Calle 4-12; mains US$4-6; ☺ breakfast, lunch & dinner, closed Wed) Really good coffee has finally made it to San Pedro thanks to this little Italian restaurant-café-bakery. Also on offer are some good basic pastas and excellent homemade breads and pastries.

Chile's (4a Av 8-12; mains US$4-7; ☺ breakfast, lunch & dinner) Chile's deck overlooking the Pana dock and lake will always be a popular option. The party starts later here, too, with

---

BUYING LOCAL

At the time of research, an anonymous poster campaign was under way in San Pedro. The gist of it was that foreigners (who constitute a large part of the business community in San Pedro) were taking away income from the locals. The advice for travelers was to only patronize restaurants and businesses that were locally owned.

It's a good argument, on the surface, and certainly an effective one in more-glamorous locations, where large multinational corporations move in and squeeze out local competition, then send the profits out of the country.

The reality is a bit more humble in San Pedro, though – the great majority of foreigners who own businesses do so because they live here. They employ locals, shop locally and often have family connections with the local community. In short, the money stays in San Pedro.

Foreign-owned businesses are often more successful because they know what travelers want, not because they have the money to squeeze out the competition. To take one example: if a local can make the best pizza in town, that's where travelers are going to eat, regardless of whose name is on the lease.

---

free salsa classes and dance music through the week.

D'Noz (4a Av 8-16; mains US$4-7; ☺ breakfast, lunch & dinner) This is upstairs above Nick's and is another popular hangout – it's about as close as San Pedro gets to a cultural center, with a global menu, free movies, a big bar, board games and a lending library.

Restaurants on the path between the two docks:

Buddha Bar (2a Av 2-24; mains US$6-8; ☺ lunch & dinner, closed Tue) An excellent place to hang out – downstairs there's a pool table, upstairs a restaurant doing convincing versions of Thai, Indian and other Asian dishes.

Mikaso (4a Callejon A 1-88; mains US$6-8; ☺ breakfast, lunch & dinner) With a real live Spanish chef, this is the place to come for Iberian delights. If you want the paella (US$8 per person) you'll have to give 24 hours' notice.

Drinking & Entertainment

El Barrio (7a Av 2-07, Zona 2; ☺ 5pm-1am) This cozy little bar on the path between the two docks has one of the most happening happy hours in town, food till midnight and drinks till one. There's a good cocktail and snacks list and a couple of chilled-out outside areas.

Alegre Lounge (8a Calle 4-10) This place has a range of ridiculous drinks specials, such as US$0.30 Cuba Libres, all through the week.

Freedom Bar (8a Calle 3-95, Zona 2; ☺ till 1am) The hardest-partying bar in town, the Freedom has good lounging areas, a pool table, a (relatively) huge dance floor and often hosts guest DJs on weekends. It's on the first street to your left coming up from the Pana dock.

At the Panajachel dock, D'Noz and the Alegre Lounge show movies most nights.

Shopping

About 100m uphill from Hotel Mansión del Lago is Caza Sueños, a leather shop owned by brothers Fernando and Pedro González. They handcraft custom leather goods, including vests, boots and bags. For a very reasonable US$35 they will craft a pair of shoes to your specifications of size, color, fringe, trim and lace style; allow a few days. Galería de Arte, on the road leading uphill from the Santiago dock, is operated by the family of celebrated primitivist artist Pedro Rafael González Chavajay. Some of his paintings and those of many of his family and students are exhibited and sold here.

Getting There & Away

Passenger boats arrive here from Panajachel (see p135) and Santiago Atitlán (see p141). Boats from San Pedro to Santiago (US$1.30, 45 minutes) leave hourly from 6am to 2pm. The last *lancha* from San Pedro to San Marcos, Jaibalito, Santa Cruz and Panajachel usually leaves around 5pm.

San Pedro is connected by paved roads to Santiago Atitlán and to the Interamericana at Km 148 (about 20km west of Los Encuentros). A paved branch off the San Pedro–Interamericana road runs along the northwest side of the lake from Santa Clara to San Marcos. Veloz San Pedro buses leave for Quetzaltenango (US$3, 2½ hours) from San Pedro's Catholic parish church, up in the town center, at 4:45am, 6am and 7am.

THE HIGHLANDS

SAN JUAN LA LAGUNA

pop 4900

Two kilometers east of San Pedro, this is a mellow little lakeside village that has escaped much of the excesses of its neighbors. There are a couple of good swimming beaches here and a trail leads to Las Cristalinas mountains – you should take an experienced guide, both for navigation and security (see Dangers & Annoyances, p123, for more details).

Two weaving cooperatives operate in town, the Asociación de Mujeres de Color on the right from the dock having the greater variety.

San Juan is famous for its *petates* – woven mats made from reeds that grow by the lakeshore. No doubt you will see them in hotel rooms and restaurants around the lake.

Accommodations here are limited compared to other lakeside villages. **Uxlabil Eco Hotel** (☎ 2366 9555; www.uxlabil.com/atitlan-ing.htm; s/d US$45/62) is the best option in town, with hand-carved stone trimmings done by local craftsmen. The hotel is set on 2 acres of coffee plantation and has a good swimming dock. It can arrange a variety of hikes and ecotours in the area. **Hospedaje Estrella del Lago** (☎ 7759 9126; s/d US$) provides simple rooms with shared bathrooms.

To get to San Juan, you can ask any boat coming from Pana to drop you off at the dock. Otherwise it's a 15-minute (US$0.30) pickup or bus ride from San Pedro.

SAN MARCOS LA LAGUNA

pop 3000 / elev 1640m

Without doubt the prettiest of the lakeside villages, the flat shoreline in San Marcos La Laguna has paths snaking though banana, coffee and avocado trees. The town has become something of a magnet for hippies with a purpose, who believe the place has a particular spiritual energy, and is an excellent place to learn or practice meditation, holistic therapies, massage, reiki and other spiritually oriented activities.

Whatever you're into, it's definitely a great place to kick back and distance the everyday world for a spell. Lago de Atitlán is beautiful and clean here, with several little docks you can swim from.

Boats usually put in at a central dock just below Posada Schumann. The path leading up to the village center from here, and a parallel one about 100m west, are San Marcos' main axes for most visitors.

The nongovernment organization (NGO) **La Cambalacha** (☎ 5590 2649; www.lacambalacha.org), which provides space, technical training and teachers for projects that get local kids involved in theater and the arts, is based here. It's always looking for volunteers.

Sights & Activities

The village's greatest claim to fame is the meditation center **Las Pirámides** (☎ 5205 7151; www.laspiramidesdelka.com). You can enter from the path that passes Posada Schumann, or walk a short distance to the left (west) from the dock below Posada Schumann. A one-month personal development course begins every full moon, with three sessions daily, Monday to Saturday: one of Hatha yoga, one of meditation, and one of introduction to the spiritual life (first week), Shaluha-Ka therapy (second week), metaphysics and astral travel (third week) and retreat (fourth week). The final week requires fasting and silence by participants, so is not recommended for novice spiritualists. If you can stay for a month to do the whole course, come in time for the full moon. Most sessions are held in English, though occasionally they'll be translated from Spanish. There's also a three-month solar course running from each equinox to the following solstice, with a whole month's silence at the end.

Other experiences available here include yoga, aura work, massage (US$20) and tarot readings. Monday through Saturday, nonguests can come for the meditation (5pm to 6pm) or Hatha yoga (7am to 8:30am) sessions for US$4.

Most structures on the property are pyramidal in shape and oriented to the four cardinal points, including the two temples where sessions are held. Accommodations are available in little pyramid-shaped houses for US$15/13/11 per day by the day/week/month and are only available to people interested in taking courses. Included in this price are the course, use of the sauna, and access to a fascinating library with books in several languages. There's also a great vegetarian restaurant here, and room to wander about in the medicinal herb garden.

Next door to Hotel El Unicornio, **San Marcos Holistic Centre** (www.sanmholisticcentre.com; 🕐 10am-5pm Mon-Sat), run by Briton Louise Rothwell

THE HIGHLANDS

with various resident and visiting practitioners, provides a whole range of massages, holistic therapies and training courses in fields such as Bach flower remedies, reiki, shiatsu, massage and reflexology. The approach is relaxed and you're welcome to discuss possibilities before committing to anything. English, Spanish, French and German are spoken. Most massages and therapies cost around US$13 an hour.

Guy (☎ 5854 5365) at Restaurant Sol y Tul (see right) offers paragliding rides (US$60) in the mornings from Santa Clara down to San Juan. It's an exhilarating ride offering some great photo opportunities.

The walks along the lake west to Santa Clara La Laguna and east to Jaibalito and Santa Cruz La Laguna are breathtaking, but attacks and robberies have made it essential to take local advice before setting out. The section between San Marcos and Jaibalito is particularly notorious and you may be advised only to try it in a large group, or not at all.

Sleeping

Hotel El Unicornio (s/d US$5/9) A favorite with the budget-conscious, El Unicornio has eight rooms in small, thatch-roofed A-frame bungalows among verdant gardens, sharing hot showers, nice hangout areas, a sauna and an equipped kitchen. Mexican owner Chus is a musician and enjoys playing with guests and making fun recordings in his little domed studio. To get here, turn left past Hotel La Paz, or walk along the lakeside path and turn right after Las Pirámides.

Hotel La Paz (☎ 5702 9168; r per person US$6) Along a side path off the track behind Posada Schumann, the mellow La Paz has rambling grounds holding two doubles and five dormitory-style rooms. All are in bungalows of traditional *bajareque* (a stone, bamboo and mud construction) with thatch roofs, and some have loft beds. Antiques, art works, the organic gardens and vegetarian restaurant, the traditional Mayan sauna and the music and book room above the restaurant all contribute to making this place a little bit special. You can join Hatha yoga sessions (US$2) in a special pavilion at 8am, or take a massage.

Hotel Paco Real (☎ 5891 1025; agutknecht54@hotmail .com; s/d US$8/13) Along the same side path as Hotel La Paz, the Paco Real has simple but tasteful rooms in thatched cottages, with shared bathrooms. Also here is a good

restaurant with some Mexican choices (mains US$4 to US$5).

Posada Schumann (☎ 5202 2216; hotel schumann@ hotmail.com; s US$11-17, d US$22-33) Set in gardens that stretch right down to the lakeside, popular Posada Schumann has neat rooms in stone or wooden cottages, some with kitchen, most with bathroom and some with an upper floor and extra bed. There's also a restaurant (meals US$6 to US$10) and sauna.

Aaculaax (☎ 5803 7243; www.aaculaax.com; s/d from US$12/15) An ecological fantasy come true, the new, German-owned Aaculaax is a five- to 10-minute walk to the left (west) along the lakeside path from the Posada Schumann dock. It's built around the living rock of the hillside, also using lots of recycled glass and plastic (plastic bottles stuffed hard with empty plastic bags form the core of many walls). Each of the seven double rooms is unique, with terrace, lake views, hot-water bathroom and compost toilets, and four have kitchens. A bar and restaurant should be open by the time you get there.

Posada del Bosque Encantado (☎ 5208 5334; gringamaya@yahoo.com; s/d US$13/21) Set in jungly grounds that could well be an enchanted forest, these rooms strike a good balance between rustic and stylish. Each room has a loft with a double bed and another bed downstairs. Walls are mud-brick, beds are big and firm and there are hammocks strewn around the place.

Eating

A couple of *comedores* around the plaza sell tasty, good-value Guatemalan standards.

Il Giardino (mains US$2.75-5.25; ⏱ lunch & dinner Tue-Sun) This excellent vegetarian restaurant, owned by a Costa Rican–Italian couple, is set in a tranquil, spacious garden reached just before Hotel Paco Real. Main dishes include pizzas, spaghetti and fondues. The burritos with salsa and melted mozzarella are a treat.

Il Forno (mains US$6-10; ⏱ lunch & dinner) Serves up delicious pizzas cooked in a wood-fired oven. To get there, follow the signs from the main path to the dock.

Sol y Tul (mains US$6-10; ⏱ breakfast, lunch & dinner) Out on the balcony at this French-influenced restaurant are some of the best lake views in town. Meals are huge and the service is friendly. To get there, turn left from the main dock and follow the path for 20m.

Getting There & Away

The last dependable boat back to Jaibalito, Santa Cruz and Panajachel usually goes about 5pm. For information on boats from Panajachel, see p135.

A paved road runs east from San Marcos to Tzununá and west to San Pablo and Santa Clara, where it meets the road running from the Interamericana to San Pedro. You can travel between San Marcos and San Pedro by pickup, with a transfer at San Pablo.

JAIBALITO

pop 400

This small village, only accessible by boat or on foot, has two marvelous places to stay. Unfortunately, the picturesque hike to San Marcos (6km) was not recommended at the time of writing, except perhaps for large groups, because of attacks on walkers in the Tzununá area. The equally picturesque 45-minute (4km) path to Santa Cruz is, however, currently safe.

Sleeping & Eating

Vulcano Lodge (☎ 5410 2237; d US$25-57) Towards the back of the village, Norwegian-owned-and-built Vulcano Lodge doesn't enjoy La Casa del Mundo's views, but its handful of trim and spotless Scandinavian-cum-Guatemalan rooms are just as appealing and its gardens just as lovely. There's also a fine restaurant with mainly European food (US$9 for the all-you-can-eat four-course dinner). The owners, Terje and Monica, are well versed in local walking routes.

La Casa del Mundo Hotel & Café (☎ 5218 5332; www.lacasadelmundo.com; r US$27, with bathroom US$55; ⊠) Perched on a secluded cliff facing the three volcanoes, this is one of Guatemala's most spectacular hotels. Designed and built by husband-and-wife team Bill and Rosie Fogarty, it has beautiful gardens, good lake swimming and even a wood-fired hot tub overhanging the lake (US$36 for up to 10 people). Every room has privacy and views and is impeccably outfitted with comfortable beds, Guatemalan fabrics and fresh flowers. The best rooms seem to be floating above the water, with no land visible beneath. All rooms are nonsmoking. The excellent restaurant is open to the public; dinner (US$9) is four courses of seriously tasty food. You can rent kayaks (US$3.50 to US$7 an hour) for exploring the lake. Room reservations (by phone only) are advisable.

Getting There & Away

Jaibalito is a 20-minute *lancha* ride from Panajachel or San Pedro. As well as the public dock roughly in the center of the village, La Casa del Mundo has a pier.

SANTA CRUZ LA LAGUNA

pop 5680 / elev 1665m

For all practical purposes four hotels spread along the lakeside, this is the earthiest of the lake options, and also the home of the lake's scuba diving outfit, ATI Divers. The main part of the village is uphill from the dock.

Amigos de Santa Cruz (www.amigosdesantacruz.org) is an excellent, grass-roots program focusing on Santa Cruz's families in need. It's always looking for mid- to long-term volunteers for projects including fuel-efficient stoves, nutritional programs, technology training, school sponsorships and medical care.

Activities

ATI Divers (☎ 7762 2621; www.laiguanaperdida.com) offers a four-day PADI open-water diving certification course (US$205), as well as a PADI high-altitude course and fun dives. It's based at La Iguana Perdida hotel.

Good walks from Santa Cruz include the beautiful lakeside walking track between Santa Cruz and San Marcos, 10km (about four hours) one way. You can stop for a beer and a meal at La Casa del Mundo en route (see Jaibalito, left). Or you can walk up the hill to Sololá, a 9km (3½-hour) walk one way.

Sleeping & Eating

Three welcoming lakeside places provide beds and meals.

La Iguana Perdida (☎ 5706 4117; www.laiguana perdida.com; dm US$3, s/d US$8/10) Some might say they're going a bit overboard on the whole rustic thing, but this is still a good place to hang out, enjoy the lake views and meet other travelers. There's no electricity and the showers in the bathrooms (all shared) are lovely and cold! Meals are served family-style, with everyone eating together; a three-course dinner is US$5.50. You always have a vegetarian choice, and everything here is on the honor system: your tab is totaled up when you leave. Don't miss the Saturday night cross-dressing, fire and music barbecues!

Arca de Noé (☎ 5515 3712; arcasantacruz@yahoo .com; s/d US$8/12, with bathroom US$22/24) Spread out along the lakeside, the rooms and bungalows here are spacious, with good views. The concrete bed bases are a bit of a letdown. Solar energy provides some hot water and electric light. It has a welcoming, sociable atmosphere and great food: the large candlelit set dinner, always with a vegetarian option, is US$8.50. For breakfast try the filling, tasty Western omelet (US$3).

Casa Rosa Hotel (☎ 5803 2531; www.la-casa-rosa .com; r/bungalows US$30/37) With gardens running down to the lake, but a little removed from the action of the other hotels, Casa Rosa is the most formal of the lakeside establishments. Rooms are spacious and cool, shaded by banana trees and decorated in a restrained, tasteful fashion. There are large picture windows overlooking the lake, and wide balconies for catching an afternoon breeze.

Getting There & Away

For information about boats travelling to Santa Cruz, see Panajachel (p135) and San Pedro La Laguna (p145).

QUICHÉ

A largely forgotten little pocket of the country, most visitors here are on a quick in-and-out for the famous market at Chichicastenango. Further north is Santa Cruz del Quiché, the departmental capital; on its outskirts lie the ruins of K'umarcaaj (or Gumarcaah), also called Utatlán, the last capital city of the Quiché Maya.

More adventurous souls come for the excellent hiking around Nebaj, a small mountain town which suffered terribly during the civil war, and the breathtaking backdoor route to Cobán.

The road into Quiché leaves the Interamericana at Los Encuentros, winding northward through pine forests and cornfields. Women sit in front of their little roadside houses weaving gorgeous pieces of cloth on backstrap looms. From Los Encuentros, it takes about half an hour to travel the 17km to Chichicastenango.

CHICHICASTENANGO

pop 49,000 / elev 2030m

Surrounded by valleys, with mountains serrating the horizons, Chichicastenango can seem isolated in time and space from the rest of Guatemala. When its narrow cobbled streets and red-tiled roofs are enveloped in mist, as they often are, it can seem magical. The crowds of crafts vendors and tour groups who flock in for the huge Thursday and Sunday markets give the place a much worldlier, commercial atmosphere, but Chichi remains beautiful and interesting, with lots of shamanistic and ceremonial overtones. *Masheños* (citizens of Chichicastenango) are famous for their adherence to pre-Christian religious beliefs and ceremonies. If you have a choice of days, come for the Sunday market rather than the Thursday one, as the *cofradías* (Mayan religious brotherhoods) often hold processions in and around the church of Santo Tomás on Sunday.

Chichi has two religious and governmental establishments. On the one hand, the Catholic Church and the Republic of Guatemala appoint priests and town officials; on the other, the indigenous people elect their own religious and civil officers to manage local matters, with a separate council and mayor, and a court that decides cases involving only local indigenous people.

Once called Chaviar, Chichi was an important Kaqchiquel trading town long before the Spanish conquest. In the 15th century the Kaqchiquel and the K'iche' (based at K'umarcaaj near present-day Santa Cruz del Quiché, 20km north) went to war. The Kaqchiquel abandoned Chaviar and moved their headquarters to the more defensible Iximché. When the Spanish conquered K'umarcaaj in 1524, many of its residents fled to Chaviar, which they renamed Chugüilá (Above the Nettles) and Tziguan Tinamit (Surrounded by Canyons). These are the names still used by the K'iche' Maya, although everyone else calls the place Chichicastenango, a name given by the Spaniards' Mexican allies.

Information

Chichi's many banks all stay open on Sunday, taking their day off (if any) on some other day of the week. Most banks change cash US dollars and traveler's checks.

ACSES (6a Calle; per hr US$0.80) Internet access; east of 5a Av.

Banco Industrial (⏰ 10am-2pm Mon, 10am-5pm Wed & Fri, 9am-5pm Thu & Sun, 10am-3pm Sat) Almost next door to Banrural; changes cash US dollars and traveler's checks.

THE HIGHLANDS

Banrural (6a Calle; ☯ 9am-5pm Sun-Fri, 9am-1pm Sat) Changes cash US dollars and traveler's checks; has a MasterCard ATM. East of 5a Av.

Hotel Santo Tomás (p153) Has a good selection of books for sale in its lobby.

Internet Digital (5a Av 5-60; per hr US$0.80) Internet access.

Post office (7a Av 8-47) On the road into town, 3½ blocks south of Hotel Santo Tomás.

Visa ATM (cnr 5a Av & 6a Calle) On the street.

Dangers & Annoyances

The cemetery on the western edge of town is an unwise place to wander, even in groups. Tourists have been robbed at gunpoint there.

Crowded markets are the favorite haunts of pickpockets, so be alert while you wander in the labyrinth of stalls here.

When you arrive in Chichi, you may be approached by touts offering guide services and assistance in finding a hotel. Showing up at a hotel with a tout in tow means you'll be quoted a higher price for a room, as the hotel has to give them a kickback – and this on top of your tip! In fact, you don't need their 'help,' because there's no difficulty finding lodgings. In addition, touts won't take you to some of the best-value hotels because the owners refuse to provide kickbacks.

Sights

Make sure you check out the fascinating mural that runs alongside the wall of the town hall on the east side of the plaza. It's dedicated to the victims of the civil war and tells the story of the war using symbology from the *Popol Vuh*.

MARKET

In the past villagers would walk for many hours carrying their wares to participate in Chichi market, one of Guatemala's largest indigenous markets. Some still do, and when they reach Chichi on the night before the market, they lay down their loads in one of the arcades or spaces around the plaza, cook some supper, spread out a blanket and go to sleep.

At dawn on Thursday and Sunday they spread out their vegetables, fruits, chunks of chalk (ground to a powder, mixed with water and used to soften dried maize), balls of wax, handmade harnesses and other merchandise and wait for customers. The plaza is now the territory of more full-time traders, with stalls covered in unsightly black plastic sheeting, but many more traders fill the streets for several blocks around the plaza on Sunday and Thursday. Tourist-oriented handicraft stalls selling masks, textiles, pottery and so on now occupy much of the plaza and the streets to the north. Things villagers need – food, soap, clothing, sewing notions, toys – cluster at the north end of the square, in the *centro comercial* off the north side, and in streets to the south.

The market starts winding down around 3pm. Prices are best just before it breaks up, as tired traders would rather sell than carry goods away with them. By this time you'll also notice quite a few drunks staggering around or lying comatose in the street.

IGLESIA DE SANTO TOMÁS

This church on the east side of the plaza dates from about 1540 and is often the scene of

---

THE MAYAN 'BIBLE'

One of the most important Mayan texts, the *Popol Vuh*, was written down after the Spanish conquest in K'iche' Maya, using Latin script. The K'iche' scribes showed their book to Francisco Ximénez, a Dominican who lived and worked in Chichicastenango from 1701 to 1703. Friar Ximénez copied the K'iche's book word for word, then translated it into Spanish. Both his copy and the Spanish translation survive, but the Mayan original has been lost. The *Popol Vuh* deals with the dawn of life and the glories of gods and kings. You'll find copies on sale throughout Guatemala. The definitive English translation is by Dennis Tedlock. Its tale is somewhat cyclical and not always consistent, but its gist is as follows: the great god K'ucumatz created humankind first from earth (mud), but these earthlings were weak and dissolved in water. The god tried again, using wood. The wood people had no hearts or minds and could not praise their creator. These too were destroyed, all except the monkeys of the forest, who are the descendants of the wood people. The creator tried once again, this time successfully, using material recommended by four animals – the grey fox, the coyote, the parrot and the crow. The substance was white and yellow corn, ground into meal to form the flesh and stirred into water to make the blood. Thus do Guatemalans think of themselves with pride as *hombres de maíz*, men of corn.

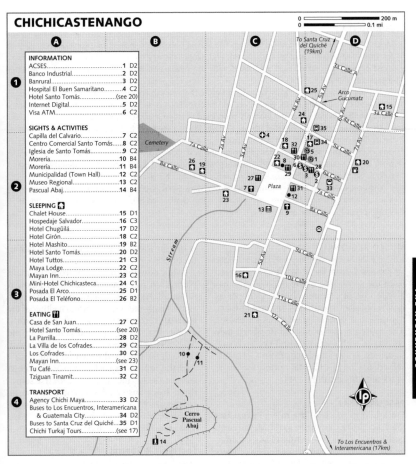

CHICHICASTENANGO

To Santa Cruz del Quiché (19km)

Arco Gucumatz

Cemetery

7a Calle

8a Calle

Stream

Plaza

5a AV

10a Calle

11a Calle

7a Calle

Cerro Pascual Abaj

To Los Encuentros & Interamericana (17km)

THE HIGHLANDS

rituals that are only slightly Catholic and more distinctly Mayan. The front steps of the church serve much the same purpose as did the great flights of stairs leading up to Mayan pyramids. For much of the day (especially on Sunday), they smolder with incense of copal resin, while indigenous prayer leaders called *chuchkajaues* (mother-fathers) swing censers (usually tin cans poked with holes) and chant magic words marking the days of the ancient Mayan calendar and in honor of their ancestors.

It's customary for the front steps and door of the church to be used only by important church officials and by the *chuchkajaues*, so you should go around to the right and enter by the side door.

Inside, the floor of the church may be spread with pine boughs and dotted with offerings of maize kernels, flowers, bottles of liquor wrapped in corn husks, and candles. Many local families can trace their lineage back centuries, some even to the ancient kings of the K'iche'. The candles and offerings on the floor are in remembrance of those ancestors, many of whom are buried beneath the church floor just as Maya kings were buried beneath pyramids. Please note that photography is not permitted in this church.

On the west side of the plaza is another whitewashed church, the **Capilla del Calvario**, which is similar in form and function to Santo Tomás, but smaller.

THE HIGHLANDS

MIXING IT UP

Much is made of the blend of Catholicism and Mayan beliefs. And indeed, one survival technique for the Maya was to 'accept' Catholicism, and simply rename their objects of worship. This is most obvious in that Mary is associated with the moon and the stars whereas God or Jesus represents the sun.

But the Maya were using the cross long before the Spanish arrived – for them the four points represent the sun, the Earth, the moon and people. Four is an especially holy number for the Maya, as they believe that the world is supported at its four corners by gods.

One Mayan creation story that obviously owes little to the bible is that of Old Jesus and Young Jesus. The story goes that one day the two Jesuses found a tree with wax at the top. The young one climbed the tree, and started dropping the wax down to the old one, who made an army from it. But young Jesus dropped too much wax, angering the old one, who ordered his army to bite off the tree trunk, causing Young Jesus to fall to his death.

Old Jesus went to tell his mother, the Virgin Mary, what happened and she banished him to a mountaintop, where he found an umbilical cord, climbed to Heaven and became the sun, at which point his mother became the moon.

MUSEO REGIONAL

Chichi's **Museo Regional** (5a Av 4-47; admission US$0.80; 8am-noon & 2-4pm Tue-Sat, 8am-2pm Sun), entered from the south side of the main square, has a collection of ceremonial masks, copper ax heads, obsidian spearheads, incense burners, figurines and *metates* (grindstones for maize). The museum also holds the Rossbach jade collection, with some beautiful necklaces and figurines. Hugo Rossbach, from Germany, served as Chichi's Catholic priest for many years until his death in 1944.

PASCUAL ABAJ

On a hilltop south of the town, **Pascual Abaj** (Sacrifice Stone) is a shrine to the Mayan earth god Huyup Tak'ah (Mountain Plain). Said to be hundreds – perhaps thousands – of years old, the stone-faced idol has suffered numerous indignities at the hands of outsiders, but local people still revere it. *Chuchkajaues* come regularly to offer incense, food, cigarettes, flowers, liquor, Coca-Cola, and perhaps even to sacrifice a chicken, in thanks and hope for the Earth's continuing fertility.

Sacrifices do not take place at regular hours. If you're in luck, you may witness one. The worshippers will not mind if you watch, but be sure to request permission before taking any photos and don't assume it will be granted. You may be asked if you want to make an offering (of a few quetzals) yourself. If there is no ceremony, you can still see the idol and enjoy the walk up the pine-clad hill. Tourists walking to visit Pascual Abaj have on occasions been robbed, so the best plan

is to join with others and go not too late in the afternoon.

Walk downhill on 5a Av from the main plaza, turn right into 9a Calle and follow it downhill. At the bottom of the hill, bear left along a path and head up through either of the **morerías** (ceremonial mask workshops, worth a visit) that are signposted here. From the back of either *morería,* follow the path uphill through the trees to the top of the hill. You'll find the idol in its rocky, smoke-blackened shrine in a clearing, looking a little like something from Easter Island. The squat stone crosses nearby have many significances for the Maya, only one of which pertains to Christ. The area is littered with past offerings.

Festivals & Events

Holidays and special events here can offer a more intriguing experience than the usual dancing, drinking and fireworks typical of Guatemalan fiestas. December 7 sees the **Quema del Diablo** (Burning of the Devil), when residents burn their garbage in the streets and usher a statue of the Virgin Mary to the steps of the Iglesia de Santo Tomás. There's lots of incense and candles, a marimba band and an ingenious and daring fireworks display that has observers running for cover. The following day is the **Feast of the Immaculate Conception**; don't miss the early-morning dance of the giant, drunken cartoon characters in the plaza.

The **fiesta of Santo Tomás** starts on December 13 and culminates on December 21 when pairs of brave (some would say mad) men fly about at high speeds suspended from a tall, vertical pole in the *palo volador* (fliers' pole) extravaganza. Traditional dances and parades also feature.

Sleeping

Chichi does not have a lot of accommodations, and it's a good idea to call or arrive fairly early on Wednesday or Saturday if you want to secure a room the night before the Thursday or Sunday market.

BUDGET

Posada El Teléfono (☎ 7756 1197; 8a Calle A 1-64; s/d US$4/8) Not exactly luxury, but the rooms here are comfortable enough and good value for the price. The view of the town's technicolor cemetery from the rooftop is a draw in itself. There's a kitchen that guests can use.

Hospedaje Salvador (☎ 7756 1329; 5a Av 10-09; s/d US$5/7, with bathroom US$8/10) Huge and crumbling, the Salvador still scrapes together a bit of character, but it's mostly just budget digs for market days. Rooms get better as you go higher: Nos 49 to 52 on the top floor are light and airy, with good views. Try negotiating for reduced prices. The entrance is an unmarked blue door on 10a Calle.

Mini-Hotel Chichicasteca (☎ 7756 2111; 5a Calle 4-42; s/d US$5/9) This hotel's adequately clean rooms with bare brick walls are a decent budget choice. It's conveniently located for both the bus stop and plaza.

Hotel Mashito (☎ 7756 1343; 8a Calle 1-72; s/d US$5.50/11, with bathroom US$7/14) Another cheapie-but-goodie, also on the road to the cemetery, offering plain but comfortable rooms in a big family house.

Hotel Tuttos (☎ 7756 1540; 12a Calle 6-29; s/d with bathroom US$10/12) Up on a hill away from the chaos of the market area, the Tuttos has good-sized, fairly clean rooms. The terrace and rooms out back have great views over the valley behind town.

Hotel Girón (☎ 7756 1156; 6a Calle 4-52; s/d with bathroom US$11/15; P) There's plenty of varnished pine going on here, but the paint job's cheery, rooms are big and spotless and the proximity to the market can't be beat for the price. There are broad, sunny walkways in front of the rooms for catching a few rays. There are a couple of cheaper rooms with shared bathroom.

Chalet House (☎ 7756 1360; www.chalethotelguatemala.com; 3a Calle C No 7-44; s/d with bathroom US$15/22) The cozy Chalet House has good beds, homey touches and private hot-water bathrooms.

Rooms get better the further upstairs you go, so ask to see a few. Rates rise in July, August and September.

MIDRANGE

Posada El Arco (☎ 7756 1255; 4a Calle 4-36; s/d US$20/26) This winner guesthouse, near the Arco Gucumatz, is the best accommodation for the price in Chichi. All seven rooms are spacious and spotless, with attractive decor, fireplace and hot-water bathroom. Rooms 6 and 7 have private balconies with great views. You can sit in lawn chairs in the garden and enjoy a great northward view of the mountains of Quiché. The friendly owners, Emilsa and Pedro Macario, speak English and Spanish. Reservations are a good idea.

Hotel Chugüilá (☎ 7756 1134; chuguila@intelnet.net.gt; 5a Av 5-24; s/d US$26/30; P) All 36 colonial-style rooms have a bathroom, and some have a fireplace, but check a few before settling in, as some are huge, with separate sitting areas. They're set around a large, pretty courtyard providing ample parking – overall, it's decent value.

Maya Lodge (☎ 7756 1167; 6a Calle A 4-08; s/d US$26/30; P) Located right on the main plaza, this hotel has a slightly colonial atmosphere. The 10 rooms have wooden ceilings, three with a fireplace and all with a hot-water bathroom, are set along a pretty pillared patio and adorned with woven rugs and Mayan-style bedspreads. You're really paying for the location on this one.

TOP END

Hotel Santo Tomás (☎ 7756 1061; hst@itelgua.com; 7a Av 5-32; s/d US$70/80; P 🏊) Chichi's most gorgeous hotel is big on plant-filled patios, tinkling fountains and decorations that include local handicrafts and religious relics. Each of the rooms has a bathroom with tub and a fireplace. There's a swimming pool, Jacuzzi and a good bar and dining room (see p154).

Mayan Inn (☎ 7756 1176; www.mayaninn.com.gt; 8a Calle A 1-91; s/d/tr US$80/92/110) A lovely old inn on a quiet street, the Mayan Inn was founded in 1932 by Alfred S Clark of Clark Tours, and is the best hotel in town. It has grown to include several restored colonial houses, their courtyards planted with exuberant tropical flora and their walls covered with bright indigenous textiles. Not all of the 30 rooms are equally charming, so look before

THE HIGHLANDS

COFRADÍAS

Chichicastenango's religious life is centered in traditional religious brotherhoods known as *cofradías*. Membership in the *cofradía* is an honorable civic duty, and election as leader is the greatest honor. Leaders must provide banquets and pay for festivities for the *cofradía* throughout their term. Though it is very expensive, a *cofrade* (brotherhood member) happily accepts the burden, even going into debt if necessary.

Each of Chichi's 14 *cofradías* has a patron saint. Most notable is the *cofradía* of Santo Tomás, Chichi's patron saint. *Cofradías* march in procession to church every Sunday morning and during religious festivals, with the officers dressed in costumes showing their rank. Before them is carried a ceremonial staff topped by a silver crucifix or sun-badge that signifies the *cofradías'* patron saint. A drum and a flute, and perhaps a few more modern instruments such as a trumpet, may accompany the procession, as do fireworks.

During major church festivals, effigies of the saints are carried in grand processions, and richly costumed dancers wearing traditional wooden masks act out legends of the ancient Maya and of the Spanish conquest. For the rest of the year, these masks and costumes are kept in storehouses-cum-workshops called *morerías*; you'll see them, marked by signs, around the town.

---

choosing. Each has a fireplace and interesting antique furnishings. The bathrooms (many with tubs) may be old-fashioned, but they are decently maintained. A staff member is assigned to answer your questions and serve you in the dining room (see right), as well as to look after your room – there are no door locks.

Eating
BUDGET
On Sunday and Thursday, eating at the cookshops set up in the center of the market is the cheapest way to go. Don't be deterred by the fried-food stalls crowding the fringe – dive into the center for wholesome fare. On other days, look for the little *comedores* near the post office on the road into town.

Casa de San Juan (4a Av, main plaza; dishes US$3-5; breakfast, lunch & dinner) The San Juan is one of the few eateries in town with style – art on the walls and the tables themselves, jugs of lilies, wrought-iron chairs – and its food is great too, ranging from burgers and tortillas to homemade cakes and more-traditional dishes. There are balcony tables overlooking the market and live music some nights.

Tu Café (5a Av, main plaza; mains US$3.50-5; lunch & dinner) The *plato vegetariano* here is soup, rice, beans, cheese, salad and tortillas, for a reasonable US$3.50. Add *lomito* (a pork fillet) and it becomes a *plato típico* (US$4.50).

Tziguan Tinamit (5 Av 5-67; mains US$3.50-6; lunch & dinner) For a more down-to-earth dining experience, check out this local eatery, with good pastas (US$4) and hit-and-miss pizzas (US$5).

La Villa de los Cofrades (6a Calle A, main plaza; dishes US$4-6; breakfast, lunch & dinner) You can't beat this location in the arcade on the north side of the plaza. This is a fine café for breakfast, crepes or larger meals with an Italian influence and good strong coffee.

La Parrilla (6a Calle 5-37; mains US$5-6; lunch & dinner) A meat lover's dream, La Parrilla serves up every cut imaginable, chargrilled, in a quiet courtyard setting.

Los Cofrades (cnr 6a Calle & 5a Av; 2-course lunch or dinner US$6-7; breakfast, lunch & dinner) This bright upstairs restaurant (enter from 6a Calle) serves up some excellent set meals and has a decent drinks list. Go for a table out on the balcony – the atmosphere inside is very 'dining hall.'

MIDRANGE
Mayan Inn (8a Calle A 1-91; set breakfast/lunch/dinner with drinks US$7/13/13; breakfast, lunch & dinner) The three dining rooms at Chichi's classiest hotel have beamed ceilings, red-tiled floors, colonial-style tables and chairs, and decorations of colorful local cloth. Waiters wear traditional costumes evolved from the dress of Spanish colonial farmers: colorful headdress, sash, black embroidered tunic, half-length trousers and squeaky leather sandals called *caïtes*. The food may not be as stellar as the costuming, however.

Hotel Santo Tomás (7a Av 5-32; 3-course dinner US$14; breakfast, lunch & dinner) Chichi's other top-end hotel has a good dining room, but you might find it crowded with tour groups. Try to get one of the courtyard tables, where you can enjoy the sun and the marimba band that plays at market-day lunchtimes and on the evenings before.

Getting There & Away

Buses heading south to Los Encuentros, Panajachel, Quetzaltenango, Guatemala City and all other points reached from the Interamericana normally arrive and depart from the corner of 5a Calle and 5a Av, one block uphill from the Arco Gucumatz. Buses heading north to Santa Cruz del Quiché stop half a block downhill on the same street. On market days, however, buses to or from the south may stop at the corner of 7a Av and 9a Calle, to avoid the congested central streets.

Antigua (3½ hours, 108km) Take any bus heading for Guatemala City and change at Chimaltenango.

Guatemala City (US$3, three hours, 145km) Buses every 20 minutes from 4am to 5pm.

Los Encuentros (US$1.50, 30 minutes, 17km) Take any bus heading south for Guatemala City, Panajachel, Quetzaltenango and so on.

Nebaj (103km) Take a bus to Santa Cruz del Quiché and change there.

Panajachel (US$2.50, 1½ hours, 37km) About eight buses, from 5am to 2pm; or take any southbound bus and change at Los Encuentros.

Quetzaltenango (US$3, 3 hours, 94km) Seven buses, mostly in the morning; or take any southbound bus and change at Los Encuentros.

Santa Cruz del Quiché (US$1.50, 30 minutes, 19km) Buses depart every 20 minutes, 5am to 8pm.

On market days, shuttle buses arrive en masse mid-morning, bringing tourists from Panajachel, Antigua, Guatemala City and Quetzaltenango. They depart around 2pm. If you're looking to leave Chichi, you can usually catch a ride out on one of these.

Chichi Turkaj Tours (☎ 5293 5480; Hotel Chugüilá, 5a Av 5-24) and **Agency Chichi Maya** (☎ 7756 1008; 6a Calle 6-45) provide shuttles to the same places and elsewhere including Huehuetenango, the Mexican border and the ruins of K'umarcaaj near Santa Cruz del Quiché. In most cases they need four or five customers unless you're prepared to rent the whole vehicle (which costs around US$30 to Panajachel, and US$65 to Antigua or Quetzaltenango).

SANTA CRUZ DEL QUICHÉ

pop 25,600 / elev 2020m

The capital of Quiché department is 19km north of Chichicastenango. As you leave Chichi heading north along 5a Av, you pass beneath the Arco Gucumatz, an arched bridge named for Ku'ucumatz, the founder of the old K'iche' Maya capital K'umarcaaj, near Santa Cruz.

Without Chichi's big market and attendant tourism, Santa Cruz – usually called El Quiché or simply Quiché – is quieter and more typical of Guatemalan towns. Travelers who come here usually do so to visit K'umarcaaj or to change buses en route further north (for Nebaj, for example).

The main market days are Thursday and Sunday, making things slightly more interesting and way more crowded.

Orientation & Information

Everything you need is within a few short blocks of the central plaza, called the Parque Central. From the bus terminal, walk three bocks north on 1a Av (Zona 5), then two blocks to the left (west), then one to the right (north) to reach the plaza's southeast corner. The church rises on the east side of the plaza, with the market behind it.

Banrural (⏰ 8:30am-6pm Mon-Fri, 9am-1pm Sat), at the plaza's northwest corner, changes cash US dollars and traveler's checks and has a MasterCard ATM. You can access the internet at Occitel on the west side of the plaza.

Sights

MUSEO MILITAR

Should you want to know the Guatemalan army's version of the civil war in Quiché department, have a look at the **Military Museum** (admission US$0.25; ⏰ 9am-noon & 2-6pm Mon-Fri) in the northeast corner of the plaza. Displays cover uniforms and weapons, the struggle against communism, and social work now being done by the military. No comment.

K'UMARCAAJ

The ruins of the ancient K'iche' Maya capital (also called Gumarcaaj or Utatlán) are 3km west of El Quiché along an unpaved road. Take a flashlight (torch) if you have one. Head west along 11a Calle, opposite the bus station, and follow this all the way to **K'umarcaaj** (admission US$2.50; ⏰ 8am-5pm). A taxi there and back from the bus station, including waiting time, costs around US$12.

The kingdom of K'iche' was established in late postclassic times (about the 14th century) by a mixture of indigenous people and invaders from the Tabasco/Campeche border area in Mexico. Around 1400, King Ku'ucumatz founded K'umarcaaj and conquered many neighboring settlements. During the long reign of his successor Q'uik'ab (1425–75), the K'iche' kingdom extended its borders to Huehuetenango, Nebaj, Rabinal and the Pacific Slope. At the same time the Kaqchiquel, a vassal people who once fought alongside the K'iche', rebelled, establishing an independent capital at Iximché.

When Pedro de Alvarado and his Spanish conquistadors hit Guatemala in 1524, it was the K'iche', under their king Tecún Umán, who led the resistance to them. In the decisive battle fought near Quetzaltenango on February 12, 1524, Alvarado and Tecún locked in mortal combat. Alvarado prevailed. The defeated K'iche' invited Alvarado to visit K'umarcaaj, secretly planning to kill him. Smelling a rat, Alvarado enlisted the aid of his Mexican auxiliaries and the anti-K'iche' Kaqchiquel, and together they captured the K'iche' leaders, burnt them alive in K'umarcaaj's main plaza and then destroyed the city.

The ruins have a fine setting, shaded by tall trees and surrounded by ravines, which failed to defend it against the conquistadors. Archaeologists have identified 100 or so large structures here, but only limited restoration or clearing has been done. The **museum** at the entrance will help orientate you. The tallest of the structures round the central plaza, the Templo de Tohil (a sky god), is blackened by smoke and has a niche where contemporary prayer-men regularly make offerings to Mayan gods. K'umarcaaj is still very much a sacred site for the Maya.

Down the hillside to the right of the plaza is the entrance to a long tunnel known as the *cueva*. Legend has it that the K'iche' dug the tunnel as a refuge for their women and children in preparation for Pedro de Alvarado's coming, and that a K'iche' princess was later buried in a deep shaft off this tunnel. Revered as the place where the K'iche' kingdom died, the *cueva* is sacred to highland Maya and is an important location for prayers, candle burning, offerings and chicken sacrifices.

If there's anyone around the entrance, ask permission before entering. Inside, the long tunnel (perhaps 100m long) is blackened with smoke and incense and littered with candles and flower petals. Use your flashlight and watch your footing: there are several side tunnels and at least one of them,

on the right near the end, contains a deep, black shaft.

Sleeping & Eating

Hotel San Pascual (☎ 7755 1107; 7a Calle 0-43, Zona 1; s/d US$5/8, with bathroom US$11/14; P) Between the bus station and plaza, this is a clean and friendly hotel with plants in its two courtyards. More-expensive rooms have big clean bathrooms and cable TV.

Hotel Leo (☎ 7765 0776; 1 Av 9-02, Zona 5; s/d US$10/12) An excellent deal right around the corner from the bus terminal, with spacious, quiet rooms and good clean bathrooms.

Hotel Rey K'iche (☎ 7755 0827; 8a Calle 0-39, Zona 5; s/d/tr US$12/22; P) Between the bus station and plaza, the Rey K'iche has 24 good, clean, modern rooms with brick and/or whitewash walls, cable TV and hot-water bathroom. There's free drinking water and a decent restaurant open 24 hours daily.

San Miguel (2 Av & 5 Calle, Zona 1; snacks US$2-3; ☯ breakfast & lunch) A little bakery-café that injects a bit of style into Santa Cruz's eating scene. A friendly, tranquil environment and some excellent baked goods and sandwiches are on offer.

Café La Torre (2a Av, Zona 1; mains US$3-5; ☯ breakfast, lunch & dinner) If you want to escape the hectic streets for a while, this little upstairs café is a good place to do it and catch some plaza views at the same time. Snacks include burgers and sandwiches and good-value set lunches (US$3) are available.

Getting There & Away

Many buses from Guatemala City to Chichicastenango continue to El Quiché. The last bus from El Quiché headed south to Chichicastenango and Los Encuentros leaves mid-afternoon.

El Quiché is the jumping-off point for the somewhat remote reaches of northern Quiché, which extend all the way to the Mexican border. Departures from the bus station include the following:

Chichicastenango (US$1.50, 30 minutes, 19km) Take any bus heading for Guatemala City.

Guatemala City (US$4, 3½ hours, 163km) Buses every 20 minutes, 3am to 5pm.

Los Encuentros (US$2.50, one hour, 36km) Take any bus heading for Guatemala City.

Nebaj (US$3, 2½ hours, 75km) Eight buses, 8:30am to 5pm

Sacapulas (US$2, one hour, 45km) Buses every 30 minutes, 8:30am to 5pm; or take any bus bound for Nebaj or Uspantán

Uspantán (US$3.50, 3 hours, 75km) Buses at approximately 9:30am, 10:30am, 1:30pm, 3pm and 3:30pm

SACAPULAS

This small, friendly town on the Río Negro is where the El Quiché–Nebaj road meets the Huehuetenango–Cobán road and so is a place where you may need to change buses or possibly stay a night. **Banrural** (8am-5pm Mon-Fri, 8am-noon Sat) on the plaza, up the hill from the bridge, changes cash US dollars.

There's a Cruz Roja (Red Cross) post on the southern bank of the river, where you'll also find the friendly **Hospedaje Tujaal** (s/d US$8/16). The rooms here are big and bright and overlook the river. Bonuses are the super-clean private bathrooms with hot showers, flat-screen cable TV and decent *comedor* downstairs.

Getting There & Away

The 45km road from El Quiché is paved; the spectacular mountain roads to Huehue, Uspantán and Nebaj are newly paved, and (at the time of writing) some of the best roads in the country. Minibuses for Nebaj, Uspantán and Aguacatán leave from the north end of the bridge whenever full. Bus schedules from Sacapulas are imprecise.

Cobán (US$6, five hours, 100km) Transportes Mejía's Aguacatán–Cobán bus stops at the north end of Sacapulas bridge at about 7:30am on Saturday and Tuesday (only). Otherwise, catch a minibus to Uspantán and either spend the night there or catch another one onward.

El Quiché (US$1.50, one hour, 45km, 12 daily, 1:30am-5:30pm) Buses stop at the south end of the bridge at erratic hours: the greatest frequency is between about 6am and 10am.

Huehuetenango (US$2, 2½ hours, 42km, two daily, 4am & 5:30am) Buses go from the north end of the bridge: later in the day, occasional pickups and other vehicles can take you as far as Aguacatán, from where buses leave for Huehue a dozen times between 4:45am and 4pm.

Nebaj (US$1, 1½ hours, 26km, eight daily, 9:30am-6pm) Catch these at the south end of the bridge.

Uspantán (US$4, 1¾ hours, 30km, five daily, 10:30am, 11:30am, 2:30pm, 4pm and 4:30pm) Catch them at the south end of the bridge.

USPANTÁN

pop 3500

You may end up spending the night in Uspantán while traveling between Nebaj/Sacapulas/Huehuetenango and Cobán. The last scheduled minibus leaves at 4pm, but

ask around – there may be somebody going later. It's a benevolent and clean town, with wide paved avenues, though it can seem distinctly eerie if you arrive after dark during one of the frequent power outages and the place is enveloped in fog! It can get very cold here, so don't hesitate to ask for extra blankets.

Rigoberta Menchú (p38) grew up a five-hour walk through the mountains from Uspantán. She is not loved by all her former neighbors, however, so don't be shocked if you get a chilly reaction on this front.

Banrural (7a Av, Zona 4; 8:30am-5pm Mon-Fri, 9am-1pm Sat), 2½ blocks from the central plaza, will change cash US dollars.

Sleeping & Eating

Pensión Galindo (5a Calle 2-09; s/d US$3.50/7) About three blocks from the plaza, Galindo offers a reasonable deal, with a dozen tiny, clean rooms round a neat little patio open to the stars. Get a room on the avenida side of the building if you can – it's quieter there.

Hotel Doña Leonar (7951 8041; 6a Calle 4-25; s/d from US$10/12) An excellent, comfortable option is this newish place a couple of blocks from the plaza. Luxuries include firm beds, reading lamps and spotless bathrooms with blasting-hot showers.

Restaurant San José (7 Calle 4-32, Zona 2; mains US$3-6; breakfast, lunch & dinner) The finest dining in town is to be had in the semitropical (in looks, anyway) surrounds at this outdoor eatery by the Hotel Montana. Meat is the go here, and the *parrillada* (mixed grill; US$5.50) is hard to beat, but there are vegetarian options available. On weekends they show movies on the big screen.

The simple *comedor* on the plaza, opposite the Municopaz office (which is next to the church), will grill slices of meat over hot coals and serve it up with rice, avocado, tortillas and hot chocolate for US$2.30.

Getting There & Away

Five or six buses daily leave Uspantán for Quiché (US$4, three hours) via Sacapulas, the first two at about 3am and 5am, the last at 4pm. For Cobán (US$4, three to four hours), buses go at 3am and 5am. On Saturday and Tuesday (only) there's also Transportes Mejía's Aguacatán–Cobán bus, at about 9am. Get to the plaza in good time for the early buses, as they fill up fast with sleepy locals.

The rest of the time, faster, more-cramped minibuses are the go, leaving whenever full up until around 4pm. For Nebaj get a Sacapulas bus and change either at the *entronque de Nebaj* (Nebaj turnoff), about 8km before Sacapulas, or at Sacapulas itself, where you might be more likely to get a seat.

Uspantán to Cobán is one of the most gorgeous rides in Guatemala and epitomizes the chicken-bus experience, as it's a difficult ride in a crowded bus on an unpaved road. You may find yourself praying to higher powers as the bus loses its grip on muddy mountain passes in the pitch black of night, but try to be awake when the sun pushes over the tops of the mountains, burning off the fog clinging to the valley below. Sit on the right for views.

NEBAJ
pop 27,200 / elev 1900m

Hidden in a remote fold of the Cuchumatanes mountains north of Sacapulas is the Triángulo Ixil (Ixil Triangle), comprising the towns of Nebaj, Cotzal and Chajul and dozens of outlying villages and hamlets. The scenery is breathtakingly beautiful, and the local Ixil Maya people, though they suffered perhaps more than anybody in Guatemala's civil war and are still very impoverished, cling proudly to many of their old traditions. Nebaj women are celebrated for their beautiful purple, green and yellow pom-pommed hair braids, and for their *huipiles* and *rebozos* (shawls) of the same colors, with many bird and animal motifs. This is a fascinating area to explore and free (to date) of crime against tourists and of the trails of trash that disfigure so much of the Guatemalan countryside.

Living in this beautiful mountain vastness has long been both a blessing and a curse. The Spaniards found it difficult to conquer and laid waste to the inhabitants when they did. The area suffered terribly during the Guatemalan civil war, especially during the brutal reign of Efraín Ríos Montt (1982–83), when the local people became the chief victims of the army's merciless measures to dislodge guerrillas from the area. Massacres and disappearances were rife, and more than two dozen villages were destroyed. The horror touched every family, and many people fled to Guatemala City, Mexico or simply to the forests. Some were settled in *polos de desarrollo* (poles of development), supposed 'strategic hamlets' whose real purpose was to enable

the army to keep their inhabitants under close control. You may hear some appalling personal experiences from locals while you are here. For a horrifying report and analysis of massacres in and around Nebaj, see the website http://shr.aaas.org/guatemala/ciidh/dts/toc.html.

The people of the Ixil Triangle are making a heroic effort to build a new future. Development organizations and NGOs have contributed to this and you'll likely encounter some of their workers too. One project of special interest to visitors, carried out with the help of the Spanish NGO Solidaridad Internacional, has been the establishment of a network of signed walking routes and *posadas comunitarias,* simple village lodgings with meals and guides available, to make it easier for travelers to hike some of the beautiful Ixil countryside and experience village life.

Orientation & Information

Coming from the south, your first view of Nebaj, set neatly at the foot of a bowl ringed by green mountains, makes the rough bus ride worthwhile. Nebaj's central plaza, known as the Parque, has a large church on its south side. From the southeast corner of the Parque, the market (daily but busiest on Sunday) is one block east, and the Terminal de Buses (bus terminal) is one longish block south then 1½ blocks east. Calzada 15 de Septiembre, sometimes simply called the Salida a Chajul, runs northeast from the Parque to become the road to Cotzal and Chajul.

The restaurant **El Descanso** (☎ 5311 9100; www.nebaj.com; 3a Calle, Zona 1; ☘ 6am-10pm) is a focal point for travelers, development workers and locals. To reach it, walk two blocks north along 5a Av from the northwest corner of the Parque, then half a block to the left. Tetz Chemol in the El Descanso building sells 1:50,000 area maps for US$8.50.

Banrural (2a Av 46; ☘ 9am-4pm Mon-Fri, 9am-1pm Sat), one block east from the northeast corner of the Parque, then half a block north, changes cash US dollars and traveler's checks and has a Visa ATM. The **post office** (5a Av 4-37) is one block north of the Parque. **La Red** (El Descanso Bldg, 3a Calle, Zona 1) has Nebaj's fastest internet connections, for US$1 per hour (US$0.70 with its discount card).

There's a heap of fascinating and helpful information about Nebaj in Spanish at www.nebaj.org. If you can't understand Spanish, the maps and listings are still useful. The Guias Ixil website (www.nebaj.com) also has good information on hiking, volunteering and studying in the area.

Activities

Guias Ixil (☎ 5311 9100; www.nebaj.com; 3a Calle, Zona 1), in the El Descanso building, offers hikes with informative young local guides. Like all the other enterprises in this building, a portion of Guias Ixil's profits goes to a community project. Short one-day hikes, costing US$6 for one person plus US$3 for each extra person, go to **Las Cataratas** (a series of waterfalls on the Río Las Cataratas north of town), or around town with visits to the **sacred sites** of the *costumbristas* (people who still practice non-Christian Mayan rites). Las Cataratas is actually easy enough to reach on your own: walk 1.25km past the Hotel Ilebal Tenam along the Chajul road to a bridge over a small river. Immediately before the bridge, turn left (north) onto a gravel road and follow the river. Walking downriver for 45 minutes to an hour (6km one way), you'll pass several small waterfalls before reaching a larger waterfall about 25m high.

Longer day hikes with Guias Ixil, costing US$10 for one person plus US$4 for each extra person, go across the mountains to **Cocop** (one of the worst hit of all villages in the civil war, 4km east of Nebaj as the crow flies), **Acul** (founded as the first *polo de desarrollo* in 1983; 4km west) or **Ak' Txumb'al**, also called La Pista, about 5km north (also founded as a *polo de desarrollo*). Ak' Txumb'al means New Mentality in the Ixil language, a name given by its military founders; La Pista (Spanish for airstrip) refers to a civil-war landing strip where you can still see bomb craters. A three-day hike to **Xeo** and **Cotzol** (northwest of Nebaj) and back to Nebaj through Ak' Txumb'al costs US$11 per day for one person plus US$6 for each extra person. Guias Ixil also offers two- to three-day treks over the Cuchumatanes to Todos Santos Cuchumatán north of Huehuetenango (US$120 per person plus US$40 per extra person).

In Cocop, Xeo and Cotzol you can stay in **posadas comunitarias** (dm US$3; veg/meat meals US$2/3) – community-run lodges with wooden-board beds, bedding, drinking water, toilets and solar electricity. Just north of Acul, in a beautiful, tranquil valley along the road leading to the Nebaj–Salquil Grande road, **Hospedaje San Antonio** (☎ 5439 3352; r per person US$10) has neat, wood-roofed and wood-floored rooms, some with a hot-water bathroom, and does meals (US$4.50). This place makes its own cheese.

Guias Ixil sells a very useful booklet, *Trekking en la Región Ixil*, full of maps and information on the above village walks, for US$2.

Pablo's Tours (☎ 7755 8287; pablostours@hotmail .com; 3a Calle 3-20, Zona 1), next door to El Descanso, also provides guided walks of up to two days, plus horse rides. It's run by a young local guy and gets good reports. Drop in to see its program and photos.

If you prefer to hike without a guide, take a copy of *Trekking en la Región Ixil* with you and organize lodging and food on arrival in villages. There are further *posadas comunitarias* at Xexocom, Chortiz and Parramos Grande, west of Nebaj, on a possible four-day hike route.

Language Courses

Nebaj Language School (☎ 5311 9100; www.nebaj.com; El Descanso Bldg, 3a Calle, Zona 1) charges US$63 for 20 hours a week of one-to-one Spanish lessons, including some hiking and cultural activities, or US$3 per hour. Staying with a local family, with two meals a day, costs US$50 a week. You can also take cooking classes here, learning how to make regional faves like *boxboles* (corn dough wrapped in *güisquil* (squash) leaves, served with a spicy peanut sauce) for US$3.50 per hour.

Festivals & Events

Nebaj's annual **festival** runs from August 12 to 15.

Sleeping

Popi's Hostel (☎ 7756 0159; 5a Calle 6-74; dm US$3.50) An excellent choice for the truly budget conscious are the comfortable if plain rooms at this popular café-bakery. Choose your bed carefully – some sag dramatically.

Media Luna Medio Sol (☎ 5311 9100; 3a Calle 6-15; dm US$3.50) The three dorm rooms upstairs here aren't a bad deal – there's six beds per dorm, with a ping pong table and kitchen facilities to keep you busy.

Hospedaje La Esperanza (☎ 7756 0098; 6a Av 2-36, Zona 1; s/d US$4/8) This reasonably friendly place has basic wooden rooms with pink walls. There's hot water in the shared showers. Upstairs rooms provide more light and air, but some beds sag.

Hotel Ilebal Tenam (☎ 7755 8039; Calzada 15 de Septiembre; s/d US$6/8, with bathroom US$8/12; **P**) Good clean rooms out on the edge of town (which is only 500m from the Parque). The quiet location and shady patio area make it a good deal.

Hotel Ixil (☎ 7756 0036; 9 Calle & 2 Av, Zona 5; s/d US$9/12) A great little budget hotel, with clean, bright rooms set around a plant-filled courtyard. Rooms have cable TV and good hot showers.

Hotel Ixil (☎ 7756 0036; cnr 2a Av & 9a Calle, Zona 5; s/d US$9/12; P) One of the best places in town, just one block south of the bus station. The clean, bright, modern rooms have cable TV and hot-water bathrooms. They're set around a leafy courtyard that offers some good hammocking opportunities.

Hotel Turansa (☎ 7755 8219; cnr 5a Calle & 6a Av; s/d US$10/15; P) Surprisingly unfriendly for this little town, but the rooms are a decent size and come with big TVs, looking out onto a cheery courtyard. It's one block west of the Parque.

Hotel Shalom (☎ 7755 8028; cnr Calzada 15 de Septiembre & 4a Calle, Zona 1; s/d US$10/16; P) If you can ignore the low-level grunge, you'll be pretty happy with this one – big rooms with cable TV, gas-fired hot water and two double beds.

Hotel Villa Nebaj (☎ 7756 0005; Av 15 de Septiembre 2-37; s/d US$12/17, with bathroom US$25/32) Nebaj's fanciest hotel is actually a pretty good deal – slate-tiled courtyards with fountains and well-decorated, comfortable rooms in a three-story building.

Eating

Popi's Restaurant (5a Calle 6-74; mains US$2-4; ☺ breakfast, lunch & dinner) For all your baked-goods needs, head straight to Popi's. It also sells a mean selection of breads and pies to take away, and some good comfort food, such as barbecued pork ribs ($US3.50).

Comedor Dámaris (Av 15 de Septiembre; meals US$2.80; ☺ lunch & dinner) A large room with six long tables, the Dámaris has such *típico* Guatemalan adornments as plastic flowers, strings of leftover Christmas decorations and stacks of Coke crates. The set lunch might be a tasty *caldo de res* (a broth with large chunks of meat and veggies), half an avocado, tortillas and a soft drink. It's one block from the Parque.

El Descanso (3a Calle, Zona 1; mains US$3-5; ☺ breakfast, lunch & dinner) Probably the most comfortable café in the entire highlands, this two-story place has a bar and lounge areas, good music and board games and serves

everything from salads to sandwiches to *churrascos*. It was started as a Peace Corps project as a sustainable way for local youth to earn money, and shares its building with Trekking Ixil and the Nebaj Language School. A portion of the profits from all these businesses goes to fund a lending library in town for children and young adults.

Pizza del César (2a Av; medium/small pizzas US$6/7, slices US$0.70-1.40; ☺ lunch & dinner) The pizza is average, but it's pizza. From the northeast corner of the Parque, go one block east then half a block north.

Shopping

You can buy local textiles at stalls on and around the Parque, or at Tetz Chemol in the El Descanso building. A *huipil* costs anywhere from US$30 to US$170, depending on quality. A *rebozo* is US$15 to US$20, and a *cinta* (the pom-pommed braid woven into Ixil women's hair) around US$20. For more variety, check out the surprisingly hassle-free **artisan's market** (cnr 7a Calle & 2a Av, Zona 1).

Getting There & Away

About eight daily buses run to/from Santa Cruz del Quiché (US$3, two hours), via Sacapulas (US$1, 1¼ hours). The best time to get one is between 5am and 8am, and the last departure may be no later than noon. After that, minibuses pick up the slack, leaving whenever full and charging roughly the same. There's an 11pm bus all the way to Guatemala City via Chichicastenango. To head west to Huehuetenango or east to Cobán, change at Sacapulas (p157). If you want to make it to Cobán in one day from Nebaj, you should definitely leave before midday.

WESTERN HIGHLANDS

The departments of Quetzaltenango, Totonicapán and Huehuetenango are more mountainous and generally less frequented by tourists than regions closer to Guatemala City. The scenery here is incredibly beautiful, and the indigenous culture vibrant, colorful and fascinating. Highlights of a visit to this area include Quetzaltenango, Guatemala's second-largest city, with an ever-growing language-school and volunteer-work scene;

the pretty nearby town of Zunil, with its Fuentes Georginas hot springs; ascents of the volcanoes around Quetzaltenango; and the remote mountain village of Todos Santos Cuchumatán, north of Huehuetenango, with a strong traditional culture and excellent walking possibilities.

CUATRO CAMINOS

Westward from Los Encuentros, the Interamericana twists and turns ever higher into the mountains, bringing still more dramatic scenery and cooler temperatures. It reaches its highest point, 3670m, after the village of Nahualá, some 42km from Los Encuentros. After a further 17km, you come to another dusty and important highway junction, Cuatro Caminos (Four Ways). You'll know the place by the many parked buses and people milling about as they change buses. The road to the southwest leads to Quetzaltenango (13km). To the east is Totonicapán (12km). Northward, the Interamericana continues to Huehuetenango (77km) and La Mesilla on the Mexican border (160km).

QUETZALTENANGO

pop 140,400 / elev 2335m

Quetzaltenango, which the locals kindly shorten to Xela (*shell*-ah), itself an abbreviation of the original Quiché Maya name, Xelajú, may well be the perfect Guatemalan town – not too big, not too small, enough foreigners to support a good range of hotels and restaurants, but not so many that it loses its national flavor. The Guatemalan 'layering' effect is at work in the city center here – once the Spanish moved out, the Germans moved in and their architecture gives the zone a somber, some would say Gothic, feel.

Xela attracts a more serious type of traveler – people who really want to learn Spanish, and then stay around and get involved in the myriad volunteer projects on offer.

It also functions as a base for a range of spectacular hikes through the surrounding countryside – the constantly active Santiaguito and highest-point-in-Central-America Tajumulco volcanoes and the picturesque, fascinating three-day trek to Lake Atitlán to name a few.

Xela is big, but by Guatemalan standards, it is an orderly, clean and safe city. It helps that the bus terminal is far removed from the center.

History

Quetzaltenango came under the sway of the K'iche' Maya of K'umarcaaj when they began their great expansion in the 14th century. Before that it had been a Mam Maya town. It was near here that the K'iche' leader Tecún Umán was defeated and killed by the Spanish conquistador Pedro de Alvarado in 1524 (p155).

The town prospered in the late-19th-century coffee boom, with brokers opening warehouses and *finca* (plantation) owners coming to town to buy supplies. The boom was shattered by a combined earthquake and eruption of Santa María in 1902, which brought mass destruction. Still, the city's position at the intersection of roads to the Pacific Slope, Mexico and Guatemala City guaranteed it some degree of prosperity. Today it's again busy with commerce, of the indigenous, foreign and ladino varieties.

Orientation

The heart of Xela is the Parque Centroamérica, shaded by old trees, graced with neoclassical monuments and surrounded by the city's important buildings. Most accommodations are within a few blocks of the park.

The main bus station is Terminal Minerva, on 7a Calle, Zona 3, on the western outskirts and next to one of the main markets. First-class bus lines have their own terminals (p173).

Information
BOOKSTORES

El Libro Abierto (Map p164; 15a Av A 1-56, Zona 1) Great selection of books in English and Spanish on Guatemala and the Maya, plus Lonely Planet guides, fiction, dictionaries, language textbooks and maps; will buy used books.

North & South (Map p163; 8 Calle & 15 Av, Zona 1) A wide range of books focusing on Latin America, politics, poetry and history. Also plenty of new and used guidebooks and Spanish student resources.

Vrisa Bookstore (Map p164; 15a Av 3-64, Zona 1) Excellent range of secondhand books in English and European languages. One of the best notice boards in town.

EMERGENCY

Bomberos (Firefighters; ☎ 7761 2002)
Cruz Roja (Red Cross; ☎ 7761 2746)
Policía Municipal (☎ 7761 5805)
Policía Nacional (☎ 7765 4991/2)

INTERNET ACCESS

Internet access here is some of the cheapest in Guatemala, at around US$0.25 to US$0.80 per hour. Some of the places its available:

Café Digital (Map p163; Diagonal 9 19-77, Zona 1)
Celas Maya (Map p164; 6a Calle 14-55, Zona 1)
Infinito Internet (Map p163; 7a Calle 15-16, Zona 1)
Xela Pages (Map p163; 4 Calle 19-48, Zona 1)

INTERNET RESOURCES

Xela Pages (www.xelapages.com) Packed with information about Xela and nearby attractions. Also a useful discussion forum.

LAUNDRY

It costs around US$0.50 to wash and dry 1kg loads at a laundry. You may have to pay a bit more for detergent.
Lavandería El Centro (Map p164; 15a Av 3-51, Zona 1; 8:30am-6pm Mon-Fri, 8:30am-5pm Sat)
Lavandería Mini-Max (Map p164; 14a Av C47)
Rapi-Servicio Laundromat (Map p164; 7a Calle 13-25A, Zona 1; 8am-6pm Mon-Sat)

MEDIA

English-language publications are available free in bars, restaurants and cafés around town.
EntreMundos (www.entremundos.org) Newspaper published every two months by the Xela-based organization of the same name. It has plenty of information on political and current events and volunteer projects in the region.
XelaWho (www.xelawho.com) Billing itself as 'Quetzaltenango's leading Culture & Nightlife Magazine' (where's the competition?), this little magazine has details of cultural events in the city, plus some fairly irreverent takes on life in Guatemala in general.

MEDICAL SERVICES

Hospital Privado Quetzaltenango (Map p163; ☎ 7761 4381; Calle Rodolfo Robles 23-51)
Hospital San Rafael (Map p163; ☎ 7761 4414; 9a Calle 10-41, Zona 1) This hospital has a 24-hour emergency service.

MONEY

Parque Centroamérica is the place to go for banks. **Banco de Occidente** (Map p164; 8:30am-7pm Mon-Fri, 8:30am-1:30pm Sat), in the beautiful building on the northern side of the plaza, changes US dollars and traveler's checks and gives advances on Visa. **Banco Industrial** (Map p164; 9:30am-5pm Mon-Fri, 9:30am-1:30pm Sat), on the east side of the plaza, changes cash US dollars and traveler's checks, and has a Visa ATM. A MasterCard ATM and another Visa ATM are next to Banrural on the west side of the plaza.

POST

Main post office (Map p164; 4a Calle 15-07, Zona 1) Central location.

TELEPHONE

Café Digital (Map p163; Diagonal 9 19-77, Zona 1) Calls to USA or Canada/Europe cost US$0.10/0.15 per minute.
Infinito Internet (Map p164; 7a Calle 15-16, Zona 1) Calls to USA or Canada/Europe cost US$0.10/0.15 per minute.
Telgua (Map p164; cnr 15a Av A & 4a Calle) Plenty of card phones outside this office.
Xela Pages (Map p163; 4 Calle 19-48, Zona 1) Calls to US or Canada/Europe cost US$0.15/0.20 per minute.

LOCAL VOICES: EDUARDO TATZAN, TREKKING GUIDE

The countryside around Xela is teeming with volcanoes, mountains and other trekking possibilities. We talked to local guide Eduardo Tatzan about what's so good about getting high.

When did you start climbing volcanoes?
About 10 years ago. Since then I've climbed Santa Maria about 300 times and Tajumulco 91 times. When I get to 101 on Tajumulco I'm going to retire.

Have you got a favorite trek?
They're all different and I like them all for different reasons. The views and the wildlife change. For walking, I like the trek from Xela to Lake Atitlán. You go through beautiful countryside and stay with local families or camp by the river.

What attracts you to the mountains?
It's getting into nature. Here in town, things can get crazy with the people and the traffic and the noise, but you get up onto the mountain and it's pure peace, pure nature.

What do the mountains mean for the Maya?
For the Maya, the mountains and volcanoes are very spiritual places. Going up high, you get closer to God. Each volcano has its *nahual* (spirit) and so Maya go up to pray for better lives, better harvests, those kinds of things. Some come from Chichi or Quiché to pray on Tajumulco, like the Catholics when they go on pilgrimage. They also pray to Juan Noj, the mountain spirit. They say he lives in a cave on Cerro Quemado, just out of Xela.

THE HIGHLANDS

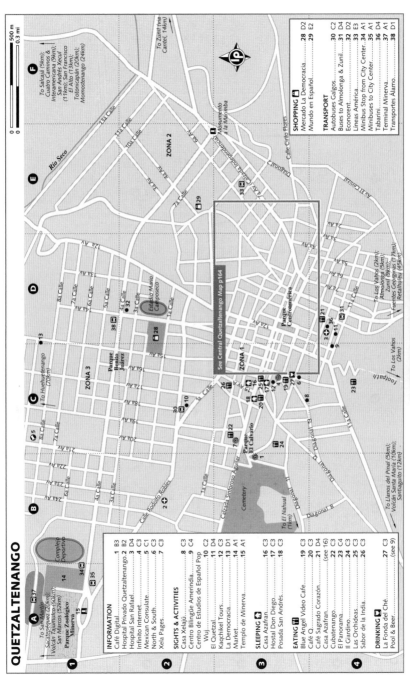

QUETZALTENANGO

INFORMATION	
Café Digital................................1	B3
Hospital Privado Quetzaltenango 2	B2
Hospital San Rafael...................3	D4
Infinito Internet.........................4	C3
Mexican Consulate.....................5	C1
North & South............................6	C3
Xela Pages................................7	C3

SIGHTS & ACTIVITIES	
Casa Xelajú...............................8	C3
Centro Bilingüe Amerindia...........9	C4
Centro de Estudios de Español Pop	
Wuj.......................................10	C2
El Quetzal...............................11	D4
Kaqchikel Tours.......................12	C3
La Democracia.........................13	D1
Market...................................14	A1
Templo de Minerva...................15	A1

SLEEPING	
Casa Azafran............................16	C3
Hostal Don Diego.....................17	C3
Posada San Andrés...................18	C3

EATING	
Blue Angel Video Cafe..............19	C3
Café Q...................................20	C3
Café Sagrado Corazón...............21	D4
Casa Azafran.....................(see 16)	
Cubatenango............................22	C3
El Panorama.............................23	C4
Il Giardino...............................24	C3
Las Orchideas..........................25	C3
Sabor de la India.....................26	C3

DRINKING	
La Fonda del Ché.....................27	C3
Pool & Beer.......................(see 9)	

SHOPPING	
Mercado La Democracia............28	D2
Mundo en Español....................29	E2

TRANSPORT	
Autobuses Galgos.....................30	C2
Buses to Almolonga & Zunil......31	D4
Econorent...............................32	D2
Lineas América........................33	E3
Minibus Stop from City Center...34	A1
Minibuses to City Center...........35	A1
Tabarini.................................36	D4
Terminal Minerva.....................37	A1
Transportes Álamo...................38	D1

CENTRAL QUETZALTENANGO

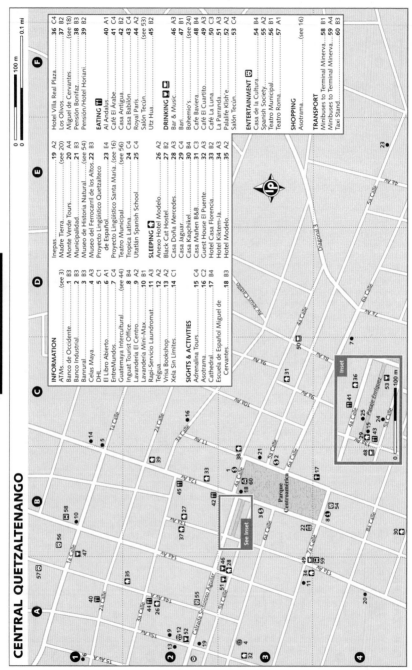

TOURIST INFORMATION

Inguat (Map p164; ☎ /fax 7761 4931; ☺ 8am-1pm & 2-5pm Mon-Fri, 8am-1pm Sat) At the southern end of Parque Centroamérica. If you're looking for a brochure, this is the place to come. For hard information, you're often better off asking Tour Operators (see p169).

TRAVEL AGENCIES

Adrenalina Tours (Map p164; ☎ 7761 4509; www .adrenalinatours.com; 13a Av, Zona 1, inside Pasaje Enríquez) Flights and package deals to anywhere in the country (and the world), a direct plane-ticket booking service, charter flights and much more.

Guatemaya Intercultural (Map p164; ☎ 7765 0040; www.xelapages.com/guatemaya; 14a Av A 3-06, Zona 1) Sells student, youth, teacher and discounted air fares; issues student, youth and teacher cards (US$9); and offers deals to Tikal and other tours within Guatemala, and to Cuba and South America.

Xela Sin Límites (Map p164; ☎ /fax 7761 6043; www .xelapages.com/xelasinlimites; 12a Av C-35, Zona 1) Does tours locally and around Guatemala and can make international travel arrangements.

Sights

PARQUE CENTROAMÉRICA

The park and the buildings surrounding it are pretty much what there is to see in Xela itself. The **Casa de la Cultura** (Map p164) at the southern end holds the funky **Museo de Historia Natural** (Map p164; admission US$0.80; ☺ 8am-noon & 2-6pm Mon-Fri, 9am -1pm Sat), which has a fascinating collection including exhibits on the Maya, the liberal revolution in Central American politics and the Estado de Los Altos, of which Quetzaltenango was the capital. Marimbas, the weaving industry, stuffed birds (frightening eagles and owls) and animals (some scary members of the cat family), and other local artifacts also claim places here.

The once-crumbling **cathedral** has been rebuilt in recent decades: the facade of the colonial building has been preserved, and a modern church built behind it.

The **Municipalidad** (Town Hall; Map p164), at the northeastern end of the park, was rebuilt after the 1902 earthquake in the grandiose neoclassical style so favored as a symbol of culture and refinement in this wild mountain country.

On the west side of the park between 4a and 5a Calles is **Pasaje Enríquez**, an imposing arcade built to be lined with elegant shops – but as Quetzaltenango has few elegant shoppers, it stands half-empty.

OTHER SIGHTS

Walk north on 14a Av to 1a Calle to see the impressive neoclassical **Teatro Municipal** (Map p164; 1a Calle), which holds regular, recommended performances. Inside are three tiers of seating, the lower two with private boxes for prominent families; each is equipped with a vanity.

Mercado La Democracia (Map p163; 1a Calle, Zona 3), about 10 blocks north of Parque Centroamérica, is an authentic Guatemalan city market with food and other necessities for city dweller and villager alike.

About 3km northwest of Parque Centroamérica, near the Terminal Minerva bus station and another big market, is the **Parque Zoológico Minerva** (Map p163; admission free; ☺ 9am-5pm Tue-Sun), a zoo-park with a few monkeys, coyotes, raccoons, deer, Barbary sheep, plus

---

SAFETY GUIDELINES FOR WALKING

Before embarking on a walking trip, consider the following points to ensure a safe and enjoyable experience:

- Pay any fees and possess any permits required by local authorities.
- Be sure you are healthy and feel comfortable walking for a sustained period.
- Obtain reliable information about physical and environmental conditions along your intended route.
- Be aware of local laws, regulations and etiquette about wildlife and the environment.
- Walk only in regions and on trails within your realm of experience.
- Be aware that weather conditions and terrain vary significantly from one region to another, or even from one trail to another. Seasonal changes can significantly alter any trail. These differences influence the way walkers dress and the equipment they carry.
- Ask before you set out about the environmental characteristics that can affect your walk and how local, experienced walkers deal with these considerations.

THE HIGHLANDS

RESPONSIBLE TREKKING

To help preserve the ecology and beauty of Guatemala, consider the following tips when trekking.

Rubbish

- Carry out *all* your rubbish. Don't overlook easily forgotten items, such as silver paper, orange peel, cigarette butts and plastic wrappers. Empty packaging should be stored in a dedicated rubbish bag. Make an effort to carry out rubbish left by others.
- Never bury your rubbish: Digging disturbs soil and ground cover and encourages erosion. Buried rubbish will likely be dug up by animals, who may be injured or poisoned by it. It may also take years to decompose.
- Minimize waste by taking minimal packaging and no more food than you will need. Take reusable containers or stuff sacks.
- Sanitary napkins, tampons, condoms and toilet paper should be carried out despite the inconvenience. They burn and decompose poorly.

Human Waste Disposal

- Contamination of water sources by human faeces can lead to the transmission of all sorts of nasties. Where there is a toilet, please use it. Where there is none, bury your waste. Dig a small hole 15cm (6in) deep and at least 100m (320ft) from any watercourse. Cover the waste with soil and a rock. In snow, dig down to the soil.
- Ensure that these guidelines are applied to a portable toilet tent if one is being used by a large trekking party. Encourage all party members, including porters, to use the site.

Washing

- Don't use detergents or toothpaste in or near watercourses, even if they are biodegradable.
- For personal washing, use biodegradable soap and a water container (or even a lightweight, portable basin) at least 50m (160ft) away from the watercourse. Disperse the waste water widely to allow the soil to filter it fully.
- Wash cooking utensils 50m (160ft) from watercourses using a scourer, sand or snow instead of detergent.

Erosion

- Hillsides and mountain slopes, especially at high altitudes, are prone to erosion. Stick to existing trails and avoid shortcuts.
- If a well-used trail passes through a mud patch, walk through the mud so as not to increase the size of the patch.
- Avoid removing the plant life that keeps topsoils in place.

a few rides for children. Outside the zoo on an island in the middle of 4a Calle stands the neoclassical **Templo de Minerva** (Map p163), built by dictator Estrada Cabrera to honor the Roman goddess of education and to inspire Guatemalans to new heights of learning.

Activities
VOLCANO ASCENTS & TREKS
There are many exciting walks and climbs to be done from Xela. **Volcán Tajumulco** (4220m), 50km northwest, is the highest point in

Central America and is a challenging trip of one long day from the city or two days with a night camping on the mountain. This includes about five hours' walking up from the starting point, Huitán, and three to four hours down. Huitán is about three hours by bus from Xela.

With early starts, **Volcán Santa María** (3772m), towering to the south of the city, and the active **Santiaguito** (2488m), on Santa María's southwest flank, can both be done in long mornings from Xela. You start walking

Fires & Low-Impact Cooking

■ Don't depend on open fires for cooking. The cutting of wood for fires in popular trekking areas can cause rapid deforestation. Cook on a light-weight kerosene, alcohol or Shellite (white gas) stove and avoid using stoves powered by disposable butane gas canisters.

■ If you are trekking with a guide and porters, supply stoves for the whole team. In highland areas, ensure that all members are outfitted with enough clothing so that fires are not a necessity for warmth.

■ If you patronize local accommodation, select those places that do not use wood fires to heat water or cook food.

■ Fires may be acceptable below the tree line in areas that get very few visitors. If you light a fire, use an existing fireplace. Don't surround fires with rocks. Use only dead, fallen wood. Remember the adage 'the bigger the fool, the bigger the fire.' Use minimal wood, just what you need for cooking. In huts, leave wood for the next person.

■ Ensure that you fully extinguish a fire after use. Spread the embers and flood them with water.

Wildlife Conservation

■ Do not engage in or encourage hunting. Even when it is legal, many animals are on the verge of joining the endangered list.

■ Don't buy items made from endangered species.

■ Don't attempt to exterminate animals in huts. In wild places, they are likely to be protected native animals.

■ Discourage the presence of wildlife by not leaving food scraps behind you. Place gear out of reach and tie packs to rafters or trees.

■ Do not feed the wildlife as this can lead to animals becoming dependent on hand-outs, to unbalanced populations and to diseases.

Environmental Organizations

If you would like to know more about environmental issues in Guatemala, the following organizations can provide information:

■ **Alianza Verde** (www.alianzaverde.org)

■ **Arcas** (www.arcasguatemala.com)

■ **ProPeten** (www.propeten.org)

■ **Rainforest Alliance** (www.rainforest-alliance.org)

THE HIGHLANDS

at the village of Llanos del Pinal, 5km south of Xela (US$6.50 by taxi from Xela; US$0.25 by bus), from which it's about four hours up to the summit of Santa María (then three hours down). Getting too close to Santiaguito is dangerous, so people usually just look at it from a *mirador* about 1½ hours' walk from Llanos del Pinal.

Kaqchikel Tours (Map p163; ☎ 5294 8828; www .kaqchikeltours.com; 7 Calle 15-36, Zona 1) is a well-run, locally owned outfit specializing in volcano ascents and other great-value hikes, with camping along the way on some trips. Two-day Tajumulco trips cost around US$40. Kaqchikel also offers full-moon ascents of Santa María (US$15) and challenging two-day Santiaguito trips (US$66 with a minimum group size of four), camping on a small hill as close as is safely possible to the active crater. A three-day Quetzaltenango–Lago de Atitlán trek is US$70, and a five-day Nebaj–Todos Santos jaunt across the Cuchumatanes mountains is US$130. Prices include transportation, food, equipment and a guide.

Adrenalina Tours (Map p164; ☎ 7761 4509; www
.adrenalinatours.com; 13a Av, Zona 1, inside Pasaje
Enríquez) Goes everywhere, with an emphasis on little-
visited parts of the Huehuetenango region.
Monte Verde Tours (Map p164; ☎ 7761 6105; www
.monte-verdetours.com; 13a Av 8-34, Zona 1) Does a
variety of volcano hikes and offbeat tours around the local
area.

CYCLING

Cycling is a great way to explore the surrounding countryside or commute to Spanish class. Fuentes Georginas, San Andrés
Xequl and the steam vents at Los Vahos
(see p174) are all attainable day trips. **Vrisa
Bookstore** (Map p164; 15a Av 3-64, Zona 1) rents
mountain and town bikes for US$3.50/9.50
per day/week, as does **Monte Verde Tours** (Map
p164; ☎ 7761 6105; www.monte-verdetours.com; 13a Av
8-34, Zona 1).

DANCE CLASSES

The highly recommended **Tropica Latina** (Map
p164; ☎ 5892 8861; www.xelawho.com/tropicalatina; 5a
Calle 12-24, Zona 1) is the longest-running dance
school in town, and gets top marks for its
fun atmosphere and professionalism. Group
and private salsa classes and private merengue classes are offered.

WEAVING CLASSES

The women's co operative **Asotrama** (Map p164;
☎ 7765 8564; www.xelapages.com/asotrama; 3a Calle 10-
56, Zona 1) offers backstrap weaving classes and
operates a fair-trade fabrics shop.

Language Courses

Xela's many language schools attract students from around the world. Unlike Antigua, which has had a similar reputation for
quite a bit longer, Xela is not overrun with
foreigners, though there is a growing social
scene revolving around language students and
volunteer workers.

Xela seems to attract altruistic types, and
most of the Spanish schools here provide
opportunities to get involved in social action programs working with the local K'iche'
Maya. Prices for the schools vary, but not
by much; the standard price is US$110/125
per week for four/five hours of instruction
per day, Monday to Friday, including room
and board with a local family, or around
US$80/95 per week without homestay. Some
schools charge up to 20% more for tuition
during the high season from June to August,
and many require nonrefundable registration
fees. College students may be able to take
classes for academic credit.

VOLUNTEERING IN XELA

The Quetzaltenango area has many nonprofit organizations working on social projects with the
local K'iche' Maya people and others that need volunteers. Volunteer jobs can range from teaching math to village children, to designing websites for indigenous organizations, to developing
sustainable agriculture, to medical work in clinics, to working in orphanages for disabled children. For anyone in a giving frame of mind, the possibilities are endless. You can volunteer part
time for a week or two while also studying Spanish, or you can live and work in a close-knit
indigenous village for a year. Obviously, the more Spanish you speak the better, but in a few
weeks at one of Xela's schools, you can learn enough to be effective. Indeed, many schools are
intimately connected with particular social projects – some in fact exist primarily to generate
funds for them – and can help students to participate in their free time. Skills in fields such as
medicine, nursing, teaching, youth work and computers are prized, but there are possibilities for
anyone with the will to help. Volunteers must normally meet all their own costs and be willing
to commit to a project for a specified minimum time. Three months is fairly typical for full-time
posts, though the minimum can be as little as a week or as long as a year.

    EntreMundos (Map p164; ☎ 7761 2179; www.entremundos.org; El Espacio, 6a Calle 7-31, Zona 1) is a
forum for social projects in Xela. Its website has details on hundreds of nonprofit projects all
over Guatemala, many of which need volunteers, and its magazine, *EntreMundos*, comes out every
couple of months with articles and ads about volunteering, volunteer opportunities and some
completely unrelated interesting stuff!

    Guatemaya Intercultural (Map p164; ☎ 7765 0040; www.xelapages.com/guatemaya; 14a Av A 3-06, Zona
1) can place volunteers in any of 15 projects including human rights and ecological organizations,
medical clinics, schools and old-people's homes.

Most schools are lively and have plenty going on. Extras (some free, some not) range from movies and free internet to dancing and cooking classes, trips out and lectures and discussions on Guatemalan politics and culture.

Reputable language schools (there are more!) include the following:

Casa Xelajú (Map p163; ☎ 7761 5954; www.casaxelaju .com; Callejón 15 D13-02, Zona 1) One of the biggest, also offering classes in K'iche', and college credits.

Celas Maya (Map p164; ☎ /fax 7761 4342; www .celasmaya.edu.gt; 6a Calle 14-55, Zona 1) Set around a pleasant garden-courtyard, Celas Maya also offers classes in K'iche'.

Centro Bilingüe Amerindia (CBA; Map p163; ☎ 7771 8049; www.languageschool.com.gt; 12a Av 10-27, Zona 1) Classes in Mayan languages as well.

Centro de Estudios de Español Pop Wuj (Map p163; ☎ /fax 7761 8286; www.pop-wuj.org; 1a Calle 17-72, Zona 1) Pop Wuj's profits go to development projects in nearby villages, in which students can participate. The school also offers medical and social work specialist language programs.

El Nahual (Map p163; ☎ 7765 2098; www.languages elnahual.com; 27 Av 8-68, Zona 1) A bit out of town, but runs some excellent, grass-roots community projects in which students can participate, such as teaching underprivileged kids and maintaining an organic community garden.

El Quetzal (Map p163; ☎ 7765 1085; www.xelawho .com/elquetzal; 10a Calle 10-29, Zona 1) One of the few indigenous-run businesses in town, offering plenty of activities and a reading room with more than 300 books.

Escuela de Español Miguel de Cervantes (Map p164; ☎ 7765 5554; www.learn2speakspanish.com; 12a Av 8-31) Friendly female owner, intimate atmosphere, also has accommodation (see Sleeping).

Inepas (Instituto de Estudios de Español y Participación en Ayuda Social; Map p164; ☎ 7765 1308; www.inepas .org; 15a Av 4-59) Offers a selection of cheap accommodations other than living with a family, also organizes worthy projects in which students are invited to participate.

La Democracia (Map p163; ☎ 7763 6895; www.lademo cracia.net; 9a Calle 15-05, Zona 3) In a residential part of town, this highly recommended school arranges volunteer work teaching English to underprivileged kids and building classrooms.

Madre Tierra (Map p164; ☎ 7761 6105; www. madre-tierra.org; 13 Av 8-34, Zona 1) Plenty of activities; runs its own reforestation project. Classes held in a pretty courtyard in classic colonial house.

Mundo en Español (Map p163; ☎ 7761 3256; www .elmundoenespanol.org; 8 Av Calle B A-61, Zona 1) Seventeen years' experience; family atmosphere; gym, garden and accommodation on premises.

Proyecto Lingüístico Quetzalteco de Español (Map p164; ☎ /fax 7763 1061; www.hermandad.com; 5a Calle 2-42, Zona 1) This very professional and politically minded school also runs the Escuela de la Montaña, a language school with a maximum enrollment of eight on an organic coffee *finca* in the mountains near Xela, where participation in local culture and volunteering are strongly encouraged.

Proyecto Lingüístico Santa Maria (Map p164; ☎ 7765 8136; 3a Calle 10-56, Zona 1) Young staff and good atmosphere. Nonprofit status since 1984. Can organize volunteer work with Maya women's weaving cooperative. The director writes books on Spanish grammar and usage.

Utatlán Spanish School (Map p164; ☎ 7763 0446; www.xelapages.com/utatlan; Pasaje Enríquez, 12a Av 4-32, Zona 1) Young and energetic with plenty of parties and activities.

Tours

A professional, knowledgeable and amiable outfit, **Adrenalina Tours** (Map p164; ☎ 7761 4509; www.adrenalinatours.com; Pasaje Enríquez, Zona 1) provides a range of trips in the Xela area, including to Zunil, Fuentes Georginas and little-visited parts of the department of Huehuetenango. Also offers shuttles around the country, international flights and personalized trips all over Central America.

Monte Verde Tours (Map p164; ☎ 7761 6105; www .monte-verdetours.com; 13a Av 8-34, Zona 1) also offers tours in the Xela area, beach trips, ecotours and tours of local coffee farms, as well as shuttle buses and guided bike tours.

Festivals & Events

Xela Music Festival Organized by the Alianza Francaise, this one- or two-day festival takes place in late March or early April, and sees city streets blocked off as local musicians play on five or six stages around the city center.

Feria de la Virgen del Rosario (Feria Centroamericana de Independencia) Held from September 15 to 22, this is Xela's big annual party. Residents kick up their heels at a fairground on the city's perimeter and there's plenty of entertainment at selected venues around town.

Juegos Florales Centroamericanos The prizes in this international Spanish-language literary competition hosted by the city are awarded at the time of Feria de la Virgen del Rosario too.

Sleeping
BUDGET

All of the places listed here are in Zona 1.

Pensión/Hotel Horiani (Map p164; ☎ 7763 5228; 12a Av 2-23; s/d US$4/6) There's very little in the way of frills on offer here, but the small plain rooms upstairs set around a plant-filled patio have a certain charm to them. Enter on 2a Calle.

Posada San Andrés (Map p163; 4 Calle D 12-41; www .guesthousesanandres.com; s/d US$4/7) Undergoing renovations at the time of writing, this old wooden house has spacious, bare rooms with shared bathrooms and kitchen access. A few sticks of furniture and some art on the walls make the place comfortable enough.

Casa Kaqchikel (Map p164; ☎ 7761 2628; 9a Calle 11-26; dm US$4, s/d US$5.50/10, with bathroom US$8/12) There's only a few rooms in this old wooden house, but they're all good value – big and comfortable. The super-friendly family who run the place can whip you up a Guatemalan meal, or you can use the kitchen.

Guest House El Puente (Map p164; ☎ 7765 4342; 15a Av 6-75; s/d US$5.50/8, with bathroom US$8/10) An intimate little place with five good-sized rooms, kitchen access and a grassy garden area. Discounts for longer stays keep the place filled with long-termers.

Hostal Don Diego (Map p163; ☎ 5511 3211; hostal dondiego@gmail.com; 6a Calle 15-12; dm US$4.50, s/d US$6/10) A beautiful little budget choice – rooms are OK, with parquetry floors and good firm beds. Kitchen access and a sunny courtyard are other bonuses. It offers reduced rates for weekly or monthly stays, with or without kitchen use.

Miguel de Cervantes (Map p164; ☎ 7765 5554; www .learn2speakspanish.com; 12 Av 8-31; s/d US$7/14) These basic but comfortable wood and concrete rooms are set around one of the cutest courtyards in Xela. When there's water pressure, the showers in the shared bathrooms rock.

Black Cat Hostel (Map p164; ☎ 5037 1871; black catxela@gmail.com; 13a Av 3-33; dm incl breakfast US$7, s/d incl breakfast US$11/17) Xela's newest hostel is a good deal, and a great place to go if you're looking to meet up with other travelers. There's a sunny courtyard, a bar-restaurant and lounge/TV area. Rates include a big breakfast.

For long-term stays, renting an apartment is an option. Read all the fine print and know the terms for deposits and gas and electricity charges before plunking down your cash. **Casa Jaguar** (Map p164; ☎ 5446 3785; Pasaje Enríquez; r/apt per person per month US$131/266) rents fully furnished apartments with cable TV and free gas for the first month. Also available are rooms with access to shared kitchen and bathroom facilities.

MIDRANGE

Casa Azafran (Map p163; ☎ 7763 0206; casababylon restauranteyhotel@yahoo.com; 15 Av A 3-33; s/d US$10/12, with bathroom US$14/20) A classic old house on a quiet street just out of the center. Each room is spacious, with two big firm beds, closets and cable TV. One room has a fireplace.

Los Olivos (Map p164; ☎ 7761 0215; 13a Av 3-32; s/d US$12/21; P) Up a side street next to the park, this one offers neat, tiled rooms with good hot-water bathrooms and carpeted floors. Beds are big and firm and there's cable TV.

Hotel Casa Florencia (Map p164; ☎ 7761 2326; www .hotelcasaflorencia.com; 12a Av 3-61, Zona 1; s/d US$15/24; P) The attractive wood-paneled rooms here are a pretty good deal. They're all carpeted, with plenty of space, big TVs with cable, and closets galore. Breakfast is available in the dining room.

Hotel Kiktem-Ja (Map p164; ☎ 7761 4304; 13a Av 7-18; s/d US$16/21; P) Set in a great old building downtown, the Kiktem-Ja is all floorboards at weird angles, and colonial touches. Rooms are spacious, with TV and fireplaces. The hot-water bathrooms don't disappoint.

Casa Doña Mercedes (Map p164; ☎ 7765 4687; 6a Calle & 14 Av; r US$20) Some of Xela's best-looking rooms are on offer here at this newish little guesthouse in the heart of downtown. Rooms have shared bathrooms, but are otherwise extremely comfortable, with carpeted floors or wooden floorboards, cable TV and closets.

Anexo Hotel Modelo (Map p164; ☎ 7763 1376; s/d US$23/27) In a surprisingly tranquil setting right in the heart of Xela's Zona Viva, rooms here are a good deal for the price – spacious, with cable TV and some well-chosen room furnishings.

Hotel Villa Real Plaza (Map p164; ☎ 7761 4045; 4a Calle 12-22, Zona 1; s/d US$35/45; P) By far the grandest-looking hotel in town, the Real Plaza started life as a prison. Looking at the stone archways, high ceilings and spacious rooms, you'd never know. There's a courtyard restaurant, bar and sauna.

Hotel Modelo (Map p164; ☎ 7761 2529; hotelmodelo 1892@yahoo.es; 14a Av A 2-31, Zona 1; s/d US$35/40; P) Set in a beautiful old colonial house, the Modelo offers some of the most atmospheric rooms in town, with wooden floorboards, firm beds and spacious bathrooms. Some are along a pretty patio at one side but tend to be noisier because they front the street.

TOP END

our pick Casa Mañen B&B (Map p164; ☎ 7765 0786; www.comeseeit.com; 9a Av 4-11; s/d from US$40/50) Most tourist towns in Guatemala have at least one hotel fit for honeymooning couples – a quiet place with romantic atmosphere, beautifully and comfortably outfitted rooms, tranquil gardens and a distinguishing style. In Xela, Casa Mañen is it. All nine rooms have traditional appointments (hand-woven woolen rugs, bed throws and wall hangings), hand-carved furniture, tiled floors, TV and a hot-water bathroom – even toweling dressing gowns folded on the beds. Upstairs units have balconies and views, as does the roof terrace/bar.

Pensión Bonifaz (Map p164; ☎ 7765 1111; bonifaz@ intel.net.gt; 4a Calle 10-50, Zona 1; s/d US$61/65; **P** **♨**) The oldest and grandest hotel in Xela, this one could try a little harder. What's with the wood-patterned linoleum, for example? Rooms are good otherwise – spacious and comfortable enough, scattered over four floors right next to the Parque Centroamérica.

Eating

Quetzaltenango has a good selection of places to eat in all price ranges. Cheapest are the food stalls in and around the small market to the left of the Casa de la Cultura, where snacks and main-course plates are sold for US$1 or less.

GUATEMALAN & LATIN AMERICAN CUISINE

Blue Angel Video Café (Map p163; 7a Calle, Zona 1; snacks US$2-4; ⊙ lunch & dinner) Economical café with excellent, healthy foods and an awesome tea selection – popular with language students.

Café Sagrado Corazón (Map p163; 14a Av 3-08, Zona 1; lunch plates US$2-2.60; ⊙ breakfast, lunch & dinner) This is an excellent place for Guatemalan home cooking. Regional specialties such as *pepian* and *jocom* are often on the menu, but there's always fried chicken and grilled beef as fallbacks. Meals are truly filling, coming with soup, tamalitos, rice, potatoes, avocado and salad.

Utz Hua (Map p164; 12a Av & 3a Calle; meals US$3.50; ⊙ breakfast, lunch & dinner Mon-Sat) Delicious, authentic Guatemalan and Quetzalteco dishes for equally yummy prices. The restaurant is well (if slightly frantically) decorated, and it's worth stopping by to check out the indoor thatched roof, if nothing else.

Restaurante Las Calas (Map p164; 14a Av A 3-21; mains US$4-5; ⊙ breakfast, lunch & dinner Mon-Sat) An artistic sort of place with lilies growing in the patio and lily-themed art on the walls (and a gallery in the back), Las Calas serves good medium-priced meals. Satisfying portions of chicken, fish or beef are creatively prepared

and served with a unique *salsa picante*. This restaurant also features cheaper vegetarian dishes and a daily regional specialty.

Cubatenango (Map p163; 19a Av 2-06; mains US$4-6; ⊙ breakfast, lunch & dinner Mon-Sat) Authentic Cuban food with a Miami twist is the go here – *ropa vieja* (shredded beef), *moros y cristianos* (black beans and rice) and *vaca frita* (fried beef). The *tostones* (fried, mashed, savory bananas) are worth the trip alone, and this place makes a mean Mojito.

INTERNATIONAL CUISINE

Café Q (Map p163; Diagonal 12 4-46; mains from US$3.50; ⊙ 7-10pm Mon-Fri) The varied international flavors at Q's include interesting vegetarian options such as falafel, soy burgers and chickpea soup.

Al Andalus (Map p164; 2a Calle 14 A-30; mains US$4-6; ⊙ breakfast, lunch & dinner) Xela's Spanish restaurant comes up with the goods in terms of paella, lentils and *chorizo* (spicy sausage) and other Spanish favorites. It's set in a charming courtyard ringed by potted plants and Moorish archways.

Sabor de la India (Map p163; 2 Calle 15 A-34; mains US$4-6; ⊙ lunch & dinner Tue-Sat, dinner Sun) Probably the most authentic Indian dishes in the country, whipped up by a friendly Indian/ Guatemalan couple. Servings are huge and there are plenty of vegetarian options.

Las Orchideas (Map p163; 4a Calle 15-45; mains US$4-6; ⊙ lunch & dinner Tue-Sat) Hanging out for some Thai food? This is the place. Green curry, pad thai, satay, oodles of noodles, and sticky rice with papaya to round things out.

Salón Tecún (Map p164; Pasaje Enríquez; burgers, salads & sandwiches US$4-6; ⊙ breakfast, lunch & dinner) On the west side of Parque Centroamérica, the Tecún, consistently Xela's busiest bar, serves good bar food including the best burgers in town.

Casa Antigua (Map p164; 12a Av 3-26; meals US$4-8; ⊙ breakfast, lunch & dinner) An excellent, tranquil spot right in the middle of downtown. Sandwiches are big, chunky affairs and there's plenty of steaks flame-grilling out front.

El Panorama (☎ 5319 3536; Map p163; 13a Av A; meals US$4-8; ⊙ dinner Wed-Fri, lunch & dinner Sat & Sun) This Swiss-owned restaurant (a 10-minute slog up the hill at the south end of town) does good set meals and raclette. The view is amazing and it's a romantic spot for that special night out.

Café El Árabe (Map p164; 4a Calle 12-22, Zona 1; mains US$4-9; ⊙ lunch & dinner Tue-Sat) Fans of Middle

THE HIGHLANDS

Eastern food will be thrilled to find such an authentic place here, just off Parque Centroamérica. The Arabic bread is made on the premises and the ingredients for all dishes are lovely and fresh. You can fill up on meat dishes but there are plenty of vegetarian choices. The falafel and dips are wonderful.

Casa Babylon (Map p164; cnr 13a Av & 5a Calle; mains US$4-12; ⟲ breakfast, lunch & dinner Mon-Sat) With the widest menu in town, the Babylon is a travelers' favorite. Dishes run from big, tasty sandwiches to Guatemalan classics such as *pepian*, to more exotic fare such as fondue and Middle Eastern choices.

Il Giardino (Map p163; 19a Callejón 8-07; mains US$5-9; ⟲ lunch & dinner Wed-Mon) The best pizzas in town are made by the Italian-descended family who run this place. It's set around a big leafy indoor garden and offers pasta, steaks and good salads and sandwiches, too.

Royal Paris (Map p164; ☎ 7761 1942; 14 Av A 3-06; meals from US$5; ⟲ lunch & dinner Tue-Sun) Xela's oldest French restaurant has some lovely cheesy steak dishes, cheap set lunches and live music on Friday and Saturday nights (reservations recommended).

Casa Azafran (Map p163; 15 Av A 3-33; mains from US$6; ⟲ lunch & dinner Wed-Sun) Serving up the most elaborate French food in town, this well-decorated, intimate restaurant is a romantic choice with some decadent options, such as lobster tails, on the menu.

Drinking

The live music scene is particularly strong in Xela. For details on what's on, pick up a copy of *XelaWho* or check www.xelawho.com. All of the following are in Zone 1.

CAFÉS

Coffee plays an important part in Xela's economy, and there are plenty of places where you can grab a cup.

Café Baviera (Map p164; 5a Calle 13-14 ⟲ 7am-8:30pm) This European-style café has good coffee, roasted on the premises, and is a decent place for breakfast or a snack (crepes, croissants, soups and salads; US$3 to US$4). The wooden walls are hung with countless photos and clippings on Xela and international themes.

Café La Luna (Map p164; 8a Av 4-11 ⟲ 9:30am-9pm Mon-Fri, 4-9pm Sat & Sun) La Luna is a comfortable, relaxed placto hang out and eat a cake, salad or sandwich (snacks US$2). The hot chocolate

is the specialty – the coffee is so-so. Choose any of several rooms: decor is in similar vein to Café Baviera but the music is classical instead of jazz.

Café Las Calas (Map p164; 14a Av A 3-21; ⟲ 7am-9:30pm Mon-Sat) Some of Xela's best coffee gets served up here in a leafy, tranquil courtyard environment. There's live music on Thursday and Friday nights. Meals from US$4.

Café El Cuartito (Map p164; 13a Av A 7-09; ⟲ 7am-midnight Wed-Mon) Xela's hippest café does a good range of snacks and juices and coffee just about any way you want it. On weekends it often has DJs spinning laid-back tracks, and there's always art on the walls by local contemporary artists.

BARS

Salón Tecún (Map p164; Pasaje Enríquez; ⟲ 8am-1am) On the west side of Parque Centroamérica, and busy all day and night with a healthy crowd of Guatemalans and foreigners, the Tecún claims to be the country's longest-running bar (since 1935). Don't miss it.

Bajo La Luna (Map p164; 8a Av 4-11; ⟲ 8pm-1am Thu-Sat) An atmospheric wine-and-cheese bar set in a cellar with exposed beams. Liters of Chilean red go for US$6.

Bar & Music (Map p164; 13a Av 5-38; ⟲ 6pm-1am Mon-Sat) The regular hotspot before hitting the dance floors, with decently priced drinks and loud Latin pop and rock music.

Pool & Beer (Map p163; 12a Av 10-21; ⟲ 5pm-midnight) An excellent place for some drinks and a few games of pool. At the time of writing, the tables hadn't been trashed and the cues were straight.

Bohemio's (Map p164; 5a Calle 12-24; ⟲ 8pm-Tue-Sat, Zona 1) Some nights it's mellow, some nights it goes berserk, but this friendly little bar a few steps away from the Parque Central is always worth a look in.

La Parranda (Map p164; 6 Calle & 14a Av) The hottest place in town for dancing and drinking. Wednesdays there's free salsa classes, other nights have guest DJs and drinks giveaways.

Bari (Map p164; 1a Calle 14-31; ⟲ 8pm-1am Thu-Sat) This little bar has live trova, pop and rock music Thursday to Saturday and sells a good selection of wine and draft beers.

La Fonda del Ché (Map p163; 15a Av 7-43; ⟲ 7pm-1am Tue-Sat) Trova and other guitar music nightly.

Palalife Klish'e (Map p164; 15a Av & 4a Calle; ⟲ 5pm-1am Tue-Sat) This 'open minded' disco-bar is always fun and attracts a mixed crowd, with good dance music, drinks specials and drag shows on Saturday night.

Entertainment

It gets chilly when the sun goes down, so you won't want to sit out in the Parque Centroamérica enjoying the balmy breezes – there aren't any. Nevertheless, it's softly lit and still a pleasant place for an evening stroll.

The **Spanish Society** (Map p164; 4a Calle & 14 Av A, Zone 1) cultural center hosts a women's theater group that stages monthly performances, and occasionally has events such as book launches and poetry readings.

Other recommendations:

Blue Angel Video Café (www.xelawho.com/blueangel; Map p163; 7a Calle 15-79, Zona 1; US$1.30) Shows Hollywood videos nightly.

Cinema Paraíso At the time of writing, this cinema, which shows a couple of interesting documentaries or movies daily, was looking for a new home. Check notice boards around town for the latest.

Teatro Municipal (Map p164; 1a Calle) Cultural performances are presented at this beautiful venue.

Teatro Roma (Map p164; 14a Av A) Facing Teatro Municipal; sometimes screens interesting movies.

Shopping

Asotrama (Map p164; ☎ 7765 8564; www.xelapages.com /asotrama; 3a Calle 10-56, Zona 1), the shop belonging to the association of Maya women weavers, is just uphill from the park.

Xela's central market (Map p163) is three floors of reasonably priced handicrafts and souvenirs. Bargain hard. For a more intense, everyday marketing experience, hit the La Democracia market (Map p164), up in Zona 3. You should be able to find everything from pirated CDs to a Sonyo TV.

Getting There & Away

BUS

For 2nd-class buses, head out to Terminal Minerva, a dusty, noisy, crowded yard on 7a Calle, Zona 3, in the west of town. Buses leave frequently for many highland destinations. Leaving or entering town, some buses make a stop east of the center at the Rotonda, a traffic circle on Calzada Independencia, marked by the Monumento a la Marimba. Getting off here when you're coming into Xela saves the 10 to 15 minutes it will take your bus to cross town to Terminal Minerva.

First-class companies operating between Quetzaltenango and Guatemala City have their own terminals. All of the buses listed here depart from Terminal Minerva, unless otherwise indicated.

Almolonga (for Los Vahos) (US$0.50, 15 minutes, 6km) Buses every 15 minutes, 5:30am to 5pm, with a stop for additional passengers at the corner of 9a Av and 10a Calle.

Antigua (170km) Take any bus heading to Guatemala City via the Interamericana and change at Chimaltenango.

Chichicastenango (US$3, three hours, 94km) Buses at 5am, 6am, 9:30am, 10:45am, 11am, 1pm, 2pm and 3:30pm. Or take a bus heading to Guatemala City by the Interamericana and change at Los Encuentros.

Ciudad Tecún Umán (Mexican border) (US$3.50, 3½ hours, 129km) Hourly buses from 5am to 2pm.

Cuatro Caminos (US$0.50, 30 minutes, 11km) Take any bus for Huehuetenango, Momostenango, Totonicapán, San Francisco El Alto and so on.

El Carmen/Talismán (Mexican border) Take a bus to Coatepeque (US$2.50, two hours, every 30 minutes) and get a direct bus to El Carmen (US$2.50, two hours).

Guatemala City (US$6, four to five hours, 205km) Línea Dorada (☎ 7767 5198; 12 Av & 5 Calle, Zona 1) Two 1st-class buses (US$8), 4am and 2:30pm; Líneas América (☎ 7761 4587; 7a Av 3-33, Zona 2) Six pullmans, 5:15am to 3:30pm; Transportes Álamo (☎ 7763 5044; 14 Av 5-15, Zona 3) Seven pullman buses, from 4:30am to 4:45pm; Transportes Galgos (☎ 7761 2248; Calle Rodolfo Robles 17-43, Zona 1) Five pullmans, 3am to 3pm. Each departs from their own terminals. Cheaper 2nd-class buses depart Terminal Minerva every 30 minutes, 3am to 4:30pm, but they have many stops and take longer.

Huehuetenango (US$2, two hours, 90km) Buses every 30 minutes, 5am to 5:30pm.

La Mesilla (Mexican border) (US$3, 3½ hours, 170km, buses at 5am, 6am, 7am, 8am, 1pm and 4pm) Or take a bus to Huehuetenango and change there.

Momostenango (US$1, 1¼ hours, 26km) Buses every 30 minutes, 6am to 5pm.

Panajachel (US$2.50, 2½ hours, 90km) Buses at 5am, 6am, 8am, 10am, noon and 3pm. Or take any bus for Guatemala City via the Interamericana and change at Los Encuentros.

Retalhuleu (US$1.50, 1 hour, 46km) Buses every 30 minutes, 4:30am to 6pm. Look for 'Reu' on the bus; 'Retalhuleu' won't be spelled out.

San Andrés Xecul (US$0.80, 40 minutes) Buses every hour or two, from 6am to 3pm. Or take any bus to San Francisco El Alto or Totonicapán, get out at the Esso station at the Moreiria junction and flag a pickup.

San Francisco El Alto (US$0.60, one hour, 15km) Buses about every 15 minutes, 6am to 6pm.

San Martín Sacatepéquez (San Martín Chile Verde) (US$0.80, 45 minutes, 22km) Various companies have buses that leave when full. Placards may say 'Colomba' or 'El Rincón.' Minibuses also serve this route.

EXPLORE MORE OF QUETZALTENANGO

The wide open spaces and mountainous countryside around Xela offer an almost endless array of opportunities for getting out there and doing a bit of solo exploration. Small villages dotted around the valley mean that you shouldn't ever have too much trouble finding somebody to ask directions from, and the relative safety of the area means that the biggest danger you're ever likely to face is that of a yapping dog (carry a stick). A few destinations to head towards:

■ the Santiaguito lookout – get a close-up view of volcanic eruptions, going off like clockwork every 20 minutes

■ the lava fields – over near Mt Candelaria, these extensive fields are a great place for a picnic and a spot of sunbathing

■ the San Cristobal waterfall – halfway between Xela and San Francisco, the falls are much more impressive in the wet season

■ Las Mojadas – the walk to this pretty flower-growing village takes you from Llanos del Pinal and past the Santiago volcano. And the best part – you can catch a bus back.

Totonicapán (US$1, one hour, 22km) Buses every 20 minutes, 6am to 5pm. Departing from the Rotonda on Calzada Independencia. Placards generally say 'Toto.'

Zunil (US$0.60, 20 minutes, 10km) Buses every 30 minutes, 7am to 7pm. With an additional stop at the corner of 9a Av and 10a Calle, southeast of Parque Centroamérica.

SHUTTLE MINIBUS

Adrenalina Tours (Map p164; ☎ 7761 4509; www .adrenalinatours.com; 13a Av, Zona 1, inside Pasaje Enríquez) runs shuttle minibuses to many destinations including Guatemala City (US$30 per person), Antigua (US$25), Chichicastenango (US$15), Panajachel (US$15), and San Cristobal Las Casas (Mexico; US$35). **Monte Verde Tours** (Map p164; ☎ 7761 6105; www.monte-verdetours.com; 13 Av 8-34, Zona 1) offers the same runs for slightly cheaper prices.

CAR & MOTORCYCLE

Rental companies in Xela:

Econorent (☎ 7765 0592; cnr 4a Calle & 14a Av, Zona 3)

Tabarini (Map p163; ☎ /fax 7763 0418; 9a Calle 9-21, Zona 1)

Getting Around

Terminal Minerva is linked to the city center by minibuses known as microbuses, charging US$0.15 for the 10- to 15-minute ride. From the terminal, walk south through the market to the intersection by the Templo de Minerva, where you'll see the vehicles waiting on the south side of 4a Calle. Inguat has information on city bus routes. City buses charge US$0.15, doubling the fare after 7pm and on public holidays. Going from the center to the terminal, you can catch the microbuses

on 13a Av at the corner of 7a or 4a Calle, or on 14a Av north of 1a Calle. Linea Dorada has a door-to-door shuttle service (US$3) for passengers getting their 4am departure. A taxi from Terminal Minerva to the city center costs around US$4.50. The Rotonda bus stop on Calzada Independencia is also served by Parque microbuses running to the center and by taxis.

There's a taxi stand at the north end of Parque Centroamérica.

AROUND QUETZALTENANGO

The beautiful volcanic country around Quetzaltenango makes for many exciting day trips. For many, the volcanoes themselves pose irresistible challenges (p166). The steam baths at Almolonga are basic but cheap and accessible. The hot springs at Fuentes Georginas are idyllic. You can feast your eyes and soul on the wild church at San Andrés Xecul, or hike to the ceremonial shores of Laguna Chicabal. Or simply hop on a bus and explore the myriad small traditional villages that pepper this part of the Highlands. Market days are great opportunities to observe locals in action, so Sunday and Wednesday in Momostenango, Monday in Zunil, Tuesday and Saturday in Totonicapán and Friday in San Francisco El Alto are good days to visit these surrounding towns.

Los Vahos

If you're a hiker and the weather is good, you'll enjoy a trip to the rough-and-ready sauna/steam baths at **Los Vahos** (the Vapors; admission US$3; ☺ 8am-6pm), 3.5km from the Parque Centroamérica. Take a bus headed for Almolonga and ask to get out at the road to Los Vahos, which is marked with a small sign reading 'A Los Vahos.' From here it's a 2.3km uphill walk (around 1½ hours) to Los Vahos. As you climb, the views of the city on a clear day are remarkable. But, better still, walk south straight out of the city center along 13a Av to its end, where you'll see the little yellow-and-red Monte Sinai evangelical church. Continue straight ahead on the road passing the right-hand side of the church. The road soon zigzags uphill, becoming a dirt track and then a good footpath. Follow the path past the dairy and school to where it joins the main track to Los Vahos. From here you'll have 1km or so more to walk uphill to the steam baths.

At Los Vahos you can have a sauna/steam bath and a picnic if you're so inclined. The saunas are just two dark stone rooms behind plastic curtains. Occasionally, the vents are carpeted with eucalyptus leaves, giving the steam a herbal quality. Straight in front of the steam-bath entrance is a rocky hillside, which you can climb to some caves.

A taxi costs US$22 for the return trip, including waiting time.

Almolonga

On the way to Zunil the road passes through Almolonga, 6km from Quetzaltenango, an indigenous town become relatively wealthy from vegetable-growing (it exports veggies to El Salvador) and with a population that is more than 90% evangelical Christian. Market days are Tuesday, Thursday and Saturday, when you'll see the most gorgeous vegetables ever. Almolonga celebrates its annual fair on June 27. Don't miss the **Iglesia de San Pedro**, which has a gilded altarpiece with a backdrop of incongruous neon lights, an inverted galleon ceiling and huge old paintings. At the lower end of the village the road passes through **Los Baños**, an area with natural hot sulfur springs. Several little places down here have bath installations; most are quite decrepit, but if a hot-water bath at low cost is your desire, you may want to stop. Rather tomb-like enclosed concrete tubs rent for US$2 to US$3 an hour. **El Recreo** and **Los Cirilos** are among the better set-ups.

Zunil

pop 10,900 / elev 2076m

Zunil is a pretty agricultural and market town in a lush valley framed by steep hills and dominated by a towering volcano. As you speed downhill toward Zunil on the road from Quetzaltenango, you will see it framed as if in a picture, with its white colonial church gleaming above the red-tiled and rusted tin roofs of the low houses.

Winding down the hill from Los Baños, the road skirts Zunil and its fertile gardens before a road on the left leads across a river bridge and, 1km further, to Zunil's plaza.

Zunil, founded in 1529, is a typical Guatemalan highland town. What makes it so beautiful is its setting in the mountains and the traditional indigenous agriculture practiced here. The cultivated plots, divided by stone fences, are irrigated by canals; you'll see the farmers scooping up water from the canals with a shovel-like instrument and throwing it over their plants. Women wash their clothes near the river bridge in pools of hot water that come out of the rocks. In Zunil, the centuries-old life cycle thrives.

SIGHTS

Another attraction of Zunil is its particularly striking **church**. Its ornate facade, with eight pairs of serpentine columns, is echoed inside by a richly worked altar of silver. On market day (Monday) the plaza in front of the church is bright with the predominantly red-and-pink traditional garb of the local K'iche' Maya people buying and selling.

Half a block downhill from the church plaza, the **Cooperativa Santa Ana** (7:30am-6pm) is a handicrafts cooperative in which more than 500 local women participate. Handicrafts, mainly superbly woven cloth, are displayed and sold here, and weaving lessons are offered.

While you're in Zunil, visit the image of **San Simón**, the name given here to the much-venerated non-Christian deity known elsewhere as Maximón. His effigy, propped up in a chair, is moved each year to a different house; ask any local where to find San Simón, everyone will know (local children will take you for a small tip). You'll be charged a few quetzals to visit him and US$0.65 for each photograph taken. For more on San Simón, see the boxed text, p140.

FESTIVALS

The **festival of San Simón** is held each year on October 28, after which he moves to a new house. The **festival of Santa Catarina Alejandrí**, official patron saint of Zunil, is celebrated on November 25. In between, November 1 sees lots of kites flying above the cemetery.

THE HIGHLANDS

SLEEPING & EATING

Eco Saunas Las Cumbres (☎ 7767 1746; Km 210; r US$34; **P**) This hotel, about 500m south of Zunil village, is built on top of natural steam vents. It's one of the most comfortable in the region. Rooms come with fireplace, sauna and Jacuzzi, as well as cable TV and all the usual comforts. There's a good restaurant (mains US$4 to US$8), open for breakfast, lunch and dinner, serving up regional specialties and generous meat platters. Also on the grounds are a squash court, gymnasium and handicrafts store. Nonguests can use the public sauna (US$3.50 per hour), which you'll have all to yourselves. It's a clean and modern pine-paneled installation and there are bathrooms, showers and change rooms attached.

GETTING THERE & AWAY

From Zunil, which is 10km from Quetzaltenango, you can continue to Fuentes Georginas (8km), return to Quetzaltenango via the Cantel road (16km), or alternatively, take Hwy 9S down through ever lusher countryside to El Zarco junction on the Carretera al Pacífico. Buses depart Zunil for Xela from the main road beside the bridge.

Fuentes Georginas

The prettiest, most popular natural spa in Guatemala is **Fuentes Georginas** (admission US$2.50; ☯ 8am-5pm Mon-Sat, 8am-4pm Sun). Four pools of varying temperatures are fed by hot sulfur springs and framed by a steep, high wall of tropical vines, ferns and flowers. Fans of Fuentes Georginas were dismayed when a massive landslide in 1998 destroyed several structures, filled the primary bathing pool with trees, mud and rubble and crushed the angelic Greek goddess that previously gazed upon the pools. But after the site was successfully restored, spa regulars realized that the landslide had opened a new vent that feeds the pools. As a result, the water here is hotter than ever. Though the setting is intensely tropical, the mountain air currents keep it deliciously cool through the day. There is a little 500m walk starting from beside the pool and worth doing to check out the birds and orchids. Bring a bathing suit, which is required.

Besides the **restaurant** (meals US$6-8; ☯ 8am-6pm), which serves great *papas*, there are three sheltered picnic tables with cooking grills (you need to bring your own fuel). Big-time soak-

ers will want to spend the night: down the valley a few dozen meters are seven rustic but cozy **cottages** (s/d/tr/q US$12/16/20/24), each with a shower, a barbecue area and a fireplace to ward off the mountain chill at night (wood and matches are provided; US$3.25 for extra wood). Included in the price of the cottages is access to the pools all day and all night, when rules are relaxed.

Trails here lead to two nearby volcanoes: **Volcán Zunil** (15km, about three hours one way) and **Volcán Santo Tomás** (25km, about five hours one way). Guides are essential if you don't want to get lost; they are available for around US$14 for either trip. Ask at the restaurant.

GETTING THERE & AWAY

Take any bus to Zunil, where pickup trucks wait to give rides up the hill 8km to the springs, a half-hour away. Negotiate the price for the ride. It's very likely they'll tell you it's US$4.50 roundtrip, and when you arrive at the top, tell you it's US$4.50 each way – this is an annoying game the pickup drivers play. If there are many people in the group, they may charge US$1 per person. Unless you want to walk back down the hill, arrange a time for the pickup driver to return to pick you up. You can walk from Zunil to Fuentes Georginas in about two hours (it's 12km). If you're the mountain-goat type, you may enjoy this; it's a strenuous climb.

Hitchhiking is not good on the Fuentes Georginas access road, as there are few cars and they are often filled to capacity with large Guatemalan families. The best days to try for a ride are Saturday and Sunday, when the baths are busiest.

If you're driving, walking or hitching, go uphill from Zunil's plaza to the Cantel road (about 60m), turn right and go downhill 100m to a road on the left marked 'Turicentro Fuentes Georginas, 8km.' (This road is near the bus stop on the Quetzaltenango–Retalhuleu road – note that there are three different bus stops in Zunil.) This road heads up to Fuentes Georginas. You'll know you're approaching the baths when you smell the sulfur in the air.

Alternatively, make it all simple and take a shuttle or a tour from Quetzaltenango. Monte Verde Tours and Adrenalina Tours (see p169) in Quetzaltenango offer shuttle services directly here from Xela for US$5, including waiting time.

El Palmar Viejo

The turnoff to El Palmar Viejo is signposted immediately before the Puente Samala III bridge, about 30km down the Retalhuleu road from Xela. It's 4km west from the main road to the village itself – or rather the overgrown remnants of the village are, for El Palmar was destroyed by a mudslide and floods emanating from Santiaguito volcano at the time of Hurricane Mitch in the 1990s. Its inhabitants were resettled at a new village, El Palmar Nuevo, east of the main highway, but some still come here to tend plantations. A river has cut a deep ravine through the heart of the old village, slicing the **church** in two. A pair of **swing bridges** cross the ravine. Downstream, to the right of the river, you can see the top of the village cemetery **chapel** poking up through the trees – but beware, reaching the cemetery involves crossing an unstable bridge. Atop the hill behind the **cemetery** is a modern Mayan **altar**. Buses bound for Retalhuleu can drop you at the El Palmar Viejo turnoff, but it's probably best to come with a guide, as this is an isolated place. Adrenalina Tours (p169) is one agency that comes here.

Salcajá

Seven kilometers from Xela, this is an apparently unremarkable town that everyone passes through en route to all points north. However, behind all the traffic and dust lurk some special qualities to which Salcajá alone can lay claim.

Salcajá's **Iglesia de San Jacinto**, two blocks west on 3a Calle from the main road (3a Av, Zona 1), dates from 1524. It was the first Christian church in Central America. The facade retains some character, with carved lions and bunches of fruit, but the real treat (if you find the church open) is inside, where you'll find several original paintings and a pretty, ornate altar.

Salcajá is famed for its traditional *ikat*-style textiles, remarkable for the hand-tied and dyed threads that are laid out in the preferred pattern on a loom. Shops selling bolts of this fabric are ubiquitous in Salcajá, and you can usually visit their workshops before purchasing.

Salcajá is also known for its production of two alcoholic beverages that locals consider akin to magic elixirs. *Caldo de frutas* (literally, fruit soup) is like a high-octane sangria that will knock your socks off. It's made by combining *nances* (cherry-like fruits), apples, peaches, and pears and fermenting them for years. You can purchase fifths of it for around US$3 after viewing the production process. *Rompopo* is an entirely different type of potent potable, made from rum, egg yolks, sugar and spices. A sickly yellow *rompopo* costs around US$4 a fifth. Little liquor shops all over Salcajá peddle the stuff, but you may like to try the friendly **Rompopo Salcajá** (4a Calle 2-02), a block east of the main road along 4a Calle.

All buses headed north from Quetzaltenango pass through Salcajá, so it's easy to hop off here en route to other destinations.

San Andrés Xecul

A few kilometers past Salcajá and less than 1km before Cuatro Caminos, the road from Quetzaltenango passes the Morería crossroads, where the road to San Andrés Xecul branches off to the west. After about 3km on this uphill spur, you'll start seeing rainbow cascades of hand-dyed thread drying on the roofs and you'll know you have arrived in San Andrés Xecul. This small town is boxed in by fertile hills and boasts the most bizarre, stunning **church** imaginable. Technicolored saints, angels, flowers and climbing vines fight for space with whimsical tigers and frolicking monkeys on the shocking yellow facade. The red, blue and yellow cones on the bell tower are straight from the circus big top.

Sitting on the wall overlooking the entire Quetzaltenango valley and contemplating this wild combination of Catholic and Mayan iconography, it's hard to believe hallucinogenic substances didn't somehow figure in. Why and how this church came to resemble the inside of a lunatic's mind has been lost, though the church doors are inscribed 1917. Inside, a carpet of candles illuminate bleeding effigies of Christ. These are unabashedly raffish, with slabs of thick makeup trying to make him look alive and boyish. In one especially campy display, a supine Jesus is surrounded by gold and satin trimmings that hang thick inside his glass coffin. The pews are generally packed with praying indigenous women. The outside of the church was vibrantly refurbished in late 1999.

Continue walking up the hill and you'll come to a smaller (and decidedly more sedate) **yellow church**. Mayan ceremonies are still held here, and the panoramic view across the valley is phenomenal. The **annual festival** is November 29 and 30 – a good time to visit this town. There are no facilities; the easiest way to get here is by taking any northbound bus from Xela, alighting at the Esso station at the Morería crossroads and hailing a pickup or walking the 3km uphill. Buses returning to Xela line up at the edge of the plaza and make the trip until about 5pm.

Totonicapán
pop 94,700 / elev 2500m
San Miguel Totonicapán is a pretty Guatemalan highland town known for its artisans. Shoemakers, weavers, tinsmiths, potters and woodworkers all make and sell their goods here. Market days are Tuesday and Saturday; it's a locals' market, not a tourist affair, and it winds down by late morning.

The ride from Cuatro Caminos is along a pine-studded valley. From Totonicapán's bus station it's a 600m walk up 4a Calle to the twin main plazas. The lower plaza has a statue of Atanasio Tzul, leader of an indigenous rebellion that started here in 1820, while the upper one is home to the requisite large **colonial church** and a wonderful **municipal theater**, built in 1924 in neoclassical style and recently restored.

ACTIVITIES
The **Casa de la Cultura Totonicapense** (☎ 7766 1575; www.larutamayaonline.com/aventura.html; 8a Av 2-17), next door to Hospedaje San Miguel 1½ blocks off the lower plaza, has displays of indigenous culture and crafts and administers a fascinating 'Meet the Artisans' program to introduce tourists to some of the town's many artisans and local families. A one-day program, usually for a minimum of four people and requiring a week's advance booking, includes visits to various craft workshops (including potters, carvers of wooden masks and musical instruments, and weavers), a concert of traditional instruments and a traditional lunch in a private home. Prices range from US$49 per person for four people down to US$24 per person for 15 to 20 people. An alternative program, costing US$15/10/6 per person for two/six/10 people, takes you on foot to nearby villages to visit community development projects, natural medicine projects, schools, artisans workshops and Mayan sacred sites. All tours are in Spanish.

FESTIVALS & EVENTS
The festival of the **Apparition of the Archangel Michael** is on May 8, with fireworks and traditional dances. The **Feria Titular de San Miguel Arcángel** (Name-Day Festival of the Archangel Saint Michael) runs from September 24 to 30, peaking on September 29. Totonicapán keeps traditional masked dances very much alive with its **Festival Tradicional de Danza** – dates vary but recently it was over a weekend in late October.

SLEEPING & EATING
Casa de la Cultura clients can stay with local families for around US$18 per person including dinner and breakfast.

Hospedaje Paco Centro (☎ 7766 2810; 3a Calle 8-22, Zona 2; s/d US$5.50/11, with bathroom US$8/16) A clean, tidy place with big bare rooms, a couple of blocks from the lower plaza. Rooms with bathroom have TV. Front rooms get a bit of street noise.

Hotel Totonicapán (☎ 7766 4458; www.hoteltotonicapan.com; 8a Av 8-15, Zona 4; s/d with bathroom US$18/30) The fanciest digs in town are reasonable for the price, with big, modern rooms featuring carpeted floors, a few bits of furniture and some good views.

Restaurante Bonanza (4a Calle 8-16, Zona 2; meals US$4-6; ☺ breakfast, lunch & dinner) Totonicapán's most formal restaurant won't blow your mind, but it will fill your stomach. Mostly meat, with a few seafood and veggie options.

GETTING THERE & AWAY
Buses between Totonicapán and Quetzaltenango (passing through Cuatro Caminos) run frequently throughout the day. Signs in the bus window say 'Toto.' The ride from Cuatro Caminos is along a beautiful pine-studded valley. The last direct bus to Quetzaltenango (US$0.50, one hour) leaves Toto at 6:30pm.

San Francisco El Alto
pop 45,000 / elev 2630m
High on a hilltop overlooking Quetzaltenango (17km away) stands the town of San Francisco El Alto.

Banco Reformador (2a Calle 2-64; ☺ 8:30am-7pm Mon-Fri, 9am-1pm Sat) changes US dollars and traveler's checks and has a Visa ATM.

San Francisco's big party is the **Fiesta de San Franciosco de Asís**, celebrated around October 4 with traditional dances such as La Danza de Conquista and La Danza de los Monos.

This whole town is Guatemala's garment district: Every inch is jammed with vendors selling sweaters, socks, blankets, jeans, scarves and more. Bolts of cloth spill from storefronts packed to the ceiling with miles of material, and this is on the quiet days! On Friday, the real market action kicks in. The large plaza in front of the 18th-century church is covered in goods. Stalls are crowded into neighboring streets, and the press of traffic is so great that a special system of one-way roads is established to avoid colossal traffic jams. Vehicles entering the town on market day must pay a small fee, and any bus ride within town is laborious.

San Francisco's market is regarded as the biggest, most authentic market in the country, and it's not nearly as heavy with handicrafts as those in Chichicastenango and Antigua. As in any crowded market, beware of pickpockets and stay alert.

Around mid-morning, when the clouds roll away, panoramic views can be had from throughout town, but especially from the roof of the **church**. The caretaker will let you go up (on the way through, have a look at the church's six elaborate gilded altarpieces and remains of what must once have been very colorful frescoes).

Hotel Vista Hermosa (2a Calle & 3a Av; s/d with bathroom US$8/16) does indeed have beautiful views, out over the valley to the Santa María volcano. Rooms are spacious, with TV, balconies and (thankfully) hot showers.

For food, **El Manantial** (☎ 738 4373; 2a Calle 2-42; mains US$2.50-3), a couple of blocks below the plaza, is pleasant and clean, serving up steaks and a few *tipica* dishes.

GETTING THERE & AWAY

Buses to San Francisco leave Quetzaltenango (passing through Cuatro Caminos) frequently throughout the day. The trip takes about one hour and costs US$0.60. Because of San Francisco's one-way streets, arriving from Quetzaltenango you'll want to get off on 4a Av at the top of the hill (unless you like walking uphill) and walk towards the church. To go back to Cuatro Caminos, buses run downhill along 1a Av.

Momostenango
pop 28,000 / elev 2200m

Beyond San Francisco El Alto, 15km from Cuatro Caminos and 26km from Quetzaltenango, this town, set in a pretty mountain valley along a road through pine woods, is famous for the making of *chamarras,* or thick, heavy woolen blankets. The villagers also make ponchos and other woolen garments. The best days to look for these are Wednesday and Sunday, the main market day. A basic good blanket costs around US$13; it's perhaps twice as much for an extra-heavy 'matrimonial.'

Momostenango is noted for its adherence to the ancient Mayan calendar and for its observance of traditional rites. Hills in the town are the scene of ceremonies enacted on the important dates of the calendar. Visits on important celestial days – such as the summer solstice, the spring equinox, the start of the Mayan solar year (February 24), or Wajshakib Batz, the start of the 260-day *cholq'ij* or *tzolkin* year – can be particularly powerful and rewarding. But few Mayan ceremonies are open to outsiders, so don't assume showing up means you'll be able to participate. Should you be so fortunate as to observe a ceremony, be sure to treat altars and participants with the utmost respect.

Banrural (1a Calle, Zona 2; ☒ 9am-4pm Mon-Fri, 9am-1pm Sun), a block south of the plaza, changes US dollars and traveler's checks and has a Visa ATM.

The **Centro Cultural** (☒ 8am-6pm Mon-Fri, 8am-1pm, 2-5pm Sat), in the *municipalidad* building, is good for tourist information. It also has interesting local art exhibitions from time to time, so it's worth dropping in and checking it out.

SIGHTS & ACTIVITIES

Los Riscos, a set of strange geological formations on the edge of town, are worth the little walk it takes to see them. Technically eroded pumice, these bunches of tawny spires rising into the air look like something from Star Trek. To get there, head downhill on 3a Av, Zona 2, from beside Kikotemal shop, which is two blocks east along 1a Calle from Banrural. Turn right after 100m at the bottom of the hill, go left at a fork (signed 'A Los Riscos'), then after 100m turn right along 2a Calle and walk 300m to Los Riscos.

Takiliben May Wajshakib Batz (☎ 7736 5537; 3a Av 'A' 6-85, Zona 3) is at the southern entrance to town – turn up a signed path just north of the Texaco station to find it. Takiliben May, a 'Maya Mission,' is dedicated to studying and teaching Mayan culture and sacred traditions. Its director, Rigoberto Itzep Chanchavac, is a *chuchkajau* (Mayan priest) responsible for advising the community on when special days of the Mayan calendars fall. Rigoberto also does Mayan horoscopes (US$5) and leads day or half-day workshops where groups of around eight can gain an understanding of customs that usually remain hidden from outsiders. His **chuj** (traditional Mayan sauna; per person US$10; ☼ 3-6pm Tue & Thu) requires advance bookings. The Takiliben May can also provide tourist guides for US$10 an hour.

FESTIVALS & EVENTS

Picturesque *diablo* (devil) **dances** are held here in the plaza a few times a year, notably on Christmas Eve and New Year's Eve. The homemade devil costumes can get quite campy and elaborate: all have masks and cardboard wings, and some go the whole hog with fake fur suits and heavily sequined outfits. Dance groups gather in the plaza with a five- to 13-piece band, drinking alcoholic refreshments during the breaks. For entertainment, they are at their best around 3pm, but the festivities go on late into the night. The annual fair, **Octava de Santiago**, is celebrated from July 28 to August 2.

SLEEPING & EATING

Accommodations here are very basic.

Posada de Doña Pelagia (☎ 7736 5175; 2a Av 'A' 2-88, Zona 1; s/d US$2/3) Very basic, door-bumps-bed type rooms set around a courtyard. They're good enough for a night.

Hospedaje y Comedor Paclom (2a Av & 1a Calle, Zona 2; d US$7) This serviceable *hospedaje,* a block uphill from the first plaza, has rooms facing a courtyard crammed with plants and birds.

Restaurante La Cascada (1a Calle 1-35, Zona 2; meals US$3; ☼ breakfast, lunch & dinner) A bright and clean upstairs eatery serving up good-value set meals. The food is simple and filling and there are some good views of the church spires and surrounding hills.

GETTING THERE & AWAY

You can get buses to Momostenango from Quetzaltenango's Terminal Minerva (US$0.80, 1½ hours), from Cuatro Caminos (US0.50, one hour), or from San Francisco El Alto (US$0.40, 45 minutes). Buses run about every half-hour, with the last one back to Quetzaltenango normally leaving Momostenango at 4:30pm.

Laguna Chicabal

This magical, sublime lake is nestled in the crater of Volcán Chicabal (2712m) on the edge of a cloud forest. Laguna Chicabal is billed as the 'Center of Maya-Mam Cosmovision' on huge signs, both on the path leading out of town and at the crater itself. As such, it is a very sacred place and a hotbed of Mayan ceremonial activity. There are two active Mayan altars on its sandy shores, and Mayan priests and worshipers come from far and wide to perform ceremonies and make offerings here, especially on and around May 3. The lake is 575m wide and 331m deep.

Adding to the atmosphere of mystery, a veil of fog dances over the water, alternately revealing and hiding the lake's placid contours. Amid the thick, pretty vegetation are picnic tables and one of Guatemala's most inviting campsites, right on the lakeshore. Because the lake and grounds have great ceremonial significance, campers and hikers are asked to treat them with the utmost respect. In addition, Laguna Chicabal is pretty much off-limits to tourists during the entire first week of May, so that ceremonial traditions can be observed without interference.

Laguna Chicabal is a two-hour hike from San Martín Sacatepéquez (also known as San Martín Chile Verde), a friendly, interesting village about 22km from Xela. This place is notable for the elaborate traditional dress worn by the village men, who sport a white tunic with red pinstripes that hangs to mid-shin and has densely embroidered red, pink and orange sleeves. A thick, red sash serves as a belt. The tunic is worn over pants that nearly reach the ankles and are similarly embroidered.

To get to the lake, head down from the highway towards the purple-and-blue church and look for the Laguna Chicabal sign on your right (you can't miss it). Hike 5km (about 45 minutes) uphill through fields and past houses until you crest the hill. Continue hiking, going downhill for 2km (15 minutes) until you reach the rangers station, where you pay the US$2.50 entrance fee. From here, it's another 3km (about 30 minutes) uphill to a *mirador* and then a whopping 615 steep steps down to the edge of the lake. Start early for best visibility. Coming back up, allow two hours.

For bus information, see p173. For the return, there are fairly frequent minibuses from San Martín or you can hail a pickup. There are a few basic cookshacks on the square in San Martín, though you may prefer to hop off in San Juan Ostuncalco for a meal. In this

THE HIGHLANDS

interesting town, halfway between San Martín and Xela, the artisans are renowned for their wicker furniture and fine handcrafted instruments. San Juan's market day is Sunday. A taxi from Quetzaltenango to San Martín Sacatepéquez costs around US$16.

HUEHUETENANGO

pop 99,300 / elev 1902m

Mostly a stopping-off point for more interesting places, Huehuetenango, or Huehue (*way*-way), offers few charms of its own, but some people do love it for its true Guatemalan character. Either way, there are enough eating and sleeping options here to keep you happy, and the sight of the Cuchumatanes mountain range (highest in Central America) in the background makes for some striking scenery.

The lively *indígena* market is filled daily with traders who come down from surrounding villages. Surprisingly, the market area is about the only place you'll see traditional costumes in this town, as most of its citizens are ladinos wearing modern clothes. Coffee growing, mining, sheep raising, light manufacturing and agriculture are the region's main activities.

For travelers, Huehue is usually a leg on the journey to or from Mexico – the logical place to spend your first night in Guatemala. The town is also the perfect staging area for forays deeper into the Cuchumatanes or through the Highlands on back roads.

History

Huehuetenango was a Mam Maya region until the 15th century, when the K'iche', expanding from their capital K'umarcaaj, which is near present-day Santa Cruz del Quiché, pushed them out. Many Mam fled into neighboring Chiapas, Mexico, which still has a large Mam population near its border with Guatemala. In the late 15th century, the weakness of K'iche' rule brought about civil war, which engulfed the Highlands and provided a chance for Mam independence. The turmoil was still unresolved in 1525 when Gonzalo de Alvarado, the brother of Pedro, arrived to conquer Zaculeu, the Mam capital, for Spain.

Orientation & Information

The town center is 4km northeast of the Interamericana, and the bus station is off the road linking the two, about 2km from each. Almost every service of interest to tourists is in Zona 1 within a few blocks of the Parque Central.

Huehue has no official tourist office, but folks in the *municipalidad* can generally answer any queries you might have.

Banrural (cnr 6a Av & 3a Calle; ☽ 9am-7pm Mon-Fri, 9am-1pm Sat) and **Corpobanco** (cnr 6a Av & 3a Calle; ☽ 8:30am-7pm Mon-Fri, 8:30am-12:30pm Sat) both change US dollars and traveler's checks. There are Visa ATMs at Bancafé and Banco Industrial, a block further north.

The **post office** (2a Calle 3-54; ☽ 8:30am-5:30pm Mon-Fri, 9am-1pm Sat) is half a block east of the Parque.

Génesis Internet (2a Calle 6-37; ☽ 8:30am-1pm & 3-7pm Mon-Sat) and **Interhuehue** (3a Calle 6-65B; ☽ 9am-12:30pm & 2-6pm) charge US$0.60 per hour for internet access.

The **Mexican Consulate** (5a Av 4-11; ☽ 9am-noon, 3-5pm Mon-Fri) is in the same building as the Farmacia del Cid.

Sights & Activities

PARQUE CENTRAL

Huehuetenango's main plaza is shaded by old trees and surrounded by the town's imposing buildings: the *municipalidad* (with its band shell on the upper floor) and the huge colonial church. For a bird's-eye view of the situation, check out the little relief map of Huehuetenango department, which lists altitudes, language groups and populations of the various municipal divisions.

ZACULEU

With ravines on three sides, the late postclassic religious center Zaculeu ('White Earth' in the Mam language) occupies a strategic defensive location that served its Mam Maya inhabitants well. It finally failed, however, in 1525, when Gonzalo de Alvarado and his conquistadors laid siege to the site for two months. It was starvation that ultimately defeated the Mam.

The park-like **Zaculeu archaeological zone** (admission US$4.50; ☽ 8am-6pm), about 200m square, is 4km west of Huehuetenango's main plaza. Cold soft drinks and snacks are available. A small museum at the site holds, among other things, skulls and grave goods found in a tomb beneath Estructura 1, the tallest structure at the site.

Restoration by the United Fruit Company in the 1940s has left Zaculeu's pyramids, ball courts and ceremonial platforms covered by a thick coat of graying plaster. It's oddly stark and clean. Some of the restoration methods were not authentic to the buildings, but the

Book accommodation online at lonelyplanet.com

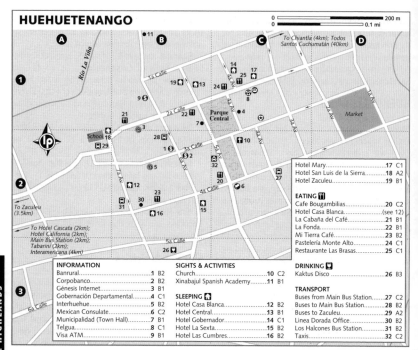

HUEHUETENANGO

Hotel Mary...**17** C1
Hotel San Luis de la Sierra..............**18** A2
Hotel Zaculeu...................................**19** B1

EATING
Cafe Bougambilias............................**20** C2
Hotel Casa Blanca.....................(see 12)
La Cabaña del Café..........................**21** B1
La Fonda...**22** B2
Mi Tierra Café...................................**23** B2
Pastelería Monte Alto.......................**24** C1
Restaurante Las Brasas......................**25** C1

DRINKING
Kaktus Disco.....................................**26** B3

TRANSPORT
Buses from Main Bus Station............**27** C2
Buses to Main Bus Station................**28** B2
Buses to Zaculeu..............................**29** A2
Linea Dorada Office..........................**30** B2
Los Halcones Bus Station..................**31** B1
Taxis..**32** C2

INFORMATION
Banrural..**1** B2
Corpobanco..**2** B2
Génesis Internet..................................**3** B1
Gobernación Departamental................**4** C1
Interhuehue..**5** B2
Mexican Consulate..............................**6** C2
Municipalidad (Town Hall)..................**7** B1
Telgua..**8** C1
Visa ATM..**9** B1

SIGHTS & ACTIVITIES
Church...**10** C2
Xinabajul Spanish Academy................**11** B1

SLEEPING
Hotel Casa Blanca.............................**12** B2
Hotel Central....................................**13** B1
Hotel Gobernador.............................**14** C1
Hotel La Sexta..................................**15** B2
Hotel Las Cumbres............................**16** B2

work goes further than others in making the
site look as it might have done to the Mam
priests and worshipers when it was still an
active religious center. What is missing, however, is the painted decoration, which must
have been applied to the wet plaster as in frescoes. The buildings show a great deal of Mexican influence and were probably designed and
built originally with little innovation.

Buses to Zaculeu (US$0.50, 20 minutes)
leave about every 30 minutes, 7am to 6pm,
from in front of the school at the corner of 2a
Calle and 7a Av. A taxi from the town center
costs US$8 one way (US$10 from the bus
station). One hour is plenty of time to look
round the site and museum.

Courses
Xinabajul Spanish Academy (☎ /fax 7764 1518; acade
miaxinabul@hotmail.com; 6a Av 0-69) offers one-to-
one Spanish courses and homestays with
local families.

Festivals & Events
Fiestas Julias This special event, held from July 13 to 20,
honors La Virgen del Carmen, Huehue's patron saint.

Fiestas de Concepción Honoring the Virgen de Concepción, this festival is celebrated on December 5 and 6.

Sleeping
BUDGET
Hotel Central (☎ 7764 1202; 5a Av 1-33; s/d US$4/8)
This rough-and-ready little number might be
to your liking. Rooms are simple, large and
plain. Bathrooms are downstairs. The pil-
lared wooden interior balcony gives the place
a sliver of charm and it sure is central.

Hotel Gobernador (☎ /fax 7764 1197; 4a Av 1-45;
s/d US$5/7, with bathroom US$7/10) A little maze of
rooms (don't get lost!), some much better
than others – check your bed for sponge
factor and your window for openability and
you should be happy.

Hotel Las Cumbres (☎ 7764 1189; 4a Calle 6-83; s/d
US$6/8, with bathroom US$8/12) You're definitely getting what you pay for here – concrete boxes
with a weird smell. Front rooms get plenty
of street noise.

Hotel La Sexta (☎ 7764 1488; 6a Av 4-29; s/d with
bathroom US$14/17; P) Judging by the parking-
garage exterior, this place doesn't look like
much, but it's one of the better deals in

town, even if the bathrooms do look like improvised afterthoughts.

Hotel Mary (☎ 7764 1618; 2a Calle 3-52; s/d with bathroom US$14/17) This is really the cutting edge of the budget hotel payoff – you can have clean, central, spacious or well equipped, but not all four. Grungy rooms and an odd smell are the only problems here.

MIDRANGE

Hotel Zaculeu (☎ 7764 1086; 5a Av 1-14; s/d US$28/32; **P**) Not a bad deal, and certainly a great location, the Zaculeu's big, clean rooms are gradually getting done up. The fresh paint-work and new beds are a welcome addition. Ground-floor rooms are darker and some are damp-affected, unfortunately including some of those around the plant-filled front patio, which is the prettiest area.

Hotel San Luis de la Sierra (☎ 7764 9216; hsan luis@intellnet.net.gt; 2a Calle 7-00; s/d US$30/40; **P**) Another good choice. The clean, medium-sized rooms have pine furniture, TV, hot-water bathroom and nice touches such as fan, reading lamp and shampoo. There's a restaurant here, too.

Hotel Casa Blanca (☎ 7769 0777; 7a Av 3-41; s/d US$32/38; **P**) The bright attractive courtyard here leads onto spacious modern rooms with pine ceilings and good hot showers. The restaurant out back serves up good-value set lunches (US$3)

There are plenty of hotels near the bus station: leave the east side of the station between the Díaz Álvarez and Transportes Fronterizos offices, and walk left up the street outside to come out on 3a Av, Zona 5. Within 300m or so in each direction here there's a total of at least seven hotels. Try **Hotel California** (☎ 7769 0500; 3a Av 4-25; s US$10, s/d with bathroom US$18/34) or **Hotel Cascata** (☎ 7764 1188; Lote 4 4-42; s/d US$10/18, with bathroom US$14/28).

Eating & Drinking

Pastelería Monte Alto (cnr 4a Av & 2a Calle; cakes & pastries US$0.50-0.80; ☒ 9am-9pm) For some fine pastry munching right on the plaza, check this place out, where your decision will probably be aided by the menus with food photos on them.

La Cabaña del Café (2a Calle 6-50; dishes US$2-3; ☒ 8am-9pm) Huehue's best coffee (and donuts, incidentally) can be found in this imitation log cabin a short walk from the plaza.

Hotel Casa Blanca (7a Av 3-41; set lunches US$2.50; ☒ breakfast, lunch & dinner) For lovely surroundings, you can't beat the two restaurants at this classy hotel, one indoors, the other in

---

LOCAL LORE: THE SACRED GRAIN

There was once a poor feather collector called Quiché Wanak, who fell in love with a beautiful weaver, Xajal mama'. Xajal's parents thought she was too good for him and opposed their marriage.

One night, Quiché, who could transform himself, turned into a bird and flew into Xajal's house so they could elope.

Xajal's parents hired a hunter to track the couple down. They ran for a long time, eventually coming to an old man's house, who was a friend of Quiché's.

Quiché asked him to hide Xajal in a cave on Mount Paxil. He said that after seven years they would reunite, and then he rose to the heavens and became the sun, as was his destiny.

The old man took Xajal to the cave where she stayed, eventually becoming corn, as was her destiny.

Years passed. There was not much food in the lands and people were starving. A mountain cat found Xajal's cave and began eating the corn.

People began to notice that the mountain cat was strong and well fed, and soon they followed him to see what he was eating. But the entrance to the cave was too narrow for people, so they asked the 13 lightning brothers to break the rock. The 12 oldest tried, but could not. The youngest tried and succeeded, but when he broke the rock, a fire started in the cave. Some of the corn was burnt, some singed and some remained white.

People rushed into the cave and took the corn to plant it. Some took the black corn, others the red and white.

Since then, Quiché Wanak, the sun, and Xajal mama', the corn, express their love every day, feeding the people.

the garden. Breakfasts cost US$3 to US$5 (on Sunday, from 8am to 11am, it's a big buffet for US$4), burgers and croissants are around US$3, and steaks (try filet mignon or cordon bleu) are around US$6.

Mi Tierra Café (4a Calle 6-46; mains US$3-5; ☯ breakfast, lunch & dinner; ☒) An informal café-restaurant serving good homemade soups and burgers. It also takes a good crack at some international dishes, muffins and a range of other goodies. Good, cheap and filling set lunches are available.

Café Bougambilias (5a Av north of 4a Calle; breakfast US$3; ☯ breakfast & lunch) One of three *comedores* in a line along the southern part of the Parque Centrale, the Bougambilias has a team of busy cooks preparing food on the ground floor, while the two upper floors have tables with views over the park and plenty of fresh air. It's good for all meals, with large serves of straightforward food.

La Fonda (2a Calle 5-35; mains US$3-5; ☯ breakfast, lunch & dinner) A few steps from the Parque Central, this clean, reliable place serves varied Guatemalan and international fare including good-value pizzas.

Restaurante Las Brasas (4a Av 1-36; mains US$5-8; ☯ breakfast, lunch & dinner) Half a block from the Parque Central, this is one of Huehue's best restaurants. With a good combination of steaks and Chinese on the menu, it should be pushing multiple buttons.

Kaktus Disco (6a Calle 6-38; ☯ 9pm-late Fri & Sat) There's not a whole lot going on in the center, nightlife-wise. This little disco is about your best bet after hours.

Getting There & Away

Linea Dorada has a central **office** (☎ 7764-1617; 4a Calle 6-62, Zona 1) inside the Hotel Imperial in the center of town.

The bus terminal is in Zona 4, 2km southwest of the plaza along 6a Calle. Buses serving this terminal include the following:

Antigua (230km) Take a Guatemala City bus and change at Chimaltenango.
Aguacatán (US$1, one hour, 22km, 12 daily, 6am to 7pm) Covered by the Mendoza and Rivas companies.
Barrillas (US$6, seven hours, 139km, 10 daily, 2am to 10pm) Run by Transportes Josué and Autobuses del Norte.
Cobán (142km) No direct service; take a minibus to Aguacatán, change there for Sacapulas, change there for Uspantán and then change there for Cobán. The road is paved up to Uspantán and the entire trip could be done in seven hours with good connections.

Cuatro Caminos (US$2, 1½ hours, 77km) Take any bus heading for Guatemala City or Quetzaltenango.
Gracias a Dios (US$4, 1½ hours) Four departures daily.
Guatemala City (Five hours, 266km) Los Halcones Pullman buses (US$8) leave at 4:30am, 7am and 2pm from their town-center terminal on 7a Av; Linea Dorada (US$10) buses leave from in front of the Hotel California opposite the terminal at 2:30pm and 11pm. From the main terminal, around 20 buses (US$4 to US$6) leave between 2am and 4pm by Transportes El Condor, Díaz Álvarez and Transportes Velásquez.
La Mesilla (Mexican border) (US$2, two hours, 84km) At least 20 buses depart from 5:45am to 6:30pm, by various companies.
Nebaj (68km) Take a bus to Sacapulas, or a bus to Aguacatán and a pickup on to Sacapulas, then another bus from Sacapulas to Nebaj.
Nentón (US$3, three hours, six daily, 3:30am to 1pm)
Panajachel (159km) Take a Guatemala City bus and change at Los Encuentros.
Quetzaltenango (US$2, two hours, 90km) At least 14 buses depart between 6am and 2:30pm, by various companies.
Sacapulas (US$2, 2½ hours, 42km) Buses at 11:30am (Rutas García) and 12:45pm (Transportes Rivas).
San Mateo Ixtatán (US$5, six hours, 111km) Take a Barillas bus.
Soloma (US$3, three hours, 70km) About 16 buses daily, from 2am to 10pm, by Transportes Josué and Autobuses del Norte.
Todos Santos Cuchumatán (US$3, three hours, 40km) Buses at approximately 3:45am, 5:30am, 11:30am, 12:45pm, 1:30pm, 1:45pm, 2pm, 2:45pm and 3:45pm by the Flor de María, Mendoza, Pérez, Todosanterita, Concepcionerita and Chicoyera companies; some buses do not run on Saturday.

Tabarini (☎ 7764 9356) has a car rental office in Sector Brasilia in the west of town.

Getting Around

For city buses from the bus station to the town center, leave the east side of the bus station through the gap between the Díaz Álvarez and Transportes Fronterizos offices. During hours of darkness until 11pm and after 2am, 'Centro' buses (US$0.40) go intermittently from the street outside; in daylight hours, cross this street and walk through the covered market opposite to a second street, where 'Centro' buses (US$0.20) depart every few minutes. To return to the bus station from the center, catch the buses outside Barbería Wilson (6a Av 2-22).

A taxi between the bus terminal and town center costs US$4, which is outrageous, but what are you gonna do?

AROUND HUEHUETENANGO

Except for Todos Santos Cuchumatán, the mountainous far northwest of Guatemala is little visited by travelers. The adventurous few will often be a novelty to the local Mayan folks they meet. Spanish skills, patience and tact will pave the way in these parts.

Chiantla

Just before the climb into the Cuchumatanes, this little village is about 5km out of Huehuetenango. Its church holds the Virgen del Rosario, a silver statue donated by the owner of a local silver mine. The virgin is believed to have mystical healing powers and people come from all over the country to seek her assistance. The main date for the pilgrimage is February 2, when the town packs out with supplicants and the infirm.

Also in the church are some interesting murals painted in the 1950s, showing local Maya having miraculous experiences while working in the silver mines. You can get here on any bus headed towards Todos Santos, Barillas or Salama.

El Mirador

Overlooking Huehuetenango, another 4km on from Chiantla, this is a lookout point up in the Cuchumatanes, 12km from town (one hour by bus). On a sunny day it offers a great view of the entire region and many volcanoes. A beautiful poem, *A Los Cuchumatanes,* is mounted on plaques here. Any bus from Huehue heading for Todos Santos, Soloma or Barillas comes past here.

Laguna Magdalena

This beautiful lagoon, 35km north of Huehuetenango, is nestled between two mountains. The scenery is dramatic – the mineral-rich waters are a deep shade of turquoise, and scattered around the lakeshore are massive boulders and ancient, gnarled trees.

It's nearly impossible to get here independently – the best you can do is get to the village of Paquix, 20km out of Huehue (regular buses depart from the terminal) and then hire a guide who can take you out on horseback (three to four hours) or foot (six to eight hours). Otherwise, **Unicornio Azul** (☎ /fax 5205 9328; www.unicornioazul.com) does horse rides out here, and Adrenalina Tours (p169) in Quetzaltenango can get you out here in a 4WD, weather and roads permitting.

Unicornio Azul

This Guatemalan- and French-run **horse riding ranch** (☎ /fax 5205 9328; www.unicornioazul.com) at Chancol, about 25km by road northeast of Huehuetenango, offers riding in the Cuchumatanes from one hour (US$15 per hour) to one/three/nine days (US$78/340/970). The nine-day trip crosses the mountains to the Ixil Triangle and back.

Todos Santos Cuchumatán

pop 3500 / elev 2450m

Way up in the Highlands, Todos Santos is as raw as Guatemalan village life gets – dramatic mountain scenery, mud streets, beans and tortillas and everything shut by 9pm. There are a couple of language schools operating here and this is the end point for the spectacular hike from Nebaj.

Todos Santos lies in the bottom of a deep valley, and the last 1¼ hours of the approach by bus are down a bone-shaking dirt road that leaves the paved Huehuetenango–Soloma road after a 1½-hour climb up from Huehue.

Traditional clothing is very much in use here and, unusually, it's the male costume that is the more eye-catching. Men wear red-and-white-striped trousers, small flat hats with blue ribbon around them, jackets with multicolored stripes and thick woven collars. Saturday is the main market day, and by the end of it the main street is half-full of inebriated *todosanteños* staggering they know not where. There's a smaller market on Wednesday.

Reasons to visit Todos Santos include good walking in the hills, learning Spanish (there are two schools) and getting to know a traditional and close-knit but friendly community. Todos Santos suffered terribly during Guatemala's civil war and is still very poor. To supplement their subsistence from agriculture, families from here still travel in the early part of the year to work for meager wages in very tough conditions on coffee, sugar and cotton plantations on the Pacific Slope. Working in the US is, however, proving a more lucrative alternative for some *todosanteños* today, as the amount of new construction in the valley demonstrates.

Todos Santos gained notoriety in 2000 when a Japanese tourist and his Guatemalan bus driver were murdered by a mob of villagers after the tourist attempted to take photos of a young village girl. By all accounts this was an isolated incident sparked by rumors that

THE HIGHLANDS

child-sacrificing Satanists were in the area at the time. But it's confirmation, if such were needed, that one should never photograph Maya people without permission

If you're coming to Todos Santos in the wet season (mid-May to November), bring warm clothes, as it's cold up here, especially at night.

ORIENTATION & INFORMATION

Todos Santos' main street is about 500m long. Towards its west end are the church and market on the north side, with the central plaza raised above street level on the south side. Buses stop at this west end of the street. A side street going uphill beside the plaza leads to most of the accommodations. No street names are in common use, but businesses and sights are either well signposted or known by everyone.

To make telephone calls look for signs saying 'Se alquila teléfono' or 'Llamadas Nacionales y Internacionales' in the area around the church.

Banrural On the central plaza; changes cash US dollars and traveler's checks.

Post office (8:30am-5pm Mon-Fri, 8am-noon Sat) On the central plaza.

Todos Santos Internet (per hr US$1.60; 9am-9pm) Located 30m off the main street, 400m back towards Huehue from the church.

SIGHTS & ACTIVITIES

A set of small ancient **ruins** is 500m up the uphill street beside the central plaza. Among trees on the left of the road, it consists of a few grassy mounds and two crosses with indications of contemporary Mayan offerings. Todos Santos' **Museo Cultural** (US$0.65 or larger donation) is in a two-story house, 125m down a dirt street off the main street. It comes to life when Fortunato, its creator and a community leader, is there to explain the assembled clothes, photos and antique artifacts.

Walking around Todos Santos provides superb opportunities to check out the rugged countryside. All the language schools offer guided walks – usually two or three mornings a week – which are free for students and usually US$1.30 for nonstudents. If you want to walk on your own, invest a few quetzals in the leaflets describing several of the best routes, with sketch maps, sold by Nuevo Amanecer language school. January to April are the best months for walking, with the best and warmest weather, but you can usually walk in the

morning, before the weather closes in, year-round (except maybe in July).

One of the most spectacular destinations is **La Torre** (3837m), the highest nonvolcanic point in Central America. Take a bus east up the valley to the hamlet of La Ventosa (US$0.60, 50 minutes) from where it's a trail walk of 8km (about 1¼ hours) through limestone and pines to the top. At the summit (marked by a radio mast), the southern horizon is dotted with almost a dozen volcanoes from Tacaná on the Mexican border to Volcán Agua near Antigua.

Las Letras, on a hillside above town, is a good morning walk (14km, about 1½ to two hours roundtrip). The 'Letters' spell out Todos Santos, but may be illegible; it depends on when the stones were last rearranged. Still, it's a hale hike and affords beautiful views, especially in the morning after the fog lifts. You can continue up beyond Las Letras to the villages of **Tuicoy** and **Tzichim** (30km, about five hours from Todos Santos). A bus leaves Tzichim for Todos Santos at noon on Thursday. From Tuicoy you can detour to the Puerta del Cielo, an outstanding lookout.

Other walk destinations include **Las Cuevas**, a sacred cave still used for Mayan rituals (this walk starts from 'La Maceta,' a tree growing out of rock, 30 minutes by bus up the Huehue road from Todos Santos), and the village of **San Juan Atitán**, over the mountains to the south of Todos Santos (32km, about five hours one way). From here you can continue on to Santiago Chimaltenango, 15km away (around 2½ hours), another small traditional village with cobbled streets where the women wear dazzling red *huipiles*.

Todos Santos' chilly climate makes it a great place to try the traditional **Mayan sauna** called a *chuj*. This is a small adobe building (traditionally with space for three small people) with wooden boards covering the entrance. A wood fire burns in a stone hearth inside, and water is sprinkled on the stones or heated in a ceramic jug to provide steam. Sometimes herbs are used to create aromatic vapors. A *chuj* can be claustrophobic, and the fire burning within the enclosed space is throat-tightening, so it's not an experience everyone will enjoy. Still, if you're into it, check out the large *chuj* at the Hotel Casa Familiar (opposite).

LANGUAGE COURSES

Todos Santos' two language schools are controlled by villagers and all make major contributions to community projects – funding a library, medicines, school materials, scholarships for village kids to go to high school in Huehue, and so on.

Academia Hispano Maya (www-personal.umich .edu/~kakenned/) Opposite Hotelito Todos Santos.

Nuevo Amanecer (escuela_linguistica@yahoo.com) Down the main street 150m, opposite the church.

The standard weekly price for 25 hours' one-on-one Spanish tuition, with lodging and meals in a village home, is US$115. Included are usually guided walks, movies, seminars on local life and issues, and saunas. The schools also offer classes in Mam and in Mayan weaving (weaving costs around US$1 an hour or US$35 for a week's course). Individual language classes are usually $4 an hour. The schools can put you in touch with volunteer work in reforestation and English teaching.

FESTIVALS & EVENTS
Todos Santos is famous for the annual **horse races** held on the morning of November 1 (El Día de Todos los Santos), which are the culmination of a week of festivities and an all-night male dancing and *aguardiente*-drinking spree on the eve of the races. Traditional foods are served throughout the day, and there are mask dances.

SLEEPING & EATING
You can arrange **rooms with families** (r per person US$2-2.50, with 3 meals US$4.50) through the language schools irrespective of whether you're studying. You'll get your own bedroom, and share the bathroom and meals with the family. A week's full board should cost US$25.

Hotel Casa Familiar (☎ 7783 0656; s/d US$4/8) The simple wooden rooms here are far from luxurious, but the place is run by a friendly family and there are plenty of extra blankets on hand. The rooms here are clean and have windows and fine views. The hotel also has a sauna and a restaurant where chicken dishes cost around US$3, and *mosh* (porridge), granola and banana costs US$2.

Hotel Mam (s/d US$8/12) Just downhill from the Hotelito Todos Santos, this is the newest hotel in town. They were still working on it at the time of research, but it looks like it will be one of the more comfortable options available once it opens.

Hotelito Todos Santos (☎ 7783 0603; s/d with bathroom US$8/12) Along a side street that goes off to the left a few meters up the hill beside the plaza, this has Todos Santos' most comfortable rooms – bare but clean, with tile floors and firm beds. Three of the four rooms with a private bathroom open onto the street, separate from the main part of the hotel upstairs. The hotel has a casual café, sinks for washing clothes, and hot water.

Comedor Martita (meals around US$2.25) This simple family-run *comedor*, opposite Hotel Mam, serves the best food in town, prepared with fresh ingredients by friendly hosts. You walk through the kitchen to get to the eating area, which has a nice view over the town and valley. A typical meal might be boiled chicken, rice, vegetables, beans, a *refresco* (soft drink or fruit juice) and coffee.

Restaurante Cuchumatlan (meals US$2-8) Todos Santos' most formal restaurant is nothing flash, but it takes a good stab at pizzas, stir fries and curries. It's also the only place in town you'd really want to have a beer, and there's a good selection of used books on sale.

ENTERTAINMENT
All the language schools show movies on Guatemalan, Mayan and Latin American themes in the evening, with a small admission charge (usually US$0.65) for nonstudents. The English-language documentaries *Todos Santos* and *Todos Santos: The Survivors*, made in the 1980s by Olivia Carrescia, are particularly fascinating to see here on the spot. They deal with the traditional life of Todos Santos and with the devastation and terror of the civil war, when by some accounts 2000 people were killed in the area.

GETTING THERE & AWAY
Buses and minibuses depart from the main street between the plaza and the church. Half a dozen buses leave for Huehuetenango (US$3, three hours) between 4:45am and 6:30am, then usually three others between noon and 1pm. Occasional minibuses leave throughout the day, whenever they fill up. Daily buses head northwest to Concepción Huista, San Antonio Huista and Jacaltenango. Times are erratic, but the 5am departure is fairly reliable.

Soloma
pop 12,700
This agricultural town, 70km north of Huehuetenango by paved road, is one of the biggest towns in the Cuchumatanes. The Maya

here speak Q'anjob'al, but most of the ladino cowboys will greet you in English! The town's prosperity and its residents' language skills can be attributed to the migratory laborers who annually make the arduous trip to the US, working as cowhands, auto detailers or landscapers. The populace is very gregarious here, and visitors will fast make friends. There's a Banrural on Soloma's plaza. For phone calls, use the international services at the Caucaso Hotel. Market day is Sunday.

The **cemetery** south of town is worth a look, as most of the colorful tombs are bigger than the average Guatemalan home. You can make good day trips to nearby villages such as **San Juan Ixcoy** (7km), where the women wear traditional white *huipiles* embroidered at the collar and hanging almost to their ankles.

A rough 10km track leads to the **Pepajaú waterfalls** from the village of San Lucas Quisil, just north of San Juan. Their 250m drop is an impressive sight, particularly after the rains. The walk itself is a delight, crossing swing bridges, with jaw-dropping scenery en route.

Closer to San Juan Ixcoy are the **Pajaj waterfalls**, a much more humble affair at 30m, but easier to get to, on a moderate 6km path. Along the way, you pass the Bacau Maya ceremonial center, where shamans gather every Thursday to perform rituals. Visitors are welcome, photography is not.

Attesting to the town's prosperity is a fine choice of accommodations. **Hotel Don Chico** (4a Calle 3-55; s/d with bathroom US$10/20), a pink-and-pastel palace, is the most comfortable option in town. Rooms are big and bare, with good firm beds and TV.

With its heavy wooden doors and black marble tiles, **Hotel Real del Valle** (☎ 7880 6412; cnr 5a Calle & 4a Av; s/d with bathroom US$8/16) pulls out a bit of class in this otherwise workaday town.

For a real cheapie, check into the basic rooms at **Hospedaje Katy** (r US$3). Rooms are arranged around a concrete courtyard and have shared bathroom. Lots of local cowboys hang out here.

A big, warm and sunny (when applicable) place right next to the park, **Comedor Chiantlequita** (mains US$2-4; ☯ breakfast, lunch & dinner) is the best and friendliest eating option in town.

See under Huehuetenango (p184) for details on buses to Soloma. Minivans serving San Juan Ixcoy and other nearby villages leave from beside the plaza.

Santa Eulalia
pop 6100

A surprisingly large village just over the hill from Soloma, Santa Eulalia is deeply traditional and can get very cold. This is sheep-farming territory, and you'll see shepherds wearing *capixays* (short woolen ponchos) in the fields. The town has a reputation for producing some of the finest marimbas in the country, and hormigo trees (from which the marimba is traditionally made) grow on the outskirts of town. Factories and workshops producing marimbas line the streets around the plaza. If you're interested in the production process, wander in and ask to be shown around – tourists are rare here and chances are you'll be treated well.

If you want to stay the night, Soloma is a much more comfortable option, but you could try the **Hotel Eulalense** (☎ 7765 9634; s/d US$4/8), which is just off the plaza and has a fine *comedor* attached.

A couple of buses per day make the run from Soloma to Santa Eulalia (US$0.30, 30 minutes) and minibuses leave from the plaza whenever full.

San Mateo Ixtatán
pop 16,850

From Santa Eulalia, the bad dirt road keeps climbing, through pasturelands and occasional pine forest – sit on the left and you can see all the way to Mexico – and after 30km reaches San Mateo Ixtatán, perched on a ridge overlooking the valley. The women of this small Chuj town wear perhaps the most colorful *huipiles* in all Guatemala – gorgeous red-dominated affairs with large concentric star patterns.

As in most of the Cuchumatanes, the mist can descend early here, wiping out visibility by early afternoon.

San Mateo is the logical place to break the journey if you're heading for Laguna Lachuá from Huehue – it's smaller but better looking than Barillas down the road, and there are a couple of interesting sights around town.

The church is worth a quick look in for its red-painted saints – the whole set-up being much more a homage to Mayan than Christian religion, as the smoking altar out in the courtyard attests.

Just to the east of town is a **salt mine** (admission free; ☯ 1-4pm) that was used by the Mam Maya, dating from the Classic period. The salt is disturbingly black in color, but is believed to have medicinal qualities.

Just below town, the unrestored ruins of **Wajxaklajunh** have excellent views out over the valley. It's a decent-sized site, featuring some stelae, a ball court and a few pyramid-shaped temples.

Hotel Ixtateco (☎ 7756 6586; s/d US$) above the police station is the best of the basic hotels in town and the showers are thankfully hot. Basic *comedores* around the plaza should keep you fed.

Buses leave regularly for Huehue (US$5, six hours) and Barillas (US$2, 45 minutes).

East to Playa Grande

Leaving San Mateo, the road drops and weather becomes slightly kinder. After 28km, you'll reach **Barillas**, an unremarkable coffee-growing town. If you're moving on (recommended), start organizing transportation immediately – at the time of writing, only one bus was leaving daily at 11am (US$6, five hours) for Playa Grande, but if you miss it, there are regular pickups and the occasional minibus. This section of the road is probably the worst, and bad weather can extend the travel time by two or three hours. Ask around to see what conditions are like before committing to this trip.

Nentón, Los Huistas & Gracias a Dios

In a lower-lying, more lushly vegetated zone between the Cuchumatanes and the Mexican border, Nentón and the Los Huistas area to its south suffered grievously during the civil war. Reconstruction is happening, including a paved road to Nentón from the Interamericana, and the area has a few archaeological remains and a distinctive culture including the Popti' (Jakalteko) Mayan language. North of Nentón it's possible to cross into Mexico (near the Lagos de Montebello) at remote Gracias a Dios, but there are no border facilities there and you would have to head to Mexican immigration at Comitán or San Cristóbal de Las Casas to get your passport stamped. There are places to stay in Gracias a Dios if you get stuck. For details on buses to Nentón and Gracias a Dios, see p184.

Huehuetenango to Cobán

This spectacular and often rugged cross-country route on mostly paved roads is an exciting way of getting into the center of the country from the northwest highlands. It can be done in a day, if you're in a hurry. You climb up out of Huehuetenango to **Aguacatán** (which has a bank and other services, including the Hospedaje Nuevo Amanecer, should you need them). Here you are treated to panoramic views of pine-studded slopes and the fertile valleys below. The trip continues via a snaking road down to Sacapulas (see p157) and climbs again to Uspantán (p157). At the time of writing, the paved road ended here, so there's six hours of dirt track ahead of you. Along the way you have the option of diverting to Nebaj (p158).

LA MESILLA

The Guatemalan and Mexican immigration posts at La Mesilla and Ciudad Cuauhtémoc are 4km apart, and you must take a collective taxi (US$0.50) between the two. This town gets chaotic on weekends – it's best to try to cross midweek. The strip in La Mesilla leading to the border post has a variety of services, including a police station, post office and a bank. There are also moneychangers who will do the deal – at a good rate if you're changing dollars, a terrible one for pesos or quetzals.

With an early start from Huehuetenango (or from Comitán or San Cristóbal de Las Casas in Mexico) you should have no trouble getting through this border and well on into Mexico (or Guatemala) in one day. During daylight hours fairly frequent buses and combis run from Ciudad Cuauhtémoc to Comitán (US$3 to US$4, 1¼ hours) and San Cristóbal (US$7, 2½ hours). From La Mesilla buses leave for Huehuetenango (US$1, two hours) at least 20 times between 5:45am and 6pm. If you get marooned in La Mesilla, try **Hotel Mily's** (d US$15), which has rooms with fan, cable TV and hot-water bathroom; bargaining may be in order here. Further down the hill is the super-basic **Hotel El Pobre Simón** (r per person US$2).

The Pacific Slope

Divided from the highlands by a chain of volcanoes, the flatlands that run down to the Pacific are known universally as La Costa. It's a sultry region – hot and wet or hot and dry, depending on the time of year – with rich volcanic soil good for growing coffee at higher elevations and palm oil seeds and sugarcane lower down.

Archaeologically, the big draws here are Abaj Takalik and the sculptures left by pre-Olmec civilizations around Santa Lucía Cotzumalguapa.

The culture is overwhelmingly ladino, and even the biggest towns are humble affairs, with low-rise wooden or concrete houses and the occasional palm thatched roof.

A fast highway, the Carretera al Pacífico (Hwy 2), roughly parallels the coast all the way from Ciudad Tecún Umán on the Mexican border to Ciudad Pedro de Alvarado on the El Salvador border. The 250km from Ciudad Tecún Umán to Guatemala City can be covered in five hours by bus – much less than the 345km of the Interamericana (Hwy 1) through the Highlands from La Mesilla.

Guatemalan beach tourism is seriously underdeveloped. Monterrico is the only real contender in this field, helped along by a nature reserve protecting mangroves and their inhabitants. Almost every town on the beach has places to stay, although more often than not they're very basic affairs. Sipacate gets the best waves and is slowly developing as a surf resort, although serious surfers find much more joy in Mexico or El Salvador.

THE PACIFIC SLOPE

TOP FIVE

- Getting away from absolutely everything at the one-hotel town of **Tilapita** (opposite)

- Investigating the bridge in history between the Olmec and the Maya while strolling through the grassy **Parque Arqueológico Abaj Takalik** (p197)

- Spotting wildlife among the mangrove-lined canal and lagoons of the **Biotopo Monterrico-Hawaii** (p206)

- Checking out the big mysterious heads carved by the non-Mayan Pipil culture at **Santa Lucía Cotzumalguapa** (p199)

- Getting wet at **Parque Acuático Xocomil** (p197) and dizzy at **Parque de Diversiones Xetulul** (p197), two fun parks near Retalhuleu.

History

Despite it being one of the first settled areas in Guatemala, relatively little is known about the Pacific region's early history. Many archaeological sites are presumed overgrown by jungle; others have been destroyed to make way for agriculture.

What *is* known is that the Olmecs were among the first to arrive, followed by the Ocós and Iztapa, whose cultures appear to have flourished around 1500 BC.

Although these cultures were much more humble than those of their northerly counterparts, they developed a level of sophistication in stone carving and ceramics. It's also thought that the coastal region acted as a conduit, passing cultural advances (like the formation of writing and the Mayan calendar) from north to south.

Between AD 400 and 900, the Pipil moved in, most likely displaced by the turmoil in the Mexican Highlands, and began farming cacao, which they used to make a (rather bitter) chocolate drink. They also used cacao beans as currency.

Towards the end of the postclassic period, the K'iche', Kaqchiquel and Tz'utujil tribes began moving in as population expansion in Guatemala's highlands had made food scarce and land squabbles common.

Pedro de Alvarado, the first Spaniard to land in Guatemala, arrived here in 1524, pausing briefly to fight the K'iche' as a sort of forerunner to a much larger battle around present-day Quetzaltenango. Franciscan missionaries were dispatched to the region and began a lengthy, largely unsuccessful attempt to convert the locals.

Further agricultural projects (mostly indigo and cacao) were started around this time, but it wasn't until independence that the region became one of the country's main agricultural suppliers, with plantations of coffee, bananas, rubber and sugarcane.

In the languid tropical climate here, not much changes, particularly the social structure. The distribution of land – a few large landholders and many poorly paid, landless farmer workers – can be traced back to these early post-independence days. You'll see the outcome as you travel around the region – large mansions and opulent gated communities alongside squalid, makeshift workers' huts.

CIUDAD TECÚN UMÁN

This is the preferable and busier of the two Pacific Slope border crossings, having better transport connections with other places in Guatemala. A bridge links Ciudad Tecún Umán with Ciudad Hidalgo (Mexico). The border is open 24 hours daily, and several basic hotels and restaurants are available, but you should aim to be clear of the border well before dark. The town has all the trademarks of the seedy border town. Banks here change US dollars and traveler's checks.

From Ciudad Tecún Umán frequent buses depart until about 6pm along the Carretera al Pacífico to Coatepeque, Retalhuleu, Mazatenango, Escuintla and Guatemala City. There are direct buses to Quetzaltenango (US$3.50, 3½ hours) up until about 2pm. If you don't find a bus to your destination, take one to Coatepeque or, better, Retalhuleu, and change buses there. On the Mexican side, buses run from Ciudad Hidalgo to the city of Tapachula (US$1.50, 45 minutes) every 20 minutes from 7am to 7:30pm.

EL CARMEN

A bridge across the Río Suchiate connects El Carmen with Talismán (Mexico). The border is open 24 hours daily. It's generally easier and more convenient to cross at Tecún Umán. There are few services at El Carmen, and those are very basic. Most buses between here and the rest of Guatemala go via Ciudad Tecún Umán, 39km south, and then along the Carretera al Pacífico through Coatepeque, Retalhuleu and Escuintla. On the way to Ciudad Tecún Umán, most stop at Malacatán on the road to San Marcos and Quetzaltenango, so you could try looking for a bus to Quetzaltenango there, but it's more dependable to change at Coatepeque (US$2.50, two hours from El Carmen) or Retalhuleu.

On the Mexican side, minibuses run frequently between Talismán and Tapachula (US$1.20, 30 minutes) until about 10pm.

TILAPITA

Just south of the Mexican border, this little fishing village is the place to come for some seriously laid-back beach time. There's exactly one hotel here (and it's a good one) and it's a world away from the often hectic, scruffy feel of other towns along the coast.

The village, which sits on a sandbar cut off from the mainland by the Ocós estuary,

THE PACIFIC SLOPE

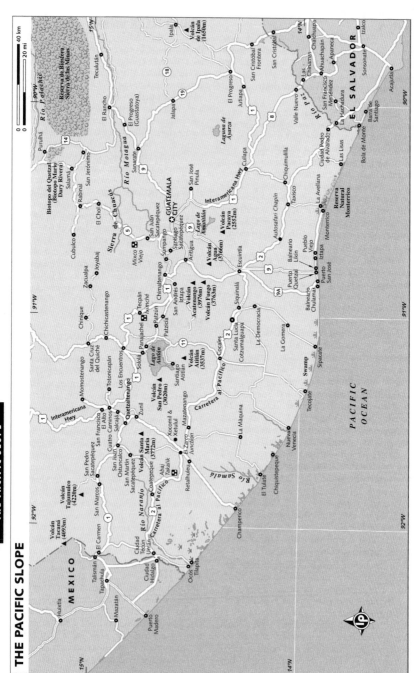

LOCAL VOICES: JUAN HERNÁNDEZ, RETURNED UNDOCUMENTED IMMIGRANT

Every year, thousands of Guatemalans make the long, dangerous journey as illegal immigrants to the United States. Juan Hernández* has done it three times. We spoke to him about his experiences.

When was the first time you went to the States?

It was about 20 years ago. It was easier then, but still hard. It took me 18 days to get there. I got caught by immigration in the States and deported to Mexico, so I crossed again and made it through.

What was the journey like?

It was tough. We were sleeping under bridges, walking at night. We went every which way – by bus, train, in cars and taxi. We did a lot of walking. We got robbed and ripped off, beaten by police and immigration. I turned 30 in the desert and ate half an orange for my birthday.

At the border it was crazy. There were 20 immigration vans waiting on the other side, with spotlights and hundreds of us waiting till nightfall. There were women selling food and drinks and clothes. Once night fell, every half-hour a group would make a run for it.

When I got caught and sent back to Mexico I had nothing. I was starving and exhausted. I went to the church but the priest kicked me out. I had no option but to keep going north.

How was life in the States?

I was really lucky. I met some good people straight away. They gave me somewhere to stay and helped me find a job. I was one of the lucky ones. I scrubbed pots in a Chinese restaurant, earning US$3.50 an hour. After seven months I saved $2000. I missed my wife and kids, so I came back to Guatemala, bought some land and built a house. A year later I went back.

Was it hard to fit in there?

You know, LA is a lot like here. You don't have to speak English to survive. Latinos there – we lived like backpackers, always doing things the cheapest, everybody sleeping in the same room.

*Not his real name

---

is only reachable by boat from the town of Tilapa. There's some excellent swimming to be had here, although as with all the beaches along this coast, the undertow can be quite serious and there are no lifeguards. If you're not a strong swimmer, don't go too far out.

There's not a whole lot to do (which is kind of the point), but local fishermen offer fascinating boat tours of the estuary, mangroves and adjoining **Reserva Natural El Manchón** for US$13 per boat per hour. There are no guarantees, but local wildlife includes iguanas, crocodiles, white herons, egrets and kingfishers.

Back in Tilapita, the **Tortugario Tilapita**, across the path from Hotel El Pacífico, is fighting an uphill battle to preserve the local sea turtle population, and would be quite happy for whatever help they can get if you're looking for some volunteer work.

One of the best accommodation deals along the coast, **Hotel El Pacífico** (☎ 5914 1524; www.playatilapa.com; r with bathroom US$8; 🏊) is nothing fancy, but it has decent-sized, clean concrete rooms. Delicious meals (US$4) are served in an oversized thatched-roof *palapa*

(thatched palm-leaf shelters), and generally consist of the catch of the day – shrimp, fish and *caldo de mariscos* are always a good bet. The good-sized swimming pool is a welcome addition as things can get slightly warm here.

Coming from the Mexican border, your best bet is to get off the bus at the turnoff and wait for a Tilapa-bound bus there. Direct buses run from Coatepeque to Tilapa (US$1.50, 1½ hours). Once you get to Tilapa, turn left down the side street and follow it to the end, where you will find *lanchas* (small boats) waiting. The 10-minute ride to Tilapita costs US$0.80 per person in a shared *lancha*, or you can hire a private one to make the trip for US$4. Tell the *lanchero* you are going to *el hotel* (although he will probably know that already). If you get stuck, there are cheap, not so lovely hotels in Tilapa.

Pullman drivers doing the Guatemala City–Tecún Umán run often stop in at Tilapa. If you're headed straight for the capital or anywhere in between, ask around to find out when the next departure is.

COATEPEQUE

pop 48,700

Set on a hill and surrounded by lush coffee plantations, Coatepeque is a brash, fairly ugly and chaotic commercial center, noisy and humid at all times. If you read the papers, the name Coatepeque should be familiar. A major stopover on the Columbia–Mexico drugs 'n' guns route, this town probably has more gang-related activity than any other outside of Guatemala City. Barely a day goes by without somebody getting shot in a turf war or revenge killing. Tourists are never the target, and rarely get caught in the crossfire (although one foreign volunteer did quite literally in 2006).

It *is* another facet of Guatemala, and probably not one you want to get too acquainted with. If you're here to see the ruins at Abaj Takalik, Retalhuleu is a much better bet. If you really want to stay here or (more likely) get stuck, there are a couple of places in the relatively quiet town center that will put you up admirably.

Maya Expeditions (see p81) runs rafting expeditions on the nearby Río Naranjo for US$85 per person per day.

Hotel Baechli (☎ 7775 1483; 6a Calle 5-45, Zona 1; s/d with bathroom US$11/15; **P**) has cool, simple rooms with fan. **Hotel Villa Real** (☎ 7775 1308; 6a Calle 6-57, Zona 1; s/d with bathroom US$15/20; **P**) is slightly more elaborate, but the payoff is in the smaller rooms. Both are a block or so uphill from the main park.

Good restaurants (mostly in the steakhouse and/or Chinese vein) are scattered around the park.

Coatepeque is a major transport hub for the Pacific slope and bus connections here are good. The bus terminal blends into the market, and has departures to El Carmen (US$2.50, two hours), Tecún Umán (US$2.50, two hours), Quetzaltenango(US$3, 2 ½ hours, Tilapa (US$2, 1½ hours) and Retalhuleu (US$2, one hour), among others. Several Pullman bus companies stop here on the Guatemala City–Tecún Umán run, providing much more comfort and possibly a welcome spot of air-conditioning in the tropical heat. They stop on the street one block east of the bus terminal and charge US$7 for the four-hour run to Guatemala City.

WELCOME HOME, GANGSTER

Talk to anyone about crime in Guatemala and the conversation will eventually turn to gangs. Gang membership and activity has skyrocketed over the last decade, despite the *'mano dura'* (iron fist) policies of successive governments.

It's got so that every year the *Prensa Libre* publishes a map of Guatemala City, showing where the respective gang territories are. There are neighborhoods where the police will not enter.

The end of the civil war played a big part in the formulation of the gangs – there were plenty of guns lying around, going cheap, and plenty more orphans and disaffected youth looking for a sense of belonging.

The two biggest gangs here are the Mara 18 and the Salvatruchas. No doubt you will see their graffiti around the place. The gangs' main activities are drugs, guns, kidnapping and extortion. Tourists are very small fry for these guys and you'd have to be very unlucky to ever bump into them.

One of the main reasons cited for the increase in gang membership is the Illegal Immigration Reform and Immigrant Responsibility Act, a US law passed in 1996 that gives wide scope to immigration officials to deport criminals – both undocumented and legally registered – who are convicted of gang-related activities.

Exacerbating the problem is a lack of information-sharing between governments, meaning that Guatemalan authorities are not told why somebody has been deported and cannot therefore keep an eye on gang members when they return to Guatemala.

It's a situation that Guatemalans view with mixed feelings – on the one hand, they'd like to deport the gangbangers, too. On the other, they see the States as a training ground for gangsters, where not enough is being done to eradicate the gang problem in Latino neighborhoods.

They feel their kids go to the States, get involved in gangs there, learn the tricks of the trade and then come back, all schooled up and ready to join the local chapter of the gang they belonged to up north.

RETALHULEU

pop 42,000 / elev 240m

Arriving at the bus station in Retalhuleu, or Reu (*ray*-oo) as it's known to most Guatemalans, you're pretty much guaranteed to be underwhelmed. The neighborhood's a tawdry affair, packed out with dilapidated wooden cantinas and street vendors.

The town center, just five blocks away, is like another world – a majestic, palm-filled plaza, surrounded by some fine old buildings. Even the city police get in on the act, hanging plants outside their headquarters.

On the outskirts are the homes of wealthy plantation owners, impressive weekend getaways and the gated communities that are springing up all over the country.

The real reason most people visit is for access to Abaj Tahalik, but if you're up for some serious downtime, a couple of world-class fun parks are just down the road (see p197).

Tourists are something of a curiosity in Reu and are treated well. The heat is fairly stifling, and if you can splurge for digs with a pool, you'll be happy for it; at the very least, make sure your room has a fan.

Orientation & Information

The town center is 4km southwest of the Carretera al Pacífico, along Calzada Las Palmas, a grand boulevard lined with towering palms. The bus terminal is on 10a Calle between 7a and 8a Avs, northeast of the plaza. To find the plaza, look for the twin church towers and walk toward them.

There is no official tourist office, but people in the Municipalidad (Town Hall), on 6a Av facing the east side of the church, will do their best to help.

Banco Industrial (cnr 6a Calle & 5a Av; ☺ 9am-7pm Mon-Fri, 10am-2pm Sat) and **Banco Occidente** (cnr 6a Calle & 6a Av) change US dollars and traveler's checks and give cash advances on Visa cards. Banco Industrial has a Visa ATM. **Banco Agromercantil** (5a Av), facing the plaza, changes US dollars and traveler's checks and has a MasterCard ATM.

Internet (cnr 5a Calle & 6a Av; per hr US$0.80) provides internet access.

Sights & Activities

The **Museo de Arqueología y Etnología** (6a Av 5-68; admission US$1.30; ☺ 8am-5:30pm Tue-Sat) is a small

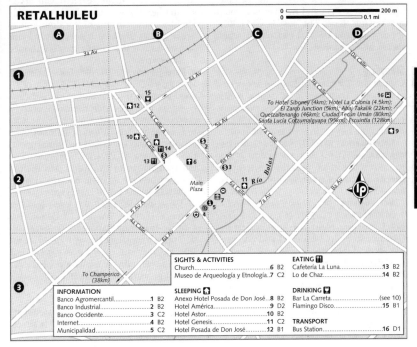

RETALHULEU

To Hotel Siboney (4km); Hotel La Colonia (4.5km); El Zarco Junction (5km); Abaj Takalik (22km); Quetzaltenango (46km); Ciudad Tecún Umán (80km); Santa Lucia Cotzumalguapa (95km); Escuintla (128km)

To Champerico (38km)

Main Plaza

INFORMATION
Banco Agromercantil...................**1** B2
Banco Industrial.........................**2** B2
Banco Occidente........................**3** C2
Internet....................................**4** B2
Municipalidad............................**5** C2

SIGHTS & ACTIVITIES
Church......................................**6** B2
Museo de Arqueología y Etnología...**7** C2

SLEEPING 🛏
Anexo Hotel Posada de Don José...**8** B2
Hotel América............................**9** D2
Hotel Astor...............................**10** B2
Hotel Genesis...........................**11** C2
Hotel Posada de Don José..........**12** B1

EATING 🍴
Cafetería La Luna......................**13** B2
Lo de Chaz...............................**14** B2

DRINKING 🍸
Bar La Carreta.....................(see 10)
Flamingo Disco.........................**15** B1

TRANSPORT
Bus Station..............................**16** D1

THE PACIFIC SLOPE

LOCAL LORE: THE STONE MERMAID

Alba Lucretia lived in Retalhuleu, back when it was just a small town. She was young and charming and much sought after by local gentlemen, but she was bored of small-town life.

One day Gunther, a German archaeologist, arrived to study the local area. Little by little they got to know each other. He was captivated by her simple charms and she thought he was handsome, and her ticket out of Retalhuleu.

Semana Santa was approaching. One of Alba's neighbors said that after the festivities, Gunther would return to the capital to marry his fiancé.

Alba was stunned. She began making a fine dress to wear on Good Friday, to capture Gunther's heart forever.

The day before Good Friday, Alba was bathing in the patio when her mother came home.

'Good thing that you're bathing today,' her mother said. 'You know it's a sin to bathe on Good Friday.'

'What do I care?' said Alba. 'Tomorrow I'll bathe as well, to smell sweet for Gunther.'

'Don't you dare!' cried her mother. 'You know you'll turn to stone.'

Early the next morning, Alba's parents heard somebody bathing in the patio. Scared, they ran outside. There was their beautiful daughter, turned into a stone mermaid.

The neighbors took her and put her in a fountain in the plaza, as a lesson to future generations to respect the holy days.

---

museum of archaeological relics. Upstairs are historical photos and a mural showing locations of 33 archaeological sites in Retalhuleu department.

You can **swim** at the Siboney and La Colonia hotels (see right and right) even if you're not staying there. The cost is US$1.30 at the Siboney and US$2 at La Colonia, where there's also a poolside bar.

Sleeping

Out on the Carretera al Pacífico are several other hotels. These tend to be 'tropical motels' by design, with bungalows, pools and restaurants. They are convenient if you have a car or can get a bus to drop you on the spot.

Hotel América (☎ 7771 1154; 8a Av 9-32, Zona 1; s/d with bathroom US$11/15) A trusty budget option just down the street from the bus terminal, the América has spotless rooms with fan and TV.

Hotel Genesis (☎ 7771 2855; 6a Calle 6-27, Zona 1; s/d with bathroom US$15/28; ✖) A good-value hotel sporting plenty of homely features (but not so many windows) and an excellent, central location.

our pick **Hotel Posada Don José** (☎ 7771 0180; posadadonjose@hotmail.com; 5a Calle 3-67, Zona 1; s/d with bathroom US$20/26; ✖ ✉ P) A beautiful colonial-style hotel built around a huge swimming pool. Swan dives from the top balcony are tempting, but probably unwise. Rooms are spacious and comfortable, if a bit dated.

Hotel Astor (☎ 7771 2559; hotelastor@terra.com.gt; 5a Calle 4-60, Zona 1; s/d with bathroom US$23/36; ✖ ✉) While the shady courtyard/pool area is by far the best thing about this place (drop in for a drink, even if you aren't staying here), the rooms are good enough. Slightly cramped, but nicely done out in ochre paints and dark woods. Cocktails can be had in the hotel's air-conditioned Bar La Carreta.

Hotel Siboney (☎ 7771 0149; Cuatro Caminos, San Sebastián; s/d US$27/34; P ✖ ☐ ✉) There's a good blend of tropical and modern themes going on here. Poolside rooms fill quickly, especially on weekends, so you might want to book ahead. You'll find it 4km northeast of town where Calzada Las Palmas meets the Carretera al Pacífico. Coming from Quetzaltenango or the south, ask the bus to drop you here to avoid backtracking.

Hotel La Colonia (☎ 7771 6482; Carretera al Pacífico Km 178; s/d US$40/50; P ✖ ✉) A few hundred meters east of the Siboney, La Colonia has a fairly luxurious layout. The sweet little duplex bungalows seem trapped in the '70s, but they still offer a pretty good deal. The big swimming pool with poolside bar doesn't go astray in this heat.

Eating & Drinking

Reu seems to be slightly obsessed with pizza – 5a Av north of the plaza is almost wall-to-wall pizzerias.

Cafetería La Luna (5a Calle 4-97; lunch incl drink US$2.90, dinner US$3.50; ⏰ breakfast, lunch & dinner) Opposite the west corner of the plaza, this is a town favorite for simple but filling meals in a low-key environment.

Lo de Chaz (5a Calle 4-65; mains US$3-4; ⏰ breakfast, lunch & dinner) A simple place, right off the plaza, serving up good breakfasts, icy beer, soups, snacks and seafood.

Bar La Carreta (5a Calle 4-50) For cocktails, check out this bar, next to the Hotel Astor.

Flamingo Disco (4a Av & 5a Calle A; ⏰ Wed-Sat 10pm-1am) Reu's biggest disco really gets going on Fridays, but Saturdays are a good bet, too.

Getting There & Away

Most buses traveling along the Carretera al Pacífico detour into Reu. Departures include the following:

Champerico (US$0.60, one hour, 38km, buses every few minutes, 6am to 7pm)

Ciudad Tecún Umán (US$2, 1½ hours, 78km, every 20 minutes, from 5am to10pm)

Guatemala City (US$6, three hours, 196km, every 15 minutes, from 2am to 8:30pm)

Quetzaltenango (US$1.50, one hour, 46km, buses every 30 minutes, from 4am to 6pm)

Santa Lucía Cotzumalguapa (US$2.50, two hours, 97km) Some Escuintla- or Guatemala City–bound buses might drop you at Santa Lucía; otherwise get a bus to Mazatenango ('Mazate') and change there.

Local buses go to El Asintal (for Abaj Takalik).

AROUND RETALHULEU
Parque Acuático Xocomil & Parque de Diversiones Xetulul

If you have children along, or simply if the heat is getting to you, head out to the **Parque Acuático Xocomil** (☎ 7772 9400; www.irtra.org.gt; Carretera CITO Km 180.5; adult/child US$10/7; ⏰ 9am-5pm Thu-Sun), a gigantic water park in the Disneyland vein, but with a distinct Guatemalan theme. Among the 10 water slides, two swimming pools and two wave pools are re-creations of Mayan monuments from Tikal, Copán and Quiriguá. Visitors can bob along a river through canyons flanked with ancient temples and Mayan masks spewing water from the nose and mouth. Three real volcanoes – Santiaguito, Zunil and Santa María – can be seen from the grounds. Xocomil is very well executed and maintained, and kids love it. Xocomil is at San Martín Zapotitlán on the Quetzaltenango road, about 12km north of Reu.

Next door to Xocomil on the same road is the even more impressive **Parque de Diversiones Xetulul** (☎ 7722 9450; www.irtra.org.gt; Carretera CITO Km 180.5; adult/child US$26/13; ⏰ 10am-6pm Thu-Sun). It's a theme park with representations of a Tikal pyramid, historical Guatemalan buildings and famous buildings from many European cities, plus restaurants and many first-class rides. You need an extra US$6.50 ticket for the rides.

These two attractions are both run by Irtra, the Instituto de Recreación de los Trabajadores de la Empresa Privada de Guatemala (Guatemalan Private Enterprise Workers' Recreation Institute), which administers several fun sites around the country for workers and their families. Between them, Xocomil and Xetulul comprise the most popular tourist attraction in Guatemala, with over a million visitors a year.

Any bus heading from Retalhuleu toward Quetzaltenango will drop you at Xocomil or Xetulul.

Parque Arqueológico Abaj Takalik

About 30km west of Retalhuleu is the **Parque Arqueológico Abaj Takalik** (admission US$4; ⏰ 7am-5pm), a fascinating archaeological site set on land now occupied by coffee, rubber and sugarcane plantations. Abaj Takalik was an important trading center in the late Preclassic era, before AD 250, and forms a historical link between Mesoamerica's first civilization, the Olmecs, and the Maya. The Olmecs flourished from about 1200 to 600 BC on Mexico's southern Gulf coast, but their influence extended far and wide, and numerous Olmec-style sculptures have been found at Abaj Takalik.

The entire 6.5 sq km site spreads over nine natural terraces, which were adapted by its ancient inhabitants. Archaeological work is continuing outside the kernel of the site, which is the Grupo Central on terrace No 2, where the most important ceremonial and civic buildings were located. Classic-era stream baths and multicolored floors were discovered here in late 2005. The largest and tallest building is Estructura 5, a pyramid 16m high and 115m square on terrace No 3, above No 2. This may have formed one side of a ball court. Estructura 7, east of Estructura 5, is thought to have been an observatory. What's most impressive as you move around the park-like grounds, with its temple mounds, ball courts and flights of steps paved with rounded river stones, is the quantity of stone sculpture dotted about, including numerous representations of animals and aquatic creatures (some in a curious pot-bellied style known as *barrigón*), miniature versions of the characteristic Olmec colossal heads, and early Mayan-style monuments depicting finely adorned personages carrying out religious ceremonies.

Abaj Takalik, which had strong connections with the city of Kaminaljuyú (in present-day Guatemala City), was sacked about AD 300 and its great monuments, especially those in Mayan style, were decapitated. Some monuments were rebuilt after AD 600 and the site retained a ceremonial and religious importance for the Maya, which it maintains to this day. Maya from the Guatemalan highlands regularly come here to perform ceremonies.

To reach Abaj Takalik by public transportation, catch a bus from Retalhuleu to El Asintal (US$0.25, 30 minutes), which is 12km northwest of Reu and 5km north of the Carretera al Pacífico. The buses leave from a bus station on 5a Av A, 800m southwest of Reu plaza, about every half-hour, 6am to 6pm. Pickups at El Asintal provide transportation on to Abaj Takalik, 4km further by paved road. You'll be shown round by a volunteer guide, whom you will probably want to tip. You can also visit Abaj Takalik on tours from Quetzaltenango (see p169).

Nueva Alianza

This fair-trade **coffee farm** (☎ 5047 2238, Quetzaltenango 5819 2282; www.comunidadnuevaalianza.org; dm/s/d US$7/10/20) was taken over by its ex-employees when the owner went bankrupt and ran off with their back wages. They now offer a range of tours around the farm and local countryside as well as workshops detailing the community's fascinating history and present. Set on a hillside overlooking the coast, the farm has gorgeous views, and the hike to the nearby waterfall comes with some very welcome swimming at the end of it. The easiest way to get here is by contacting the office in Quetzaltenango and coming when a Spanish school comes on tour (most weekends). Otherwise it's easy enough from Retalhuleu. Buses leave at midday (but get there early) from the main terminal – look for the one that says 'Hochen' – it's about a one-hour ride out to the farm.

CHAMPERICO
pop 7900
Built as a shipping point for coffee during the boom of the late 19th century, Champerico, 38km southwest of Retalhuleu, is a tawdry, sweltering, dilapidated place that sees few tourists. Nevertheless, it's one of the easiest ocean beaches to reach on a day trip from Quetzaltenango, and beach-starved students still try their luck here. Beware of strong waves and an undertow if you go in the ocean, and stay in the main, central part of the beach: if you stray too far in either direction you put yourself at risk from impoverished, potentially desperate shack dwellers who live towards the ends of the beach. Tourists have been victims of violent armed robberies here. Most beachgoers come only to spend the day, but there are several cheap hotels and restaurants. **Hotel Neptuno** (☎ 7773 7206; s/d US$6/8), on the beachfront, is the best bet. The last bus back to Retalhuleu leaves at about 6:30pm.

MAZATENANGO
pop 46,800 / elev 370m
Mazatenango, 23km east of Retalhuleu, is the capital of the Suchitepéquez department . It's a center for the farmers, traders and shippers of the Pacific Slope's agricultural produce. There are a few serviceable hotels if you need to stop in an emergency. Otherwise just keep on keeping on.

TULATE
Another beach town that's yet to make it onto travelers' radar is Tulate. The great thing about this beach is that, unlike others along the coast, the water gets deep very gradually, making it a great place to swim and just hang around and have some fun. The waves rarely get big enough to surf, but bodysurfers should be able to get a ride any time of the year. To get to the beach you have to catch a boat (US$0.50) across the estuary. Once on the other side, the water's 500m in front of you, straight down the only paved street.

There are two hotels in Tulate worth mentioning. Both have restaurants, but the best, most atmospheric dining is at the little shacks right on the beach front where good fresh seafood meals start at around US$4.

Villa Victoria (☎ 5704 6825; r US$17, with bathroom & air-con US$33; ☒ ☒), on the main street, halfway between the boat landing and the beach, is a

---

EXPLORE MORE OF THE PACIFIC COAST

The coast is, logically, all about the beach. The two most popular beach spots for travelers happen to be the ones closest to Quetzaltenango and Antigua – Champerico and Monterrico respectively, and they suffer for their popularity, both with foreign and Guatemalan tourists.

There are, however, plenty of little beach towns that are worth considering, where quite often you'll have the place to yourself:

- Tilapita – literally a one-hotel village, this is a great place to get away from it all and take a couple of mangrove tours while you're at it (p191).
- Tulate – the coastline's gentle slope into the ocean makes this one of Guatemala's best swimming beaches (opposite).
- Sipacate – Guatemala's surf capital goes off year round, especially between December and April (p203).
- Chicago – a mellow little beach town with an excellent community project that's always looking for volunteers.

---

reasonable deal. Rooms are fresh and simple, with two double beds. It also doubles as a Turicentro, meaning that local kids come and use the pool (which has an awesome waterslide, by the way) and they crank up the music ridiculously early on weekends.

Playa Paraíso (☎ 5985 0300; bungalows US$47; 🖭), by far the more refined of the two, is about 1km down the beach to the left. The extremely comfortable bungalows here have two double beds, a sitting room and laid-back little balconies out front. There are hammocks strung around the property and a good, if somewhat pricey, restaurant serves meals any time. Things can get a little hectic on weekends, but midweek you may just have the place to yourself.

Buses run direct to Tulate from Mazatenango (US$1.80, two hours) along a good, newly paved road. Coming from the west, it's tempting to get off at Cuyotenango and wait for a bus there to avoid backtracking. The only problem with this is that buses tend to leave Mazatenango when full, so you might miss out on a seat.

CHIQUISTEPEQUE

On a virtually untouched stretch of beach, this little fishing village is home to the **Hamaca y Pescado Project** (☎ 7858 2700; www.hamacaypescadoesp .blogspot.com; s/d US$15/30), a grass-roots education and environmental awareness project. You can come to volunteer in one of the many programs they have running, or you can just hang out on the beach. Accommodation is in comfortable rustic beachside cabanas, and

rates include three meals daily. If you're coming from Tulate, get off at La Máquina and change buses there. Otherwise, it's best to get to Mazatenango for one of the two daily buses (10:30am and 1:30pm) to Chiquistepeque (three hours, US$1.50).

SANTA LUCÍA COTZUMALGUAPA
pop 26,500 / elev 356m

Another 71km eastward from Mazatenango is Santa Lucía Cotzumalguapa, an important stop for anyone interested in archaeology. In the fields and *fincas* (plantations) near the town stand great stone heads carved with grotesque faces and fine relief scenes, the product of the enigmatic Pipil culture that flourished here from about AD 500 to 700. In your explorations you get to see a Guatemalan sugarcane *finca* in full operation.

The town, though benign enough, is unexciting. The local people around here are descended from the Pipil, an ancient culture that had linguistic and cultural links with the Nahuatl-speaking peoples of central Mexico. In early Classic times, the Pipil who lived here grew cacao, the money of the age. They were obsessed with the ball game and with the rites and mysteries of death. Pipil art, unlike the flowery, almost romantic style of the Maya, is cold, grotesque and severe, but still very finely done. When these 'Mexicans' settled in this pocket of Guatemala, and where they came from, is not known, though connections with Mexico's Gulf Coast area, whose culture was also obsessed with the ball game, have been suggested.

THE PACIFIC SLOPE

Orientation & Information

Santa Lucía is now bypassed to the south by Hwy 2, but the original highway running through the south of town is still known as the Carretera al Pacífico, and the best places to stay are on and just off it. The main plaza is 400m north from the highway, along 3a or 4a Avs.

There are three main sites to visit, all outside town: El Baúl hilltop site, about 4.5km north; the museum at Finca El Baúl, 2.75km further north; and the Museo Cultura Cotzumalguapa, off the highway 2km northeast of town.

Taxi drivers in Santa Lucía's main square will take you round all three sites for about US$25 without too much haggling. In this hot and muggy climate, riding at least part of the way is the least you can do to help yourself.

Banco Industrial (cnr 4a Av & 4a Calle), a block north of the plaza, changes US-dollar cash and traveler's checks and has a Visa ATM.

El Baúl Hilltop Site

This site has the additional fascination of being an active place of pagan worship for local people. Mayan people regularly, and especially on weekends, make offerings, light fires and candles and sacrifice chickens here. They will not mind if you visit as well, and may be happy to pose with the idols for photographs in exchange for a small contribution.

Of the two stones here, the great, grotesque, half-buried head is the most striking, with its elaborate headdress, beaklike nose and 'blind' eyes with big bags underneath. The head is stained with wax from candles, splashes of liquor and other drinks, and with the smoke and ashes of incense fires, all part of worship. People have been coming here to pay homage for more than 1400 years.

The other stone is a relief carving of a figure with an elaborate headdress, possibly a fire god, surrounded by circular motifs that may be date glyphs.

To get there you leave town northward on the road passing El Calvario church. From the intersection just past the church, go 2.7km to a fork in the road just beyond a bridge; the fork is marked by a sign saying 'Los Tarros.' Buses heading out to Finca El Baúl, the plantation headquarters, pass this sign. Take the right-hand fork, passing a settlement called Colonia Maya on your right. After you have gone 1.5km from the Los Tarros sign, a dirt track crosses the road: turn right here, between two concrete posts. Ahead now is a low mound topped by three large trees: this is the hilltop site. After about 250m, fork right between two more identical concrete posts, and follow this track round in front of the mound to its end after some 150m, and take the path up on to the mound, which is actually a great ruined temple platform that has not been restored.

THE PACIFIC SLOPE

A CHICKEN BUS IS HATCHED

If you rode the bus to school 10 years ago or more in the US, you might just end up meeting an old friend in Guatemala, resurrected and given new life as a chicken bus. Love 'em or hate 'em, chicken buses (*camionetas* or *parrillas* to Guatemalans) are a fact of life in traveling around Guatemala. A lot of times there is no alternative.

As you can probably tell by the signs that sometimes remain in these buses ('anyone breaking the rules will lose their bus riding privileges'), these buses really did used to carry school kids. In the US, once school buses reach the ripe old age of 10 years, or they do 150,000 miles, they're auctioned off. This is just the first step in the long process to hitting the Guatemalan road. They then get towed through the States and Mexico, taken to a workshop here where they are refitted (bigger engine, six-speed gearbox, roof rack, destination board, luggage rack, longer seats) and fancied up with a paint job, CD player and chrome detailing.

Drivers then add their individual touches – anything from religious paraphernalia to stuffed toys and Christmas lights dangling around the dashboard area.

Thus, the chicken bus is ready to roll, and roll they do. The average bus works 14 hours a day, seven days a week – more miles in one day than it covered in a week back on the school run.

If you've got a choice of buses to go with, looks *are* important – chances are that if the paint is fresh and the chrome gleaming, the owner also has the cash to spend on new brakes and regular maintenance. And, with a conservative estimate of an average of one chicken-bus accident per week in Guatemala, this is something you may want to keep in mind.

Museo El Baúl

About 2.75km on foot, or 5km by vehicle, from the hilltop site is **Museo El Baúl** (admission free; 8am-4pm Mon-Fri, 8am-noon Sat). It comprises a very fine open-air collection of Pipil stone sculpture collected from around Finca El Baúl's sugarcane fields. A large stone jaguar faces you at the entrance. Other figures include four humans or monkeys with arms folded across their chests, a grinning, blank-eyed head reminiscent of the one at the hill-top site, carvings of skulls, and at the back a stela showing a personage wearing an animal headdress, standing over a similarly attired figure on the ground: seemingly winner and loser of a ball game. Unfortunately, nothing is labeled.

To get there, if driving, return to the fork with the Los Tarros sign. Take the other fork this time (what would be the left fork as you come from Santa Lucía), and follow the paved road 3km to the headquarters of the Finca El Baúl sugarcane plantation. Buses trundle along this road every few hours, shuttling workers between the refinery and the town center. (If you're on foot, you can walk from the hilltop site back to the crossroads with the paved road. Cross the road and continue along the dirt track. This will eventually bring you to the asphalt road that leads to the *finca* headquarters. When you reach the road, turn right.)

Approaching the *finca* headquarters (6km from Santa Lucía's main square), you cross a bridge at a curve. Continue uphill and you will see the entrance on the left, marked by a guard post and a sign 'Ingenio El Baúl Bienvenidos.' Tell the guards that you would like to visit the *museo*, and you should be admitted. Pass the sugar refinery buildings to arrive at the museum on the right.

Museo Cultura Cotzumalguapa

At the headquarters of another sugarcane plantation, Finca Las Ilusiones, is **Museo Cultura Cotzumalguapa** (admission US$1.30; 8am-4pm Mon-Fri, 8am-noon Sat). The collection here, of sculptures found around Las Ilusiones' lands, has some explanatory material and you'll probably be shown around by the caretaker. It includes a reconstruction of a sacrificial altar with the original stones, and photos of some fine stelae that were removed to the Dahlem Museum in Berlin in 1880. The most impressive exhibit, Monumento 21, is actually a glass-fiber copy

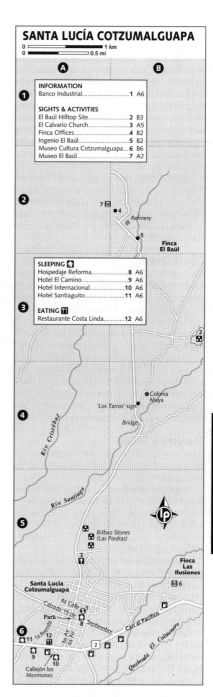

SANTA LUCÍA COTZUMALGUAPA

INFORMATION	
Banco Industrial	1 A6

SIGHTS & ACTIVITIES	
El Baúl Hilltop Site	2 B3
El Calvario Church	3 A5
Finca Offices	4 B2
Ingenio El Baúl	5 B2
Museo Cultura Cotzumalguapa	6 B6
Museo El Baúl	7 A2

SLEEPING	
Hospedaje Reforma	8 A6
Hotel El Camino	9 A6
Hotel Internacional	10 A6
Hotel Santiaguito	11 A6

EATING	
Restaurante Costa Linda	12 A6

THE PACIFIC SLOPE

of a stone that still stands in the fields of Finca Bilbao (part of Las Ilusiones' plantations), depicting what may be a shaman holding a sort of puppet on the left, a ball-game player in the middle with a knife in one hand, and a king or priest on the right holding what may be a heart. Another copy of this stone, along with one of Monumento 19, lie on the ground across the street from the museum. Along the road just before the bridge to the *finca* house are copies of some of the sculptures from the El Baúl museum.

About 1.5km east of the town center on Carretera al Pacífico (Hwy 2), shortly before an Esso station on the left (not to be confused with other Esso stations on the right), take a side track 400m to the left (north) to find the museum.

Bilbao Stones

Monumento 21, whose copy is in the Museo Cultura Cotzumalguapa, still stands with three other fine sculpted stones dotted about the Finca Bilbao cane fields to the northeast of El Calvario church, on the north edge of Santa Lucía town. In the past, tourists have regularly visited these stones, often guided through the tall cane to Las Piedras (the Bilbao Stones) by local boys. Unfortunately, locals say it is now dangerous for tourists to go into these fields because of recent assaults. So unless you receive convincing information to the contrary, we don't recommend it.

Sleeping & Eating

The best hotels around are out on the entrance to town. You're not missing much by being out here.

Hospedaje Reforma (4a Av 4-71; s/d US$4/7) This hotel has exactly three things going for it: it's cheap, central and the patio is decorated with stuffed boars' heads. And if you like sleeping in dark and airless little concrete cells, make that four.

Hotel Internacional (☎ 7882 5504; Callejón los Mormones; s/d US$10/12.50; P ☒) Down a short lane (signposted) off Carretera al Pacífico is the best budget hotel in town. It has clean, good-sized rooms with a fan, cold showers and a TV. Air conditioning costs US$10 extra.

Hotel El Camino (☎ 7882 5316; Carretera al Pacífico Km 90.5; s/d with fan US$14/18; P ☒) About 200m east along the highway from the Santiaguito, Hotel El Camino's rooms are almost ridiculously large, with a few sticks of furniture

like clothes racks and writing tables. You could organize a game of five a side with the rest of the floor space, but don't tell management it was our idea.

Hotel Santiaguito (☎ 7882 5435; Carretera al Pacífico Km 90.4; s/d US$50/60; P ☒ ☒) On the highway on the west edge of town, the Santiaguito is fairly lavish for Guatemala's Pacific Slope, with spacious tree-shaded grounds and a nice swimming pool (open to nonguests for US$2.50). The large rooms have huge, firm beds and are set around a jungly patio/parking area. The spacious restaurant is cooled by ceiling fans and serves up slightly overpriced meals and good cheeseburgers (US$4).

Restaurante Costa Linda (Carretera al Pacífico; ☒ lunch & dinner) On the highway about 150m east of Hotel el Camino, this friendly and clean place serves tasty meat and seafood at reasonable prices.

The Hotel Santiaguito has a good **restaurant** (mains US$10-12) and a swimming pool that nonguests can use for US$2.50 per day.

Getting There & Away

As Hwy 2 now bypasses Santa Lucía, a lot of buses along it do not come into town. Coming to Santa Lucía from the east, you will almost certainly need to change buses at Escuintla (US$0.80, 30 minutes). From the west you will probably have to change at Mazatenango (US$1.50, 1¼ hours). At Cocales, 23km west of Santa Lucía, a road down from Lago de Atitlán meets Hwy 2, providing a route to or from the Highlands. Eight buses daily run from Cocales to Panajachel (US$2, 2½ hours, 70km, between about 6am and 2pm).

LA DEMOCRACIA

pop 5800 / elev 165m

La Democracia, a nondescript Pacific Slope town 10km south of Siquinalá, is hot day and night, rainy season and dry season. During the late Preclassic period (300 BC to AD 250), this area, like Abaj Takalik to the northwest, was home to a culture showing influence from southern Mexico.

Sights

Facing the plaza, along with the church and the modest Palacio Municipal, is the small, modern **Museo Regional de Arqueología** (admission US$3; ☒ 9am-4pm Tue-Sat), which houses some fascinating archaeological finds. The star of the show is an exquisite jade mask. Smaller figures, yokes used in the ball game, relief carvings and other objects make up the rest of this small but important collection.

At the archaeological site called Monte Alto, on the outskirts of La Democracia, huge basalt heads and pot-bellied sculptures have been discovered. These heads resemble crude versions of the colossal heads that were carved by the Olmecs on Mexico's southern gulf coast some centuries previously.

Today, these great **Olmecoid heads** are arranged around La Democracia's main plaza. As you come into town from the highway, follow signs to the Museo.

Sleeping & Eating

Guest House Paxil de Cayala (☎ 7880 3129; s/d with bathroom US$7/10) Half a block from the plaza, La Democracia's only place to stay is OK for the night, with big, mosquito-proofed rooms.

Burger Chops (mains US$3-5; ☻ breakfast, lunch & dinner) Also just off the square, this is as close as the town gets to a restaurant.

The flour tortillas stuffed with meat from the little roadside stands around the plaza are delicious, and a bargain at US$2.50.

Getting There & Away

The Chatía Gomerana company runs buses every half-hour, 6am to 4:30pm, from Guatemala City's Terminal de Autobuses to La Democracia (US$2.50, two hours) via Escuintla. From Santa Lucía Cotzumalguapa, catch a bus 8km east to Siquinalá (8km) and change there.

SIPACATE

An hour and a half down the road from Santa Lucía is Guatemala's surf capital. Waves here average 6ft, the best time being between December and April. The town is separated from the beach by the Canal de Chiquimulilla. Oddly unexploited, the beach here has only a couple of hotels, the most accessible being **Rancho Carillo** (☎ 5517 1069; www.marmaya.com; cabins from US$40; ☒), a short boat ride (US$2.80 return) from town. The only trouble you'll have sleeping is from the noise of crashing waves. Call ahead and you'll probably be able to get a better price. Surfboards are available for rent here. There are a couple of cheaper, basic *hospedajes* (budget hotels; single/double US$4/7) in town, but remember you'll be paying for the boat ride every day. Buses from Guatemala City (US$4,

3½ hours) pass through La Democracia en route to Sipacate every two hours.

ESCUINTLA

pop 116,100

Surrounded by rich green foliage, Escuintla should be a tropical idyll where people swing languidly in hammocks and concoct pungent meals of readily available exotic fruits and vegetables. In fact, it's a hot, shabby commercial and industrial city that's integral to the Pacific Slope's economy but not at all important to travelers, except for making bus connections.

Banco Reformador (cnr 4a Av & 12a Calle; ☻ 9am-6pm Mon-Fri, 9am-1pm Sat), two blocks north of the bus station, changes US-dollar cash and traveler's checks and has a Visa ATM. Escuintla has some marginal hotels and restaurants. If stranded, try the **Hotel Costa Sur** (☎ 5295 9528; 12a Calle 4-13; s/d with private bathroom US$12/16; ☒), a couple of doors from Banco Reformador, which has decent, cool rooms with TV and fan. Air-con costs an extra US$3.

All buses from the terminal pass along 1a Av, but if you really want to get a seat, head to the main bus station in the southern part of town, just off 4a Av. The station entrance is marked by a Scott 77 fuel station. Buses depart for Antigua (US$1.20, one hour) about every half-hour, from 5:30am to 4:30pm. Buses going to Guatemala City (US$2.30, 1½ hours) go about every 20 minutes from the street outside, from 5am to 6pm. Buses to Puerto San José (US$1, 45 minutes), some continuing to Iztapa, have similar frequency. Buses coming along the Carretera al Pacífico may drop you in the north of town, necessitating a sweaty walk through the hectic town center if you want to get to the main station.

AUTOSAFARI CHAPÍN

About 25km southeast of Escuintla, **Autosafari Chapín** (☎ 2363 1105; Carretera al Pacífico Km 87.5; admission adult/child US$6/4.50; ☻ 9:30am-5pm Tue-Sun) is a drive-through safari park and animal conservation project earning high marks for its sensitivity and success breeding animals in captivity. Species native to Guatemala here include white-tailed deer, tapir and macaws. Around the grounds also roam non-native species such as lions, rhinos and leopards. There is a restaurant and pool, and it makes a good day if you're traveling with kids. It's more fun if you have your own vehicle, but if not, a 20-minute cruise through the park in a minibus is included in the admission price. **Delta y Tropical** (cnr 1a Calle & 2a Av, Zona 4, Guatemala City) runs buses here from the capital (US$2, 1½ hours), every 30 minutes, from 6am to 6:30pm, via Escuintla.

PUERTO SAN JOSÉ & LIKÍN

Guatemala's most important seaside resort leaves a lot to be desired. But if you're eager to get into the Pacific surf, head 50km south from Escuintla to Puerto San José and neighboring settlements.

Puerto San José (population 14,000) was Guatemala's most important Pacific port in the latter half of the 19th century and well into the 20th. Now superseded by the more modern Puerto Quetzal to the east, Puerto San José languishes and slumbers, except at weekends and holidays when thousands of Guatemalans pour into town. The beach, inconveniently located across the Canal de Chiquimulilla, is reached by boat.

It's smarter to head west along the coast 5km (by taxi or car) to Balneario Chulamar, which has a nicer beach and also a suitable hotel or two.

About 5km east of Puerto San José, just past Puerto Quetzal, is Balneario Likín, Guatemala's only upmarket Pacific resort. Likín is much beloved by well-to-do families from Guatemala City who have seaside houses on the tidy streets and canals of this planned development.

IZTAPA

About 12km east of Puerto San José is Iztapa, Guatemala's first Pacific port, used by none other than Pedro de Alvarado in the 16th century. When Puerto San José was built in 1853, Iztapa's reign as the port of the capital city came to an end, and it relaxed into a tropical torpor from which it has yet to emerge.

Iztapa has gained renown as one of the world's premier **deep-sea fishing** spots. World records have been set here, and enthusiasts can fish for marlin, sharks and yellowfin tuna, among others. November through June is typically the best time to angle for sailfish. **B&B Worldwide Fishing Adventures** (☎ in the US 888 479 2277; www.wheretofish.com; 14161/2 E 10th Pl, Dalles, OR 97058) and **Fishing International** (☎ in the US 800 950 4242; www.fishinginternational.com; 184 S Fourth St, Santa Rosa, CA 95404) run all-inclusive deep-sea fishing tours to Iztapa from the USA. It is also possible to

contract local boat owners for fishing trips, though equipment and comfort may be nonexistent and catch-and-release could prove a foreign concept. The boat owners hang out at the edge of the Río María Linda – bargain hard. Yellowfin tuna will likely be out of reach for the local boats, as these fish inhabit the waters some 17km from Iztapa.

There's not much to do in Iztapa. The best thing to do is get a boat across the river to the sandbar fronting the ocean, where the waves pound and a line of palm-thatch restaurants offer food and beer.

Sleeping

Rancho Maracaibo (s/d US$7/14) On the beach, Maracaibo offers probably the worst accommodation deal in Guatemala, with very basic *cabañas*, sporting a bed with reed mat instead of a mattress.

Sol y Playa Tropical (☎ 7881 4365/6; 1a Calle 5-48; s/d with bathroom US$10/20; ☒) Should you want to stay, the Tropical has tolerable rooms with fan and a bathroom, on two floors around a swimming pool that monopolizes the central patio.

Getting There & Away

The bonus about Iztapa is that you can catch a bus from Guatemala City all the way here (US$3, three hours). They leave about every half-hour, from 5am to 6pm, traveling via Escuintla and Puerto San José. The last bus heading back from Iztapa goes around 5pm.

You can reach Monterrico by paved road from Iztapa: follow the street 1km east from Club Cervecero bar, where the buses terminate, and get a boat across the river to Pueblo Viejo (US$0.80 per person in passenger *lanchas;* US$4 per vehicle, including passengers, on the vehicle ferry). From the far side buses leave for the pretty ride to Monterrico (US$1.50, one hour) at 8am, 11:30am, 2pm, 4pm and 6pm.

MONTERRICO

The coastal area around Monterrico is a totally different Guatemala. Life here is steeped with a sultry, tropical flavor – it's a place where hanging out in a hammock is both a major endeavor and goal. Among the main cash crops here is *pachete* (loofah), which get as big as a man's leg. In season, you see them everywhere growing on trellises and drying in the sun. The architecture, too, is different,

---

THE ONE THAT DIDN'T GET AWAY

Somewhere between 5 and 40 miles off the coast of Iztapa, chances are that right now a sport fisher is hauling in a billfish. This area is recognized as one of the world's top sport fishing locations – the coastline here forms an enormous, natural eddy and scientists who have studied the area have concluded this might be the largest breeding ground for Pacific sailfish in the world.

Catches of 15 to 20 billfish per day are average throughout the year. During high season (October to May) this number regularly goes over 40.

Guatemala preserves its billfish population by enforcing a catch-and-release code on all billfish caught. Other species, such as dorado and tuna, are open game, and if you snag one, its next stop could well be your frying pan.

If you'd like to get lessons, or you're looking for an all-inclusive accommodations-and-fishing package, check www.greatsailfishing.com.

Fish here run in seasons. There's fishing all year round, but these are the best months:

- May to October – dorado
- June to September – roosterfish
- September to December – marlin
- September to January – yellowfin tuna
- October – sea bass
- October to May – sailfish

As in any part of the world, overfishing is a concern in Guatemala. The prime culprits here, though, are the commercial fishers, who use drag netting. Another concern, particularly for inland species and shrimp, is the practice of chemical-intensive agriculture. Runoff leeches into the river system, decimating fish populations and damaging fragile mangrove ecosystems.

It's estimated that Guatemala's Pacific coast has lost more than 90% of its original mangrove forests. The mangroves serve as nurseries for fish and shellfish and the trees maintain water quality and prevent erosion. They also provide food and income for local populations, but all along the Pacific coast, commercial shrimp farming is moving in. Over the past decade, commercial shrimp farms have consumed about 5% of all the remaining mangroves in the world.

---

with rustic wooden slat-and-thatched roofed houses instead of the dull cinder block, corrugated-tin models common elsewhere. When the sky is clear, keep your eyes peeled for the awesome volcanoes that shimmer in the hinterland. This part of Guatemala is also treated to sensational lightning storms from around November to April.

Monterrico is a coastal village with a few small, inexpensive hotels right on the beach, a large wildlife reserve and two centers for the hatching and release of sea turtles and caimans. The beach here is dramatic, with powerful surf crashing onto black volcanic sand at odd angles. The odd-angled wave-print signals that there are rip tides; deaths have occurred at this beach, so swim with care. Strong swimmers, however, can probably handle and enjoy the waves. Behind the town is a large network of mangrove swamps and canals, part of the 190km Canal de Chiquimulilla.

Monterrico is probably the best spot for a weekend break at the beach if you're staying in Antigua or Guatemala City. It's fast becoming popular with foreigners. On weekdays it's relatively quiet, but on weekends and holidays it teems with Guatemalan families, and everything seems a bit harried. Monterrico has a real problem with trash, something that local businesses are trying to sort out.

Orientation & Information

From where you alight from the La Avellana boat, it's about 1km to the beach and the hotels. You pass through the village en route. From the *embarcadero* (jetty) walk straight ahead and then turn left. Pickups (US$0.25) meet scheduled boats or *lanchas*.

If you come by bus from Pueblo Viejo, from the stop walk about 300m toward the beach on Calle Principal. At the beach, head left to reach the cluster of hotels.

There is no bank, but there is a **post office** (Calle Principal) on the one real road in Monterrico. Internet access is available from **Walfer** (per hr US$1.80) on the main street.

Biotopo Monterrico-Hawaii

Sometimes called the Reserva Natural Monterrico, **Biotopo Monterrico-Hawaii** is administered by Cecon (Centro de Estudios Conservacionistas de la Universidad de San Carlos), and is Monterrico's biggest attraction. This 20km-long nature reserve of coast and coastal mangrove swamps is bursting with avian and aquatic life. The reserve's most famous denizens are the endangered leatherback and ridley turtles, who lay their eggs on the beach in many places along the coast. The mangrove swamps are a network of 25 lagoons, all connected by mangrove canals.

Boat tours of the reserve, passing through the mangrove swamps and visiting several lagoons, take around 1½ to two hours and cost US$10 for one person, US$6.50 for additional people. It's best to go just on sunrise, when you're likely to see the most wildlife. If you have binoculars, bring them along for bird-watching. January and February are the best months for bird-watching. Locals will approach you on the street (some with very impressive-looking ID cards), offering tours, but if you want to support the Tortugario (who incidentally have the most environmentally knowledgeable guides), arrange a tour directly through the Tortugario Monterrico (see below).

Some travelers have griped about the use of motorboats (as opposed to the paddled varieties), because the sound of the motor scares off the wildlife. If you're under no time pressure, ask about arranging a paddled tour of the canal.

Tortugario Monterrico

The Cecon-run **Tortugario Monterrico** (admission US$1.20; ☼ 8am-noon & 2-5pm) is just a short walk east down the beach from the end of Calle Principal and then a block inland. Several endangered species of animals are raised here, including leatherback, olive ridley and green sea turtles, caimans and iguanas. There's an interesting interpretative trail and a little museum with pickled displays in bottles. The staff offer lagoon trips (see above) and will accept volunteers.

Parque Hawaii

This nature reserve operated by **Arcas** (Asociación de Rescate y Conservación de Vida Silvestre, Wildlife Rescue & Conservation Association; ☎ in Guatemala City 2478 4096; www.arcasguatemala.com) comprises a sea-turtle hatchery with some caimans 8km east along the beach from Monterrico. It is separate from and rivals Cecon's work in the same field. Volunteers are welcome year round, but the sea turtle nesting season is from June to November, with August and September being the peak months. Volunteers are charged US$50 a week for a room, with meals extra and homestay options. Jobs for volunteers include hatchery checks and maintenance, local school education sessions, mangrove reforestation, basic construction and data collection. Most of the egg collection happens at night. It's a way out of town, but there are usually other volunteers to keep you company and while you're here you can use the kayaks, go on village trips and go fishing in the sea and mangroves.

A bus (US$0.50, 30 minutes) leaves the Monterrico jetty at 6am, 11am, 1:30pm and 3:30pm (and 6:30pm, except Saturday) for the bumpy ride to the reserve. Pickups also operate on this route, charging US$3.25 per person. Check out the Arcas website for more information.

Language Courses

Proyecto Lingüístico Monterrico (☎ 5558 9039; Calle Principal), about 250m from the beach, is quite professional. Classes are generally held outdoors in a shady garden area. You can study in the morning or afternoon, depending on your schedule. Courses here run at US$125 per week with 20 hours of tuition, and accommodation with access to a kitchen, or US$75 for classes only. It has useful maps of the town.

Sleeping

All hotels listed here are on the beach, unless otherwise stated. To save a difficult, hot walk along the beach, take the last road to the left before you hit the beach. All these hotels either front or back onto it. The majority have restaurants serving whatever is fresh from the sea that day. Many accommodations offer discounts for stays of three nights or more. Reserve for weekends if you want to avoid a long hot walk while you cruise around asking for vacancies. Weekend prices are given here. Midweek, you'll have plenty more bargaining power.

Johnny's (☎ 7762 0015; johnnys@backpackamericas .com; dm US$6, s & d with bathroom US$23, bungalows for 4 US$43; P 🖥 🏊) A lot of people are unimpressed by Johnny's – it's the first place you come to turning left on the beach, and one of the biggest operations here. It's got a decent atmosphere though, and attracts a good mix of backpackers and family groups. Every pair of bungalows shares a barbecue and a small swimming pool. There's also a larger general swimming pool. The rooms are not glamorous but have fans and screened windows. Its bar-restaurant overlooks the sea and is a popular hangout: the food is not gourmet but there are plenty of choices and imaginative *licuados* and other long cool drinks.

Brisas del Mar (☎ 5517 1142; s/d with bathroom US$7/14; P 🏊) Behind Johnny's, one block back from the beach, this popular newcomer offers good-sized rooms and a 2nd-floor dining hall with excellent sea views.

El Kaiman (☎ 5517 9285; r per person with bathroom US$7; 🏊 P) Further along the beach you'll find this other cheapie, which is much more worn around the edges. Rooms are in a two-story concrete block set back from the beach. The beachfront area is much more appealing, with hammocks and a decent restaurant.

El Mangle (☎ 5514 6517; r with bathroom & fan US$26, with bathroom & air-con US$50; P 🍴 🏊) Eclectic decorations fill the grounds of this friendly little place 100m further along the beach. Rooms are decent sized, with hammocks strung on individual porches. There's a big open space, with a very pleasant pool, for hanging out and it's quiet. The seafront restaurant here pumps out some very tasty wood-fired pizza.

Dulce y Salado (☎ 5817 9046; cabins with bathroom per person, incl breakfast & lunch US$27; P 🏊) The furthest from town, about 2km east of the center. Neat little thatched-roof cabins are set around a good-sized swimming pool. The place is Italian owned, so the restaurant out front does good pastas (US$6) and excellent coffee. Midweek, prices halve, but don't include meals.

Hotel Pez de Oro (☎ 5204 5249; s/d US$50/60; P 🏊) Further down the beach, this is the funkiest looking place in town, with comfortable little huts and bungalows scattered around a shady property. The color scheme is a cheery blue and yellow and the rooms have some tasteful decorations and big overhead fans. The excellent restaurant, with big sea views, serves up great Italian cuisine and seafood dishes. Pastas cost from US$6, whole fish from US$6.50.

FREE AT LAST?

A local tradition in Monterrico is the Saturday night baby turtle race, hosted by the Tortugario Monterrico. You buy a baby turtle, let it go and the first person's turtle to reach the finish line wins dinner in a local restaurant.

On the surface, it's a good deal. The *tortugario* (turtle sanctuary) raises funds, the turtles go free and the punters go home with a warm fuzzy feeling.

There's a problem here, though. Turtles can hatch on any day of the week, so the tortugario keeps them in holding tanks until race day on Saturday.

Now, turtles are born with their tiny metabolisms racing, biologically amped up to make it from their nests, across the sand, through the waves and out into the currents that will (hopefully) carry them to safety. In the holding tanks, they burn off a good deal of body fat and energy swimming aimlessly around, waiting to be released. By the time they finally make it down the beach and into the ocean, they're worn out, and if you pay attention, you'll notice that many can't even make it past the breaking waves and keep getting washed back up on shore.

And given that, under perfect conditions, baby turtles stand about a one in 1000 chance of making it to adulthood, giving them an extra obstacle hardly seems fair.

The *tortugario* doesn't want to stop the Saturday night races because it's an excellent fundraiser, but if you really want to save a turtle, there are a few alternatives:

▪ Donate the money to the *tortugario* and explain why you aren't interested in the race.

▪ Buy a turtle and release it on your own, explaining why you don't want to wait till Saturday.

▪ Donate your time and/or money to the other turtle sanctuary in the area, at Hawaii (see opposite), which takes a much more low-key, serious approach to conservation issues.

Dos Mundos Pacific Resort (☎ 5847 4840; 2mundos pacific@yahoo.com; bungalows with bathroom US$100; P ✖ ☎) The biggest complex around is pushing resort status – manicured grounds, two swimming pools, a gorgeous beachfront restaurant. The bungalows are spacious and simply but beautifully presented, with wide shady balconies out front.

Going in the opposite direction from these hotels, heading right from Calle Principal, are more options.

Set all under one big thatched roof, the rooms at **Café del Sol** (☎ 5810 0821; www.café-del-sol .com; s/d US$24/27; P ☎) are a bit disappointing compared to the rest of the place. Still, they're good enough – spacious, with a few sticks of furniture. The restaurant's menu has some original dishes; try risotto with mushrooms (US$6) or fish fillet with tomatoes, peppers (capsicums) and olives (US$8). Eat on the terrace or in the big *palapa* dining area.

A cheery little option right on the beachfront, **Eco Beach Place** (☎ 5611 6637; ecobeachplace@hotmail .com; s/d US$24/31; P ☎) has rooms of a decent size, with huge clean bathrooms, and the place is very secure. There's also a steakhouse restaurant (mains US$7 to US$17) on the premises and a bright, shady terrace overlooking the beach.

Eating

There are many simple seafood restaurants on Calle Principal. For the best cheap eats, hit either of the two nameless *comedores* on the last road to the right before the beach, where you can pick up an excellent plate of garlic shrimp, rice tortillas, fries and salad for US$4.

All of the hotels have restaurants. See listings for details.

OUR PICK **Taberna El Pelicano** (mains US$7-10; ✓ lunch & dinner Wed-Sat) By far the best place to eat in town, with the widest menu and most interesting food, like seafood risotto (US$8), beef carpaccio (US$6) and a range of jumbo shrimp dishes (US$14).

Drinking

El Animal Desconicido (✓ 8pm-late Thu-Sat) Really the only bar in town, this gets very happening on weekends, with happy hours, cocktails and electronic music. Comfy seating fills up early out front, and the rest of the place starts rocking around 11pm. To find it, go down the main street till you hit the beach, then walk 200m to your right.

Getting There & Away

There are two ways to get to Monterrico. You can take a bus to Iztapa (four hours from Guatemala City), then catch a *lancha* across the canal to Pueblo Viejo and hop on another bus to Monterrico (US$1, one hour). This is the longer alternative, but it's a pretty journey, revealing local life at a sane pace.

The other option is to head to La Avellana, where *lanchas* and car ferries depart for Monterrico. The Cubanita company runs a handful of direct buses to and from Guatemala City (US$4, four hours, 124km). Alternatively, you reach La Avellana by changing buses at Taxisco on Hwy 2. Buses operate half-hourly from 5am to 4pm between Guatemala City and Taxisco (US$3, 3½ hours) and roughly hourly from 7am to 6pm between Taxisco and La Avellana (US$1, 40 minutes), although taxi drivers will tell you that you've missed the last bus, regardless of what time you arrive. A taxi between Taxisco and La Avellana costs around US$6.50.

Shuttle buses also serve La Avellana. You can take a round-trip from Antigua, coming on one day and returning the next (2½ hours, US$9 one way). Voyageur Tours (see p101) comes to La Avellana three or four times weekly in the low season, daily in high season, with a minimum of three passengers. On Saturday and Sunday they pick up in Monterrico (not La Avellana) from outside Proyecto Lingüístico Monterrico at 3pm, for the round-trip. They charge US$6.50 from Monterrico to Antigua, so it's best not to buy a round-trip ticket in Antigua; they'll take you on to Guatemala City (US$11) if you wish. Other shuttle services also make the Antigua–Monterrico trip.

From La Avellana catch a *lancha* or car ferry to Monterrico. The collective *lanchas* charge US$0.60 per passenger for the half-hour trip along the Canal de Chiquimulilla, a long mangrove canal. They start at 4:30am and run more or less every half-hour or hour until late afternoon. From Monterrico they leave at 3:30am, 5:30am, 7am, 8am, 9am, 10:30am, noon, 1pm, 2:30pm and 4pm. You can always pay more and charter your own boat. The car ferry costs US$13 per vehicle.

AROUND MONTERRICO

East down the coast from Monterrico, near Las Lisas, is the Guatemalan Pacific coast's best-kept secret, **Isleta de Gaia** (☎ 7885-0044;

www.isleta-de-gaia.com; 2-/4-person bungalows US$80/160; 🖥 🐾). It's a bungalow-hotel built on a long island of sand and named for the Greek earth goddess. Overlooking the Pacific on one side and a romantic and silent lagoon with mangroves on the other, this small, friendly, ecological, French-owned resort is constructed from natural materials. There are 12 bungalows, on one and two levels, with sea, lagoon or pool views. Each has good beds, fan, a bathroom, balcony and hammock; decorations are Mexican and Costa Rican. The seafront restaurant offers Italian, Spanish and French cuisine with fresh fish naturally the star. It has boogie boards and kayaks for rent and a big boat for fishing trips (US$140 for two people). Reserve your stay in this little paradise by email four days in advance. The staff run a shuttle service to and from Guatemala City and Antigua. From Monterrico there is no road east along the coast beyond Hawaii, so you have to backtrack to Taxisco and take Carretera al Pacífico for about 35km to reach the turnoff for Las Lisas. From the turnoff it's 20km to Las Lisas, where you take a boat to Isleta de Gaia.

Chiquimulilla & the El Salvador Border

Surfers found in this part of Guatemala will likely be heading to or from La Libertad in El Salvador. Most people shoot straight through Escuintla and Taxisco to Chiquimulilla and on to the Salvadoran border at Ciudad Pedro de Alvarado/La Hachadura, from where it is about 110km along the coast of El Salvador to La Libertad. Be sure about whether or not you need a visa to enter El Salvador.

Buses leave Taxisco for the border every 15 minutes until 5pm. There are two serviceable *hospedajes* in La Hachadura on the El Salvador side of the border, but the *hostales* (budget hotels) in Ciudad Pedro de Alvarado on the Guatemalan side are not recommended. Should you need to stop for the night before crossing the border, you could do worse than head to the friendly cowboy town of Chiquimulilla, some 12km east of Taxisco. There isn't much going on here, but it's a decent enough place to take care of errands and regroup. The new bus terminal is way out on the outskirts of town – ask to be dropped off in *el centro*. Failing that, shared *tuk tuks* take you anywhere you want to go in town for US$0.25.

The family-run **Hotel San Juan de Letrán** (☎ 7885 0831; cnr 2a Av & 2a Calle; s/d US$8/12; **P**) is a clean place offering fair-sized rooms with a fan and bathroom. There are also less-attractive rooms with a shared bathroom. Drinking water is provided and there are nice plantings. The *cafétería* attached serves some of the iciest drinks in Guatemala, which are very welcome in this sweltering heat, and big plates of tasty, cheap food. Buses run every hour between Taxisco and Chiquimulilla, and also hourly, until 6pm, from Chiquimulilla to the border (US$1.50, 45 minutes).

The other option for getting to El Salvador is to turn north from Chiquimulilla and take local buses through Cuilapa to the border at Valle Nuevo/Las Chinamas, traveling inland before veering south to La Libertad.

CUILAPA
pop 18,300

Surrounded by citrus and coffee plantations, the capital of Santa Rosa department isn't much of a tourist attraction in its own right, although the area's fame for woodcarvings, pottery and leather goods may turn up a couple of decent souvenirs.

People coming this way are usually headed for the border with El Salvador, but there are a couple of volcanoes just out of town that are easily climbed and afford some excellent views. Cuilapa is connected by a good road with Guatemala City. Buses (US$2.50, 2½ hours) leave from the bus terminal in Zona 4.

Volcán Cruz Quemado

This dormant volcano towers 1700m over the tiny village of Santa María Ixhuatán at its base. Coffee plantations reach about one third of the way up its slopes, after which you move into thick rainforest. The summit, littered with radio towers, offers excellent views of the land running down to the coast, the Cerro la Consulta mountain range and the nearby Tecuamburro volcanic complex (see p210).

From Santa María it's an easy-to-moderate climb to the top that should take about three hours. The 12km hike is possible to do on your own, asking plenty of directions along the way. Alternatively, guides can be hired in Santa María – ask at the taxi stand on the main square.

To get to Santa María, catch a bus to Cuilapa, then a minibus (US$0.80, 25 minutes) from there.

THE PACIFIC SLOPE

Tecuamburro

The Tecuamburro volcanic complex comprises various peaks, including Cerro de Miraflores (1950m), Cerro la Soledad (1850m) and Cerro Peña Blanca (1850m). This last, which has several small vents releasing steam and sulfur, provides the most interesting climb, although thick forest on its slopes means you'll have to wait till you're almost at the top for views of the surrounding fields, the coastline and nearby volcanoes.

Buses and minibuses (US$2, 1½ hours) leave regularly for the village of Tecuamburro from Cuilapa. From there it's a two- to three-hour hike (14km) to the summit.

LAGO DE AMATITLÁN

Lago de Amatitlán is a placid lake backed by a looming volcano, and situated a mere 25km south of Guatemala City, making it a good day trip. After suffering years of serious neglect, the lake is slowly being rejuvenated, thanks mainly to local community groups who hope to see it once again function as a tourist attraction. On weekends, people from Guatemala City come to row boats on the lake (its waters are too polluted for swimming) or to rent a hot tub for a dip. Many people from the capital own second homes here.

A **teleférico** (chairlift; adult/child return US$2/0.80; ☯ 9am-5pm Fri-Sun) heads out over the lakeshore then pretty much straight up the hillside. It's a half-hour ride with some stunning views of the surrounding countryside from the top.

Boat tours are about the only other thing to do here – full boats can be rented for tours of the lake (US$7/13 per half-hour/two hours). If you're feeling energetic, rowboats rent from US$4 per hour.

If you have a car and some spare time, a drive around the lake offers some pretty scenery.

Down on the waterfront several *comedores* and small restaurants serve up tasty, filling meals from US$3. Placita Nilda seems to be the one favored by locals.

Getting There & Away

The lake is situated just off the main Escuintla–Guatemala City highway (Hwy 9). Coming from Guatemala City (one hour, US$0.80), just ask to be dropped at the *teleférico*. The waterfront is about half a kilometer from the signposted turnoff. Coming from Escuintla, or heading back to Guatemala City, buses stop on the main road, about 1km away. It's an easy 10- to 15-minute walk, and taxis are rare.

THE PACIFIC SLOPE

Central & Eastern Guatemala

Stretching from the steamy lowland forests of El Petén to the dry tropics of the Río Motagua valley, and from the edge of the western Highlands to the Caribbean, this is the country's most diverse region.

The Carretera al Atlántico (Hwy 9) shoots eastward to the sea from Guatemala City. Along the way are numerous attractions – side trips to the pilgrim town of Esquipulas, and beyond to the wonderfully preserved ruins of Copán in Honduras. Further along the highway is Quiriguá, boasting impressive stelae more than 10m tall.

Another short detour brings you to Río Dulce, a favored resting spot for Caribbean sailors and gateway to the wilds of the Bocas del Polochic. While you're here, don't miss the gorgeous boat ride down the Río Dulce to the Garífuna enclave of Lívingston.

The north of the region is lush and mountainous coffee-growing country. As you climb, you enter cloud forest where rain or at least mist will become a guaranteed daily part of your travels.

The limestone crags around Cobán attract cavers the world over, but those at Lanquín, Rey Marcos and elsewhere are easily accessible for amateurs.

The two must-sees in the Cobán area are the beautiful pools and cascades of Semuc Champey and the Biotopo del Quetzal, a nature reserve where you stand a reasonable chance of seeing the elusive national bird, the quetzal.

TOP FIVE

- Splashing around the turquoise waters of **Semuc Champey** (p225) and getting deep in the caves at **Grutas de Lanquín** (p224)

- Admiring the impressive carvings at **Copán** (p236) and **Quiriguá** (p249) and relaxing in the Antigua-rivaling beauty of **Copán Ruinas** (p242)

- Going bush in the jungle hideaway of **Las Conchas** (p226), where waterfalls, jungle treks and village tours await

- Getting down with the Garífuna in the unique Caribbean town of **Lívingston** (p261)

- Taking in the natural beauty of such little-visited protected areas as **Parque Nacional Laguna Lachuá** (p228) and the **Bocas del Polochic** (p256)

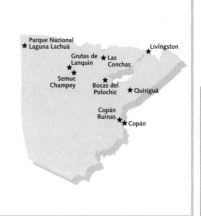

CENTRAL & EASTERN GUATEMALA

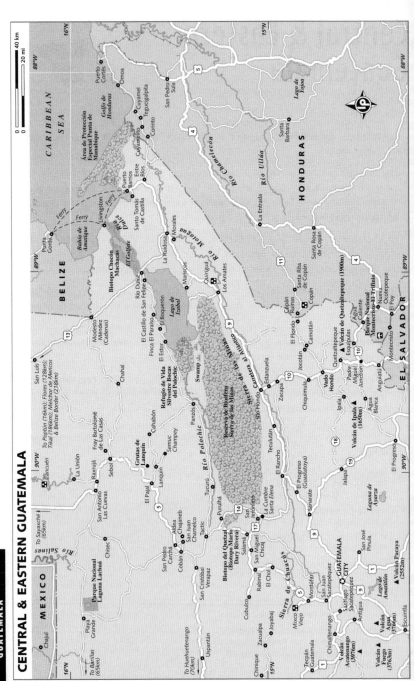

CENTRAL & EASTERN GUATEMALA

SALAMÁ

pop 24,200 / elev 940m

A wonderful introduction to Baja Verapaz's not-too-hot, not-too-cold climate, Salamá is a smallish town with a couple of attractions. Excellent information on the area is available at www.laverapaz.com.

Hwy 14 (also marked Hwy 17) leaves the Carr al Atlántico at El Rancho, 84km from Guatemala City. It heads west through a dry, desert-like lowland area, then turns north and starts climbing up into the forested hills. After 47km, at the junction called La Cumbre Santa Elena, Hwy 17 to Salamá divides from Hwy 14 for Cobán. Descending the other side of the ridge, Hwy 17 winds down into the broad valley of the Río Salamá, and enters Salamá town, 17km from the highway.

Before the Spanish conquest, the mountainous departments of Baja Verapaz and Alta Verapaz were populated by the Rabinal Maya, noted for their warlike habits and merciless victories. They battled the powerful K'iche' Maya for a century but were never conquered.

When the conquistadors arrived, they too had trouble defeating the Rabinal Maya. It was Fray Bartolomé de Las Casas who convinced the Spanish authorities to try peace where war had failed. Armed with an edict that forbade Spanish soldiers from entering the region for five years, the friar and his brethren pursued their religious mission, and succeeded in pacifying and converting the Rabinal Maya. Their homeland thus was renamed Verapaz (True Peace) and is now divided into Baja Verapaz, with its capital at Salamá, and Alta Verapaz, which is centered on Cobán. The Rabinal Maya have remained among the most dedicated and true to ancient Mayan customs, and there are many intriguing villages to visit in this part of Guatemala, including Rabinal itself (p214).

Information

Banrural (🕓 9am-5pm Mon-Fri, 9am-1pm Sat) On the south side of the plaza (opposite the church), changes cash and traveler's checks and has a Visa and MasterCard ATM.

Cafe Deli-Donas (15a Calle 6-61) Has useful free maps of the town (without street names).

Police station One block west of the plaza.

Telgua Has internet access (per hour US$0.80). East of the plaza.

Sights

Salamá has some attractive reminders of colonial rule. The main plaza, for instance, boasts an ornate **church** with gold-encrusted altars and a carved pulpit, which is located just to the left before the altar. Be sure to check out Jesus lying in a glass coffin with cotton bunting in his stigmata and droplets of blood seeping from his hairline. His thick mascara and the silver lamé pillow where he rests his head complete the scene. The Salamá **market** is impressive for its colorful, local bustle, particularly on Sunday.

Tours

EcoVerapaz (☎ 7940 0146; ecoverapaz@hotmail.com; 8a Av 7-12, Zona 1; 1-day tours per person US$40) is in the shop Imprenta, Mi Terreno – a block west of the plaza on the road to La Cumbre. Its local, trained naturalists offer interesting tours throughout Baja Verapaz including caving, birding, hiking, horse riding and orchid trips. EcoVerapaz also goes to Rabinal (p214) to check out its museum and crafts and arrange trips to see the famous rodeos of Baja Verapaz. Guides speak some English. Group discounts are offered.

Sleeping

Turicentro Las Orquídeas (☎ 7940 1622; Carr a Salamá Km 147; campsite US$4.50) Travelers with tents may want to check out this place, a few kilometers east of Salamá on Hwy 17. It has a grassy area for camping, plus a café, pool and open spaces hung with hammocks. You can use the pool (US$2 per person per day) even if you're not camping here.

Hotel Rosa de Sharon (☎ 5774 8650; 5a Calle 6-39; s/d with bathroom US$7.50/12; **P**) The neat, bright rooms here loom over the busy market area, but they're set back from the road, so remain peaceful. They're big and clean, with whacky decorations such as wrought-iron hat stands made to look like trees.

Posada de Don Maco (☎ 7940 0083; 3a Calle 8-26; s/d with bathroom US$8/14; **P**) This clean, family-run place has simple but spacious rooms with fan and good bathrooms. The courtyard boasts a collection of caged squirrels.

Hotel San Ignacio (☎ 7940 0186; 4a Calle 'A' 7-09; s/d US$8/14; **P**) Not the loveliest place you're ever likely to stay, but it's a reasonable deal for the price, and super-close to the park. Look for the big *palapa* (open-sided palm-leaf shelter) sitting area up on the rooftop.

CENTRAL & EASTERN GUATEMALA

Hotel Real Legendario (☎ 7940 1751; 8a Av 3-57, Zona 1; s/d with bathroom US$12/19; P) You'll recognize this place, three blocks east of the plaza, by the stands of bamboo in the car park. The clean, secure rooms have fan, hot-water bathroom and cable TV.

Eating

You don't have to step far from the plaza to eat well.

Café Deli-Donas (15a Calle 6-61; cakes US$1.30, sandwiches US$2, licuados US$0.90; 8am-6pm Mon-Sat) This exceedingly pleasant little café (where even the bathrooms smell good) is like an oasis in Salama's busy market zone. Excellent coffee, homemade cakes and light meals are the go here.

Antojitos Zacapanecos (cnr 6a Calle & 8a Av; mains US$2-3; lunch & dinner) For something a little different in the fast-food vein, check out the huge flour tortillas filled with pork, chicken or beef from this place. Better yet, grab one to go and have a picnic in the plaza.

Cafetería Central (cnr 15a Calle & 9a Av; lunches US$2.40; breakfast & lunch) Try the savory, filling lunches at this place a few doors back towards the plaza from Cafe Deli-Donas. The chicken broth followed by grilled chicken, rice and salad, with perhaps a mango to finish, is a worthy feast.

Restaurante El Balcón de los Recuerdos (8a Av 6-28; mains US$5-7; breakfast, lunch & dinner Mon-Sat) This restaurant, a half-block west of the plaza on the road to La Cumbre, is spacious, fan-cooled and has a central fountain. Here you can choose from a typical list of grilled meats, fish, prawns, and seafood soup.

Getting There & Away

Buses going to Guatemala City (US$3 to US$4.50, three hours, 151km) depart hourly between 3am and 8pm from the northeast corner of the park. There is a Pullman at 4am. Arrive early for a seat. Buses coming from Guatemala City continue west from Salamá to Rabinal (US$1.50, 40 minutes, 19km) and then 15km further along to Cubulco. Buses for San Jerónimo leave from in front of the *municipalidad* (town hall; east side of the plaza) every half-hour from 6am to 5:30pm (US$0.40, 25 minutes). Buses for La Cumbre (US$0.60, 25 minutes) and Cobán (US$2.50; 1½ to two hours) leave just downhill from the corner of 15 Calle and 6a Av about every 30 minutes from early morning to 4pm.

AROUND SALAMÁ

A few kilometers along the road to Salamá from Hwy 14, you come to the turnoff for **San Jerónimo**. Behind the town's beautiful church is a 16th-century sugar mill now used as a **museum** (admission free; 8am-4pm Mon-Fri, 10am-noon & 1-4pm Sat & Sun) displaying a decent collection of artifacts and photographs, though none of the former is labeled. The grounds here are immaculate and there's a playground to keep the kids out of trouble. On the plaza are some large stones that were carved in ancient times.

About a five-minute walk from the town center are **Los Arcos**, a series of 124 arches in various states of decay. These formed a sophisticated aqueduct system to power the sugar mill. To get there, take the main road heading east (away from Salamá), bear right and slightly downhill, where you'll see a 'Barrio El Calvario' sign. Keep an eye to your right along this road and you'll start to see the arches. A second set of arches can be seen by going right at the second dirt alley on this road. If you continue straight ahead for about 50m, rather than going right, you'll see more arches through gaps in the trees. Continue straight on this road to reach **Finca San Lorenzo**, a coffee farm open to the public. The last bus of the day returning to Salamá leaves San Jerónimo at 4pm.

Nine kilometers west of Salamá along Hwy 5 is the village of **San Miguel Chicaj**, known for its weaving and for its traditional fiesta from September 25 to 29. Continue along the same road for another 10km to reach the colonial town of **Rabinal**, founded in 1537 by Fray Bartolomé de Las Casas as a base for his proselytizing. Rabinal has gained fame as a pottery-making center (look especially for the hand-painted chocolate cups), and for its citrus fruit harvest (November and December). Rabinal is also known for its adherence to pre-Columbian traditions, folklore and dance. If you can make it here for the annual fiesta of San Pedro, between January 19 and 25 (with things reaching a fevered pitch on January 21), or Corpus Cristi (40 days after Easter), do so. Market day here is Sunday. Rabinal also has the **Museo Communitario Rabinal Achi'** (cnr 4a Av & 2a Calle, Zona 3), which is devoted to history, culture and the Achi' Maya who live in the district. Two small hotels, the Pensión Motagua and the Hospedaje Caballeros, can put you up.

COURTING THE QUETZAL

The resplendent quetzal, which gave its name to Guatemala's currency, was sacred to the Maya. Its feathers grace the plumed serpent Quetzalcoatl and killing one was a capital offence. Unfortunately, in modern times it enjoys no such protection and hunting (mostly for the male's long, emerald-green tail feathers) and habitat loss have made the bird a rarity in Guatemala. You'd stand a much better chance of seeing one in Costa Rica or Panama.

The best place to look for a quetzal here is in the cloud forests of the Alta Verapaz, especially in the hopefully named Biotopo del Quetzal (below).

Avocado and fruit trees are what you're looking for here – that's the preferred food of the quetzal (along with insects, snails, frogs and lizards). But you'll have to look closely – the quetzal's green plumage is dull unless in direct sunlight, providing perfect camouflage, and it often remains motionless for hours.

The females lay two eggs per year, from March to June, and this is the best time to go looking, as the males' tail feathers grow up to 75cm long during this period. Keep an ear out for their distinctive call – sharp cackles and a low, burbling whistle: *keeeoo-keeeoo*.

It's possible to continue on from Rabinal another 15km to the village of **Cubulco**. Or, from Rabinal you can follow Hwy 5 all the way to Guatemala City, a trip of about 100km passing through several small villages. Buses ply this mostly unpaved route, albeit very slowly. Along the way you could detour 16km north from Montúfar to the ruins of **Mixco Viejo** (admission US$4), which was the active capital of the Poqomam Maya when the Spaniards came and crashed the party. The location of this ceremonial and military center is awesome, wedged between deep ravines, with just one way in and one way out. To further fortify the site, the Poqomam built impressive rock walls around the city. It took Pedro de Alvarado and his troops more than a month of concerted attacks to conquer Mixco Viejo. When they finally succeeded, they furiously laid waste to this city, which scholars believe supported close to 10,000 people at its height. There are several temples and two ball courts here. Self-sufficient campers can overnight here for free. It's difficult to reach this site by public transportation. From Guatemala City you need to get a Servicios Unidos San Juan bus from the Zona 4 Terminal de Autobuses to San Juan Sacatepéquez (US$0.80, one hour, departures every few minutes from 4am to 6pm) then change to onward transportation there. It's 12km north from San Juan to Montúfar.

BIOTOPO DEL QUETZAL

Along the main Cobán highway (Carretera a Cobán or Hwy 14), 34km beyond the La Cumbre turnoff for Salamá, you reach the Biotopo

Mario Dary Rivera nature reserve, commonly called the **Biotopo del Quetzal** (admission US$2.50; 7am-4pm), at Km 161, just east of the village of Purulhá.

You need a fair bit of luck to see a quetzal – they're rare and shy. For more about the quetzal, see the boxed text, above. You have the best chance of seeing them from March to June. If you're really keen to see Guatemala's national bird in the wild, contact Proyecto EcoQuetzal in Cobán (p220).

It's well worth stopping to explore and enjoy this lush high-altitude cloud-forest ecosystem that is the quetzal's natural habitat at any time – and you may get lucky! Early morning or early evening when the quetzals feed on *aguacatillo* trees are the best times to watch out for them – try around the Hotel y Comedor Ranchito del Quetzal (p216).

Trail guide maps in English and Spanish (US$0.70) are available at the visitors center. They contain a checklist of 87 birds commonly seen here. Other animals include spider monkeys and *tigrillos*, which are similar to ocelots. Good luck spotting either of these.

Two excellent, well-maintained nature trails wind through the reserve: the 1800m Sendero los Helechos (Fern Trail) and the 3600m Sendero los Musgos (Moss Trail). As you wander through the dense growth, treading on the rich, spongy humus and leaf-mold, you'll see many varieties of epiphytes (air plants), which thrive in the *biotopo*'s humid atmosphere.

Both trails pass by waterfalls, most of which cascade into small pools where you can take a dip; innumerable streams have their headwaters here, and the Río Colorado pours

CENTRAL & EASTERN GUATEMALA

CARDAMOM

The world's coffee drinkers know that high-quality coffee is important to Guatemala's export trade, but few know that Guatemala is the world's largest exporter of the spice cardamom. In Alta Verapaz, cardamom is more important to the local economy than coffee, providing livelihood for some 200,000 people. Cardamom *(Elettaria cardamomum)*, a herbaceous perennial of the ginger family native to the Malabar Coast of India, was brought to Alta Verapaz by German coffee plantation owners.

The plants grow to a height of between 1.5m and 6m and have coarse leaves up to 76cm long that are hairy on the underside. The flowers are white, and the fruit is a green, three-sided oval capsule holding 15 to 20 dark, hard, reddish-brown to brownish-black seeds. Though the cardamom plant grows readily, it is difficult to cultivate, pick and sort the best grades, so fragrant cardamom commands a high price. That does not seem to bother the people of Saudi Arabia and the Arabian Gulf states, who purchase more than 80% of the world supply. They pulverize the seeds and add the powder to the thick, syrupy, pungent coffee that is a social and personal necessity in that part of the world.

---

through the forest along a geological fault. Deep in the forest is **Xiu Gua Li Che** (Grandfather Tree), some 450 years old, which germinated around the time the Spanish fought the Rabinal in these mountains.

The reserve has a visitors center, a little shop for drinks and snacks, and a camping and barbecue area. The ruling on camping changes from time to time. Check by contacting Cecon (Centro de Estudios Conservacionistas de la Universidad de San Carlos) in Guatemala City (see p68), which administers this and other *biotopos*.

Sleeping & Eating

There are three lodging places close to the reserve.

Hotel y Comedor Ranchito del Quetzal (☎ 5368 6397; s/d US$5/10, with bathroom US$7.50/15; P) Carved out of the jungle on a hillside 200m away from the Biotopo del Quetzal entrance, this place has good-sized, simple rooms with cold showers in the older wooden building and hot showers in the newer concrete one. Reasonably priced, simple meals (mains US$3.50) are served, and there are vegetarian options.

Posada Montaña del Quetzal (☎ 6620 0709; www .hposadaquetzal.com; Hwy 14 Km 156.5; s/d with bathroom US$30/40, 2-bedroom bungalows US$40/50; P ✆) This comfortable place is 5km before the Biotopo del Quetzal if you're coming from Guatemala City. Accommodations are rustically styled, but extremely comfortable. It's set on a huge property that includes an orchid nursery, fishing holes, forest walks and a 30-minute mountain bike track out to a private waterfall. The bungalows are a real steal, featuring living

rooms with huge open fireplaces. The restaurant is popular with tour groups, mainly for its excellent *cack'ik* (turkey stew; US$4).

Hotel Restaurant Ram Tzul (☎ 5908 4066; www .m-y-c.com.ar/ramtzul; Hwy 14 Km 158; s/d US$30/40; P) Quite likely the most beautiful hotel in either of the Verapaces, this place is about halfway between the Posada Montaña del Quetzal and the *biotopo* entrance. The restaurant/sitting area is in a tall, thatched-roofed structure with fire pits and plenty of atmosphere. The rustic, upmarket theme extends to the rooms and bungalows, which are spacious and elegantly decorated. The hotel property includes waterfalls and swimming spots.

Getting There & Away

Any bus to/from Guatemala City will set you down at the park entrance. Heading in the other direction, it's best to flag down a bus or microbus to El Rancho and change there for your next destination.

COBÁN

pop 57,600 / elev 1320m

Not so much an attraction in itself, but an excellent jumping-off point for the natural wonders of Alta Verapaz, Cobán is a prosperous city with an upbeat air. Return visitors will marvel at how much (and how tastefully) the town has developed since their last visit.

As you enter Cobán, a sign says 'Bienvenidos a Cobán, Ciudad Imperial,' referring to the city charter granted in 1538 by Emperor Carlos V.

The town was once the center of Tezulutlán (Tierra de Guerra, or 'Land of War'), a stronghold of the Rabinal Maya.

In the 19th century, when German immigrants moved in and founded vast coffee and cardamom *fincas* (plantations), Cobán took on the aspect of a German mountain town, as the *finca* owners built town residences. The era of German cultural and economic domination ended during WWII, when the USA prevailed upon the Guatemalan government to deport the powerful *finca* owners, many of whom actively supported the Nazis.

Today, Cobán is an interesting town to visit, though dreary weather can color your impression. Most of the year it is either rainy or overcast, dank and chill. You can count on sunny days in Cobán for only about three weeks, in April. In the midst of the 'dry' season (January to March) it can be misty and sometimes rainy, or bright and sunny with marvelous clear mountain air.

Guatemala's most impressive festival of Indian traditions, the national folklore festival of **Rabin Ajau** with its traditional dance of the Paabanc, takes place here in the latter part of July or in the first week of August. The **national orchid show** is hosted here every December.

There is not a lot to do in Cobán itself except enjoy the local color and mountain scenery, but the town is a base for marvelous side trips, including to the Grutas de Lanquín (p224) and the pools and cascades of Semuc Champey (p225).

Orientation

Most of the services you'll need are within a few blocks of the main plaza and the cathedral. The shopping district is around and behind the cathedral, and you'll smell the savory cardamom, which vendors come from the mountains to sell, before you see it.

Most buses will drop you at the terminal north of town. It's a 15-minute walk (2km) or US$1 taxi ride to the plaza from there.

There is a **tourist office** (1a Calle, Zona 1; 10am-5pm Mon-Sat) on the plaza, but unless your questions are very basic, you will probably send you to the tourism people in the **municipalidad** (1a Calle, Zona 1; ☎ 7952 1305, 7951 1148), where some switched-on young staff work in an office behind the police office. Casa D'Acuña (p221) can also give you loads of information.

The heart of Cobán is built on a rise, so unless what you're looking for is in the dead center, be prepared to walk uphill and down.

Information

INTERNET ACCESS

Plenty of places offer internet access. The going rate is US$0.80 an hour.

Access Computación (Oficinas Profesionales Fray Bartolomé de las Casas, 1a Calle 3-13; 9am-7pm Mon-Fri, 8am-6pm Sat)

Cybercobán (3a Av 1-11, Zona 4; 8:30am-7pm Mon-Sat) East (200m) of the plaza.

COFFEE: FROM THE BEAN TO THE CUP

It's a long way from the farm to the table for the humble coffee bean. First, they have to wait until they're ripe – a sunburst red color – then they're picked and put in water. Those that float are skimmed off and sold as second-grade beans. The rest soak in the water for 12 to 24 hours (depending on the altitude) until they ferment and shed their outer skin.

Then it's into the wash to remove any residues and the fleshy substance that covers the kernel, before being baked in an oven to dry.

All the above, from picking to drying, should take place in around one day to maintain flavor, but at this point the bean can be stored for months without any loss in quality.

Many small-scale producers sell the beans at this point – buyers often prefer to take over from here, as the rest of the process influences the flavor of the finished product greatly.

A machine is now used to remove a fine, transparent skin that covers the inner kernel. This is done just prior to toasting. A lighter toast makes for a more aromatic, less flavorsome brew. Longer toasting means more flavor but less aroma.

The degree of acidity in a coffee bean is directly related to the altitude it's grown at – the higher the altitude, the greater the acidity.

Of Guatemala's main coffee-growing regions, Huehuetenango and Cobán produce the most acidic beans, Lake Atitlán and Antigua produce a medium acidity, and the smoothest beans come from the Pacific Slope and El Petén.

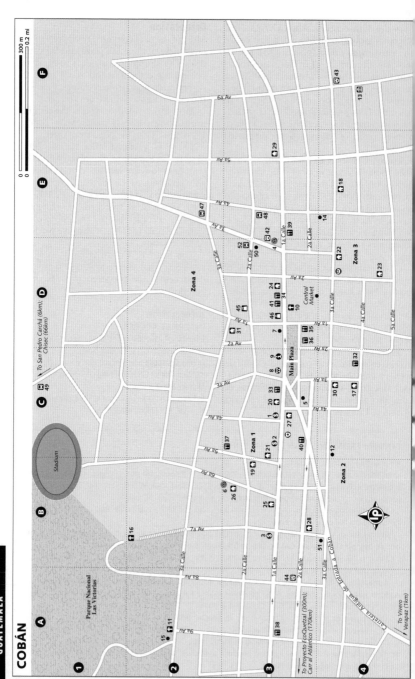

COBÁN

CENTRAL & EASTERN
GUATEMALA

Mayan Internet (6a Av 2-28; 8:30am-8pm Mon-Sat, 2:30-9pm Sun) Fast connections; 500m west of the plaza.

LAUNDRY
Lavandería Providencia (8am-noon & 2-5pm Mon-Sat) On the south side of the plaza. A 7lb (3.2kg) wash costs US$1.50; drying costs US$2.20 per hour.

MONEY
The banks listed here change cash US dollars and traveler's checks.

Banco G&T (1a Calle) Opposite Hotel La Posada, has a MasterCard ATM.

Banco Industrial (1a Calle 4-36) Has another branch (corner of 1a Calle and 7a Av) with a Visa ATM.

POST & TELEPHONE
Post office (cnr 2a Av & 3a Calle) A block southeast from the plaza.

Telgua On the plaza; has plenty of card phones outside.

Sights
TEMPLO EL CALVARIO
You can get a fine view over the town from this church atop a long flight of stairs at the north end of 7a Av. Indigenous people leave offerings at outdoor shrines and crosses in front of the church. Don't linger here after 4pm!

The **Ermita de Santo Domingo de Guzmán**, a chapel dedicated to Cobán's patron saint, is 150m west of the bottom of the stairs leading to El Calvario.

PARQUE NACIONAL LAS VICTORIAS
This forested 0.82-sq-km **national park** (admission US$0.80; 8am-4:30pm, walking trails 9am-3pm), right in town, has ponds, barbecue, picnic areas, children's play areas, a lookout point and kilometers of trails. The entrance is near the corner of 9a Av and 3a Calle, Zona 1. Beware: readers have reported violent crime here. Consider hiking in a group.

VIVERO VERAPAZ
Orchid lovers mustn't miss the chance to see the many thousands of species at this famous **nursery** (7952 1133; Carr Antigua de Entrada a Cobán; US$1.80; 9am-noon & 2-4pm). The rare *monja blanca* (white nun orchid), Guatemala's national flower, can be seen here; there are also hundreds of species of miniature orchids, so small that you'll need the magnifying glass they will loan you to see them. Visits are by guided tour. The national orchid show is held here each December, and by all accounts, it's spectacular. Otherwise, try to visit between October and February, when many flowers are in bloom.

Vivero Verapaz is about 2km from the town center – a 30-minute walk southwest from the plaza. You can hire a taxi for around US$2.

FINCA SANTA MARGARITA
A working coffee farm, **Finca Santa Margarita** (7952 1586; 3a Calle 4-12, Zona 2; admission US$2.50; guided tours 8am-12:30pm & 1:30-5pm Mon-Fri, 8am-

noon Sat) offers stellar guided tours. From propagation and planting to roasting and exporting, the 45-minute tour will tell you all you ever wanted to know about these powerful beans. At tour's end, you're treated to a cup of coffee and can purchase beans straight from the roaster for US$2.60 to US$5 a pound (0.45kg). The talented guide speaks English and Spanish.

MUSEO EL PRÍNCIPE MAYA
This private **museum** (☎ 7952 1541; 6a Av 4-26, Zona 3; admission US$1.30; ⏰ 9am-6pm Mon-Sat) features a collection of pre-Columbian artifacts, with an emphasis on jewelry, other body adornments and pottery. The displays are well designed and maintained.

Language Courses
The **Oxford Language Center** (☎ 5892 7718; www .olcenglish.com; 4a Av 2-16, Zona 3) charges around US$170 for 20 hours of Spanish lessons,

with discounts for groups. Its rationale for charging more than the competition is that it pays its teachers better.

Tours
Aventuras Turísticas (☎ /fax 7951 4213; www.aventuras turisticas.com; 3a Calle 2-38, Zona 3) In the Hostal de Doña Victoria, Aventuras leads tours to Laguna Lachuá, the Grutas de Lanquín, Rey Marcos and Candelaria, as well as to Semuc Champey, Tikal, Ceibal, and anywhere else you may want to go; it will customize itineraries. French-, English- and Spanish-speaking guides are available. Prices ranges from US$16 to US$200, per person.

Casa D'Acuña (☎ 7951 0484; casadacuna@yahoo .com; 4a Calle 3-11, Zona 2) offers tours to Semuc Champey, the Grutas de Lanquín and other places further afield. Its guides are excellent.

Proyecto EcoQuetzal (☎ /fax 7952 1047; www .ecoquetzal.org; 2a Calle 14-36, Zona 1; ⏰ 8:30am-1pm

---

WAKE UP & SMELL THE EXPLOITATION

Coffee is not just a drink in Guatemala. For many, it's a livelihood. It's also a neat analogy to the country's history and society.

The majority of coffee *fincas* (plantations) are large landholdings, many passed down for generations since the Spanish came and took over the land. Others have been 'gifted' from the government – often to ex-military types for…services rendered.

Wages and conditions on coffee farms are pitiful. Around harvest time, subsistence farmers from the area are brought in to live on the farm in crude dormitory-style buildings. Workers are paid by weight of beans picked, and you will often see entire families – including small children – out in the fields.

Minimum wage (around US$100 per month for rural workers) is not a relevant concept here.

The unsteady world coffee market means that farm owners sometimes get rich, but workers barely scrape by.

A small group of owners and workers have come up with an alternative model. Working on a cooperative basis, they shun the exploitative model and market their produce as fair-trade coffee.

For a product to claim fair-trade status, it must be certified by the **Fair Trade Labeling Organization** (www.fairtrade.net). The main requisites for certification are that the producer:

- respects the human rights of workers
- grants equal pay and conditions to men and women
- doesn't use child labor
- assists in community development.

There are around 24 communities producing fair-trade coffee in Guatemala. The vast majority of their produce is exported, and much of it is organic, using natural, plant-based herbicides and pesticides.

To find out more about fair-trade coffee, log on to www.caféconciencia.org. You can visit, stay and even volunteer at a fair-trade coffee farm at Nueva Alianza (see p198).

& 2-5:30pm Mon-Fri) is an innovative project offering 'ethnotourism' trips in which participants hike to nearby villages nestled in the cloud forest and stay with a Q'eqchi' Maya family. To maximize the experience, travelers are encouraged to learn some Q'eqchi' words and stay with their host family for at least two days. For US$42 you'll get a guide for three days, lodging for two nights, and six meals. Your guide will take you on hikes to interesting spots. The men of the family are the guides, providing them an alternative, sustainable way to make a living. Reservations are required at least one day in advance. The Proyecto also rents boots, sleeping bags and binoculars at reasonable prices, so you need not worry if you haven't come prepared for such a rugged experience. Participants should speak at least a little Spanish. With a month's notice, this outfit also offers quetzal-viewing platforms; contact the office for full details.

Sleeping

When choosing a room in Cobán, you may want to ensure that the showers have hot water; it can be cold in these parts.

BUDGET

Parque Nacional Las Victorias Camping (campsites per person per night US$3) Camping is available at Parque Nacional Las Victorias, right in town. Facilities include water and toilets but no showers.

Chipi Chipi Hostel (☎ 5226 0235; 1a Calle 3-25, Zona 1; dm US$3.50) This new hostel is a total winner in terms of location, and offers decent shared rooms, sleeping four in two bunks. The patio has hammocks and the young staff are full of info and tips.

Hotel La Paz (☎ 7952 1358; 6a Av 2-19, Zona 1; s US$4, s/d with bathroom US$6/10; P) This cheerful, clean hotel, 1½ blocks north and two blocks west of the plaza, is an excellent deal. It has many flowers, and a good *cafetería* next door.

Casa Luna (☎ 7951 3528; 5a Av 2-28, Zona 1; dm US$6; r per person US$7.50) Modern rooms set around a pretty, grassy courtyard. Dorms have lockers and private rooms are well decorated. The shared bathrooms are spotless.

Guest House Cobán (5a Av & 2a Calle, Zona 1; s/d incl breakfast US$6/12, with bathroom US$7.50/15) A basic but comfortable little guesthouse in a good location. The beds are firm and the family who runs it is super friendly.

Hostel Jam Bamboo (2a Av 4-33, Zona 2; dm US$6) Definitely party central in Cobán's hostel scene, this one isn't for your retiring types. But if you're looking to meet people and listen to live music (Tuesday to Sunday), this is your place. Rooms are spacious, with three beds per room and a bathroom in each.

Posada de Don Pedro (☎ 7951 0562; 3a Calle 3-12, Zona 2; s/d US$6/12) This family-run place has spacious rooms with terracotta-tiled floors around a happy little courtyard. There are good sitting areas to while the day away.

Casa D'Acuña (☎ 7951 0482; casadacuna@yahoo.com; 4a Calle 3-11, Zona 2; dm/d US$6.50/13) This clean, very comfortable European-style hostel has four dormitories (each with four beds) and two private doubles, all with shared bathroom with good hot-water showers. Also here is a fabulous restaurant called El Bistro (p222), a gift shop, laundry service and reasonably priced local tours.

Hotel Central (☎ 7952 1442; 1a Calle 1-79, Zona 1; s/d with bathroom & TV US$16/20) Reasonable-sized rooms, with just a touch of mold on the walls, and lovely outdoor sitting areas make this a decent choice.

MIDRANGE

Posada Don Matalbatz (☎ /fax 7951 0811; www .discoveryguate.com; 3a Calle 1-46, Zona 1; s/d US$8/16, with bathroom US$22/27; P) This friendly place has a selection of rooms, including big, clean units facing a pretty courtyard with hot-water bathroom and cable TV. Upstairs, the attic room has the most light and character, and sleeps five. Also on this level are a couple of rooms with clean, shared bathroom and little balconies. There's also a pool table. Stuck in the middle of markets, this isn't the best area in town, especially after dark.

Pensión Monja Blanca (☎ 7952 1712; 2a Calle 6-30, Zona 2; s/d US$7/15, with bathroom US$15/30; P) This place is peaceful despite being on busy 2a Calle. After walking through two courtyards, you come to a lush garden packed with fruit and hibiscus trees around which the spotless rooms are arranged. Each room has an old-time feel to it and is furnished with two good-quality single beds with folksy covers, and has cable TV; the light switches are on the outside. This is a good place for solo women travelers.

ourpick Posada de Don Antonio (☎ 7951 4287; 5a Av 1-51, Zona 4; s/d US$14/28; P) This atmospheric two-story place provides some of the best value in town. Rooms are spacious with two (or even three!) double beds, high ceilings and loving attention to detail. Breakfast (US$4 to US$6) in the lush patio area is a great way to start the day.

Hostal de Doña Victoria (☎ /fax 7951 4213; www .adventurasturisticas.com; 3a Calle 2-38, Zona 3; s/d US$20/25; **P**) This lovely hotel in a restored mansion more than 400 years old is jam-packed with eye-catching decorations varying from an old copper coffee machine to wooden masks to antique religious statues. Eight brightly painted comfortable rooms, with bathroom and TV, surround a central courtyard with lush plants and a restaurant-bar.

Casa Duranta (☎ 7951 4188; www.casaduranta.com; 3a Calle 4-46, Zona 3; s/d US$40/47) Some rooms at this carefully restored, eclectically decorated place are excellent value, while others are a bit cramped for the price. Have a look around if you can.

Hotel La Posada (☎ 7952 1495; www.laposadacoban .com; 1a Calle 4-12, Zona 2; s/d with bathroom US$40/50) Just off the plaza, this colonial-style hotel is Cobán's best, though rooms streetside suffer from traffic noise. Its colonnaded porches are dripping with tropical flowers and furnished with easy chairs and hammocks from which you can enjoy the mountain views. The rooms are a bit austere, with plenty of religious relics around the place, but they have nice old furniture, fireplaces and wall hangings of local weaving, and a bathroom. La Posada has a restaurant and café (right).

Eating

Most of the hotels in Cobán come with their own restaurants. In the evening, food trucks (kitchens on wheels) park around the plaza and offer some of the cheapest dining in town. As always, the one to go for has the largest crowd of locals hanging around and chomping down.

Xkape Koba'n (2a Calle 5-13, Zona 2; snacks US$2; ⏰ 10am-7pm) The perfect place to take a breather or while away a whole afternoon, this beautiful, artsy little café has a lush garden out back. The cakes are homemade, the coffee delectable and there are some interesting handicrafts on sale.

Café El Tirol (Oficinas Profesionales Fray Bartolomé de las Casas, 1a Calle 3-13; breakfasts US$2-4; ⏰ Mon-Sat) Another good central café, the Tirol claims to have Cobán's 'best coffee' (we disagree) and offers several types of hot chocolate. It's a cozy little place in which to enjoy breakfasts,

pastries and coffee or light meals, with a pleasant terrace away from the traffic.

El Cafeto (2a Calle 1-36 B, Zona 2; mains US$3-4; ⏰ breakfast, lunch & dinner) This cute little café right on the square does good, light set lunches (US$3), has a half-decent wine selection and serves delicious coffee.

Sonic Burger (1a Calle 3-50, Zona 3; burgers from US$3, set meals US$3-5; ⏰ lunch & dinner) The best burgers in town in a young, almost-hip environment. The food is cheap, the drinks expensive… go figure.

Café La Posada (1a Calle 4-12, Zona 2; ⏰ 1-9pm; snacks under US$4; ⏰ 11am-7pm) This café has tables on a veranda overlooking the square, and a comfortable sitting room inside with couches, coffee tables and a fireplace. All the usual café fare is served. Snacks comprise nachos, tortillas, sandwiches, burgers, tacos, tostadas, fruit salad and more.

Bokatas (4a Calle 2-34, Zona 2; mains US$4-10; ⏰ dinner) This large outdoor eatery pumps out big juicy steaks and loud disco music in equal portions. Also on offer is a decent paella for two or three people (US$24) and a range of seafood and Mediterranean options.

Restaurant Kam Mun (1a Calle 8-12, Zona 2; mains US$5-11; ⏰ lunch & dinner) Here you will find Chinese fare, served in a nice, clean atmosphere, 500m west of the plaza. Enjoy your meal surrounded by Chinese dragons, Buddhas and floral paintings.

El Peñascal (5a Av 2-61; mains US$8-10; ⏰ lunch & dinner) Probably Cobán's finest dining option, this one has plenty of regional specialties, Guatemalan classics, mixed meat platters, seafood and snacks in a relaxed, upmarket setting.

El Bistro (4a Calle 3-11; fish, steak & chicken mains US$8.50-13; ⏰ from 7am) Casa D'Acuña's restaurant offers authentic Italian and other European-style dishes served in an attractive oasis of tranquility to background classical music. In addition to protein-oriented mains, there is a range of pastas (US$4 to US$5.25), salads, homemade breads, cakes and outstanding desserts.

Entertainment

Cobán has several places where you can get down and boogie. **Bar Milenio** (3a Av 1-11, Zona 4) has a bar, food, a pool table and mixed music disco.

La Casona (8a Av & 2 Calle, Zona 2; admission US$2-3; ⏰ Thu-Sat) A mega-disco with balcony seating and bowtied waiters.

Keops (3a Calle 4-71, Zona 3; admission US$4) A popular disco. Wear your best gear.

Getting There & Away

BUS

The highway connecting Cobán with Guatemala City and the Carr al Atlántico is the most traveled route between Cobán and the outside world. The road north through Chisec to Sayaxché and Flores has almost all been paved in recent years, providing much easier access than before to El Petén. The off-the-beaten-track routes west to Huehuetenango and northeast to Fray Bartolomé de Las Casas and Poptún are mostly paved and still provide a bit of an adventure. Always double-check bus departure times, especially for less frequently served destinations. Tourism staff at the *municipalidad* try to keep up with the frequent schedule changes and display bus details in the foyer.

Many buses leave from Cobán's new bus terminal, southeast of the stadium. Buses to Guatemala City, Salamá, Lanquín and many other destinations depart from completely different stations (see the list, above).

Minibuses, known as microbuses, are replacing, or are additional to, chicken buses on many routes. Many buses do a circuit of the plaza before leaving town and stop outside Oficinas Profesionales Fray Bartolomé de Las Casas.

Bus departures from Cobán:

Biotopo del Quetzal (US$1, 1¼ hours, 58km) Any bus heading for Guatemala City will drop you at the entrance to the Biotopo.

Cahabón (US$3.20, 4½ hours, 85km) Same buses as to Lanquín.

Chisec (US$1.95, two hours, 66km, 10 buses from Campo 2, from 6am to 5pm)

El Estor (US$6, seven hours, 166km) This road gets washed out in heavy rains – check at the *municipalidad* to see if the bus is running.

Flores (five to six hours, 224km) Go to Sayaxché and take an onward bus or minibus from there.

Fray Bartolomé de Las Casas (via Chisec US$4, three hours, 121km; via San Pedro Carchá US$4.50, four hours, 101km) Several buses and minibuses depart from Campo 2, from 5am to 3:30pm. Buses might just say 'Las Casas.'

Guatemala City (US$4 to US$6, four to five hours, 213km) Transportes Monja Blanca (☎ 7951 3571; 2a Calle 3-77, Zona 4) has buses leaving for Guatemala City every 30 minutes from 2am to 6am, then hourly until 5pm.

Lanquín (US$2 to US$3, 2½ to three hours, 61km) Minibuses depart from the corner of 3a Calle and 3a Av, in Zona 4, from 7am to 4pm. Do check these times, though, as they seem to be fluid.

Playa Grande (for Laguna Lachuá) (US$6.50, four hours, 141km) Frequent buses and minibuses from Campo 2. Playa Grande is sometimes called Cantabal.

Puerto Barrios (6½ hours, 335km) Take any bus headed to Guatemala City and change at El Rancho junction.

Raxrujá (US$3, 2½ to three hours, 81km) Take a bus or microbus heading to Fray Bartolomé de Las Casas via Chisec; some Sayaxché-bound buses go through Raxrujá too. Or go to Chisec and change.

Río Dulce (6½ hours, 318km) Take any bus headed to Guatemala City and change at El Rancho junction. You may have to transfer again at La Ruidosa junction, 169km past El Rancho, but there is plenty of transportation going through to Río Dulce and on to Flores.

Salamá (US$3, 1½ hours, 57km) Frequent minivans leave from Campo 2, or take any bus to Guatemala City and change at La Cumbre.

San Pedro Carchá (US$0.40, 20 minutes, 6km) Buses every 10 minutes, from 6am to 7pm, from the lot in front of the Monja Blanca terminal.

Sayaxché (US$7, four hours, 84km) Buses at 6am and noon, and microbuses from early until 1pm, from Campo 2.

Tactic (US$0.60, 40 minutes, 32km) Frequent buses from Campo 2.

Uspantán (US$4.50, 4½ hours, 94km) Microbuses go from Campo 2 with a stop at Oficinas Fray Bartolomé de Las Casas.

CAR

Cobán has a couple of places that rent cars. Reserve your choice in advance. If you want to go to the Grutas de Lanquín or Semuc Champey, you'll need a 4WD vehicle. Rental companies include **Inque Renta Autos** (☎ 7952 1994, 7952 1172; 3a Av 1-18, Zona 4) and **Tabarini Rent A Car** (☎ 7952 1504; fax 7951 3282; 7a Av 2-27, Zona 1).

AROUND COBÁN

Cobán, and indeed all of Alta Verapaz, has become a magnet for Guatemalan adventure travel, both independent and organized. Not only are there scores of villages where you can experience traditional Mayan culture in some of its purest extant forms, there are also caves running throughout the department, waterfalls, pristine lagoons and many other natural wonders yet to be discovered. Go find them!

San Cristóbal Verapaz is an interesting Poqomchi' Maya village set beside Lake Chicoj, 19km west of Cobán. During Semana Santa (Easter Week), San Cristóbal artists design elaborate *alfombras* (carpets) of colored sawdust and flower petals rivaled only by those in Antigua. In addition, San Cristóbal is home to the **Centro Communitario Educativo Pokomchi** (Cecep; ☎ 7950 4039; www.ajchicho.50g.com), an organization dedicated to preserving traditional and modern ways of Poqomchi' life. To this end, Cecep inaugurated the **Museo Katinamit** (Calle del Calvario; admission US$1; ✆ 8am-5pm Mon-Sat, 9am-noon Sun), which re-creates a typical Poqomchi' house, with well-ordered displays of household items and everyday products. Other rooms feature art, tools and textiles still in daily use, and an introduction and orientation on the Poqomchi'. Cecep also offers volunteer and ethnotourism opportunities and runs the **Aj Chi Cho Language Center** (courses incl homestay per week US$120) for teaching Spanish. **El Portón Real** (☎ 7950 4604) is a Poqomchi'-owned and -operated hostelry.

Tactic is a small town 32km south of Cobán that offers myriad opportunities to experience traditional Mayan culture. On the plaza is the **Cooperativa de Tejadores**, where women demonstrate weaving techniques and sell their wares. On the outskirts of Tactic, atop the hill called Chi Ixhim, is an altar to the God of Maiz; anyone in town can point you in the right direction. There are a few places to stay, but none as nice as **Country Delight** (☎ 7909 1149; ecotdms@latinmail.com; Hwy 14 Km 166.5), where there are hiking trails, camping facilities, rooms and a restaurant. Staff can supply information on the area and its attractions. Tactic celebrates the **Fiesta de la Virgen de la Asunción** from August 11 to 16.

Balneario Las Islas

At the town of San Pedro Carchá, 6km east of Cobán on the way to Lanquín, is the Balneario Las Islas, with a river coming down past rocks and into a natural pool that's great for swimming. It's a five- to 10-minute walk from the bus stop in Carchá; anyone can point the way. Buses operate frequently between Cobán and Carchá (US$0.50, 20 minutes).

San Juan Chamelco

About 8km southeast of Cobán is the village of San Juan Chamelco, where you can swim at the Balneario Chio. The **church** here sits on top of a small rise, providing awesome views of the villages below. The colonial church may have been the first in Alta Verapaz. Paintings inside depict the arrival of the conquistadors. Mass is still held here in both Spanish and Q'eqchi'.

Buses to San Juan Chamelco leave from 4a Calle, Zona 3, in Cobán. To reach Don

Jerónimo's, take a bus or pickup from San Juan Chamelco towards Chamil and ask the driver to let you off at Don Jerónimo's. When you get off, take the footpath to the left for 300m, cross the bridge and it's the first house on the right. Alternatively, hire a taxi from Cobán (US$6.50).

Grutas Rey Marcos

This **cave system** (admission US$3; ✆ 9am-5pm) is set in the **Balneario Cecilinda** (admission US$2), which is, incidentally, a great place to go for a swim or a hike on scenic mountain trails. The caves themselves go for more than 1km into the earth, although chances are you won't get taken that far. A river runs through the cave (you have to wade through it at one point) and there are some impressive stalactites and stalagmites. According to local legend, any wishes made in the cave are guaranteed to come true. The Balneario Cecilinda is located a few hundred meters down the road from Don Jerónimo's.

In Aldea Chajaneb, only 12km from Cobán, **Don Jerónimo's** (☎ 2308 2255; www.dearbrutus .com/donjeronimo; s/d US$25/45), owned by Jerry Makransky (Don Jerónimo), rents comfortable, simple bungalows. The price includes three ample, delicious vegetarian meals fresh from the garden. Jerry also offers many activities, including tours to caves and the mountains, and inner-tubing on the Río Sotzil. He dotes on his guests, and the atmosphere is friendly.

Grutas de Lanquín

One of the best excursions to make from Cobán is to the caves near Lanquín, a pretty village 61km to the east.

The **Grutas de Lanquín** (admission US$3; ✆ 8am-4pm) are about 1km northwest of the town, and extend for several kilometers into the earth. There is now a ticket office here. The first cave has lights, but do take a powerful flashlight (torch) anyway. You'll also need shoes with good traction, as inside it's slippery with moisture and bat crap.

Though the first few hundred meters of cavern have been equipped with a walkway and are lit by diesel-powered electric lights, most of this subterranean system is untouched. If you are not an experienced spelunker, you shouldn't wander too far into the caves; the entire extent has yet to be explored, let alone mapped.

As well as featuring funky stalactites, mostly named for animals, these caves are crammed with bats; at sunset, they fly out of the mouth of the cave in formations so dense they obscure the sky. For a dazzling display of navigation skills, sit at the entrance while they exit. The river here gushes from the cave in clean, cool and delicious torrents. You can swim in the river, which has some comfortably hot pockets close to shore.

Tours to the Grutas de Lanquín and Semuc Champey, offered in Cobán for US$35 per person (see p220), are the easiest way to visit these places. Tours take about two hours to reach Lanquín from Cobán; the price includes a packed lunch.

Maya Expeditions (see p81), based in Guatemala City, offers exciting one- to five-day rafting expeditions on the Río Cahabón.

If you're driving, you'll need a 4WD vehicle. The road from San Pedro Charca to El Pajal, where you turn off for Lanquín, is paved. The 11km from El Pajal to Lanquín is not. You can head on from Lanquín to Flores in 14 to 15 hours via El Pajal, Sebol, Raxrujá and Sayaxché. The road from El Pajal to Sebol is not paved. Or you can head from Lanquín to Sebol and Fray Bartolomé de Las Casas and on to Poptún.

SLEEPING & EATING

El Retiro (☎ 7983 0009; hammock/dm US$3/4, s/d US$6/12, with bathroom US$22; 🖳) This sublimely located hotel is about 500m along the road beyond Rabin Itzam. *Palapa* buildings look down over the greenest of green fields to a beautiful wide river – the same river that flows out from the Lanquín caves. It's safe to swim, and to inner-tube if you're a confident swimmer. The place is Guatemalan- and English-owned. Attention to detail in every respect makes this a backpackers' paradise. Dorm rooms have only four beds. Individual decor includes some clever use of tiles, shells, strings of beads and local fabrics. Excellent vegetarian food (three-course dinner US$4.50) is available in the hammock-lined restaurant. Plenty of info is provided for onward journeys and there are organized activities such as jungle walks.

La Divina Providencia (s/d US$3.50/7) In the center of Lanquín village, the plain wooden rooms here will do at a stretch if you're just stopping over and need a place to sleep. Upstairs rooms are much cheerier.

Rabin Itzam (s/d US$3.50/7, with bathroom US$13/16) The most comfortable option in the center, although the beds sag a bit. Rooms upstairs at the front (with shared bathroom) have good valley views.

El Recreo (☎ 7983 0057; hotel_el_recreo@hotmail .com; s/d US$10/20, with bathroom US$20/29; 🅿 🖳) Between the town and the caves, this place has that 'made for tour groups' feel to it, but the bungalows set around forested grounds are a good deal – spacious and well decorated. The rooms set in the basement with shared bathrooms might be a bit grim for some.

La Estancia de Alfaro (mains US$3-5; ⏲ breakfast, lunch & dinner) This large outdoor eatery halfway between town and El Retiro serves up good-sized plates of steak, eggs and rice and gets rowdy and beerish at night.

GETTING THERE & AWAY

Buses operate several times daily between Cobán and Lanquín, continuing to Cahabón. Buses leave Lanquín to return to Cobán at 3am, 4am, 5:30am and 1pm, and there are assorted microbuses with no fixed timetable. Since the last reliable return bus departs so early, it's best to stay the night.

Road to El Estor

If you're heading towards Río Dulce, a back road exists, although it's unpaved for most of the way and gets washed out in heavy rains. Transportation schedules along here are flexible at best. Ask around to see what the current situation is. Five minibuses daily leave Lanquín for Cahabón (US$2, one hour). The last of these leaves at 4pm, although you'll want to leave earlier to avoid getting stuck here. From Cahabón, one bus leaves daily for El Estor at 1pm (US$5, four hours), although if you miss it you should be able to get a ride in a pickup without too much trouble.

Semuc Champey

Nine kilometers south of Lanquín, along a rough, bumpy, slow road, is **Semuc Champey** (admission US$4), famed for its great 300m-long natural limestone bridge, on top of which is a stepped series of pools with cool, flowing river water good for swimming. The water is from the Río Cahabón, and much more of it passes underground, beneath the bridge. Though this bit of paradise is difficult to reach, the beauty of its setting and the perfection of the pools, ranging from turquoise to emerald-green,

CENTRAL & EASTERN GUATEMALA

make it worth it. Many people consider this the most beautiful spot in all Guatemala.

If you're visiting on a tour, some guides will take you down a rope ladder from the lowest pool to the river, which gushes out from the rocks below. Plenty of people do this and love it, though it is a bit risky.

It's possible to camp at Semuc Champey, but be sure to pitch a tent only in the upper areas, as flash floods are common down below. It's risky to leave anything unattended, as it might get stolen. The place now has 24-hour security, which may reassure potential campers, but you should keep your valuables with you. You will also need to bring all supplies, as there's no shop of any kind nearby.

Las Marías (☎ 7861 2209; www.posadalasmarias.com; dm US$3, s/d US$6/9.50, with bathroom US$9.50/14) is a rustic, laid-back place by the road 1km short of Semuc Champey. There are a couple of dorm rooms and three private rooms, all in wooden buildings in a verdant setting. Cool drinks and vegetarian food are available (full dinner US$2.60) from the restaurant, where you can see the Río Cahabón flowing past. This place offers cave tours (US$4/5.50 for guests/nonguests), tubing, walking tours and shuttles to Cobán for US$4. You can camp here for US$1.50 and rent a hammock for US$2.

Pickups run from the plaza in Lanquín to Semuc Champey – your chances of catching one are better in the early morning and on market days: Sunday, Monday and Thursday. If there are a lot of local people traveling, expect to pay US$0.65; otherwise, it's US$1.95. Minibuses also serve this route – they leave when full (or get bored of waiting) from the main street in Lanquín.

Fray Bartolomé de Las Casas

This town, often referred to simply as Fray, is a way station on the backdoor route between the Cobán/Lanquín area and Poptún on the Río Dulce–Flores highway. This route is nearly all along unpaved roads and is dotted with traditional Mayan villages where only the patriarchs speak Spanish, and then only a little. This is a great opportunity for getting off the 'gringo trail' and into the heart of Guatemala.

Fray is pretty substantial for being in the middle of nowhere, but don't let its size fool you. This is a place where the weekly soccer game is the biggest deal in town,

chickens languish in the streets and siesta is taken seriously.

The town itself is fairly spread out, with the plaza and most tourist facilities at one end and the market and bus terminus at the other. Walking between the two takes about 10 minutes. Coming from Cobán, you'll want to hop off at the central plaza.

The **post office** and **police station** are just off the plaza. Nearby, **Banrural** changes cash US dollars and traveler's checks. The **municipalidad** is on the plaza.

The friendly **Hotel La Cabaña** (☎ 7952 0352; 2a Calle 1-92 Zona 3; s/d US$3.50/7, with bathroom US$8/16) has the best accommodations in town. Eating options are limited here – you could try in the restaurant of the **Hotel Bartolo**, behind the plaza. Otherwise, grab a steak (with tortillas and beans; US$1.50) at the informal barbecue shacks that open up along the main street at night.

One daily bus departs from the plaza at 3am for Poptún (US$5, five to six hours, 100km). Buses for Cobán leave hourly between 4am and 4pm. Some go via Chisec (3½ hours, US$4). Others take the slower route via San Pedro Carchá.

LAS CONCHAS

From Fray you can visit Las Conchas, a series of limestone pools and waterfalls (admission US$3) on the Río Chiyú, which some say are better than those at Semuc Champey. The pools are up to 8m deep and 20m wide and connected by a series of spectacular waterfalls. The pools are not turquoise like those at Semuc.

Oasis Chiyú (☎ 5839 4473; www.naturetoursguatemala .com; dm incl breakfast & dinner US$20), a newish place right by the pools, has a wonderful tropical feel to it. Accommodations are in big, new rustic thatched-roof huts. Reservations are absolutely essential. The whole place has an atmosphere of serenity and seclusion. There's plenty to do here: kayaking (free for guests), 10m-high waterfalls to jump from, caves to explore, jungle trekking and visits to nearby Q'eqchi' communities. Volunteer work on community projects is also available. Tierra Madre Nature Tours operates out of here, and can arrange all-inclusive tours from Antigua or anywhere else in the country to Las Conchas. Local tour prices start at US$15 per person.

Regular minibuses (US$1, one hour) leave Fray for Chahal when full. From there you must change buses for Las Conchas (US$0.80). If you're in your own vehicle, look for the marked sign to Las Conchas, a few kilometers east of Chahal. Minibuses also go to Chahal direct from Cobán (US$5, five hours). If you're coming south from El Petén, get off in Modesto Mendez (known locally as Cadenas), catch a Chahal-bound minibus to Sejux (*Say*-whoosh) and wait for another minibus to take you the remaining 3km to Las Conchas. Whichever direction you're coming from, travel connections are always easiest in the morning and drop off severely in the late afternoon.

CHISEC

pop 20,600

The town of Chisec, 66km north of Cobán, is becoming a center for reaching several exciting destinations. This is thanks to the paving of nearly all the road from Cobán to Sayaxché and Flores, which runs through here, and some admirable community tourism programs aiming to help develop this long-ignored region, the population of which is almost entirely Q'eqchi' Maya.

Chisec has a few places to stay. The best hotel, **Hotel La Estancia** (☎ 5514 7444; s/d with bathroom US$15/20; P)), on the main road at the northern exit from town, has neat and sensible rooms with fan and cable TV. It has a restaurant and the swimming pool has some excellent waterslides in the shape of fallen tree trunks. **Hotel Nopales** (central plaza; s/d US$6/10) has surprisingly large rooms (with smell) set around a courtyard dominated by a permanently empty (unless it's been raining) swimming pool.

In Raxrujá, **Pensión Gutiérrez** (r per person US$4), a two-story wooden house, has decent rooms with mosquito net, fan and shared bathroom.

Buses leave Chisec for Cobán (US$1.95, two hours) eight times daily, from 3am to 2pm. Buses or minibuses to San Antonio and Raxrujá (one hour) go hourly, from 6am to 4pm. Some of these continue to Fray Bartolomé de Las Casas. There are also two services daily, morning and afternoon, to La Isla (1¼ hours) and two to Playa Grande (two hours), for the Parque Nacional Laguna Lachuá. Some Cobán–Sayaxché minibuses and buses pass through Chisec. There are at least five scheduled departures daily to both Sayaxché and Cobán from Raxrujá.

AROUND CHISEC

Lagunas de Sepalau

Surrounded by pristine forest, these turquoise **lagoons** (admission US$4; 8am-3pm) are 8km west of Chisec. Recently developed as a community ecotourism project by local villagers, tours of the area include a fair bit of walking and some rowboat paddling. The area is rich in wildlife: jaguars, tapir, iguanas, toucans and howler monkeys are all in residence.

There are three lagoons, the most spectacular of which is the third on the tour, Q'ekija, which is ringed by steep walls of thick jungle. This is a water source for the local community and swimming is prohibited at certain times of the year.

Pickups leave Chisec's plaza for the village of Sepalau Cataltzul throughout the day and there's usually a bus (US$1, 45 minutes) at 10:30am. On arrival at the village, you pay the entrance fee and a guide will take you on the 2km walk to the first lagoon.

Cuevas de B'ombi'l Pek

A mere 3km north of Chisec, these **painted caves** (admission US$3; 8am-3pm) remained undiscovered until 2001. They haven't been fully mapped yet, but it's thought that they connect to the Candelaria caves. The community-run guide office is by the roadside. Pay the entrance fee and the guide will take you on the 1.5km walk through cornfields to the entrance. The first, main cavern is the most impressive for its size (reaching 50m in height), but a secondary cave – just 1m wide – features paintings of monkeys and jaguars.

Any bus running north from Chisec can drop you at the guide office.

Cuevas de Candelaria

This 18km-long cave system, dug out by the subterranean Río Candelaria, holds some monstrous proportions – the main chamber is 30m high, 200m wide and has stalagmites measuring up to 30m in length. Natural apertures in the roof allow sunlight in, creating magical, eerie reflections.

The caves were used by the Q'eqchí Maya and you'll see some platforms and ladders carved into the stone. A two-hour guided tour costs US$3 per person. Two-day boat tours of the complex cost around US$35 per person.

The **Complejo Cultural de Candelaria** (☎ 5710 8753; cuevascandelarias@aol.com; cabins per person from US$50) offers supremely comfortable accommodation in stylishly decorated cabins. Excellent, French-influenced meals are included in the rates. Some slightly cheaper cabins with shared bathrooms are available.

Another couple of caves can be visited nearby at the **Comunidad Candelaria** (Km 309.5; guided tours per person US$1.30). Guides can be organized at the roadside *tienda* (store) for the short walk to the caves. Any bus running between Chisec and Raxrujá can drop you at either of these two places.

CANCUÉN

This large Mayan site hit the papers when it was 'discovered' in 2000, even though it had already been 'discovered' back in 1907. Excavations are still under way, but estimates say that Cancuén may rival Tikal (see p288) for size.

It's thought that Cancuén was a trading, rather than religious, center, and the usual temples and pyramids are absent. In their place is a grand palace boasting more than 150 rooms set around 11 courtyards. Carvings here are impressive, particularly on the grand palace, but also along the ball courts and the two altars that have been excavated to date.

Cancuén's importance seems to stem from its geographical/tactical position. Hieroglyphics attest to alliances with Calakmul (Mexico) and Tikal, whereas its relative proximity to the southern Highlands would have given it access to pyrite and obsidian, prized minerals of the Maya.

Artisans certainly worked here – their bodies have been discovered found dressed, unusually, in royal finery. Several workshops have also been uncovered, one containing a 17kg piece of jade.

Cobán tour companies (see p220) make day trips to Cancuén. To get here independently, catch a pickup (leaving hourly) from Raxrujá to La Unión (US$1, 40 minutes), from where you can hire a boat (US$4 per person) to the site.

PARQUE NACIONAL LAGUNA LACHUÁ

This **national park** (☎ 5704 1508; park admission US$5.50, campsites US$3.50, bunks with mosquito net US$9) is renowned for the perfectly round, pristine turquoise lake (220m deep) for which it was named. Until recently, this Guatemalan gem was rarely visited by travelers because it was an active, violent area during the civil war and the road was in pathetic disrepair. Now it fills

up quickly on weekends and public holidays, and if you're thinking about coming during these times it's a good idea to call and reserve a space. Overnight visitors can use the cooking facilities, so come prepared with food and drink. There is only one shower. You can no longer rent canoes for exploring the lake, but there are hiking trails. The Cobán tour outfits (p220) offer two-day and one-night trips for US$90 per person. Proyecto EcoQuetzal, also in Cobán, does jungle hikes (US$45, three days) to the **Río Ikbolay** in the Laguna Lachuá vicinity.

Outside the park, about 7km southwest of the park entrance, is **Finca Chipantún** (www .geocities.com/chipantun/main.html; campsites per person US$1.50, beds per person US$4), 4 sq km of private land bordering the Río Chixoy (Negro). It has teak and cardamom plantations plus virgin tropical rain forest, and some uncovered Mayan ruins. In addition to accommodations, there are horse-riding opportunities, forest trails, river trips, kayaking, and bird- and wildlife-watching. The owners can take you by boat on the Río Negro to El Peyan, a magical gorge. Meals cost US$2.50 to US$4.

A new road (though unpaved most of the way from Chisec) means you can get to the park entrance from Cobán in four hours by bus. Take a Playa Grande (Cantabal) bus from Cobán via Chisec and ask the driver to leave you at the park entrance, from which it's about a 4km walk to the lake.

WEST TO THE HIGHLANDS

From Playa Grande, a couple of buses a day make the tortuous journey across to Barillas (US$6, five hours), the first stop on the backdoor route to Huehuetenango in the western Highlands. The road here is unmade and liable to get washed out in the wet season, but it's a spectacular, fascinating journey well off the beaten track. Check with locals for current road conditions. For details on the onward journey from Barillas, see p189.

RÍO HONDO
pop 6900

Río Hondo (Deep River), 50km east of El Rancho junction and 130km from Guatemala City, is where Hwy 10 to Chiquimula heads south off the Carr al Atlántico (Hwy 9). Beyond Chiquimula are turnoffs to Copán, just across the Honduras border; to Esquipulas and on to Nueva Ocotepeque (Honduras); and a remote border crossing between Guatemala and El Salvador at Anguiatú, 12km north of Metapán (El Salvador).

The actual town of Río Hondo is northeast of the junction. Lodging places hereabouts may list their address as Río Hondo, Santa Cruz Río Hondo or Santa Cruz Teculután. Nine kilometers west of the junction are several attractive motels right on Hwy 9, which provide a good base for explorations of this region if you have your own vehicle. By car, it's an hour from here to Quiriguá, half an hour to Chiquimula and 1½ hours to Esquipulas. These motels are treated as weekend resorts by locals and residents of Guatemala City, so they are heavily booked on weekends. They're all modern, pleasant places, with well-equipped bungalows (all have cable TV and bathroom), spacious grounds with large or giant swimming pools, and good restaurants, open from 6am to 10pm daily. You can find other eateries along the highway.

The town is home to the **Parque Aquatico Longarone** (adult/child US$5/7; ☉ daylight hours) with giant waterslides, an artificial river and other water-based fun.

The motels are near each other at Km 126 on Hwy 9. **Hotel Santa Cruz** (☎ 7934 7112; ysik6780@yahoo.com; s/d with air-con US$16/20; P ⚇ ⚒), the most laid-back option here, has modern, comfortable rooms set in duplex bungalows spread over a large area with plenty of foliage. Its popular **restaurant** (breakfast US$3-5, 3-course lunches US$5.50; ☉ breakfast, lunch & dinner) is cheaper than those at the other motels.

On the north side of the highway, **Hotel Nuevo Pasabién** (☎ 934 7201; pasabien@infovia.com .gt; s/d/tr US$20/39/42; P ⚒ ⚇) has large rooms with big windows. This hotel is a good choice for people traveling with children who can enjoy the three pools with all manner of fancy slides.

Hotel El Atlántico (☎ 7933 0598; s/d US$30/40; P ⚇ ⚒ ⚇), the best-looking place in town, has plenty of dark wood fittings and well-spaced bungalows. The pool area is tranquil, with some shady sitting areas.

Valle Dorado

Another attraction of Río Hondo is the Valle Dorado **aquatic park and tourist center** (☎ 7943 6666; www.hotelvalledorado.com; Hwy 9 Km149; d/tr/f US$58/68/108). This large complex 14km past the Hwy 10 junction and 23km from the other Río Hondo hotels includes an **aquatic park** (adult/child US$7/6; ☉ 8:30am-5:30pm Tue-Sun) with giant pools, waterslides, toboggans and other entertainment. Make reservations on weekends.

ESTANZUELA
pop 9300

Traveling south from Río Hondo along Hwy 10, you are in the midst of the Río Motagua valley, a hot expanse of what is known as 'dry tropic,' which once supported a great number and variety of dinosaurs. Three kilometers south of Hwy 9 you'll see a small monument on the right-hand (west) side of the road commemorating the earthquake disaster of February 4, 1976.

Less than 2km south of the earthquake monument is the small town of Estanzuela, with its **Museo de Paleontología, Arqueología y Geología Ingeniero Roberto Woolfolk Sarvia** (admission free; ☉ 9am-5pm), a startling museum filled with dinosaur bones – some reconstructed and rather menacing-looking. Most of the bones of three giant creatures are here, including those of a huge ground sloth some 30,000 years old and a prehistoric whale. Other exhibits include early Mayan artifacts. To find the museum, go west from the highway directly through the town for 1km, following the small blue signs pointing to the *museo*.

ZACAPA
pop 40,800 / elev 230m

Capital of the department of the same name, Zacapa is just east of Hwy 10 a few kilometers south of Estanzuela. This town offers little to travelers, though the locals do make cheese, cigars and superb rum. The few hotels in town are basic and will do in an emergency, but better accommodations are available in Río Hondo, Esquipulas and Chiquimula. The bus station is on the road into town from Hwy 10.

CHIQUIMULA
pop 44,200 / elev 370m

Another departmental capital, this one set in a mining and tobacco-growing region, Chiquimula is on Hwy 10, 32km south of the Carr al Atlántico. It is a major market town for all of eastern Guatemala, with lots of daily buying and selling activity. For travelers it's not a destination but a transit point. Your goal is probably the fabulous Mayan ruins at Copán in Honduras, just across the border from El Florido. There are also some interesting journeys between Chiquimula and Jalapa, 78km to the west (p232). Among other things, Chiquimula is famous for its sweltering climate and its decent budget hotels (a couple have swimming pools).

Orientation & Information

Though very hot, Chiquimula is easy to get around on foot.

Banco G&T (7a Av 4-75, Zona 1; ☼ 9am-8pm Mon-Fri, 10am-2pm Sat) Half a block south of the plaza. Changes cash US dollars and traveler's checks, and gives cash advances on Visa and MasterCard.

Biblioteca El Centro (cnr 4a Calle & 8a Av; per hr US$0.80; ☼ 8am-7pm Mon-Fri, 8am-6pm Sat & Sun) For email and internet access.

Post office (10a Av) In a dirt alley between 1a and 2a Calles, around to the side of the building opposite the bus station.

Telgua (3a Calle) Plenty of card phones, a few doors downhill from Parque Ismael Cerna.

Viajes Tivoli (☎ 7942 4915; 8a Av 4-71, Zona 1) Can help you with travel arrangements.

Sleeping

Hotel Dario (☎ 7942 0192; 8a Av 4-40, Zona 1; s/d US$4/6, with bathroom US$9/12) Big, plain rooms around a leafy courtyard. Upstairs rooms share a breezy sitting area, but have shared bathrooms.

Hotel Hernández (☎ 7942 0708; 3a Calle 7-41, Zona 1; s/d US$5.50/8, with bathroom US$11/13; ⊠ ⊠ ℙ) It's hard to beat the Hernández – it's been a favorite for years, and keeps going strong, with its central position, spacious, simple rooms and good-sized swimming pool. Check out the carp pond in the *pila* (laundry trough).

Posada Doña Eva (☎ 7942 4956; 2a Calle 9-61, Zona 1; s/d with bathroom US$8/12) Set way back from the busy streets, the cool clean rooms here offer a minimalist approach to comfort, with TV and fans.

Hotel Victoria (☎ 7942 2732; cnr 2a Calle & 10a Av; s/d with bathroom US$9/12) If you're just looking for somewhere to crash close to the bus terminal, these rooms are a pretty good bet. Clean and not too cramped, with TV and a decent *comedor* (cheap eatery) downstairs. Get one at the back – the street noise can be insane.

Hotel Casa (☎ 7942 5357; 6a Calle 6-20, Zona 1; s/d with bathroom US$12/16; ℙ ⊠) Neat rooms done out

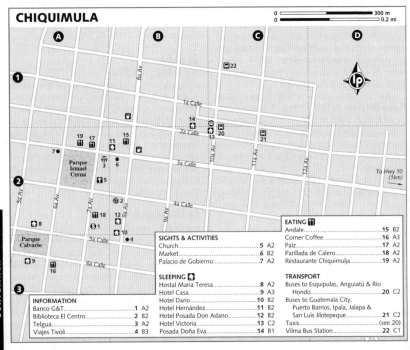

CHIQUIMULA

0 ———— 300 m
0 ———— 0.2 mi

To Hwy 10 (1km)

SIGHTS & ACTIVITIES
Church..5 A2
Market...6 B2
Palacio de Gobierno.............................7 A2

SLEEPING
Hostal Maria Teresa..............................8 A2
Hotel Casa...9 A3
Hotel Dario..10 B2
Hotel Hernández...................................11 B2
Hotel Posada Don Adano......................12 B2
Hotel Victoria.......................................13 C2
Posada Doña Eva..................................14 B1

INFORMATION
Banco G&T..1 A2
Biblioteca El Centro.................................2 B2
Telgua...3 A2
Viajes Tivoli...4 B3

EATING
Andale..15 B2
Corner Coffee.......................................16 A3
Paíz..17 A2
Parillada de Calero................................18 A2
Restaurante Chiquimulja.......................19 A2

TRANSPORT
Buses to Esquipulas, Anguiatú & Río
Hondo...20 C2
Buses to Guatemala City,
Puerto Barrios, Ipala, Jalapa &
San Luís Jilotepeque...........................21 C2
Taxis...(see 20)
Vilma Bus Station................................22 C1

in pleasant shades of mustard and blue, in a quiet location just off the Parque Calvario. Air-conditioning costs an extra US$5.

Hotel Posada Don Adano (☎ 7942 3924; 8a Av 4-30, Zona 1; s/d with bathroom US$13/20; P 🔀) The Don offers the best deal in this price range – neat, complete rooms with TV, fan, air-conditioning, a couple of sticks of furniture and good, firm beds.

Hostal Maria Teresa (☎ 7942 0177; 5a Calle 6-21, Zona 1; s/d with bathroom US$25/45; 🔀) Set around a gorgeous colonial courtyard with wide shady passageways. The single rooms are a bit poky, but the doubles are generous and all the comforts are here: cable TV, hot showers and air-conditioning.

Eating

There's a string of cheap *comedores* on 8a Av behind the market. At night, snack vendors and taco carts set up along 7a Av opposite the plaza, selling the cheapest eats in town.

Andale (8a Av 2-34, Zona 1; mains US$3-5; 🍽 lunch & dinner) For that late-night (until 11pm) Tex-Mex munchout, this is the place to be – big burritos, tacos three for US$1.50 and cheap beer in a relaxed, clean environment.

Restaurante Chiquimulja (3a Calle 6-51; breakfasts US$2-3.25, mains US$4-7; 🍽 breakfast, lunch & dinner) In the Hotel Chiquimulja, this is an impressive palm-roofed building on two levels. Relax with a lovely drink and choose from the list of pasta dishes, prawns and grilled meats. The *parrillada* (mixed grill) platter for two is a real heart-stopper, in more ways than one.

Corner Coffee (6a Calle 6-70, Zona 1; mains US$4-8; 🍽 lunch & dinner) You could argue with the syntax, but this air-con haven right on the lovely Parque Calvario serves up the best range of steaks, pasta, burgers and bagels in town.

Parillada de Calero (7a Av 4-83; mains US$5-8; 🍽 breakfast, lunch & dinner) An open-air steak-house, serving the juiciest flame-grilled cuts in town. This is also the breakfast hotspot – the Tropical Breakfast (pancakes with a mound of fresh fruit; US$4.50) goes down well in this climate.

Paíz (3a Calle) On the plaza, this grocery store is tremendous and sells close to everything under the sun. Stock up here for a picnic, or stop in to enjoy the air-con.

Getting There & Away

Several companies operate buses to Guatemala City and Puerto Barrios; all of them arrive and depart from the bus station area on 11a Av, between 1a and 2a Calles. Ipala and San Lúis Jilotepeque microbuses and the Jalapa bus also go from here. Minibuses to Esquipulas, Río Hondo and Anguiatú and buses to Flores arrive and depart a block away, on 10a Av between 1a and 2a Calles. **Vilma** (☎ 7942-2064), which operates buses to El Florido, the border crossing on the way to Copán, has its own bus station a couple of blocks north.

Agua Caliente (Honduras border) Take a minibus to Esquipulas and change there.

Anguiatú (Salvador border) (US$2, one hour, 54km) Hourly minibuses, from 5am to 5:30pm.

El Florido (Honduras border) (US$2, 1½ hours, 58km) Minibuses depart from the Vilma bus station every 30 minutes, from 5:30am to 4:30pm.

Esquipulas (US$2, 45 minutes, 52km) Minibuses run every 10 minutes, from 4am to 8pm. Sit on the left for the best views of the basilica.

Flores (US$10, seven to eight hours, 385km) Transportes María Elena (☎ 7942 3420) goes at 6am, 10am and 3pm.

Guatemala City (US$5, three hours, 169km) Rutas Orientales and other companies depart at least hourly, from 3am to 3.30pm. The 3am bus leaves from the plaza, the rest from the bus station.

Ipala (US$1.50, 1½ hours) Microbuses depart half-hourly, from 5am to 6pm.

Jalapa (US$3, 3½ hours, 78km) One direct bus at 6am daily. Otherwise take a microbus to Ipala or San Luís Jilotepeque (US$1, one hour) and change.

Puerto Barrios (US$5, 4½ hours, 192km) Buses run every 30 minutes, from 4am to 6pm.

Quiriguá (US$4, two hours, 103km) Take a Puerto Barrios bus.

Río Dulce (US$4.50, three hours, 144km) Take a Flores bus, or a Puerto Barrios bus to La Ruidosa junction and change there.

Río Hondo (US$2, 35 minutes, 32km) There are mini-buses every 30 minutes, from 5am to 6pm. Or take any bus heading for Guatemala City, Flores or Puerto Barrios. On Sunday, Guatemala City buses won't let you on for Río Hondo – take a minibus.

AROUND CHIQUIMULA
Volcán de Ipala

Volcán de Ipala is a 1650m volcano, notable for its especially beautiful clear crater lake measuring nearly a kilometer around and nestled below the summit at 1493m. The dramatic hike to the top takes you from 800m to 1650m in about two hours, though you can drive halfway up in a car. There are trails, a visitors center and a campsite on the shores of the lake. To get there, take a bus

---

LOCAL LORE: HOW THE LAGUNA DE GÜIJA WAS FORMED

In the beginning of time, powerful beings lived on Earth. One created the volcanoes, each of which had an owner, except for the Suchítan volcano. Devils began to argue over who should be the owner.

Some said they deserved it because they were younger. Others said it was theirs because they were older. All were liars and cheats. The slyest of them all said he would give his crown to whoever won ownership of the volcano.

Then the argument really began. One devil said he deserved it because he had invented sickness. Another said he deserved it because he invented floods. A third said it was his because he invented envy.

The argument raged on. The oldest devil said he was the rightful owner because he had invented laziness, so that humans could do no good. The other devils applauded, and the old devil thought he had won.

But the devil who invented envy still thought he was the winner, and soon a fight started – devils were gouging eyes, hitting each other with tree trunks and throwing stones. The fight would never end because they were all equally powerful.

Just then, a group of angels came down from Heaven. The old devil said to their leader, San Miguel, 'I deserve the crown because I invented laziness.'

'Show me the crown,' said San Miguel.

They showed him the crown, which was beautiful, made of thousands of stars.

'None of you shall have this crown,' said San Miguel. 'Now go back to Hell, and never return.'

With this, he threw the crown on the ground, where the stars turned into water and the Laguna de Güija was formed.

---

from Chiquimula (1½ hours) or Jalapa (two hours) to Ipala and transfer to a microbus to Agua Blanca (US$0.60, every 15 minutes). The trailhead is at El Sauce just before Agua Blanca; look for the blue Inguat sign. There are several banks and serviceable (but basic) *hospedajes* (budget hotels) in Ipala if you want to stay overnight there.

Jalapa

pop 50,800

Jalapa is a small, friendly town 78km west of Chiquimula, and the route is a stunning one: verdant gorges choked with banana trees alternate with fog-enveloped valleys. Crossing the rugged mountain passes you'll see waterfalls, rivers and creeks flowing through the undergrowth. Though there isn't much going on in Jalapa proper, it's a good stopover before or after Volcán Ipala. There are plenty of services for travelers. Banks that change cash US dollars and traveler's checks are clustered around the bus terminal.

SLEEPING & EATING

Hotel Recinos (☎ 9722 2580; s/d US$5/10, with bathroom US$9/18) If you're just passing through, this pink palace on the west side of the terminal is your best bet. The clean rooms with fan and shared bathroom are a good deal. More-expensive rooms come with cable TV.

Pensión Casa del Viajero (☎ 7922 4086; 1a Av 0-64; s/d US$5/10, with bathroom US$8.50/17) Four longish blocks from the bus terminal, this is a safe, clean place to stay, and definitely the pick of the budget joints. Some rooms are better than others – have a look around. There's a restaurant here that serves up big steaks and snacks all day.

Posada de Don José Antonio (☎ 7922 5751; Av Chipilapa A 0-64, Zona 2; s/d with bathroom US$15/18; P) The big, clean rooms here are bare and simple, but offer a cool sanctuary from the heat outside; they're set around a small courtyard and come with TV. There's also a restaurant.

Hotel Villa Plaza (☎ 7922 4841; 1a Calle 0-70, Zona 2; s/d US$15/22;) This modern hotel offers the most comfortable deal in town. The big rooms have hot-water bathroom (not that you're ever likely to need it) and cable TV. Air-con costs US$5 extra.

Restaurante Casa Real (1a Calle; mains US$4; breakfast, lunch & dinner) Next door to the Hotel Villa Plaza and serving up grilled meat, soups and snacks, this humble eatery is an excellent choice for meals.

GETTING THERE & AWAY

Buses leave Jalapa for Chiquimula hourly from 5am. Plenty of microbuses head to Ipala, where you can change for Chiquimula. For Esquipulas, change in Chiquimula. Buses to Guatemala City leave half-hourly between 2am and 3pm. Transportes Melva travels via Jutiapa and Cuilapa (US$4, 3½ hours, 167km). Other buses take the quicker route via Sanarate and the Carr al Atlántico.

PADRE MIGUEL JUNCTION & ANGUIATÚ

Between Chiquimula and Esquipulas (35km from Chiquimula and 14km from Esquipulas), Padre Miguel junction is the turnoff for Anguiatú, the border of El Salvador, which is 19km (30 minutes) away. Minibuses pass by frequently, coming from Chiquimula, Quetzaltepeque and Esquipulas.

The border at Anguiatú is open from 6am to 7pm daily. Plenty of trucks cross here. Across the border there are hourly buses to San Salvador, passing through Metapán and Santa Ana.

VOLCÁN DE QUETZALTEPEQUE

About 10km east of the village of Quetzaltepeque, this volcano tops out at 1900m. The walk to the top is tough going, through thick subtropical pine forest, and the trail disappears in sections. From the summit are excellent views of the nearby Ipala and Suchítan volcanoes and the surrounding countryside. Due to the condition of the trail, you really need a guide to undertake this trek – you should be able to pick one up in Quetzaltepeque for around US$15 per person.

Buses running between Chiquimula and Esquipulas pass through Quetzaltepeque. There are no hotels here – you're better off basing yourself in Esquipulas.

ESQUIPULAS

pop 22,300

From Chiquimula, Hwy 10 goes south into the mountains, where it's a bit cooler. After an hour's ride through pretty country, the highway descends into a valley ringed by mountains, where Esquipulas stands. Halfway down the slope, about a kilometer from the center of town, there is a *mirador* (lookout) from which to get a good view. The reason for a trip to Esquipulas is evident as soon as you catch sight of the place, dominated by the great Basílica de Esquipulas towering

above the town, its whiteness shimmering in the sun. The view has changed little in over 150 years since explorer John L Stephens saw it and described it in his book *Incidents of Travel in Central America, Chiapas and Yucatan* (1841):

> Descending, the clouds were lifted, and I looked down upon an almost boundless plain, running from the foot of the Sierra, and afar off saw, standing alone in the wilderness, the great church of Esquipulas, like the Church of the Holy Sepulchre in Jerusalem, and the Caaba in Mecca, the holiest of temples…I had a long and magnificent descent to the foot of the Sierra.

History

This town may have been a place of pilgrimage before the Spanish conquest. Legend has it that the town takes its name from a noble Mayan lord who ruled this region when the Spanish arrived, and who received them in peace.

With the arrival of the friars, a church was built, and in 1595 an image of Christ carved from black wood was installed behind the altar. The steady flow of pilgrims to Esquipulas became a flood after 1737, when Pedro Pardo de Figueroa, Archbishop of Guatemala, came here on pilgrimage and went away cured of a chronic ailment. Delighted with this development, the prelate commissioned a huge new church to be built on the site. It was finished in 1758, and the pilgrimage trade has been the town's livelihood ever since.

Esquipulas has assured its place in modern history as well: in 1986, President Vinicio Cerezo Arévalo spearheaded a series of meetings here with the other Central American heads of state to negotiate regional agreements on economic cooperation and peaceful conflict resolution. The resulting pact, known as the Esquipulas II Accord, became the seed of the Guatemalan Peace Accords, which were finally signed in 1996.

Orientation & Information

The basilica is the center of everything. Most of the good hotels are within a block or two of it, as are numerous small restaurants. The town's most luxurious hotel, the Gran Chortí, is on the outskirts, along the road to Chiquimula. The highway does not enter town;

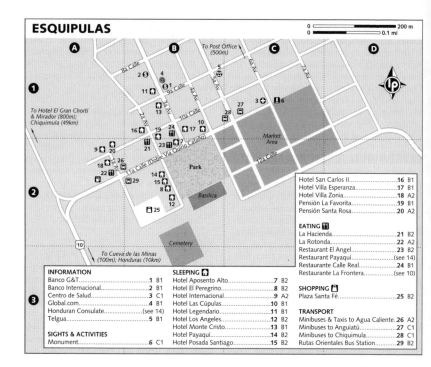

11a Calle, also sometimes called Doble Vía Quirio Cataño, comes in from the highway and is the town's main drag.

Banco Internacional (3a Av 8-87, Zona 1) Changes cash and traveler's checks, gives cash advances on Visa and MasterCard, is the town's American Express agent and has a Visa ATM.

Global.com (3a Av; per hr US$0.80) Opposite Banco Internacional; check your email here.

Post office (6a Av 2-15) About 10 blocks north of the center.

Telgua (cnr 5a Av & 9a Calle) Plenty of card phones.

Basilica

A massive pile of stone that has resisted the power of earthquakes for almost 250 years, the basilica is approached through a pretty park and up a wide flight of steps. The impressive facade and towers are floodlit at night.

Inside, the devout approach the surprisingly small (with all the fuss, you'd think it was life-sized) El Cristo Negro with extreme reverence, many on their knees. Incense, murmured prayers and the scuffle of sandaled feet fills the air. When there are throngs of pilgrims, you must enter the church from the

side to get a close view of the famous Black Christ. Shuffling along quickly, you may get a good glimpse or two before being shoved onward by the crowd behind you. On Sundays, religious holidays and (especially) during the festival around January 15, the press of devotees is intense. Guatemalan tourist authorities estimate that one million visitors a year come to Esquipulas to see the Black Christ. On weekdays, you may have the place to yourself, which can be very powerful and rewarding. On weekends, you'll probably feel very removed from the intensity of emotion shown by the majority of pilgrims whose faith is very deep.

The annual **Cristo de Esquipulas festival** (January 15) sees mobs of devout pilgrims coming from all over the region to worship at the altar of the Black Christ.

When you leave the church and descend the steps through the park and exit right to the market, notice the vendors selling straw hats that are decorated with artificial flowers and stitched with the name 'Esquipulas,' perfect for pilgrims who want everyone to know they've made the trip. These are very popular rearview mirror accessories for chicken bus drivers countrywide. Cruising the religious kitsch sold by the throngs of vendors around the basilica is an entertaining diversion.

Cueva de las Minas

The **Centro Turístico Cueva de las Minas** (admission US$1.50; ⏲ 6:30am-4pm) has a 50m-deep cave (bring your own light), grassy picnic areas and the Río El Milagro, where people come for a dip and say it's miraculous. The cave and river are half a kilometer from their entrance gate, which is behind the basilica's cemetery, 300m south of the turnoff into town on the road heading towards Honduras. Refreshments are available.

If you've got kids along (or even if you don't), **Parque Chatun** (☎ 7943 4164; www.parque chatun.com; adult/child US$6.50/4; ⏲ 9am-6pm Tue-Sat), a fun park 3km out of town, should provide some light relief from all the religious business. There are swimming pools, a climbing wall, campgrounds, a petting zoo and a mini bungee jump. If you don't have a vehicle, look for the miniature train doing rounds of the town – it will take you out there for free.

Sleeping

Esquipulas has an abundance of places to stay. On holidays and during the annual festival, every hotel in town is filled, whatever the price; weekends are super busy as well, with prices substantially higher. These higher prices are the ones given here. On weekdays when there is no festival, there are *descuentos* (discounts). For cheap rooms, look in the streets immediately north of the towering basilica.

BUDGET

Pensión Santa Rosa (☎ 7943 2908; cnr 10a Calle & 1a Av, Zona 1; s/d US$5/8, with bathroom US$14/17) Some splashes of color make this a cheerier-than-usual budget choice. Rooms with shared bathroom are plainer; those with bathroom have a bit of furniture and cable TV. There are several, similar budget hotels on this street.

Hotel Monte Cristo (☎ 7943 1453; www.hotelmonte cristo.i8.com; 3a Av 9-12, Zona 1; s/d US$10/12, with bathroom US$15/18; P) Good-sized rooms with a bit of furniture and super-hot showers. A policy of not letting the upstairs rooms until the downstairs ones are full might see you on the ground floor.

Hotel Posada Santiago (☎ 7943 2023; 2a Av; s/d US$10/14, with bathroom & cable TV US$20; P) With

some interesting (but don't get excited) architecture, these rustic-chic rooms are some of the most attractive in town. They're spacious and clean, with good showers and cable TV.

Hotel El Peregrino (☎ 7943 1054; 2a Av 11-94, Zona 1; s/d US$10/15, with bathroom US$15/20; 🖳) Motel-style rooms looking out onto plant-filled balconies. The rooftop pool is what makes this place.

Hotel Aposento Alto (☎ 7943 1115; 3a Av 10-35, Zona 1; r with bathroom US$20; P) Kinda cramped, but comfortable enough. The paintjob goes a bit heavy on the yellow, but touches such as funky tile work and dark wood trims offset that. Some rooms have balconies.

Hotel Villa Esperanza (☎ 7943 0281; 3a Av 10-29, Zona 1; s/d US$20; P) Just a few steps from the basilica, this place has bright, modern rooms with a few sticks of furniture. Rooms at the back are bigger but get less ventilation.

MIDRANGE

Hotel Internacional (☎ 7943 1131; 10a Calle 0-85, Zona 1; s/d US$20/30, with air-con US$25/35; P 🏊 🖳) This establishment is on three levels around a covered courtyard. Rooms are comfortable and plain. It wouldn't be such a good deal if it weren't for the big covered swimming pool out back.

Hotel Los Angeles (☎ 7943 1254; 2a Av 11-94, Zona 1; s/d US$20/35; P) Spacious rooms face a plant-filled balcony. Somebody obviously got a bulk deal on tiles, but these are good-value rooms, and have some of the only bathtubs on offer around town.

Hotel Villa Zonia (☎ 7943 1133; 10a Calle 1-84, Zona 1; s/d from US$24/37; P) With two big beds squeezed into smallish rooms, what you've got here is pretty much wall-to-wall bed. The rooms are nicely done, though, and have private balconies looking out onto a quiet street.

Hotel Las Cúpulas (☎ /fax 7943 1570; cnr 11a Calle & 4a Av; s/d US$30/40) If you can ignore the inordinate amount of leather lounge suites in the lobby here, this is a reasonable place. Bonuses include big, firm beds, those little courtesy shampoo bottles and balconies with tables and chairs for taking in the street action. Prices drop drastically from Monday to Thursday when there's no religious festival.

Hotel Payaquí (☎ 7943 1143; www.hotelpayaqui .com; 2a Av 11-56; s/d US$45/55; P 🏊 🖳) Once the fanciest hotel in town, this one's showing a bit of wear. It *is* trying, though, with a decent restaurant, a couple of swimming pools and a day spa offering massages, facials and so on.

TOP END

Hotel El Gran Chortí (☎ 7943 1148; Carr Internacional a Honduras Km 222; s/d US$46/61, 4-person ste US$92; 🅿 ⛌ 🈂) One kilometer west of the church on the road to Chiquimula, this hotel's lobby floor is composed of a hectare of black marble; behind it a serpentine swimming pool is set amid lawns, gardens and umbrella-shaded café tables. There's a games room and, of course, a good restaurant, bar and *cafetería*. The rooms have all comforts.

Hotel Legendario (☎ 7943 1824; www.portahotels .com; cnr 3a Av & 9a Calle, Zona 1; s/d US$50/58; 🅿 🈂) The fanciest hotel in town goes all out on the services, right down to a separate kids swimming pool. Rooms are reasonable – big enough, with new beds, large windows opening onto a grassy courtyard and all the comforts you'd expect for the price.

Eating

Restaurants are slightly more expensive here than in other parts of Guatemala. Budget restaurants are clustered at the north end of the park, where hungry pilgrims can find them readily. Most eateries open from 6:30am until 9pm or 10pm daily.

The street running north opposite the church – 3a Av – has several eateries. All of the midrange and top-end hotels have their own dining rooms.

Restaurante Calle Real (3a Av; breakfasts US$2-4; mains US$4-6; ☟ breakfast, lunch & dinner) Typical of many restaurants here, this big eating barn turns out cheap meals for the pilgrims. There's a wide menu, strip lighting and loud TV.

Restaurant El Angel (☎ 7943 1372; cnr 11a Calle & 2a Av; mains US$4-8; ☟ lunch & dinner) This main-street Chinese eatery does all the standard dishes, plus steaks and a good range of *licuados* (milkshakes). Home delivery is available.

ourpick La Hacienda (cnr 2a Av & 10a Calle, Zona 1; mains from US$6; ☟ breakfast, lunch & dinner) The best steakhouse in town also serves up some decent seafood and pasta dishes. There's a café-bakery attached and the breakfasts (US$5.50) are a good (but slightly pricey) bet.

La Rotonda (11a Calle; breakfasts from US$2.50, large pizzas US$10; ☟ breakfast, lunch & dinner) Opposite Rutas Orientales bus station, this is a round building with chairs arranged around a circular open-air counter under a big awning. It's a welcoming place, clean and fresh. There are plenty of selections to choose from, including pizza, pasta and burgers.

Restaurant Payaquí (breakfasts US$3, mains US$8; ☟ breakfast, lunch & dinner) On the west side of the park in the hotel of the same name, this is a bright and clean *cafetería* with big windows looking out onto the park. Prices are reasonable, and there's a good selection.

Restaurante La Frontera (breakfast US$3-5, mains US$5-11; ☟ breakfast, lunch & dinner) Opposite the park and attached to the Hotel Las Cúpulas, this is a spacious, clean place serving up a good variety of rice, chicken, meat, fish and seafood dishes for good prices.

Getting There & Away

Buses to Guatemala City arrive and depart from the **Rutas Orientales bus station** (☎ 7943 1366; cnr 11a Calle & 1a Av), near the entrance to town. Minibuses to Agua Caliente arrive and depart across the street; taxis also wait here, charging the same as the minibuses, once they have five passengers.

Minibuses to Chiquimula and to Anguiatú depart from the east end of 11a Calle; you'll probably see them hawking for passengers along the main street.

Agua Caliente (Honduran border) (US$1.80, 30 minutes, 10km) Minibuses every 30 minutes, from 6am to 5pm.

Anguiatú (Salvador border) (US$1.50, one hour, 33km) Minibuses every 30 minutes, from 6am to 6pm.

Chiquimula (US$1.50, 45 minutes, 52km) Minibuses every 15 minutes, from 5am to 6pm.

Flores (US$12, eight to 10 hours, 437km) Transportes María Elena (☎ 7943 0448) buses depart at 4am, 8am and 1pm from east of the basilica, amid the market.

Guatemala City (US$7, four hours, 222km) Rutas Orientales *servicio especial* buses depart at 6:30am, 7:30am, 1:30pm and 3pm; ordinary buses depart every 30 minutes, from 4:30am to 6pm.

COPÁN SITE (HONDURAS)

The ancient city of **Copán** (admission US$15; ☟ 8am-4pm), 13km from the Guatemala border in Honduras, is one of the most outstanding Mayan achievements, ranking in splendor with Tikal, Chichén Itzá and Uxmal. To fully appreciate Mayan art and culture, you must visit Copán. This can be done on a long day trip by private car, public bus or organized tour, but it's better to take at least two days, staying the night in the town of Copán Ruinas. This is a sweet town, with good facilities, so unless you're in a huge rush, try to overnight here. Get to the site around opening time to avoid the heat and the crowds.

There are two Copáns: the town and the ruins. The town is about 12km east of the Guatemala–Honduras border. Confusingly, the town is named Copán Ruinas, though the actual ruins are just over 1km further east. Minivans coming from the border may take you on to the ruins after a stop in the town. If not, the *sendero peatonal* (footpath) alongside the road makes for a pretty 20-minute walk, passing several stelae and unexcavated mounds along the way to the Copán ruins and Las Sepulturas archaeological site, a couple of kilometers further.

Crossing the Border

The Guatemalan village of El Florido, which has no services beyond a few soft-drink stands, is 1.2km west of the border. At the border crossing are a branch of **Banrural** (7am-6pm Mon-Sat), the Vilma bus office and one or two snack stands. The border crossing is open from 6am to 7pm daily but it closes to vehicles at 6pm.

Money changers will approach you on both sides of the border anxious to change quetzals for Honduran lempiras, or either for US dollars. Usually they're offering a decent rate because there's a Guatemalan bank right there and the current exchange rate is posted in the Honduran immigration office – look for it. There's no bank on the Honduran side of the border. Still, if the money changers give you a hard time, change enough at the border to get you into Copán Ruinas and then hit one of the banks there. Of course, if it's Sunday, you're beholden to the money changers. Though quetzals and US dollars may be accepted at some establishments in Copán Ruinas, it's best to change some money into lempiras.

At the crossing you must present your passport to the Guatemalan immigration and customs authorities, pay fees (although there is no official fee for leaving Guatemala) of up to US$4, then cross the border and do the same thing with the Honduran authorities. Guatemala and Honduras (along with Nicaragua and El Salvador) are members of the CA-4, a trade agreement much like the EU but with more infighting and chaos. *Supposedly*, the CA-4 is designed to facilitate the movement of people through the region. Having entered the CA-4, you should be authorized to move throughout the region freely for 90 days (or as long as your visa stipulates). In practice, the reality is somewhat more Central American.

Basically, border officials are bored, unsupervised and underpaid. Most likely you'll end up paying a few dollars to get across. Travelers have tried playing the waiting game here and lost – all you do is end up standing around for a few hours, then paying the fee anyway. The Hondurans, at least, issue a nice, official-looking receipt. For more on the CA-4, see p318.

When you return through this border point, you must again pass through both sets of immigration and customs. Whether you pay fees again is up to the whims of the officials, but you could point out that you've already done so and see where that gets you.

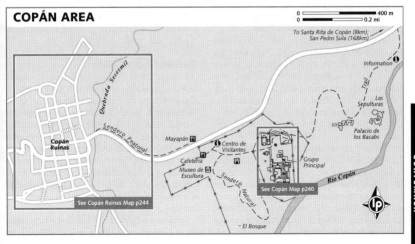

COPÁN AREA

For information on transportation to and from Copán Ruinas, see p247.

History

PRE-COLUMBIAN

People have been living in the Copán valley at least since around 1400 BC; ceramic evidence has been found from around that date. Copán must have had significant commercial activity since early times, as graves showing marked Olmec influence have been dated to around 900 to 600 BC.

In the 5th century AD one royal family came to rule Copán, led by a mysterious king named Mah K'ina Yax K'uk' Mo' (Great Sun Lord Quetzal Macaw), who ruled from AD 426 to 435. Archaeological evidence indicates that he was a great shaman, and later kings revered him as the semidivine founder of the city. The dynasty ruled throughout Copán's florescence during the classic period (AD 250–900).

Of the subsequent kings who ruled before AD 628 we know little. Only some of their names have been deciphered: Mat Head, the second king (no relation to Bed Head); Cu Ix, the fourth king; Waterlily Jaguar, the seventh; Moon Jaguar, the 10th; and Butz' Chan, the 11th.

Among the greatest of Copán's kings was Smoke Imix (Smoke Jaguar), the 12th king, who ruled from 628 to 695. Smoke Imix built Copán into a major military and commercial power in the region. He may have taken over the nearby princedom of Quiriguá, as one of the famous stelae at that site bears his name and image. By the time he died in 695, Copán's population had grown substantially.

Smoke Imix was succeeded by Uaxaclahun Ubak K'awil (18 Rabbit; r 695–738), the 13th king, who willingly took the reins of power and pursued further military conquest. In a war with his neighbor from Quiriguá, King Cauac Sky, 18 Rabbit was captured and beheaded. He was succeeded by K'ak' Joplaj Chan K'awiil (Smoke Monkey; r 738–49), the 14th king, whose short reign left little mark on Copán. Smoke Monkey's son, K'ak' Yipyaj Chan K'awiil (Smoke Shell; (r 749–63), was, however, one of Copán's greatest builders. He commissioned the city's most famous and important monument, the great Escalinata de los Jeroglíficos (Hieroglyphic Stairway), which immortalizes the achievements of the dynasty from its establishment until 755,

when the stairway was dedicated. It is the longest inscription ever discovered in the Mayan lands.

Yax Pac (Sunrise or First Dawn; r 763–820), Smoke Shell's successor and the 16th king, continued the beautification of Copán. The final occupant of the throne, U Cit Tok', became ruler in 822, but it is not known when he died.

Until recently, the collapse of the civilization at Copán had been a mystery. Now, archaeologists have begun to surmise that near the end of Copán's heyday the population grew at an unprecedented rate, straining agricultural resources. In the end, Copán was no longer agriculturally self-sufficient and had to import food from other areas. The urban core expanded into the fertile lowlands in the center of the valley, forcing both agricultural and residential areas to spread onto the steep slopes surrounding the valley. Wide areas were deforested, resulting in massive erosion that further decimated food production and brought flooding during rainy seasons. Interestingly, this environmental damage of old is not too different from what is happening today – a disturbing trend, but one that meshes with the Mayan belief that life is cyclical and history repeats itself. Skeletal remains of people who died during Copán's final years show marked evidence of malnutrition and infectious diseases, as well as decreased life spans.

The Copán valley was not abandoned overnight – agriculturists probably continued to live in the ecologically devastated valley for maybe another one or two hundred years. But by the year 1200 or thereabouts, even the farmers had departed, and the royal city of Copán was reclaimed by the jungle.

EUROPEAN DISCOVERY

The first known European to see the ruins was a representative of Spanish King Felipe II, Diego García de Palacios, who lived in Guatemala and traveled through the region. On March 8, 1576, he wrote to the king about the ruins he found here. Only about five families were living here at the time, and they knew nothing of the history of the ruins. The discovery was not pursued, and almost three centuries went by until another Spaniard, Colonel Juan Galindo, visited the ruins and made the first map of them.

It was Galindo's report that stimulated John L Stephens and Frederick Catherwood to come to Copán on their Central American journey in 1839. When Stephens published the book *Incidents of Travel in Central America, Chiapas and Yucatán* in 1841, illustrated by Catherwood, the ruins first became known to the world at large.

TODAY

The history of Copán continues to unfold today. The remains of 3450 structures have been found in the 24 sq km surrounding the Grupo Principal (Principal Group), most of them within about half a kilometer of it. In a wider zone, 4509 structures have been detected in 1420 sites within 135 sq km of the ruins. These discoveries indicate that at the peak of civilization here, around the end of the 8th century AD, the valley of Copán had more than 27,500 inhabitants, a population figure not reached again until the 1980s.

In addition to examining the area surrounding the Grupo Principal, archaeologists continue to make new discoveries in the Grupo Principal itself. Five separate phases of building on this site have been identified; the final phase, dating from AD 650 to 820, is what we see today. But buried underneath the visible ruins are layers of other ruins, which archaeologists are exploring by means of underground tunnels. This is how the Templo Rosalila (Rosalila Temple) was found, a replica of which is now in the Museo de Escultura (p242). Below Rosalila is yet another, earlier temple, Margarita. Two of the excavation tunnels, including Rosalila, are open to the public.

Archaeologists also continue to decipher more of the hieroglyphs, gaining greater understanding of the early Maya in the process. In 1998, a major discovery was made when archaeologists excavated a burial chamber beneath the Acrópolis presumed to be that of the great ruler Mah K'ina Yax K'uk' Mo' (Great Sun Lord Quetzal Macaw).

Information

Admission to Copán includes entry to **Las Sepulturas** archaeological site but not to the two **excavation tunnels** (⊗ 8am-3:30pm), for which admission is US$15.

Also at the site is the **Museo de Escultura** (admission US$7), where many of the original stelae are housed, as well as an awesome replica of the impressive and colorful Rosalila Temple.

The **Centro de Visitantes** (Visitors Center) at the entrance to the ruins houses the ticket office and a small exhibition about the site and its excavation. Nearby are a *cafetería*, and souvenir and handicrafts shops. There's a picnic area along the path to the Principal Group of ruins. A **Sendero Natural** (Nature Trail) entering the forest several hundred meters from the visitors center passes by a small ball court.

Pick up a copy of the booklet *History Carved in Stone: A guide to the archaeological park of the ruins of Copán* by noted archaeologists William L Fash and Ricardo Agurcia Fasquelle; it's available at the visitors center for US$4. It will help you to understand and appreciate the ruins. It's also a good idea to go with a guide, who can help to explain the ruins and bring them to life. Guides are US$20 no matter the size of the group; packs of trained guides hang out at the visitors center.

Visitors should not touch any of the stelae or sit on the altars at Copán.

Grupo Principal

The Principal Group of ruins is about 400m beyond the visitors center across well-kept lawns, through a gate in a strong fence and down shady avenues of trees. A group of resident macaws loiters along here. The ruins themselves have been numbered for easy identification and a well-worn path circumscribes the site.

Stelae of the Gran Plaza

The path leads to the Gran Plaza (Great Plaza; Plaza de las Estelas) and the huge, intricately carved stelae portraying the rulers of Copán. Most of Copán's best stelae date from AD 613 to 738. All seem to have originally been painted; a few traces of red paint survive on Stela C. Many stelae had vaults beneath or beside them in which sacrifices and offerings could be placed.

Many of the stelae on the Gran Plaza portray King 18 Rabbit, including stelae A, B, C, D, F, H and 4. Perhaps the most beautiful stela in the Gran Plaza is Stela A (AD 731); the original has been moved inside the Museum of Sculpture, and the one outdoors is a reproduction. Nearby and almost equal in beauty are Stela 4 (731); Stela B (731), depicting 18 Rabbit upon his accession to the throne; and Stela C (782), with a turtle-shaped altar in front. This last stela has figures on both sides. Stela E (614), erected on top of Estructura 1

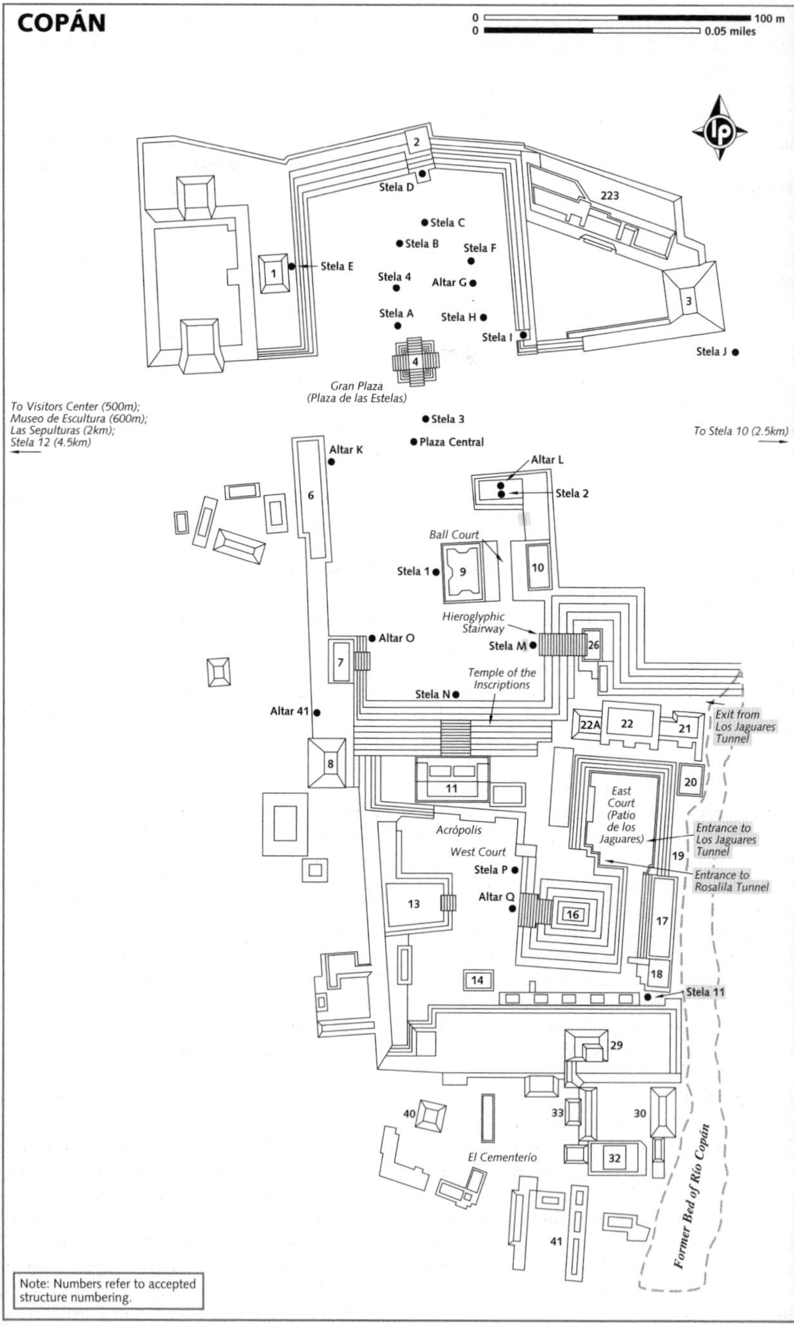
COPÁN
0 100 m
0 0.05 miles
Stela D
Stela C
Stela B
Stela F
Stela E
Stela 4
Altar G
Stela A
Stela H
Stela I
Stela J
223
Gran Plaza (Plaza de las Estelas)
To Visitors Center (500m); Museo de Escultura (600m); Las Sepulturas (2km); Stela 12 (4.5km)
Stela 3
Plaza Central
To Stela 10 (2.5km)
Altar K
Altar L
Stela 2
Ball Court
Stela 1
Hieroglyphic Stairway
Altar O
Stela M
Temple of the Inscriptions
Stela N
Altar 41
Exit from Los Jaguares Tunnel
22A
East Court (Patio de los Jaguares)
Entrance to Los Jaguares Tunnel
Entrance to Rosalila Tunnel
Acrópolis
West Court
Stela P
Altar Q
Stela 11
El Cementerio
Former Bed of Río Copán
Note: Numbers refer to accepted structure numbering.

(Structure 1) on the west side of the Great Plaza, is among the oldest.

At the northern end of the Gran Plaza at the base of Estructura 2, Stela D (736) also portrays King 18 Rabbit. On its back are two columns of hieroglyphs; at its base is an altar with fearsome representations of Chac, the rain god. In front of the altar is the burial place of Dr John Owen, an archaeologist with an expedition from Harvard's Peabody Museum who died during excavation work in 1893.

On the east side of the plaza is Stela F (721), which has a more lyrical design than other stelae here, with the robes of the main figure flowing around to the other side of the stone, where there are glyphs. Altar G (800), showing twin serpent heads, is among the last monuments carved at Copán. Stela H (730) may depict a queen or princess rather than a king. Stela I (692), on the structure that runs along the east side of the plaza, is of a person wearing a mask. Stela J, further off to the east, resembles the stelae of Quiriguá in that it is covered in glyphs, not human figures.

Juego de Pelota

South of the Great Plaza, across what is known as the Plaza Central, is the Juego de Pelota (Ball Court; 731), the second largest in Central America. The one you see is the third one on this site; the other two smaller courts were buried by this construction. Note the macaw heads carved atop the sloping walls. The central marker in the court is the work of King 18 Rabbit.

Escalinata de los Jeroglíficos

South of the ball court is Copán's most famous monument, the Escalinata de los Jeroglíficos (Hieroglyphic Stairway; 743), the work of King Smoke Shell. Today it's protected from the elements by a roof. The flight of 63 steps bears a history (in several thousand glyphs) of the royal house of Copán; the steps are bordered by ramps inscribed with more reliefs and glyphs. The story told on the inscribed steps is still not completely understood because the stairway was partially ruined and the stones jumbled.

At the base of the Hieroglyphic Stairway is Stela M (756), bearing a figure (probably King Smoke Shell) dressed in a feathered cloak; glyphs tell of the solar eclipse in that year. The altar in front shows a plumed serpent with a human head emerging from its jaws.

Beside the stairway, a tunnel leads to the tomb of a nobleman, a royal scribe who may have been the son of King Smoke Imix. The tomb, discovered in June 1989, held a treasure-trove of painted pottery and beautiful carved jade objects that are now in Honduran museums.

Acrópolis

The lofty flight of steps to the south of the Hieroglyphic Stairway mounts the Templo de las Inscripciones (Temple of the Inscriptions). On top of the stairway, the walls are carved with groups of hieroglyphs. On the south side of the Temple of the Inscriptions is the Patio Occidental (West Court), with the Patio Oriental (East Court), also called the Patio de los Jaguares (Court of the Jaguars) to its east. In the West Court, be sure to see Altar Q (776), among the most famous sculptures here; the original is inside the Museum of Sculpture. Around its sides, carved in superb relief, are the 16 great kings of Copán, ending with its creator, Yax Pac. Behind the altar is a sacrificial vault in which archaeologists discovered the bones of 15 jaguars and several macaws that were probably sacrificed to the glory of Yax Pac and his ancestors.

The East Court also contains evidence of Yax Pac – his tomb, beneath Estructura 18. Unfortunately, the tomb was discovered and looted long before archaeologists arrived. Both the East and West Courts hold a variety of fascinating stelae and sculptured heads of humans and animals. To see the most elaborate relief carving, climb Estructura 22 on the northern side of the East Court. This was the Templo de Meditación (Temple of Meditation) and has been heavily restored over recent years.

Túnel Rosalila & Túnel de los Jaguares

In 1999, exciting new additions were made to the wonders at Copán when two excavation tunnels were opened to the public. The Túnel Rosalila (Rosalila Tunnel) exposes the Rosalila Temple below Estructura 16, and the Túnel de los Jaguares (Jaguar Tunnel) shows visitors the Tumba Galindo (Galindo Tomb), below Estructura 17 in the southern part of the Patio Oriental.

Descending into these tunnels is interesting, but not so exciting as when they were opened in 1999; at the time of writing you could only visit 25m of the Rosalila Tunnel and 95m of the longer Jaguar Tunnel. The Rosalila Tunnel reveals a little of the actual temple over which Estructura 16 was built; the carvings are remarkably crisp and vivid, especially the Sun God mask looming over the doorway. This is considered by some scholars to be the best-preserved stucco edifice in the Mayan world. Everything is behind Plexiglas to protect it from natural and human elements. Under the Rosalila Temple is the Margarita Temple, built 150 years earlier. Beneath that, there are other even earlier platforms and tombs.

The Túnel de los Jaguares is less dramatic, with its burial tombs and niches for offerings. The Galindo Tomb was one of the first tombs discovered at Copán, in 1834. Bones, obsidian knives and beads were found here, and archaeologists date the tomb's antebase mask to AD 540. The decorative macaw mask here is incredible. The full extent of this tunnel is 700m.

Though the US$15 price of admission is dear for a short-lived pair of highlights, these tunnels are worth a look if you're into history.

Museo de Escultura

Copán is unique in the Mayan world for its sculpture, and the **Museo de Escultura** (Museum of Sculpture; admission US$7; 8am-3:40pm) is fittingly magnificent. Just entering the museum is an impressive experience in itself. Walking through the mouth of a serpent, you wind through the entrails of the beast, then suddenly emerge into a fantastic world of sculpture and light.

The highlight of the museum is a true-scale replica (in full color) of the Rosalila Temple, discovered in nearly perfect condition by archaeologists in 1989 by means of a tunnel dug into Estructura 16, the central building of the Acrópolis (p241). Rosalila, dedicated in AD 571 by Copán's 10th ruler, Moon Jaguar, was apparently so sacred that when Estructura 16 was built over it, the temple was not destroyed but was left completely intact. The original Rosalila Temple is still in the core of Estructura 16.

The other displays in the museum are stone carvings, brought here for protection from the elements. All the important stelae may eventually be housed here, with detailed reproductions placed outdoors to show where the stelae originally stood. So far, at least Altar Q and Stelae A, N, P and Estructura 2 have

been brought into the museum, and the ones you see outdoors are reproductions.

El Bosque & Las Sepulturas

Excavations at El Bosque and Las Sepulturas have shed light on the daily life of the Maya in Copán during its golden age.

Las Sepulturas, once connected to the Gran Plaza by a causeway, may have been the residential area where rich and powerful nobles lived. One huge, luxurious residential compound seems to have housed some 250 people in 40 or 50 buildings arranged around 11 courtyards. The principal structure, called the **Palacio de los Bacabs** (Palace of the Officials), had outer walls carved with the full-sized figures of 10 males in fancy feathered headdresses; inside was a huge hieroglyphic bench.

To get to Las Sepulturas you have to go back to the main road, turn right, then right again at the sign (2km from the Gran Plaza).

The walk to get to El Bosque is the real reason for visiting it, as it is removed from the main ruins. It's a one-hour (5km) walk on a well-maintained path through foliage dense with birds, though there isn't much of note at the site itself save for a small ball court. Still, it's a powerful experience to have an hour-long walk on the thoroughfares of an ancient Mayan city all to yourself. To get to El Bosque, go right at the hut where your ticket is stamped. There have been no reports of crimes against tourists here.

COPÁN RUINAS
pop 6000

The town of Copán Ruinas, often simply called Copán, is just over 1km from the famous Mayan ruins of the same name. It's a beautiful place paved with cobblestones and lined with white adobe buildings with red-tiled roofs. There's even a lovely colonial church on the recently remodeled plaza. The Maya have inhabited this valley, which has an aura of timeless harmony, for about 2000 years. Copán has become a primary tourist destination, but this hasn't disrupted the town's integrity to the extent one might fear.

Orientation & Information

The Parque Central, with the church on one side, is the heart of town. Copán is very small, and everything is within a few blocks of the plaza. This is fortunate for visitors, since

---

CALLING COPÁN

The Honduras telephone country code is ☎ 504. Like Guatemala, Honduras has no area or city codes. So when dialing a number in Copán Ruinas from Guatemala, or any other country, you dial the international access code (usually 00), then 504, then the local number.

---

the town doesn't use street signs. The ruins are on the road to La Entrada. Las Sepulturas archaeological site is a few kilometers further along.

Internet services cost around US$1 per hour:

Copán Net One block south and one block west of the plaza.

Maya Connections Two locations, one across from Vamos a Ver restaurant, the other in La Casa de Todo, one block east of the plaza. International phone and fax services are also available, and both branches offer laundry service (US$0.50 to wash, dry and fold each pound; US$1 per kg), plus book exchange.

For US dollars, the banks give a better rate than the money changers at the border, but slightly less than banks elsewhere in Honduras.

Banco Atlántida (☽ 8:30am-3:30pm Mon-Fri, 8:30am-noon Sat) On the plaza, changes cash US dollars and traveler's checks and gives cash advances on Visa cards.

Banco Credomatic Also on the plaza; has a Visa and MasterCard ATM.

Banco de Occidente (☽ 8:30am-4:30pm Mon-Fri, 8:30am-noon Sat) On the plaza, changes cash US dollars and traveler's checks, and quetzals, and gives cash advances on Visa and MasterCard.

Honduran immigration office (Palacio Municipal; ☽ 7am-4:30pm Mon-Fri) On the plaza; come here for visa matters.

Hondutel Telephone office around the corner from the post office.

Post office A few doors from the plaza.

Tourist office (www.copanhonduras.org; ☽ 11am-7pm) Run by a chamber of commerce; down the hill half a block east of the plaza.

Sights & Activities

Though the main attraction of the Copán region is the archaeological site, there are other fine places to visit in the area. The **Museo de Arqueología Maya** (admission US$3; ☽ 8am-4pm Mon-Sat), on the town plaza, is well worth a visit. It contains the original Stela B, portraying King

18 Rabbit. Other exhibits of painted pottery, carved jade, Mayan glyphs and a calendar round are also interesting and informative, as is the Tumba del Brujo, the tomb of a shaman or priest who died around AD 700 and was buried with many items under the east corner of the Plaza de los Jaguares. **Casa K'inich** (admission free; ☽ 8am-noon & 1-5pm Mon-Sat), on the north side of the plaza, inside the little artisan market, is an interactive museum for kids all about the Maya.

About four blocks north of the plaza is the **Mirador El Cuartel**, the old jail, with a magnificent view over town.

A pleasant, easy walk on the road on the south side of town provides a fine view over the corn and tobacco fields surrounding Copán. On this same side of town is an agreeable walk to the river.

The **Macaw Mountain Bird Park** (☎ 651 4245; www.macawmountain.com; admission US$10; ☽ 9am-5pm), 2.5km out of town, is an extensive private reserve aimed at saving Central American macaws. There's plenty of them in evidence, along with toucans, motmots, parrots, kingfishers and orioles, all flying around freely. Even if you're not a bird freak, it's a lovely place to wander around, with plenty of walking trails weaving through the lush forest and over boardwalks to various lookout points and swimming holes. The entrance ticket – which includes a guided tour in English – is valid for three days and there's a café-restaurant on the property.

The **Enchanted Wings Butterfly House** (☎ 651 4133; www.hondurasecotours.com; adult/child US$6/2; ☽ 8am-5pm) is a nature center about a 10-minute walk west of the plaza on the road back to Guatemala. It has beautiful live and preserved butterflies, and numerous tropical flowers including around 200 species of orchids. With such a pretty name, how could you miss it?

Horse rides can be arranged by any of the town's tour companies and most hotels. You can ride to the ruins or make other, lengthier excursions. You will most likely be approached on the street by somebody wanting to rent you a horse. Unfortunately, there have been a number of incidents of payment without delivery, and it's recommended that you go through an agency. The Hacienda El Jaral (p248) also offers horse riding. Three-hour rides (US$10 to US$15) out of Café ViaVia and the Tunkul Bar (both in the second block west of the plaza) visit a local school sponsored by Spaniards.

A popular horseback excursion is to **Los Sapos** (US$2), 5km from town. The *sapos* (toads) are old Mayan stone carvings in a spot with a beautiful view over the town. This place is connected with Mayan fertility rites. You can get there by horseback in about half an hour or walk in about an hour, all uphill. From Los Sapos you can walk to a stela. Nearby is **Hacienda San Lucas**, a century-old farmhouse that has been converted into a B&B and restaurant (p248). There are walking trails here too.

Language Courses

Ixbalanque Spanish School (☎ /fax 651 4432; www .ixbalanque.com), a short walk out of town, offers

20 hours of one-on-one instruction in Spanish for US$210 per week, including homestay with a local family that provides three meals a day. Instruction only costs US$130 per week. **Guacamaya Spanish Academy** (☎ /fax 651 4360; www.guacamaya.com), across the road from the Manzana Verde hostel, offers much the same deal.

Tours

A huge number of tours can be organized from Copán Ruinas. Local companies promote these widely. You can cave, tube a river, visit a Mayan village and make tortillas or manufacture ceramics, plunge into hot springs, visit a coffee plantation or head off into the wilds of Honduras.

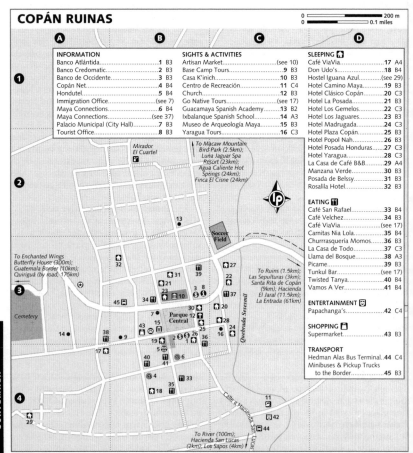

COPÁN RUINAS

0   200 m
0   0.1 miles

INFORMATION
Banco Atlántida.................................1 B3
Banco Credomatic..............................2 B3
Banco de Occidente............................3 B3
Copán Net...4 B4
Hondutel...5 B4
Immigration Office.........................(see 7)
Maya Connections.............................6 B4
Maya Connections......................(see 37)
Palacio Municipal (City Hall)...............7 B3
Tourist Office....................................8 B3

SIGHTS & ACTIVITIES
Artisan Market..............................(see 10)
Base Camp Tours...............................9 B3
Casa K'inich....................................10 B3
Centro de Recreación.......................11 C4
Church...12 B3
Go Native Tours.............................(see 17)
Guacamaya Spanish Academy...........13 B2
Ixbalanque Spanish School...............14 A3
Museo de Arqueología Maya.............15 B3
Yaragua Tours..................................16 C3

SLEEPING
Café ViaVia......................................17 A4
Don Udo's.......................................18 B4
Hostel Iguana Azul.......................(see 29)
Hotel Camino Maya..........................19 B3
Hotel Clásico Copán.........................20 B3
Hotel La Posada...............................21 B3
Hotel Los Gemelos...........................22 C3
Hotel Los Jaguares...........................23 B3
Hotel Madrugada..............................24 C3
Hotel Plaza Copán............................25 B3
Hotel Popol Nah...............................26 B3
Hotel Posada Honduras....................27 C3
Hotel Yaragua..................................28 C3
La Casa de Café B&B.........................29 A4
Manzana Verde.................................30 B3
Posada de Belssy..............................31 B3
Rosalila Hotel...................................32 B3

EATING
Café San Rafael................................33 B4
Café Velchez.....................................34 B3
Café ViaVia..................................(see 17)
Carnitas Nia Lola..............................35 B4
Churrrasquería Momos......................36 B3
La Casa de Todo...............................37 C3
Llama del Bosque.............................38 A3
Picame...39 B3
Tunkul Bar...................................(see 17)
Twisted Tanya..................................40 B4
Vamos A Ver....................................41 B4

ENTERTAINMENT
Papachanga's...................................42 C4

SHOPPING
Supermarket.....................................43 B3

TRANSPORT
Hedman Alas Bus Terminal..44 C4
Minibuses & Pickup Trucks
to the Border....................45 B3

Mirador El Cuartel

To Macaw Mountain Bird Park (2.5km); Luna Jaguar Spa Resort (23km); Agua Caliente Hot Springs (24km); Finca El Cisne (24km)

Soccer Field

To Enchanted Wings Butterfly House (300m); Guatemala Border (10km); Quiriguá (by road, 175km)

Cemetery

To Ruins (1.5km); Las Sepulturas (3km); Santa Rita de Copán (9km); Hacienda El Jaral (11.5km); La Entrada (61km)

Parque Central

Quebrada Sesesmil

Calle a Hacienda San Lucas

To River (100m); Hacienda San Lucas (2km); Los Sapos (4km)

Xukpi Tours (☎ 651 4435), operated by Jorge Barraza, also runs several ecological tours both locally and further afield. His ruins and bird-watching tours are justly famous, and he'll do trips to all parts of Honduras and to Quiriguá (Guatemala). Most days Jorge can be found at the archaeological site. You can also contact him through Café ViaVia.

Yaragua Tours (☎ 651 4147; fax 651 4695) is opposite the Hotel Yaragua. Samuel from Yaragua leads local tours, horse-riding trips and excursions to Lago de Yojoa. Caving trips are another option.

Base Camp Tours, across the road from Café ViaVia, offers a range of original and adventurous tours around the local area on foot, motorcycle and horseback. One horse-riding tour goes up to nearby San Rafael, where you have the option of whizzing back down on a 22 zip-line canopy tour (US$30). An excellent two-hour walking tour delves beneath the glossy surface of the town and investigates the reality of life for many Hondurans.

Sleeping
BUDGET
Manzana Verde (☎ 651 4652; dm US$4) A beautifully decked-out hostel, run by the same people as the Café ViaVia, with six beds in bunks per dorm. Common areas are comfortably set up, there's heaps of free, reliable tourist advice and kitchen access for guests.

Hostel Iguana Azul (☎ 651 4620; www.iguanaazul copan.com; dm/s/d US$4/8/11) This funky place three blocks west and two blocks south of the plaza is next door to La Casa de Café B&B (p246) and operated by the same friendly people. It has eight comfy bunk beds in two rooms with shared piping-hot, terrific bathroom in a colonial-style ranch home. Three private rooms sleep two. There's also a pretty garden. The common area has books, magazines, travel guides and lots of travel information. This is backpacking elegance at its finest.

Hotel Posada Honduras (☎ 651 4082; s/d US$4.50/5.50, with bathroom US$6/8; **P**) There's not a whole lot of joy in this, the cheapest hotel in town, but if you're looking for a bargain bed, these aren't the worst in the country. The courtyard at least is pretty: full of mango, mamey and lemon trees. Shared bathrooms have hot water, private bathrooms have cold.

Hotel Los Gemelos (☎ 651 4077; s/d US$5.50/8; **P**) A longtime budget-watcher's favorite,

a block northeast from the plaza. The simple rooms look out onto a leafy garden patio with flowers and birds. The shared bathrooms are gender-specific.

Posada de Belssy (s/d US$11/15; ⊠) Run by a charming local family, this place has great rooms with balconies overlooking the mountains on the outskirts of town. All the mod cons – cable TV, hot showers, air-conditioning – are here.

Café ViaVia (☎ 651 4652; www.viaviacafé.com; s/d US$12/14) This small European-style hotel is run by two young, energetic, helpful, travel-loving Belgian couples. (It's part of the Joker group, a Belgian-led organization of cafés with a travel theme around the world including at Louvain, Zanzibar, Kathmandu and Yogyakarta.) Café ViaVia Copán has five spotless rooms with private hot-water bathroom, tiled floors and great beds (2m long for the tall folks reading this!) There are hammocks, a small garden and enough space to chill out. It's a great place to come for tourist information, and has an art gallery and lively bar attached. English, French, German and Dutch are spoken here.

Rosalila Hotel (☎ 651 4235; s/d US$14/20) Despite the technicolor paint job, this is one of the better budget deals in town. Rooms look out onto a leafy courtyard and have super-hot showers, big TVs and firm beds.

Hotel Clásico Copán (☎ 651 4040; s/d with bathroom US$13/15; **P**) Good-sized standard rooms set upstairs around a lush courtyard. If you don't want TV, they'll take a couple of bucks off the price.

Hotel La Posada (☎ 651 4059; laposada@hotelmarina copan.com; s/d US$15/25) Good-value, tranquil and comfortable, La Posada is only half a block from the plaza. Its 19 rooms with hot-water bathroom, fan and TV are set around two leafy patios. There's very tasty, free black coffee first thing in the morning.

Hotel Yaragua (☎ 651 4147; www.yaragua.com; s/d US$20/25) The bright-yellow paint job and jungly patio area give this place a cheery feel. Rooms are smallish but comfortable and you can't beat the central location.

MIDRANGE & TOP END
Hotel Madrugada (☎ 651 4092; s/d US$25/50; **P**) This beautiful little hotel is tucked away in a corner, but actually has one of the best locations in town, overlooking a babbling creek. Rooms are generously sized and fitted out with period touches such as four-poster

beds. There are plenty of armchairs and hammocks on the wide wooden balcony.

Hotel Popol Nah (☎ 651 4645; r US$25) Right off the park, this tranquil little spot has comfortable, modern rooms with tiled floors. Try to get one upstairs with a balcony.

La Casa de Café B&B (☎ 651 4620; www.casadecafecopan.com; s/d incl breakfast US$35/45) This classy B&B four blocks from the plaza has loads of character in a beautiful setting – the garden area with tables and hammocks has a view over cornfields to the mountains of Guatemala. The 10 rooms with hot-water bathroom have wooden ceilings, antique ceiling fans and other nice touches, and all prices include a hearty breakfast. This place has a good library pertaining to Honduras. It also rents comfortable, fully equipped two-bedroom houses, starting from US$70 per night, with discounts for longer stays. You can check them out at www.casajaguarcopan.com.

Hotel Los Jaguares (☎ 651 4451; jaguares@copanhonduras.org; s/d US$36/40; P ⊠) A surprisingly good deal right on the plaza. The rooms don't have views, but are clean and cheery enough, without being overly stylish.

Don Udo's (☎ 553 2675; www.donudos.com; s/d US$40/60; ⊠) A lovely little B&B run by a Dutch-Honduran couple (and guess which one decided that all the tap water – even in the showers – should be purified?). Rooms are decently sized and well decorated, and set around a cheery courtyard patio.

Hotel Camino Maya (☎ 651 4518; www.caminomayahotel.com; s/d US$48/54; P ⊠ ▫ ▣) Shades of old British colonial rule run through this place – the decor's all very stiff upper lip, with a bit of exotic native carving thrown in. The restaurant downstairs lays on a big fry-up breakfast (US$5.50), just to drive the point home. The swimming pool area set in large gardens is gorgeous.

Hotel Plaza Copán (☎ 651 3832; www.plazacopanhotel.com; s/d US$49/55; P ⊠ ▫ ▣) This classically styled hotel right on the plaza has a range of good-smelling, atmospheric but modern rooms. The dark wood furniture and Spanish tiling give it that extra boost of class. Some rooms have private balconies and views of the church. Each room differs, so look at a few before choosing. The hotel has a restaurant and a terrace with views.

Eating

The town's little food market is right by the Parque Central.

Café San Rafael (snacks US$1; ⊗ 9am-7:30pm) This café serves organic coffee grown at the *finca* of the same name, just out of town. There's also a yummy range of teas and homemade snacks on offer.

Café Velchez (breakfasts US$0.90-3.50, cakes per slice US$1.80; ⊗ 8am-8pm) This pleasant, wood-paneled café has good views out over the plaza from the upper floor. The menu doesn't go much beyond coffee, cakes, juice and breakfast, but it does them all well.

Café ViaVia (breakfasts US$1.40-2.40, mains US$3-5; ⊗ 7am-10pm) This terrific restaurant serves breakfast, lunch and dinner in a convivial atmosphere, with tables overlooking the street and a replica of Altar Q behind the bar. The organically grown coffee it prepares is excellent, bread is homemade and there's always a good selection of vegetarian and meat-based dishes on offer.

La Casa de Todo (mains US$3-5; ⊗ breakfast, lunch & dinner) This restaurant/café/gift shop/stationery store has a lush backyard, perfect for sipping a cold *licuado* or sampling the healthy, innovative breakfasts and salads on offer.

Llama del Bosque (mains US$3-6; ⊗ breakfast, lunch & dinner) This large, popular place has a bit of a dining hall feel to it, but the side balcony is lush and cool. The menu has a good selection of Honduran meals and snacks; the *anafre* (fondue cooked in a clay pot; US$4) is especially tasty.

Picame (mains US$3-6; ⊗ breakfast, lunch & dinner) This cute little café-restaurant does a seriously full breakfast, yummy roast chicken and an assortment of burgers and sandwiches.

Churrasquería Momos (mains US$4.50-7; ⊗ lunch & dinner) With one of the best settings in town, this big open-air steakhouse occupies a huge *palapa*. It's popular with tourists and locals alike.

Carnitas Nia Lola (dishes US$3-6.20; ⊗ 7am-10pm) Two blocks south of the plaza, this open-air restaurant has a beautiful view toward the mountains over corn and tobacco fields. It's a relaxing place with simple and economical food; the specialties are charcoal-grilled chicken and beef. Happy hour starts at 6:30pm.

Vamos A Ver (mains US$6-10; ⊗ breakfast, lunch & dinner) Although the outdoor jungly setting is a bit more imaginative than the food on offer, this place is popular for its large portions and laid-back atmosphere. Homemade breads, a variety of international cheeses, tasty soups, fruit or vegetable salads, rich coffee, fruit *licuados*, a wide variety of teas and always something for vegetarians are just a taste of what's on offer.

Twisted Tanya (mains US$15; ☻ lunch & dinner) Set upstairs, with a lovely balcony sporting views out to the mountains, Tanya's serves up some good versions of Italian and Asian-influenced dishes. Cardboard Moroccan-style lampshades add an artistic flourish. A starter of soup or salad is included in the price.

Entertainment

Café ViaVia and the bar in Carnitas Nia Lola are happening spots in the evening. Café ViaVia also shows movies on Sunday night in low season, nightly in high season; proceeds go to Cine Campesino – an innovative grassroots project that projects educational and cultural films in rural locations in Honduras. The Hotel Camino Maya's **Centro de Recreación** (admission $US1.80; ☻ disco 6am-2am Fri & Sat) has a disco that's popular with locals and a few tourists. It's beside the Quebrada Sesesmil, two blocks south and one block east of the plaza. Also down here is **Papachanga's** (☻ from midnight Thu-Sat), a popular, laid-back reggae bar. It heats up around midnight, when all the bars in the center are required by a town council ordnance to close.

Getting There & Away

If you need a Honduran visa in advance, you can obtain it at the Honduran consulate in Esquipulas or Guatemala City (p313).

Several Antigua travel agencies offer weekend trips to Copán (US$125), which may include stops at other places, including Quiriguá. All-inclusive day trips from Antigua to Copán cost around US$90 and are very rushed. Check with the agencies in Antigua (p107).

BUS

It's 227km (five hours) from Guatemala City to El Florido, the Guatemalan village on the Honduras border. **Hedman Alas** (☎ 651 41037) runs direct 1st-class services daily in both directions between Copán Ruinas and Guatemala City (US$35), leaving its office in Copán Ruinas at 1pm and 5:30pm and Guatemala City at 5am. Coming from

other places, you have to take a bus to Chiquimula, and change there for a connecting service to the border.

If you're coming from Esquipulas, you can get off the bus at Vado Hondo, the junction of Hwy 10 and the road to El Florido, and wait for a bus there. As the buses to El Florido usually fill up before departing from Chiquimula, it may be just as well to go the extra 8km into Chiquimula and secure your seat before the bus pulls out. Traveling from the border to Esquipulas, there's no need to go into Chiquimula; minibuses ply the route to Esquipulas frequently.

Minivans and some pickups depart for Copán Ruinas from the Honduras side of the border regularly throughout the day. They should charge around US$1.50, payable before you depart, for the 20-minute ride. Drivers may hassle you about the fare but late in the day they have the trump card.

Minibuses and pickups from Copán Ruinas to Guatemala depart from the intersection one block west of the plaza. They leave every 40 minutes (or when full), from 6am to 6pm, and charge around US$2 – check the price beforehand. On the Guatemala side, buses to Chiquimula (US$2, 1½ hours, 58km) leave the border hourly from 5:30am to 11:30am then hourly from noon to 4pm and at 4:30pm.

Buses serving points further afield in Honduras depart from a few different places in Copán Ruinas. Hedman Alas goes to San Pedro Sula (US$9, three hours) and on to Tegucigalpa (US$17, seven hours) at 5:30am daily.

SHUTTLE MINIBUS

Base Camp Tours (p245) in Copán Ruinas and nearly every Antigua travel agency (p100) run shuttles between those two towns. Scheduled shuttles leave Copán for Antigua (US$16, minimum four passengers, six hours) at 2pm daily and can drop you in Guatemala City (five hours) en route. Base Camp also offers direct shuttles to San Salvador, El Salvador, on Saturday and Sunday at 3pm (US$18, five hours).

CAR

You could conceivably visit the ruins as a day trip from Guatemala City by car, but it's exhausting and far too harried. From Río Hondo, Chiquimula or Esquipulas, it still takes a full day to get to Copán, tour the ruins and return, but it's easier. It's better to spend at least one night in Copán Ruinas if you can.

Drive 10km south from Chiquimula (or 48km north from Esquipulas) and turn eastward at Vado Hondo (Km 178.5 on Hwy 10). Just opposite the turnoff there is a small motel, which will do if you need a bed. A sign reading 'Vado Hondo Ruinas de Copán' marks the way on the one-hour, 50km drive along the paved road that runs from this junction to El Florido.

Twenty kilometers northeast of Vado Hondo are the Ch'orti' Maya villages of Jocotán and Camotán, set in mountainous tropical countryside dotted with thatched huts in lush green valleys. Jocotán has a small *centro de salud* (medical clinic) and the **Hotel Katú Sukuchuje** (☎ /fax 7941 2431; s/d with hot-water bathroom US$6/8; P), which also has a restaurant.

If you are driving a rented car, you will have to present the Guatemalan customs authorities at the border with a special letter of permission to enter Honduras, written on the rental company's letterhead and signed and sealed by the appropriate company official. If you do not have such a letter, you'll have to leave your car at El Florido and continue to Copán by minivan or pickup.

AROUND COPÁN RUINAS

Hacienda San Lucas (☎ 651 4106; www.haciendasanlucas.com; s/d US$50/60) is a magical place 5km south of town. Phone beforehand or enquire at Café ViaVia. The recently restored adobe hacienda is solar-powered, but the rooms are candlelit at night, adding to the serene atmosphere. The food here is highly praised. Los Sapos archaeological site (p244) is on the property.

Visiting **Finca El Cisne** (☎ 651 4695; www.fincaelcisne.com; overnight packages per person US$85), 24km from Copán Ruinas, is more like an agro-eco experience than a tour. Founded in the 1920s and still operating, the *finca* mainly raises cattle and grows coffee and cardamom, but it also produces corn, avocados, beans, breadfruit and star fruit, among other things. Day-long (US$65 per person) and overnight packages include guided horse riding through the forests and pastures (with a stop to swim in the Río Blanco) and tours of the coffee and cardamom fields and processing plants. If you come in February or October you can help with the harvest. Lodging is in a homey,

solar-powered cabin, with meals and a visit to nearby hot springs included.

Hacienda El Jaral (☎ 552 4457; www.haciendaeljaral.com; campsite per person US$4, s/d/tr US$55/60/80; ✕ ☎ P), a lush ecotourism resort offering many activities, is 11km from town on the way to La Entrada. The luxurious rooms with aircon, hot-water bathroom, cable TV and fridge are all in duplex cabins with outdoor terraces. The resort has a shopping mall, cinema, water park, children's play area and a couple of restaurants. The activities offered to guests and nonguests alike include bird-watching in a bird-sanctuary lagoon (thousands of herons reside here from November to May), horse riding, bicycling, hiking, river swimming, inner-tubing, canoeing and 'soft rafting' on the Río Copán.

Santa Rita de Copán

Nine kilometers from town (20 minutes by bus) on the road towards La Entrada, Santa Rita de Copán is a lovely village at the confluence of two rivers. Just outside Santa Rita – but unfortunately out of bounds due to a sequence of nasty incidents – is **El Rubí** waterfall, with an inviting swimming hole. It's about a half-hour uphill walk (3km) on a trail departing from opposite the Esso fuel station beside the bridge on the highway. Yaragua Tours (p245) in Copán Ruinas comes out here with armed guards – not your most tranquil swimming experience, but unfortunately the most sensible way to do it until the situation improves.

Agua Caliente

The attractively sited **Agua Caliente** (hot springs; admission US$1; ☼ 8am-8pm), not to be confused with Agua Caliente in Honduras, not far from Esquipulas, are 23km north of Copán Ruinas via the road running north out of town. Here hot water flows and mingles with a cold river. There are facilities for changing, a basketball court and bathrooms plus a *tienda* for soft drinks and snacks. To get to the springs, you can drive (45 minutes), hire a pickup (US$25) or catch a ride early with farmers going out there (US$1.50). Base Camp Tours (p245) in Copán Ruinas hires a minibus with a capacity of 15 people for US$30 return – a good deal if you can get a group together.

LUNA JAGUAR SPA RESORT

Directly across the river from the hot springs, this is a high-concept Mayan **day spa** (admission

US$10, with treatment US$30; ⊗ 8am-5pm). The idea is that this is what the Maya kings would have done to relax if they had the chance.

Thirteen 'treatment stations' (offering massage, hot tub, herbal steam baths and so on) are scattered around the hillside, connected by a series of stone pathways. The jungle here has been left as undisturbed as possible, and reproduction Mayan sculptures dot the landscape. The water used in the hot tub and steam baths comes directly from the volcanic spring. It's an amazing and beautiful spot, and worth checking out even if you aren't a spa junkie.

QUIRIGUÁ

From Copán it is only some 50km to Quiriguá as the crow flies, but the lay of the land, the international border and the condition of the roads make it a journey of 175km. Quiriguá is famed for its intricately carved stelae – the gigantic brown sandstone monoliths that rise as high as 10.5m, like ancient sentinels, in a quiet, well-kept tropical park.

From Río Hondo junction it's 67km along the Carr al Atlántico to the village of Los Amates, where there are a couple of hotels, a restaurant, food stalls, a bank and a little bus station. The village of Quiriguá is 1.5km east of Los Amates, and the turnoff to the ruins is another 1.5km to the east. The 3.4km access road leads south through banana groves.

History

Quiriguá's history parallels that of Copán, of which it was a dependency during much of the classic period. Of the three sites in this area, only the present archaeological park is of interest.

Quiriguá's location lent itself to the carving of giant stelae. Beds of brown sandstone in the nearby Río Motagua had cleavage planes suitable for cutting large pieces. Though soft when first cut, the sandstone dried hard in the air. With Copán's expert artisans nearby for guidance, Quiriguá's stone carvers were ready for greatness. All they needed was a great leader to inspire them – and to pay for the carving of the huge stelae.

That leader was K'ak' Tiliw Chan Yo'at (Cauac Sky; r 725–84), who decided that Quiriguá should no longer be under the control of Copán. In a war with his former suzerain, Cauac Sky took King 18 Rabbit of Copán prisoner in 737 and later had him beheaded. Independent at last, Cauac Sky commissioned his stonecutters to go to work, and for the next 38 years they turned out giant stelae and zoomorphs dedicated to the glory of King Cauac Sky.

Cauac Sky's son Sky Xul (r 784–800) lost his throne to a usurper, Jade Sky. This last great king of Quiriguá continued the building boom initiated by Cauac Sky, reconstructing Quiriguá's Acrópolis on a grander scale.

Quiriguá remained unknown to Europeans until John L Stephens arrived in 1840. Impressed by its great monuments, Stephens lamented the world's lack of interest in them in his book *Incidents of Travel in Central America, Chiapas and Yucatan* (1841):

> Of one thing there is no doubt: a large city once stood there; its name is lost, its history unknown; and…no account of its existence has ever before been published. For centuries it has lain as completely buried as if covered with the lava of Vesuvius. Every traveler from Yzabal to Guatemala has passed within three hours of it; we ourselves had done the same; and yet there it lay, like the rock-built city of Edom, unvisited, unsought, and utterly unknown.

Stephens tried to buy the ruined city in order to have its stelae shipped to New York, but the owner, Señor Payes, naturally assumed that Stephens (being a diplomat), was negotiating on behalf of the US government and that the government would pay. Payes quoted an extravagant price, and the deal was never made.

Between 1881 and 1894, excavations were carried out by Alfred P Maudslay. In the early 1900s all the land around Quiriguá was sold to the United Fruit Company and turned into banana groves (see boxed text, p252). The company is gone, but the bananas and Quiriguá remain. Restoration of the site was carried out by the University of Pennsylvania in the 1930s. In 1981, Unesco declared the ruins a World Heritage Site, one of only three in Guatemala (the others are Tikal and Antigua).

Ruins

The beautiful park-like **archaeological site** (admission US$4; ⊗ 7:30am-5pm) has a small *tienda* near the entrance selling cold drinks and snacks, but you'll be better off bringing your own picnic.

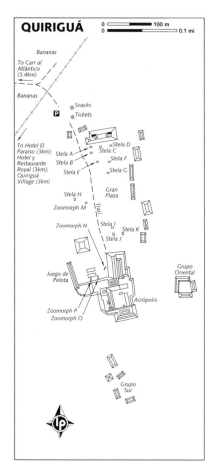

QUIRIGUÁ

0 .... 100 m
0 .... 0.1 mi

Bananas

To Carr al
Atlántico
(3.4km)

Bananas

Snacks
Tickets
P

To Hotel El
Paraiso (3km);
Hotel y
Restaurante
Royal (3km);
Quiriguá
Village (3km)

Stela D
Stela C
Stela A
Stela F
Stela B
Stela E
Stela G

Stela H
Gran
Plaza
Zoomorph M
Trail
Zoomorph N
Stela I
Stela K
Stela J

Grupo
Oriental

Juego de
Pelota

Acrópolis
Zoomorph P
Zoomorph O

Grupo
Sur

Note the exuberant, elaborate headdresses; the beards on some of the figures (an oddity in Mayan art and life); the staffs of office held in the kings' hands; and the glyphs on the sides of the stela.

At the far end of the plaza is the **Acrópolis**, far less impressive than the one at Copán. At its base are several **zoomorphs**, blocks of stone carved to resemble real and mythic creatures. Frogs, tortoises, jaguars and serpents were favorite subjects. The low zoomorphs can't compete with the towering stelae in impressiveness, but as works of art, imagination and mythic significance, the zoomorphs are superb.

Sleeping & Eating

Both of the hotels listed here have restaurants. There seems to be a bit of a price war going on in Quiriguá – just mention that you're going to have a look at the other place and listen to the prices plummet. To get to them both, walk down the main street, veering right at the first fork and then follow the road around to the left at the bend.

Hotel El Paraiso (s/d US$5.50/8, with bathroom US$8/11) The better of the two hotels in town, the rooms with shared bathroom here are fine, plus you get to use the shower with the awesome mountain views.

Hotel y Restaurante Royal (☎ 7947 3639; s/d US$5.50/8, with bathroom US$8/11) The first hotel you come to, this one has small but adequate rooms – those with bathroom are a lot nicer. The restaurant serves both meat and vegetarian meals (US$4 to US$6).

Getting There & Around

The turnoff to Quiriguá village is 205km (four hours) northeast of Guatemala City, 70km northeast of the Río Hondo junction, 41km southwest of La Ruidosa junction (for Río Dulce and Flores) and 90km southwest of Puerto Barrios.

Buses running from Guatemala City to Puerto Barrios, Guatemala City to Flores, Esquipulas to Flores or Chiquimula to Flores will drop you off or pick you up here. They'll also drop you at the turnoff to the archaeological site if you ask.

From the highway it's 3.4km to the archaeological site – US$0.25 by bus or pickup, but if one doesn't come, don't fret: it's a pleasant walk (without luggage) on a dirt road running through banana plantations to get there. You

Despite the sticky heat and (sometimes) bothersome mosquitoes, Quiriguá is a wonderful place. The giant stelae on the **Gran Plaza** (Great Plaza) are all much more worn than those at Copán. To impede further deterioration, each has been covered by a thatched roof. The roofs cast shadows that make it difficult to examine the carving closely and almost impossible to get a good photograph, but somehow this does little to inhibit one's sense of awe.

Seven of the stelae, designated A, C, D, E, F, H and J, were built during the reign of Cauac Sky and carved with his image. **Stela E** is the largest Mayan stela known, standing some 8m above ground, with another 3m or so buried in the earth. It weighs almost 60,000kg.

may have to wait to get from the ruins back to the main highway, but eventually some transportation will turn up.

If you're staying in the village of Quiriguá or Los Amates and walking to the archaeological site, you can take a shortcut along the railway branch line that goes from the village through the banana fields, crossing the access road very near the entrance to the archaeological site. There have been no reports of safety issues here.

To head on to Río Dulce (US$3, two hours) if you don't want to wait for a bus to Flores (around 20 daily coming from Guatemala City), you can take any bus or minibus to Morales (the transportation hub for the area) and a bus on from there to Río Dulce. This is a bit of a detour off the main road, but at least you'll get a seat from Morales. Alternatively, take a Puerto Barrios bus and get off at La Ruidosa, where you can wait for a minivan or bus for the 34km to Río Dulce. For Chiquimula, take any bus the 3km from the turnoff to the ruins to Los Amates and wait for the next bus through to Chiquimula (US$3, two hours).

LAGO DE IZABAL

Guatemala's largest lake, to the north of the Carr al Atlántico, is just starting to register on travelers' radar screens. Most visitors checking out the lake stay at Río Dulce town, by the long, tall bridge where Hwy 13, heading north to Flores and Tikal, crosses the Río Dulce emptying out of the east end of the lake. Downstream, the beautiful river broadens into a lake called El Golfete before meeting the Caribbean at Lívingston. River trips are a highlight of a visit to eastern Guatemala. If you're looking for lakeside ambience minus the Río Dulce congestion and pace, head to Denny's Beach at Mariscos (p257) or, closer, El Castillo de San Felipe (p254), about 3km west of the bridge. The neat town of El Estor near the west end of the lake gives access to the Bocas del Polochic river delta, where there is lots of wildlife (see p256). There are many undiscovered spots in this area waiting to be explored, so don't limit yourself.

Río Dulce

At the east end of the Lago de Izabal where it empties into the Río Dulce, this town still gets referred to as Fronteras. It's a hangover from the days when the only way across the river was by ferry, and this was the last piece

of civilization before embarking on the long, difficult journey into El Petén.

Times have changed. A huge bridge now spans the water and El Petén roads are some of the best in the country. The town sees most tourist traffic from yachties – the US coast guard says this is the safest place on the western Caribbean for boats during hurricane season. The rest of the foreigners here are either coming or going on the spectacular river trip down to Lívingston (see p264).

ORIENTATION & INFORMATION

Unless you're staying at Hotel Backpacker's (p253) or volunteering at its Casa Guatemala, get off the bus on the north side of the bridge. The Fuente del Norte and Litegua bus offices are both here, opposite each other. Otherwise you'll find yourself trudging over what is believed to be the longest bridge in Central America – it's a very hot 30-minute walk (3.5km).

The main dock is now under the bridge on the opposite side of the main road from Bruno's (p253) – you'll see a side road leading down to it.

The website www.mayaparadise.com has loads of information about Río Dulce.

Cap't Nemo's Communications (☎ 7930 5174; www .mayaparadise.com; internet access per hr US$2; ⏲ 7am-8pm Mon-Sat, 9am-2pm Sun) Beside Bruno's on the river, Nemo's offers email and international phone and fax services. Tijax Express, Hacienda Tijax and Hotel Backpacker's are hooked up too, all charging US$3 per hour.

Tijax Express (⏲ daily) In the little lane between the river and the Fuente del Norte bus office, this is Río Dulce's unofficial tourist information center. English is spoken here. There are two similar places near the Tijax, Otitours and Atitrans. You can book *lanchas*, tours, sailing trips and shuttles with all three.

If you need to change cash or traveler's checks, hit one of the banks in town, all on the main road.

Banco Agromercantil Will give cash advances on credit cards if there is a problem with the ATMs.

Banco Industrial (⏲ 9am-5pm) Has a Visa ATM.

Banrural Has Visa and MasterCard ATMs.

TOURS

Aventuras Vacacionales (☎ /fax 7832 5938; www.sailing -diving-guatemala.com; Centro Comercial María, 4a Calle Poniente 17, Antigua) runs fun sailing trips on the sailboat *Las Sirenas* from Río Dulce to the Belize reefs and islands (US$400, seven days)

BANANA REPUBLIC

In 1870, the first year that bananas were imported to the US, few Americans had ever seen a banana, let alone tasted one. By 1898 they were eating 16 million bunches annually.

In 1899 the Boston Fruit Company merged with the interests of the Brooklyn-born Central American railroad baron Minor C Keith to form the United Fruit Company. The aim was to own large areas of Central America and cultivate them by modern methods, providing predictable harvests of bananas that Keith, who controlled virtually all of the railroads in Central America, would then carry to the coast for shipment to the USA.

Central American governments readily granted United Fruit rights at low prices to large tracts of undeveloped jungle. The company created access to the land by road and/or rail, cleared and cultivated it, built extensive port facilities for the export of fruit and offered employment to large numbers of local workers.

By 1930, United Fruit was capitalized at US$215 million and was the largest employer in Central America. The company's Great White Fleet of transportation ships was one of the largest private navies in the world. In Guatemala, by controlling Puerto Barrios and the railroads serving it, all of which it had built, United Fruit effectively controlled all the country's international commerce, banana or otherwise.

The company came to be referred to as El Pulpo, 'the Octopus,' by local journalists, who accused it of corrupting government officials, exploiting workers and in general exercising influence far beyond its role as a foreign company in Guatemala.

United Fruit's treatment of its workers was paternalistic. Though they worked long and hard for low wages, these wages were higher than those of other farm workers, and they received housing, medical care and in some cases schooling for their children. Still, indigenous Guatemalans were required to give right of way to whites and remove their hats when talking to them. And the company took out of the country far more in profits than it put in: between 1942 and 1952 the company paid stockholders almost 62 cents (US) in dividends for every dollar invested.

The US government, responding to its rich and powerful constituents, saw its role as one of support for United Fruit and defense of its interests.

On October 20, 1944, a liberal military coup paved the way for Guatemala's first-ever free elections. The winner and new president was Dr Juan José Arévalo, a professor who, inspired by the New Deal policies of Franklin Roosevelt, sought to remake Guatemala into a democratic, liberal nation guided by 'spiritual socialism.' His successor, Jacobo Arbenz, was even more vigorous in undertaking reform. Among Arbenz' many supporters was Guatemala's small communist party.

Free at last from the repression of past military dictators, labor unions clamored for better conditions, with almost constant actions against la Frutera, United Fruit. The Guatemalan government demanded more-equitable tax payments from the company and divestiture of large tracts of its unused land.

Alarm bells sounded in the company's Boston headquarters and in Washington, where powerful members of Congress and the Eisenhower administration – including Secretary of State John Foster Dulles – were convinced that Arbenz was intent on turning Guatemala communist. Several high-ranking US officials had close ties to United Fruit, and others were persuaded by the company's expensive and effective lobbying campaign that Arbenz was a threat.

In 1954, the CIA arranged an invasion from Honduras by 'anti-communist' Guatemalan exiles, which resulted in Arbenz' resignation and exile. The CIA's hand-picked 'liberator' was Carlos Castillo Armas, a military man of the old caste, who returned Guatemala to rightist military dictatorship. The tremendous power of the United Fruit Company had set back democratic development in Guatemala by at least half a century.

A few years after the coup, the US Department of Justice brought suit against United Fruit for operating monopolistically in restraint of trade. In 1958 the company was ordered to reduce its size by two-thirds within 12 years. It began by selling some of its Guatemalan holdings to Guatemalan entrepreneurs and its US rival Standard Fruit. It yielded its monopoly on the railroads as well.

Caught up in the 'merger mania' of the 1960s, United Fruit became part of United Brands, which in the early 1970s sold all of its remaining land in Guatemala to the Del Monte corporation. Standard Fruit (now part of the Dole Corporation) and Del Monte are still active in Guatemala.

and Lago Izabal (US$180, four days). The office is in Antigua but you can also hook up with this outfit in Río Dulce. It makes the Belize and lake trips in alternate weeks.

The Río Dulce–based **Wizard of Oz** (☎ 5733 0516; www.sailthewiz.com; tours per person per day US$75) offers sailing tours to Belize, Honduras and Cayes from Guatemala. Trips include snorkeling, kayaking and also basic sail training if you are interested.

That Boat (www.that-boat.com; tours per person from US$10), a 60-footer, offers various day and half-day trips (including sunset tours, splash lunches and waterparties) on the Río Dulce and its lakes. For more information visit the Sundog Café (see p254) or the website.

SLEEPING
Many places in Río Dulce communicate by radio. Tijax Express, the bar at Bruno's, and Restaurant Río Bravo will radio your choice of place to stay if necessary.

On the Water
The places listed here are out of town on the water, which is the best place to be. You can call or radio them from Tijax Express and they'll come and pick you up.

Hotel Backpacker's (☎ 7930 5169; casaguatemal@ guate.net; dm US$4, s/d US$8/16, with bathroom US$10/20) Across the bridge, this is a business run by Casa Guatemala and the orphans it serves. It's an old (with the emphasis on old) backpacker favorite, set in a rickety building with very basic rooms. Volunteer work is available here, either working in the hotel or the nearby children's refuge. The bar kicks on here at night. If you're coming by *lancha* or bus, ask the driver to let you off here to spare yourself the walk across the bridge.

Casa Perico (☎ 7930 5666; VHF channel 68; dm US$5.50, s/d US$6/7, with bathroom US$20/27) One of the more low-key options in the area, this is set on a little inlet about 200m from the main river. Cabins are well built and connected by boardwalks. The Swiss guys who run it offer tours all up and down the river and put on an excellent buffet dinner (US$6) or you can choose from the menu (mains US$3 to US$4). The place has a good book exchange and a young, fun atmosphere.

Nutria Marina (☎ 5863 9365; www.nutriamarina .com; dm/s/d US$7/20/30) Set right across the water from the Castillo San Felipe and a bit up on the hillside, this place catches some cool breezes and good views. Bungalows are simple and well built and the nine-person dorm is popular with groups who come for art workshops.

Hacienda Tijax (☎ 7930 5505/7; VHF channel 09; www.tijax.com; campsite per person US$3, s US$8-34, d US$13-39; **P** **⋈**) This 500-acre hacienda, a two-minute boat ride across the cove from Bruno's, is a special place to stay. Activities include horse riding, hiking, birding, sailboat trips and tours around the rubber plantation. Accommodation is in lovely little cabins connected by a boardwalk. Most cabins face the water and there's a very relaxing pool/bar area. Access is by boat or by a road that turns off the highway about 1km north of the village. The folks here speak Spanish, English, Dutch, French and Italian, and they'll pick you up from across the river; ask at the Tijax Express office.

El Tortugal (☎ 5306 6432; www.tortugal.com; bungalows US$20) The best-looking bungalows on the river are located here, a five-minute *lancha* ride east from town. There are plenty of hammocks, the showers are seriously hot and kayaks are free for guest use.

Hotel Catamaran (☎ 7930 5494; www.catamaran island.com; s/d from US$71/91; **⋈** **▢** **⋈**) Built on its own little island, this is the most upmarket option on the river. Bungalows are surprisingly plain, but comfortable enough and the grounds strike a neat balance between lush and manicured.

In Town
Bruno's (☎ 7930 5721; www.mayaparadise.com/brunoe .htm; dm US$5, s/d US$6/12, with bathroom US$23/33; **P** **⋈** **⋈**) A path leads down from the northwest end of the bridge to this riverside hang-out for yachties needing to get some land under their feet. The cheapest rooms here are barely worth looking at, but the dorms are clean and spacious and the new building offers some of the most comfortable rooms in town, with air-con and balconies overlooking the river. They're well set up for families and sleep up to six, charging US$10 per additional person over the doubles rate.

Hospedaje Golding (☎ 7930 5123; Carr a San Felipe; r per person US$5, with bathroom US$8) A yellow building with no sign, just off the main road, Golding is a simple place. It has some pretty trees and its brightly colored upstairs rooms have a bit of a view.

Hospedaje Marilu (☎ 7930 5403; s/d US$5/8, with bathroom US$6/10) A clean, cheap option on the main drag, opposite Las Brisas. Rooms have a double bed, fan and mosquito screen.

Las Brisas Hotel (☎ 7930 5124; s/d with bathroom US$10/13; ✷) This hotel is opposite Tijax Express. All rooms are clean enough and have three beds and fans. Three rooms upstairs have private bathroom and air-con (US$40). It's central and good enough for a night, but there are much better places around.

EATING

Sundog Café (sandwiches US$3, meals from US$4; ✷ lunch & dinner) Down the hill a bit from Tijax express, this open-air bar-restaurant makes great sandwiches on homemade bread, a good selection of vegetarian dishes and fresh juices. It's also the place to come for unbiased information about the area.

Restaurante La Carreta (breakfast US$2, mains US$5-8; ✷ lunch & dinner) While most of the waterside joints are serving up pricey food with romantic views, this *palapa*-style restaurant off the highway on the road towards San Felipe (with charming views of the neighbor's backyard) is keeping it real for the locals with big serves at low prices. The surf 'n' turf (US$9.50) comes highly recommended.

Restaurant Los Pinchos (breakfasts US$3, mains US$6-10; ✷ breakfast, lunch & dinner) With an open-air deck over the lake, this place has some good eats and a very local flavor. It doesn't get too fancy, but there is a good range of steaks, seafood and Chinese dishes on offer in a relaxed environment.

Bruno's (breakfasts US$2.60-4, mains US$10; ✷ breakfast, lunch & dinner) Another open-air place right beside the water, Bruno's is a restaurant–sports bar with satellite TV and video; its floating dock makes it popular with yachties.

GETTING THERE & AWAY

Beginning at 7am, 14 Fuente del Norte buses a day head north along a paved road to Poptún (US$4, two hours, 99km) and Flores (US$6.50, four hours, 208km). The 12:30pm, 7:30pm, 9:30pm and 11:30pm buses continue all the way to Melchor de Mencos (US$12) on the Belize border. With good connections you can get to Tikal (279km) in a snappy six hours. In the other direction, at least 17 buses daily go to Guatemala City (US$6.50, six hours, 280km) with Fuente del Norte and Litegua. Línea Dorada/Fuente del Norte has

1st-class buses departing at 1:30pm for Guatemala City and at 2:30pm for Flores (both US$18). This shaves up to an hour off the journey times.

Minibuses leave for Puerto Barrios (US$2.50, two hours) when full, from the roadside opposite Tijax Express.

Atitrans' shuttle minibus operates from the Atitrans office on the highway. Shuttles to Antigua cost US$37, to Copán Ruinas US$30 and Guatemala City US$30, with a minimum of four passengers in each case. Otitours and Tijax Express offer much the same service.

Dilapidated Fuente del Norte buses leave for El Estor (US$1.30, 1½ hours, 43km) from the Pollolandia restaurant at the San Felipe and El Estor turnoff in the middle of town, hourly from 7am to 4pm. The road is only paved for 15km.

Colectivo lanchas go down the Río Dulce (from the new dock) to Lívingston, usually requiring eight to 10 people, charging US$12 per person. The trip is a beautiful one and they usually make a 'tour' of it, with several halts along the way (see p264). If everyone wants to get there as fast as possible, it takes one hour without stops. Boats usually leave from 9am to about 2pm. The three tour offices (see p251) offer *lancha* service to Lívingston and most other places you'd care to go, but they charge more.

El Castillo de San Felipe

The fortress and castle of San Felipe de Lara, **El Castillo de San Felipe** (admission US$2.80; ✷ 8am-5pm), about 3km west of the bridge, was built in 1652 to keep pirates from looting the villages and commercial caravans of Izabal. Though the fortress deterred the buccaneers a bit, a pirate force captured and burned it in 1686. By the end of the next century, pirates had disappeared from the Caribbean, and the fort's sturdy walls served as a prison. Eventually, though, the fortress was abandoned and became a ruin. The present fort was reconstructed in 1956.

Today the castle is protected as a park and is one of the Lago de Izabal's principal tourist attractions. In addition to the fort itself, there are grassy grounds, barbecue and picnic areas, and the opportunity to swim in the lake. The place rocks from April 30 to May 4 during the **Feria de San Felipe**.

SLEEPING & EATING

Hotel Don Humberto (☎ /fax 7930 5051; s/d US$8/11; **P**) Near the Castillo, offering basic rooms with big beds and good mosquito netting. It's nothing fancy, but more than adequate for a cheap sleep.

Viñas del Lago (☎ 7930 5053; www.infovia.com .gt/hotelvinasdellago; s/d US$32/40; **P** ✘ ✎) The much fancier del Lago, near the Hotel Don Humberto, has 18 spacious, plain rooms, all with hot-water bathroom, air-con and TV. Rooms out the back have good views. The grounds are large and there's a restaurant (mains US$7.75 to US$10.50) with views of Lago de Izabal.

Between the turnoff from the El Estor–Río Dulce road and the castle are a couple of good-value places:

La Cabaña del Viajero (☎ 7930 5062; s/d with bathroom US$10/17; **P** ✘ ✎) The smallish rooms in these two-story cabins are an excellent deal. They're clean and colorfully decorated and there's a shady pool area to splash around in. Air-conditioning costs an extra US$7.

Hotel Changri-la (☎ 7930 5467; hotelchangrila@yahoo .com; s/d with bathroom US$25/37, 6-person bungalows US$152; **P** ✘ ✎) These pretty rooms provide some comfortable touches. There are no water views, but there is a relaxed little pool/restaurant/bar area.

GETTING THERE & AWAY

San Felipe is on the lakeshore, 3km west of Río Dulce. It's a beautiful 45-minute walk between the two towns, or take a minivan (US$0.80, every 30 minutes). In Río Dulce it stops on the corner of the highway and road to El Estor; in San Felipe it stops in front of the Hotel Don Humberto, at the entrance to El Castillo.

Boats coming from Lívingston will drop you in San Felipe if you ask. The Río Dulce river tours usually come to El Castillo, allowing you to get out and visit the castle if you like. Or you can come over from Río Dulce by private *lancha* for US$8.

Finca El Paraíso

On the north side of the lake, between Río Dulce and El Estor, **Finca El Paraíso** (☎ 7949 7122; admission US$1.30) makes a great day trip from either place. This working ranch's territory includes an incredibly beautiful spot in the jungle where a wide, hot waterfall drops about 12m into a clear, deep pool. You can bathe in the hot water, swim in the cool pool or duck under an overhanging promontory and enjoy a jungle-style sauna.

Also on the *finca* are a number of interesting caves and a restaurant by a sandy lake beach. If you like you can stay on in comfortable bungalows for around US$30 for two people.

The *finca* is on the Río Dulce–El Estor bus route, about one hour (US$0.90) from Río Dulce and 30 minutes (US$0.60) from El Estor. The last bus in either direction passes at around 4:30pm to 5pm.

El Estor

pop 17,100

The major settlement on the northern shore of Lago de Izabal is El Estor. The nickel mines a few kilometers to the northwest (for which the town grew up) closed in 1980 but are set to be reopened by Canadian companies as world nickel stocks run low. A friendly, somnolent little town with a lovely setting, El Estor is the jumping-off point for the Bocas del Polochic, a highly biodiverse wildlife reserve at the west end of the lake. The town is also a staging post on a possible route between Río Dulce and Lanquín.

ORIENTATION & INFORMATION

The main street, running parallel to the lakeshore two blocks back from the water, is 3a Calle. Buses from Río Dulce terminate at Tienda Cobanerita on the corner of 3a Calle and 4a Av. Walk one block west from here along 3a Calle to find the Parque Central.

Asociación Feminina Q'eqchi' sells clothes, blankets and accessories that are made from traditional cloth woven by the association's members. To find it go two blocks north along 5a Av from the Parque Central, then two blocks west. All profits benefit the women involved in the program.

Banrural (cnr 3a Calle & 6a Av; ☘ 8:30am-5pm Mon-Fri, 9am-1pm Sat) Changes US dollars and Amex traveler's checks.

Café Portal (5a Av 2-65; ☘ 6:30am-10pm) On the east side of Parque Central, this place provides information, tours and transportation.

Municipal police (cnr 1a Calle & 5a Av) Near the lakeshore.

SLEEPING & EATING

Hotel Santa Clara (☎ 7949 7244; 5a Av 2-11; s/d US$3/6, with bathroom US$4/8) You'd have to be really penny-pinching to find the downstairs rooms with shared bathroom here attractive.

Upstairs (with bathroom), the situation improves slightly, as rooms get a breeze at least and some have lake views.

Hotel Villela (☎ 7949 7214; 6a Av 2-06; s/d US$5/9) The rooms are less attractive than the neat lawn and trees they're set around, but some are airier and brighter than others. All have fan and bathroom.

Hotel Central (☎ 7949 7497; 5a Av; s/d with bathroom US$7/10; **P**) This hotel provides rooms with fan at the northeast corner of the Parque Central.

Restaurante Típico Chaabil (☎ 7949 7272; 3a Calle; r with bathroom per person US$10; **P**) Although they go a bit heavy on the log cabin feel, the rooms at this place, at the west end of 3a Calle, are the best deal in town. Get one upstairs for plenty of light and good views. The restaurant here, on a lovely lakeside terrace, cooks up delicious food, such as *tapado* (the Garífuna seafood and coconut stew; US$8). The water here is crystal clear and you can swim right off the hotel's dock.

Hotel Vista al Lago (☎ 7949 7205; 6a Av 1-13; s/d with bathroom US$10/20) Set in a classic, historic building down on the waterfront, this place has plenty of style, although the rooms themselves are fairly ordinary. Views from the upstairs balcony are superb.

The Chaabil apart, the best place to look for food is around the Parque Central, where Café Portal and Restaurante Hugo's both serve a broad range of fare with some vegetarian options. Main dishes are around US$3 to US$4 at either.

GETTING THERE & AWAY

See Río Dulce (p254) for information on buses from there. The schedule from El Estor to Río Dulce is hourly, from 6am to 4pm.

The road west from El Estor via Panzós and Tucurú to Tactic, south of Cobán, has had a bad reputation for highway holdups and robberies in the past, especially around Tucurú. It's also prone to getting flooded out during the wet season, so it's very advisable to ask around on the current situation. You can get to Lanquín by taking the truck that leaves El Estor's Parque Central at 9am for Cahabón (US$2, four to five hours), and then a bus or pickup straight on from Cahabón to Lanquín the same day. Two buses go direct to Cobán (US$8, six hours) on this route, leaving at the very unfriendly times of 1am and 4am from the El Estor's Central Park.

There are no public boat services between El Estor and other lake destinations. Private *lanchas* can be contracted, though this can be pricey. Ask at your hotel.

Around El Estor
REFUGIO BOCAS DEL POLOCHIC & RESERVA DE BIOSFERA SIERRA DE LAS MINAS

The Refugio Bocas del Polochic (Bocas del Polochic Wildlife Reserve) covers the delta of the Río Polochic, which provides most of Lago de Izabal's water. A visit here provides great bird-watching and howler monkey observation. The reserve supports more than 300 species of birds – the migration seasons, September to October and April to May, are reportedly fantastic – and many varieties of butterflies and fish. You may well see alligators and, if you're very lucky, glimpse a manatee. Café Portal (p255) can set up early-morning trips with local boatman Benjamín Castillo costing US$60 for two people plus US$13 for each extra person for 3½ hours. The reserve is managed by the **Fundación Defensores de la Naturaleza** (☎ 7949 7130; www.defensores.org.gt in Spanish; cnr 5a Av & 2a Calle, El Estor), whose research station, the **Estación Científica Selempim**, just south of the Bocas del Polochic reserve, in the Reserva de Biosfera Sierra de las Minas, is open for ecotouristic visits. Contact Defensores' El Estor office for bookings and further information: ask for Luis Pérez, who speaks English. You can get to the station on a local *lancha* service leaving El Estor at 11am Monday, Wednesday and Saturday (US$7 round-trip, 1¼ hours each way) or by special hire (US$65 to US$90 for a boatload of up to 12 people), and stay in attractive wood-and-thatch *cabañas* (per person US$7) or camp (US$4 per person). Meals are available for US$3.50 each or you can use the Estación Científica's kitchen. To explore the reserves you can use canoes free of charge, take boat trips (US$20 to US$32) or walk any of the three well-established trails.

El Boquerón

This beautiful, lushly vegetated canyon abutting the tiny Mayan settlement of the same name is about 6km east of El Estor. For around US$2, villagers will paddle you up the Río Sauce through the canyon, drop you at a small beach, where you can swim and if you like scramble up the rocks, and return for you at an agreed time. Río Dulce–bound buses from El Estor will drop you at El Boquerón (US$0.50, 15 minutes), as will El Estor–bound buses from Río Dulce.

Mariscos

Mariscos is the principal town on the lake's south side. Ferries from here used to be the main access to El Estor and the north side of the lake, but since a road was built from Río Dulce to El Estor, Mariscos has taken a back seat. As a result, **Denny's Beach** (☎ 2337 4946; VHF channel 63; www.dennysbeach.com; campsites per tent US$4, hammocks US$2, cabañas per person US$5-10), 10 minutes by boat from Mariscos, is a good place to get away from it all. Dennis Gulck and his wife, Lupe, offer tours, hiking and swimming, and host full-moon parties. When you arrive in Mariscos, you can radio them on VHF channel 63 – many people and businesses in Mariscos use radios – and they'll come to pick you up. Otherwise, you can hitch a ride in a *cayuco* (dugout canoe) at the market for US$2 or go to Shop-n-Go and hire a speedboat for US$15, fine if you're a group. In Río Dulce, you can radio from Cap't Nemo's Communications (p251) and they'll send someone to pick you up.

PUERTO BARRIOS

pop 62,800

The country becomes even more lush, tropical and humid heading east from La Ruidosa junction toward Puerto Barrios. Port towns have always had a fame for being slightly dodgy, and those acting as international borders doubly so. Perhaps the town council wants to pay homage to that here. Or perhaps the edgy, slightly sleazy feel is authentic. Either way, for foreign visitors, Puerto Barrios is mainly a jumping-off point for boats to Punta Gorda (Belize) or Lívingston, and you probably won't be hanging around.

The powerful United Fruit Company once owned vast plantations in the Motagua valley and many other parts of Guatemala. The company built railways to ship its produce to the coast, and it built Puerto Barrios early in the 20th century to put that produce onto ships sailing for New Orleans and New York (see the boxed text, p252). Laid out as a company town, Puerto Barrios has long, wide streets arranged neatly on a grid plan, and lots of Caribbean-style wood-frame houses, many of which have seen better days.

When United Fruit's power and influence declined in the 1960s, the Del Monte company became successor to its interests. But the heyday of the imperial foreign firms was past, as was that of Puerto Barrios. A more modern and efficient port was built a few kilometers to the southwest at Santo Tomás de Castilla, and Puerto Barrios sank into tropical torpor. In the last few years, however, things have started to look up again with the construction of a huge new truck container depot where the old railway yards were.

Orientation & Information

Because of its spacious layout, you must walk or ride further in Puerto Barrios to get from place to place. For instance, it's 800m from the bus terminals by the market in the town center to the Muelle Municipal (Municipal Boat Dock) at the end of 12a Calle, from which passenger boats depart.

Banco Industrial (7a Av; 9am-5pm Mon-Fri, 9am-1pm Sat) Changes cash US dollars and traveler's checks, and has Visa ATMs.

Banrural (8a Av; 8:30am-5pm Mon-Fri, 9am-1pm Sat) Changes cash dollars only and has a MasterCard ATM.

Cybernet del Atlántico (7a Calle; per hr US$0.80) Internet access; west of 2a Av.

El Muñecón (intersection 8a Av, 14a Calle & Calz Justo Rufino Barrios) A statue of a dock worker; this is a favorite landmark and monument in the town.

Immigration office (cnr 12a Calle & 3a Av; 24hr) A block from the Muelle Municipal. Come here for your entry or exit stamp if you're arriving from or leaving for Belize: if you're leaving, there is a US$10 departure tax to pay. If you are heading to Honduras, you can get your exit stamp at another immigration office on the road to the border.

Red Virtu@l (cnr 17a Calle & Calz Justo Rufino Barrios; per hr US$0.80; 8am-9:30pm) Internet access.

Sleeping

Hotel Xelajú (☎ 7948 0482; 9a Calle; s/d US$5/8, with bathroom US$8/12) The Xelajú is right in the town center, between 6a and 7a Avs, facing the market, but it's secure: no rooms are let after 10pm and *'señoritas de clubes nocturnos'* are not allowed. It has clean fan-cooled rooms and its own generator for when the electricity fails.

Hotel Lee (☎ 7948 0685; 5a Av; s/d US$5/9, with bathroom US$8/14) This is a friendly, family-owned place, between 9a and 10a Calles, close to the bus terminals. The rooms are a bit cramped but clean, and have fans, TV, drinking water and Chinese art.

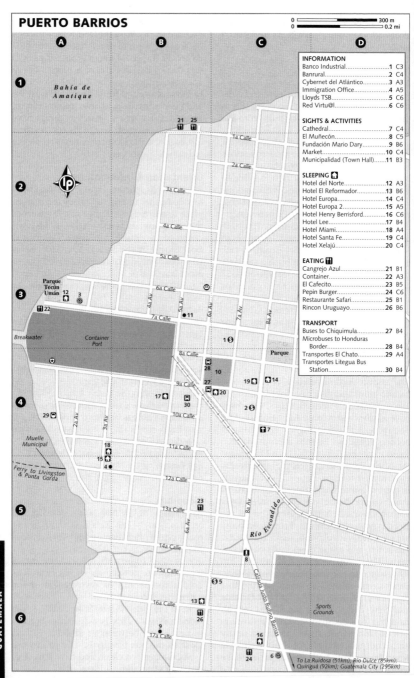

PUERTO BARRIOS

| 0 | 300 m |
| 0 | 0.2 mi |

INFORMATION
Banco Industrial........................1 C3
Banrural...................................2 C4
Cybernet del Atlántico.............3 A3
Immigration Office...................4 A5
Lloyds TSB................................5 C6
Red Virtu@l.............................6 C6

SIGHTS & ACTIVITIES
Cathedral..................................7 C4
El Muñecón...............................8 C5
Fundación Mario Dary...............9 B6
Market...................................10 C4
Municipalidad (Town Hall)......11 B3

SLEEPING
Hotel del Norte......................12 A3
Hotel El Reformador...............13 B6
Hotel Europa..........................14 C4
Hotel Europa 2.......................15 A5
Hotel Henry Berrisford............16 C6
Hotel Lee...............................17 B4
Hotel Miami...........................18 A4
Hotel Santa Fe.......................19 C4
Hotel Xelajú..........................20 C4

EATING
Cangrejo Azul.........................21 B1
Container...............................22 A3
El Cafecito.............................23 B5
Pepin Burger.........................24 C6
Restaurante Safari..................25 B1
Rincon Uruguayo....................26 B6

TRANSPORT
Buses to Chiquimula..............27 B4
Microbuses to Honduras
    Border...............................28 B4
Transportes El Chato..............29 A4
Transportes Litegua Bus
    Station..............................30 B4

Bahía de Amatique

Breakwater

Container Port

Muelle Municipal

Ferry to Livingston & Punta Gorda

Parque Tecún Umán

1ª Calle
2ª Calle
3ª Calle
4ª Calle
5ª Calle
6ª Calle
7ª Calle
8ª Calle
9ª Calle
10ª Calle
11ª Calle
12ª Calle
13ª Calle
14ª Calle
15ª Calle
16ª Calle
17ª Calle

Parque

Río Escondido

Calzada Justo Rufino Barrios

Sports Grounds

To La Ruidosa (51km); Río Dulce (85km);
Quiriguá (92km); Guatemala City (295km)

Hotel Miami (☎ 7948 0537; 3a Av; s/d with bathroom US$5.50/8, with air-con US$12/24; **P** ✴) Not bad if you want to save your pennies to spend elsewhere…otherwise a bit grim.

Hotel Europa (☎ 7948 0127; 8a Av; s/d US$7/12; **P**) Not quite up to the standards of the Europa 2 (and they aren't setting the bar that high, either), the Europa, between 8a and 9a Calles, scrapes in thanks to its quiet rooms and firm beds.

Hotel Europa 2 (☎ 7948 1292; 3a Av; s/d with bathroom US$8/10; **P**) The best of the budget options in the port area, this hotel, between 11a and 12a Calles, just 1½ blocks from the Muelle Municipal, is run by a friendly family and has clean rooms with fan and TV, arranged around a parking courtyard.

Hotel Henry Berrisford (☎ 7948 7289; cnr 9a Av & 17a Calle; s/d with bathroom US$11/22) A big four-story modern concrete construction offering decent-sized rooms with cable TV. The lobby is an impressive sight and there are plenty of sitting areas scattered around.

Hotel El Reformador (☎ 7948 0533; reformador@ intelnet.net.gt; cnr 7a Av & 16a Calle; s/d with bathroom US$13/18.50, with air-con US$22/28; **P** ✴) Like a little haven away from the hot busy streets outside, the Reformador offers big, cool rooms set around leafy patios. Air-con rooms lead onto wide interior balconies. There is a restaurant (meals US$5 to US$8) here.

Hotel del Norte (☎ 7948 2116; 7a Calle; s/d with bathroom US$16/21; **P** ✴ ☍) A large, classically tropical wooden construction with mosquito-screened corridors wide enough to run a banana train through, the century-old Hotel del Norte is in a class by itself. Its weathered and warped frame is redolent of history and most of the floorboards go off at crazy angles. In the airy dining room overlooking the Bahía de Amatique you can almost hear the echoing conversation of bygone banana moguls and smell their pungent cigars. Spare, simple and agreeably dilapidated, this is a real museum piece. Meals are served with old-fashioned refinement by white-jacketed waiters, though the food isn't always up to the same standard. Pick a room carefully – some are little more than a wooden box, others have great ocean views and catch good breezes. There's a swimming pool beside the sea.

Hotel Santa Fe (☎ 7948 8799; hotelsanta-fe56@hotmail .com; 8a Av; s/d with bathroom US$30/35; **P** ✴) Going heavy on the pastels, this hotel's a bit on the twee side, particularly for this town, but decent midrange options are scarce here. Rooms are spacious enough, with big, clean bathrooms and cable TV. It's located between 8a and 9a Calles.

Eating

Pepín Burger (17a Calle; snacks from US$2; ☽ closed Tue) Come here, between 8a and 9a Avs, for an almost mind-boggling array of snacks, fajitas, good-value burgers and more serious meals on an open-air upstairs terrace.

El Cafecito (13a Calle 6-22; mains US$4-10; ☽ breakfast, lunch & dinner) This sweet little air-conditioned spot whips up some of the most interesting food in town. Portuguese dishes such as *feijoda* (stewed beans, pork, beef, chicken and other stuff; US$6) and a good range of seafood and sandwiches.

Rincon Uruguayo (cnr 7a Av & 16a Calle; mains US$4-12; ☽ lunch & dinner) Given that the concepts of 'big' and 'juicy' are so rarely applied to Guatemalan steak, this outdoor eatery comes as a relief. Chorizo, barbecue chicken and *chivitos* (steak sandwiches) are also available.

Restaurante Safari (☎ 7948 0563; cnr 1a Calle & 5a Av; seafood US$6.50-10; ☽ 10am-9pm) The town's most enjoyable restaurant is on a thatch-roofed, open-air platform right over the water about 1km north of the town center. Locals and visitors alike love to eat and catch the sea breezes here. Excellent seafood of all kinds including the specialty *tapado* – that great Garífuna casserole (US$6.50); chicken and meat dishes are less expensive (US$3 to US$6). There's live music most nights. If the Safari is full, the Cangrejo Azul next door offers pretty much the same deal, in a more relaxed environment.

Container (7a Calle; snacks US$3; ☽ lunch & dinner) The oddest café in town – made from two shipping containers, at the west end of 7a Calle, with fine bay views, thatched huts out over the water and plenty of cold, cold beer.

Getting There & Around
BUS & MINIBUS
Transportes Litegua (☎ 7948 1172; cnr 6a Av & 9a Calle) leaves for Guatemala City (US$7, five to six hours, 295km), via Quiriguá and Río Hondo, 15 times between 1am and noon, and also at 4pm. *Directo* services avoid a half-hour detour into Morales.

Buses for Chiquimula (US$4, 4½ hours, 192km), also via Quiriguá, leave every half-hour, from 4am to 4pm, from the corner of 6a Av and 9a Calle.

For Río Dulce, take a Chiquimula bus to La Ruidosa junction (US$1, 50 minutes) and change to a bus or minibus (US$1, 35 minutes) there.

Minibuses leave for the Honduras frontier (US$1.30, 1¼ hours) every 20 minutes, from 5:30am to 6pm, from 6a Av outside the market. The paved road to the border turns off Hwy 9 at Entre Ríos, 13km south of Puerto Barrios. Buses and minibuses going in all directions wait for passengers at Entre Ríos, meaning that you can get to or from the border fairly easily, whichever direction you are traveling in. The minibuses from Puerto Barrios stop en route to the border at Guatemalan immigration, where you may be required to pay US$1.30 for an exit stamp. Honduran entry formalities may leave you US$1 to US$3 lighter. Pickups shuttle between the border and the small Honduran town of Corinto, nearby, for about US$1 (or you can walk the 2km, in about 15 minutes). From Corinto buses leave for Omoa and Puerto Cortés (US$2.50, two hours) about every two hours. You can continue by bus from Puerto Cortés to San Pedro Sula and from there to La Ceiba, but it's touch and go whether you would make the 3pm ferry from La Ceiba to Roatán island in one day from Puerto Barrios, even if you took the first vehicle out in the morning.

BOAT

Boats depart from the Muelle Municipal at the end of 12a Calle.

A ferry departs for Lívingston (US$2, 1½ hours) every day at 10am and 5pm. From Lívingston, it leaves for Puerto Barrios at 5am and 2pm. Get to the dock from 30 to 45 minutes before departure for a seat, otherwise you could end up standing.

Smaller, faster *lanchas* depart from both sides whenever they have about a dozen people ready to go; they cost US$4.50 and take 30 minutes.

Most of the movement from Lívingston to Puerto Barrios is in the morning, returning in the afternoon. From Lívingston, your last chance of the day may be the 2pm ferry, especially during the low season when fewer travelers are shuttling back and forth.

A *lancha* service of **Transportes El Chato** (☎ 7948 5525; 1a Av) departs from the Muelle Municipal at 10am daily for Punta Gorda, Belize (US$18, one hour), arriving in time for the noon bus from Punta Gorda to Belize City.

Tickets are sold at El Chato's office. Before boarding you also need to get your exit stamp at the nearby immigration office (p257). The return boat leaves Punta Gorda at 4pm.

If you want to leave a car in Puerto Barrios while you visit Lívingston for a day or two, hotels such as the Europa 2 (p259) and Miami (p259) provide off-street parking for US$2.50 to US$3 a day.

TAXI

Most cabs charge around US$3 for ridiculously short rides around town.

PUNTA DE MANABIQUE

The Punta de Manabique promontory, which separates the Bahía de Manabique from the open sea, along with the coast and hinterland all the way southeast to the Honduran frontier, comprise a large, ecologically fascinating, sparsely populated wetland area. Access to the area, which is under environmental protection as the Área de Protección Especial Punta de Manabique, is not cheap, but the attractions for those who make it there include pristine Caribbean beaches, boat trips through the mangrove forests, lagoons and waterways, bird-watching, fishing with locals, and crocodile and possible manatee sightings. To visit, get in touch – a week in advance, if possible – with the nongovernment organization (NGO) involved in the reserve's management, **Fundary** (Fundación Mario Dary; ☎ 7948 0435, in Guatemala City 2232 3230; www.guate.net/fundarymanabique; 17a Calle, Puerto Barrios).

Fundary is helping to develop several ecotouristic possibilities in the reserve. It offers accommodation for groups of two to four people at the **Estación Biológica Julio Obiols** (1/2/3 nights per person US$65/90/115) at the small community of Cabo Tres Puntas on the north side of the promontory, near a lovely beach. The price includes round-trip transportation from Puerto Barrios or Lívingston (one hour each way from either place by *lancha*) and meals. Rooms have two to four beds and mosquito nets. If you want a program of trips around the reserve from here, you're looking at a total of about US$100 per person per day. Another option is **camping** (per person US$3), at the Estación Biológica or at the small community of Estero Lagarto on the south side of the promontory, or at El Quetzalito near the mouth of the Río Motagua at the eastern end of the reserve. At **Estero Lagarto**, villagers will provide a fresh fish lunch (US$3.25) or take you on a boat trip through the lagoons and mangroves (per person US$7). Accommodations in local homes may become available here for about US$6.50 per person. A visitors center offering information and meals is located at **Santa Isabel** on the Canal de los Ingleses, a waterway connecting the Bahía de Manabique with the open sea. Canoe trips along the canal are offered as well as fishing with locals and demonstrations of the local charcoal-making process. **El Quetzalito** – about one hour by pickup from Puerto Barrios then half an hour by boat down the Río Motagua – is a good area for bird-watching and crocodile spotting, and for fishing with locals.

If you want to organize your own transportation, a *lancha* from Puerto Barrios or Lívingston will cost between US$65 and US$125 round-trip depending on the deal you strike. A small boat (four passengers) to Estero Lagarto might be US$50.

LÍVINGSTON

pop 17,000

Quite unlike anywhere else in Guatemala, this largely Garífuna town is fascinating in itself, but also an attraction for a couple of good beaches, and its location at the end of the river journey from Río Dulce.

Unconnected by road from the rest of the country (the town is called 'Buga' – mouth – in Garífuna, for its position at the river mouth), boat transportation is logically quite good here, and you can get to Belize, the Cayes, Honduras and Puerto Barrios with a minimum of fuss.

The Garífuna (Garinagu, or Black Carib) people of Caribbean Guatemala, Honduras, Nicaragua and southern Belize trace their roots to the Caribbean island of St Vincent, where shipwrecked African slaves mixed with the indigenous Carib in the 17th century. It took the British a long time, and a lot of fighting, to establish colonial control over St Vincent, and when they finally succeeded in 1796 they decided to deport its surviving Garífuna inhabitants. Most of the survivors wound up, after many had starved on Roatán island off Honduras, in the Honduran coastal town of Trujillo. From there, they have spread along the Caribbean coast. Their main concentration in Guatemala is in Lívingston but there are also a few thousand in Puerto Barrios and elsewhere. The Garífuna language is a unique mélange of Caribbean and African languages with a bit of French. Other people in Lívingston include the indigenous Q'eqchi' Maya – who have their own community a kilometer or so upriver from the main dock – ladinos and a smattering of international travelers.

Orientation & Information

Lívingston stands where the Río Dulce opens out into the Bahía de Amatique. After being here half an hour, you'll know where everything is. The main street, Calle Principal, heads straight ahead, uphill, from the main dock, curving round to the right at Hotel Río Dulce. The other most important streets head to the left off this: Calle Marcos Sánchez Díaz heading southwest, parallel to the river, to the Q'eqchi' Maya community, and another street leading northwest from the town center to several places to stay, eat and drink. Though we use such street names here for ease of orientation, in reality no one uses them.

Several private businesses around the town will change cash US dollars and traveler's checks.

Banrural (Calle Principal; ☼ 9am-5pm Mon-Fri, 9am-1pm Sat) Changes cash US dollars and traveler's checks. Several private businesses do, too.

Happy Fish (Calle Principal; per 30min/hr US$1.30/2.60) Internet access available.

Immigration office (Calle Principal; ☼ 6am-7pm) Issues entry and exit stamps for travelers arriving direct from or going direct to Belize or Honduras, charging US$10 for exit stamps. Outside business hours, you can knock for attention at any time.

Labug@net (Calle Principal; per 30min/hr US$2/3) Internet access.

Laundry (Hotel Casa Rosada; per load US$4) It can be difficult to get laundry properly dry in the rainy season.

Use mosquito repellent and other sensible precautions here, especially if you go out into the jungle; mosquitoes here on the coast carry both malaria and dengue fever.

Dangers & Annoyances

Lívingston has its edgy aspects and a few hustlers operate here, trying to sweet-talk tourists into 'lending' money, paying up front for tours that don't happen and the like. Take care with anyone who strikes up conversation for no obvious reason on the street or elsewhere.

Like many coastal locations in Guatemala, Lívingston is used as a *puente* (bridge) for northbound drug traffic. There's very little in the way of turf wars, and so on – the industry is fairly stable – but there are some big-time players around, and a lot of money at stake. Keep your wits about you.

The beachfront between Lívingston and the Río Quehueche and Siete Altares had a bad reputation for some years, but locals 'took care' of the troublemakers (we don't really want to know details). It now makes a fine walk, with some great swimming at the end of it. You can go independently or as part of a tour.

Sights & Activities

The **Museo Multicultural de Lívingston** (admission US$2; 9am-6pm Tue-Sun), upstairs on the municipal park in front of the public dock, has some excellent displays on the history and culture of the area, focusing on the ethnic diversity, with Garífuna, Q'eqchi, Hindu and Ladino cultures represented. While you're down here, check out the open-air alligator enclosure in the middle of the park.

Beaches in Lívingston itself are disappointing, as buildings or vegetation come right down to the water's edge in most places. Those beaches that do exist are often contaminated. However, there are better beaches within a few kilometers to the northwest. You can reach **Playa Quehueche** by taxi (US$2) in about 10 minutes: this beach near the mouth of the Río Quehueche has been cleaned up by Exotic Travel (opposite). The best beach in the area is **Playa Blanca** (admission US$2), around 12km from Lívingston. This is privately owned and you need a boat to get there (see opposite).

LOS SIETE ALTARES

About 5km (1½-hour walk) northwest of Lívingston along the shore of Bahía de Amatique, Los Siete Altares (The Seven Altars) is a series of freshwater falls and pools. It's a pleasant goal for a beach walk and is a good place for a picnic and swim. Follow the shore northward to the river mouth and walk along the beach until it meets the path into the woods (about 30 minutes). Follow this path all the way to the falls.

Boat trips go to the Seven Altars, but locals say it's better to walk there to experience the natural beauty and the Garífuna people along the way. About halfway along, next to the rope bridge is **Gaviota's Restaurant** (mains US$5-7; lunch & dinner), serving decent food and ice-cold beers and soft drinks.

LOCAL VOICES: JORGE LUÍS BALTHAZAR SALDAÑAS, GARÍFUNA PERCUSSIONIST

The most easily accessible aspect of Garífuna culture is the music. Heavily influenced by West African rhythms, Garífuna music relies greatly on percussion. We talked to master percussionist Jorge Balthazar about how it is to be a musician in Lívingston.

When did you start playing music?

When I was a kid. My mother's a music and dance teacher, so I was always around music. I started playing the maraca, then the turtle shell. I still play them, but now I like the *primera* (bass drum) best.

Where do you play?

Sometimes we play in bars, but mostly we play at parties or at funerals, where we play the dead person's favorite songs. We also play at festivals, to keep the old songs alive.

Who writes the songs?

A lot of times, the songs come together very organically – somebody starts playing something, then somebody else joins in. It's more like a jam session with people listening and coming together than somebody saying 'OK, let's sit down and write a song now.'

Do you go on tour?

We do, but it's complicated. People get us to play, but then they don't want to pay us – they say we're doing what we love, so why do we have to get paid?

Is Garífuna culture strong in Guatemala?

In some ways it is, but technology means that the culture is changing. Traditionally, we were fishers and farmers – now we're losing that. The language is another thing. They teach English in schools here, but not Garífuna. A lot of my friends can't speak Garífuna. Some can read, but not speak, for others it's the other way around. It's not that they don't respect it, just that the opportunities to learn aren't there.

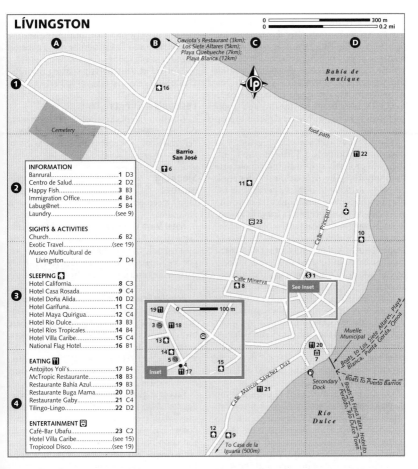

LÍVINGSTON

Bahía de Amatique

Cemetery

Barrio San José

INFORMATION
Banrural.................................1 D3
Centro de Salud....................2 D2
Happy Fish............................3 B3
Immigration Office...............4 B4
Labug@net...........................5 B4
Laundry..........................(see 9)

SIGHTS & ACTIVITIES
Church..................................6 B2
Exotic Travel...................(see 19)
Museo Multicultural de
   Lívingston.........................7 D4

SLEEPING
Hotel California.....................8 C3
Hotel Casa Rosada.................9 C4
Hotel Doña Alida.................10 D2
Hotel Garífuna....................11 C2
Hotel Maya Quirigua............12 C4
Hotel Río Dulce...................13 B3
Hotel Ríos Tropicales...........14 B4
Hotel Villa Caribe................15 C4
National Flag Hotel..............16 B1

EATING
Antojitos Yoli's...................17 B4
McTropic Restaurante..........18 B3
Restaurante Bahía Azul.........19 B3
Restaurante Buga Mama........20 D3
Restaurante Gaby.................21 C4
Tilingo-Lingo......................22 D2

ENTERTAINMENT
Café-Bar Ubafu...................23 C2
Hotel Villa Caribe...........(see 15)
Tropicool Disco..............(see 19)

Gaviota's Restaurant (3km);
Los Siete Altares (5km);
Playa Quehueche (7km);
Playa Blanca (12km)

Calle Principal

Calle Minerva

See Inset

Calle Marcos Sánchez Díaz

Muelle Municipal

Boats to Los Siete Altares, Playa Blanca, Punta Gorda, Omoa

Secondary Dock

Boats to Puerto Barrios

Boats to Finca Tatín, Hotelito Perdido, Río Dulce Town

Río Dulce

To Casa de la Iguana (500m)

Inset

Tours

A few outfits in Lívingston offer tours that let you get out and experience the natural wonders of the area. **Exotic Travel** (☎ 7947 0048; www .bluecaribbeanbay.com; Restaurante Bahía Azul, Calle Principal) is a well-organized operation with several good trips. Its popular Ecological Tour/Jungle Trip takes you for a walk through town, out west up to a lookout spot and on to the Río Quehueche, where you take a half-hour canoe trip down the river to Playa Quehueche (see opposite). Then you walk through the jungle to Los Siete Altares (see opposite), hang out there for a while, then you walk down to the beach and back along it to Lívingston. The trip leaves the Restaurant Bahía Azul on Calle Principal every day at 9am and arrives back around 4:30pm;

it costs US$10 including a box lunch. This is a great way to see the area, and the friendly local guides can also give you a good introduction to the Garífuna people who live here.

Exotic Travel's Playa Blanca tour goes by boat first to the Seven Altars, then on to the Río Cocolí, where you can swim, and then on to Playa Blanca for two or three hours at the best beach in the area. This trip goes with a minimum of six people and costs US$13.

It also offer day trips to the **Cayos Sapodillas** (or Zapotillas), well off the coast of southern Belize, where there is great snorkeling (US$40 plus US$10 to enter the cayos, plus US$10 exit tax), and to Punta de Manabique for US$16 per person. A minimum of six people is needed for each of these trips.

CENTRAL & EASTERN GUATEMALA

RÍO DULCE TOURS

Tour agencies in town offer day trips up the Río Dulce to Río Dulce town, as do most local boatmen at the Lívingston dock. Many travelers use these tours as one-way transportation to Río Dulce, paying around US$10. If you want to return to Lívingston the cost is US$15 to US$18. It's a beautiful ride through tropical jungle scenery, with several places to stop on the way.

Shortly after you leave Lívingston, you pass the tributary Río Tatín on the right, then will probably stop at an indigenous arts museum set up by Asociación Ak' Tenamit, an NGO working to improve conditions for the Q'eqchi' Maya population of the area. The river enters a gorge called **La Cueva de la Vaca**, its walls hung with great tangles of jungle foliage and the humid air noisy with the cries of tropical birds. Just beyond that is **La Pintada**, a rock escarpment covered with graffiti. Local legend says people have been tagging this spot since the 1700s, though the oldest in evidence is from the 1950s. If you're lucky, you might spot a freshwater dolphin in these parts. Further on, a **thermal spring** forces sulfurous water out of the base of the cliff, providing a chance for a warm swim. The river widens into **El Golfete**, a lake-like body of water that presages the even vaster expanse of Lago de Izabal further upstream.

On the northern shore of El Golfete is the **Biotopo Chocón Machacas**, a 72-sq-km reserve established within the Parque Nacional Río Dulce to protect the beautiful river landscape, the valuable forests and mangrove swamps and their wildlife, which includes such rare creatures as the tapir and above all the manatee. The huge, walrus-like manatees are aquatic mammals weighing up to a ton, yet they glide effortlessly beneath the calm surface of the river. They are very elusive, however, and the chances of seeing one are very slim. A network of 'water trails' (boat routes around several jungle lagoons) provide ways to see other bird, animal and plant life of the reserve. A nature trail begins at the visitors center (US$2.50) and winds its way through forests of mahogany, palms and rich tropical foliage.

Boats will probably visit the **Islas de Pájaros**, a pair of islands where thousands of waterbirds live, in the middle of El Golfete. From El Golfete you continue upriver, passing increasing numbers of expensive villas and boathouses, to the town of Río Dulce, where the soaring Hwy 13 road bridge crosses the river, and on to El Castillo de San Felipe on Lago de Izabal (p254).

You can also do this trip starting from Río Dulce with *colectivo lanchas* (p254).

Festivals & Events

Lívingston is packed with merrymakers during **Semana Santa. Garífuna National Day** is celebrated on November 26 with a variety of cultural events.

Sleeping

BUDGET

Don't sleep on the beach in Lívingston – it isn't safe.

Hotel Maya Quirigua (☎ 7947 0674; Calle Marcos Sánchez Díaz; s/d US$3/6, with bathroom US$4.50/9) Run by a friendly family, the basic rooms here are good enough for the price. There's a shady garden area and good views from the rooftop. Downstairs rooms are a bit grim.

Hotel Río Dulce (☎ 7947 0764; Calle Principal; r per person US$4, with bathroom US$6) This authentic Caribbean two-story wood-frame building has bare but clean wooden rooms, in various colors, with fans. The wide verandas are great for watching the street life and catching a breeze, and the food in the restaurant below (mains from US$4) is superb.

Casa de la Iguana (☎ 7947 0064; Calle Marcos Sánchez Díaz; dm US$4.50, s/d with bathroom US$8/13) Five minutes' walk from the main dock, this newcomer has some of the best-value cabins in the country. They're clean, wooden affairs, with simple but elegant decoration. Happy hour here rocks on and you can camp for US$2 per person.

Hotel California (☎ 7947 0178/6; Calle Minerva; s/d with bathroom US$6/8) Down a quiet street, the California offers good, basic rooms on the 2nd floor (ones on the 1st floor are a little stuffy). There's an OK restaurant and some shady places to hang out.

Hotel Ríos Tropicales (☎ 7947 0158; www.mctropic .com; Calle Principal; s/d US$7/14, with bathroom US$13/25) The Ríos Tropicales has a variety of big, well-screened rooms facing a central patio with plenty of hammocks and chill-out space. Rooms with shared bathroom are bigger, but others are better decorated.

Hotel Garífuna (☎ 7947 0183; Barrio San José; s/d with bathroom US$7/10) About a five-minute walk from the main street, these big breezy rooms are a solid budget choice. Beds are good, bathrooms are spotless and the folks are friendly.

National Flag Hotel (☎ 7947 0247; Barrio San José; s/d with bathroom US$8) The big tiled rooms here are an excellent deal, even if the location is a bit remote. There are good views from the shady rooftop terrace.

MIDRANGE & TOP END

Hotel Casa Rosada (☎ 7947 0303; www.hotelcasarosada .com; Calle Marcos Sánchez Díaz; r US$20) The Casa Rosada (Pink House) is an attractive place to stay right on the river, 500m upstream from the main dock; it has its own pier where boats will drop you if you ask. The charming little wooden cabins are jammed up against each other, so there's not much privacy. But the garden area is pretty and the restaurant (mains from US$5) has great views out over the water. The shared bathrooms are very clean. Also available are a laundry service and tours.

Hotel Doña Alida (☎ /fax 7947 0027; s/d with bathroom US$27/40; ❄) In a great position just above the sea a few blocks from the center of town, the Doña Alida has a variety of rooms spread out over the cliff face. They're big and airy, with some charming decorations. As far as atmosphere goes, it's one of the best places to stay in town.

Hotel Villa Caribe (☎ 7947 0072; www.hotelvillacaribe guatemala.com; Calle Principal; s/d US$71/87, bungalows s/d US$85/95; ❄ ☐ ☒) The 45-room Villa Caribe is a luxurious anomaly among Livingston's laid-back, low-priced Caribbean lodgings. Modern but still Caribbean in style, it has many conveniences and comforts, including extensive tropical gardens, a big swimming pool and a large poolside bar. Rooms are fairly large, with modern bathrooms, ceiling fans and little balconies overlooking the gardens and river mouth.

Eating

Food in Livingston is relatively expensive because most of it (except fish and coconuts) must be brought in by boat. There's fine seafood here and some unusual flavors for Guatemala, including coconut and curry. *Tapado*, a rich stew made from fish, shrimp, shellfish and coconut milk, spiced with coriander, is the delicious local specialty. A potent potable is made by slicing off the top of a green coconut and mixing in a healthy dose of rum. These *coco locos* hit the spot.

Calle Principal is dotted with many open-air eateries.

Antojitos Yoli's (Calle Principal; items US$0.50-2; ☻ 8am-5pm) This is the place to come for baked goods. Especially recommended are the coconut bread and pineapple pie.

Restaurante Gaby (Calle Marcos Sánchez Díaz; mains US$3-5; ☻ breakfast, lunch & dinner) For a good honest feed in underwhelming surrounds, you can't go past Gaby's. She serves up the good stuff: lobster, tapado, rice and beans and good breakfasts at good prices. The *telenovelas* (soap operas) come free.

McTropic Restaurante (Calle Principal; mains US$4-10; ☻ breakfast, lunch & dinner) Some of the best-value seafood dishes in town are on offer at this laid-back little place. Grab a table streetside for people-watching and sample some of the good Thai cooking.

Tilingo-Lingo (Calle Principal; mains US$5-10; ☻ breakfast, lunch & dinner) An intimate little place down near the beach. It advertises food from 10 countries, and makes a pretty good job of it, with the Italian and East Indian dishes being the standouts.

Restaurante Bahía Azul (Calle Principal; mains US$6-12; ☻ breakfast, lunch & dinner) The Bahía's central location, happy decor and good fresh food keep it popular. The menu's wide, with a good mix of Caribbean, Guatemalan and Asian influences. It opens early for breakfast.

Restaurante Buga Mama (Calle Marcos Sánchez Díaz; mains US$8-11; ☻ breakfast, lunch & dinner) This place enjoys the best location of any restaurant in town, and profits go to the Asociación Ak Tenemit. There's a wide range of seafood and other dishes on the menu, including a very good *tapado* (US$9). Most of the waiters here are trainees in a community sustainable tourism development scheme, so service can be sketchy, but forgivable.

Drinking

Adventurous drinkers should try *guifiti*, a local concoction made from coconut rum, often infused with herbs. It's said to have medicinal as well as recreational properties.

A handful of bars down on the beach to the left of the end of Calle Principal pull in travelers and locals at night (after about 10pm or 11pm). It's very dark down here, so take care. The bars are within five minutes' walk from each other, so you should go for a wander and see what's happening. Music ranges from punta to salsa, merengue and electronica. Things warm up on Friday but Saturday is the party night – often going 'til 5am or 6am.

Happy hour is pretty much an institution along the main street, with every restaurant getting in on the act. One of the best is at **Casa de la Iguana** (Calle Marcos Sánchez Díaz).

Entertainment

A traditional Garífuna band is composed of three large drums, a turtle shell, some maracas and a big conch shell, producing throbbing, haunting rhythms and melodies. The chanted words are like a litany, with responses often taken up by the audience. *Punta* is the Garífuna dance; it's got a lot of gyrating hip movements.

Quite often a roaming band will play a few songs for diners along the Calle Principal around dinnertime. If you like the music, make sure to sling them a few bucks. Several places around town have live Garífuna music, although schedules are unpredictable.

Café-Bar Ubafu Probably the most dependable. Supposedly has music and dancing nightly, but liveliest on weekends.

Hotel Villa Caribe Diners can enjoy a Garífuna show each evening at 7pm.

Tropicool Disco Next door to the Restaurante Bahía Azul, this is a small mainstream disco that sometimes pulls a crowd.

Getting There & Away

Frequent boats come downriver from Río Dulce (p254) and across the bay from Puerto Barrios (p260). There are also international boats from Honduras and Belize.

Exotic Travel (p263) operates combined boat and bus shuttles to La Ceiba (the cheapest gateway to Honduras' Bay Islands) for US$45 per person, with a minimum of six people. Leaving Lívingston at 7:30am or earlier will get you to La Ceiba in time for the boat to the islands, making it a one-day trip, which is nearly impossible to do independently.

There's also a boat that goes direct to Punta Gorda on Tuesday and Friday at 7am (US$20, one hour), leaving from the public dock. In Punta Gorda, the boat connects with a bus to Placencia and Belize City. The boat waits for this bus to arrive from Placencia before it sets off back for Lívingston from Punta Gorda at about 10:30am.

If you are taking one of these early international departures, get your exit stamp from immigration in Lívingston (see p261) the day before.

AROUND LÍVINGSTON

Hotelito Perdido (☎ 5725 1576; www.hotelitoperdido .com; dm US$4, bungalows s/d US$17/20), a beautiful new place a five-minute boat ride from Finca Tatín, is run buy a couple of young travelers. The

---

CATCH THE RHYTHM OF THE GARÍFUNA

Lívingston is the heartland of Guatemala's Garífuna community, and it won't take too long before you hear some of their distinctive music. A Garífuna band generally consists of three drums (the *primera* takes the bass part, the other two play more melodic functions), a shaker or maraca, a turtle shell (hit like a cowbell) and a conch shell (blown like a flute).

The lyrics are often call and response – most often sung in Garífuna (a language with influences from Arawak, French and West African languages) but sometimes composed in Spanish. Most songs deal with themes from village life – planting time, harvests, things that happen in the village, honoring the dead and folktales of bad sons made good. Sometimes they simply sing about the beauty of the village.

Traditional Garífuna music has given birth to an almost bewildering array of musical styles, among them Punta Rock, Jugujugu, Calachumba, Jajankanu, Chumba, Saranda, Sambé and Parranda.

There are many local groups who play in Lívingston, the best known of which are Ubafu, Gayuza, Ibimeni and Zugara. Unlike some of Belize's Garífuna musicians, no musician from Lívingston has ever become famous in the 'outside world.'

Punta Rock is by far the most widely known adaptation of traditional Garífuna rhythms, and you can hear 'Punta' in most discos throughout Central America. The dance that accompanies it (also called *punta*) is a frenzied sort of affair, following the nature of the percussion. The left foot swivels back and forth while the right foot taps out the rhythm. Perhaps coincidentally, this movement causes the hips to shake wildly, leading some observers to comment on the sexual nature of the dance.

ambience is superb – relaxed and friendly. The whole place is solar powered and constructed in such a way as to cause minimal impact on the environment. The two-story bungalows are gorgeous – simple yet well decorated, with a sleeping area upstairs and a small sitting area downstairs. At the time of writing, there were three (so book ahead!), with plans to construct one more. You can organize many of the activities available at Finca Tatín (see below) from here as well. Call to get picked up from Lívingston (US$4) or get dropped off by any boat going between there and Río Dulce.

Finca Tatín (☎ 5902 0831; www.fincatatin.centramerica .com; dm US$5, s/d US$8/13, with bathroom US$15/20), a wonderful, rustic B&B at the confluence of Ríos Dulce and Tatín, about 10km from Lívingston, is a great place for experiencing the forest. Four-hour guided walks and kayak trips, some visiting local Q'eqchi' villages, are offered. Accommodation is in funky wood-and-thatched cabins scattered through the jungle. There are trails, waterfalls and endless river tributaries that you can explore with one of the *cayucos* available for guest use (US$10 per day). Guided night walks through the jungle offer views of elusive nightlife, and cave tours are good for swimming and soaking in a natural sauna. You can walk to Lívingston from here in about four hours, or take a kayak and staff from Finca Tatín will come pick you up (US$13).

Lanchas traveling between Río Dulce and Lívingston (or vice versa) will drop you here. It costs around US$4 from Lívingston, 20 minutes away. Or the *finca* may be able to send its own *lancha* to pick you up at Lívingston (per person US$4, minimum two people).

El Petén

Vast, sparsely populated and jungle-covered, Guatemala's largest department is ripe for further exploration.

Two things really stand out about El Petén – the well-preserved (and often unrestored) archaeological sites and the abundance of wildlife that inhabits the jungle surrounding them.

There are so many Mayan ruins here that you can take your pick depending on ease of access. The towering temples of Tikal can be reached by tour from just about anywhere in the country, minimizing your time outside of air-conditioned comfort. Other, more remote sites like El Mirador and Piedras Negras require days of planning, and further days of jungle trekking.

Wherever you go, you'll be accompanied by a jungle symphony – the forests are alive with parrots, monkeys and larger, more elusive animals.

In 1990 Guatemala established the 21,000 sq km Reserva de Biosfera Maya (Maya Biosphere Reserve), occupying approximately the whole northern third of El Petén. This Guatemalan reserve adjoins the vast Calakmul Biosphere Reserve in Mexico and the Río Bravo Conservation Area in Belize, forming a huge multinational reserve totaling more than 30,000 sq km. The great variety of animal, bird and plant life is as exciting as the mysteries of the ancient Mayan cities – and many sites in El Petén combine both.

TOP FIVE

- Taking in the majesty of the jungle-shrouded ruins at **Tikal** (p288)

- Getting right out there to little-excavated ruins such as **El Mirador** (p306) and **Piedras Negras** (p304)

- Spotting rare birds, monkeys and other **rainforest wildlife** (p294) at Tikal and other sites

- Taking a break at super-mellow **El Remate** (p285) or the picturesque island town of **Flores** (p272)

- Boating, horse riding and trekking your way to ancient Mayan ruins around **Sayaxché** (p299)

HISTORY

Often referred to as the cradle of Mayan civilization, El Petén has historically been isolated from the rest of present-day Guatemala, a situation that continued until quite recently.

The major Mayan population centers here – Tikal and El Mirador – almost certainly had more contact with neighboring settlements in Belize and Mexico than with those down south.

The arrival of the Spanish changed little in this regard. The Itzá, who lived on the island now known as Flores, earned an early reputation for cruelty and ferocity and this, along with El Petén's impenetrable jungles and fierce wildlife, kept the Spanish out of the region until 1697, about 150 years after the rest of the country had been conquered.

Even after conquest, the Spanish had no great love for El Petén. The island of Flores was a penal colony for a couple of years, then a small city was founded, mostly to facilitate the growing trade in chicle, hardwood, sugarcane and rubber that had been planted in the region.

The big change didn't come until 1970, when the Guatemalan government saw the opportunity to market Tikal as a tourist destination and work was initiated on a decent road network.

El Petén's population boom – largely a result of government incentives for farmers to relocate – has been staggering, having gone from 15,000 to 500,000 in the last 50 years.

Some of the new neighbors are not entirely welcome, however – large tracts of land, particularly in the northwest corner and in the Parque Nacional Laguna del Tigre, have been taken over by drug traffickers and people smugglers, capitalizing on the unpatroled border with Mexico.

CLIMATE

If you visit from December to February, expect some cool nights and mornings. Weather-wise this can be the best time to visit El Petén. March and April are the hottest and driest months. The rains begin in May or June, and with them come the mosquitoes – bring rain gear, repellent and, if you plan on slinging a hammock, a mosquito net. July to September is muggy and buggy. October and November see the end of the occasional rains and a return to cooler temperatures.

GETTING THERE & AROUND

El Petén's main tourism node is at the twin towns of Flores and Santa Elena, about 60km southwest of Tikal. The main roads to Flores from Río Dulce to the southeast, from Cobán and Chisec to the southwest, from Melchor de Mencos on the Belize border to the east, and from El Naranjo to the northwest are now all paved and in good condition, except for a few short stretches. Frequent buses and minibuses ferry travelers along these routes. Flores also has the only functioning civil airport in the country except for Guatemala City.

POPTÚN

pop 19,500 / elev 540m

The small town of Poptún is about halfway between Río Dulce and Flores. The reason most travelers come here is to visit Finca Ixobel (below).

On the corner of 5a Calle, just south of the Flores minibus stop, **Banco Reformador** (5a Calle 7-98; ☺ 9am-5pm Mon-Fri, 9am-1pm Sat) has a Visa ATM and changes cash US dollars and Visa and American Express traveler's checks. One block along 5a Calle, **Banrural** (☺ 8:30am-5pm Mon-Fri, 9am-1pm Sat) has a MasterCard ATM and changes cash US dollars as well as American Express traveler's checks.

Sleeping & Eating

Finca Ixobel (☎ 5892 3188; www.fincaixobel.com; campsites per person US$3, dm US$4, tree houses, rooms & bungalows s US$10-17, d US$13-30; P ☐ ☎) With by far the best facilities, this 2 sq km venue is 5km south of Poptún. For several decades Carole DeVine has offered travelers tent sites, *palapas* (thatched palm-leaf shelters) for hanging hammocks, beds and lip-smacking homemade meals, with veggie options galore. Carole founded this bohemian hideaway in the 1970s with her husband Michael, who was tragically murdered in 1990 during the civil war, when Poptún was a training ground for the vicious antiguerrilla forces called Kaibiles. Finca Ixobel is a special place, with large and beautiful grounds and famous for its friendly, relaxed atmosphere – a great place for meeting other travelers from all parts of the globe. It's also renowned for its food and its activities. The grounds contain a lovely natural pool for swimming, and horse riding (from two hours to four days), treks, cave trips and inner-tubing on the Río Machaquilá (in the rainy season) are all organized on a daily basis, at reasonable prices. The six-hour Cueva del Río outing, to an underground river complete with rapids and waterfalls, costs US$9. Internet use is US$2.50 an hour.

The camping area is large and grassy, with good bathrooms and plenty of shade. Dotted around it are several tree houses (actually mostly cabins on stilts), which are fun places to sleep. The assorted other accommodations range from a couple of dormitories to rooms with shared and private bathroom, and a bungalow. The rooms and bungalow all have a fan, mosquito nets and mosquito-screened windows. Meals here are excellent, including the eat-all-you-like buffet dinner for US$3.50 (salads, garlic bread, drinks) or US$7 (with a main dish too). Finca Ixobel

has its own bakery, grows its own salads and produces its own eggs. You can cook in the campground if you bring your own supplies. After 9pm many people move on to the pool bar, where reasonably priced cocktails and other drinks are served.

Everything at Finca Ixobel works on the honor system: guests keep an account of what they eat and drink and the services they use. Watch your budget and don't neglect the tip box for the staff when you settle your account! There are often volunteer opportunities for fluent English and Spanish speakers in exchange for room and board. If the *finca* (ranch) suits your style and you want to help/hang out for six weeks minimum, ask about volunteering.

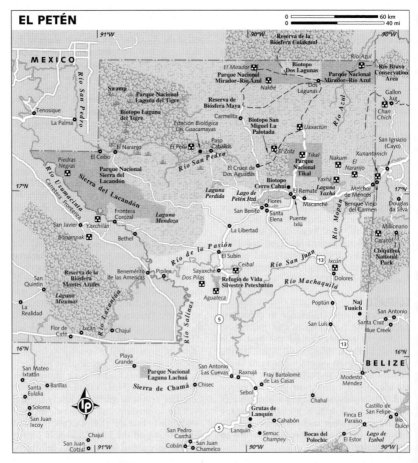

THE RESERVA DE BIOSFERA MAYA

The Reserva de Biosfera Maya, occupying 21,000 sq km stretched right across the north of El Petén, is part of the Unesco world biosphere reserve network, which recognizes that the many human demands on this planet's land require innovative strategies if nature is to be conserved. In this vein, the Maya reserve is split into three spheres. Along its southern fringe is a buffer zone where economic activities are permitted, supposedly within a framework of environmental protection. The main part of the reserve is divided into a multiple use zone, composed of tropical forest and supposedly dedicated to the sustainable harvest of *xate* ferns, chicle gum and timber, and eight core areas (the Sierra del Lacandón, Tikal, Laguna del Tigre and Mirador-Río Azul national parks, and the Cerro Cahuí, San Miguel La Palotada, Laguna del Tigre and Dos Lagunas biotopes) for scientific research, conservation of the natural environment and/or archaeological sites, and tightly controlled ecological and cultural tourism. Unfortunately, the theory is prettier than the reality: the forest is still being ravaged by people illegally harvesting timber on a massive scale, looters desecrating tombs and tourists (no matter how conscientious) negatively impacting on the fragile ecosystem. Even some core areas have been subject to illegal settlements by land-hungry peasants from further south. In 1998 the environmental organization Conservation International had a camp in the reserve burned down by angry settlers. At least two conservationists who have spoken out about abuses in the reserve have been shot dead. The buffer zone is rapidly changing from a forested landscape with scattered agricultural patches to an agricultural landscape with scattered forest patches.

Meanwhile the remaining forests of southern Petén are falling at an alarming rate to the machetes of subsistence farmers. Sections of forest are felled and burned off, crops are grown for a few seasons until the fragile jungle soil is exhausted, and then the farmer moves deeper into the forest to slash and burn new fields. Cattle ranchers, also slashing and burning the forest in order to make pasture, have also contributed to the damage, as have resettled refugees and urban Guatemalans moving from the cities to El Petén in their endless struggle to make a living.

The turnoff for the *finca* is marked on Hwy 13. In the daytime you can ask the bus or minibus driver to let you off there; it's a 15-minute walk to the *finca*. At night, or if you don't feel like making the walk, get off the bus in Poptún and take a taxi for US$4. It's not advisable to walk to the *finca* at night – it's an isolated spot. When you leave Finca Ixobel, most buses will stop on the highway to pick you up, but not after dark. The *finca* offers shuttles to Flores for US$5.50. Shuttles coming from Flores should drop you at the gate, but check first. Other recommendations in Poptún town include the following:

Hotel Izalco (☎ 7927 7372; 4a Calle 7-11; s/d US$5.50/11, with bathroom US$7/14) Small but clean rooms with TV and good mosquito netting. Some of those with private bathroom don't have a fan. And you want a fan.

Hotel Posada de los Castellanos (☎ 7927 7222; cnr 4a Calle & 7a Av; s/d with bathroom US$7/14) In the center of town, this hotel has average rooms with TV, arranged around a shady courtyard.

Getting There & Away

Most buses and minibuses stop on the main road through town: Fuente del Norte buses stop by the Shell station; minibuses to San Luís, 16km south, go from the next corner south, and minibuses to Flores start half a block further along.

Bus departures from Poptún include the following:

Flores/Santa Elena Fuente del Norte buses (US$3, two hours, 113km) go every hour or two almost around the clock. The other option is a minibus (US$3.50, about every 30 minutes, 6am to 6pm).

Fray Bartolomé de Las Casas (US$6, five hours, 100km) One bus departs at 10am from the market area. If you want to push on from Las Casas to Lanquín the same day, try getting a Guatemala City–bound bus as far as Modesto Méndez (also called Cadenas), 60km south on Hwy 13. Change there for a westbound bus or minibus to Las Casas.

Guatemala City (US$7 to US$10.50, six to seven hours, 387km) Fuente del Norte buses go about every 30 minutes, from 5:30am to midnight.

Río Dulce (US$3.25 to US$4, two hours, 99km) Fuente del Norte buses leave about every 30 minutes, from 5:30am to midnight.

NAJ TUNICH

When they were discovered in 1979, these caves created about as close to a stir as you get in the archaeological world. They only measure 3km long, but they're packed out with hieroglyphic texts and Mayan murals, depicting religious ceremonies, ball games and erotic scenes (a detail not found elsewhere in the Mayan world). Scribes and artists traveled from as far away as Calakmul in Mexico to contribute to the murals.

The caves were closed in 1984, due to vandalism, reopened briefly, then closed in 2004 for conservation purposes. Fortunately, a superbly executed replica has been created in a nearby cave. Reproductions of the murals were painted by local artists under the supervision of archaeological and cultural authorities.

Independent access to the site is near impossible at this time – your best bet is to go with one of the very reasonably priced tours from Finca Ixobel (see p269), proceeds of which go to development projects in local communities.

MACHAQUILÁ

This unremarkable little town 7km north of Poptún is worth considering as a halt because of the **Hotel Ecológico Villa de los Castellanos** (☎ 7927 7541; ecovilla@intelnet.net.gt; s/d/tr US$20/25/30; P), by the highway at the north end of town. The hotel is right by the Río Machaquilá, which is good for swimming, and its large grounds – through which you can take a 3km circuit tour or walk – are dedicated to cultivating over 60 medicinal plants. Accommodations are in wooden, thatch-roofed bungalows, each with two four-poster beds, mosquito nets, hot-water bathroom and TV, and there's a good, medium-priced restaurant.

Machaquilá is served by the same buses and minibuses as Poptún.

FLORES & SANTA ELENA

pop Flores 23,700, Santa Elena 29,000 / elev 110m

The town of Flores is built on an island in Lago de Petén Itzá. A 500m causeway connects Flores to its sister town of Santa Elena on the lakeshore, which merges into San Benito to the west. The three towns actually form one large settlement, often referred to simply as Flores.

Flores proper is by far the more attractive place to base yourself. Small hotels and restaurants line the lakeside streets, meaning you don't have to shell out the big bucks to get a room with some awesome views. It does have a slightly twee, built-up edge to it, though, and many Tikal-bound shoestringers opt for the natural surrounds and tranquility of El Remate (p285), just down the road.

LOCAL LORE: THE STONE HORSE

There was a time when the waters of Lago Petén Itzá rose and fell drastically. When it rained, the islands would flood and the crops would be destroyed.

Many people left the region, feeling that the gods were punishing them, but some remained. One holy man pierced his ears, tongue and nose and with his blood the gods were calmed and there were no more floods.

After a time, Cortés' army came through. They were headed south and didn't attack the locals, but Cortés' horse got sick and they had to leave it behind.

The horse was beautiful and strong, but it soon became weak and died. The villagers decided to throw it intro the lake as an offering to the gods.

The gods were again appeased and there were no more floods, so the villagers made a stone statue of the horse and began to leave offerings for it.

Generations later, more foreigners came, this time to conquer. Their priest said they could not worship the horse any more and had it destroyed. The floods began again and continued for many years. The people were distraught, until one of the ancient ones remembered the offerings to the horse, and suggested that they make offerings again – not to the lake, or the horse, but to the new god the foreigners had brought. They threw offerings into the lake and the waters calmed.

Now the waters rise and fall occasionally, because there are some who still make offerings and some who are lazy and do nothing.

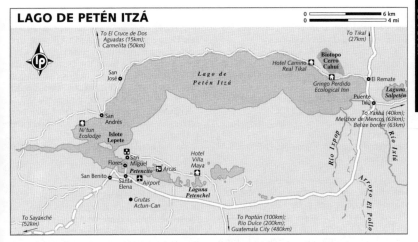

LAGO DE PETÉN ITZÁ

Santa Elena is where you'll find banks, supermarkets and buses. Adjoining Santa Elena is San Benito (population 35,600). There's not really much for the average traveler here, unless you're up for a night of slumming it in one of the town's numerous *cantinas*.

History

Flores was founded on an island (*petén*) by a people called the Itzáes who came here after being expelled from Chichén Itzá on Mexico's Yucatán Peninsula, maybe in the 13th century AD, maybe in the 15th. Flores was originally named Tayasal. Hernán Cortés dropped in on King Canek of Tayasal in 1525 on his way to Honduras, but the meeting was, amazingly, peaceable. Cortés left behind a lame horse, which the Itzáes fed on flowers and turkey stew. When it died, the Itzáes made a statue of it which, by the time a couple of Spanish friars visited in 1618, was being worshiped as a manifestation of the rain god Chac. It was not until 1697 that the Spaniards brought the Itzáes of Tayasal – by some distance the last surviving independent Mayan kingdom – forcibly under their control. The God-fearing Spanish soldiers destroyed its many pyramids, temples and statues, and today you won't see a trace of them, although the modern town is doubtless built on the ruins and foundations of Mayan Tayasal. Confusingly, the overgrown ruins named Tayazal, on the mainland peninsula just north of the island, date mostly from the Classic period, well before the Itzáes came to Flores.

Orientation

The airport is on the eastern outskirts of Santa Elena, 2km from the causeway connecting Santa Elena and Flores. Long-distance buses drop passengers on or just off Santa Elena's main drag, 4a Calle.

Information

AIRLINE OFFICES

The following airlines are at Flores airport:

Inter/Grupo TACA (☎ 7926 1238)
Maya Island Air (☎ 7926 3386)
Tropic Air (☎ 7926 0348)

EMERGENCY

Hospital San Benito (☎ 7926 1459)
Policía Nacional (☎ 7926 1365)

INTERNET ACCESS

You can access the web at the following places:

Flores.Net (Map p276; Av Barrios, Flores, per hr US$1.10)
Internet Petén (Map p276; Calle Centroamérica, Flores; per hr US$1.20; ☺ 8am-10pm)
Naomi's Café (Map p276; Calle Centroamérica, Flores; per hr US$1.20)

LAUNDRY

Mayan Princess Travel Agency (Map p276; Calle 30 de Junio, Flores; ☺ 8am-8pm) US$3.25 to wash and dry a load.

MONEY

At the airport, **Banquetzal** (☺ 7am-noon & 2-5pm) changes US-dollar cash and traveler's checks. **Banrural** (Map p276; Avenida Flores), just off the Parque Central in Flores, changes US-dollar cash and traveler's checks.

Other banks are on 4a Calle in Santa Elena. The following all change cash US dollars and at least American Express US-dollar traveler's checks:

Banco Agromercantil (Map p275; ☽ 9am-6pm Mon-Fri, 9am-1pm Sat) Has a MasterCard ATM.

Banco Industrial (Map p275; ☽ 9am-7pm Mon-Fri, 10am-2pm Sat) Has a Visa ATM.

Banquetzal (Map p275; ☽ 9am-1pm & 2-5:30pm Mon-Fri, 9am-1pm Sat)

Many travel agencies and places to stay will change cash US dollars, and sometimes traveler's checks, at poor rates. San Juan Travel (right) will also change Belize dollars and Mexican pesos, and give Visa, Master-Card, Diner's Club and American Express cash advances.

POST

Post office Flores (Map p276; Av Barrios); Santa Elena (Map p275; 4a Calle east of 7a Av)

TELEPHONE & FAX

Martsam Travel (Map p276; ☎ /fax 7926 3225; www .martsam.com; Calle 30 de Junio, Flores) Offers domestic and international telephone and fax services.

TOURIST OFFICES

Asociación Alianza Verde (Map p276; ☎ /fax 7926 0718; www.alianzaverde.org) This association dedicated to sustainable, responsible, low-impact tourism in the Reserva de Biosphera Maya runs Cincap. Its Green Deal program (www.greendeal.org) awards a seal of excellence to tourism businesses that meet stringent environmental and social standards.

Cincap (Map p276; Centro de Información Sobre la Naturaleza, Cultura y Artesanía de Petén; Petén Nature, Culture & Handicrafts Information Center; ☎ 7926 0718; mercadeo@peten.net; Parque Central, Flores; ☽ 9am-noon & 2-9pm) Has interesting displays on archaeological sites, conservation areas and the local way of life in El Petén. It also sells handicrafts from the region and has an information desk, where you can ask about visits to some of the region's more remote natural and archaeological sites.

Inguat (☎ 7926 0533; airport; ☽ 7am-noon & 3-5pm) The only official tourist information around is at this office out at the airport.

TRAVEL AGENCIES

Several travel agencies in Flores and Santa Elena offer trips to archaeological sites, shuttle minibuses and other services. **Martsam Travel** (Map p276; ☎ /fax 7926 3225; www.martsam.com; Calle 30 de Junio, Flores) is a well-established, well-organized agency with a particularly wide range of services, as you'll see from the frequency with which its name crops up in this chapter. **San Juan Travel** (☎ 7926 0041; sanjuant@internetdetelgua .com.gt; Flores Map p276, Playa Sur; Santa Elena Map p275, 2a Calle) provides various shuttles and tours and offers the most regular service to Tikal and Palenque.

Several hotels can book you on tours, shuttles, buses and flights.

Volunteer Work

The Estación Biológica Las Guacamayas (p304), in the Parque Nacional Laguna del Tigre, and the rehabilitation center at Arcas (p283) both offer the chance of volunteer work with wildlife. At Las Guacamayas you pay US$9 a day for the first two weeks, US$8 a day the third week and US$7 a day the fourth week, and provide your own food. If you're interested, contact **ProPetén** (Map p276; Proyecto Petenero para un Bosque Sostenible; ☎ 7926 1370; www.propeten.org; Calle Central, Flores; ☽ 9am-5pm Mon-Fri), the Guatemalan NGO that owns the station. At Arcas you pay US$110 a week including food. The language schools in San Andrés (p283) and San José (p284) provide the chance to get involved in community and environmental projects.

Tours

Many travel agencies in Flores offer day tours to the more accessible archaeological sites such as Tikal, Uaxactún, Yaxhá and Ceibal. Day trips to these places with a guide and lunch cost US$40 to US$60 with agencies such as Martsam Travel, Hotel Posada Tayazal and San Juan Travel (see left).

Maya Expeditions (see p81), based in Guatemala City, offers mild (ie good for families or inexperienced rafters) one- to three-day rafting expeditions on the Río Chiquibul, with options to visit lesser-known sites like Yaxhá, Nakum and Topoxte for US$85 to US$430 per person.

Martsam also offers more demanding hiking-and-camping ecotrails and ecotours to exciting, more remote archaeological sites such as Nakum, El Perú, El Zotz, El Mirador, Nakbé, Wakná and La Muralla, working with local Comités Comunitarios de Ecoturismo (Community Ecotourism Committees), which provide guides to these sites deep in El Petén

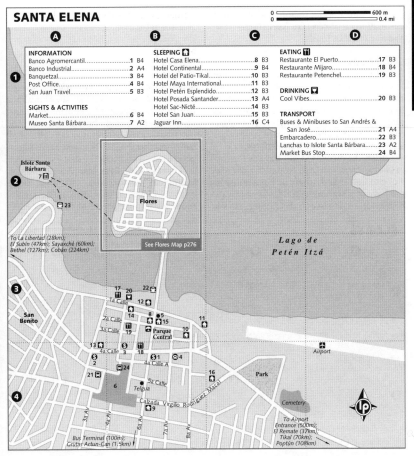

SANTA ELENA

INFORMATION
Banco Agromercantil...........................**1** B4
Banco Industrial.................................**2** A4
Banquetzal......................................**3** B4
Post Office......................................**4** B4
San Juan Travel.................................**5** B3

SIGHTS & ACTIVITIES
Market...**6** B4
Museo Santa Bárbara........................**7** A2

SLEEPING
Hotel Casa Elena...............................**8** B3
Hotel Continental..............................**9** B4
Hotel del Patio-Tikal.........................**10** B3
Hotel Maya International....................**11** B3
Hotel Petén Esplendido......................**12** B3
Hotel Posada Santander......................**13** A4
Hotel Sac-Nicté................................**14** B3
Hotel San Juan................................**15** B3
Jaguar Inn.......................................**16** C4

EATING
Restaurante El Puerto.........................**17** B3
Restaurante Mijaro...........................**18** B4
Restaurante Petenchel........................**19** B3

DRINKING
Cool Vibes......................................**20** B3

TRANSPORT
Buses & Minibuses to San Andrés &
   San José.....................................**21** A4
Embarcadero....................................**22** B3
Lanchas to Islote Santa Bárbara.......**23** A2
Market Bus Stop...............................**24** B4

jungles. The three ecotourism committees, in the villages of El Cruce de Dos Aguadas (about 45km north of Flores by dirt road), Carmelita (some 35km beyond El Cruce de Dos Aguadas) and Paso Caballos (west of El Cruce de Dos Aguadas), were set up with the help of Conservation International and ProPetén, with the aim of fostering low-impact tourism benefiting local jungle communities. Comité guides are usually *xateros* (collectors of *xate,* a palm used in flower bouquets) or *chicleros* (collectors of chicle, used to make chewing gum) who know the forest very well, but may be light on the archaeological significance of the sites. There's no luxury on these trips: participants should be in good shape mentally and physically, as they'll sleep in hammocks,

hike for long stretches through thick jungle, eat what's fed them and be munched by whatever ants, mosquitoes and ticks they're sharing the forest with.

The sample prices following are per person for two-/four-/five-plus people, normally including food, water, sleeping gear and Spanish-speaking guide:

Location	Duration	Cost
El Zotz and Tikal	3 days	US$200/150/140
El Perú	3 days	US$240/170/155
	2 days	US$230/140/130
El Mirador-Nakbé-Wakná	7 days	US$475/460/415
Yaxhá-Nakum-Tikal	3 days	US$250/178/165
Yaxhá & Nakum	2 days	US$180/125/110
Dos Pilas, Aguateca & Ceibal	2 days	US$290/190/175

Another outfit going to some adventurous destinations is **Monkey Eco Tours** (☎ 5201 0759; www.nitun.com; Ni'tun Ecolodge).

LAKE TOURS

Boats at the *embarcaderos* (docks) opposite Hotel Petenchel and beside Hotel Santana in Flores, and beside the Hotel Petén Espléndido in Santa Elena, can be hired for lake tours. Prices are very negotiable. You might pay US$25 for an hour on board, with stops and waiting time at no extra charge.

Carlos, the owner of Café-Bar Las Puertas in Flores, offers boat trips around the lake and along to the far end, where he has a house in the form of a Mayan pyramid, with a private beach for swimming and sunning. He's a former guide at Tikal and very knowledgeable about the area.

Sleeping

FLORES
Budget

Hostel los Amigos (Map p276; ☎ 5584 8795; www.amigoshostel.com; Calle Central; dm US$3.50; 🖳) Flores' one true hostel, with eight-bed dorms and hammocks on offer, could be a disaster, but the place has such a cool atmosphere that it all hangs together. Nightly bonfires, happy hours, good food – you know the deal…

Hospedaje Doña Goya (Map p276; ☎ 7926 3538; hospedajedonagoya@yahoo.com; Calle Unión; dm/s/d US$3.50/8/11, s/d with bathroom US$11/13) This family-room guesthouse is one of the best budget

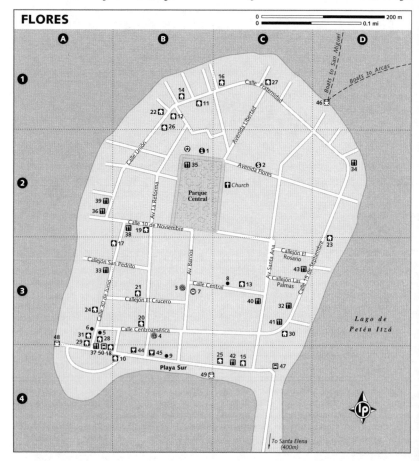

FLORES

choices in town and often full as a result. The beds are comfortable, the water's hot and there's a roof terrace with a palm-thatched shelter and plenty of hammocks from which to enjoy lake views. The eight-person dorms are spacious and clean.

Hospedaje Doña Goya 2 (Map p276; ☎ 7926 3538; hospedajedonagoya@yahoo.com; Calle Unión; dm/ s/d US$3.50/8/11, s/d with bathroom US$11/13) Doña Goya's second effort is even better than her first – there's a definite jungle theme running through this one, with banisters made to look like climbing vines. Rooms are good sized and spotless, most of them with some sort of view.

Hotel Mirador del Lago (Map p276; ☎ 7926 3276; s/d with bathroom US$6/8; Calle 15 de Septiembre) Compared to what else is on offer for these prices on the island, this is a good deal. Rooms are bare but functional and upstairs they catch good afternoon breezes.

Hotel Santa Rita (Map p276; ☎ 7926 3224; Calle 30 de Junio; s/d with bathroom US$7/12) It's never going to be beautiful, but someone is at least trying with this place, keeping it clean and freshly painted. Smallish rooms with shared balconies and a couple of good hang-out areas.

Hotel Casablanca (Map p276; ☎ 5699 1371; Playa Sur; s/d with bathroom US$7.50/13) The first hotel you reach coming off the causeway is one of the best in the budget game – simple, spacious rooms and a great terrace for lake-gazing.

Hotel Petenchel (Map p276; ☎ 7926 3359; Playa Sur; s/d with bathroom US$7.50/13) Eight rooms set around a lush little courtyard just off the causeway. Rooms are spacious, with firm beds. In the event that

El Petén ever experiences a chilly night, have no fear – showers here are superhot.

Hotel Casa del Lacandón (Map p 276; ☎ 7926 4359; Calle Unión; s/d US$8/13) If you can get one of the upstairs rooms at the back, this is one of the best budget deals in town. Rooms have a couple of beds, a clothes rack (!) and windows with sweeping views of the lake.

Mayab Hotel (Map p276; ☎ 7926 4094; mcestra@gmail .com; Calle 30 de Junio; s/d with bathroom US$12/16; 🖳) Decent-sized rooms with cable TV and hot showers. The real bonus here is the upstairs balcony overlooking the lake and the back gate, leading directly to the shoreline.

There are two further budget hotels with respectable, fan-cooled rooms:

Hotel Itzá 2 (Map p276; ☎ 7926 3654; Av La Reforma; s/d with cold-water bathroom US$6/8)

Hotel La Unión (Map p276; ☎ 7926 3584; Calle Unión; s/d US$8/13, d with view US$16)

Midrange

Hotel La Mesa de los Maya (Map p276; ☎ /fax 7926 1240; mesamayas@hotmail.com; Callejon El Crucero; s/d US$15/20, with air-con US$20/25; 🍴) The Mesa's one of the stalwarts in the Flores hotel scene – it's been around (nearly) forever and they know what they're doing. Rooms are smallish, but well decorated, with good touches like reading lamps and pleasant paint jobs.

Hotel Villa del Lago (Map p276; ☎ /fax 7926 508; www.hotelvilladelago.com; Calle 15 de Septiembre; s/d US$25/30; 🍴 🖳) Stern and blockish from the outside, this place has a cool tiled interior that runs a little heavy on the potted plants and Grecian column work. Rooms are comfortable, with good furnishings and big ceiling fans. Breakfast is available, there's a breezy upstairs terrace, and the staff can do your laundry, exchange books and book flights.

Hotel El Itzá 1 (Map p276; ☎ 7926 3666; uniglob@guate .net.gt; Playa Sur; s/d US$30/40; 🛏) The owners of this place must have been bleeding when somebody whacked up that monster hotel in front, killing all the lake views. Still, rooms here are clean and big – get one upstairs for the afternoon breezes.

Hotel Sabana (Map p276; ☎ /fax 7926 1248; Calle Fraternidad; s/d US$30/40; 🛏 🛏) On the north side of the island, this is a larger, 28-room, less personal place with a small pool (featuring family-sized Jacuzzi) and a super chilled terrace area overlooking the lake. Rooms have bathroom, air-con and cable TV.

Hotel Petén (Map p276; ☎ 7926 0692; www.hoteles depeten.com; Calle 30 de Junio; s/d US$30/46; 🛏 🛏 🛏) There's a bit of chintz going on here, but it's not overwhelming – rooms are cheerily decorated and there's a good-sized indoor/outdoor swimming pool downstairs in the small courtyard with tropical plants, a pleasant lakeside terrace and restaurant. Try to get a room on the top floor with a lake view: the interior ones can be a little gloomy.

Hotel Casazul (Map p276; ☎ 7926 1138; www.corpetur .com; Calle Fraternidad; s/d US$35/45; 🛏) They're not kidding when they call this the blue house – there's shades of it everywhere, from the pleasing plantation-style balconies to the individually decorated, spacious and comfortable rooms. A couple have their own balconies and everyone can enjoy the 3rd-floor terrace.

Hotel Casona de la Isla (Map p276; ☎ 7926 0593; www.hotelesdepeten.com; Calle 30 de Junio; s/d from US$40/48; 🛏 🛏 🛏) There are some pleasing nautical themes running through this place, augmented by the cheery blue and yellow paint job. The tile work in the lobby and stairs is worth a look in on its own. Rooms are clean and large and decorated with restraint. Rooms 31, 303 and 304 have windows facing right out to the lake and gorgeous sunsets.

Hotel Santana (Map p276; ☎ /fax 7926 3305; www.santana peten.com; Calle 30 de Junio; s/d US$40/50; 🛏 🛏 🛏) We're going with 'eclectic' when it comes to describing the decor here – a mix of concrete, wood, thatch and wickerwork. It all hangs together somehow, though. Rooms are generously sized, and if you get one out the back you'll have a sweet little balcony looking over the lake onto Isla Santa Barbara.

Top End

Hotel Isla de Flores (Map p276; ☎ 7926 0614; www .junglelodge.guate.com; Av La Reforma; s/d US$50/70; 🛏) From the overload of white wicker furniture and grandfather clock in the lobby, you know this isn't any run-of-the-mill Flores hotel. Rooms are big and businesslike, with a few homey touches softening the effect. Many have little balconies with a view of the lake.

Gran Hotel de La Isla (Map p276; ☎ 7926 0686; www .hoteldelaisla.com; Playa Sur; s/d US$70/80; 🅿 🛏 🛏 🛏) Everything about this place is big, down to the lobby/dining-room windows overlooking the lake and the swimming pool out back. Rooms are well presented, with the touches you would expect, like individual reading lamps. Make sure you get one on the lakefront, so you can take advantage of the (oddly) skimpy balconies overlooking the water.

CHICLE & CHEWING GUM

Chicle, a pinkish to reddish-brown gum, is actually the coagulated milky sap, or latex, of the sapodilla tree *(Achras zapota)*, a tropical evergreen native to the Yucatán Peninsula and Central America. *Chicleros* (chicle workers) cut large gashes in the sapodillas' trunks, making a pattern of V-shaped cuts as high as 9m. The sap runs from the wounds and down the trunk to be collected in a container at the base. After being boiled, it is shaped into blocks for shipping. The cuts can kill the tree, and thus chicle harvesting tends to result in the serious depletion of sapodilla forests. Even if the tree survives the first round of cuts, a typical tree used for harvesting chicle has a life span of just 10 years.

First used as a substitute for natural rubber (to which the sapodilla is related), by about 1890 chicle was best known as the main ingredient in chewing gum.

As a result of war research for a rubber substitute during the 1940s, synthetic substitutes were developed for chicle. Now chewing gum is made mostly from these synthetic substitutes. However, in the northern reaches of El Petén, *chicleros* still live in the forest for months at a time harvesting the sap for gum.

SANTA ELENA
Budget

Hotel Continental (Map p275; ☎ 7926 0095; 6a Av south of Calzada Virgilio Rodríguez Macal; s/d US$5/9, with fan, bathroom & TV US$9/12 ⓟ ☒) A 51-room hotel with friendly reception staff, the Continental has a range of rooms on three floors along a courtyard painted in vaguely refreshing shades of blue and green. Private bathrooms are good and clean, but there's no hot water.

Hotel San Juan (Map p275; ☎ 7926 2146; 2a Calle; s/d from US$6/8, with bathroom US$9/11) Another cheap Santa Elena hotel, but less attractive.

Hotel Posada Santander (Map p275; ☎ 7926 0574; 4a Calle; s/d with bathroom US$6/9.50) A simple, spotless and friendly family-run hostelry in a convenient but loud location. The rooms are definitely secure (there are bars on the windows *and* the TVs) and have cold-water bathrooms. The attached *comedor* (restaurant) serves good basic meals for US$2.

Hotel Sac-Nicté (Map p275; ☎ 7926 0092, 7926 1731; 1a Calle; s/d from US$9/11) The rooms here are tolerably clean and will do in a pinch. They all have private bathroom and fan, and those upstairs have small balconies from which you might just glimpse the lake. They'll pick you up free from the airport, where they have a desk.

Jaguar Inn (Map p275; ☎ 7926 0002; Calzada Virgilio Rodríguez Macal 8-79; s/d with fan US$15/18, with air-con US$18/20; ⓟ ☒) Comfortable without being fancy, the Jaguar Inn has rooms with cable TV, bright bedspreads and hot-water bathrooms set along a garden patio. It's a better deal than most of the hotels around here, probably due to its inconvenient location, 150m off the main road near the airport – good if you have a vehicle.

Midrange

Hotel Casa Elena (Map p275; ☎ 7926 2239; 6a Av; s/d US$27/30; ⓟ ☒ ☒) Just south of the causeway, Casa Elena has nice, clean, air-conditioned rooms that are short on character but long on comfort. Each is equipped with hot-water bathroom, cable TV and telephone. Some rooms overlook Santa Elena's plaza, others overlook the big pool (with waterslide). There's a bar, restaurant and roof terrace.

Top End

Hotel Maya International (Map p 275; ☎ 7926 2083; www.villasdeguatemala.com; 1a Calle; s/d US$50/70; ⓟ ☒ ☐ ☒) A wooden boardwalk snakes through lush vegetation to bring you to the airy thatched-roof reception area/restaurant here. There's wi-fi, espresso and staff dress in loose, flowing white cotton. This chic/savage vibe runs throughout the place, all to a very pleasing effect. A lot of the rooms don't have lake views, but all are well designed, with good use of tiles and tasteful, restrained decorations.

Hotel del Patio-Tikal (Map p275; ☎ 7926 1229; www.hoteldelpatio.com.gt; cnr 8a Av & 2a Calle; s/d US$55/62; ⓟ ☒ ☒) There are touches of colonial charm going on at this two-story hotel a short walk from the lakeside. Rooms are spacious and feature tasteful furnishings and luxurious showers.

Hotel Petén Espléndido (Map p275; ☎ 7926 0880; www.petenesplendido.com; 1a Calle 5-01; s/d US$100/110; ⓟ ☒ ☒ ☒) The most formal hotel in the region pulls out all the stops, with room safes, bathroom telephones, great balcony views and what may be the only elevator in all of El Petén. The rooms could be bigger, but they're definitely comfortable and there are a couple of good restaurants and a poolside bar to keep you happy. If you're flying in, you can hook up a free shuttle from the airport.

Eating

On the menu at many places is a variety of local game, including *tepescuintle* (agouti, a rabbit-sized jungle rodent), *venado* (venison), armadillo, *pavo silvestre* (wild turkey) and *pescado blanco* (white fish). You may want to avoid dishes that may soon jump from the menu to the endangered species list (for more on endangered species on menus, see p57).

FLORES

Cool Beans (Map p276; Calle 15 de Septiembre; mains US$3-6; ⓥ lunch & dinner Wed-Mon) An earthy sort of place with a thatched roof and hammocks. Good coffee, decent breakfasts and tasty snacks what's on offer here. You can just make out the lake by peering through the lush garden down the back. Be warned – the kitchen closes at 9:01pm sharp.

La Villa del Chef (Map p276; Calle Unión; mains US$3-6; ⓥ breakfast, lunch & dinner) Go out the back (keep going) to reach the rustic little deck built out over the water in this newish place with a varied menu. You can choose from a good selection of Arabic, seafood, Guatemalan and international dishes. Don't miss the 6pm happy hour.

Restaurante Peche's (Map p276; Playa Sur; mains US$3.50-4.50; 4am-10pm) Busy Peche's serves inexpensive plates of meat, rice, tortillas and salad – and it's open for early breakfast.

Capitán Tortuga (Map p276; Calle 30 de Junio; mains US$3.50-7; breakfast, lunch & dinner) A long, barn-like place stretching down to a small lakeside terrace, 'Captain Turtle' serves large plates of a wide variety of tasty food – pizzas, steaks, chicken, pasta, salads, sandwiches, tacos – at medium prices. Big tour groups turn up here from time to time.

ourpick Café Yax-ha (Map p276; Calle 15 de Septiembre; mains US$4-5; breakfast, lunch & dinner Wed-Mon) Literally wallpapered with photos and articles relating to archaeology and Mayan sites, this café-restaurant serves up the standard range of dishes. What's really special here is the prehispanic menu items and Itza dishes – the spicy chicken with yuca (US$4) comes recommended.

Suico Café (Map p 276; Calle 15 de Septiembre; mains US$4-6; lunch & dinner) Japanese food in El Petén? Well, why not. The Japanese owners take a fair stab at all your faves (miso soup, tempura, sushi) and only come up short when ingredients are lacking. Definitely worth a look in.

Restaurante & Pizzería Picasso (Map p276; Calle 15 de Septiembre; pizza US$4-6; lunch & dinner Tue-Sun) Still going strong after all these years, this Italian-owned pizzeria does the best pizzas in town, with artwork on the walls courtesy of you-know-who and a cool little courtyard area.

Jalapeños (Map p276; Calle Unión; mains US$4-10; breakfast, lunch & dinner) Maybe you don't need any more Mexican food, but if you do, this is the place – airy and breezy, serving all your (Tex) Mex faves with a couple of international dishes thrown in. The zucchini chicken in creamy sauce with black olives (US$7) is one good example.

La Luna (Map p276; cnr Calle 30 de Junio & Calle 10 de Noviembre; mains US$7-11; lunch & dinner Mon-Sat) In a class by itself, this very popular restaurant cultivates a classic tropical ambience, with potted palms to catch the breeze from the whirling overhead fans. The food is Continental and delectable, with innovative chicken, fish and beef dishes the likes of which you'll be hard pressed to find anywhere else in Guatemala. There are also good pasta and vegetarian options, such as falafel, salad and rice, for US$4 to US$5.

Las Puertas (Map p276; cnr Calle Central & Av Santa Ana; mains US$8-9; 8am-late Mon-Sat) This popular restaurant and bar has good, if pricey, food. There's live music some nights (mainly weekends). The *camarones a la oriental* (prawns served with vegetables and rice) are a treat. For something cheaper Las Puertas has 10 ways of doing spaghetti and nine types of salad. Round it off with a crepe (US$2). Breakfasts (US$3 to US$4) are good here, too.

La Hacienda del Rey (Map p276; south end Calle 30 de Junio; mains US$8-15; 4am-evening) This spacious two-story wooden affair, open to the air and invitingly strung with white lights, specializes in meat. It's one of the more atmospheric places to eat on the island (except for their terrible radio selection) They do big juicy steaks, Argentinean or American style. Steaks aren't cheap (US$13 for a 16oz T-bone), but there's a range of tacos and snacks (US$2 to US$3) in case you're feeling like taking advantage of the US$1 Tecate beer deal.

At the breezy northwest corner of the plaza, the **food stalls** (Map p276; Parque Central; tacos & burritos US$1) are a good place to dine cheap on *antojitos* (snacks/light dishes).

SANTA ELENA

Restaurante Petenchel (Map p275; 2a Calle 4-20; mains US$3-7; lunch & dinner) This little place (and its sister across the road) is trying hard enough – there are checked tablecloths and a wide selection of dishes including Chinese, ceviches, pastas and steak.

Restaurante Mijaro (Map p275; 4a Calle; mains US$3.50-4.25; breakfast, lunch & dinner) Cool off at this friendly *comedor* on the main street, which has fans not only inside but also in its little thatch-roofed garden area. It does good long *limonadas* (lime-juice drink) and snacks like sandwiches and burgers (US$1.30 to US$2) as well as weightier food.

Restaurante El Puerto (Map p275; 1a Calle 2-15; mains US$5-8; lunch & dinner) With its lakefront position, this open-air beer barn–steak house serves up a mean steak and packs out weekends when the Cool Vibes (see Drinking) next door fires up.

For a splurge, try one of the two fancy restaurants overlooking the water at the Hotel Petén Espléndido (see p279).

Drinking

Flores doesn't exactly jive at night but there are a couple of places to hang out. Flores' little Zona Viva is a strip of bars along the Playa Sur, and nearly all of the lakeside restaurants in Santa Elena have afternoon happy hours, a great way to unwind and watch the sunset.

Adictos (Map p276; Playa Sur) If you're up for dancing, this was the place to be at time of writing.

Cool Vibes (Map p275; 1a Calle 2-25; ☺ 7pm-1am Thu-Sat) This open-air bar–dance club was Santa Elena's hotspot at time of writing. And it *is* kind of fun to be out shaking your thing in the fresh air, lakeside.

El Trópico (Map p276; Playa Sur) This is a popular place to start the night.

Hotel La Unión (Map p276; Calle Unión) The terrace overlooking the lake is a magnificent spot to watch the sun go down over a Cuba libre (US$1) or a piña colada (US$2).

Entertainment

Locals gather in the cool of the evening for long drinks, snacks and relaxation in the Parque Central, where a marimba ensemble plays some nights.

Café Yax-ha (Map p276; Calle 15 de Septiembre; lunch & dinner Wed-Mon) There are occasional archaeological/cultural lectures here.

Las Puertas (Map p276; cnr Calle Central & Av Santa Ana; movies US$1.50; ☺ 8am-late Mon-Sat) Shows movies every night.

Getting There & Away
AIR

The airport at Santa Elena is usually called Flores airport and sometimes Tikal airport. TACA is the only airline with regularly scheduled flights between here and the capital (US$127/204 oneway/return). Two Belizean airlines, Tropic Air and Maya Island Air, each fly twice a day from and to Belize City, both charging US$103 each way for the one-hour trip.

BUS & MINIBUS

In Santa Elena, the following buses all stop at the main bus terminal:

Fuente del Norte (☎ 7926 0517),
Transportes María Elena, Línea Dorada/Mundo Maya (☎ 7926 1788)
Transportes Rosita (☎ 7926 1245)

Flores has a second office of **Línea Dorada/Mundo Maya** (☎ 7926 3649; Playa Sur), where its buses also pick up passengers.

Santa Elena's terminal is also used by the chicken buses of Transportes Pinita and Transportes Rosío and minibuses (or microbuses) to El Remate, Melchor de Mencos, Poptún, El Naranjo and Sayaxché. Buses and minibuses to San Andrés and San José go from 5a Calle just west of the market. Buses of **San Juan Travel** (☎ 7926 0041) leave from its office on 2a Calle, Santa Elena.

Bus and minibus departures include the following:

Belize City (four to five hours, 220km) Línea Dorada/Mundo Maya (US$15.50) leaves at 5am and 7am, returning from Belize City at 2pm and 5pm. San Juan Travel (US$20) goes at 5am, returning from Belize City at 9:30am and 4:30pm. These buses to Belize City all connect with boats to Caye Caulker & Ambergris Caye. It's cheaper but slower from Flores to take local buses to the border and on from there (see Melchor de Mencos).

Bethel (Mexican border) (US$4, four hours, 127km) Fuente del Norte departs at 5am; Pinita goes at 5am, 8am, noon and 1pm. Returning, Fuente del Norte leaves Bethel at 4pm and Pinita leaves at 5am, noon and 2pm.

Chetumal (Mexico) (seven to eight hours, 350km) Via Belize City, Línea Dorada/Mundo Maya (US$23) leaves at 6am, returning from Chetumal at 2pm. San Juan Travel (US$25) goes at 5am, with departures for Flores from Chetumal at 9:30am and 4:30pm. Check Belizean visa regulations before you set off.

Cobán (US$6.50, six hours, 245km) Transportes Rosío leaves the market bus stop at 10:30am. Or take a bus or minibus to Sayaxché, from where a bus leaves for Cobán at 10am. (See also the Shuttle Minibus section, p282.)

El Naranjo (Río San Pedro) (US$4, four hours, 151km) Minibuses go about every hour, from 5am to 6pm.

El Remate (US$2, 40 minutes, 29km) Minibuses go about hourly, 6am to 1pm, plus a few times between 1pm and 6pm. Buses and minibuses to and from Melchor de Mencos will drop you at Puente Ixlú junction, 2km south of El Remate.

Esquipulas (US$11, 10 hours, 440km) Transportes María Elena goes at 6am, 10am and 2pm via Chiquimula (US$9, nine hours).

Fray Bartolomé de Las Casas (US$5.50, five hours, 178km) Transportes Rosío departs the market at 10:30am.

Guatemala City (eight to 10 hours, 500km) Fuente del Norte has 29 departures between 3:30am and 11pm, costing US$10 to US$12, except for the 10am and 9pm buses (US$19) and the 2pm, 8pm and 10pm departures (US$15). Línea Dorada/Mundo Maya has deluxe buses at 10am and 9pm (US$30), plus an *económico* (US$16) at 10pm. Transportes Rosita goes at 7pm (US$8) and 8pm (US$11).

La Técnica (Mexican border) (US$6, five hours, 140km) Pinita leaves at 5am and 1pm; starts back from La Técnica at 4am and 11am.

Melchor de Mencos (Belizean border) (two hours, 100km) Minibuses (US$3.50) go about every hour, 5am to 6pm. Transportes Rosita buses (US$2.50) go at 5am, 11am, 2pm, 4pm and 6pm. A Pinita bus (US$3) goes at 8am. See p299 for more information on crossing the border here.

Palenque (Mexico) See Shuttle Minibus, below.

Poptún (two hours, 113km) Take a Guatemala City–bound Fuente del Norte bus (US$3) or a minibus (US$3.60), leaving about every 30 minutes, 5am to 6pm.

Puerto Barrios Take a Guatemala City–bound Fuente del Norte bus and change at La Ruidosa junction, south of Río Dulce.

Río Dulce (4½ hours, 212km) Take a Guatemala City–bound bus with Fuente del Norte (US$8) or Línea Dorada (US$11.50/US$22 *económico*/deluxe).

San Andrés (US$1, 30 minutes, 20km) Buses and mini-buses depart about hourly, 5am to 5pm.

San José (US$1, 45 minutes, 25km) Buses and minibuses depart about hourly, 5am to 5pm.

Sayaxché (US$2, 1½ hours, 60km) Minibuses about every 30 minutes, 5am to 6pm; Pinita buses go at 11am, 2pm and 2:30pm.

Tikal See Shuttle Minibus, below.

CAR & MOTORCYCLE
Several car-rental companies have desks at the airport, including the following:

Hertz (☎ 7926 0332)
Nesa (☎ 7926 0082)
Payless (☎ 7926 0455)
Tabarini (airport ☎ 7926 0277; Santa Elena ☎ 7926 0253)

San Juan Travel (☎ 7926 0041; sanjuant@internetdetelgua .com.gt; Flores Map p276, Playa Sur; Santa Elena Map p275, 2a Calle) rents 4WD vehicles, the cheapest being a Suzuki Jeep (US$70 a day).

SHUTTLE MINIBUS
San Juan Travel (☎ 7926 0041; sanjuant@internetdetel gua.com.gt; Flores Map p276, Playa Sur; Santa Elena Map p275, 2a Calle) operates shuttle minibuses to Tikal (US$4/6 oneway/round-trip, 1¼ hours each way). They leave hourly from 5am to 10am and usually at 2pm. Most hotels and travel agencies can book these shuttles for you and the vehicles will pick you up where you're staying. Returns leave Tikal at 12:30pm, 2pm, 3pm, 4pm, 5pm and 6pm. If you know which round-trip you plan to be on, ask your driver to hold a seat for you or arrange a seat in an-other minibus. If you stay overnight in Tikal and want to return to Flores by minibus, it's a good idea to reserve a seat with one of the drivers when they arrive in the morning. Outside the normal timetable, you can rent a whole minibus for US$35.

San Juan also does shuttles to Cobán (US$20), Palenque (Mexico; US$30) and Corozal (the border crossing for Bonampak, Mexico; US$25).

On the Palenque run (in either direction) make sure you get a ticket, receipt or other documentation that proves you have paid for the whole trip from Flores to Palenque or vice-versa. Occasionally travelers find that the driver waiting on the far side of the Río Usu-macinta to take them on to their destination attempts to extract an extra payment.

Getting Around
A taxi from the airport to Santa Elena or Flores costs US$2. Tuk tuks will take you anywhere between or within Flores and Santa Elena for US$0.80. La Villa del Chef (see p279) rents mountain bikes for US$6 for up to four hours and US$8 for four to 12 hours.

BOAT
Motor launches making tours around Lago de Petén Itzá depart from the Santa Elena end of the causeway. *Colectivo* (shared) boats to San Andrés and San José, villages across the lake, depart from San Benito, on the west side of Santa Elena and alongside the Hotel Santana in Flores (US$0.40 if the boat is full; US$8 for one passenger, private hire). You can also contract the *lancheros* for lake tours; bargain hard.

AROUND FLORES
Museo Santa Barbara
On a small island just to the west of Flores, this **museum** (Map p275; admission US$1.50; ☁ 8am-noon & 2-5pm) shows a collection of ceramics found in nearby archaeological sites. It's not a huge collection, but it is well presented – the boat ride over and just hanging out on the island are as much fun as the museum itself. To get there you can try haggling with any lakeside *lanchero* down by the Hotel Santana (where you might rent a boat for US$14). If you want to scrimp it, you'll have to go to San Benito, where boats will take you for US$2 per person.

El Mirador & Tayazal
Boats (US$0.25 per person) make the five-minute crossing to San Miguel village from beside Restaurante La Guacamaya on the northeast side of Flores whenever they have a boatload. San Miguel itself is a quiet, slow-

moving place. To reach the lookout point called El Mirador (1.75km west), walk 250m to the left along the shore from where the boat drops you, then turn up the street to the right, which passes the Iglesia Evangélica Príncipe de Paz. After 200m turn left, passing a football field on your right to reach a sign telling you that you are entering the Tayazal archaeological site, which is a set of chiefly Classic-era mounds scattered around this western end of the peninsula and largely overgrown by vegetation. Some 180m downhill beyond this sign, fork left following a 'Mirador' sign (the straight-on road leads to the **Playita**, a small lake beach). After 200m the track enters a clearing surrounded by low mounds with an upright rock carved with a skull in the middle. Fork right onto a single-track path passing the left side of the **skull rock** and winding on through the trees. After some 450m the track bends sharp left then forks: choose the right-hand path here and continue for some 230m, mainly downhill, till you see steps mounting the hillside on your right. The hillside is actually one of the **pyramids** of ancient Tayazal and on its summit wooden steps have been built up to a platform around a tree: this is El Mirador, with fine views of Flores and around Lago de Petén Itzá. The walk is best done in the morning, to avoid afternoon heat and the danger of being overtaken by dusk.

Arcas

The **Asociación de Rescate y Conservación de Vida Silvestre** (Wildlife Rescue & Conservation Association; ☎ 5476 6001; www.arcasguatemala.com; Biblioteca Arcas, Barrio La Ermita, San Benito), a Guatemalan NGO, has a rescue and rehabilitation center on the mainland northeast of Flores for wildlife such as macaws, parrots, jaguars, monkeys, kinkajous and coatis that have been rescued from smugglers and the illegal pet trade. The rehabilitation center itself is closed to visitors but a Centro de Educación e Interpretación Ambiental (CEIA, Environmental Education & Interpretation Center) has been set up for visitors, with a 1.5km interpretative trail featuring medicinal plants and animal tracks, an area for viewing animals that cannot be returned to the wild, a beach and a bird observation deck. A boat leaves from beside Restaurante La Guacamaya, on the northeast side of Flores, at 4pm daily for tours of the CEIA. It costs US$7 per person for one or two people, US$6 for three to five people and US$4 for six or more. It's best to call the Arcas office in San Benito beforehand to confirm that the boat is going. You can also reach Arcas by walking 5km (about 45 minutes) east from San Miguel; tours for people who arrive independently between 9am and 3pm cost US$2 each.

Grutas Actun-Can

The **Actun-Can caves** (La Cueva de la Serpiente; Cave of the Serpent; admission US$2; ⌚ 8am-5pm) are of standard limestone. No serpents are in evidence, but the cave-keeper will turn on the lights for you and may give you the rundown on the cave formations, which suggest animals, humans and various scenes. Bring your own flashlight if you have one, and adequate shoes – it can be slippery. Explorations take about 30 to 45 minutes.

At the cave entrance is a shady picnic area. Actun-Can makes a good goal for a long walk from Santa Elena. To find it, walk south on 6a Av past the Telgua office. About 1km from the center of Santa Elena, turn left, go 300m and turn right at the electricity generating plant. Go another 1km to the site. A taxi from Santa Elena costs US$3.

Laguna Petenchel

Hotel Villa Maya (☎ in Guatemala City 2334 1818; www.villasdeguatemala.com; s/d/ US$85/93; ⓟ ⓡ), on Laguna Petenchel, a small lake east of Santa Elena, is one of the best hotels in the area, with 36 double rooms in bungalows with bathroom, ceiling fan, hot water, beautiful views of the lake, and blissful quiet. There's a patio restaurant, tennis court, two swimming pools, two lagoons and a wildlife refuge. It's 4km north of the crossroads where the Guatemala City road diverges from the Tikal road, 8km east of Flores.

San Andrés

This small town on the northwest side of the lake is home to two Spanish-language schools:

Eco-Escuela de Español (☎ 5940 1235; www.ecoescuelaespanol.org) This community-owned school emphasizes ecological and cultural issues and organizes environmentally related trips and volunteer opportunities; cost is US$100 a week plus US$75 for room and board with a local family.

Nueva Juventud Spanish School (☎ 5711 0040; www.volunteerpeten.com; Restaurant La Troja, San Andrés) Also environmentally oriented, this school is closely tied to a volunteer program that cares for the ecological park where the school is sited, and encourages volunteers to develop community projects. Classes cost US$150 a week, with homestay included.

A few kilometers west of San Andrés, **Ni'tun Ecolodge** (☎ 5201 0759; www.nitun.com; s US$100-150 d US$170-235; **P** 💻) is a beautiful property, set on 350,000 sq meters of grounds where six species of hummingbird nest year-round. There are only four huts (although small houses is a better description) and the capacity for the whole place is 12 people, which may rise to 16 with planned construction. Accommodations are in the rustic/spacious vein, and from the little patio areas in front of the rooms you can just see the lake water's tinkling reflection. The room rates include airport transfers and breakfast. Bernie and Lore, who built and operate the lodge, are adventurers and conservationists who also operate Monkey Eco Tours, which offers adventure trips with transport in Land Cruisers. Portable showers, inflatable mattresses and crystalware are provided, and they employ specialized guides such as birders, archaeologists and biologists. Tours go to El Mirador, Río Azul, Ceibal, Dos Pilas and Tikal, among other sites, with prices ranging from US$90 to US$200 a day.

For information on minibuses and buses to San Andrés, see p281.

San José

San José, a town of about 3000 a few kilometers along the lake from San Andrés, is peopled by Itzá Maya, descendants of the Flores area's prehispanic inhabitants. It has one of the best beaches on the lake. The community-owned **Escuela Bio-Itzá** (☎ 7928 8056; www.bioitza.org) is part of an association working to keep Itzá traditions and language alive. Cost for the usual 20 hours of one-on-one Spanish classes is US$200 per week if you live with a local family, or US$125 if you camp and organize your own meals. Students can participate with the Itzá community on projects such as their medicinal plant garden and Itzá language academy.

San José is a special place to be on the night of October 31, when perfectly preserved human skulls that are housed in the church are paraded around town on a velvet pillow followed by devotees in traditional dress, carrying candles.

Throughout the night, the skulls make visits to predetermined houses, where blessings are sought, offerings made and a huge feast eaten.

VILLAGE JUSTICE

Here's a sticky one for you: take it as given that the Guatemalan justice system is broken, perhaps beyond repair. Lawyers get shot in broad daylight on downtown streets and nobody saw anything.

Now translate that to the villages, where the police drop in every week or so to see that everything's OK.

Tired of living with known rapists, murderers, baby sellers and thieves in their midst, villagers often take justice into their own hands, rather than wait for a lengthy and often inconclusive court case.

The most extreme form of 'village justice' is the lynching – a mob grabs a criminal and strings them up from the nearest tree. And nobody saw anything.

But there are less extreme forms. Traditional Mayan society had its own set of punishments – mostly along the lines of public humiliation – shaving women's heads, tying them to a post half naked, making them walk through town on their knees carrying a heavy rock. Which is all fine up to this point – in fact the Guatemalan constitution guarantees the indigenous population the right to continue with their customs as long as they don't conflict with national law.

And that's where it gets sticky – these same criminals have been turning up at the offices of the Protector of Human Rights, claiming that their human rights have been violated.

So the choice boils down to this: an ineffective system, which doesn't deter and rarely catches criminals, or a more improvised approach, without formal process, meting out punishments that, to the outside world, seem cruel and unusual.

For information on minibuses and buses to San José, see p281. There is no regular boat service. Renting a boat from beside the Hotel Santana in Flores or Hotel Petén Espléndido in Santa Elena costs around US$15 for the 30-minute crossing.

Parque Natural Ixpanpajul

At **Parque Natural Ixpanpajul** (☎ 7863 1317; www .ixpanpajul.com; admission adult/child US$25/15, campsites per person US$5; ⏰ 7:30am-6:30pm) you can ride horses, mountain bikes or tractors, or zip line your way through the jungle canopy. The big attraction is the Sky Way, a 3km circuit of stone paths and six linked suspension bridges through the upper levels of the forest. Early morning and late afternoon are your best times for wildlife viewing. It's 2km south down the Guatemala City road from its junction with the Tikal road, 8km east of Flores. You can get here by catching any Guatemala City-bound bus from Santa Elena, or else call the park's **shuttle service** (☎ 5897 6766; US$5) to arrange transportation.

EL REMATE

The closest decent accommodation to Tikal can be found in this enchanting village on the shores of Lago de Petén Itzá. It's a mellow little place – two roads, basically – much more relaxed and less built up than Flores. Most hotels here are set up for swimming in – and watching the sun set over – the lake.

El Remate is known for its wood carving. Several handicrafts shops on the lakeshore opposite La Mansión del Pájaro Serpiente sell local handicrafts and rent canoes, rafts and kayaks.

El Remate begins 1km beyond Puente Ixlú (also called El Cruce), the village where the road to Melchor de Mencos on the Belize border diverges from the Tikal road. El Remate is strung along the Tikal road for 1km to another junction, where an unpaved road branches west along the north shore of the Lago de Petén Itzá to the Biotopo Cerro Cahuí and beyond. Several more places to stay and eat are dotted along this road, which continues all the way to the villages of San José and San Andrés near the west end of the lake, making it possible to go all the way around the lake by road.

If you're stuck for cash, you can change US dollars and traveler's checks and Belize dollars, at low rates, at La Casa de Don David just north of the junction.

EXPLORE MORE OF EL PETÉN

The Petén region is literally brimming with smaller, largely unexcavated archaeological sites. Some are hard to get to, some are right by the highway. Here are a few of the more accessible ones that you might want to check out:

■ El Chal – right by the Poptún–Flores highway, this site with a ballcourt and some carvings is built on a ridge, with some good views.

Ixcun – an hour's walk out of Dolores, this rarely visited site is made up of eight plazas. Its sister city, Ixtontón, is another 6km along the river.

■ Ixlú – 2km south of El Remate on the shore of Lago de Salpetén.

■ Machaquilá – some finely preserved stelae are left from this mysterious city.

With their newfound prosperity, Rematecos have built a *balneario municipal* (municipal beach) just off the highway; several cheap pensiones and small hotels have opened here as well.

Sights & Activities
BIOTOPO CERRO CAHUÍ

The entrance to the 6.5 sq km subtropical forest reserve, **Biotopo Cerro Cahuí** (admission US$2.50; ⏰ 6:30am-dusk), is 1.75km west along the north-shore road from El Remate. The vegetation here ranges from *guamil* (regenerating slash-and-burn land) to rain forest. Trees here include mahogany, cedar, ramón, broom, sapodilla and cohune palm, and you'll also see many species of liana and epiphyte, these last including bromeliads, ferns and orchids. The hard wood of the sapodilla was used in Mayan temple door lintels, some of which have survived from the Classic period to our own time. This is also the tree from which chicle is sapped.

More than 20 mammal species roam the reserve, including spider and howler monkeys, ocelots, white-tailed deer, raccoons and armadillos. The bird life, of course, is rich and varied. Some 179 species have been identified. Depending upon the season and migration patterns, you might see kingfishers, ducks, herons, hawks, parrots, toucans, woodpeckers and the famous ocellated (or Petén) turkey, a beautiful big bird resembling a peacock.

A network of loop trails starts at the road and goes up the hill, affording a view of the whole lake and of Laguna Salpetén to the east and Laguna Petenchel to the south. The one called Los Escobos (6km long – it takes about 2¼ hours) is good if you want to see monkeys. The guards at the entrance can give you directions.

The admission fee includes the right to camp or sling your hammock under small thatch shelters inside the entrance. There are toilets and showers.

The dock opposite the entrance is one of the best places to swim along the generally rather muddy shore of the lake.

OTHER ACTIVITIES

Most El Remate accommodations can book you on five-hour **horseback rides** to Laguna Salpetén and a small archaeological site there (US$18 per person) or two-hour boat trips for **bird-watching** or nocturnal **crocodile spotting** (each US$8 per person). Casa Mobego and Casa Yaikán do five-hour **walking tours** to Laguna Salpetén for US$10 per person.

Ask around about **bicycle**, **kayak** and **canoe rental**. Casa Mobego rents double kayaks for

US$4/5/10 for one/two/four hours. Various places rent bicycles at US$2/3.25/4.50 for two/four/24 hours, with a deposit of US$30.

Tours

The Hotel Mon Ami (opposite) and Hotel Sak-Luk (below) offer reasonably priced jungle treks to El Mirador, Yaxhá and Nakum.

La Casa de Don David (☎ 7928 8469; www .lacasadedondavid.com), just north of the junction, offers tours to Yaxhá (US$15 to US$20 per person), Uaxactún (US$20 per person) and Ceibal (US$35 to US$40 per person). Prices do not include guides.

Sleeping

ALONG THE MAIN ROAD

These establishments are listed in south-to-north order.

Hotel Sak-Luk (☎ 5494 5925; main road; dm/hammock/ bungalow per person US$2/3/4) This little slice of hippieheaven offers huts, dorms and hammocks in adobe constructions scattered around a lush hillside. There's a good restaurant offering Italian and vegetarian dishes and it can organize jungle treks and trips to the Biotopo Cerro Cahuí.

Posada Ixchel (☎ 7928 8475; s/d US$4/6.50, with bathroom US$6.50/11) This friendly, family-owned

---

A BIOLOGICAL POWERHOUSE

Rainforests are an amazing thing, and those of the Petén are no exception. Apart from providing a much-needed source of oxygen for the region, the Petén jungles play host to a staggering array of life forms.

This diversity is what sets a rainforest apart – the canopy is composed of hundreds of species of trees – ebony, sapodilla, mahogany and ramón to name just a few. They provide the moist, shady climate that's perfect for the mosses, fungi and microorganisms that thrive on the forest floor. In between, smaller shrubs and fruit-bearing trees live off the nutrients stored in this fecund base.

Plant life in the rainforests has a secondary purpose – every year new medicinal uses are discovered (some from age-old knowledge) for jungle plants, and many extracts are then synthesized and sold as pharmaceuticals.

All of this makes a wonderful habitat for animals, of course, and the Petén won't let you down on that score. Amongst the birdlife are toucans, motmots, scarlet macaws, ocellated turkeys, buzzards and hawks.

Larger animals are plentiful, too, although sometimes harder to spot. You'll definitely see (and hear) howler monkeys and coatis, and if you're patient you might get a glimpse of wild pigs. With your luck running hot, you'll be able to tick off ocelots, pumas and maybe even a jaguar. Jaguarundis are common and get around during the day – you're pretty much guaranteed to see at least one.

Throw in a few species of turtles, a plethora of frogs, 40 or so species of snake and the very occasional crocodile and you'll see that, while the Petén may be under populated in human terms, it's not such a lonely place after all.

MOSQUITOES ARE MEAN AND EVIL

One of the joys of traveling in an area that has both dengue fever and malaria is that you can never completely relax. Dengue-carrying mosquitoes typically bite during the daytime; their malaria-carrying colleagues come out from dusk to dawn.

To avoid getting bitten, all the classic tactics hold true – wear light-colored, long-sleeved garments. Avoid the use of heavy perfumes and colognes. Stay inside around dusk and dawn and don't sleep near stagnant bodies of water.

Apart from slathering yourself in DEET, there are a few natural ways you can deter these pesky little suckers and a few natural remedies in case you do get stung.

One deterrent is to make yourself smell bad to them. Overloading on garlic or vitamin B will make your sweat smell terrible to mosquitoes (and possibly your travel companions) and they'll just steer clear. The Maya used the herb called *tres puntas* (jackass bitters in English) in much the same way. Another, slightly less offensive method is to boil basil leaves in water, then splash the water on. This has the advantage that you end up smelling like a pizza.

As far as relief from bites goes, there are various local remedies. One is basil again – crush the leaves and rub them on the affected areas. Another is *ix'can'aan* (*chichibe* in Spanish), which you can also crush and rub directly onto bites.

If you do happen to contract dengue or malaria, it's best to contact a doctor immediately – the former can be extremely uncomfortable and the latter fatal. The traditional remedy for these and other blood-related ailments was the *sorosí* plant, a blood purifier, ground up and made into tea.

place another 200m north has spotless rooms set around a stone cobbled courtyard. The comfy little private sitting areas out front of the rooms are a nice touch.

Hotel Sun Breeze (☎ 5807 1487; s/d US$4/7) This is a pleasant little place down the lane toward the lake, nearly at the turnoff for the north road. The clean, bare rooms sport mosquito nets and share cold-water bathrooms.

Hostal Hermano Pedro (☎ 2332 4474; www.hhpedro .com; s/d with bathroom US$7/14) Set in a great two-story wood-and-stone house 20m off to the right from the main road. The basic, spacious rooms here are how budget hotels should be – clean, simple and comfortable, with just a couple of frills. They offer guests free transport to Tikal.

Hotel La Mansión del Pájaro Serpiente (☎ 7928 8498; s/d US$40/48; 🏊) Dotted along a steep hillside and connected by winding stone paths, these cabins are more like little houses, with black-and-white tiled floors, lounge/sitting areas and spacious bathrooms. All have lake views, sport colorful textiles and netted windows. There's a gorgeous pool too, with hammocks under *palapa* shelters nearby, and a reasonably priced restaurant-bar.

ALONG THE NORTH-SHORE ROAD

Casa de Doña Tonita (☎ 5701 7114; s/d US$4/8) Just past Casa Mobego, Doña Tonita's has four simple rooms with two single beds each, in a two-story wood-and-thatch *rancho*. There's an inexpensive restaurant with vegetarian food available.

our pick Mon Ami (☎ 7928 8413; www.hotelmonami .com; dm US$5, d with bathroom US$15-25) This place, 1200m from the main Tikal road, has a good balance of jungle wild and French sophistication. The cabins and dorms are just rustic enough, the gardens are full of local plant life and the restaurant (see p288) offers some of the best food for miles around.

Casa Mobego (Casa Roja; ☎ 7909 6999; dm US$7.50) Fairly bursting with character, this secluded little spot has a collection of two-story, open-walled thatched houses spread out over a hillside. Bathrooms are shared and beds have mosquito nets. Breakfast, snacks and sandwiches are served in a pleasant restaurant area dotted with curious sculptures and paintings. The friendly owner, Gonzalo, is an artist and sculptor who worked for 10 years restoring monuments at Tikal and other sites. There's a swimming dock across the road.

Gringo Perdido Ecological Inn (☎ 2334 2305 in Guatemala City; www.hotelgringoperdido.com; r per person with bathroom US$40; 🅿) Waking up here is like waking up in paradise, with no sound but the lake lapping at the shore a few steps from your door. The rooms have one double and one single bed, stone walls and floors, mosquito nets and full-wall canvas roll-up blinds that can almost give you the sensation of sleeping in the open air. When there are only a few guests, the Inn doesn't switch on the generator, meaning no hot water and no cold drinks, but plenty of soothing, romantic candlelight. The Gringo Perdido is 3km along the north-shore road from the main Tikal road. Rates include dinner and breakfast.

Hotel Camino Real Tikal (☎ 7926 0204/09; www .caminorealtikal.com.gt; s & d US$150; P ⊠ ⊠) Two kilometers further along the lake is the luxury Camino Real, the fanciest hotel in El Petén, with 72 air-con rooms with balconies, lake views and all the comforts. Two restaurants, a bar and a coffee shop keep guests happy, as do the Tikal and Cerro Cahuí tours, pool, kayaking, sailing, windsurfing and beach sports. This hotel is rather remote: check out its special packages, which include airport transfers.

Eating

Most hotels have their own restaurants and there are simple *comedores* scattered along the main road.

Las Orquideas (pasta US$4-6, mains US$8-12; ⊠ lunch & dinner) Almost next door to Casa de Doña Tonita, Las Orquideas has a genial Italian owner-chef cooking up genuine Italian fare, with tempting desserts too.

Restaurante Cahuí (mains US$4-6; ⊠ breakfast, lunch & dinner) While most people eat in their hotels here, this restaurant on the main road is a popular option. People come for the big, wholesome meals and stay for the lake views from the big wooden deck overlooking the water and the extensive wine and beer list.

Mon Ami (mains US$5-8, crepes US$2; ⊠ breakfast, lunch & dinner) Further along the north-shore road (1200m from the main Tikal road), Mon Ami serves good French and Guatemalan food in a peaceful palm-thatched, open-walled area. Try the *carne al vino* with rice and tomato salad, or the big *ensalada francesa*.

Getting There & Around

El Remate is linked to Flores by a public minibus service (see p281).

A minibus leaves El Remate at 5:30am for Tikal, starting back from Tikal at 2pm (US$4 round-trip). Any El Remate accommodations can make reservations. Or you can catch one of the shuttles or regular minibuses passing through from Flores to get to Tikal. They normally charge US$2.50 per person.

For taxis, ask at Hotel Sun Breeze or Hotel Don Juan. A one-way ride to Tikal or Flores costs about US$18.

For Melchor de Mencos on the Belizean border, get a minibus or bus from Puente Ixlú, 2km south of El Remate.

MACANCHÉ

Set on the banks of the lagoon of the same name, this little village is home to one of the finer accommodations options in the region, **El Retiro** (☎ 5751 1876; www.retiro-guatemala.com; campsites per person US$20, cabins per person US$30). Comfortable cabins are set on leafy grounds down by the water's edge. There's an excellent dock for swimming and a good restaurant here, as well as a snake house and walking trails through the ruin-dotted rain forest.

What's unique about the property (apart from the location) is the presence of a series of chultuns – holes carved into the ground rock with a circular capping stone. Their purpose remains a mystery, but educated guesses suggest they were used either for food storage or religious rituals.

The hotel offers boat tours of the lagoon, crocodile-spotting night tours (US$40 per person) and jungle walks (US$30 per person).

Any bus heading for the Belize border can drop you at Macanché village, from where it's a 2km walk to the hotel. Taxis are sometimes on hand in the village, or you can call and get picked up.

TIKAL

Towering pyramids poke above the jungle's green canopy to catch the sun. Howler monkeys swing noisily through the branches of ancient trees as brightly colored parrots and toucans dart from perch to perch in a cacophony of squawks. When the complex warbling song of some mysterious jungle bird tapers off, the buzz of tree frogs fills the background and it will dawn on you that this is indeed hallowed ground.

Certainly the most striking feature of **Tikal** (☎ 2361 1399; www.parque-tikal.com; admission US$7; ⊠ 6am-6pm) is its steep-sided temples, rising to heights of more than 44m. But Tikal is different from Copán, Chichén Itzá, Uxmal, and most other great Mayan sites, because it is fairly deep in the jungle. Its many plazas have been cleared of trees and vines, its temples uncovered and partially restored, but as you walk from one building to another you pass beneath the dense canopy of rainforest. Rich, loamy smells of earth and vegetation, a peaceful air, and animal noises all contribute to an experience not offered by other Mayan sites.

You can, if you wish, visit Tikal on a day trip from Flores or El Remate. You can even make a literally flying visit from Guatemala City in one day, using the daily flights between there and Flores airport. But you'll get more out of Tikal if you spend a night here, enabling you to visit the ruins twice and to be here in the late afternoon and early morning, when other tourists are fewest and the wildlife is more active.

History

Tikal is set on a low hill, which becomes evident as you walk up to the Gran Plaza from the entry road. The hill, affording relief from the surrounding low-lying swampy ground, may be why the Maya settled here around 700 BC. Another reason was the abundance of flint, the valuable stone used by the ancients to make clubs, spear points, arrowheads and knives. The wealth of flint meant good tools could be made, and flint could be traded for other goods. Within 200 years the Maya of Tikal had begun to build stone ceremonial structures, and by 200 BC there was a complex of buildings on the site of the Acrópolis del Norte.

CLASSIC PERIOD

The Gran Plaza was beginning to assume its present shape and extent by the time of Christ. By the dawn of the early Classic period, around AD 250, Tikal had become an important religious, cultural and commercial city with a large population. King Yax Moch Xoc, in power about AD 230, is looked upon as the founder of the dynasty that ruled Tikal thereafter.

Under Chak Toh Ich'ak I (King Great Jaguar Paw), who ruled in the mid-4th century, Tikal adopted a new and brutal method of warfare, used by the rulers of Teotihuacán in central Mexico. Rather than meeting their adversaries on the plain of battle in hand-to-hand combat, the army of Tikal used auxiliary units to encircle the enemy and throw spears to kill them from a distance. This first use of 'air power' among the Maya of Petén enabled Siyah K'ak' (Smoking Frog), the Tikal general, to conquer the army of Uaxactún; thus Tikal became the dominant kingdom in El Petén.

By the middle of the Classic period, in the mid-6th century, Tikal's military prowess and its association with Teotihuacán allowed it to grow until it sprawled over 30 sq km and had a population of perhaps 100,000. But in 553, Yajaw Te' K'inich II (Lord Water) came to the throne of Caracol (in southwestern Belize), and by 562, using warfare methods learned from Tikal, he had conquered Tikal and sacrificed its king. Tikal and other Petén kingdoms suffered under Caracol's rule until the late 7th century.

TIKAL'S RENAISSANCE

A powerful king named Ah Cacau (682–734, also called Moon Double Comb or Lord Chocolate), 26th successor of Yax Moch Xoc, restored not only Tikal's military strength but also its primacy in the Mayan world. He conquered the greatest rival Mayan state, Calakmul in Mexico, in 695, and his successors were responsible for building most of the great temples around the Gran Plaza that survive today. King Moon Double Comb was buried beneath the staggering height of Templo I.

Tikal's greatness waned around 900, but it was not alone in its downfall, which was part of the mysterious general collapse of lowland Mayan civilization.

REDISCOVERY

No doubt the Itzáes, who occupied Tayasal (now Flores), knew of Tikal in the late post-Classic period (1200–1530). Perhaps they even came here to worship at the shrines of old gods. Spanish missionary friars who moved through El Petén after the conquest left brief references to these junglebound structures, but their writings moldered in libraries for centuries.

It wasn't until 1848 that the Guatemalan government sent out an expedition, under the leadership of Modesto Méndez and Ambrosio Tut, to visit the site. This may have been inspired by John L Stephens' bestselling accounts of fabulous Mayan ruins, published in 1841 and 1843 (though Stephens never visited Tikal). Like Stephens, Méndez and Tut took an artist, Eusebio Lara, to record their archaeological discoveries. An account of their findings was published by the Berlin Academy of Science.

In 1877, the Swiss Dr Gustav Bernoulli visited Tikal. His explorations resulted in the removal of carved wooden lintels from Templos I and IV and their shipment to Basel, where they are still on view in the Museum für Völkerkunde.

Scientific exploration of Tikal began with the arrival of English archaeologist Alfred P Maudslay in 1881. Others continued his work, Teobert Maler, Alfred M Tozzer and RE Merwin among them. Tozzer worked tirelessly at Tikal on and off from the beginning

of the 20th century until his death in 1954. The inscriptions at Tikal were studied and deciphered by Sylvanus G Morley.

Since 1956 archaeological research and restoration have been carried out by the University Museum of the University of Pennsylvania (until 1969) and the Guatemalan Instituto de Antropología y Historia. Since 1991, a joint

TIKAL

Guatemalan-Spanish project has worked on conserving and restoring Templos I and V.

In the mid-1950s an airstrip was built at Tikal. In the early 1980s the road between Tikal and Flores was improved and paved, and direct flights to Tikal were abandoned. The Parque Nacional Tikal (Tikal National Park) was declared a Unesco World Heritage Site in 1979.

Orientation & Information

The 550 sq km Parque Nacional Tikal contains thousands of separate ruined structures. The central area of the city occupied about 16 sq km, with more than 4000 structures.

The road from Flores enters the national park 17km south of the ruins. The gate opens at 6am. Here you must pay a fee of US$7 for

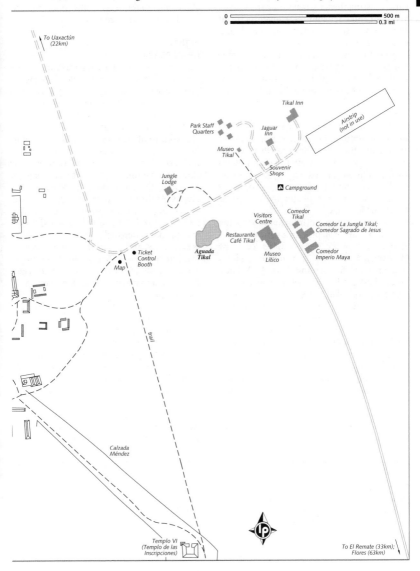

To Uaxactún (22km)

Tikal Inn

Airstrip (not in use)

Park Staff Quarters

Jaguar Inn

Museo Tikal

Souvenir Shops

Jungle Lodge

Campground

Comedor Tikal

Visitors Centre

Comedor La Jungla Tikal; Comedor Sagrado de Jesus

Restaurante Café Tikal

Aguada Tikal

Ticket Control Booth

Map

Museo Lítico

Comedor Imperio Maya

trail

Calzada Méndez

Templo VI (Templo de las Inscripciones)

To El Remate (33km); Flores (63km)

0   500 m
0   0.3 mi

EL PETÉN

the day; if you enter after about 3pm, your ticket should be stamped with the following day's date, meaning that it will be valid for the next day too. Multilingual guides are available at the visitors center (US$40 for a half-day tour for up to four people, plus US$5 for each extra person). These authorized guides always display their accreditation carnet, listing the languages they speak. The visitors center sells books, souvenirs, print film, hats, insect repellent, sun block and other necessities.

Near the visitors center are Tikal's three hotels, a camping area, a few small *comedores,* a tiny post office, a police post, two museums and a disused airstrip. From the visitors center it's a 1.5km walk (20 to 30 minutes) southwest to the Gran Plaza.

The walk from the Gran Plaza southeast to the Templo de las Inscripciones is over 1km; from the Gran Plaza north to Complejo P, it's 800m; from the Gran Plaza west to Templo IV it's over 600m. To visit all the major building complexes, you must walk at least 10km, probably more, so wear comfortable shoes.

For more complete information on the monuments at Tikal, pick up a copy of *Tikal – A Handbook of the Ancient Maya Ruins,* by William R Coe, which is available in Flores and at Tikal for around US$14. A book you're best off finding before you come is *The Lords of Tikal,* by Peter D Harrison, a vivid, cogent summary of the city's history. *The Birds of Tikal: An Annotated Checklist,* by Randell A Beavers, and *The Birds of Tikal,* by Frank B Smythe, also available at Tikal, are good resources for bird-watchers.

The ruins are open from 6am to 6pm daily. Tickets are checked at a booth on the approach track between the visitors center and the ruins. Seeing sunrise from Templo IV at the west end of the main site is possible from about October to March, but you need to leg it from this ticket booth!

It's a good idea to wear shoes with good rubber treads that grip well. The ruins here can be very slick from rain and organic material, especially during the wet season. Bring plenty of water, as dehydration is a real danger if you're walking around all day in this heat. Please don't feed the coatis *(pisotes)* that wander about the site.

The Jaguar Inn will exchange US-dollar cash and traveler's checks at a poor rate.

Dangers & Annoyances

The number of guards and rangers at Tikal has been stepped up since several robberies and rapes happened there a few years ago. On our visit it seemed safe and secure enough, but when visiting the more isolated parts of the site, such as the Templo de las Inscripciones, it still pays to be on your guard and not to go alone. If in doubt, you can always ask a guard whether it is safe to go there.

Sights
GRAN PLAZA

The path comes into the Gran Plaza around the awesome **Templo I**, the Templo del Gran Jaguar (Temple of the Grand Jaguar). This was built to honor – and bury – King Moon Double Comb. The king may have worked out the plans for the building himself, but it was actually erected above his tomb by his son, who succeeded to the throne in 734. The king's rich burial goods included stingray spines, which were used for ritual bloodletting, 180 beautiful jade objects, pearls and 90 pieces of bone carved with hieroglyphs. At the top of the 44m-high temple is a small enclosure of three rooms covered by a corbeled arch. The sapodilla-wood lintels over the doors were richly carved; one of them was removed and is now in a Basel museum. The lofty roofcomb that crowned the temple was originally adorned with reliefs and bright paint. It may have symbolized the 13 realms of the Mayan heavens.

Visitors used to be allowed to make the dangerous climb to the top, but since (at least) two people tumbled to their deaths, the stairs have been closed. Don't fret, though, the views from **Templo II** just across the way are nearly as awe-inspiring. Templo II, also known as the Temple of the Masks, was at one time almost as high as Templo I, but it now measures 38m without its roofcomb.

Nearby, the **Acrópolis del Norte** (North Acropolis), while not as immediately impressive as the twin temples, is of great significance. Archaeologists have uncovered about 100 different structures, the oldest of which dates from before the time of Christ, with evidence of occupation as far back as 400 BC. The Maya built and rebuilt on top of older structures, and the many layers, combined with the elaborate burials, added sanctity and power to their temples. Look especially for the two huge, powerful wall masks, uncovered from an earlier structure and now protected by roofs. The final version of the acropolis, as it stood around AD 800, had more than 12 temples atop a vast platform, many of them the work of King Moon Double Comb.

On the plaza side of the North Acropolis are two rows of stelae. Though hardly as bowl-you-over as the magnificent stelae at Copán or Quiriguá, these served the same purposes: to record the great deeds of the kings, to sanctify their memory and to add power to the temples and plazas that surrounded them.

ACRÓPOLIS CENTRAL

South and east of the Gran Plaza, this maze of courtyards, little rooms and small temples is thought by many to have been a palace where Tikal's nobles lived. Others think the tiny rooms may have been used for sacred rites and ceremonies, as graffiti found within them suggest. Over the centuries the configuration of the rooms was repeatedly changed, suggesting that perhaps this 'palace' was in fact a noble or royal family's residence changed to accommodate different groups of relatives. A hundred years ago, one part of the acropolis, called the Palacio de Maler, provided lodgings for archaeologist Teobert Maler when he worked at Tikal.

PLAZA OESTE

The West Plaza is north of Templo II. On its north side (obscured by vegetation) is a large late Classic temple. To the southwest, across the Calzada Tozzer (Tozzer Causeway), is **Templo III**, 55m high. Yet to be uncovered, it allows you to see a temple the way the last Tikal Maya and first white explorers saw them. The Tozzer Causeway leading west to Templo IV was one of several sacred byways built in the temple complexes of Tikal, no doubt for astronomical as well as aesthetic purposes.

ACRÓPOLIS DEL SUR & TEMPLO V

Due south of the Gran Plaza is the South Acropolis. Excavation has hardly even begun on this huge mass of masonry. The palaces on top are from late Classic times (the time of King Moon Double Comb), but earlier constructions probably go back 1000 years.

Templo V, just east of the South Acropolis, is 58m high and was built around AD 600. Unlike the other great temples, this one has slightly rounded corners, and one very tiny room at the top. The room is less than 1m deep, but its walls are up to 4.5m

thick. The view from the top is wonderful, giving you a 'profile' of the temples on the Gran Plaza.

PLAZA DE LOS SIETE TEMPLOS

To the west of the Acrópolis del Sur is the Plaza of the Seven Temples. The little temples, all in a line and now most sprouting trees, were built in late Classic times. On the north side of the plaza is an unusual triple ballcourt; another, larger version in the same design stands just south of Templo I.

EL MUNDO PERDIDO

About 400m southwest of the Gran Plaza is El Mundo Perdido (Lost World), a large complex of 38 structures with a huge pyramid in its midst. Unlike the rest of Tikal, where late Classic construction overlays work of earlier periods, El Mundo Perdido exhibits buildings of many different periods: the large pyramid is thought to be essentially Preclassic (with some later repairs and renovations); the Templo del Talud-Tablero, early Classic; and the Templo de las Calaveras (Temple of the Skulls), late Classic.

The pyramid, 32m high and 80m along the base, has a stairway on each side and had huge masks flanking each stairway, but no temple structure at its top. Each side of the pyramid displays a slightly different architectural style. Tunnels dug into the pyramid by archaeologists reveal four smaller pyramids beneath the outer face; the earliest (Structure 5C-54 Sub 2B) dates from 700 BC, making this pyramid the oldest Mayan structure at Tikal.

TEMPLO IV & COMPLEJO N

Complex N, near Templo IV, is an example of the 'twin-temple' complexes popular with Tikal's rulers during the late Classic period. These complexes are thought to have commemorated the completion of a *katun,* or 20-year cycle in the Mayan calendar. This one was built in 711 by King Moon Double Comb to mark the 14th *katun* of *baktun* 9. (A *baktun* equals 400 years.) The king himself is portrayed on Stela 16, one of the finest stelae at Tikal.

Templo IV, at 64m, is the highest building at Tikal and the second highest pre-Columbian building known in the western hemisphere, after El Tigre at El Mirador. It was completed about 741, in the reign of King Moon Double Comb's son. From the base it looks like a precipitous little hill. Steep wooden steps will take you to the top. The view is almost as good as from a helicopter – a panorama across the jungle canopy. If you stay up here for the sunset, climb down immediately thereafter, as it gets dark on the path very quickly.

TEMPLO DE LAS INSCRIPCIONES (TEMPLO VI)

Compared to Copán or Quiriguá, there are relatively few inscriptions on buildings at Tikal. The exception is this temple, 1.2km southeast of the Gran Plaza. On the rear of the 12m-high roofcomb is a long inscription; the sides and cornice of the roofcomb bear glyphs as well. The inscriptions give us the date AD 766. Stela 21 and Altar 9, standing before the temple, date from 736. The stela had been badly damaged (part of it was converted into a *metate* for grinding corn!) but has now been repaired.

NORTHERN COMPLEXES

About 1km north of the Gran Plaza is **Complejo P**. Like Complejo N, it's a late Classic twin-temple complex that probably commemorated the end of a *katun*. **Complejo M**, next to it, was partially torn down by the late Classic Maya to provide building materials for a causeway, now named after Alfred Maudslay, which runs southwest to Templo IV. **Grupo H**, northeast of Complexes P and M, with one tall, cleared temple, had some interesting graffiti within its temples (we're not talking about the moronic modern scrawls now disfiguring them).

Complejo Q and **Complejo R**, about 300m due north of the Gran Plaza, are very late Classic twin-pyramid complexes with stelae and altars standing before the temples. Complex Q is perhaps the best example of the twin-temple type, as it has been partly restored. Stela 22 and Altar 10 are excellent examples of late Classic Tikal relief carving, dated 771.

MUSEUMS

Tikal has two museums. The **Museo Lítico** (Museum of Stone; admission US$1.30; ☺ 9am-5pm Mon-Fri, 9am-4pm Sat & Sun), the larger of the two, is in the visitors center. It houses a number of stelae and carved stones from the ruins. Outside is a large model showing how Tikal would have looked around AD 800. The photographs taken by Alfred P Maudslay and Teobert Maler of the jungle-covered temples in various stages of discovery, in the late 19th century, are particularly striking.

The **Museo Tikal** or **Museo Cerámico** (Museum of Ceramics; admission US$1.30; ☺ 9am-5pm Mon-Fri, 9am-4pm Sat & Sun) is near the Jaguar Inn. It has some fascinating exhibits, including the burial goods of King Moon Double Comb, carved jade, inscribed bones, shells, stelae, ceramics and other items recovered from the excavations.

Activities
BIRDING

As well as howler and spider monkeys romping through the trees of Tikal, the plethora of birds flitting through the canopy and across the green expanses of the plazas is sure to impress you. Around 300 bird species (migratory and resident) have been recorded at Tikal. Early morning is the best time to go birding, and even amateur bird-watchers will have their share of sightings here. Bring binoculars if you have them, tread quietly and be patient, and you will probably see some of the following birds in the areas specified:

- Tody motmots, four trogon species and royal flycatchers around the Templo de las Inscripciones.
- Two oriole species, keel-billed toucans and collared aracaris in El Mundo Perdido.
- Great curassows, three species of woodpecker, crested guans, plain chachalacas and three tanager species around Complejo P.
- Three kingfisher species, jacanas, blue herons, two species of sandpiper, and great kiskadees at the Aguada Tikal (Tikal Reservoir) near the entrance. Tiger herons sometimes nest in the huge ceiba tree along the entrance path.
- Red-capped and white-collared manakins near Complejo Q; emerald toucanets near Complejo R.

In addition, look for several hawk species near the reservoirs, hummingbirds and ocellated turkeys (resembling a cross between a turkey and peacock) throughout the park, and several parrot species and Aztec parakeets while exploring the ruins.

TIKAL CANOPY TOUR

At the national park entrance, you can take a fairly expensive one-hour treetop tour through the forest by harness attached to a series of cables linking trees up to 300m apart, with **Tikal Canopy Tour** (☎ 7926 4270; www.canopytikal .com; admission US$25; ☼ 7am-5pm).

Sleeping & Eating

The days when intrepid visitors could convince park guards (with a US$5 'tip') to let them sleep atop Templo IV are over. If you are caught in the ruins after hours, you're likely to be escorted out for your own safety. Your best bet to catch some solitude at the ruins and get an early glimpse of the wildlife is to stay overnight and be at the ticket control booth at opening time.

Other than camping, there are only three places to stay at Tikal, all overpriced, and tour groups often have many of the rooms reserved. But staying here does enable you to relax and savor the dawn and dusk, when most of the jungle birds and animals can be seen and heard (especially the howler monkeys). The chances of getting a room depend a lot on the season. In the low season (from after Easter to late June, and from early September to Christmas), you will probably secure a room without reservation. At other times it's advisable to book. It's always advisable to arrive by early afternoon so that you have time to sort out any difficulties – and to get back to El Remate if everything fails. One way of ensuring a room is to become a group tourist yourself. Almost any travel agency in Guatemala offers Tikal tours, including lodging, a meal or two, a guided tour and transportation, and they needn't be prohibitively expensive.

Jaguar Inn (☎ 7926 0002; www.jaguartikal.com; campsites per person US$3.25, hammocks per person US$5, s/d US$33/53; ☷ ☐ ℗) Although the little duplex bungalows here are kinda jammed together, it still makes a decent and (relatively) cheap sleep in the park. Hammocks on the little porches are a bonus, but nobody's likely to get excited about paying US$6 for an hour of internet. If you don't have a tent, you can rent one for US$6.50 per person. The electricity goes off at 9pm.

Jungle Lodge (☎ 7861 0446; www.junglelodge.guate .com; s/d US$35/40, with bathroom US$69/86; ℗ ℞) This largest and most attractive of the three hotels was built originally to house archaeologists excavating and restoring Tikal. It's by far the sweetest of the accommodation options in the park, with mostly self-contained bungalows well-spaced throughout the jungly grounds. There's a swimming pool, large garden grounds, and a restaurant-bar with breakfast for US$5 and lunch or dinner for US$10.

Tikal Inn (☎ 7926 1917; www.tikalinn.com; s/d US$40/60, bungalows US$60/80; ℗ ☐ ℞) If you're going to do it here, you may as well do it in style, and go with the bungalows. They're bright and spacious and set well enough apart to give you a bit of privacy, with little sitting areas out front. All the accommodations are simple but clean and quite large. Rates on the rooms in the main building drop substantially when the hotel decides it isn't high season. You can pay an extra US$7.50 for the breakfast and dinner package.

There's no need to make reservations if you want to stay at Tikal's **campground** (campsite per person US$4), opposite the visitors center. This is a large, grassy area with a clean bathroom block, plenty of space for tents and *palapa* shelters for hanging hammocks.

As you arrive in Tikal, look on the right-hand side of the road to find the little *comedores:* Comedor Imperio Maya, Comedor La Jungla Tikal, Comedor Tikal, Comedor Sagrado de Jesús and Tienda Angelita. Comedor Tikal seems to be the most favored one. These *comedors* offer rustic and agreeable surroundings and are run by local people serving huge plates of fairly tasty food at low prices. Chicken or meat dishes cost around US$4.50, pasta and burgers a little less. All these places are open from 5am to 9pm daily.

Picnic tables beneath shelters are located just off Tikal's Gran Plaza, with soft-drink and water peddlers standing by, but no food is sold. If you want to spend all day at the ruins without having to make the 20- to 30-minute walk back to the *comedors,* carry food and water with you.

In the visitors center, **Restaurant Café Tikal** (mains US$6.50-10) serves fancier food at fancier prices. *Lomito* (tenderloin of beef) and steaks are featured. Plates of fruit cost less. All the hotels also have restaurants.

Getting There & Away

For details of transport to and from Flores and Santa Elena, see p281. Coming from Belize, you could consider taking a taxi from the border to Tikal for around US$40. Otherwise, get a bus to Puente Ixlú, sometimes called El Cruce, and switch there to a northbound minibus or bus for the remaining 36km to Tikal. Note that there is little northbound traffic after lunch. Heading from Tikal to Belize, start early in the morning and get off at Puente Ixlú to catch a bus or minibus eastward. Be wary of shuttles to Belize advertised at Tikal: these have been known to detour to Flores to pick up passengers!

UAXACTÚN

Uaxactún (wah-shahk-*toon*), 23km north of Tikal along an unpaved road through the jungle, was Tikal's political and military rival in late Preclassic times. It was conquered by Tikal's Chak Toh Ich'ak I (King Great Jaguar Paw) in the 4th century, and was subservient to its great sister to the south for centuries thereafter.

Uaxactún village lies either side of a disused airstrip, which now serves as pasture and a football field. Villagers make an income from collecting chicle, *pimienta* (all- spice) and *xate* in the surrounding forest. A recently started timber extraction operation is supposedly employing sustainable methods but critics have their doubts about this.

About halfway along the airstrip, roads go off to the left and right to the ruins. Village boys will want to guide you: you don't need a guide to find the ruins, but you might want to let one or two of them earn a small tip.

Ruins

The pyramids at Uaxactún were uncovered and stabilized so that no further deterioration would result, but they were not restored. White mortar is the mark of the repair crews, who patched cracks in the stone to prevent water and roots from entering.

Head south from the airstrip to reach Grupo E, a 10- to 15-minute walk. Perhaps the most significant temple here is E-VII-Sub, among the earliest intact temples excavated, with foundations going back perhaps to 2000 BC. It lay beneath much larger structures, which have been stripped away. On its flat top are holes, or sockets, for the poles that would have supported a wood-and-thatch temple. The pyramid is part of a group with astronomical significance: seen from it, the sun rises behind Templo E-I on the longest day of the year and behind Templo E-III on the shortest day. Also look for the somewhat deteriorated jaguar and serpent masks on this pyramid's sides.

About a 20-minute walk to the northwest of the runway are Grupo B and Grupo A. At Grupo A, early excavators sponsored by Andrew Carnegie simply cut into the sides of the temples indiscriminately, looking for graves. Sometimes they used dynamite. This unfortunate work destroyed many of the temples, which are now in the process of being reconstructed.

If you are visiting Uaxactún from Tikal, no fee is charged. But if you are going to Uaxactún without stopping to visit Tikal, you still have to pass through the Parque Nacional Tikal and will have to pay a US$2 Uaxactún-only fee at the park entrance.

Tours

Tours to Uaxactún can be arranged in Flores or at the hotels in Tikal. The Jungle Lodge has a trip departing daily at 8am and returning at 1pm, costing US$60 for one to four people.

Sleeping & Eating

Aldana's Lodge (campsites per person US$2.50, r per person US$4) To the right off the street leading to Grupos B and A, Aldana's has alternative, cheaper accommodations, and also offers tours to other sites, but has erratic water supplies. Camping using Aldana's equipment costs US$3 per person.

Campamento, Hotel & Restaurante El Chiclero (☎ /fax 7926 1095; campsites US$5, s/d US$14/17) On the north side of the airstrip, El Chiclero has 10 small and very basic rooms, but with good mattresses and mosquito-netted ceilings and windows, and does the best food in town (US$6 for soup and a main course with rice). Accommodation prices are very negotiable. Also here is a small museum with shelves full of Mayan pottery from Uaxactún and around. Neria, the owner, can organize trips to more remote sites such as El Mirador, Xultún, Río Azul, Nakbé and La Muralla.

A few basic *comedores* also provide food: Comedor Uaxactún, Comedor La Bendición and Comedor Imperial.

Getting There & Away

A Pinita bus supposedly leaves Santa Elena for Uaxactún (US$3) at 1pm, passing through Tikal about 3pm to 3:30pm, and starting back for Santa Elena from Uaxactún at 6am. But its schedule is rubbery and it can arrive in Tikal any time up to about 5pm and in Uaxactún up to about 6:30pm. During the rainy season (from May to October, sometimes extending into November), the road from Tikal to Uaxactún can become pretty muddy: locals say it

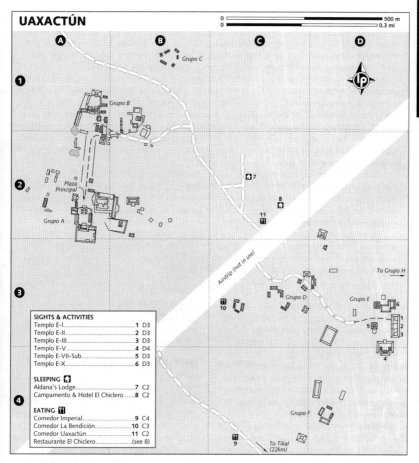

UAXACTÚN

0   500 m
0   0.3 mi

Grupo C

Grupo B

Plaza Principal

Grupo A

Grupo D

Grupo E

Grupo H

Grupo F

Airstrip (not in use)

To Grupo H

To Tikal (22km)

SIGHTS & ACTIVITIES		
Templo E-I	1	D3
Templo E-II	2	D3
Templo E-III	3	D3
Templo E-V	4	D4
Templo E-VII-Sub	5	D3
Templo E-X	6	D3
SLEEPING		
Aldana's Lodge	7	C2
Campamento & Hotel El Chiclero	8	C2
EATING		
Comedor Imperial	9	C4
Comedor La Bendición	10	C3
Comedor Uaxactún	11	C2
Restaurante El Chiclero	(see 8)	

is always passable but a 4WD vehicle might be needed during the wet.

If you're driving, the last chance to fill your fuel tank as you come from the south is at Puente Ixlú, just south of El Remate. A taxi from El Remate to Uaxactún and back, including waiting time, should cost about US$40; bargain hard.

From Uaxactún, unpaved roads lead to other ruins at El Zotz (about 30km southwest), Xultún (35km northeast) and Río Azul (100km northeast).

YAXHÁ

A beautiful and quite large classic Mayan ceremonial site, **Yaxhá** (admission US$1.80; 6am-5pm) may be familiar as it was used as the setting for *Survivor Guatemala*. The site is 11km north of the Puente Ixlú-Melchor de Mencos road, accessed from a turnoff 32km from Puente Ixlú and 33km from Melchor de Mencos. The access road is unpaved. Yaxhá's setting, on a hill overlooking two sizable lakes, Laguna Yaxhá and Laguna Sacnab, makes it particularly worth visiting. It takes about 1½ hours to wander round the main groups of ruins, which are gradually being cleared and restored, though many mounds are still under vegetation. The high point (literally), towering above all else, is **Templo 216** in the Acrópolis Este (Eastern Acropolis), which affords magnificent views in every direction. On an island near the far (south) shore of Laguna Yaxhá is a separate,

NOW WE'VE DUG IT UP, LET'S BURY IT AGAIN!

In the bad old days, archaeology was all about getting in there, digging up as much as possible and carrying the loot off to some foreign museum (or auction house). The field has become a lot more conservation-minded lately, and an interesting debate has developed.

It's all got to do with erosion and the way that some sites are literally falling apart due to exposure to wind, rain and weather in general. Originally, these structures would have been covered in stucco, the stones thus protected from the elements. After falling into disuse, many sites have been covered by soil, which acts as a natural shield. Now, having been excavated, they lie exposed and every year takes its toll. Some archaeologists and conservationists are calling for structures to be buried again once they have been examined for archaeological purposes. Others argue that, without tourist revenue, governments will not be able to afford even what meager resources they now contribute to excavation projects.

Ironically, tourism has played a part in some of the major archaeological finds in this century. The hugely popular (and much maligned) sound-and-light shows that are installed at some of the more popular ruins are pretty much the only time that anybody does any kind of heavy work around the ruins, and there are many stories of lighting technicians falling through roofs and into previously undiscovered chambers.

Either way, regardless of whether you're a tourist, archaeologist or conservationist, the argument raises some interesting questions: What are the ruins for? Are they just tourist eye candy, or should they be left solely to people studying them for academic reasons? And if we are going to bury them again, who exactly is allowed to dig them up?

late Postclassic archaeological site, Topoxté, whose dense covering of ruined temples and dwellings may date back to the Itzá culture that occupied Flores island at the time the Spanish came. On the northern lake shore below the Yaxhá ruins is **Campamento Yaxhá**, where you can camp for free on raised platforms with thatched roofs and where you might be able to find a boatman to take you over to Topoxté.

Campamento Ecológico El Sombrero (☎ 7926 5529; www.ecosombrero.com; s/d US$20/30, with bathroom US$30/40; **P**), on the southern shore and 250m off the approach road, is an excellent place to stay. It has good-sized, neat and clean rooms in mosquito-netted bungalows overlooking the lake. There's a good restaurant here, with a small library on local archaeology, and *lancha* tours to Topoxté are offered (US$20 for up to three people, US$26 for four to nine people) as well as horse riding and day trips to Nakum and El Naranjo, other Classic period sites to the north and northeast of Yaxhá. You can call here in advance and the friendly owner will come pick you up from the bus stop.

Don't swim in the lakes, by the way – there are crocodiles!

Agencies in Flores (see p274) and El Remate (see p286) offer organized trips to Yaxhá, some combined with Nakum and/or Tikal. To get there independently get a Melchor de Mencos-bound bus or minibus as far as the Yaxhá turnoff (and be prepared to walk the 11km to the site) – or find a taxi in El Remate, Puente Ixlú (about US$30 round-trip) or elsewhere.

MELCHOR DE MENCOS
pop 12,200

Right on the Belize–Guatemala border, Melchor is your classic border town – plenty of moneychangers and suspect dudes hanging around, and not a lot to beautify it. The one exception is the **Río Mopan Lodge** (☎ 7926 5196; www.tikaltravel.com; s/d with bathroom from US$16/20), the last (or first, depending on which way you're going) beautiful hotel you'll find in Guatemala. Set back from the road in lush, jungly grounds, you could be anywhere. The rooms are big, cool and well decorated, with balconies overlooking the Río Mopan. The Swiss-Spanish couple who run it offer trips to Tikal and other, lesser-known sites in the area. It's across the river from Melchor proper, in between the bridge and Guatemalan immigration.

MEXICAN BORDER (CHIAPAS & TABASCO)
Via Bethel/La Técnica & Frontera Corozal

The only route with regular transportation connections is via Bethel or La Técnica on the eastern (Guatemalan) bank of the Río

Usumacinta and Frontera Corozal on the Mexican bank. For details of bus services to and from Bethel and La Técnica and shuttle minibus services all the way through to Palenque, see p282. Guatemalan immigration is in Bethel: bus drivers to La Técnica will normally stop and wait for you to do the formalities in Bethel.

See below for information on river crossings: it's cheaper and quicker from La Técnica than from Bethel, but crossing at La Técnica means a longer bus journey on the Guatemalan side. Minibuses leave Frontera Corozal for Palenque at about 5am, 10am, noon and 3pm (US$5, three hours).

If you should want to stay in the Usumacinta area, perhaps to visit the Mayan ruins at Yaxchilán on the Mexican side of the river, the riverside **Posada Maya** (☎ 7861 1799; s/d/tr US$9/18/28), 1km outside Bethel, has a great location and comfortable thatched bungalows, plus tent and hammock shelters. Boats from Bethel to Yaxchilán cost from US$15 to US$25 per person for four to 12 people, round-trip.

Other Routes

You can also cross into Mexico by boat down the Río de la Pasión from Sayaxché to Benemérito de las Américas or down the Río San Pedro from El Naranjo to La Palma. But there are no regular passenger services on either river and you will probably have to rent a boat privately for around US$80 on the Río San Pedro or US$100-plus on the Río de la Pasión. Both trips take around four hours. La Palma has transportation connections with Tenosique, Tabasco, from where minibuses leave for Palenque up to 5:30pm. Benemérito has good bus and minibus connections with Palenque. Both Sayaxché and El Naranjo have bus and minibus connections with Flores (see p282).

A possible alternative on the Río San Pedro route is to get a boat from El Naranjo only as far as El Ceibo, on the border, for around US$35. From El Ceibo there are a few buses on to Tenosique (US$3, 1½ hours), the last one leaving about 5:30pm. Mexico has no immigration facilities at Benemérito or El Ceibo: you have to get your passport stamped at Frontera Corozal or Tenosique, or failing that, Palenque.

El Naranjo, Tenosique and Benemérito all have a few basic accommodations.

SAYAXCHÉ
pop 10,500

Sayaxché, on the south bank of the Río de la Pasión, 61km southwest of Flores, is the closest town to nine or 10 scattered Mayan archaeological sites, including Ceibal, Aguateca, Dos Pilas, Tamarindito and Altar de Sacrificios (p300). Otherwise, for travelers it's little more than a transportation halt between Flores and the Cobán area.

Minibuses and buses from Santa Elena drop you on the north bank of the Río de la Pasión. Frequent ferries (US$0.15 for pedestrians, US$2 for cars) carry you across to the town.

GETTING TO THE BELIZE BORDER

It's 100km from Flores to Melchor de Mencos, the Guatemalan town on the border with Belize. For information on bus services to the border and also on more expensive services going right through to Belize City and Chetumal, Mexico, see p282.

The road to the border diverges from the Flores–Tikal road at Puente Ixlú (also called El Cruce), 27km from Flores. It continues paved until about 25km short of the border. The stretch between Puente Ixlú and the border has been the scene of a few highway robberies.

There should be no fees at the border for entering or leaving Guatemala, and none for entering Belize. But travelers leaving Belize usually have to pay a US$15 departure tax and a US$3.75 protected areas conservation fee.

There are money changers at the border with whom you can change sufficient funds for immediate needs. Taxis run between the border and the nearest town in Belize, Benque Viejo del Carmen, 3km away, for around U$2.50. Buses run from Benque to Belize City (US$4, three hours) about every half-hour from 11am to 4pm. You might want to stop over at San Ignacio, 13km beyond Benque: there are many serviceable hotels and interesting things to do around San Ignacio. If you arrive in Benque early enough in the day, you may have sufficient time to visit the Mayan ruins of Xunantunich on your way to San Ignacio.

Banrural (🕑 9am-4pm Mon-Fri, 10am-1pm Sat), just up the main street from Hotel Guayacán, changes US-dollar cash and traveler's checks.

Sleeping & Eating

Hotel Yaxkin (☎ 7928 6429; s/d with bathroom US$7.50/15) Surprisingly big rooms in a brick and concrete wonderland 50m up from the boat landing. Try to get one away from the front as the street noise is formidable.

Hotel Petexbatún (☎ 7928 6166; s/d with bathroom US$9/16) This is the second-best place. All rooms have fan and TV. Go one block up the street past the Hotel Guayacán, then three blocks to the right. It overlooks the Río Petexbatún.

Hotel Guayacán (☎ 7928 6111; s/d with bathroom US$16/20; P 🞬) Right on the south bank of the river in Sayaxché, the Guayacán is the best place in town, with good rooms equipped with solid wooden beds and tile floors. It also has the best restaurant, on a terrace overlooking the river. Chicken, fish or beef with salad and fries costs US$4 to US$6. Air-con costs an extra US$4.

Café del Río (mains US$3-5; 🕑 breakfast, lunch & dinner) The most atmospheric place to eat in town is actually across the river on the big wooden dock built out over the water. Forget about the US$0.50 return trip and enjoy the wholesome food, sweet breezes and icy beer.

Restaurant Yaxkin (mains US$3-5; 🕑 breakfast, lunch & dinner) A pleasant and clean family-run restaurant a couple of doors from Hotel Mayapán. It serves up good-value set lunches (US$2.50) and does picnic boxes (US$3) in case you're going somewhere.

Getting There & Away

Southbound from Sayaxché, buses and minibuses leave at 5am, 6am, 10am and 3pm for Cobán (US$7, five hours). Most if not all of these go via Raxrujá and Sebol, not via Chisec. Other minibuses and buses go just to Raxrujá (US$3.50), about hourly from 7am to 3pm. For Chisec, you can change in Raxrujá or at San Antonio Las Cuevas. Vehicles may start from the southern riverbank or they may start from the Texaco station opposite Hotel Guayacán.

For river transportation, talk to any of the boatmen on the riverbank, or to **La Gaviota Tours** (☎ 7928 6461), with an office 200m to the left of where boats dock. A trip all the way down the Río de la Pasión to Benemérito de las Américas (Mexico), with stops at the ruins of Altar de Sacrificios and Guatemalan immigration at Pipiles, should cost between US$130 and US$180.

AROUND SAYAXCHÉ

Of the archaeological sites reached from Sayaxché, Ceibal and Aguateca are the most interesting to the amateur visitor. Ceibal is fairly well restored, Aguateca has an impressive location, and both are reached by boat trips along jungle-fringed rivers and/or lakes followed by forest walks.

Ceibal

Unimportant during most of the Classic period, Ceibal (sometimes spelt Seibal) grew rapidly in the 9th century AD under the rule of the Putun Maya merchant-warrior culture from the Tabasco area of Mexico. It attained a population of perhaps 10,000 by AD 900, then was abandoned shortly afterwards. Its low, ruined temples were quickly covered by a thick carpet of jungle.

Some interesting carvings are on display here – one shows the presence of strangely dressed men with distinctly un-Mayan features, which has lead to all sorts of wild speculation that foreigners once inhabited the area. Another shows a finely dressed king holding his war club upside down in a classic gesture of submission – believed to be a reference to the site's surrender to neighboring Dos Pilas.

Ceibal is not one of the most impressive Mayan sites, but the river journey to it is among the most memorable. A one-hour ride up the Río de la Pasión from Sayaxché brings you to a primitive dock. After landing, you clamber up a narrow, rocky path beneath gigantic ceiba trees and ganglions of jungle vines to reach the archaeological zone.

Smallish temples, many of them still (or again) covered with jungle, surround two principal plazas. In front of a few temples, and standing seemingly alone on paths deeply shaded by the jungle canopy, are magnificent stelae, their intricate carvings still in excellent condition. It takes about two hours to explore the site.

For information on tours to Ceibal, see p274. Otherwise, talk to any of the boatmen by the river at Sayaxché. For a round-trip including waiting time, they charge around US$40 for one person plus US$3 for each extra person. You should hire a guide to see the site, as some of the finest stelae are off the plazas

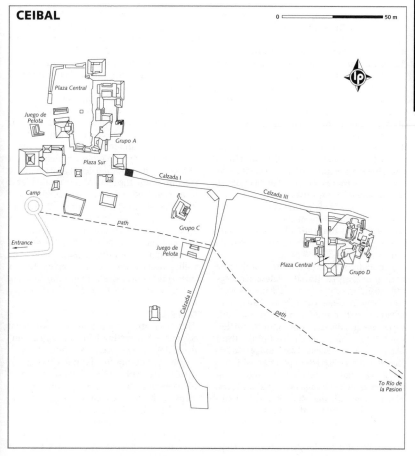

CEIBAL

Plaza Central

Juego de Pelota

Grupo A

Plaza Sur

Camp

Calzada I

Calzada III

Entrance

path

Grupo C

Juego de Pelota

Calzada II

Plaza Central

Grupo D

path

To Río de la Pasion

in the jungle. Most *lancheros,* conveniently, also serve as guides.

If you wish, you can get to Ceibal cheaper by land: get any bus, minibus or pickup heading south from Sayaxché on Hwy 5 (toward Raxrujá and Chisec) and get off after 9km at Paraíso (US$0.80), from which a dirt track leads 8km east to Ceibal. You may have to walk the last 8km. In the rainy season check first that this stretch is passable.

LAGUNA PETEXBATÚN

Laguna Petexbatún is a 6km-long lake southwest of Sayaxché approached by an hour's *lancha* ride up the Río Petexbatún, a tributary of the Río de la Pasión, from Sayaxché. The lake, river and surrounding forests harbor many

birds, including kingfishers, egrets, vultures, eagles, cormorants and herons. Within reach of the waterways are five archaeological sites (Dos Pilas, Tamarindito, Arroyo de Piedra, Punta de Chiminos and Aguateca), and three jungle-hideaway accommodations close to the waters' edge. What we know of the history of these archaeological sites has mostly been unraveled by archaeologists since the late 1980s. Dos Pilas was founded about AD 640 by a prince who had left Tikal and later defeated Tikal in two wars, capturing its ruler Nuun Ujol Chaak (Shield Skull) in 679, according to inscriptions at Dos Pilas. Dos Pilas' second and third rulers carried out monumental building programs, waged wars of conquest and came to dominate most of the territory between the Pasión and Chixoy rivers, but in AD 761 their vassal Tamarindito rebelled and killed the fourth ruler, causing the Dos Pilas nobility to relocate to the naturally fortified site of Aguateca, which was already functioning as a twin capital. Aguateca in turn was abandoned in the early 9th century, at around the same time as three defensive moats were cut across the neck of the Chiminos peninsula on the edge of Laguna Petexbatún. Archaeologists surmise that Punta de Chiminos was the last refuge of the Petexbatún dynasty founded at Dos Pilas.

The first landmark you reach, on the river a few kilometers before the lake, is **Posada Caribe** (☎ 7928 6114; posadacaribe@peten.net; s/d US$50/60), with thatched bungalows. From here you can walk to the **Dos Pilas** ruins in about three hours, including stops at the lesser ruins of **Tamarindito** and **Arroyo de Piedra** en route. You can organize horses for this trip at Posada Caribe for around US$8 each.

Just up from the western shore of the lake itself is the fairly comfortable **Petexbatún Lodge** (☎ 7926 0501; philippe_petex@yahoo.fr; r per person with bunks US$10, bungalows with bathroom US$40), with mosquito-netted rooms and meals available if you ask in advance. Two minutes further south by *lancha* is the choicest of the three places to stay, **Chiminos Island Lodge** (☎ 2335 3506; www.chiminosisland.com; r per person incl 3 meals US$75). This has just five lovely, large, comfortable, thatched bungalows set along forest paths, each with one double and two single beds, hot-water bathroom, fan, electric light, mosquito screens, balcony and lake view. Good food is served in an open-air restaurant and the lodge shares its promontory with the Punta de Chiminos ruins, where you can make out a ballcourt, stela and several mounds. Fat folders full of absorbing archaeological information and articles about the area are available to peruse as you chill out here.

AGUATECA

If you have limited time and funds, this site, just off the far south end of the lake, is both the easiest reached and the most immediately impressive. It's a 1¼-hour *lancha* trip direct from Sayaxché. It's a five-minute walk up from the dock to the office of the rangers, who will guide you round the site in about 1½ hours (a tip of a few dollars is in order). The ruins are on a hilltop, defended by cliffs facing the lake and by a ravine. Pottery shards

dating from as far back as 200 BC have been found here. Carved stelae suggest that the city enjoyed military successes (including one over nearby Ceibal) up until about AD 735. It's fairly certain that rulers from Dos Pilas abandoned that city for the better-fortified Aguateca around AD 761, and that the city was finally overrun by unknown attackers around 790 – a wealth of arrowheads and skeletons have been found dating back to that time. There was no new building after that and the city was abandoned shortly afterwards.

There are two main groups, both in process of restoration: the Grupo del Palacio where the ruler lived, and the Plaza Mayor (Main Plaza) to its south, where glass fiber copies of several stelae showing finely attired rulers stand beside the fallen originals. The two groups are connected by a causeway. The rangers are usually happy to let people camp at Aguateca (bring supplies with you). They might even be willing to show you the way overland to Dos Pilas (11km northwest). Howler monkeys are much in evidence early and late in the day.

DOS PILAS

This fascinating site is a mere 16 km from Sayaxché, but getting here is a serious undertaking. If you have the time, it's well worth considering for the fine carvings on display, particularly the partially excavated hieroglyphic staircase, with five 6m-wide steps, each with two rows of superbly preserved glyphs, climbing to the base of the royal palace near the main plaza.

The city began life as a breakaway from the Tikal group when that city was taken by Calakmul. Dos Pilas appears to have been governed by a set of very aggressive rulers – it clashed with Tikal, Ceibal, Yaxhilán and Motul all within 150 years, often ignoring the traditional 'war season,' which finished in time for the harvest.

Dos Pilas was virtually abandoned in 760 AD, but some farmers hung on into the 9th century when the city was overrun and subsequently evacuated.

A few caves nearby are thought to have been used for human sacrifices, having contained skeletons, altars and ceremonial bloodletting objects.

Many stelae at this site have been relocated to museums and replaced by crushed-rock and fiberglass replicas, in a pilot program designed to deter looters.

The best way to reach Dos Pilas is by tour from Sayaxché (p299) or by staying at the Posada Caribe (opposite) and organizing a tour there. Either way, you'll be up for about three hours of jungle trekking on foot or horseback from the Posada, passing the sites of Tamarandito (which also features a hieroglyphic stairway) and the smaller site of Arroyo de Piedra, which has a plaza and some well-preserved stelae.

GETTING AROUND

Getting to all these places involves making your own arrangements with boatmen at Sayaxché, or taking a tour. A straightforward half-day return trip from Sayaxché to Aguateca costs around US$45 for one person plus US$5 for each extra person. You could, for example, arrange to be dropped at one of the lodges afterwards and to be picked up the next afternoon after making a trip to Dos Pilas. Martsam Travel (see p274) offers tours to these sites, with camping at Aguateca.

REMOTE MAYAN SITES

Several Mayan sites buried in the Petén forest, of interest to archaeology buffs and adventurous travelers, are open for limited tourism. They're exciting not just because of the ruins but because of the jungle and its wildlife that you encounter en route. Few of these sites can be visited without a guide because of their remote location, the difficult jungle terrain you must brave to get there and the lack of water (potable or otherwise), but several businesses in Flores, El Remate and San Andrés offer trips to these sites. Few of these tours offer anything approaching comfort, and you should be prepared for buggy, basic conditions. People reluctant to use a mosquito repellent containing DEET may want to reconsider taking one of these trips.

If you take a trip with an outfit that works with the local Comités Comunitarios de Ecoturismo (Community Ecotourism Committees) in the remote villages that serve as starting points for these treks, you will be participating in a considered program of low-impact, sustainable tourism and you will have a guide who is highly knowledgeable about local conditions. Freelance guides can lead tourists to some of these sites, which may save you some money, but they may have little concept of responsible tourism and little knowledge of what you are seeing. Nor is there any assurance, given the difficulty of these treks, that your freelance trip will come off successfully, and in case of failure, you'll have no claim to any money you may have paid up front.

El Perú & Around

Trips to this site 62km northwest of Flores in the Parque Nacional Laguna del Tigre are termed La Ruta Guacamaya (the Scarlet Macaw Trail), because the chances of seeing

---

THE LONG ROAD NORTH

Every year, thousands of Guatemalans pass through the Petén jungle. They're not ecotourists or archaeologists – they go in search of the American Dream.

Figures are obviously hard to nail down, but the International Organization for Migration (IOM) in Guatemala estimates that between 6000 and 12,000 Guatemalans arrive in the United States each year. The Pew Hispanic Center estimates there are 320,000 Guatemalans living there illegally.

It's not easily done. Guatemalans pay US$5000 to a *coyote* (people smuggler) to be taken on the hazardous journey up north. Rape, robbery and murder of illegal immigrants en route are commonplace.

It's not just Guatemalans, either – people from as far as Bolivia, Brazil and even China pass through here to take advantage of the long, relatively unpatroled land borders.

Getting to the States may be the easy part. Once there, they're subjected to racist slurs – 'wetback' or *'mojado'* (for having swum across the Río Grande) and 'beaner' or *'frijolero'* (for obvious reasons) and offered only the lowest-paying work. It's generally accepted that the economies of the entire west coast and much of Florida would collapse without the cheap labor supplied by undocumented immigrants. In 2006 the Bush administration started pushing for tighter border controls (including the construction of a fence along much of the US–Mexico border) alongside a Guest Worker Scheme, which critics say gives the US the best of both worlds – unlimited cheap (taxpaying) labor without the burdens associated with granting citizenship.

these magnificent birds are high, chiefly during their February-to-June nesting season. You normally journey by road to Paso Caballos (2½ hours from Flores) then travel by boat an hour down the Río San Pedro to El Perú, making various trips out from a camp in the area, including night-time observation of El Petén's endangered endemic crocodile, *Cocodrilo moreletti*. There are several important Classic-period structures at El Perú, including the Mirador de los Monos (Monkey Lookout). Despite its proximity to Tikal, archaeologists believe El Perú may have allied with Tikal's great rival Calakmul in Mexico.

Another destination in Parque Nacional Laguna del Tigre that is sometimes combined with El Perú trips is the **Estación Biológica Las Guacamayas** (Scarlet Macaw Biological Station) on the Río San Juan. This is a scientific station surrounded by rainforest, where among other things, scarlet macaws and white tortoises are observed.

A further site that may start to be combined with El Perú trips is **La Joyanca**, 20km west of El Perú, a Classic-period site where several structures have recently been restored and walking trails and information panels installed.

Piedras Negras

On the banks of the Río Usumacinta, which forms the border with Mexico, these little-visited ruins have been mercifully untouched by looters, despite their impressive size and wealth of carvings. Several of the finest pieces found here – including a carved throne – are now in the National Archaeological Museum in Guatemala City (see p79).

The entrance to the site is probably its most impressive aspect – black cliffs (from which it gets its name) loom over the river banks. A large rock protrudes, carved with a kneeling man making an offering to a female figure. A (now crumbling) stairway leads up the riverbank to the building complex 100m above.

The best-preserved buildings here are the sweat baths and acropolis complex, which incorporates rooms, courtyards and passageways. Other buildings show a mix of styles, often with Classic structures built on top of Preclassic ones.

It was here in the 1930s that part-time archaeologist Tatiana Proskouriakoff deciphered the Mayan hieroglyphic system, recognizing patterns between the glyphs and certain dates, events and people. Although her theory played out when she tested it at nearby Yaxchilán, it was not accepted by the wider archaeological community until the 1960s.

The original name of the city, Yokib' ('the entrance'), is believed to be a reference to a large cenote found in the center of the city.

RESPONSIBLE TOURISM

Visitors to sites deep in the Petén forest need to be very conscious of their impact on the ecological balance. Observing a few basic guidelines and insisting your guides do the same will help protect this area. All nonorganic garbage should be carried out, human waste and toilet paper should be buried in a pit at least 15cm deep and 100m from a water source, and only dead wood should be used to build fires.

One issue of particular concern is the use of pack animals on these trips. Generally, a four-person expedition (two tourists, a guide and a cook) requires four mules or horses. Mules eat copious amounts of sapodilla tree leaves; nearly an entire mature tree will be stripped of its branches to feed four mules for one day. Multiply this over a three-day trip with four paying participants, and you begin to see the scope of the problem. If you can avoid using mules on your trip, do so. Otherwise, inquire about alternative food sources for the animals.

Another nagging problem is mud. There's lots of it between May and November (halfway up a mule's leg is the norm), and machete-wielding guides hacking trails around mud patches kills new forest growth. Walking around a mud patch also makes it bigger. Hiking in these muddy conditions is no treat anyway, so try to arrange your trip for the dry season.

Trekking in El Petén in a responsible way gets really tricky when tourists contract freelance guides. While the Comité guides are required to do courses pertaining to responsible tourism, independent guides won't necessarily adhere to ecotouristic ideals. Indeed, they're often unaware of rudimentary concepts of low-impact travel. In this case, it is up to you, the traveler, to ensure that basic tenets of responsible tourism are respected.

LOCAL VOICES: NORA LÓPEZ – LABORATORY DIRECTOR, THE MIRADOR PROJECT

One of the major archaeological excavations being undertaken in Guatemala is at El Mirador, a remote Mayan site in El Petén (see p306). This megacity has been buried in jungle for centuries, and its importance is only just starting to be understood. We caught up with Ms López to find out how the dig's going.

What are you working on at the moment?

It's the rainy season now, so pretty much the whole team is back in the lab, classifying and cataloging finds, looking for connections and similarities, establishing timelines. I'm also involved in bibliographical research.

What's special about El Mirador?

For one thing, it's huge. We're still mapping, but it looks like El Mirador occupied 23 sq km. Around the city were others like Nakbé and Florida, connected by stone 'highways' that are up to 23km long. Altogether, we're looking at an area of around 2000 sq km. Another is that, because there wasn't much water near the site, hydraulic irrigation systems were used to grow crops needed to feed so many workers.

What's a typical day like for an archaeologist?

It depends. In the field, there's plenty of digging, note taking, and classifying. That all goes into the field report. Back in the lab, we wash everything and reclassify it. We use pottery finds to establish dating, so we classify it by color and material, frequency and chronology.

What's the most exciting thing you've found?

Plenty of little things. Small things contribute to the big picture. I'm interested in bones, so I like finding burials, even though it implies more work. Once a body is uncovered we have to work around the clock or else it can get damaged by weather or stolen by thieves.

How do you see the relation between tourism and archaeology?

It can be excellent, but it has to be managed. What you see at more popular sites is a lot of damage – crowds trampling things and not understanding what they're looking at. If you keep the groups small, visitors can be informed and educated. Mass tourism doesn't really do anything but provide photo opportunities.

Due to its remote location and the drug smuggling activity in the area, it's neither easy nor wise to visit Piedras Negras on your own. Martsam Travel (see p274) in Flores, Monkey Eco Tours, operating out of the Ni'tun Ecolodge (see p284) in San Andrés and Maya Expeditions (see p81) in Guatemala City can all organize trips here. The cheapest way to do it is to make your way to Bethel independently, then organize a tour with the Posada Maya (see p299).

El Zotz

Completely unrestored and barely excavated, the large site of El Zotz ('bat' in many Mayan languages) occupies its own *biotopo* abutting the Tikal National Park. The three major temples here are all covered in soil and moss, but you can scramble to the top of the tallest, the Pirámide del Diablo, for views of Tikal's temples, 24km to the west. If you're here around dusk, you'll see where the place gets its name, as thousands of bats come pouring out of nearby caves.

Tour operators in Flores (see p274) and El Remate (see p286) offer jeep/horse/trekking tours here, often incorporating Tikal – see those sections for details. Coming independently, it's a 30km (five-hour) trek (with the possibility of a ride in a *xate* truck) from Cruce Dos Aguadas, which is connected to Santa Elena by bus. You can also take the longer route from Uaxactún (p296). Camping is permitted near the site – talk to the guards at the Cecon station when you arrive and bring all supplies with you.

Río Azul

This medium-sized site (its population is believed to have peaked at around 5000) is located in the Parque Nacional Mirador-Río Azul, up near the corner where the Belize, Guatemala and Mexico borders meet. Once an independent city, it fell under the domain of Tikal in the early Classic period and became a key trading post for cacao from the Caribbean on its way to Tikal and Central Mexico. The city was overrun in 530 AD by forces from Calakmul, then regained by Tikal during its resurgence in the late Classic era before being finally destroyed by the Puuc Maya from the Yucatán.

There are over 350 structures here, but most notable are the tombs, with vibrant red glyphs painted inside, as well as three round altars, with carvings depicting ritual executions.

Looting reached a frenzy point here during the 1960s and '70s – international treaties banning the trafficking in Mayan artifacts were precipitated, in part, by the volume of ceramics and other objects stolen from Río Azul – one archaeological team returned to the site after the rainy season to find 150 trenches dug in their absence.

We can only guess at the full extent of the treasures carted away, but some of the documented losses include jade masks, murals, pendants and other carved objects.

The tallest temple, AIII, a smaller replica of those found at Tikal, stands 47m high, high enough to give a panoramic view out over the jungle canopy.

There's no public transportation anywhere near Río Azul. If you've got a 4WD, you could make the trip in as little as five hours from Uaxactún. Walking or on horseback, it's more like four days. Tours here leave from Flores, Uaxactún and El Remate.

El Mirador

This archaeological site is buried within the furthest reaches of the Petén jungle, just 7km south of the Mexican border. A visit here involves an arduous jungle trek of at least five days and four nights (it's about 60km each way), with no facilities or amenities aside from what you carry in and what can be rustled from the forest. The trip departs from a cluster of houses called Carmelita – the end of the line.

The metropolis at El Mirador, dated to 150 BC to AD 150, contains the largest cluster of buildings in any single Mayan site, among which is the biggest pyramid ever built in the Mayan world: El Tigre. This pyramid measures 18 stories high (more than 60m) and its base covers 18,000 sq meters – six times the area of Tikal's biggest structure, Templo IV. El Tigre's twin, La Danta (the Tapir), though technically smaller, soars higher because it's built on a rise. From atop La Danta, some 105m above the forest floor, virgin canopy stretches into the distance as far as your eye can see. The green bumps hovering on the horizon are other pyramids still buried under dense jungle. There are hundreds of buildings at El Mirador, but a major ongoing excavation has never been tackled, so almost everything is still hidden beneath the jungle. You'll have to use your imagination to picture this city that at its height spread over 16 sq km and supported tens of thousands of citizens.

Scholars are still figuring out why and how El Mirador thrived (there are few natural resources and no water sources save for the reservoirs built by ingenious, ancient engineers) and what led to its abandonment. It was certainly the greatest Mayan city of the Preclassic era.

Trips to El Mirador can include a couple of extra days to see Nakbé, another Preclassic site 13km southeast of El Mirador (and joined to it by an ancient causeway) and other sites. Trekking to El Mirador is not for the faint of heart. Conditions are rudimentary: there are no toilets, beds, cold beverages or bathrooms. The ants, ticks and mosquitoes never relent, the mud is knee-deep and the hiking is strenuous and dirty. That said, folks who make this journey will never forget it.

Directory

CONTENTS

ACCOMMODATIONS

Guatemalan accommodations range from luxury hotels to budget hotels to ultra-budget guesthouses called *hospedajes, casas de huéspedes* or *pensiones*.

This book's budget category covers places where a typical double costs US$20 or less. Doubles under US$10 are generally small, dark and not particularly clean. Security may not be the best in such places. An exception is the low-priced dormitories that exist alongside other rooms in generally better establishments. A US$20 double should be clean, sizable and airy, with a bathroom, TV and, in hot parts of the country, a fan.

Midrange covers establishments with doubles between US$20 and US$50. These rooms are always comfortable: private hot-water bathroom, TV, decent beds, fan and/or aircon are standard. Good midrange hotels have attractive public areas such as dining rooms, bars and swimming pools. In hot regions, the rooms may be attractive wooden bungalows, with thatch roofs, verandas and hammocks; in cooler areas they may be in beautiful old colonial-style houses with antique furnishings and lovely patios. The smaller the establishment, the better the attention to guests is likely to be. Many B&Bs in Guatemala fit this description.

Anything more expensive than US$50 is top end. Guatemala City's international-class business-oriented hotels, Antigua's very finest hostelries, and a few resort hotels elsewhere constitute nearly the whole of the top end options.

Room rates often go up in places tourists go during Semana Santa (the week leading up to Easter Sunday), Christmas–New Year and July and August. Semana Santa is the major Guatemalan holiday week of the year, and prices can rise by anything from 30% to 100% on the coast and in the countryside – anywhere Guatemalans go to relax – as well as in international-tourism destinations such as Antigua. At this time advance reservations are a very good idea. We indicate throughout this book where and when you should expect seasonal price hikes.

Be aware that room rates are subject to two large taxes – 12% IVA (value-added tax) and 10% to pay for the activities of the Guatemalan Tourism Institute (Inguat). All prices in this book include both taxes. Some of the more

BOOK ACCOMMODATIONS ONLINE

For more accommodations reviews and recommendations by Lonely Planet authors, check out the online booking service at www.lonelyplanet.com. You'll find the true, insider lowdown on the best places to stay. Reviews are thorough and independent. Best of all, you can book online.

expensive hotels forget to include them when they quote their prices.

Camping

In Guatemala, camping can be a hit-or-miss affair, as there are few designated campgrounds and safety is rarely guaranteed. Where campsites are available, expect to pay from US$3 to US$5 per person per night.

Homestays

Travelers attending Spanish school have the option of living with a Guatemalan family. This is usually a pretty good bargain – expect to pay between US$35 and US$60 a week for your own room, shared bathrooms, and three meals a day except Sunday. It's important to find a homestay that gels with your goals. For example, some families host several students at a time, creating more of an international hostel atmosphere than a family environment.

ACTIVITIES
Climbing, Trekking & Hiking

The many volcanoes are irresistible challenges, and many of them can be done in one day from Antigua (p104) or Quetzaltenango (p161). There's further great hill country in the Ixil Triangle and the Cuchumatanes mountains to the north of Huehuetenango, especially around Todos Santos Cuchumatán (p185). The Lago de Atitlán (p123) is surrounded by spectacular trails, though robberies here have made some

routes inadvisable. Treks of several days are perfectly feasible, and agencies in Antigua, Quetzaltenango and Nebaj (p158) can guide you. In the Petén jungles, treks to remote archaeological sites such as El Mirador and El Perú (p303) offer an exciting challenge.

Cycling

There's probably no better way to experience the Guatemalan highlands than by bicycle. Panajachel (p125), Quetzaltenango (p161) and Antigua (p105) in particular are the best launch points, with agencies offering trips and equipment.

Horse Riding

Opportunities for a gallop, a trot or even a horse trek are on the increase in Guatemala. There are stables in Antigua (p105), Santiago Atitlán (p137), Quetzaltenango (p161), El Remate (p285) and Río Dulce (p251). Unicornio Azul (p185), north of Huehuetenango, offers treks of up to nine days in the Cuchumatanes.

Spelunking

Guatemala attracts cavers from the world over. The limestone area around Cobán is particularly riddled with cave systems whose full extents are unknown. The caves of Lanquín (p224), B'omb'il Pek (p227), Candelaria (p227) and Rey Marcos (p224) are all open for tourist visits. There are also exciting caves to visit from Finca Ixobel (p269), near Poptún.

PRACTICALITIES

- Guatemalans use the metric system for weights and measures, except that they pump gasoline by the *galón* (US gallon) and occasionally weigh things such as laundry and coffee in pounds.

- Videos and DVDs on sale use the NTSC image registration system.

- Electrical current is 115V to 125V, 60Hz, and plugs are two flat prongs, all the same as in the US and Canada.

- The most respected of Guatemala's many newspapers are *La Prensa Libre* (www.prensalibre .com), *Siglo Veintiuno* (www.sigloxxi.com), *La Hora* (www.lahora.com.gt) and *El Periódico* (www .elperiodico.com.gt). For Guatemala-related articles from around the world and Guatemala in English, check the *Guatemala Post* (www.guatemalapost.com).

- The *Revue* is Guatemala's free, widely distributed, monthly English-language magazine – a lot of ads, a few interesting articles.

- Almost every TV is cable, which ensures reception and brings a number of US stations to hotel TVs.

Water Sports

You can dive inside a volcanic caldera at Lago de Atitlán (p123), raft the white waters of the Río Cahabón (p225) near Lanquín, sail from the yachtie haven of Río Dulce (p251), and canoe or kayak the waterways of Monterrico (p204), Lívingston (p261), the Bocas del Polochic (p256) or Punta de Manabique (p260).

Wildlife Viewing & Bird-Watching

National parks and nature reserves generally have few tourist facilities, but they do offer lots of wildlife and bird-watching opportunities. Fine locations in the Petén jungles for bird-watching include Tikal (p288), El Mirador (p306), Cerro Cahuí (p285), Laguna Petexbatún (p301) and (for scarlet macaws) the Estación Biológica Las Guacamayas (p303) and the Macaw Mountain Bird Park (p243). Elsewhere, the wetlands of Bocas del Polochic (p256), Punta de Manabique (p260) and Monterrico (p204), the Río Dulce (p251) and Laguna Lachuá (p228) national parks and the Biotopo del Quetzal (p215) also provide lots of avian variety. Mammals tend to prove more elusive but you should see several species at Tikal. Monkey fans will also be happy at the Reserva Natural Atitlán (p129), the Bocas del Polochic (p256) and Cerro Cahuí (p285).

BUSINESS HOURS

Guatemalan shops and businesses are generally open from 8am to noon and 2pm to 6pm, Monday to Saturday, but there are many variations. Banks typically open 9am to 5pm Monday to Friday (again with variations), and 9am to 1pm Saturday. Government offices usually open 8am to 4pm, Monday to Friday. Official business is always better conducted in the morning.

Restaurant hours are typically 7am to 9pm, but can vary by up to two hours either way. Most bars open from 10am or 11am to 10pm or 11pm. The *Ley Seca* (dry law) stipulates that bars and discotecas must close by 1am, except on nights before public holidays. It is rigidly adhered to in large cities and universally laughed at in smaller towns and villages. If restaurants or bars have a closing day, it's usually Sunday. Typical shopping hours are 8am to noon and 2pm to 6pm, Monday to Saturday.

CHILDREN

Young children are highly regarded in Guatemala and can often break down barriers and open the doors to local hospitality. However, Guatemala is so culturally dense, with such an emphasis on history and archaeology, that children can get easily bored. To keep kids entertained, parents will need to make a point of visiting some of the more kid-friendly sites like Guatemala City's Museo de los Niños (p79) and La Aurora Zoo (p79), Autosafari Chapín (p203) south of the capital, and Retalhuleu's Xocomil water park (p197) and Xetulul theme park (p197). Most Spanish courses are open to kids, too. Many older kids will enjoy activities such as kayaking and horse riding.

Facilities such as safety seats in hired cars are rare but nearly every restaurant can rustle up something resembling a high chair. If you need supplies such as diapers (nappies) and creams, bring what you can with you and stock up in Guatemala City or, failing that, Antigua or Quetzaltenango. Fresh milk is rare and may not be pasteurized. Packet UHT milk and, even more so, milk powder to which you must add purified water are much more common. If your child has to have some particular tinned or packaged food, bring supplies with you. Public breast-feeding is not common and, when done, is done discreetly.

For a wealth of good ideas, get hold of Lonely Planet's *Travel with Children*.

CLIMATE CHARTS

For climatic considerations concerning your trip, see the charts on p310 and when to Go (p19).

COURSES

Dance

Dancing is *everything* in Guatemala (a party is thought to be a flop unless people are dancing). The most popular formal style is merengue, with salsa coming more or less second. Dance schools in Quetzaltenango (p168) and Antigua (p115) can help you get your groove on at a fraction of the price you'd pay back home.

Language

Guatemala is celebrated for its many language schools. A spot of study here is a great way not only to learn Spanish but also to meet locals and get an inside angle on the culture. Many travelers heading down through Central America to South America make

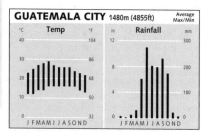

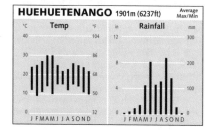

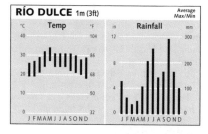

Guatemala an early stop so they can pick up the Spanish skills they need for their trip.

Guatemalan language schools are a lot cheaper than those in Mexico, but few people go away disappointed. There are so many schools to choose from that it's essential to check out a few before deciding. It's not hard to see whether a school is professional and well organized, or whether its teachers are qualified and experienced.

Antigua is the most popular place to study, with about 75 schools (see p106). Quetzaltenango (p168), the second most popular, perhaps attracts a more serious type of student; Antigua has a livelier students' and travelers' social scene. San Pedro La Laguna (p143) and Panajachel (p129) on the Lago de Atitlán both have a handful of language schools, and if you'd like to learn Spanish while hanging out in a remote mountain town, there are schools in Todos Santos Cuchumatán (p186)

and Nebaj (p159). On average, schools charge US$110 to US$120 for four hours of one-on-one classes five days a week and accommodation with a local family.

Studying in a small town has its pros and cons. On the upside, you may be the only foreigner around, so you won't be speaking any English. On the downside, Spanish may be the second language of the inhabitants of the village (including your teacher), meaning that you could pick up all sorts of bad habits.

You can start any day at many schools, any week at all of them, and study for as long as you like. All decent schools offer a variety of elective activities from salsa classes to movies to volcano hikes. Many schools offer classes in Mayan languages as well as Spanish.

Weaving

Guatemalan fabrics are famed worldwide, mostly because they are produced by a traditional method known as back strap weaving. If you'd like to learn this craft, lessons are available in San Pedro La Laguna (p143) and Quetzaltenango (p168).

CUSTOMS

Customs officers only get angry and excited about a few things: weapons, drugs and paraphernalia, large amounts of currency, and automobiles and other expensive items that might be sold while you're in the country. It is also illegal to bring fruit, vegetables or plants through the international airports at Guatemala City and Flores.

Normally customs officers won't look seriously in your luggage and may not look at all. At some border points the amount of search is inversely proportional to the amount of 'tip' you have provided: big tip no search, no tip big search.

Whatever you do, keep it formal. Anger, hostility or impoliteness can get you thrown out of the country or into jail, or worse.

DANGERS & ANNOYANCES

No one could pretend that Guatemala is a very safe country. There are just too many stories of robbery, often armed robbery, for that. Rapes and murders of tourists have also happened. The two most frequently reported types of nasty incident involving tourists are highway robbery, when a vehicle is stopped and its occupants relieved of their belongings,

GOING BACK TO SCHOOL? BETTER DO YOUR HOMEWORK

Choosing between the mass of Spanish schools in Antigua and elsewhere can be tough. Many schools don't have in-house teacher training programs, so there aren't so many 'good schools' as there are 'good teachers.' It's best to pay for as little time as possible (a week, usually) so you can change if you're really unhappy. You should be completely up-front about what your goals (conversation, grammar, vocabulary etc) are when starting, as well as any specialized interests that you have (politics, medical, legal etc) so the school can design a curriculum and assign you a teacher to best suit your needs. If you end up liking like the school, but not the teacher, ask for a new teacher as soon as possible – personality conflicts occur, and four or five hours of one-on-one with someone you don't like can soon turn into hard work.

Here are some questions to think about when you're looking at schools. Some you can find out just by turning up, some you should ask the school, others you'll have to talk to current and ex-students to get a feel for.

- Where do the classes take place – on a quiet, shaded patio or in hot classrooms with buses roaring along the street outside?
- What experience and qualifications do the teachers have in teaching Spanish as a second language?
- Is Spanish your teacher's first language?
- What afternoon and evening activities are available (many schools offer activities like salsa classes, movies and excursions – some of them free)?
- Many schools offer gimmicks to get you in, like a half hour of free internet per day, which ends up saving you around US$0.30 per day – should these little perks really sway your judgment?
- What is the general atmosphere of the school? Serious students probably won't fit in at a school whose activities include all-night bar crawls, and party animals may feel out of place at schools with names like the Christian Spanish Academy.
- Can the school provide opportunities for voluntary work in your free time – for example, assisting in local schools, visiting hospitals or playing with children at orphanages?
- If the school claims to be involved in social/community projects, is it a serious commitment, or just a marketing ploy?

and robberies on walking trails. For a scary litany of recent incidents, visit the website of Guatemala City's **US embassy** (http://guatemala .usembassy.gov) and click on 'Recent Crime Incidents Involving Foreigners.' Further, marginally less alarming, information is on the website of the **US Department of State** (http://travel .state.gov) and the website of the **UK Foreign and Commonwealth Office** (www.fco.gov.uk).

Vehicles carrying tourists, such as shuttle minibuses and buses, along heavily touristed routes seem to be a prime target for highway robbery. On this basis, some people argue that chicken buses are the most risk-free way to travel, but chicken buses are certainly not exempt from holdups. No road in the country is exempt from this risk, but those that are most frequently mentioned include the Interamericana (Hwy 1) between the Antigua and Panajachel turnoffs and near the Salva-doran border, Carretera al Pacífico (Hwy 2) near the Salvadoran and Mexican borders, and Hwy 13 between the Belizean border and the Puente Ixlú (El Cruce) junction.

Robberies against tourists on walking trails tend to occur in isolated spots on well-known walks. Some trails around the Lago de Atitlán (see p123) and on Volcán Agua outside Antigua are particularly notorious. The Tikal archaeological site, Volcán Pacaya and Cerro de la Cruz (Antigua), all the scenes of several incidents in the past, have become, for now, safer because of increased police and ranger presence designed to protect tourism.

Other potential dangers are pickpocketing, bag-snatching, bag-slitting and the like in crowded bus stations, buses, streets and markets, but also in empty, dark city streets.

It is impossible to remove the element of risk from traveling in Guatemala, but it is

DIRECTORY

possible to reduce that risk by always staying alert to the behavior of people around you (watch out for people who get unwarrantedly close to you in any situation) and by following a few simple precautions:

■ Only carry on your person the money, cards, checks and valuables that you have immediate need of. Leave the rest in a sealed, signed envelope in your hotel's safe, and obtain a receipt for the envelope. If your hotel doesn't have a safe, it is usually safer to secrete your money and valuables in three or four different stashes among your locked luggage in your room than to carry them with you.

■ Be aware that any purse or bag in plain sight may be slashed or grabbed. At ticket counters in bus stations, keep your bag between your feet.

■ Don't flaunt jewelry, cameras or valuable-looking watches. Keep your wallet or purse out of view.

■ On buses keep your important valuables with you, and keep a close hold on them.

■ Don't wander alone in empty city streets or isolated areas, particularly at night.

■ When using ATMs (cash machines), keep alert to people nearby. Don't accept help from strangers when using ATMs.

■ Keep informed by talking to travelers, hotel staff and others, and consulting official information sources such as the US and UK government websites mentioned on p311, your country's embassy in Guatemala City, and Inguat (see p76).

■ Hiking in large groups and/or with a police escort reduces the risk of robbery.

■ Resisting or trying to flee from robbers usually makes the situation worse.

Hiking on active volcanoes obviously has an element of risk. Get the latest story before you head out. In the wet season, go up volcanoes in the morning before rain and possible thunderstorms set in. A Canadian tourist was killed by lightning on Volcán Pacaya in 2002.

There have been a few bizarre incidents in which foreign visitors have been unjustly suspected of malicious designs against Guatemalan children; see the boxed text, p44. Be careful not to put yourself in any situation that might be misinterpreted.

Any crowd can be volatile, especially when drunk or at times of political tension.

Scams

One common scenario is for someone to spray ketchup or some other sticky liquid on your clothes. An accomplice then appears to help you clean up the mess and robs you in the process. Other methods of distraction, such as dropping a purse or coins, or someone appearing to faint, are also used by pickpockets and bag snatchers.

EMBASSIES & CONSULATES
Guatemalan Embassies & Consulates

You'll find a full listing of Guatemala's embassies and consulates at www.minex.gob.gt (in Spanish). The following listings are for embassies unless noted:

Australia Consulate in Sydney(☎ 02-9327 7348; 5 Weldodon Lane, Woolahra, NSW, 2025)

Canada Ottawa (☎ 613-233 7237; embguate@ottawa .net; 130 Albert St, Suite 1010, Ontario K1P 5G4)

REPORTING A CRIME

Reporting a crime is always a toss-up in Guatemala. If you're the victim of something really serious, of course you should take it to the police – the phrase you're looking for here is *'Yo quisiera denunciar un crimen'* ('I'd like to report a crime'). If you've been robbed, get a statement filed so you can show your insurance company.

If it's a minor thing, on the other hand, sometimes the police are better off avoided – sometimes their services don't come cheap.

Specially trained tourist police (often English speaking) operate in some major tourist areas – you can call them in Antigua (☎ 7832 7290) and Guatemala City (☎ 2232 0202).

Outside of those areas (and normal office hours) your best bet is to call Asistur (☎ 1500), which operates a 24-hour nationwide toll-free hotline in English and Spanish. It can give you information and assistance and help with dealing with the police and even arranging a lawyer if need be.

France Paris (☎ 01 42 27 78 63; embguafr@easynet.fr;
73 rue de Courcelles, 75008)
Germany Bonn (☎ 49-228 358609; embaguate_bonn@
compuserve.com; Zietenstrasse, 16, 5300 Bonn 2)
Ireland Contact the Guatemalan embassy in London.
Japan Tokyo (☎ 3340-1830; fax 3340-1820; 38 Kowa
Bldg, Rm 905, 4-12-24 Nishi-Azabu, 106-0031)
Mexico Mexico City (☎ 55-5540 7520; meroldan@iserve
.net.mx; Av Explanada 1025, Lomas de Chapultepec,
11000); consulate in Chetumal (☎ 983 832 30 45; Av
Independencia 326); consulate in Ciudad Hidalgo, Chiapas
(☎ 962 628 01 84; 5a Calle Oriente s/n entre 1a & 3a
Norte); consulate in Comitán, Chiapas (☎ 963 632 04 91;
fax 963 632 26 69; 1a Calle Sur Poniente 26); consulate in
Tapachula, Chiapas (☎ 962 625 63 80; 3a Av Norte 85).
There are also consulates in Puebla and Tijuana.
Netherlands Appeldoorn (☎ 31 355 74 21; PO Box
10224, 7301 GE)
New Zealand Contact the Guatemalan consulate in Sydney
Spain Madrid (☎ 913 44 14 17; embespaña@minex.gob
.gt; Calle Rafael Salgado 3, 100 derecha, 28036)
UK London (☎ 020 7351 3042; embgranbretana@minex
.gob.gt; 13 Fawcett St, SW10 9HN)
USA Washington, DC (☎ 202-745 4952/53/54; www
.guatemala-embassy.org; 2220 R St NW, 20008); consulates
in Chicago, Houston, Los Angeles (www.guatemala
-consulate.org); Miami, New York, San Francisco (www
.sfconsulguate.org)

Embassies & Consulates in Guatemala

All the following are embassies in Guatemala
City:
Belize (☎ 2367 3883; embelguate@yahoo.com; 5a Av
5-55, Zona 14, Europlaza 2, Office 1502)
Canada (☎ 2363 4348; gtmla@international.gc.ca; 8th
fl, Edificio Edyma Plaza, 13a Calle 8-44, Zona 10)
El Salvador (☎ 2360 7660; emsalva@intel.net.gt; Av Las
Américas 16-46, Zona 13)
France (☎ 2421 7370; www.ambafrance.org.gt; 5a Av
8-59, Zona 14)
Germany (☎ 2364 6700; embalemana@intelnet.net.gt;
Edificio Plaza Marítima, 20a Calle 6-20, Zona 10)
Honduras (☎ 2366 5640; embhond@intelnet.net.gt;
19a Av A 20-19, Zona 10)
Mexico (☎ 2420 3400; 2a Av 7-57, Zona 10)
Spain (☎ 2379 3530; embaespa@terra.com.gt.es; 6a
Calle 6-48, Zona 9)
UK (☎ 2367 5425/6/7/8/9; embassy@intelnett.com; 11th
fl, Torre Internacional, 16a Calle 00-55, Zona 10)
USA (☎ 2326 4000; www.usembassy.state.gov/guatemala;
Av La Reforma 7-01, Zona 10)

FESTIVALS & EVENTS

The following events are of national significance in Guatemala.

January
El Cristo de Esquipulas On January 15 this festival in
Esquipulas brings pilgrims from all over Central America for
a glimpse of the Black Jesus housed in the Basilica.

March/April
Semana Santa Easter week – the week leading up to
Easter Sunday – sees statues of Jesus and Mary carried
around the streets of towns all round the country,
followed by devout, sometimes fervent crowds, to mark
Christ's crucifixion. The processions walk over and destroy
alfombras, elaborate carpets of colored sawdust and flower
petals. The week peaks on Good Friday.

August
Fiesta de la Virgen de la Asunción Peaking on
August 15, this fiesta is celebrated with folk dances
and parades in Tactic, Sololá, Guatemala City and
Jocotenango.

November
Día de Todos los Santos All Saints' Day, November
1, sees giant kite festivals in Santiago Sacatepéquez and
Sumpango, near Antigua, and the renowned drunken horse
races in Todos Santos Cuchumatán.

December
Quema del Diablo On December 7 the Burning of the
Devil starts at around 6pm throughout the country when
everyone takes to the streets with their old garbage,
physical and psychic, to stoke huge bonfires of trash. This is
followed by impressive fireworks displays.

FOOD

See the Food & Drink chapter (p55) for the
lowdown on what you can eat where and when
and what it will cost. Where we have divided
city eating sections into different price ranges,
you can expect a main dish to cost under US$5
in a budget eatery, US$5 to US$9 in the midrange and more than US$9 in the top end.

GAY & LESBIAN TRAVELERS

Few places in Latin America are outwardly
gay-friendly, and Guatemala is no different.
Technically, homosexuality is legal for persons 18 years and older, but the reality can be
another story, with harassment and violence
against gays too often poisoning the plot.
Don't even consider testing the tolerance
for homosexual public displays of affection
here.

Though Antigua has a palatable – if sub-
dued – scene, affection and action are still
kept behind closed doors; the chief exception

is the gay-friendly club La Casbah (p115). In Guatemala City, Genetic and Ephebus are the current faves (see p89). Mostly, though, gays traveling in Guatemala will find themselves keeping it low-key and pushing the twin beds together.

The websites of the **Gully** (www.thegully.com) and **Gay.com** (www.gay.com) have some articles and information relevant to Guatemala. The best site, **Gay Guatemala** (www.gayguatemala.com), is in Spanish.

HOLIDAYS

The main Guatemalan holiday periods are Semana Santa, Christmas–New Year and July and August. During Semana Santa room prices rise in many places and it's advisable to book all accommodation and transport in advance.

Guatemalan public holidays include the following:

New Year's Day (Año Nuevo) January 1
Easter (Semana Santa; Holy Thursday to Easter Sunday inclusive) March/April
Labor Day (Día del Trabajo) May 1
Army Day (Día del Ejército) June 30
Assumption Day (Día de la Asunción) August 15
Independence Day (Día de la Independencia) September 15
Revolution Day (Día de la Revolución) October 20
All Saints' Day (Día de Todos los Santos) November 1
Christmas Eve afternoon (Víspera Navidad) December 24
Christmas Day (Navidad) December 25
New Year's Eve afternoon (Víspera de Año Nuevo) December 31

INSURANCE

Signing up for a travel insurance policy to cover theft, loss and medical problems is a good idea. Some policies specifically exclude dangerous activities, which can include scuba diving, motorcycling, even trekking.

You may prefer a policy that pays doctors or hospitals directly, rather than your having to pay on the spot and claim later. If you have to claim later, ensure you keep all documentation.

Check that the policy covers ambulances or an emergency flight home.

For more information on insurance, see p322 and p326.

INTERNET ACCESS

Most travelers make constant use of internet cafés and free web-based email such as Yahoo (www.yahoo.com) or **Hotmail** (www.hotmail .com). Most medium-size towns have cybercafés with fairly reliable connections. Internet cafés typically charge between US$0.50 and US$1 an hour.

To access your own specific account, you'll need to know your incoming (POP or IMAP) mail server name, your account name and your password. Get these from your internet service provider (ISP) or network supervisor.

If you're traveling with a notebook or handheld computer, be aware that your modem may not work once you leave home. The safest option is to buy a reputable 'global' modem before you leave home, or buy a local PC-card modem if you're spending an extended time in any one country. A second issue is the plug: Guatemala uses 110V, two-pronged, flat plugs like those found in the US. A third issue is that unless you're sporting a completely wireless system, you'll have to hunt down a hotel room with a phone jack to plug into – or find a jack somewhere else.

If you really want to travel with a laptop, consider using a local ISP, unless you use an international server with access numbers in Guatemala such as AOL or CompuServe. A good bet for a Guatemalan ISP is Conexion in Antigua (see p99), which charges US$7.75/18/36/62 for five/24/72/unlimited hours online a month, plus a US$3.25 setup fee.

For more information on traveling with a portable computer, see www.roadnews.com. See p22 for a few Guatemala-related websites to start on.

LEGAL MATTERS

Police officers in Guatemala are sometimes part of the problem rather than the solution. The less you have to do with the law, the better.

Whatever you do, don't get involved in any way with illegal drugs: don't buy or sell, use or carry, or associate with people who do – even if the locals seem to do so freely. As a foreigner, you are at a distinct disadvantage, and you may be set up by others. Drug laws in Guatemala are strict, and though enforcement may be uneven, penalties are severe. If you do get caught buying, selling, holding or using drugs, your best first defense might be to suggest that you and the officer 'work things out.'

MAPS

International Travel Maps' *Guatemala* (1:500,000) is overall the best country map for travelers, costing around US$10 in Guatemala. The cheaper *Mapa Turístico Guatemala,* produced locally by Intelimapas, tends to be the most up to date on the state of Guatemala's roads, many of which have been newly paved in recent years. It also includes plans of many cities. Inguat's *Mapa Vial Turístico* is another worthwhile map. Bookstores that sell these maps can be found in Guatemala City (p71), Antigua (p99), Panajachel (p128) and Quetzaltenango (p161). For 1:50,000 and 1:250,000 topographical sheets of all parts of Guatemala, head to the Instituto Geográfico Nacional (p71).

MONEY

Guatemala's currency, the quetzal (ket-*sahl,* abbreviated to Q), is fairly stable at around Q7.5 = US$1. The quetzal is divided into 100 centavos. For exchange rates, see the inside front cover; for information on costs in Guatemala, see p19.

You'll find ATMs (cash machines, *cajeros automáticos*) for Visa/Plus System cards in all but the smallest towns, and there are MasterCard/Cirrus ATMs in many places too, so one of these cards is the best basis for your supplies of cash in Guatemala. In addition, many banks give cash advances on Visa cards, and some on MasterCard. And you can pay for many purchases with these cards or with American Express (Amex) cards.

If you don't have one of these cards, a combination of Amex US-dollar traveler's checks and a limited amount of cash US dollars is the way to go. Take some of these as a backup even if you do have a card. Banks all over the country change cash US dollars, and many of them also change US-dollar traveler's checks too. Amex is easily the most recognized traveler's check brand.

In many places you can make payments with cash dollars, and a few places will accept traveler's checks. Currencies other than the US dollar are virtually useless in any form, although a small handful of places will now change cash euros.

Banks generally give the best exchange rates on both cash and traveler's checks. If you can't find an open bank you can often change cash (and occasionally checks) in travel agencies, hotels or shops.

Some towns suffer from change shortages: always try to carry a stash of small bills.

See p310 for security tips about your money.

Tipping

A 10% tip is expected at restaurants and automatically added to your bill in places like Antigua. In small *comedors* (basic, cheap eateries) tipping is optional, but follow the local practice of leaving some spare change. Tour guides are generally tipped, around 10%, especially on longer trips.

PHOTOGRAPHY & VIDEO

Ubiquitous film stores and pharmacies sell film, though you may not find the brand you like without a hunt. A 36-exposure, 100-ASA print film normally costs around US$4. There are quick processing labs in the main cities. Internet cafés in well-touristed areas have card readers *(lectores de tarjeta)*, so you can upload your digital photos or burn them onto CD.

Photographing People

Photography is a sensitive subject in Guatemala. Always ask permission before taking portraits, especially of Mayan women and children. Don't be surprised if your request is denied. Indigenous children often request payment (usually Q1) in return for posing. In certain places, such as the church of Santo Tomás in Chichicastenango, photography is forbidden. Mayan ceremonies (should you be so lucky to witness one) are off limits for photography unless you are given explicit permission to take pictures. If local people make any sign of being offended, you should put your camera away and apologize immediately, both out of decency and for your own safety. Never take photos of army installations, men with guns or other sensitive military subjects.

POST

The Guatemalan postal service was privatized in 1999. Generally, letters take eight to 10 days to travel to the US and Canada and 10 to 12 days to reach Europe. Almost all cities and towns (but not villages) have a post office where you can buy stamps and send mail. A letter sent to North America costs around US$0.40 and to anywhere else around US$0.50.

The Guatemalan mail system no longer holds poste restante or general delivery mail. The easiest and most reliable way to receive mail is through a private address. Language schools and some hotels will be happy to do this. If you want to get a package couriered to you, it's best to make sure the courier company has an office in the town where you are staying, otherwise you will be charged some hefty 'handling fees' along with taxes, etc.

SHOPPING
Bargaining
Be aware that bargaining is essential in some situations and not done in others. It's standard practice when buying handicrafts: the first price you're told may be double or triple what the seller really expects. Remember that bargaining is not a fight to the death. The object is to arrive at a price agreeable to both you and the seller, thereby creating a win-win situation.

Coffee
Although most of Guatemala's finest beans are exported, some are (thankfully) held back for the tourist trade. To ensure you're getting the finest, freshest coffee beans available, visit a coffee farm and/or roaster and buy from them directly. Cobán and Antigua produce some of the world's greatest coffee and both towns support growers and roasters. For more on coffee and fair trade, see p217 and p220.

Jade
Beloved of the ancient Maya, jade is mined in Guatemala today and you'll find it both as jewelry and as miniature sculpture. For more on jade, see p116.

Leather Goods
Guatemala has some terrific leather goods. Fine briefcases, duffel bags, backpacks and belts are sold in most handicrafts markets. Cowboy boots and hats are a specialty in some areas, and custom work is welcome – the best place to head for is the village of Pastores just outside of Antigua. The prices and craftsmanship of these items are usually phenomenal.

Shipping
It's best to use an international shipping service if you want to ensure the relatively safe, timely arrival of your goods. You'll find information on such courier services in this book's city sections, under Post. A 1kg package sent from Antigua to California by UPS, for example, will cost you up to US$218 for express (two-day) service. See www.ups.com for more information.

Textiles
Guatemala's intricate and brilliantly colored textiles are world famous. Weaving is a traditional and thriving art of the Maya here. Clothing – especially the beautiful embroidered *huipiles* (tunics), *cortes* (skirts) and *fajas* (belts) of the Mayan women – as well as purses, tablecloths, blankets, hacky-sacks and many other woven items, are ubiquitous and good value, some for practical use, some more for souvenirs.

The largest crafts markets are the Thursday and Sunday markets in Chichicastenango, the permanent stalls lining Calle Santander in Panajachel, Mercado Central and Mercado de Artesanías in Guatemala City, and the Mercado de Artesanías in Antigua. Fine textiles of an infinite variety are also available in Antigua's shops. Elsewhere, in places such as Nebaj, Sololá, Santa Catarina Palopó, Santiago Atitlán and Todos Santos Cuchumatán, you can obtain local textiles at weekly markets or a few permanent stalls.

Wooden Masks
Ceremonial masks are fascinating, eye-catching and still in regular use. In Chichicastenango you can visit the artists in their *morerías* (workshops).

SOLO TRAVELERS
On your own, you need to be even more alert to what's going on around you than other travelers, and you need to be more cautious about where you go.

Guatemala is a pretty good place for meeting people, both locals and other travelers. Language schools, group tours, volunteer work, dormitory accommodations and sociable lodgings where everyone eats together are just a few of the situations where travelers are thrown together with other people.

Since single rooms cost more per person than doubles and triples, solo travelers face higher accommodation costs than others unless they sleep in dormitories (available in a number of places) or find others to share with.

TELEPHONE
Guatemala has no area or city codes. Calling from other countries, you just dial the international access code (☎ 00 in most countries), then the Guatemala country code (☎ 502),

then the eight-digit local number. Calling within Guatemala, just dial the eight-digit local number. The international access code from Guatemala is ☎ 00.

Many towns and cities frequented by tourists have privately run call offices where you can make local and international calls for reasonable rates. If the telephone connection is by internet, the rates can be very cheap (US$0.15 a minute to the USA, US$0.30 to Europe), but line quality is unpredictable.

A number of companies provide public phone services. The most common street phones, found all over Guatemala, are those of Telgua, for which you need to buy a Telgua phone card *(tarjeta telefónica de Telgua)* from shops, kiosks and the like. Card sales points may advertise the fact with red signs saying *'Ladatel de Venta Aquí.'* The cards come in denominations of Q20, Q30 and Q50: you slot them into a Telgua phone, dial your number, and the display will tell you how much time you have left. The second most common street phones are those of Telefónica, which require a Telefónica card, also sold by shops and kiosks. Telefónica cards are not meant to be inserted into the phone, but simply bear codes to be keyed in and instructions to be followed. Telgua is cheaper than Telefónica for local calls (about US$0.01 per minute against US$0.05) and for calls to Europe (about US$1 a minute against US$1.60), but Telefónica is cheaper for calls to the USA (about US$0.20 a minute against US$0.50 with Telgua).

Unless it's an emergency, don't use the black phones placed strategically in tourist towns that say 'Press 2 to call the United States free!' This is a bait and switch scam; you put the call on your credit card and return home to find you have paid between US$8 and US$20 per minute.

Telgua street phones bear instructions to dial ☎ 147110 for domestic collect calls and ☎ 147120 for international collect calls. The latter number is usually successful for the USA and Canada, less so for the rest of the world.

Cell phones are widely used. It is possible to bring your cell phone, have it 'unlocked' for use in Guatemala then substitute your SIM card for a local one. This works on some phones and not others and there doesn't appear to be a logic behind it. This, and the possibility of theft (cell phones, particularly high-end ones from overseas, are a pickpocket's delight) makes most people either rent in the long term, or buy a cheap prepaid phone on arrival.

Prepaid phones are available pretty much everywhere and cost around US$25, often coming with US$15 or so in free calls. Cards to restock the credit on your phone are on sale in nearly every corner store. Calls cost US$0.15 per minute anywhere in the country, the same for the US (depending on the company you're with) and up to five times that for the rest of the world.

At the time of writing, Movistar had the cheapest rates (with coverage limited to major cities) and Tigo and Claro had the best coverage.

If you want to rent a phone, try Guatemala Ventures in Antigua (p100) or Xela Pages in Quetzaltenango (p162).

TIME

North American Central Standard Time (GMT/UTC minus six hours) is the basis of time in Guatemala. At the time of writing, daylight saving time was being trialed in Guatemala. From the end of March to the end of September, clocks are put forward one hour. You should bear in mind that, rural folks being somewhat independent types, the daylight savings concept has yet to catch on in many villages, meaning that there is a dual time system running – the *hora ofical* (official time) and the *hora de Dios* (God's time) – and it's always best to check which one people are referring to.

The 24-hour clock is often used, so 1pm may be written as 13 or 1300. When it's noon in Guatemala, it's 1pm in New York, 6pm in London, 10am in San Francisco and 4am next day in Sydney (add one hour to those times during daylight saving).

TOILETS

You cannot throw anything into Guatemalan toilets, including toilet paper. For this reason, bathrooms are equipped with some sort of receptacle (usually a small wastebasket) for soiled paper. Toilet paper is not always provided, so always carry some. If you don't have any and need some, asking a restaurant worker for *un rollo de papel* (a roll of paper), accompanied by a panicked facial expression, usually produces fast results.

Public toilets are few and far between. Use the ones at cafés, restaurants, your hotel and the archaeological sites. At bus stations you can pay US$0.15 to use the toilets in bus company offices. Buses rarely have toilets on board.

TOURIST INFORMATION

Guatemala's national tourism institute, **Inguat** (www.visitguatemala.com), has information offices in Guatemala City, Antigua, Panajachel, Quetzaltenango and Santa Elena airport; a few other towns have departmental, municipal or private-enterprise tourist information offices. See city sections for details. **Asistur** (www.asisturcard.com), a joint private-government initiative, operates a 24-hour toll free advice and assistance hotline on ☎ 1500.

The Guatemalan embassies in the US, Germany, France, Italy, Spain and the UK can provide some tourist information. From the US you can call Inguat toll-free at ☎ 800 464 8281.

TRAVELERS WITH DISABILITIES

Guatemala is not the easiest country to negotiate with a disability.

Although many sidewalks in Antigua have ramps and cute little inlaid tiles depicting a wheelchair, the streets are cobblestone, so the ramps are anything but smooth and the streets worse!

Many hotels in Guatemala are old converted houses with rooms around a courtyard; such rooms are wheelchair accessible. The most expensive hotels have facilities such as ramps, elevators and accessible toilets. Transportation is the biggest hurdle for travelers with limited mobility: travelers in a wheelchair may consider renting a car and driver as the buses will prove especially challenging due to lack of space.

Mobility International USA (www.miusa.org) advises disabled travelers on mobility issues, runs exchange programs (including in Guatemala) and publishes some useful books. Also worth consulting are **Access-Able Travel Source** (www.access-able.com) and **Accessible Journeys** (www.disabilitytravel.com).

Transitions (☎ 832-4261; transitions@guate.net; Colonia Candelaría 80, Antigua) is an organization aiming to increase awareness and access for disabled persons in Guatemala.

VISAS

Citizens of the US, Canada, EU countries, Norway, Switzerland, Australia, New Zealand, Israel and Japan are among those who do not need visas for tourist visits to Guatemala. On entry into Guatemala you will normally be given a 90-day stay. (The number 90 will be written in the stamp in your passport.)

In August of 2006 Guatemala joined the Centro America 4 (CA-4), a trading agreement with Nicaragua, Honduras and El Salvador. Designed to facilitate the movement of people and goods around the region, it has one major effect on foreign visitors – upon entry to the CA-4 region, travelers are given a 90-day stay *for the entire region*. This can be extended *once* at the **Departamento de Extranjería** (Foreigners' Office; ☎ 2411 2411; 6a Av 3-11, Zona 4, Guatemala City; ⊙ 8am-2:30pm Mon-Fri). For an extension take with you *one* of the following:

- A credit card with a photocopy of both of its sides.
- An airline ticket out of Guatemala with a photocopy.
- US$500 worth of traveler's checks.

The extension will normally be issued in the afternoon of the working day after the day you apply.

Citizens of some Eastern European countries are among those who do need visas to visit Guatemala. Inquire at a Guatemalan embassy well in advance of travel.

Visa regulations are subject to change and it's always worth checking them with a Guatemalan embassy before you go.

If you have been in the CA-4 for your original 90 days and a 90-day extension, you must leave the region for 72 hours (Belize and Mexico are the most obvious, easiest options), after which you can return to the region to start the process all over again. Some foreigners have been repeating this cycle for years.

WOMEN TRAVELERS

Women should encounter no special problems traveling in Guatemala. In fact, solo women will be pleasantly surprised by how gracious and helpful most locals are. The primary thing you can do to make it easy for yourself while traveling here is to dress modestly. Modesty in dress is highly regarded, and if you practice it, you will usually be treated with respect.

Specifically, shorts should be worn only at the beach, not in town, and especially not in the Highlands. Skirts should be at or below the knee. Wear a bra, as going braless is considered provocative. Many local women swim with T-shirts over their swimsuits; in places where they do this, you may want to follow suit to avoid stares.

VOLUNTEERING: OUR TOP PICKS

There's a wealth of volunteering opportunities in Guatemala. A lot of them center on education and environmental issues. Here are a few off-beat ones that may appeal:

AIDG (www.aidg.org) Works with Guatemalan engineering students to make renewable energy solutions from recycled materials.

Ak' Tenamit (www.aktenamit.org) A grassroots organization working to promote ecotourism around the Río Dulce area.

Arcas (www.arcasguatemala.com) Works to protect the endangered sea turtle population on the southern coast. Also has projects in El Petén.

Entre Mundos (www.entremundos.org) Produces a bi-monthly newspaper and acts as a bridge between volunteers and NGOs.

Ix Canaan (www.ixcanaan.org) A community library and literacy project in El Remate in El Petén.

Proyecto Payaso (www.proyectopayaso.org) A traveling clown troupe specializing in community AIDS awareness and education.

Safe Passage (www.safepassage.org) Provides education, health care and opportunities for kids working scavenging in Guatemala City garbage dumps.

Women traveling alone can expect plenty of attempts by men to talk to them. Often the men are just curious and not out for a foreign conquest. It is, of course, up to you how to respond, but there's no need to be intimidated. Consider the situation and circumstances (on a bus is one thing, on a barstool another) and stay confident. Try to sit next to women or children on the bus if that makes you more comfortable. Local women rarely initiate conversations, but usually have lots of interesting things to say once the ball is rolling.

Nasty rumors about Western women kidnapping Guatemalan children for a variety of sordid ends have all but died down. Still, women travelers should be cautious around children, especially indigenous kids, lest misunderstandings occur.

While there's no need to be paranoid, the possibility of rape and assault does exist. Use your normal traveler's caution – avoid walking alone in isolated places or through city streets late at night, and skip hitchhiking.

WORK

Some travelers find work in bars, restaurants and places to stay in Antigua, Panajachel or Quetzaltenango, but the wages are just survival pay. If you're looking to crew a yacht, there's always work being offered around the Río Dulce area, sometimes for short trips, sometimes to the States and further afield. Check notice boards (Bruno's, p253, has the best one) for details.

Volunteering

If you really want to get to the heart of Guatemalan matters and you've altruistic leanings, consider volunteer work. It's rewarding and exposes foreigners to the local culture typically out of reach for the average traveler. Opportunities abound, from caring for abandoned animals and kids to writing grant applications to tending fields. Travelers with specific skills such as nurses, doctors, teachers and website designers are particularly encouraged to investigate volunteering in Guatemala.

Most volunteer posts require basic or better Spanish skills and a minimum time commitment. Depending on the position and the organization, you may have to pay for room and board for the duration of your stay. Before making a commitment, you may want to talk to past volunteers and read the fine print associated with the position.

Four excellent sources of information on volunteer opportunities are Proyecto Mosaico Guatemala and AmeriSpan Guatemala, both in Antigua (see p101), and EntreMundos and Guatemaya Intercultural, both based in Quetzaltenango (see p168). You only have to visit the websites of Entremundos or Proyecto Mosaico to realize what a huge range of volunteer action is happening in Guatemala. Many language schools have close links to volunteer projects and can introduce you to the world of volunteering. Well-established volunteer organizations include Tortugario Monterrico and Reserva Natural Hawaii, Casa Guatemala, Arcas and Estación Biológica Las Guacamayas.

Transportation

TRANSPORTATION (sidebar)

THINGS CHANGE...

The information in this chapter is particularly vulnerable to change. Check directly with the airline or a travel agent to make sure you understand how a fare (and ticket you may buy) works and be aware of the security requirements for international travel. Shop carefully. The details given in this chapter should be regarded as pointers and are not a substitute for your own careful, up-to-date research.

GETTING THERE & AWAY

ENTERING THE COUNTRY

When you enter Guatemala, by land, air, sea or river, you should simply have to fill out straightforward immigration and customs forms. In the normal course of things you should not have to pay a cent.

However, immigration officials sometimes request unofficial fees from travelers. To determine whether these are legitimate, you can ask for *un recibo* (a receipt). You may find that the fee is dropped. When in doubt, try to observe what, if anything, other travelers are paying before it's your turn.

To enter Guatemala, you need a valid passport. For information on visas, see p318.

AIR
Airports & Airlines

Guatemala City's Aeropuerto La Aurora (GUA) is the country's major international airport. The only other airport with international flights (from Cancún, Mexico and Belize City) is Flores (FRS). The Guatemalan national airline, Aviateca, is part of the regional Grupo TACA, along with El Salvador's TACA, Costa Rica's Lacsa and Nicaragua's Nica. The US Federal Aviation Administration has assessed Guatemala's and El Salvador's civil aviation authorities as Category 2, which means they are not in compliance with international aviation safety standards.

Airlines flying to and from Guatemala:
American Airlines (AA; ☎ 2260 6550; www.aa.com; hub Dallas & Miami)
Aviateca See Grupo TACA.
Continental Airlines (CO; ☎ 2385 9601; www.continental.com; hub Houston)
Copa Airlines (CM; ☎ 2385 5555; www.copaair.com; hub Panama City)
Cubana (CU; ☎ 2367 2288/89/90; www.cubana.cu; hub Havana)
Delta Air Lines (DL; ☎ 1 800 300 0005; www.delta.com; hub Atlanta)
Grupo TACA (TA; ☎ 2260 6497; www.taca.com; hub San Salvador)
Iberia (IB; ☎ 2260 6337; www.iberia.com; hub Madrid)
Inter See Grupo TACA.
Lacsa See Grupo TACA.
Maya Island Air (MW; ☎ 7926 3386; www.mayaairways.com; hub Belize City)
Mexicana (MX; ☎ 2260 6335; www.mexicana.com; hub Mexico City)
TACA See Grupo TACA.
Tropic Air (PM; ☎ 7926 0348; www.tropicair.com; hub Belize City)
United Airlines (UA; ☎ 2336 9900; www.united.com; hub Los Angeles)

From Guatemala

The best place to buy flight tickets out of Guatemala is Antigua, which has many agencies offering good fares (see p100). Some agencies also issue the student, youth and teacher cards needed to obtain the best fares.

From Australia & New Zealand

The cheapest routings usually go via the USA (often Los Angeles). Many Australasians visiting Guatemala are doing so as part of a longer trip through Latin America, so the most suitable ticket might be an open-jaw (into one city, out of another) or even a round-the-world ticket. From Sydney, you'll pay approximately A$2700 return to Guatemala City via LA or San Francisco.

The following are well-known agents for cheap fares, with branches throughout Australia and New Zealand:

Flight Centre Australia (☎ 133 133; www.flightcentre.com .au); New Zealand (☎ 09 355 7550; www.flight centre.co.nz)
STA Travel Australia (☎ 134 782; www.statravel.com.au); New Zealand (☎ 0800 474 400; www.statravel.co.nz).

From Canada

There are no direct flights. Routings are usually via the USA. Montreal to Guatemala City costs in the region of C$900 return. **Travel Cuts** (☎ 1 866 246 9762; www.travelcuts.com) is Canada's national student travel agency. For online bookings try www.expedia.ca and www.travelocity.ca.

From Central America & Cuba

Grupo TACA flies from San Salvador (economy return fare US$300 to US$400); Tegucigalpa, Honduras (US$330) via San Pedro Sula; Managua, Nicaragua (US$395); and San José, Costa Rica (US$310 to US$370). Copa flies direct from Panama City (US$285), and from San José (US$200). United Airlines also flies from San José to Guatemala City. Cubana flies twice weekly to/from Havana. Return fares cost around US$410.

From Europe

Iberia is the only airline flying direct from Europe to Guatemala at the time of writing (with a stop in Miami), and the cheapest fares from many European cities are usually with Iberia via Madrid. Depending on the season, you can expect to pay from £800 (round-trip) from London and from €950 to €1200 from Frankfurt.

Recommended UK ticket agencies include the following:

Journey Latin America (☎ 020 8747 3108; www .journeylatinamerica.co.uk)
STA Travel (☎ 0870 160 0599; www.statravel.co.uk) For travelers under the age of 26.

For online bookings try www.dialaflight.com or www.lastminute.com.

From Mexico

Grupo TACA and Mexicana both fly daily direct between Mexico City and Guatemala City, with round-trip fares starting around

---

CLIMATE CHANGE & TRAVEL

Climate change is a serious threat to the ecosystems that humans rely upon, and air travel is the fastest-growing contributor to the problem. Lonely Planet regards travel, overall, as a global benefit, but believes we all have a responsibility to limit our personal impact on global warming.

Flying & Climate Change

Pretty much every form of motorized travel generates CO_2 (the main cause of human-induced climate change) but planes are far and away the worst offenders, not just because of the sheer distances they allow us to travel, but because they release greenhouse gases high into the atmosphere. The statistics are frightening: two people taking a return flight between Europe and the US will contribute as much to climate change as an average household's gas and electricity consumption over a whole year.

Carbon Offset Schemes

Climatecare.org and other websites use 'carbon calculators' that allow travelers to offset the level of greenhouse gases they are responsible for with financial contributions to sustainable travel schemes that reduce global warming – including projects in India, Honduras, Kazakhstan and Uganda.

Lonely Planet, together with Rough Guides and other concerned partners in the travel industry, support the carbon offset scheme run by climatecare.org. Lonely Planet offsets all of its staff and author travel.

For more information check out our website: lonelyplanet.com.

US$430. Inter, part of Grupo TACA, flies most days from Guatemala City to Flores to Cancún and back. Round-trip fares from Cancún to Flores/Guatemala City are US$342/334.

From South America

Lacsa (with transfers in San José, Costa Rica) and Copa (with transfers in Panama City) both fly to Guatemala City from Bogotá, Caracas, Quito and Lima.

From the USA

Nonstop flights to Guatemala City arrive from Atlanta (US$800) with Delta; from Dallas with American; from Houston (US$390) with Continental; from Los Angeles (US$825) with United and Grupo TACA; from Miami (US$680) with American, Grupo TACA and Iberia; and from New York (US$600) with American and Grupo TACA.

The following websites are recommended for online bookings:

- www.cheaptickets.com
- www.expedia.com
- www.lowestfare.com
- www.orbitz.com
- www.sta.com

DEPARTURE TAX

Guatemala levies a departure tax of US$30 on outbound air passengers. This has to be paid in cash US dollars or quetzals at the airline check-in desk.

LAND

Bus is the most common way to enter Guatemala, though you can also do so by car, river or sea. It's advisable to get through all borders as early in the day as possible. Onward transportation tends to wind down in the afternoon and border areas are not always the safest places to hang around late. You'll find more detail on the services mentioned here in the destination sections of this book. There is no departure tax when you leave Guatemala by land.

Car & Motorcycle

The mountain of paperwork and liability involved in driving into Guatemala deters most travelers. You will need the following documents, all clear and consistent, to enter Guatemala with a car:

- current and valid registration
- proof of ownership (if you don't own the car, you'll need a notarized letter of authorization from the owner that you are allowed to take it)
- your current and valid driver's license or an International Driving Permit (IDP), issued by the automobile association in your home country
- temporary import permit available free at the border and good for a maximum 30 days.

Insurance from foreign countries is not recognized by Guatemala, forcing you to purchase a policy locally. Most border posts and nearby towns have offices selling liability policies. To deter foreigners from selling cars in Guatemala, the authorities make you exit the country with the vehicle you used to enter it. Do not be the designated driver when crossing borders if you don't own the car, because you and it will not be allowed to leave Guatemala without each other.

From Belize

The border is at Benque Viejo del Carmen/ Melchor Mencos. **Línea Dorada/Mundo Maya** (☎ 7926 3649; Playa Sur, Flores) runs two direct daily buses from Belize City to Flores (US$15.50, four to five hours) and back. **San Juan Travel** (☎ 7926 0041; sanjuant@internetdetelgua.com.gt; Flores Map p276; Playa Sur; Santa Elena Map p275; 2a Calle) also covers this route daily. Otherwise, buses depart Belize City for Benque (US$4 to US$6, three hours) and vice versa about every half-hour from 11am to 4pm. Buses and minibuses run between Melchor Mencos and Flores (US$3 to US$3.50, two hours). There are also a few buses daily between Melchor Mencos and Guatemala City via Poptún and Río Dulce.

From El Salvador

There are road borders at La Hachadura/ Ciudad Pedro de Alvarado on the Carretera al Pacífico (Hwy 2), Las Chinamas/Valle Nuevo (Hwy 8), San Cristóbal/San Cristóbal (Interamericana Hwy, or Hwy 1) and Anguiatú/ Anguiatú (Hwy 10). Several companies run buses between San Salvador and Guatemala City, taking five to six hours and costing from US$8 to US$45 depending on the service. One of them, Tica Bus, has buses between San Salvador and all other Central American capitals except Belize City. Crossing at the other border points is usually a matter of taking one bus to the border and another onward from it.

From Honduras

The main road crossings are at Agua Caliente (between Nueva Ocotepeque, Honduras, and Esquipulas, Guatemala), El Florido (between Copán Ruinas, Honduras, and Chiquimula, Guatemala) and Corinto (between Omoa, Honduras, and Puerto Barrios, Guatemala). **Hedman Alas** (Copán Ruinas ☎ 651 4037; La Ceiba ☎ 441 5348; San Pedro Sula ☎ 557 3477; Tegucigalpa ☎ 237 7143) runs daily 1st-class buses via El Florido to Guatemala City from Tegucigalpa (US$68 one way, 11½ hours), La Ceiba (US$68, 12 hours), San Pedro Sula (US$59, eight hours) and Copán Ruinas (US$46, 4½ hours). Cheaper local transportation serves all three border points. Shuttle minibus services run between Copán Ruinas, Guatemala City and Antigua.

From Mexico

The main border points are at Ciudad Hidalgo/Ciudad Tecún Umán and Talismán/El Carmen, both near Tapachula, Mexico, and Ciudad Cuauhtémoc/La Mesilla, on the Interamericana between Comitán, Mexico, and Huehuetenango, Guatemala. All these borders are linked by plentiful buses to nearby cities within Guatemala and Mexico, and a few buses run all the way between Tapachula and Guatemala City by the Pacific Slope route through Mazatenango and Escuintla. There are also direct buses between Guatemala City and all three border points. **Línea Dorada/Mundo Maya** (☎ 7926 3649; Playa Sur, Flores) runs two direct daily buses from Chetumal, Mexico, to Flores (US$25, seven to eight hours) and back, via Belize City. **San Juan Travel** (☎ 7926 0041; sanjuant@internetdetelgua.com.gt; Flores Map p276 Playa Sur; Santa Elena Map p275 2a Calle) also covers this route daily for US$28.

See p281 for information on routes between Mexico and Guatemala's Petén department.

RIVER

Autotransportes Río Chancalá (5 de Mayo 120, Palenque) and **Transportes Montebello** (Calle Velasco Suárez, Palenque) run from Palenque, Mexico, to Frontera Corozal (US$5, three to four hours) on the Río Usumacinta, which divides Mexico from Guatemala. Boats across the river to Guatemala cost US$0.80 per person to La Técnica (five minutes) and US$5 to US$7 per person to Bethel (40 minutes). From La Técnica buses leave for Flores at 4am and 11am (US$6, five to six hours); from Bethel, buses leave for Flores at 5am, noon, 2pm and 4pm (US$4, four hours). Travel agencies in Palenque and Flores offer bus-boat-bus packages between the two places for US$30 to US$35. If you're making this trip it's well worth the time and expense of detouring to the outstanding Mayan ruins at Yaxchilán, near Frontera Corozal; packages incorporating this are available too.

There are other river routes from Mexico into Guatemala's Petén department: up the Río de la Pasión from Benemérito de las Américas, south of Frontera Corozal, to Sayaxché; and up the Río San Pedro from La Palma, Tabasco, to El Naranjo. There are no reliable passenger services along either river, however. You may have to hire your own boat, which can be expensive. Both Sayaxché and El Naranjo have bus and minibus connections with Flores. La Palma has transport from Tenosique, and Benemérito has good bus and minibus connections with Palenque.

SEA

Exotic Travel (☎ 7947 0048; www.bluecaribbeanbay.com) operates boat and minibus packages to and from La Ceiba in Honduras (US$35) and Punta Gorda in Belize (US$20, 1¼ hours) every Tuesday and Friday. **Transportes El Chato** (☎ 9948 5525) operates a daily boat to and from Punta Gorda in Belize (US$18, one hour). The Punta Gorda services connect with bus services to/from Belize City.

There is a US$10 departure tax when leaving Guatemala by sea.

GETTING AROUND

AIR

At the time of writing the only scheduled internal flights were between Guatemala City and Flores, a route operated daily by TACA with one-way/return fares costing around US$130/200. For further details, see p90.

BICYCLE

Bike rentals are available in a few places: the most professional outfits include Old Town Outfitters and Guatemala Ventures/Mayan

Bike Tours in Antigua (p105), and Vrisa Bookshop in Quetzaltenango (p168).

BOAT

The Caribbean town of Lívingston is only reachable by boat, across the Bahía de Amatique from Puerto Barrios or down the Río Dulce from the town of Río Dulce – great trips both. In Lago de Atitlán fast fiberglass launches zip across the waters between villages.

BUS, MINIBUS & PICKUP

Buses go almost everywhere in Guatemala. Guatemala's buses will leave you with some of your most vivid memories of the country. Most of them are ancient school buses from the US and Canada. It is not unusual for a local family of five to squeeze into seats that were originally designed for two child-sized bottoms. Many travelers know these vehicles as chicken buses, after the live cargo accompanying many passengers. They are frequent, crowded and cheap. Expect to pay US$1 (or less!) for an hour of travel.

Chicken buses will stop anywhere, for anyone. Helpers will yell '*hay lugares!*' (eye loo-*gar*-ays), which literally means 'there are places.' Never mind that the space they refer to may be no more than a sliver of air between hundreds of locals mashed against one another. These same helpers will also yell their bus's destination in voices of varying hilarity and cadence; just listen for the song of your town. Tall travelers will be especially challenged on these buses. To catch a chicken bus, simply stand beside the road with your arm out parallel to the ground.

Some routes, especially between big cities, are served by more comfortable buses with the luxury of one seat per person. The best buses are labeled *pullman, especial* or *primera clase*. Occasionally, these may have bathrooms, televisions and even food service.

In general, more buses leave in the morning (some leave as early as 3am) than the afternoon. Bus traffic drops off precipitously after about 4pm; night buses are rare and not generally recommended. An exception is Línea Dorada's overnight *de lujo* from Guatemala City to Flores, which has not experienced (to our knowledge) any trouble of note in several years (we hope we're not tempting fate here).

Distances in Guatemala are not huge and you won't often ride for more than four hours at a time. On a typical four-hour bus trip you'll cover 175km to 200km for US$5 to US$6.

For a few of the better services you can buy tickets in advance, and this is generally worth doing as it ensures that you get a place.

On some shorter routes minibuses, usually called microbuses, are replacing chicken buses. These are operated on the same cram-'em-all-in principles and can be even more uncomfortable because they have less leg room. Where neither buses nor minibuses roam, pickup (*picop*) trucks serve as de facto buses; you hail them and pay for them as if they were the genuine article.

At least a couple of times a month, a bus plunges over a cliff or rounds a blind bend into a head-on collision. Newspapers are full of gory details and diagrams of the latest wreck, which doesn't foster affectionate feelings toward Guatemalan public transportation. Equally if not more often, buses are held up by armed robbers and the passengers are relieved of their money and valuables. If this happens to you, do not try to resist or get away. You could end up losing more than your valuables. For more information on this unpleasant subject, see p310.

CAR & MOTORCYCLE

You can drive in Guatemala with your home-country driver's license or with an International Driving Permit (IDP). Gasoline (petrol) and diesel are widely available. Motor parts may be hard to find, especially for modern vehicles with sophisticated electronics and emissions-control systems. Old Toyota pickups are ubiquitous, though, so parts and mechanics will be more widely available.

Guatemalan driving etiquette will probably be very different from what you're used to back home: passing on blind curves, ceding the right of way to vehicles coming uphill on narrow passes and deafening honking for no apparent reason are just the start. Expect few road signs and no indication from other drivers of what they are about to do. A vehicle coming uphill always has the right of way. *Tumulos* are speed bumps that are generously (sometimes oddly) placed throughout the country, usually on the main drag through a town. Use of seat belts is obligatory, but generally not practiced.

In Guatemala driving at night is a bad idea for many reasons, not the least of which are armed bandits, drunk drivers and decreased visibility.

Every driver involved in an accident that results in injury or death is taken into custody until a judge determines responsibility.

Rental

You can rent cars in Guatemala City (see p92), Antigua (see p117), Quetzaltenango (see p174), Huehuetenango (see p184), Cobán (see p223) and Flores (see p282). A four-door, five-seat, five-gear vehicle with air-con such as a Mitsubishi Lancer will normally cost around US$50 a day including insurance and unlimited kilometers. The smallest cars start at around US$40 a day. Discounts may apply if you rent for three days or more.

To rent a car or motorcycle you need to show your passport, driver's license and a major credit card. Usually, the person renting the vehicle must be 25 years or older. Insurance policies accompanying rental cars may not protect you from loss or theft, in which case you could be liable for hundreds or even thousands of dollars in damages. Be careful where you park, especially in Guatemala City and at night.

Motorcycles are available for rent in Antigua (see p117) and Panajachel (see p136). Bringing safety gear is highly recommended.

HITCHING

Hitchhiking in the strict sense of the word is not practiced in Guatemala because it is not safe. However, where the bus service is sporadic or nonexistent, pickup trucks and other vehicles serve as public transport. If you stand beside the road with your arm out, someone will stop. You are expected to pay the driver as if it were a bus and the fare will be similar. This is a safe and reliable system used by locals and travelers, and the only inconvenience you're likely to encounter is full to overflowing vehicles – get used to it.

LOCAL TRANSPORT
Bus

Public transportation within towns and cities and to nearby villages is chiefly provided by aged, polluting, crowded and loud buses. They're useful to travelers chiefly in the more spread-out cities such as Guatemala City, Quetzaltenango and Huehuetenango. Quetzaltenango has a lovely fleet of quiet, smooth, comfortable, modern minibuses.

Taxi

Taxis are fairly plentiful in most significant towns. A 10-minute ride normally costs about US$4.50, which is relatively expensive – expect to hear plenty of woeful tales about the price of gasoline. Except for some taxis in Guatemala City, they don't use meters: you must agree upon the fare before you set off – best before you get in, in fact. Taxis will also often take you to out-of-town archaeological sites and other places for reasonable round-trip fares, including waiting time while you look around.

SHUTTLE MINIBUS

Shuttle minibuses run by travel agencies provide comfortable and quick transport along the main routes plied by tourists. You'll find these heavily advertised wherever they are offered. They're much more expensive than buses (anywhere between five and 15 times as expensive), but more convenient: they usually offer a door-to-door service. The most popular shuttle routes include Guatemala City airport–Antigua, Antigua–Panajachel, Panajachel–Chichicastenango and Flores–Tikal.

TRANSPORTATION

Health Dr David Goldberg

CONTENTS

Travelers to Central America need to be concerned about food- and water-borne, as well as mosquito-borne, infections. Most of these illnesses are not life-threatening, but they can certainly ruin your trip. Besides getting the proper vaccinations, it's important that you bring along a good insect repellent and exercise great care in what you eat and drink.

BEFORE YOU GO

Since most vaccines don't produce immunity until at least two weeks after they're given, visit a physician four to eight weeks before departure. Ask your doctor for an international certificate of vaccination (otherwise known as the yellow booklet), which will list all the vaccinations you've received. This is mandatory for countries that require proof of yellow fever vaccination upon entry, but it's a good idea to carry it wherever you travel.

INSURANCE

If your health insurance does not cover you for medical expenses abroad, strongly consider getting supplemental insurance. Check the Bookings & Services section of www.lonely planet.com for more information. See also the **US State Department website** (www.travel.state .gov) for a list of medical evacuation and travel insurance companies. Find out in advance if your insurance plan will make payments directly to providers or reimburse you later for overseas health expenditures.

MEDICAL CHECKLIST

- antibiotics
- antidiarrheal drugs (eg loperamide)
- acetaminophen/paracetamol (Tylenol) or aspirin
- anti-inflammatory drugs (eg ibuprofen)
- antihistamines (for hay fever and allergic reactions)
- antibacterial ointment (eg Bactroban) for cuts and abrasions
- steroid cream or cortisone (for poison ivy and other allergic rashes)
- bandages, gauze, gauze rolls
- adhesive or paper tape
- scissors, safety pins, tweezers
- thermometer
- pocket knife
- DEET-containing insect repellent for the skin
- permethrin-containing insect spray for clothing, tents and bed nets
- sunblock
- oral-rehydration salts
- iodine tablets (for water purification)
- syringes and sterile needles

INTERNET RESOURCES

There is a wealth of travel health advice available on the internet. For further information, the **Lonely Planet website** (www.lonelyplanet.com) is a good place to start. A superb book called *International Travel and Health,* which is revised annually and is available online at no cost, is published by the **World Health Organization** (www .who.int/ith/). Another website of general interest is **MD Travel Health** (www.mdtravelhealth.com), which provides complete travel health recommendations for every country, updated daily, also at no cost.

It's usually a good idea to consult your government's travel health website before departure, if one is available.

Australia (www.smartraveller.gov.au)
Canada (www.hc-sc.gc.ca)
UK (www.doh.gov.uk)
United States (www.cdc.gov/travel/)

FURTHER READING

For further information, see *Healthy Travel Central & South America*, also from Lonely Planet. If traveling with children, Lonely Planet's *Travel with Children* may be useful. The *ABC of Healthy Travel*, by E Walker et al, and *Medicine for the Outdoors*, by Paul S Auerbach, are other valuable resources.

IN TRANSIT

DEEP VEIN THROMBOSIS (DVT)

Blood clots may form in the legs during plane flights, chiefly because of prolonged immobility. The longer the flight, the greater the risk. Though most blood clots are reabsorbed uneventfully, some may break off and travel through the blood vessels to the lungs, where they could cause life-threatening complications.

The chief symptom of deep vein thrombosis is swelling or pain of the foot, ankle or calf, usually but not always on just one side. When a blood clot travels to the lungs, it may cause chest pain and difficulty breathing. Travelers with any of these symptoms should immediately seek medical attention.

To prevent the development of deep vein thrombosis on long flights, you should walk about the cabin, perform isometric compressions of the leg muscles (ie contract the leg muscles while sitting), drink plenty of fluids, and avoid alcohol and tobacco.

JET LAG & MOTION SICKNESS

Jet lag is common when crossing more than five time zones, and can result in insomnia, fatigue, malaise or nausea. To avoid jet lag try drinking plenty of fluids (nonalcoholic) and eating light meals. Upon arrival, get exposure to natural sunlight and readjust your schedule (for meals, sleep etc) as soon as possible.

RECOMMENDED VACCINATIONS

The only required vaccine is yellow fever, and that's only if you're arriving in Guatemala from a yellow fever–infected country in Africa or South America. However, a number of vaccines are recommended. Note that some of these are not approved for use by children and pregnant women – check with your physician.

Vaccine	Recommended for	Dosage	Side effects
hepatitis A	all travelers	1 dose before trip; booster 6-12 months later	soreness at injection site; headaches; body aches
typhoid	all travelers	4 capsules, 1 taken every other day	abdominal pain; nausea; rash
yellow fever	required for travelers arriving from a yellow fever–infected area in Africa or the Americas	1 dose lasts 10 years	headaches; body aches; severe reactions are rare
hepatitis B	long-term travelers in close contact with the local population	3 doses over 6 months	soreness at injection site; low-grade fever
rabies	travelers who may have contact with animals and may not have access to medical care	3 doses over 3-4 weeks	soreness at injection site; headaches; body aches
tetanus-diphtheria	all travelers who haven't had a booster within 10 years	1 dose lasts 10 years	soreness at injection site
measles	travelers born after 1956 who've had only 1 measles vaccination	1 dose	fever; rash; joint pains; allergic reactions
chickenpox	travelers who've never had chickenpox	2 doses 1 month apart	fever; mild case of chickenpox

Bring medications in their original containers, clearly labeled. A signed, dated letter from your physician describing all medical conditions and medications, including generic names, is also a good idea. If carrying syringes or needles, be sure to have a physician's letter documenting their medical necessity.

HEALTH

Antihistamines such as dimenhydrinate (Dramamine) and meclizine (Antivert or Bonine) are usually the first choice for treating motion sickness. Their main side-effect is drowsiness. A herbal alternative is ginger, which works like a charm for some people.

IN GUATEMALA

AVAILABILITY & COST OF HEALTH CARE

Good medical care is available in Guatemala City, but options are limited elsewhere. In general, private hospitals are more reliable than public facilities, which may experience significant shortages of equipment and supplies. Many travelers use **Hospital Herrera Llerandi** (☎ 2384 5959; 6a Av 8-71, Zona 10; www.herrera llerandi.com). For an online list of hospitals and physicians in Guatemala, go to the **US embassy website** (http://guatemala.usembassy.gov /medical_information.html).

Many doctors and hospitals expect payment in cash, regardless of whether you have travel health insurance. If you develop a life-threatening medical problem, you'll probably want to be evacuated to a country with state-of-the-art medical care. Since this may cost tens of thousands of dollars, be sure you have insurance to cover this before you depart.

Many pharmacies are well-supplied, but important medications may not be consistently available. Be sure to bring along adequate supplies of all prescription drugs.

INFECTIOUS DISEASES

Cholera

Cholera is an intestinal infection acquired through ingestion of contaminated food or water. The main symptom is profuse, watery diarrhea, which may be so severe that it causes life-threatening dehydration. The key treatment is drinking oral rehydration solution. Antibiotics are also given, usually tetracycline or doxycycline, though quinolone antibiotics such as ciprofloxacin and levofloxacin are also effective.

Cholera outbreaks occur periodically in Guatemala, but the disease is rare among travelers. Cholera vaccine is no longer required, and is in fact no longer available in some countries, including the US, because the old vaccine was relatively ineffective and caused side effects. There are new vaccines that are safer and more effective, but they're not available in many countries and are only recommended for those at particularly high risk.

Dengue Fever (Breakbone Fever)

Dengue fever is a viral infection found throughout Central America. Thousands of cases occur each year in Guatemala. Dengue is transmitted by aedes mosquitoes, which bite predominantly during the daytime and are usually found close to human habitations, often indoors. They breed primarily in artificial water containers, such as jars, barrels, cans, cisterns, metal drums, plastic containers and discarded tires. As a result, dengue is especially common in densely populated, urban environments.

Dengue usually causes flu-like symptoms, including fever, muscle aches, joint pains, headaches, nausea and vomiting, often followed by a rash. The body aches may be quite uncomfortable, but most cases resolve uneventfully in a few days. Severe cases usually occur in children under the age of 15 who are experiencing their second dengue infection.

There is no treatment for dengue fever except to take analgesics such as acetaminophen/ paracetamol (Tylenol) and drink plenty of fluids. Severe cases may require hospitalization for intravenous fluids and supportive care. There is no vaccine. The cornerstone of prevention is protecting against insect bites; see p331.

Hepatitis A

Hepatitis A occurs throughout Central America. It's a viral infection of the liver that is usually acquired by ingestion of contaminated water, food or ice, though it may also be acquired by direct contact with infected persons. The illness occurs all over the world, but the incidence is higher in developing nations. Symptoms may include fever, malaise, jaundice, nausea, vomiting and abdominal pain. Most cases resolve uneventfully, though hepatitis A occasionally causes severe liver damage. There is no treatment.

The vaccine for hepatitis A is extremely safe and highly effective. If you get a booster six to 12 months after the initial vaccination, it lasts for at least 10 years. You really should get it before you go to Guatemala or any other developing nation. Because the safety of hepatitis A vaccine has not been established for pregnant women or children under the age of two, they should instead be given a gammaglobulin injection.

Hepatitis B

Like hepatitis A, hepatitis B is a liver infection that occurs worldwide but is more common in developing nations. Unlike hepatitis A, the disease is usually acquired by sexual contact or by exposure to infected blood, generally through blood transfusions or contaminated needles. The vaccine is recommended only for long-term travelers (on the road more than six months) who expect to live in rural areas or have close physical contact with the local population. Additionally, the vaccine is recommended for anyone who anticipates sexual contact with the local inhabitants or a possible need for medical, dental or other treatments while abroad, especially if a need for transfusions or injections is expected.

Hepatitis B vaccine is safe and highly effective. However, a total of three injections are necessary to establish full immunity. Several countries added hepatitis B vaccine to the list of routine childhood immunizations in the 1980s, so many young adults are already protected.

Malaria

Malaria occurs in every country in Central America. It's transmitted by mosquito bites, usually between dusk and dawn. The main symptom is high spiking fevers, which may be accompanied by chills, sweats, headache, body aches, weakness, vomiting or diarrhea. Severe cases may involve the central nervous system and lead to seizures, confusion, coma and death.

Taking malaria pills is strongly recommended for all rural areas in Guatemala except at altitudes greater than 1500m. The risk is high in the departments of Alta Verapaz, Baja Verapaz, El Petén and San Marcos, and moderate in the departments of Escuintla, Huehuetenango, Izabal, Quiché, Retalhuleu, Suchitepéquez and Zacapa. Transmission is greatest during the rainy season (June through November). There is no risk in Antigua or Lago de Atitlán.

For Guatemala, the first-choice malaria pill is chloroquine, taken once weekly in a dosage of 500mg, starting one to two weeks before arrival and continuing through the trip and for four weeks after departure. Chloroquine is safe, inexpensive and highly effective. Side effects are typically mild and may include nausea, abdominal discomfort, headache, dizziness, blurred vision and itching. Severe reactions are uncommon.

Protecting yourself against mosquito bites is just as important as taking malaria pills (see the recommendations on p331), since no pills are 100% effective.

If you may not have access to medical care while traveling, you should bring along additional pills for emergency self-treatment, which you should undergo if you can't reach a doctor and you develop symptoms that suggest malaria, such as high spiking fevers. One option is to take four tablets of Malarone once daily for three days. If you start self-medication, you should try to see a doctor at the earliest possible opportunity.

If you develop a fever after returning home, see a physician, as malaria symptoms may not occur for months.

Rabies

Rabies is a viral infection of the brain and spinal cord that is almost always fatal if not treated. The rabies virus is carried in the saliva of infected animals and is typically transmitted through an animal bite, though contamination of any break in the skin with infected saliva may result in rabies. Rabies occurs in all Central American countries. In Guatemala the risk is greatest in the northern provinces along the Mexican border. Most cases are related to dog bites.

Rabies vaccine is safe, but a full series requires three injections and is quite expensive. Those at high risk for rabies, such as animal handlers and spelunkers (cave explorers), should certainly get the vaccine. In addition, you should consider asking for the vaccine if you might be traveling to remote areas and might not have access to appropriate medical care if needed. The treatment for a possibly rabid bite consists of rabies vaccine with rabies immune globulin. It's effective, but must be given promptly. Most travelers don't need rabies vaccine.

All animal bites and scratches must be promptly and thoroughly cleansed with large amounts of soap and water and local health authorities must be contacted to determine whether or not further treatment is necessary (see opposite).

Typhoid

This fever is caused by ingestion of food or water contaminated by a species of salmonella known as *Salmonella typhi*. Fever occurs in virtually all cases. Other symptoms may include headache, malaise, muscle aches, dizziness, loss of appetite, nausea and abdominal pain. Either diarrhea or constipation may occur. Possible complications include intestinal perforation, intestinal bleeding, confusion, delirium or (rarely) coma.

Unless you expect to take all your meals in major hotels and restaurants, typhoid vaccine is a good idea. It's usually given orally, but is also available as an injection. Neither vaccine is approved for use in children under the age of two.

The drug of choice for typhoid fever is usually a quinolone antibiotic such as ciprofloxacin (Cipro) or levofloxacin (Levaquin), which many travelers carry for treatment of travelers' diarrhea. However, if you self-treat for typhoid fever, you may also need to self-treat for malaria, since the symptoms of the two diseases may be indistinguishable.

Yellow Fever

Yellow fever no longer occurs in Central America, but many countries in this region, including Guatemala, require yellow fever vaccine before entry if you're arriving from a country in Africa or South America where yellow fever is known to occur. If you're not arriving from a country with yellow fever, the vaccine is neither required nor recommended. Yellow fever vaccine is given only in approved yellow fever vaccination centers, which provide validated international certificates of vaccination (also known as yellow booklets). The vaccine should be given at least 10 days before departure and remains effective for approximately 10 years. Reactions to the vaccine are generally mild and may include headaches, muscle aches, low-grade fevers, or discomfort at the injection site. Severe, life-threatening reactions have been described but are extremely rare.

Other Infections

CHAGAS' DISEASE

This is a parasitic infection that is transmitted by triatomine insects (reduviid bugs), which inhabit crevices in the walls and roofs of substandard housing in South and Central America. The triatomine insect lays its feces on human skin as it bites, usually at night. A person becomes infected when he or she unknowingly rubs the feces into the bite wound or any other open sore. Chagas' disease is extremely rare in travelers. However, if you sleep in a poorly constructed house, especially one made of mud, adobe or thatch, you should be sure to protect yourself with a bed net and a good insecticide.

HISTOPLASMOSIS

Caused by a soil-based fungus, histoplasmosis is acquired by inhalation, often when the soil has been disrupted. Initial symptoms may include fever, chills, dry cough, chest pain and headache, sometimes leading to pneumonia. Histoplasmosis has been reported in European travelers returning from Mazatenango.

HIV/AIDS

This has been reported in all Central American countries. Be sure to use condoms for all sexual encounters.

LEISHMANIASIS

This occurs in the mountains and jungles of all Central American countries. The infection is transmitted by sandflies, which are about one third the size of mosquitoes. Leishmaniasis may be limited to the skin, causing slowly growing ulcers over exposed parts of the body, or (less commonly) disseminate to the bone marrow, liver and spleen. The disease may be particularly severe in those with HIV. In Guatemala, most cases of cutaneous leishmaniasis are reported from the northern parts of the country at elevations less than 1000m. The greatest risk occurs in the forested areas of El Petén. The disseminated form may occur in the semiarid valleys and foothills in the east central part of the country. There is no vaccine for leishmaniasis. To protect yourself from sandflies, follow the same precautions as for mosquitoes (opposite), except that netting must be of finer mesh (at least 18 holes to the linear inch).

HEALTH

LEPTOSPIROSIS

This is acquired by exposure to water contaminated by the urine of infected animals. Outbreaks often occur at times of flooding, when sewage overflow may contaminate the water sources. The initial symptoms, which resemble a mild flu, usually subside uneventfully in a few days, with or without treatment, but a minority of cases are complicated by jaundice or meningitis. There is no vaccine. You can minimize your risk by staying out of bodies of fresh water that may be contaminated by animal urine. If you're visiting an area where an outbreak is in progress, as occurred in Guatemala after flooding in 1998, you can take 200mg of doxycycline once weekly as a preventative measure. If you actually develop leptospirosis, the treatment is 100mg of doxycycline twice daily.

ONCHOCERCIASIS (RIVER BLINDNESS)

Onchocerciasis is caused by a roundworm that may invade the eye, leading to blindness. The infection is transmitted by black flies, which breed along the banks of rapidly flowing rivers and streams. In Guatemala, the disease occurs in heavily forested areas between 500m and 1500m, chiefly the Pacific slope of the Sierra Madre and in Escuintla along the Verde and Guachipilín rivers.

TYPHUS

This may be transmitted by lice in scattered pockets of the country.

TRAVELER'S DIARRHEA

To prevent diarrhea, avoid tap water unless it has been boiled, filtered or chemically disinfected (see p332); only eat fresh fruits or vegetables if cooked or peeled; be wary of dairy products that might contain unpasteurized milk; and be highly selective when eating food from street vendors.

If you develop diarrhea, be sure to drink plenty of fluids, preferably an oral rehydration solution containing lots of salt and sugar. A few loose stools don't require treatment, but if you start having more than four or five stools a day, you should start taking an antibiotic (usually a quinolone drug) and an antidiarrheal agent (such as loperamide). If diarrhea is bloody or persists for more than 72 hours or is accompanied by fever, shaking chills or severe abdominal pain, you should seek medical attention.

ENVIRONMENTAL HAZARDS
Animal Bites

Do not attempt to pet, handle or feed any animal, with the exception of domestic animals known to be free of any infectious disease. Most animal injuries are directly related to a person's attempt to touch or feed the animal.

Any bite or scratch by a mammal, including bats, should be promptly and thoroughly cleansed with large amounts of soap and water, followed by application of an antiseptic such as iodine or alcohol. The local health authorities should be contacted immediately for possible postexposure rabies treatment, whether or not you've been immunized against rabies. It may also be advisable to start an antibiotic, since wounds caused by animal bites and scratches frequently become infected. One of the newer quinolones, such as levofloxacin (Levaquin), which many travelers carry in case of diarrhea, would be an appropriate choice.

Mosquito Bites

To prevent mosquito bites, wear long sleeves, long pants, hats and shoes (rather than sandals). Make sure you bring along a good insect repellent, preferably one that contains DEET, which should be applied to exposed skin and clothing, but not to eyes, mouth, cuts, wounds or irritated skin. Products containing lower concentrations of DEET are effective, but for shorter periods of time. In general, adults and children over 12 should use preparations containing 25% to 35% DEET, which usually lasts about six hours. Children between two and 12 years of age should use preparations containing no more than 10% DEET, applied sparingly, which will usually last about three hours. Neurologic toxicity has been reported from DEET, especially in children, but appears to be extremely uncommon and generally related to overuse. Compounds containing DEET should not be used on children under the age of two.

Insect repellents containing certain botanical products, including oil of eucalyptus and soybean oil, are effective but last only 1½ to two hours. Repellents containing DEET are preferable for areas where there is a high risk of malaria or yellow fever. Products based on citronella are not effective.

HEALTH

TRADITIONAL MEDICINE

The following are some traditional remedies for common travel-related conditions.

- Jet lag – melatonin
- Mosquito-bite prevention – oil of eucalyptus or soybean oil
- Motion sickness – ginger

For additional protection, you can apply permethrin to clothing, shoes, tents and bed nets. Permethrin treatments are safe and remain effective for at least two weeks, even when items are laundered. Permethrin should not be applied directly to skin.

Don't sleep with the window open unless there is a screen. If sleeping outdoors or in an accommodation that allows entry of mosquitoes, use a bed net, preferably treated with permethrin, with edges tucked in under the mattress. The mesh size should be less than 1.5mm. If the sleeping area is not otherwise protected, use a mosquito coil, which will fill the room with insecticide through the night. Repellent-impregnated wristbands are not effective.

Snake Bites

Snakes are a hazard in some areas of Central America. In Guatemala the chief concern is *Bothrops asper,* the Central American or common lancehead, also called the fer-de-lance and known locally as *barba amarilla* (yellow beard) or *terciopelo* (velvet skin). This heavy-bodied snake reaches up to 2m in length and is commonly found along fallen logs and other small animal runs, especially in the northern provinces.

In the event of a venomous snake bite, place the victim at rest, keep the bitten area immobilized and move the victim immediately to the nearest medical facility. Avoid tourniquets, which are no longer recommended.

Sun

To protect yourself from excessive sun exposure, you should stay out of the midday sun, wear sunglasses and a wide-brimmed sun hat, and apply sunscreen with SPF 15 or higher, with both UVA and UVB protection. Sunscreen should be generously applied to all exposed parts of the body approximately 30 minutes before sun exposure and should

be reapplied after swimming or vigorous activity. Travelers should also drink plenty of fluids and avoid strenuous exercise when the temperature is high.

Water

Tap water in Guatemala is not safe to drink. Vigorous boiling for one minute is the most effective means of water purification. At altitudes greater than 2000m, boil for three minutes.

Another option is to disinfect water with iodine pills. Instructions are usually enclosed and should be carefully followed. Or you can add 2% tincture of iodine to 1 quart or liter of water (five drops to clear water, 10 drops to cloudy water) and let stand for 30 minutes. If the water is cold, longer times may be required. The taste of iodinated water may be improved by adding vitamin C (ascorbic acid). Iodinated water should not be consumed for more than a few weeks. Pregnant women, those with a history of thyroid disease and those allergic to iodine should not drink iodinated water.

A number of water filters are on the market. Those with smaller pores (reverse osmosis filters) provide the broadest protection, but they are relatively large and are readily plugged by debris. Those with somewhat larger pores (microstrainer filters) are ineffective against viruses, although they remove other organisms. Manufacturers' instructions must be carefully followed.

Safe-to-drink, inexpensive purified water *(agua pura)* is widely available in hotels, shops and restaurants. Salvavida is a universally trusted brand.

CHILDREN & PREGNANT WOMEN

In general, it's safe for children and pregnant women to go to Guatemala. However, because some of the vaccines listed on p327 are not approved for use in children and pregnant women, these travelers should be particularly careful not to drink tap water or consume any questionable food or beverage. Also, when traveling with children, make sure they're up-to-date on all routine immunizations. It's sometimes appropriate to give children some of their vaccines a little early before visiting a developing nation. You should discuss this with your pediatrician. Lastly, if pregnant, you should bear in mind that should a complication such as premature labor develop while abroad, the quality of medical care may not be comparable to that in your home country.

Since yellow fever vaccine is not recommended for pregnant women or children less than nine months old, these travelers, if arriving from a country with yellow fever, should obtain a waiver letter, preferably written on letterhead stationery and bearing the stamp used by official immunization centers to validate the international certificate of vaccination.

Language

CONTENTS

There are 21 Mayan indigenous languages used in and around Guatemala, but Spanish is still the most commonly spoken language, and what visitors will encounter on a daily basis. If you're keen to try out some Mayan languages, see the short and sweet Mam and K'iche' sections at the end of this chapter.

It's easy enough to pick up some basic Spanish, but for those who want to delve a little deeper, courses are available in Antigua (p106), Panajachel (p129), San Pedro La Laguna (p143), Nebaj (p158), Quetzaltenango (p168), Todos Santos Cuchumatán (p186), Monterrico (p206), Cobán (p220) and near Flores (p283 and p284). Alternatively, before you leave home you can study books, records and tapes, resources that are often available free at public libraries. Evening or college courses are also an excellent way to get started. For food-related words and phrases, see p59.

For a more comprehensive guide to the Spanish of Guatemala, get a copy of Lonely Planet's *Latin American Spanish Phrasebook*.

PRONUNCIATION

Spanish spelling is phonetically consistent, meaning that there's a clear and consistent relationship between what you see in writing and how it's pronounced.

Vowels

a	as in 'father'
e	as in 'met'
i	as in 'marine'
o	as in 'or' (without the 'r' sound)
u	as in 'rule'; the 'u' is not pronounced after **q** and in the letter combinations **gue** and **gui**, unless it's marked with a diaeresis (eg *argüir*), in which case it's pronounced as English 'w'
y	at the end of a word or when it stands alone, it's pronounced as the Spanish **i** (eg *ley*); between vowels within a word it's as the 'y' in 'yonder'

Consonants

Most Spanish consonants are pronounced much the same way as their English counterparts. A few of the exceptions are listed below.

While the consonants **ch**, **ll** and **ñ** are generally considered distinct letters, **ch** and **ll** are now often listed alphabetically under **c** and **l** respectively. The letter **ñ** is still treated as a separate letter and comes after **n** in dictionaries.

b	similar to English 'b,' but softer; referred to as 'b larga'
c	as in 'celery' before **e** and **i**; otherwise as English 'k'
ch	as in 'church'
d	as in 'dog,' but between vowels and after **l** or **n**, the sound is closer to the 'th' in 'this'
g	as the 'ch' in the Scottish *loch* before **e** and **i** ('kh' in our guides to pronunciation); elsewhere, as in 'go'
h	invariably silent. If your name begins with this letter, listen carefully if you're waiting for public officials to call you.
j	as the 'ch' in the Scottish *loch* (written as 'kh' in our guides to pronunciation)
ll	as the 'y' in 'yellow'
ñ	as the 'ni' in 'onion'

r   a short **r** except at the beginning of a word, and after **l**, **n** or **s**, when it's often rolled

rr   very strongly rolled

v   similar to English 'b,' but softer; referred to as 'b corta'

x   usually pronounced as **j** above; in some indigenous place names it's pronounced as an 's'; as in 'taxi' in other instances

z   as the 's' in 'sun'

Word Stress

In general, words ending in vowels or the letters **n** or **s** have stress on the next-to-last syllable, while those with other endings have stress on the last syllable. Thus *vaca* (cow) and *caballos* (horses) both carry stress on the next-to-last syllable, while *ciudad* (city) and *infeliz* (unhappy) are both stressed on the last syllable.

Written accents will almost always appear in words that don't follow the rules above, eg *sótano* (basement), *América* and *porción* (portion).

GENDER & PLURALS

In Spanish, nouns are either masculine or feminine, and there are rules to help determine gender (there are of course some exceptions). Feminine nouns generally end with -**a** or with the groups -**ción**, -**sión** or -**dad**. Other endings typically signify a masculine noun. Endings for adjectives also change to agree with the gender of the noun they modify (masculine/feminine -**o**/-**a**). Where both masculine and feminine forms are included in this language guide, they are separated by a slash, with the masculine form first, eg *perdido/a*.

If a noun or adjective ends in a vowel, the plural is formed by adding **s** to the end. If it ends in a consonant, the plural is formed by adding **es** to the end.

ACCOMMODATIONS

I'm looking for ...	*Estoy buscando ...*	e·stoy boos·*kan*·do ...
Where is ...?	*¿Dónde hay ...?*	*don*·de ai ...
a hotel	*un hotel*	oon o·*tel*
a boarding house	*una pensión/ residencial/ un hospedaje*	*oo*·na pen·*syon*/ re·see·den·*syal*/ oon os·pe·*da*·khe
a youth hostel	*un albergue juvenil*	oon al·*ber*·ge khoo·ve·*neel*

MAKING A RESERVATION

(for phone or written requests)

To ...	*A ...*
From ...	*De ...*
Date	*Fecha*
I'd like to book ...	*Quisiera reservar ... (see*
the list under 'Accommodations' for bed and room options)	
in the name of ...	*en nombre de ...*
for the nights of ...	*para las noches del ...*
credit card ...	*tarjeta de crédito ...*
number	*número*
expiry date	*fecha de vencimiento*
Please confirm ...	*Puede confirmar ...*
availability	*la disponibilidad*
price	*el precio*

Are there any rooms available?
¿Hay habitaciones libres?   ai a·bee·ta·*syon*·es *lee*·bres

I'd like a room.	*Quisiera una habitación*	kee·*sye*·ra oo·na a·bee·ta·*syon* ...
double	*doble*	*do*·ble
single	*individual*	een·dee·vee·*dwal*
twin	*con dos camas*	kon dos *ka*·mas
How much is it per ...?	*¿Cuánto cuesta por ...?*	*kwan*·to *kwes*·ta por ...
night	*noche*	*no*·che
person	*persona*	per·*so*·na
week	*semana*	se·*ma*·na
full board	*pensión completa*	pen·*syon* kom·*ple*·ta
private/shared bathroom	*baño privado/ compartido*	*ba*·nyo pree·*va*·do/ kom·par·*tee*·do
too expensive	*demasiado caro*	de·ma·*sya*·do *ka*·ro
cheaper	*más económico*	mas e·ko·*no*·mee·ko
discount	*descuento*	des·*kwen*·to

Does it include breakfast?
¿Incluye el desayuno?   een·*kloo*·ye el de·sa·*yoo*·no

May I see the room?
¿Puedo ver la habitación?   *pwe*·do ver la a·bee·ta·*syon*

I don't like it.
No me gusta.   no me *goos*·ta

It's fine. I'll take it.
OK. La alquilo.   o·*kay* la al·*kee*·lo

I'm leaving now.
Me voy ahora.   me *voy* a·o·ra

CONVERSATION & ESSENTIALS

In their public behavior, South Americans are very conscious of civilities, sometimes to the point of ceremoniousness. Never approach a stranger for information without extending a greeting, and use only the polite form of address, especially with the police and public officials. Young people may be less likely to expect this, but it's best to stick to the polite form unless you're quite sure you won't offend by using the informal mode. The polite form is used in all cases in this guide; where options are given, the form is indicated by the abbreviations 'pol' and 'inf.'

Saying *por favor* (please) and *gracias* (thank you) are second nature to most Guatemalans and a recommended tool in your travel kit. The three most common Spanish greetings are often shortened to simply *buenos* (for *buenos días*) and *buenas* (for *buenas tardes* and *buenas noches*).

Hello.	Hola.	o·la
Good morning.	Buenos días.	bwe·nos dee·as
Good afternoon.	Buenas tardes.	bwe·nas tar·des
Good evening/ night.	Buenas noches.	bwe·nas no·ches
Goodbye.	Adiós.	a·dyos (rarely used)
See you soon.	Hasta luego.	as·ta lwe·go
Yes.	Sí.	see
No.	No.	no
Please.	Por favor.	por fa·vor
Thank you.	Gracias.	gra·syas
Many thanks.	Muchas gracias.	moo·chas gra·syas
You're welcome.	De nada.	de na·da
Pardon me.	Perdón.	per·don
Excuse me.	Permiso.	per·mee·so

(used when asking permission)

| Forgive me. | Disculpe. | dees·kool·pe |

(used when apologizing)

How are things?
¿Qué tal?   ke tal
What's your name?
¿Cómo se llama?   ko·mo se ya·ma (pol)
¿Cómo te llamas?   ko·mo te ya·mas (inf)
My name is ...
Me llamo ...   me ya·mo ...
It's a pleasure to meet you.
Mucho gusto.   moo·cho goos·to
The pleasure is mine.
El gusto es mío.   el goos·to es mee·o
Where are you from?
¿De dónde es/eres?   de don·de es/er·es (pol/inf)

I'm from ...
Soy de ...   soy de ...
Where are you staying?
¿Dónde está alojado?   don·de es·ta a·lo·kha·do (pol)
¿Dónde estás alojado?   don·de es·tas a·lo·kha·do (inf)
May I take a photo?
¿Puedo sacar una foto?   pwe·do sa·kar oo·na fo·to

DIRECTIONS

How do I get to ...?
¿Cómo puedo llegar a ...?   ko·mo pwe·do ye·gar a ...
Is it far?
¿Está lejos?   es·ta le·khos
Go straight ahead.
Siga/Vaya derecho.   see·ga/va·ya de·re·cho
Turn left.
Voltée a la izquierda.   vol·te·e a la ees·kyer·da
Turn right.
Voltée a la derecha.   vol·te·e a la de·re·cha
I'm lost.
Estoy perdido/a.   es·toy per·dee·do/a
Can you show me (on the map)?
¿Me lo podría indicar (en el mapa)?   me lo po·dree·a een·dee·kar (en el ma·pa)

SIGNS

Entrada	Entrance
Salida	Exit
Información	Information
Abierto	Open
Cerrado	Closed
Prohibido	Prohibited
Comisaria	Police Station
Servicios/Baños	Toilets
Hombres/Varones	Men
Mujeres/Damas	Women

---

north	norte	nor·te
south	sur	soor
east	este/oriente	es·te/o·ryen·te
west	oeste/occidente	o·es·te/ok·see·den·te
here	aquí	a·kee
there	allí	a·yee
avenue	avenida	a·ve·nee·da
block	cuadra	kwa·dra
street	calle/paseo	ka·lye/pa·se·o

HEALTH

I'm sick.
Estoy enfermo/a.   es·toy en·fer·mo/a
I need a doctor.
Necesito un médico.   ne·se·see·to oon me·dee·ko
Where's the hospital?
¿Dónde está el hospital?   don·de es·ta el os·pee·tal

EMERGENCIES

Help!	¡Socorro!	so·ko·ro
Fire!	¡Incendio!	een·sen·dyo
I've been robbed.	Me robaron.	me ro·ba·ron
Go away!	¡Déjeme!	de·khe·me
Get lost!	¡Váyase!	va·ya·se

Call ...!	¡Llame a ...!	ya·me a
an ambulance	una ambulancia	oo·na am·boo·lan·sya
a doctor	un médico	oon me·dee·ko
the police	la policía	la po·lee·see·a

It's an emergency.
Es una emergencia.   es oo·na e·mer·khen·sya
Could you help me, please?
¿Me puede ayudar,   me pwe·de a·yoo·dar
  por favor?   por fa·vor
I'm lost.
Estoy perdido/a.   es·toy per·dee·do/a
Where are the toilets?
¿Dónde están los baños?   don·de es·tan los ba·nyos

I'm pregnant.
Estoy embarazada.   es·toy em·ba·ra·sa·da
I've been vaccinated.
Estoy vacunado/a.   es·toy va·koo·na·do/a

I'm allergic to ...	Soy alérgico/a (a) ...	soy a·ler·khee·ko/a (a) ...
antibiotics	los antibióticos	los an·tee·byo·tee·kos
nuts	las nueces	las nwe·ses
penicillin	la penicilina	la pe·nee·see·lee·na
peanuts	al maní	al ma·nee

I'm ...	Soy ...	soy ...
asthmatic	asmático/a	as·ma·tee·ko/a
diabetic	diabético/a	dya·be·tee·ko/a
epileptic	epiléptico/a	e·pee·lep·tee·ko/a

I have ...	Tengo ...	ten·go ...
altitude sickness	soroche	so·ro·che
diarrhea	diarrea	dya·re·a
nausea	náusea	now·se·a
a headache	un dolor de cabeza	oon do·lor de ka·be·sa
a cough	tos	tos

LANGUAGE DIFFICULTIES

Do you speak (English)?
¿Habla/Hablas (inglés)?   a·bla/a·blas (een·gles) (pol/inf)

Does anyone here speak English?
¿Hay alguien que hable   ai al·gyen ke a·ble
  inglés?   een·gles
I (don't) understand.
Yo (no) entiendo.   yo (no) en·tyen·do
How do you say ...?
¿Cómo se dice ...?   ko·mo se dee·se ...
What does ...mean?
¿Qué quiere decir ...?   ke kye·re de·seer ...

Could you please ...?	¿Puede ..., por favor?	pwe·de ... por fa·vor
repeat that	repetirlo	re·pe·teer·lo
speak more slowly	hablar más despacio	a·blar mas des·pa·syo
write it down	escribirlo	es·kree·beer·lo

NUMBERS

0	cero	se·ro
1	uno	oo·no
2	dos	dos
3	tres	tres
4	cuatro	kwa·tro
5	cinco	seen·ko
6	seis	says
7	siete	sye·te
8	ocho	o·cho
9	nueve	nwe·ve
10	diez	dyes
11	once	on·se
12	doce	do·se
13	trece	tre·se
14	catorce	ka·tor·se
15	quince	keen·se
16	dieciséis	dye·see·says
17	diecisiete	dye·see·sye·te
18	dieciocho	dye·see·o·cho
19	diecinueve	dye·see·nwe·ve
20	veinte	vayn·te
21	veintiuno	vayn·tee·oo·no
30	treinta	trayn·ta
31	treinta y uno	trayn·ta ee oo·no
40	cuarenta	kwa·ren·ta
50	cincuenta	seen·kwen·ta
60	sesenta	se·sen·ta
70	setenta	se·ten·ta
80	ochenta	o·chen·ta
90	noventa	no·ven·ta
100	cien	syen
101	ciento uno	syen·to oo·no
200	doscientos	do·syen·tos
1000	mil	meel
5000	cinco mil	seen·ko meel
10,000	diez mil	dyes meel
50,000	cincuenta mil	seen·kwen·ta meel

SHOPPING & SERVICES

I'd like to buy ...
Quisiera comprar ...   kee·sye·ra kom·prar ...
I'm just looking.
Sólo estoy mirando.   so·lo es·toy mee·ran·do
May I look at it?
¿Puedo mirarlo/la?   pwe·do mee·rar·lo/la
How much is it?
¿Cuánto cuesta?   kwan·to kwes·ta
That's too expensive.
Es demasiado caro.   es de·ma·sya·do ka·ro
Could you lower the price?
¿Podría bajar un poco   po·dree·a ba·khar oon po·ko
el precio?   el pre·syo
I don't like it.
No me gusta.   no me goos·ta
I'll take it.
Lo llevo.   lo ye·vo

Do you   ¿Aceptan ...?   a·sep·tan ...
accept ...?
  American   dólares   do·la·res
  dollars   americanos   a·me·ree·ka·nos
  credit cards   tarjetas de   tar·khe·tas de
    crédito   kre·dee·to
  traveler's   cheques de   che·kes de
  checks   viajero   vya·khe·ro

less   menos   me·nos
more   más   mas
large   grande   gran·de
small   pequeño/a   pe·ke·nyo/a

I'm looking   Estoy buscando ...   es·toy boos·kan·do ...
for (the) ...
ATM   el cajero   el ka·khe·ro
  automático   ow·to·ma·tee·ko
bank   el banco   el ban·ko
bookstore   la librería   la lee·bre·ree·a
embassy   la embajada   la em·ba·kha·da
exchange house   la casa de   la ka·sa de
  cambio   kam·byo
general store   la tienda   la tyen·da
laundry   la lavandería   la la·van·de·ree·a
market   el mercado   el mer·ka·do
pharmacy/   la farmacia/   la far·ma·sya/
chemist   la droguería   la dro·ge·ree·a
post office   los correos   los ko·re·os
supermarket   el supermercado   el soo·per·
  mer·ka·do
tourist office   la oficina de   la o·fee·see·na de
  turismo   too·rees·mo

What time does it open/close?
¿A qué hora abre/cierra?   a ke o·ra a·bre/sye·ra

I want to change some money/traveler's checks.
Quiero cambiar dinero/   kye·ro kam·byar dee·ne·ro/
cheques de viajero.   che·kes de vya·khe·ro
What is the exchange rate?
¿Cuál es el tipo de cambio?   kwal es el tee·po de kam·byo
How many quetzals per dollar?
¿Cuántos quetzals por   kwan·tos ket·za·les por
dólar?   do·lar
I want to call ...
Quiero llamar a ...   kye·ro lya·mar a ...

airmail   correo aéreo   ko·re·o a·e·re·o
letter   carta   kar·ta
registered mail   certificado   ser·tee·fee·ka·do
stamps   estampillas   es·tam·pee·lyas

TIME & DATES

What time is it?   ¿Qué hora es?   ke o·ra es
It's one o'clock.   Es la una.   es la oo·na
It's six o'clock.   Son las seis.   son las says
midnight   medianoche   me·dya·no·che
noon   mediodía   me·dyo·dee·a
half past two   dos y media   dos ee me·dya

now   ahora   a·o·ra
today   hoy   oy
tonight   esta noche   es·ta no·che
tomorrow   mañana   ma·nya·na
yesterday   ayer   a·yer

Monday   lunes   loo·nes
Tuesday   martes   mar·tes
Wednesday   miércoles   myer·ko·les
Thursday   jueves   khwe·ves
Friday   viernes   vyer·nes
Saturday   sábado   sa·ba·do
Sunday   domingo   do·meen·go

January   enero   e·ne·ro
February   febrero   fe·bre·ro
March   marzo   mar·so
April   abril   a·breel
May   mayo   ma·yo
June   junio   khoo·nyo
July   julio   khoo·lyo
August   agosto   a·gos·to
September   septiembre   sep·tyem·bre
October   octubre   ok·too·bre
November   noviembre   no·vyem·bre
December   diciembre   dee·syem·bre

TRANSPORTATION
Public Transportation

What time does   ¿A qué hora ...   a ke o·ra ...
... leave/arrive?   sale/llega?   sa·le/ye·ga

the bus	el autobus/	el ow·to·*boos*/
	la camioneta	la ka·mee·o·ne·ta
the pickup	el picop/	el *pee*·kop/
	la camioneta	la ka·mee·o·ne·ta
the bus (long	el autobus/	el ow·to·*boos*/
distance)	la flota	la *flo* ta
the plane	el avión	el a·*vyon*
the ship	el barco/buque	el *bar*·ko/boo·*ke*
airport	el aeropuerto	el a·e·ro·*pwer*·to
bus station	la estación de	la es·ta·*syon* de
	autobuses	ow·to·*boo*·ses
bus stop	la parada de	la pa·*ra*·da de
	autobuses	ow·to·*boo*·ses
luggage check	la guardería/	la gwar·de·*ree*·a/
room	el equipaje	el e·kee·*pa*·khe
ticket office	la boletería	la bo·le·te·*ree*·a

I'd like a ticket to ...
 Quiero un boleto a ... kye·ro oon bo·*le*·to a ...
What's the fare to ...?
 ¿Cuánto cuesta hasta ...? kwan·to *kwes*·ta *a*·sta ...

student's	de estudiante	de es·too·*dyan*·te
1st class	primera clase	pree·me·ra *kla*·se
2nd class	segunda clase	se·*goon*·da *kla*·se
single/one-way	ida	ee·da
return/round-	ida y vuelta	ee·da ee *vwel*·ta
trip		
taxi	taxi	tak·see

Private Transportation

I'd like to	Quisiera	kee·*sye*·ra
hire a/an ...	alquilar ...	al·kee·*lar* ...
bicycle	una bicicleta	oo·na bee·see·
		kle·ta
car	un auto	oon *ow*·to
4WD	un todo terreno	oon to·do te·*re*·no
motorbike	una moto	oo·na mo·to
pickup (truck)	camioneta	ka·myo·*ne*·ta
truck	camión	ka·myon
hitchhike	hacer dedo	a·ser de·do

Is this the road to (...)?
 ¿Se va a (...) por esta se va a (...) por *es*·ta
 carretera? ka·re·*te*·ra

Where's a petrol station?
 ¿Dónde hay una don·de ai oo·na
 gasolinera/un grifo? ga·so·lee·*ne*·ra/oon *gree*·fo
Please fill it up.
 Lleno, por favor. ye·no por fa·*vor*
I'd like (20) liters.
 Quiero (veinte) litros. kye·ro (*vayn*·te) *lee*·tros

ROAD SIGNS

Acceso	Entrance
Aparcamiento	Parking
Ceda el Paso	Give Way
Despacio	Slow
Dirección Única	One-Way
Mantenga Su Derecha	Keep to the Right
No Adelantar/	No Passing
No Rebase	
Peaje	Toll
Peligro	Danger
Prohibido Aparcar/	No Parking
No Estacionar	
Prohibido el Paso	No Entry
Pare/Stop	Stop
Salida de Autopista	Exit Freeway

diesel	diesel	dee·sel
leaded (regular)	gasolina con	ga·so·*lee*·na kon
	plomo	*plo*·mo
gas/petrol	gasolina	ga·so·*lee*·na
unleaded	gasolina sin	ga·so·*lee*·na seen
	plomo	*plo*·mo

(How long) Can I park here?
 ¿(Por cuánto tiempo) (por kwan·to *tyem*·po)
 Puedo aparcar aquí? pwe·do a·par·kar a·kee
Where do I pay?
 ¿Dónde se paga? don·de se pa·ga
I need a mechanic.
 Necesito un mecánico. ne·se·*see*·to oon me·*ka*·nee·ko
The car has broken down (in ...).
 El carro se ha averiado el *ka*·ro se a a·ve·*rya*·do
 (en ...). (en ...)
The motorbike won't start.
 No arranca la moto. no a·*ran*·ka la *mo*·to
I have a flat tyre.
 Tengo un pinchazo. ten·go oon peen·*cha*·so
I've run out of petrol.
 Me quedé sin gasolina. me ke·*de* seen ga·so·*lee*·na
I've had an accident.
 Tuve un accidente. too·ve oon ak·see·*den*·te

TRAVEL WITH CHILDREN

I need ...	Necesito ...	ne·se·*see*·to ...
Do you have ...?	¿Hay ...?	ai ...
a car baby seat	un asiento de	oon a·*syen*·to de
	seguridad	se·goo·ree·*da*
	para bebés	pa·ra be·*bes*
a child-minding	un servicio de	oon ser·*vee*·syo de
service	cuidado de	kwee·*da*·do de
	niños	*nee*·nyos
a children's	una carta	oona *kar*·ta
menu	infantil	een·fan·*teel*

a creche	una guardería	oo·na gwar·de·ree·a
(disposable) diapers/nappies	pañoles (de usar y tirar)	pa·nyo·les de oo·sar ee tee·rar
an (English-speaking) babysitter	una niñera (de habla inglesa)	oo·na nee·nye·ra (de a·bla een·gle·sa)
formula (milk)	leche en polvo	le·che en pol·vo
a highchair	una trona	oo·na tro·na
a potty	una pelela	oo·na pe·le·la
a stroller	un cochecito	oon ko·che·see·to

Do you mind if I breast-feed here?

| ¿Le molesta que dé de pecho aquí? | le mo·les·ta ke de de pe·cho a·kee |

Are children allowed?

| ¿Se admiten niños? | se ad·mee·ten nee·nyos |

MODERN MAYAN

Since the classic period, the two ancient Mayan languages, Yucatecan and Cholan, have subdivided into 35 separate Mayan languages (such as Yucatec, Chol, Chortí, Tzeltal, Tzotzil, Lacandón, Mam, K'iche' and Kaqchiquel), some of them unintelligible to speakers of others, some not. Indigenous languages are seldom written, but when they are, the Roman alphabet is used. Most literate Maya will only be able to read and write Spanish, the language of government, schools, the church and the media – they may not be literate in Mayan.

Pronunciation

There are several rules to remember when pronouncing Mayan words and place names. Mayan vowels are pretty straightforward, but consonants can be tricky.

c	always hard, as in 'cat'
j	an aspirated 'h' sound, eg *jipijapa* is pronounced 'hee·pee·haa·pa' and *abaj* is pronounced 'a·bah'; to get the 'ah' sound, imagine the 'h' sound from 'half' at the end of a word
u	as in 'prune', except when it occurs at the beginning or end of a word, in which case it's like English 'w'; thus *baktun* is 'bak·toon,' but *Uaxactún* is 'wa·shak·toon' and *ahau* is 'a·haw'
x	as English 'sh'

Mayan glottalized consonants (indicated by an apostrophe: **b'**, **ch'**, **k'**, **p'**, **t'**) are similar to normal consonants, but are pronounced

more forcefully and 'explosively.' An apostrophe following a vowel signifies a glottal stop (like the momentary stop between the syllables in 'oh-oh!'), not a more forceful vowel.

Another rule to remember is that in most Mayan words the stress falls on the last syllable. Sometimes this is indicated by an acute accent, sometimes not. The following place names are useful guides to pronunciation:

Abaj Takalik	a·bah ta·ka·leek
Acanceh	a·kan·keh
Ahau	a·haw
Kaminaljuyú	ka·mee·nal·hoo·yoo
Pop	pope
Tikal	tee·kal
Uaxactún	wa·shak·toon

K'ICHE'

K'iche' is widely spoken throughout the Guatemalan Highlands, from around Santa Cruz del Quiché to the area adjacent to Lake Atitlán and around Quetzaltenango. There are estimated to be around two million K'iche' Maya living in Guatemala, giving you plenty of opportunity to practice some of the common terms and phrases listed below.

Greetings & Civilities

These are great icebreakers, and even if you're not completely and accurately understood, there'll be goodwill and smiles all around just for making the effort.

Good morning.	Saqarik.
Good afternoon.	Xb'eqij.
Good evening/night.	Xokaq'ab'.
Goodbye.	Chab'ej.
Bye. See you soon.	Kimpetik ri.
Thank you.	Uts awech?
Excuse me.	Kyunala.
What's your name?	Su ra'b'i?
My name is ...	Nu b'i ...
Where are you from?	Ja kat pewi?
I'm from ...	Ch'qap ja'kin pewi ...

Useful Words & Phrases

Where is (a/the) ...?	Ja k'uichi' ri ...?
bathroom	b'anb'al chulu
bus stop	tek'lib'al
doctor	ajkun
hotel	jun worib'al
police station	ajchajil re tinamit

Do you have ...?	K'olik ...?
boiled water	saq'li
coffee	kab'e
copal	kach'
a machete	choyib'al
rooms	k'plib'al

| We have it. | K'olik. |
| We don't have it. | K'otaj. |

blanket	k'ul
soap	ch'ipaq
vegetables	ichaj
good	utz
bad	itzel
open	teb'am
closed	tzapilik
hard	ko
soft	ch'uch'uj
hot	miq'in
cold	joron
sick	yiwab'
north (white)	saq
south (yellow)	k'an
east (red)	kaq
west (black)	k'eq

Numbers

1	jun
2	keb'
3	oxib'
4	kijeb'
5	job'
6	waq'ib'
7	wuqub'
8	wajxakib'
9	b'elejeb'
10	lajuj
11	julajuj
12	kab'lajuj
13	oxlajuj
14	kajlajuj
15	o'lajuj
16	waklajuj
17	wuklajuj
18	wajxaklajuj
19	b'elejlajuj
20	juwinak
30	lajuj re kawinak
40	kawinak
50	lajuj re oxk'al
60	oxk'al
70	lajuj re waqk'al
80	waqk'al
90	lajuj re o'k'al

100	o'k'al
200	lajuj k'al
400	omuch'

MAM

Mam is spoken in the department of Huehuetenango, in the western portion of the country. This is the indigenous language you'll hear in Todos Santos Cuchumatán, which is nestled among the Cuchumatanes mountains.

Greetings & Civilities

Luckily, in Mam you only need two phrases for greeting folks, no matter what time of day it is.

Good morning/ afternoon/evening.	Chin q'olb'el teya. (informal singular) Chin q'olb'el kyeyea. (informal plural)
Goodbye.	Chi nej.
Bye. See you soon.	Chi nej. Ak qli qib'.
Thank you.	Chonte teya.
How are you?	Tzen ta'ya?
Excuse me.	Naq samy.
What's your name?	Tit biya?
My name is ...	Luan bi ...
Where are you from?	Jaa'tzajnia?
I'm from ...	Ac tzajni ...

Useful Words & Phrases

Where is (a/the) ...?	Ja at ...?
bathroom	bano
doctor	medico/doctor
hotel	hospedaje

Many words in Mam have been in disuse for so long that the Spanish equivalent is now used almost exclusively.

| Where is the bus stop? | Ja nue camioneta? (literally, where does the pickup stop?) |
| How much is the fruit and vegetables? | Je te ti lobj? |

Do you have ...?	At ...?
boiled water	kqa'
coffee	café
rooms	cuartos

Is there somewhere we can sleep?	Ja tun kqta'n?
We have it.	At.
We don't have it.	Nti'.
I'm cold.	At xb'a'j/choj.

I'm sick.	*At yab'*
good	*banex/g'lan*
bad	*k'ab'ex/nia g'lan*
open	*jqo'n*
closed	*jpu'n*
hard	*kuj*
soft	*xb'une*
hot	*kyaq*
north (white)	*okan*

south (yellow)	*eln*
east (red)	*jawl*
west (black)	*kub'el*

Numbers

The numbers from one to 10 are the same as in K'iche' (p341). For numbers higher than 10, Mam speakers use the Spanish equivalents.

Also available from Lonely Planet:
Latin American Spanish Phrasebook

Glossary

abrazo – embrace, hug; in particular, the formal, ceremonial hug between political leaders

alux, aluxes – Mayan for gremlin, leprechaun, benevolent 'little people'

Apartado Postal – post-office box; abbreviated Apdo Postal

Ayuntamiento – often seen as H Ayuntamiento (Honorable Ayuntamiento) on the front of town hall buildings; translates as 'Municipal Government'

barrio – district, neighborhood

billete – bank note (unlike in Spain, where it's a ticket)

boleto – ticket (bus, train, museum etc)

bolo – colloquial term for drunk (noun)

cabañas – cabins

cacique – Mayan chief; also used to describe provincial warlord or strongman

cafétería – literally 'coffee-shop,' but refers to any informal restaurant with waiter service; not usually a cafétería in the North American sense of a self-service restaurant

cajero automático – automated teller machine(ATM)

callejón – alley or narrow or very short street

camión – truck or bus

camioneta – bus or pickup truck

cardamomo – cardamom; a spice grown extensively in the Verapaces and used as a flavor enhancer for coffee and tea, particularly in the Middle East

casa de cambio – currency exchange office; offers exchange rates comparable to those of banks and is much faster to use (uncommon in Guatemala)

cazuela – clay cooking pot; usually sold in a nested set

cenote – large, natural limestone cave used for water storage (or ceremonial purposes)

cerveza – beer

Chac – Mayan god of rain

chac-mool – Mayan sacrificial stone sculpture

chapín – citizen of Guatemala

charro – cowboy

chicle – sap of the sapodilla tree; used to manufacture chewing gum

chicleros – men who collect *chicle*

chingar – literally 'to rape' but in practice a word with a wide range of colloquial meanings similar to the use of 'to screw' in English

Chinka' – small, non-Mayan indigenous group living on the Pacific Slope

chuchkajau – Mayan prayer leader

chuj – traditional Mayan sauna; see also *tuj*

chultún – artificial Mayan cistern

cigarro – cigarette

cocina – kitchen; also used for a small, basic one-woman place to eat, often located in or near a municipal market, and in the phrases *cocina económica* (economical kitchen) or a *cocina familiar* (family kitchen)

cofradía – religious brotherhood, most often found in the Highlands

colectivo – jitney taxi or minibus (usually a Kombi or minibus) that picks up and drops off passengers along its route

comal – hot griddle or surface used to cook tortillas

comedor – basic and cheap eatery, usually with a limited menu

completo – full; a sign you may see on hotel desks in crowded cities

conquistador – explorer-conquerer of Latin America from Spain

copal – tree resin used as incense in Mayan ceremonies

correos – post office

corte – Mayan wraparound skirt

costumbre – traditional Mayan rites

criollos – people born in Guatemala of Spanish blood

cruce – crossroads, usually where you make bus connections; also known as *entronque*

curandero – traditional indigenous healer

damas – ladies; the usual sign on toilet doors

dzul, dzules – Mayan for foreigners or 'townsfolk'

encomienda – Spanish colonial practice of putting indigenous people under the 'guardianship' of landowners; practically akin to medieval serfdom

entronque – see *cruce*

faja – Mayan waist sash or belt

ferrocarril – railroad

finca – plantation, farm

galón, galones – US gallons; fluid measure of 3.79L

glyph – symbolic character or figure; usually engraved or carved in relief

gringo/a – a mildly pejorative term applied to a male/female North American visitor; sometimes applied to any visitor of European heritage

gruta – cave

guayabera – man's thin fabric shirt with pockets and appliquéd designs on the front, over the shoulders and down the back; often worn in place of a jacket and tie on formal occasions

hacienda – estate; also 'treasury,' as in Departamento de Hacienda, Treasury Department

hay – pronounced like 'eye,' meaning 'there is' or 'there are'; you're equally likely to hear *no hay,* meaning 'there isn't' or 'there aren't'

hombre/s – man/men

huipil – Mayan woman's woven tunic; often very colorful and elaborately embroidered

IVA – impuesto al valor agregado or value-added tax; on hotel rooms it is 12%

juego de pelota – ball game

kaperraj – Mayan woman's all-purpose cloth; used as a head covering, baby sling, produce sack, shawl and more

Kukulcán – Mayan name for the Aztec-Toltec plumed serpent Quetzalcóatl

ladino – person of mixed indigenous and European race; a more common term in Guatemala than *mestizo*

lancha – motorboat used to transport passengers; driven by a lanchero

larga distancia – long-distance telephone

lavandería – laundry; a *lavandería automática* is a coin-operated laundry

leng – in the highlands, a colloquial Mayan term for coins

libra – pound; weight measurement of 0.45kg

lleno – full (fuel tank)

machismo – maleness, masculine virility

malecón – waterfront boulevard

manglar – mangrove

manzana – apple; also a city block; see also *supermanzana*

mariachi – small group of street musicians featuring stringed instruments, trumpets and often an accordion; sometimes plays in restaurants

marimba – Guatemala's xylophone-like national instrument

mestizo – person of mixed indigenous and European blood; the word *ladino* is more common in Guatemala

metate – flattish stone on which corn is ground with a cylindrical stone roller

milla – mile; distance of 1.6km

milpa – maize field

mirador – lookout, vista point

mochilero – backpacker

mordida – 'bite'; small bribe paid to keep the wheels of bureaucracy turning

mudéjar – Moorish architectural style

mujer/es – woman/women

na – thatched Mayan hut

onza – ounce; weight of 28g

pachete – a squash-type vegetable; can be eaten or used as a loofah

palacio de gobierno – building housing the executive offices of a state or regional government

palacio municipal – city hall; seat of the corporation or municipal government

palapa – thatched shelter with a palm-leaf roof and open sides

panza verde – literally 'green belly,' a nickname given to Antigua residents who are said to eat lots of avocados

parada – bus stop; usually for city buses

picop – pickup truck

pie – foot; measure of 0.30m

pisto – colloquial Mayan term for money, quetzals

posada – guesthouse

propino, propina – a tip, different from a *mordida,* which is really a bribe

punta – sexually suggestive dance enjoyed by the Garífuna of the Caribbean coast

puro – cigar

Quetzalcóatl – plumed serpent god of the Aztecs and Toltecs; see also *Kukulcán*

rebozo – long woolen or linen scarf covering the head or shoulders

refago – Mayan wraparound skirt

retablo – ornate, often gilded altarpiece

retorno – 'return'; used on traffic signs to signify a U-turn or turnaround

roofcomb – a decorative stonework lattice atop a Mayan pyramid or temple

rutelero – jitney

sacbé, sacbeob – ceremonial limestone avenue or path between great Mayan cities

sacerdote – priest

sanatorio – hospital, particularly a small private one

sanitario – literally 'sanitary'; usually means toilet

secadora – clothes dryer

Semana Santa – Holy Week preceding Easter

stela, stelae – standing stone monument(s); usually carved

supermanzana – large group of city blocks bounded by major avenues; see also *manzana*

supermercado – supermarket; anything from a corner store to a large, US-style supermarket

taller – shop or workshop

taller mecánico – mechanic's shop, usually for cars

teléfono comunitario – community telephone; found in the smallest towns

tepezcuintle – edible jungle rodent the size of a rabbit

tequila – clear, distilled liquor produced, like pulque and mescal, from the maguey cactus

tienda – small store that may sell anything from candles and chickens to aspirin and bread

típico – typical or characteristic of a region; particularly used to describe food

tocoyal – Mayan head covering

traje – traditional clothing worn by the Maya

tuj – traditional Mayan sauna; see also *chuj*

túmulos – speed bumps found in many towns; sometimes indicated by a highway sign bearing a row of little bumps

tzut – Mayan man's equivalent of a *kaperraj*

viajero – traveler

vulcanizadora – automobile tire repair shop

xate – low-growing fern native to the Petén region and exported for use in floral arrangements, particularly in the US

xateros – men who collect *xate*

zonas – zones

zotz – bat (the mammal) in many Mayan languages

Behind the Scenes

THIS BOOK

This guidebook was commissioned in Lonely Planet's Oakland office, and produced by the following:

Commissioning Editors Greg Benchwick, Elizabeth Anglin, David Zingarelli
Coordinating Editors Sarah Stewart, Louise Clarke
Coordinating Cartographer Andy Rojas
Coordinating Layout Designers Jim Hsu, Clara Monitto
Managing Editor Melanie Dankel
Senior Editor Helen Christinis
Managing Cartographer Alison Lyall
Assisting Editors Kim Hutchins, Andrea Dobbin, Phillip Tang
Assisting Cartographer Joanne Luke
Cover Designer Karina Dea
Project Manager Rachel Imeson
Language Content Coordinator Quentin Frayne

Thanks to Sally Darmody, Mark Germanchis, Kate McLeod, Malcolm O'Brien, Stephanie Pearson, Averil Robertson, Celia Wood

CONTRIBUTING AUTHORS

Dr Allen J Christenson wrote the Ancient Mayan Culture chapter. He earned his PhD in Pre-Colombian Art History at the University of Texas at Austin, and now works in the Humanities, Classics and Comparative Literature department at Brigham Young University. He is the author of *Art and Society in a Highland Maya Community*, published in 2001, as well as a translation of the great K'iche-Maya epic, the *Popol Vuh*, published in 2003. The text was adapted from his original submission to Lonely Planet's *Belize 2*.

Dr David Goldberg MD wrote the Health chapter. David completed his training in internal medicine and infectious diseases at Columbia-Presbyterian Medical Center in New York City, where he has also served as voluntary faculty. At present he is an infectious-diseases specialist in Scarsdale, New York state, and the editor-in-chief of the website MDTravelHealth.com.

LONELY PLANET: TRAVEL WIDELY, TREAD LIGHTLY, GIVE SUSTAINABLY

The Lonely Planet Story

The story begins with a classic travel adventure: Tony and Maureen Wheeler's 1972 journey across Europe and Asia to Australia. There was no useful information about the overland trail then, so Tony and Maureen published the first Lonely Planet guidebook to meet a growing need.

From a kitchen table, Lonely Planet has grown to become the largest independent travel publisher in the world, with offices in Melbourne (Australia), Oakland (USA) and London (UK). Today Lonely Planet guidebooks cover the globe. There is an ever-growing list of books and information in a variety of media. Some things haven't changed. The main aim is still to make it possible for adventurous individuals to get out there – to explore and better understand the world.

The Lonely Planet Foundation

The Lonely Planet Foundation proudly supports nimble nonprofit institutions working for change in the world. Each year the foundation donates 5% of Lonely Planet company profits to projects selected by staff and authors. Our partners range from Kabissa, which provides small nonprofits across Africa with access to technology, to the Foundation for Developing Cambodian Orphans, which supports girls at risk of falling victim to sex traffickers.

Our nonprofit partners are linked by a grass-roots approach to the areas of health, education or sustainable tourism. Many projects we support – such as one with BaAka (Pygmy) children in the forested areas of Central African Republic – choose to focus on women and children as one of the most effective ways to support the whole community.

Sometimes foundation assistance is as simple as helping to preserve a local ruin like the Minaret of Jam in Afghanistan; this incredible monument now draws intrepid tourists to the area and its restoration has greatly improved options for local people.

Just as travel is often about learning to see with new eyes, so many of the groups we work with aim to change the way people see themselves and the future for their children and communities.

THANKS
LUCAS VIDGEN

This was such a huge project it's hard to know where to start. On the home front, Brian Benson and Ann Marie Madison for keeping it all together and América and Sofia Celeste just for being there. On the road, Tom Lingenfelter, Geert from Copán, Pedro Méndez, Eduardo Vasquez, Eduardo Tatzan, Juan Hernández, Jorge Luís Balthazar Saldañas, Nora López and the hundreds of travelers who I bumped into and who wrote in with snippets of information – you guys make the job a whole lot easier and we really do read every letter and email. In LP land, Sarah Stewart for her eagle eye and John Noble and Susan Forsythe for doing such excellent work on the previous edition.

OUR READERS

Many thanks to the travelers who used the last edition and wrote to us with helpful hints, useful advice and interesting anecdotes:

A Janneke Abels, Dorothy Adams, Elizabeth Adams, Samar Al-Bulushi, Dane Alderfer, Jeff Allen, Antonio Amaral, Alice Ambrose, Betsy Ames, Marilyn Amick, **B** Barbara Ancheta, Julie Andersen, Garret Atlakson, Jorg Ausfelt, Aria Avdal, Brian Baker, Elizabeth Barbeira, James Barr, Gino Baruffol, E Baumgartner, Sofie De Bauw, Josef Bayer, Charles Beckman, Anette Benzinger, Teresa Bernardo, Eliza Berries, Regina Biemel, Doreen Bierbrier, Allison Biggs, Lyne Bissonnette, Erica Boas, Mike Bodily, Henk Boelman, Sanne Bogers, Eberhard Bopp, Anna Bosch, Pierre Bourgeois, Claire Bourgin, Kate Bow, Erin Boyer, Judy Brad, Will Braun, D Brenne, Ali Briggs, Miriam Brodersen, Eric Brouwer, Roel Brouwer, Anita Brown, Louise Brown, Karen Browne, Malte Bräutigam, Stephen Bubul, Gerald Buechter, Jim Buskirk, Carol Butcher, Charlotte Buys, **C** Brigitte Cannuel, Colin Cape, Terri Carmichael, James Carson, Gwyneth Wendy Carsten, Juan Francisco Pinto Casasola, Ken & Barbara Cerotsky, Peter Chance, Julio Chew, Cheryl Clark, E M Clark, John Clark, Richard Clark, Elizabeth Claverie, Lilli Cloud, Tamar Cohen, Roxane Coleman, Joe Collins, Darcy Constans, Paula Cormack, Paola Corradini, Mª José Couto, Sarah Cowan, Stirling Cox, Kenneth G Crosby, Nick Crossling, Gaspar Cruanes, Amy Czarnecki, **D** Glo-Ann D'Souza, Elizabeth Daly, John Damaschke, Amy Davis, Jim Davis, Matthew Davis, Matthew John Davis, Traci Day, Clare Death, Ilana Debare, Kerin G Deeley, Daniel Desjardins, Sinead Devlin, Melanie Dickson, Carol Digiovanni, Marketa Doberska, Loren Donelson, Michaela Donnelly, Erica Doran, Colin Doyle, Seam Drakon, Aniela Dunin, Simon Dunne, Rachel Dwosh, **E** Erin Elder, Natasha Ell, Troy Ellis, Geertje Engel, Laura Erickson-Schroth, Tandi Erlmann, Claire Eustace, **F** Paul Farrell, Erich Feldbauer, Anat & Gil Feldman, Louise Fernandez, David Finkelstein, David & Mary Finkelstein, Amir Firer, Karly Ford, Christine Forgo, Barbara Fossati, Jan Fraser, Walter Fuchs, Andreas Funke, **G** Christina Galitsky, Kristen Gardella, Merav Gazit, Michelle Geber, Johan & Marola Gebuis, Yohai Genzer,

Daniele Ginanneschi, Richard E Ginnold, Christian Glossner, Hayley Glover, Christian Gogolin, Allan Gonzalez, Peter Gradjansky, Denise Gray, Stephanie Greenwood, Genevieve Grenon, Amy Grey, Carolyn De Groot, Anita Grunst, Laura Guenther, **H** Lukas Haehnel, Katie Hambly, Glenn Hamburger, Eric Hameister, Taili Hardiman, Arthur Harris, David Haskell-Craig, Briana Havey, Lucinda Hawksley, Sebastian Hejnowski, Jeffrey Henigson, Marian Henss, Bob Heston, Catherine Heuberger, Brian Hicks, Matthias Hillenkamp, Guy Hilson, Mark Hoddle, William Hodges, Keil Horst, Pauline Hsu, Andrew Hudson, Helen Humphreys, Jane Hørrmann, **I** Karen Immerso, Karma Ingersoll-Thorp, Chiyo Ishikawa, Helga Itulah, **J** Tor Jacobsen, Barbara Janker, Pepijn Jansen, Luis Carlos Montero Jimenez, Katherine Jo, Charlie Johnston, Ulrike Jordan, **K** Erich Keefe, Andrea De Keijzer, Jim Keller, Willem Kemp, Brian Kemsley, Charles Kenny, David Kerkhoff, Ruth Ann Kern, Femke Keunen, Priscilla Kibbee, Bob King, Dieter Klippstein, Sharon Kol, Mary Kopf, Josef Kraeuter, Lucy Kreidich, Henriette Kruimel, Janina Kugel, Sarah Kulla, **L** Juan Lagenge, Frederic Lanier, Madeline Lasko, Kathy Lassiter, Anna Lazar, Sue Leach, Anthony Lee, David Leeds, Ellen Legator, Arian Lemal, Matt Leshure, Matt Lieber, Theo Linssen, Jennifer Longfellow, Marie Lucas, Tino Luinstra, **M** Susan Madison, Caroline Maere, Carolina Magdalene Maier, Lily Manne, Martin Maranus, Roni Markovitz, M Martinez, Elger Matthes, Debiie Mattina, Brent Maupin, Scott & Narelle Mayer, Shirley Mccaughey, Mark Mccracken, Fergus Mcgaugh, Andrew Mcgeary, Stuart Mcgrow, Isabel Mendiguren, Sandra Merz, Juanita Metzger, Maria Midböe, Anze Mihelic, David Miller, Andrea Milne, Ariane Minnaar, Manuel Chirouze Montenegro, Jerry Moody, Ron Moore, Basem Morris, Darren Mossman, Anni Mountjoy, Simone Mousel, Hans Muechler, Johannes Mueller, Ekkehard Muenzing, Ekkehard Dr Muenzing, **N** Dana Nagle, Loren Nava, Vy Nguyen, Toni & Nicole, Michal Ben Noah, Jen Noone, Mirjam Novak, **O** Stu O'Brien, Elizabeth Oakes, Alex Ogle, Michal Omri, Andrew Oost, Olivier Ordonez, Knut Nesland Ose, Paül Osoy, Bessie Owen, **P** Mareike Paessler, Laura Paidock, Patrycja Pajak, John Palov, Asit Panwala, Douglas Parker, Lorinda Parks, Diane Patrick, Sena Patrick, Valerie Patrick, William Paul, Jane Pedersen, Candice Peggs, Abby Greenwald Peklo, Patti Perkins, Tim Peterson, Karl Pichler, Mike Piekey, Pablo Pitcher, Heikki Poussa, Anibal Pozuelos, Folkert Praamstra, Rebecca Profit, Kevin Puloski, **R** Ilana Raburn, Ron & Joan Raymond, Cait Read, Axel Rebenich, Lexi Reese, Deborah J Rhodes, Jasmine Rickards, Jaime Robeck, Becky Roberts, Dave Roberts, John Roberts, Michael Roberts, Shadrock Roberts, Chipper Robideau, Jemma Robinson, Friedhelm Rodermund, Justin Rose, Nick Rose, Avi Rotem, Richard Roth, Karl Ruppenthal, **S** David Russell, Laura Salcido, Ezzio Samayoa, Kristin Sanne, Rigoberto Morales Santiago, Gregor Schaefer, Reto Schaerli, Richard Scheerer, China Scherz, Arne Schirkonyer, Marc Schlichtner, Allan Scholsk, Christian Schott, René Schueler, Patrick Schwizer, Sandro Schäer, Ana San Sebastian, Harald Seemann, Gerdi Seidl, Maret Shelver, Michael Simone, George Skarbek, Luz Sluijter, Katrina Smallwood, Ineke De Smidt, Lindsay Smith, Sarah Smith, Tom Sobhani, Michiel Soede, Marynell Sorenson, Simone Stahel, Dominic Stanley, Sander Steijnis, Romoan Stoop, Martin

Stump, Shawna Suffriti, Jennifer Sugg, Anna Suggett, Christina Sundbeck, Phairoj Suntaree, Tom Sweeney, **T** Noriko Tanaka, Deniz Tanin, Travis Taylor, Texas Tea, James Thackray, Carolyn Theobald, Heinz Thogersen, Ingrid Trebisky, Anna Treurniet, Aviad Tsuck, Ricardo Turcios, Bret Turner, **V** Teuntje Der van Aalst, Sytze Der van Kooy, Gioni van Passarelli, Pieter Der van Vlugt, Fenna van Zeilen, Cees van Zoest, Linda Veldmeijer, Eddy Veliz, Emmanuel Verrier-Choquette, Linda De Voogd, **W** James Wagner, Kristen Walbran, Sarah Waldron, Tara Waldron, Mary Beth Watrous, Meredith Webb, Tjefa Wegener, Jonas Wernli, Carien Wernsen, Matt Whipple, Hoppy Whitman, Thomas De Wijn, Bruce Willis, Brian Wilson, Paul Wilson, Shane Wilson, Roel De Winter, Mindy Wise, Michaela Witzel, Birgitta Wodke, Dietmar Wuelfing, **X** Sean Xix, **Y** Greg Yanagihara, K Youngblood, Mark Younger, **Z** Klaas-Jan Zuidam

ACKNOWLEDGMENTS

Many thanks to the following for the use of their content:

Globe on title page ©Mountain High Maps 1993 Digital Wisdom, Inc.

Internal photographs p9, Sergio Pitamitz/Photolibrary. All other photographs by Lonely Planet Images, and by Jeffrey Becom p10 (#5); Richard I'Anson p6 (#3), p11 (#2); Ralph Hopkins p7 (#3); Kraig Lieb p8 (#2); Alfredo Maiquez p6 (#2), p7 (#6); Aaron McCoy p9 (#1); Doug McKinlay p10 (#1); Jane Sweeney p5.

All images are the copyright of the photographers unless otherwise indicated. Many of the images in this guide are available for licensing from Lonely Planet Images: www.lonelyplanetimages.com.

SEND US YOUR FEEDBACK

We love to hear from travelers – your comments keep us on our toes and help make our books better. Our well-traveled team reads every word on what you loved or loathed about this book. Although we cannot reply individually to postal submissions, we always guarantee that your feedback goes straight to the appropriate authors, in time for the next edition. Each person who sends us information is thanked in the next edition – and the most useful submissions are rewarded with a free book.

To send us your updates – and find out about Lonely Planet events, newsletters and travel news – visit our award-winning website: **www.lonelyplanet.com/contact**.

Note: we may edit, reproduce and incorporate your comments in Lonely Planet products such as guidebooks, websites and digital products, so let us know if you don't want your comments reproduced or your name acknowledged. For a copy of our privacy policy visit www.lonelyplanet.com/privacy.

Index

INDEX

000 Map pages
000 Photograph pages

000 Map pages
000 Photograph pages

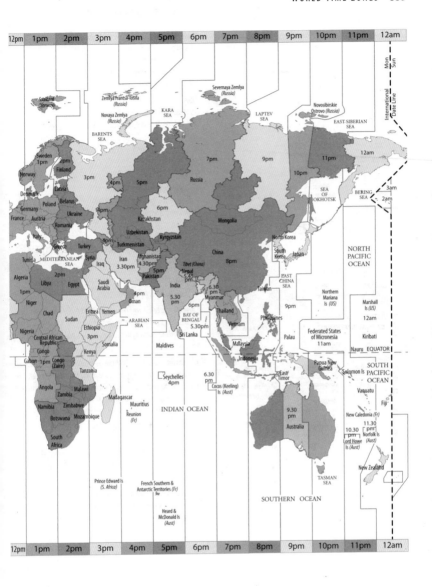

12pm 1pm 2pm 3pm 4pm 5pm 6pm 7pm 8pm 9pm 10pm 11pm 12am

International Date Line

Mon
Sun

Svalbard
(Norway)

Zemlya Frantsa-Iosifa
(Russia)

Severnaya Zemlya
(Russia)

Novosibirskie
Ostrovo (Russia)

Novaya Zemlya
(Russia)

KARA
SEA

LAPTEV
SEA

EAST SIBERIAN
SEA

BARENTS
SEA

12am

Sweden
1pm

2pm

Finland

7pm

9pm

11pm

10pm

Norway

3pm

SEA
OF
OKHOTSK

BERING
SEA

3am

2am

Denmark

Latvia

4pm

5pm

Russia

Germany
Poland
Belarus

France
Austria
Ukraine

4pm

NORTH
PACIFIC
OCEAN

Italy

Romania

6pm

Kazakhstan

Tunisia
Greece
Turkey

4pm

Turkmenistan

Uzbekistan

Kyrgyzstan

Mongolia

North Korea

Algeria
Libya
Egypt

Syria
Iraq

Iran
3.30pm

Afghanistan
4.30pm

China

South
Korea
Japan

8pm

East
China
Sea

Taiwan

MEDITERRANEAN
SEA

2pm

Saudi
Arabia

Tibet (China)

Nepal
5.45
pm

5pm

Pakistan

India

1pm

Niger
Chad

Oman

4pm

5.30 pm

Myanmar

6.30
pm

Northern
Mariana
Is (US)

Marshall
Is (US)

Nigeria

Eritrea
Yemen

3pm

ARABIAN
SEA

6pm

Thailand

Vietnam

Philippines

9pm

12am

Central African
Republic

Ethiopia

Sudan

BAY OF
BENGAL

5.30pm

Palau

Federated States
of Micronesia
11pm

Kiribati

Congo

Somalia

Sri Lanka

Malaysia

Kenya

Maldives

Indonesia

Nauru EQUATOR

Gabon
Congo
(Zaire)

1pm

Seychelles
4pm

6.30
pm

East
Timor

Papua New
Guinea

Solomon Is

SOUTH
PACIFIC
OCEAN

Tanzania

Cocos (Keeling)
Is (Aust)

Angola

Malawi
Zambia

Madagascar

Vanuatu

Namibia

Zimbabwe

Mauritius

9.30
pm

New Caledonia (Fr)

Fiji

Botswana
Mozambique

Reunion
(Fr)

INDIAN OCEAN

Australia

11.30
pm

Norfolk Is
(Aust)

South
Africa

10.30
pm
Lord Howe
Is (Aust)

Prince Edward Is
(S. Africa)

French Southern &
Antarctic Territories (Fr)

New Zealand

TASMAN
SEA

Heard &
McDonald Is
(Aust)

SOUTHERN OCEAN

12pm 1pm 2pm 3pm 4pm 5pm 6pm 7pm 8pm 9pm 10pm 11pm 12am

MAP LEGEND

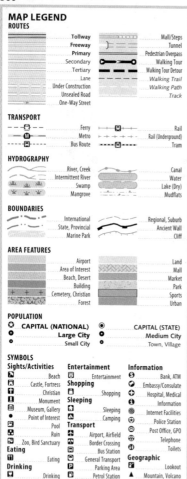

LONELY PLANET OFFICES

Australia

Head Office
Locked Bag 1, Footscray, Victoria 3011
☎ 03 8379 8000, fax 03 8379 8111
talk2us@lonelyplanet.com.au

USA

150 Linden St, Oakland, CA 94607
☎ 510 893 8555, toll free 800 275 8555
fax 510 893 8572
info@lonelyplanet.com

UK

72-82 Rosebery Ave,
Clerkenwell, London EC1R 4RW
☎ 020 7841 9000, fax 020 7841 9001
go@lonelyplanet.co.uk

Published by Lonely Planet Publications Pty Ltd

ABN 36 005 607 983

© Lonely Planet Publications Pty Ltd 2007

© photographers as indicated 2007

Cover photograph: Horse race, Day of the Dead, Todos Santos Cuchumatán, James Nelson/Getty Images. Many of the images in this guide are available for licensing from Lonely Planet Images: www.lonelyplanet images.com.

All rights reserved. No part of this publication may be copied, stored in a retrieval system, or transmitted in any form by any means, electronic, mechanical, recording or otherwise, except brief extracts for the purpose of review, and no part of this publication may be sold or hired, without the written permission of the publisher.

Printed by Hang Tai Printing Company
Printed in China

Lonely Planet and the Lonely Planet logo are trademarks of Lonely Planet and are registered in the US Patent and Trademark Office and in other countries.

Lonely Planet does not allow its name or logo to be appropriated by commercial establishments, such as retailers, restaurants or hotels. Please let us know of any misuses: www.lonelyplanet.com/ip.

Although the authors and Lonely Planet have taken all reasonable care in preparing this book, we make no warranty about the accuracy or completeness of its content and, to the maximum extent permitted, disclaim all liability arising from its use.